STRUCTURING MERGERS & ACQUISITIONS:

A Guide to Creating Shareholder Value

Second Edition

by

Peter A. Hunt

1185 Avenue of the Americas, New York, NY 10036
www.aspenpublishers.com

This publication is designed to provide accurate and authoritative information in regard to the subject matter covered. It is sold with the understanding that the publisher is not engaged in rendering legal, accounting, or other professional services. If legal advice or other professional assistance is required, the services of a competent professional should be sought.

—From a *Declaration of Principles* jointly adopted by
a Committee of the American Bar Association and
a Committee of Publishers and Associations

© 2004 Aspen Publishers, Inc.
A Wolters Kluwer Company
www.aspenpublishers.com

Printed in the United States of America

1 2 3 4 5 6 7 8 9 0

Library of Congress Cataloging-in-Publication Data
Hunt, Peter (Peter A.)
Structuring mergers & acquisitions: a guide to creating shareholder value/by Peter Hunt. — 2nd ed.
    p. cm.
  Includes bibliographical references and index.
  ISBN 0-7355-4204-X
    1. Consolidation and merger of corporations — United States — Management.
  2. Consolidation and merger of corporations — United States — Finance.
  3. Corporations — Valuation — United States. 4. Consolidation and merger of corporations — Law and legislation — United States. I. Title: Structuring mergers and acquisitions. II. Title.

  HG4028.M4H86 2004
  658.1′62 — dc22
                                      2004052671

About Aspen Publishers

Aspen Publishers, headquartered in New York City, is a leading information provider for attorneys, business professionals, and law students. Written by preeminent authorities, our products consist of analytical and practical information covering both U.S. and international topics. We publish in the full range of formats, including updated manuals, books, periodicals, CDs, and online products.

Our proprietary content is complemented by 2,500 legal databases, containing over 11 million documents, available through our Loislaw division. Aspen Publishers also offers a wide range of topical legal and business databases linked to Loislaw's primary material. Our mission is to provide accurate, timely, and authoritative content in easily accessible formats, supported by unmatched customer care.

To order any Aspen Publishers title, go to *www.aspenpublishers.com* or call 1-800-638-8437.

To reinstate your manual update service, call 1-800-638-8437.

For more information on Loislaw products, go to *www.loislaw.com* or call 1-800-364-2512.

For Customer Care issues, e-mail *CustomerCare@aspenpublishers.com;* call 1-800-234-1660; or fax 1-800-901-9075.

Aspen Publishers
A Wolters Kluwer Company

SUBSCRIPTION NOTICE

This Aspen Publishers product is updated on a periodic basis with supplements to reflect important changes in the subject matter. If you purchased this product directly from Aspen Publishers, we have already recorded your subscription for the update service.

If, however, you purchased this product from a bookstore and wish to receive future updates and revised or related volumes billed separately with a 30-day examination review, please contact our Customer Service Department at 1-800-234-1660, or send your name, company name (if applicable), address, and the title of the product to:

ASPEN PUBLISHERS
A Division of Aspen Publishers, Inc.
7201 McKinney Circle
Frederick, MD 21704

ABOUT THE AUTHOR

Peter A. Hunt is Managing Director at Shattuck Hammond Partners LLC, a boutique investment banking firm with offices in New York, San Francisco, Chicago, and Atlanta. At Shattuck Hammond, he focuses on mergers and acquisitions, strategic advisory, and capital raising for start-up and high growth companies in the health care industry. He is a former Senior Managing Director in Corporate Finance of Banc of America Securities, Inc. where he was also a Director of Mergers and Acquisitions. Peter joined Bank of America Securities as a result of two acquisitions: first, the acquisition by Nations Bank of Montgomery Securities, and then the merger between NationsBank and Bank of America. Prior to Banc of America Securities, Peter was a Vice President at Lehman Brothers in the Mergers and Acqusitions Group and a Vice President in the Strategic Advisory/M&A Group at J. P. Morgan & Co., Inc. Peter is the co-founder and former President and COO of CornerHardware.com, a business-to-customer Internet home improvement company. He started the company in early 1999, raising approximately $30 million capital, and then sold the company to iFloor.com in February 2001.

ACKNOWLEDGMENTS

It is rare that someone gets the opportunity to thank those friends and colleagues who have played a role in shaping one's development. It is also hard to remember to thank people along the way. I'd like to extend my heartfelt thanks to all of you who in some way, shape, or form have contributed to my growth and inspired me to write this book. Your inspiration, guidance, support, and mentorship have been instrumental in helping me build a career and develop as a human being. I am eternally grateful to all of you.

To the late Keith Shillington and to John Goldstein, John Gunn, Pamela Simpson, Bob Nye, and Jim Starling, you set me on the right path.

To Mike Lobdell, Tony Mayer, Monty Cerf, David Wakefield, Stephen Schaible, Fran Carr, Bob Sroka, the late Josh Rosenthal, Kyun Hee Choi, Todd Baker, Steve Tonsfeldt, Ned Ruffin, Cathey Edwards, Rich Takata, Joe Schell, and all my friends and colleagues from J.P. Morgan, Montgomery Securities, Shattuck Hammond Partners, and CornerHardware.com, each of you helped shepherd me through the years. I am sure there are many more people to whom I owe a debt of gratitude. Thank you.

To all my great clients who over the years have placed their trust in me, thank you.

To my parents, family, wife, and children, I'd like to thank you for your never-ending love, support, and encouragement. Without your ceaseless patience, I could never have finished this book.

To all the folks at Aspen including Ron Sinesio, Lisa Butkiewicz, Elizabeth Murphy, Mary Stevenson, and Shawn Hood, I'd like to thank you for your encouragement, expert advice, professional approach, and most importantly, the opportunity to work with you. I owe a special thanks to Christiane Pelz for her dedication to getting the numbers right.

And finally, to Patrick Grace of Grace Associates, Brad Bunning, and Mike Litchfield, thank you for all your help, support, and encouragement.

SUMMARY OF CONTENTS

TABLE OF CONTENTS

PART I.   A SHAREHOLDER VALUE FRAMEWORK

Chapter 1

OVERVIEW OF SHAREHOLDER VALUE 3

Chapter 2

OVERVIEW OF VALUATION AND FINANCIAL ANALYSIS . . . 15

Chapter 3

FINANCIAL STATEMENT ANALYSIS 21

Chapter 4

DISCOUNTED CASH FLOW ANALYSIS 41

Chapter 5

COMPARABLE COMPANY ANALYSIS 61

Chapter 6

COMPARABLE TRANSACTIONS ANALYSIS 71

Chapter 7

MERGER ANALYSIS 85

Chapter 8

LEVERAGED BUYOUT ANALYSIS 101

Chapter 9

STOCK PRICE ANALYSIS 117

Chapter 10

PRIVATE COMPANY VALUATION 125

Chapter 11

VALUATION CASE STUDY: TROPICAL PRODUCTS CORP. ACQUISITION OF GLOBAL SNACKS, INC. 139

PART II.   M&A ACCOUNTING

Chapter 12

M&A ACCOUNTING 171

PART III. TRANSACTION TYPES

Chapter 13

Chapter 14

DIVESTITURES AND ASSET SALES 241

Chapter 15

JOINT VENTURES AND ALLIANCES 261

Chapter 16

GOING PRIVATE TRANSACTIONS 279

Chapter 17

FAIRNESS OPINIONS 327

PART IV. RESTRUCTURING ALTERNATIVES

Chapter 18

OVERVIEW OF CORPORATE RESTRUCTURINGS 351

Chapter 19

RECAPITALIZATIONS AND SHARE REPURCHASES 371

Chapter 20

SPIN-OFFS, SPLIT-OFFS, EQUITY CARVE-OUTS, AND TRACKING STOCK 417

PART V.   LEGAL ASPECTS OF MERGERS & ACQUISITIONS

Chapter 21

BUSINESS JUDGMENT RULE **497**

Chapter 22

LEGAL ASPECTS OF MERGERS & ACQUISITIONS 519

Chapter 23

ANTI-TAKEOVER MEASURES 551

Chapter 24

HOSTILE ACQUISITIONS 583

PART VI. STRUCTURING, NEGOTIATING, AND EXECUTING THE DEAL

Chapter 25

THE FUNDAMENTALS OF NEGOTIATION 615

Chapter 26

FORMULATING AN OFFER 625

Chapter 27

STRUCTURING THE LETTER OF INTENT
AND DEFINITIVE AGREEMENT 639

Chapter 28

COLLARS AND WALK-AWAYS 661

Chapter 29

TERMINATION FEES, LOCK-UP OPTIONS,
AND NO-SHOP CLAUSES 671

Chapter 30

EARNOUTS AND CONTINGENT PAYMENTS 681

Chapter 31

DUE DILIGENCE 691

LIST OF EXHIBITS

Chapter 20

Chapter 21 (No Exhibits)

Chapter 22

Chapter 23

Chapter 24

Chapter 25 (No Exhibits)

Chapter 26

INTRODUCTION

Pick up a newspaper on any given day and you will invariably read of a number of merger, acquisition, and restructuring transactions. From the noteworthy mergers of global industry leaders to the sale of ailing dot coms, we are reminded daily of the significance of mergers and acquisitions in corporate America.

To the uninitiated, however, the mere mention of the words "mergers and acquisitions" conjures up images of over-dressed investment bankers flying around in private jets and talking on cell phones. From Michael Douglas in the movie Wall Street walking along the shores of Long Island, speaking the words "This is your wake-up call" into his cell phone, to the notorious Michael Milken, who became known as the man who made more money shaving each morning than the average family of four made in an entire year, the field of mergers and acquisitions has spawned movies, sitcoms, mysteries, legends, heroes, and criminals. And to many, despite the press, the topic is still largely misunderstood.

Recent History of Mergers and Acquisitions

Mergers, acquisitions, and restructurings have been prevalent in the United States for over a hundred years. Periods of intense M&A activity have usually been followed by periods where little M&A activity has taken place. The peaks and troughs have been driven by greed as well as market, economic, and fiscal shifts. Likewise, each renewed period of merger and acquisition growth has led to certain regulatory and other changes designed to temper M&A activity. In recent history, there have been three major periods during which mergers and acquisitions have been strong: the conglomerate era of the 1960s, the hostile acquisitions of the 1980s, and the strategic mergers of the 1990s. Each of these periods can be characterized by certain factors, whether it's low interest rates, a booming stock market, or changes in the tax code.

The 1960s Conglomerate Era and the P/E Game

The first of the merger spurts occurred in the 1960s, which became known as the "conglomerate era." This period was characterized by a strong economy and stock market. Companies went beyond simply diversifying their business; they made acquisitions outside of their core business in far-flung sectors. Two companies symbolize the conglomeratization of the 1960s. Most notable of these was ITT, a multi-national conglomerate, which acquired businesses quite unrelated to its traditional business. These included companies in baked goods, hotels, rental cars, and insurance. Another example is LTV Corporation, started in the late 1940s as an electronics company in Texas. By the end of the 1960s, the company had acquired businesses in such far-flung industries as steel, airlines, meat packing, and sporting goods. At its peak, LTV was one of the largest companies in the world.

One of the significant forces behind this trend was strict antitrust regulations that were in place at the time. The antitrust climate was such that companies had a hard time making acquisitions if the resulting company served to reduce competition in the market. In addition, modifications to antitrust policy eliminated a company's ability to even acquire assets that were in the same industry if the end result was reduced competition. This tough stance on in-industry mergers was a driving factor behind companies acquiring outside of their core industries. Another factor responsible for the heightened merger activity in the 1960s was the strength of the stock market coupled with high interest rates. The rapidly expanding economy witnessed a tightening of the credit markets which made financing an acquisition with debt a difficult proposition. However, the strong stock market provided companies with an attractive currency with which to make acquisitions. As multiples tend to be an indicator of forward-looking growth, the high multiples conveyed on companies in the 1960s led them to capitalize on their currencies and make acquisitions.

Unfortunately, a pattern evolved where high multiple companies acquired lower multiple companies. Consequently, the 1960s became known as an era when the "P/E Game" was played. This game entailed companies with high multiples acquiring companies with low multiples and witnessing their earnings per share rise. This is a temporary phenomenon that results purely from the mathematics involved in combining two companies, rather than from making an attractive acquisition that results in increased earnings. Once an acquirer made a few low growth — and low multiple — acquisitions, the core earnings of the surviving company became affected. Over time, the once high multiple proffered on the large acquirers contracted to match their growth rates.

Another factor that contributed to the 1960s merger phenomenon was certain accounting practices at the time. For example, it was possible to sell assets in order to generate accounting income that was used to prop up earnings. Another example was the accounting for convertible securities. It was possible to issue convertible debt to a target in a transaction, and consolidate the earnings of the target while using the same number of shares outstanding at the acquirer. Consequently, the accounting earnings for the acquirer would rise. The increased earnings would signal an increase in earnings growth, affording the acquirer a higher multiple.

The 1960s merger wave finally came to an end late in the decade. The P/E game took its toll as the market recognized the fallacy of the strategy. In 1969, the stock market took a sharp turn for the worse, and the high-flying stocks of the 1960s boom came back down to earth. Multiples began to reflect true earnings growth, and acquisition currencies no longer provided an attractive vehicle for acquisitions.

In 1968, the Williams Act was enacted, drastically altering the way acquisitions took place. The Act was designed to limit coercive or abusive takeover tactics. In addition, the Attorney General at the time, Richard McLaren, made a push to reduce the number of conglomerates that were forming because he felt they were anti-competitive. This further added to the downward pressure on stock prices. Furthermore, the 1969 Tax Reform Act brought to an end many of the detrimental accounting practices that had artificially inflated earnings. For example, the use of convertible debt in takeovers was severely restricted by forcing companies to account for this debt as common stock for earnings per share purposes.

The conglomerate era was a period of rising stock prices, diversification, and mergers and acquisitions driven by paper returns, not real economic gains. These disappointments coupled with a depressed stock market resulted in a fairly prolonged period of declining merger and acquisition activity that lasted through the 1970s. The 1970s are noted, however, for a number of precedent setting transactions that set the stage for aggressive hostile M&A activity in the 1980s.

Three transactions in particular opened the doors for what became considered an acceptable means to acquire or takeover a transaction. The first of these transactions was the 1974 announcement by International Nickel Company that it would launch a tender offer for Electronic Storage Battery Company. International Nickel was the largest firm in the nickel industry, controlling over 40% of the market. Electronic Storage was the world's largest maker of batteries in the world, in particular automobile and consumer batteries.

At the time, International Nickel was faced with increasing competition in its core nickel business, and saw Electronic Storage as a way to diversify its cash flows and enter the more attractive battery business. Electronic Storage's stock price had been suffering, providing International Nickel with an attractive acquisition opportunity from a financial and a strategic perspective. The unwanted public tender offer was launched despite Electronic Storage having turned down a number of other suitors. International Nickel was backed by Morgan Stanley, one of the leading investment banks at the time, lending credence to the transaction. While Electronic Storage mounted a defense, hiring Goldman Sachs to assist it in looking at alternatives to the International Nickel deal, the company was essentially caught off guard and eventually capitulated to International Nickel, selling the company by the end of 1974. While the transaction ultimately was not viewed as a success, it was precedent setting in that the suitor was a large, internationally respected firm that was backed by a premier investment banking firm. This transaction opened the door to further hostile M&A activity.

In 1975, another well-respected firm, United Technologies, launched an unsolicited offer for Otis Elevator. United Technologies was a large manufacturing concern that had been involved in aircraft parts manufacturing. Otis manufactured and serviced elevators. Its stock was trading at a discount to its book value and was perceived as undervalued in the market. Its management team was strong and its cash flows were strong and stable, in part because of its servicing component as well as its international focus. For United Technologies, an acquisition of Otis added a strong international component without acquiring overseas, brought a well-managed company into the fold, and could be achieved at an attractive price. It launched the tender offer in late 1975, despite having been rebuffed in a friendly transaction. The tender offer led to a hotly contested transaction with Dana

Corporation being brought in by Otis to serve as a white knight. Ultimately, United Technologies prevailed when it substantially increased its offer price and closed the transaction in early 1996.

The United Technology hostile acquisition of Otis Elevator built on the International Nickel acquisition of Electronic Storage partly because it validated the approach as a viable acquisition technique and also because, unlike the International Nickel transaction, the Otis acquisition turned out to be a success from a financial and strategic standpoint. Otis and United went on to build a highly successful company.

In 1975, Colt Industries launched a hostile tender offer for Garlock Industries. Colt was a diversified conglomerate that had made numerous acquisitions in the 1960s, resulting in a company with over $1 billion in revenue. During the early 1970s, the company had divested many of the poorly performing businesses in its portfolio, optimizing its financial performance and hording a lot of cash in the process. Garlock, a manufacturer of packing and sealing products, had revenues of less than $200 million and a book value less than its stock price. Its earnings per share had steadily grown but were not reflected in its stock price.

As a result of the prior hostile takeovers, Garlock had put in place various takeover defenses including a staggered board. Colt launched its offer, and instantly the transaction became hotly contested, with Garlock pursuing all the means then at its disposal to defend itself. It filed suit against Colt in federal court, alleging that Colt had not abided by federal disclosure laws. In addition, it maintained that the transaction would be anti-competitive. Finally, Colt prevailed, as the litigation and other tactics proved to be no match for a fully priced offer. These three precedent-setting transactions set the stage for the resurgence in takeover activity in the 1980s.

The 1980s Hostile M&A Era

The 1980s became an era when mergers and acquisitions came into full bloom. Sophisticated financing structures, hostile M&A, and litigation became mainstream. During the early 1980s, the weak economy served to limit the growth in the stock market and the volume of M&A transactions did not pick up until 1983–84. The mid- to late 1980s witnessed some of the largest transactions ever completed. Among others, these transactions included the Kohlberg Kravis & Roberts $25 billion leveraged buyout of RJR Nabisco, the largest LBO ever completed; Gulf Oil's $13 billion acquisition of Chevron; and Kraft's $13 billion acquisition of Philip Morris.

Leveraged buyouts became de rigeur with the advent and rise of the junk bond market in the 1980s. In addition, the Tax Reform Act of 1986 facilitated corporate restructurings, resulting in numerous restructurings of companies in tax-free transactions. Conglomerates were disassembled and divisions were sold, spun-off, or split-off. As these companies restructured, the divested subsidiaries were then acquired by companies in stock-for-stock transactions, creating integrated companies that could exploit internal synergies.

Hostile acquisitions became everyday events with corporate raiders leading the charge. Individuals like Victor Posner, Paul Bilzerian, T. Boone Pickens, and Carl Icahn acquired company after company, financing their acquisitions with substantial amounts of leverage with the use of the increasingly popular junk bonds or high-yield debt, and busting these companies up, reaping huge profits in the process. In the 1980s, the investment bank Drexel Burnham Lambert is credited with inventing the modern junk bond market. Michael Milken, the firm's west-coast chief, was hailed as the "junk bond king" and the central figure responsible for financing much of the corporate raider activity of the 1980s.

The hostile transactions of the 1980s were driven by short-term profits rather than strategic merit. The excesses of this period came to an end as Milken was later charged with securities fraud, and Drexel Burnham, the company, folded. The outstanding Drexel Burnham high-yield bonds, which largely had been invested in by savings and loan institutions, went into financial distress and were partly responsible for the savings and loan crisis of the late 1980s. As a symbol of the greed of the 1980s hostile environment, Ivan Boesky emerged as yet another villain in the drama, the most renowned insider trader, first making millions on insider trades and then being convicted of securities fraud and going to jail.

Despite the negative undertone and short-term profit mentality of the 1980s, the era was helpful in developing the mergers and acquisitions market from a number of perspectives. First, there was a critical mass of legal precedents that were established, setting the framework for acceptable and unacceptable mergers and acquisitions practices, and reinforcing disclosure requirements that were designed to protect shareholders. Second, even though the junk bond market was tainted by the savings and loan crisis, it created a financing vehicle that today is legitimized and has become widely used in mergers and acquisitions. Third, it established investment bankers as necessary players in the M&A equation. Whether in financing the transaction, devising a takeover strategy, or defending the target, investment bankers became central figures in the business.

The 1990s Strategic Driven Era

The 1990s merger era saw a strong rise in M&A activity that was strategic minded rather than short-term profit driven. As the economy emerged from a recession in 1991, mergers and acquisition became popular again as a way to spur growth. Exhibit 1 shows the trend in domestic mergers and acquisitions between 1990 and 2003.

The pace of mergers and acquisitions in the United States accelerated in the mid-1990s thanks to a number of factors. The strong economy produced an overabundance of investment capital, driving the stock market higher and fueling acquisition activity. Regulatory changes across industries and a relaxing of antitrust regulations spurred inter- and intra-industry mergers. International competition encouraged economies of scale. Technology innovation created a slew of new companies ripe for acquisition, and forced older companies to stay apace with change. Finally, higher stock prices created strong acquisition currencies, further

Exhibit 1
Domestic Announced Mergers and Acquisitions: 1990–2003[1]
($ in billions)

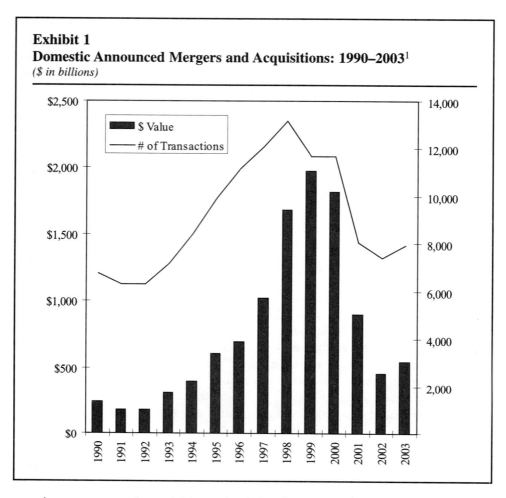

spurring mergers and acquisitions. At all levels, corporations were excited about the opportunities to capitalize on joint synergies.

In addition to these macro factors, there were numerous industry specific trends that led to consolidation. For example, in the auto industry, severe excess capacity led to large scale mergers, e.g., Chrysler/Daimler. In the banking industry, deregulation spurred a number of mergers and acquisitions, most notably, Citicorp's merger with Travelers to create CitiGroup. In the pharmaceutical industry, the high cost of drug research and development led to numerous mergers, including the SmithKline Beckman merger with Beecham to form SKB.

The Current Environment

Today, the mergers and acquisitions environment can be characterized as follows: Strategic acquisitions dominate the landscape. Leveraged buyouts continue to proliferate but are more dependent on the availability and cost of debt capital.

---

1. Thomson Financial.

INTRODUCTION

Hostile mergers and acquisitions have become accepted as a viable means to take over a company—hostile is no longer a dirty word in M&A. However, hostile acquisitions today tend to be more strategic in nature. Restructurings continue to be in vogue as companies continually reassess their portfolios of businesses, divesting non-core or unprofitable companies. In addition, with the enhanced scrutiny of public company boards, management teams and corporate performance, restructurings have become vogue. Creating shareholder value has become a central focus of managers and boards of directors, as institutional investors have put pressure on companies to deliver returns. Mergers, acquisitions and restructurings continue to play an important role in value creation.

Why M&A Is Significant

So, why is it then that the subject of mergers and acquisitions has generated millions in legal and illegal gains, helped build and destroy markets, and become the stuff from which movies and sitcoms have been made? The first answer is that the mergers and acquisitions business is enormous; in 2003, domestic dollar volume of announced merger and acquisition transactions was approximately $547 billion, an increase of 19% from $457 billion in 2002.[2] There were 7,928 announced deals in 2003, up from $7,395 in 2002.[3] It has involved some of the largest and most high-profile companies in the world. From J.P. Morgan's $58 billion merger with Bank One, to Daimler's $40 billion merger with Chrysler, whole industries have been turned upside down. The second answer is that the value created and the fees generated in mergers and acquisitions have attracted some of the brightest minds in the world and have spawned some of the most interesting personalities. The cast of characters begins before the turn of the 20th century with the rise of the Morgan empire. John Pierpont Morgan, famous for advising families like the Du Ponts and the Vanderbilts, as well as financing companies like U.S. Steel, was also well known for his numerous mistresses, behemoth art collection, and large yacht. By contrast, more recently are personalities such as Ivan Boesky, a former investment banker who made hundreds of millions trading on inside information. Quite recently, Victor Posner, the archetypal corporate raider of the 1980s, passed away. He was 83 years old, and even in the last years of his life, he was embroiled in contentious battles over companies he had acquired in his prime. Mr. Posner was known for conspiring with Ivan Boesky and Michael Milken to gain control of Fischbach Corporation, an electrical company in New York, in 1984. In 1994, Judge Milton Pollak of the Federal District Court of New York banned Mr. Posner from any further involvement with public companies.

The regular businessperson however, is unlikely ever to star in a $100 billion mega-merger or in a movie. Nor are they likely to conspire with others to take over and exploit other companies, let alone spend time in prison. It is more probable that he or she will be faced with having to sell a subsidiary, buy a division, merge

---

2. Thomson Financial.
3. Thomson Financial.

with a competitor, or restructure a company. The reason the field of mergers and acquisitions is so important is not the size and importance of the market or the fees that the transactions generate; but rather, because mergers, acquisitions, and restructurings can play a starring role in the creation of shareholder value. Companies can acquire a competitor in order to grow, merge with a partner to diversify, or spin-off a subsidiary to rationalize a balance sheet.

What Are Mergers, Acquisitions, and Restructurings?

The topics covered are broad-ranging, from the mundane accounting rules for purchase transactions, through the more exciting legal aspects of negotiations, to the more specialized areas of takeover defense. Success in this field requires a basic knowledge of a number of disciplines, including accounting, finance, and securities and corporate law. The M&A specialist couples these disciplines with sound business judgment and good negotiation skills. The practice of mergers and acquisitions combines the skills of the accountant, the lawyer, the banker, and the arbitrator.

Many books in this field focus specifically on the most common types of transactions — mergers, acquisitions, and divestitures. However, these three topics tell only part of the story. A separate but related field has not been well explored — restructurings. This refers to any type of deal that reconfigures a company's assets, ownership, or leverage. A pure restructuring is often thought of as one that modifies a company's debt-to-equity mix. However, there are a number of transactions that serve the same purpose but cross over between pure mergers and acquisitions and pure restructurings. The more common of these transactions are spin-offs, split-offs, equity carve-outs, and share repurchases. Throughout this book therefore, you will read of restructurings as well as mergers and acquisitions. Since there is so much overlap between these concepts, for simplicity sake, all three topics will often be referred to as mergers and acquisitions, or M&A.

Mergers and Acquisitions and the Creation of Shareholder Value

A sound mergers and acquisitions strategy is fundamental to the creation of shareholder value. The finest way to assess what type of transaction is right for you or your company is in the context of value creation. Each alternative should be evaluated in terms of how it can either create value today or position a company to build value tomorrow. Well-conceived transactions will reward shareholders with an increase in stock price. *Chapter 1: Overview of Shareholder Value* provides a framework for thinking about shareholder value and a basis for evaluating mergers and acquisitions.

What this Book Is

This book provides a practical overview of various merger, acquisition, and restructuring topics. It offers background in the accounting and legal concepts required to understand different transactions. It explores examples that analyze different deals and suggests ways to solve problems. Each chapter gives hints and tips on what to look out for and how to avoid the various pitfalls in a transaction.

Part I: A Shareholder Value Framework looks at the shareholder value concept and different valuation methodologies. These include financial statement analysis, discounted cash flow, comparable company, comparable transactions, merger, contribution, and leveraged buyout analyses, price/volume relationships, and private company valuation. It provides a framework for how to analyze a transaction in the context of creating shareholder value.

Part II: M&A Accounting discusses the various types of accounting methodologies that are used in mergers and acquisitions. A fundamental knowledge of these accounting approaches is critical to understanding and structuring various deal types.

Part III: Transaction Types provides an overview of the basic types of transactions that you may encounter — mergers, acquisitions, divestitures, joint ventures, leveraged buyouts, and going private transactions. It also discusses the importance of fairness opinions.

Part IV: Restructuring Alternatives discusses in depth the different restructuring alternatives that are used to enhance shareholder value without necessarily merging or selling the company. These include spin-offs, split-offs, equity carveouts, share repurchases, and recapitalizations.

Part V: Legal Aspects of Mergers & Acquisitions offers a description of the various legal considerations in mergers and acquisitions, including structural approaches and the business judgment rule. The section also discusses how companies can protect themselves from takeover threats. It provides both legal and structural defenses, and includes a discussion of the most common form of legal defense, the shareholder rights plan. Finally, this section addresses how companies go about making an aggressive or hostile offer for a company. Not to be taken lightly, this section should make you think twice before trying to go it alone in attempting a hostile acquisition.

Part VI: Structuring, Negotiating, and Executing the Deal discusses how to prepare for and manage the negotiation process, as well as structure and execute the transaction. It presents how to formulate an initial offer and structure the letter of intent. Additionally, it discusses pertinent issues in developing a definitive agreement. Other topics include collars, break-up fees, lock-ups, walk-aways, earnouts, due diligence, and financial modeling.

What this Book Is Not

This book is not for investment bankers who have spent years at their craft. It is, however, for people who would like to learn a little about this difficult topic, who want to make sure they understand what's happening to their company as they are bought or sold, or who would like to execute one of the transactions that are commonly used in mergers and acquisitions. It will also explain, for those who never quite understood it, what Michael Douglas was talking about on the beaches of Long Island.

The purpose of this guide is to take some of the mystery out of mergers and acquisitions and give readers the basic knowledge and confidence to embark on their own transactions, change careers, or challenge their investment banker. My goal is to provide a framework for analyzing transactions.

This book is not meant to be the definitive treatise on every aspect of M&A. There are many books in print that delve more deeply into one or the other topic. Should you find yourself in the midst of one of the transactions discussed in this guide, you would be well advised to seek the guidance of an expert in the area and go out and buy the definitive work on the subject you are faced with.

Revisions for Second Edition

From the perspective of mergers, acquisitions and restructurings, the years 2002 and 2003 were marked by a number of factors. The equity markets continued their slide with the number of initial public offerings, follow-on offerings, and other equity-related financings declining precipitously to the point of all but drying up in early 2003. As a consequence, investment banks restructured, laying off thousands of employees across the board. The lending market became more difficult, as banks focused on deteriorating credits and tightening up lending practices. The economy remained soft as the geopolitical landscape became more tenuous surrounding the aftermath of the Iraq war. Corporate scandals abounded with notable companies such as Integrated Health, HealthSouth, Enron, and Tyco International witnessing their stock prices plummet. Enhanced disclosure requirements revealed numerous accounting improprieties. The implementation of the Sarbanes-Oxley Act of 2002 initiated a radical change in mindset and accountability at the board and management level. The level of merger and acquisition activity continued to drop in 2002 and early 2003 with all of the above factors playing a role.

The second edition of *Structuring Mergers & Acquisitions: A Guide to Creating Shareholder Value* takes into consideration all the events that have shaped the M&A environment for the past few years. It includes a number of enhancements that are the result of feedback from many interested readers and to whom I am most grateful. First, all charts and exhibits have been updated to the present, and are current for the most recent quarter prior to this edition going to print. For example, tables depicting different types of merger and acquisition activity are current through 2003. In addition, where appropriate, the evidence behind certain types of transactions has been updated with the most current research.

Second, a new chapter entitled *Financial Statement Analysis* was added. This chapter goes beyond the typical valuation methodologies relied upon by investment bankers and others, and incorporates a broader approach to understanding and evaluating industries, companies and their individual income statements, balance sheets and cash flow statements. The comprehensive valuation case study has been enhanced to include a section on financial statement analysis.

Third, a section on the Sarbanes-Oxley Act of 2002 has been added to *Chapter 21: Business Judgment Rule*. The dramatic escalation in corporate scandals in recent history, coupled with the enhanced disclosure requirements and the implementation of the Sarbanes-Oxley Act of 2002, make a solid understanding of corporate governance crucial to mergers and acquisitions.

Fourth, a comprehensive glossary has been added as a quick-reference tool for readers.

Fifth, where appropriate, new case studies of recent transactions have been added to highlight certain merger and acquisition techniques.

Sixth, for simplification, three chapters, *Going Private Transactions, Leveraged Buyouts* and *Minority Squeezeouts*, have been condensed into one— *Chapter 16: Going Private Transactions*.

I trust these enhancements make the second edition a better read and provide the reader with more ways to take advantage of the text. I look forward to your continued feedback.

A Hypothetical Case Study

To assist the reader in understanding certain concepts, I have provided a case study that assumes two hypothetical companies enter into merger discussions. These companies, Tropical Products Corp. and Global Snacks, Inc., will be referred to throughout the book. *Chapter 11: Valuation Case Study: Tropical Products Corp. Acquisition of Global Snacks, Inc.* provides an overview of the proposed transaction and a complete valuation and financial analysis.

Some Common Terms

Throughout the book terms are used that are common to the investment banking industry, but may or may not be used everyday in the reader's vocabulary. Following is a quick overview of these terms and what they mean in the context of mergers, acquisitions, and restructurings.

Target: This is the company that is the primary subject of the transaction. For example, if Company A is attempting to acquire Company B, B would be the target corporation or simply, the target. The target could also be a subsidiary that is sold or spun-off.

Surviving Corporation: A given transaction can be structured so that different parties can be the ultimate legal surviving entity. In our example above, it is possible that even though Company B is the target, it could be the surviving corporation. Therefore, the surviving corporation is the legal entity that remains as the ongoing company once a transaction is complete.

Pro Forma: When two companies get together in the form of an acquisition or merger, or if a division or subsidiary is sold, split-off, or spun-off, it is common to develop financial statements that evaluate the impact of the transaction on the surviving corporation. The financial statements are calculated on a pro forma basis, incorporating the outcome of the transaction. For example, putting together the financial statements of Company A and B results in pro forma financial statements.

Going Concern: As we discuss valuation methodologies, it is common to distinguish between companies that operate on an ongoing, or going concern, basis and those that do not. Essentially, this simply means that the company continues to operate in fundamentally the same way as it has in the past.

Stand Alone: When a company is analyzed, it is common to look at it by itself, absent any transaction. This evaluation is considered a stand alone analysis. The company is known as the stand alone company.

Consideration: In a transaction, a company can offer different types of currency to finance an acquisition or merger. This consideration can be stock, cash, a combination of both, or even other types of securities such as preferred stock or notes.

The Market, Equity Market, or Wall Street: Throughout the book references are made to the market or Wall Street. Essentially, these are the individuals and institutions that acquire and trade public companies' stock and/or provide an opinion regarding a company's performance. These can include the media, research analysts, investment bankers, financial institutions, mutual funds, hedge funds, and the like.

Control: Control has a number of meanings; however, in most cases it means the acquirer purchasing greater than 50.1% of the target. In cases where control is any other than 50.1%, it is usually defined in the text.

Summary

As a long-time investment banker, I have had the good fortune of working on the vast majority of transaction types discussed in this book. I have also had the benefit of working with some of the sharpest people in the mergers and acquisition business, whether lawyer, accountant, consultant, or investment banker, and to all of them I am eternally grateful. I have helped shepherd many younger bankers through the M&A minefield, and these are the insights that I would like to pass on to you. I'm also always happy to provide you with additional advice or point you in the direction of someone who can help.

GLOSSARY

A

Absolute Price Performance
Evaluates a company's stock price by itself for a period of time prior to presenting the offer.

Absolute Walk-Away Provision
If the stock of the acquirer declines below a pre-determined level, e.g., 15%, the target has the absolute right to walk away from the transaction without penalty.

Accretion (Accretive)
In a transaction, if the earnings per share for the surviving company are greater than the earnings per share of that company stand alone or prior to the transaction, the amount by which the earnings per share exceeds the stand alone earnings per share is known as the accretion in the deal.

Accretion/Dilution Analysis
Analyzes the impact of a proposed merger or acquisition on the earnings of the acquirer or surviving company.

Acquirer
The company that is the acquiring or purchasing entity in the transaction.

Acquisition
The purchase of another company, business or asset.

Acquisition at Various Prices Analysis (AVP)
An analysis that translates a range of potential purchase prices for a target company into multiples of its revenues, operating profits, cash flows and other financial metrics.

Action by Written Consent
Allows shareholders to submit an action to the board and shareholders by written consent.

Aggregate Value
Market value is the value of the company's equity plus its net debt, i.e., total debt minus cash. It is also sometimes known as market capitalization, firm value, enterprise value or aggregate value.

Alliance	An alliance is a simple form of joint venture that may not involve the creation of a new entity to undertake the enterprise, and may not involve equity ownership or a contribution of capital by either party.
Alphabet Stock (also, Tracking Stock, Targeted Stock or Letter Stock)	Specially designated stock of a company where the stock that trades publicly reflects the earnings and financial performance of a specific business.
Announcement Effect	A term used to describe the impact of the announcement of a transaction on a company's stock price.
Anti-Greenmail Provision	Prohibits the payment of greenmail to a potential unwanted suitor who owns a stake in the company.
Appraisal Rights	These appraisal rights allow the dissenting shareholders to receive a third party appraisal of their shares as a means to potentially increase the price paid by the company.
A Reorganization	In an A reorganization, also known as a statutory merger, two corporations combine subject to the procedures established by the corporate laws of the state(s) where the parties are incorporated. The parties merge via a merger agreement that is signed by both parties.
As Converted Basis	Includes in the total number of shares outstanding, shares that would be issued if a security such as convertible preferred stock or convertible debt are converted into common equity.
Asset Appraisal	An approach to valuing a company that analyzes the value of each asset in the company on a discrete basis.
Asset Lock-Up Option	The target gives the favored bidder the right to acquire certain assets in the target.
Auction	The sale of a company, subsidiary, division or assets in a process whereby the seller engages in the sale process with a broad group of potential purchasers.

B

Basis
A shareholder's basis in a company is the net investment that the shareholder has in the stock or assets of the company. Basis may be viewed on an accounting or tax basis.

Best Price Rule
The consideration to be paid in a tender offer should be the highest consideration paid to any stockholder during the tender offer.

Beta
A measure of risk determined by correlating the performance of a company's stock to the general performance of the market.

Blank Check Preferred Stock
Preferred stock that is issuable in series. The terms of blank check preferred stock can be dictated by the board of directors and can be used for multiple purposes. For example, it can be used to backstop a shareholder rights plan, or it can be issued to a white knight in the face of a takeover offer.

Block Purchase
The purchase of a large number of shares of a company, typically in a share repurchase.

Blue Book Analysis
The analysis contained in an investment banker's presentation or "blue book" to the board of directors.

Break-Up Fee
Fees paid to one party to a transaction by the other party in the event the transaction is "broken up" by a third party bidder offering a higher price.

Break-Up Valuation
The valuation of a company in which each of its respective business units are valued independently and added together. From the total value of each business, the net liabilities and an allocation for corporate overhead are deducted to realize a net value, the break-up value, of the company.

B Reorganization
B reorganizations are stock acquisitions whereby the stock of one company is acquired using exclusively the voting stock of another company in a stock-for-stock exchange. After the exchange of stock, the acquirer must have control of the target, in this case, greater than 80% of the voting

stock plus 80% of the total shares of the nonvoting stock. No more than 20% of the consideration can be in the form of cash.

Bring Down Opinion

A fairness opinion drafted after the initial fairness opinion, usually delivered either when a proxy is mailed to shareholders or just prior to the closing of a transaction.

Business Combination Statute

Generally prevents a hostile acquirer from merging with a target company after the bidder has acquired a substantial stake in it without having obtained prior approval from the target's board. Specifically, if a bidder crosses over a defined threshold, say 10%–20%, it is prohibited from entering into a business combination with the target for a proscribed period of time unless prior to reaching the threshold, the bidder had received approval from the target's board to acquire the stock or to enter into the business combination.

Business Judgment Rule (Doctrine)

A doctrine that maintains that a board director is protected unless shareholders can establish that the director has violated his duty of care, duty of loyalty and good faith to a corporation.

C

Capitalization

The value of a company's total debt and equity securities outstanding, either on a market or book basis.

Capital Structure

The composition of a company's balance sheet in terms of how it is financed with debt and equity.

Cash Out Statute

A cash out statute maintains that a stockholder acquiring over a certain percentage of a target's stock, e.g., 20%, must notify the other shareholders and they must be given the right to have their shares acquired at the highest price paid by the acquirer in the last 90 days.

Cash Ratio

Cash plus marketable securities divided by current liabilities.

C Corporation	A business that is a completely separate entity from its owners.
Chewable Pill	A provision in a poison pill that nullifies the pill in the event of an all-cash tender offer for all of a target's outstanding shares.
Collar	A mechanism in the purchase or merger agreement whereby the buyer and seller are protected in the event there are significant changes in either party's stock price, such that the negotiated terms of the transaction are no longer attractive to the parties.
Common Size Analysis	Analyzes the various components of a company's income statement as a percent of sales and analyzes the various components of a company's balance sheet as a percent of total assets.
Common Stock	Securities that represent a form of common equity ownership in an entity and convey certain rights on the stockholder.
Common Stock Equivalents (CSE's)	The designation for certain securities, for example convertible debt securities, that are "in-the-money" and thus are viewed on the same basis as common stock on an as converted basis.
Comparable Trading Multiples Analysis (Comparable Company Analysis)	A going concern valuation methodology that uses the trading multiples of comparable companies to value the target company by applying those multiples to the target's own financial metrics.
Comparable Transaction Multiples Analysis	A transaction based valuation methodology that uses the transaction multiples from transactions comparable to the transaction under review and applies the multiples to the target's own financial metrics.
Confidentiality Agreement	Otherwise known as a non-disclosure agreement, it is a binding letter that outlines the restrictions and usage of confidential material provided to the parties to the confidentiality agreement. It is designed to prevent the misuse of such information.

Consideration	The type of currency that is offered in a transaction, i.e., stock, cash or a combination or both.
Consolidated Accounting	The acquisition of greater than 50% of a target but less than 100% is generally treated under consolidation accounting rules. Under consolidated accounting, the target's balance sheet is consolidated with the acquirer for accounting purposes but the net income that is "not-acquired" is backed out of the acquirer's income statement.
Contingent Payment	A form of earnout or deferred payment used to bridge a valuation or other gap in a transaction.
Contribution Analysis	Analyzes the relative contribution to revenues, operating profits and other metrics, of a target and acquirer to the combined company, and compares it to the pro forma ownership of each company's shareholders in the combined entity.
Control	Where greater than 50% of a company is owned.
Controlled Competitive Sale	The sale of a company, subsidiary, division or assets in a process whereby the seller engages in the sale process with a select number of potential purchasers.
Control Share Acquisition Statute	Generally require that a bidder receive shareholder approval prior to acquiring a significant stake in a company. The benefit of a control share acquisition statute to the target company is that it potentially delays the time period during which an unwanted acquirer may purchase the company.
Control Transaction	A "control" transaction is one where an acquirer purchases greater than 50.1% of a target.
Convertible Security	A security, such as convertible debt or convertible preferred stock, that is convertible into another form of security, such as common stock.
Corporate Restructuring	A transaction that involves the reorganization of a company's business, stock or assets.

Cost Accounting	When less that 20% of the voting stock of the target is acquired, the acquirer must use cost accounting. In cost accounting, the acquirer simply records the investment on its balance sheet at cost.
Cost of Capital	The cost at which a target company can raise debt and equity capital at any given moment in time. (See weighted average cost of capital.)
Cost of Debt (k_d)	The after-tax cost of a company's debt based on its ability to seek incremental financing at the point at which the analysis is undertaken.
Cost of Equity (k_e)	The implied cost of a company's cost of equity capital as determined by the Capital Asset Pricing Model (CAPM)
C Reorganization	C Reorganizations are asset acquisitions whereby the assets of one company are acquired using exclusively the voting stock of another company. After the transaction is complete, the target typically liquidates and distributes the stock received in the transaction to its shareholders. As a result of the transaction, the shareholders of the target become shareholders of the acquirer.
Cumulative Voting	The ability for a shareholder to vote all of his/her stock for one or a handful of directors, rather than allocating the votes among the directors.
Current Ratio	Current assets divided by current liabilities.

D

Days Payables Outstanding	365 divided by payables turnover.
Days Sales Outstanding	365 divided by receivables turnover.
Dead Hand Pill	A provision in a poison pill that mandates that only a majority of the continuing directors that were on the board prior to the removal of the board of directors may redeem or modify a pill.
Debt Capacity	The amount of debt a company can reasonably assume without incurring financial

distress or reducing its debt rating below acceptable levels.

Debt-to-Equity Ratio	Total debt divided by total equity.
Debt-to-Total Capital Ratio	Total debt divided by total capital.
Definitive Agreement	The binding agreement that sets forth the terms between the parties to the agreement.
Dilution (Dilutive)	In a transaction, if the earnings per share for the surviving company are less than the earnings per share of that company stand alone or prior to the transaction, the amount by which the earnings per share are less than the stand alone earnings per share is known as the dilution in the deal.
Direct Merger	In a direct merger, the target merges directly into the acquirer, or vice versa. In this scenario, the target's shareholders are generally not taxed, as long as they receive stock in the surviving corporation for their stock in the target, and that stock of the acquirer comprises at least 50% of the total consideration.
Discounted Cash Flow (DCF) Analysis	Values the future cash flows of a company by discounting the cash flows to present using a discount rate that reflects the target company's cost of financing.
Discount Rate	This is the rate of return required by an investor, given the level of risk associated with the investment. Also, the rate at which the cash flows of a target company are discounted in order to derive a present value for the company. (See cost of capital; weighted average cost of capital.)
Divestiture	A form of corporate restructuring that ranges from the sale of 100% of the stock or assets of a company, the 100% initial public offering of a company or subsidiary, or a spin-off, split-off or targeted stock.
Dividend	The periodic payment made by a company from after-tax earnings to shareholders of the company's equity, most commonly thought of in terms of dividends on common stock.

Double Trigger   The use of both an absolute and a relative walk-away provision.

D Reorganization   A D reorganization is one in which one corporation transfers part or all of its assets to another corporation such that immediately after the transfer, the transferor or its shareholders are in control of the corporation to which the assets where transferred. In addition, the stock of the corporation to which the assets were transferred is distributed in a transaction that meets the requirements of Sections 354, 355 or 356 of the Internal Revenue Code.

Dual Capitalization   Companies with two classes of common stock bearing different voting and other rights.

Due Diligence   The formal strategic, legal and financial investigation of a company prior to the consummation of a transaction.

Dutch Auction   A form of share repurchase in which the issuer offers to acquire its stock from shareholders at a range of prices.

Duty of Care   A director's duty of care means that he should make decisions on behalf of shareholders after taking into consideration all available information and after deliberate consideration of all the information at his disposal.

Duty of Loyalty   A director's duty of loyalty means that he should act in the best interests of the shareholders or for the entity of which he is a fiduciary.

E

Earnout   A form of contingent payment designed to provide additional value to a seller based on the target company meeting certain target performance or other objectives.

EBIAT   Earnings before interest and goodwill amortization, but after taxes.

EBITDA Margin   Earnings before interest, taxes, depreciation and amortization divided by sales.

EBIT Margin	Earnings before interest and taxes divided by sales.
Enterprise Value (also, Aggregate Value or Firm Value)	Also known as aggregate value, market value or firm value, it is the value of a company's total capitalization, i.e., debt and equity.
Equity Accounting	Equity accounting is used when more than 20% but less than 50% of the voting stock of the target is acquired. In equity accounting, the acquirer reflects its percentage ownership of the target on its income statement and balance sheet.
Equity Capitalization	Equity value is simply the value of the company's equity. It is also sometimes known as equity capitalization.
Equity Carve-Out	An equity carve-out is a sale of a stake in a subsidiary to the public in an initial public offering.
Equity Market Premium	The premium investors expect to derive from investing in common stocks over risk free securities.
Equity Risk Premium	See Equity Market Premium.
Equity Value (also, Equity Capitalization)	Equity value is simply the value of the company's equity. It is also sometimes known as equity capitalization.
ESOP	An ESOP is an employee stock ownership plan.
Exchange Offer	A form of transaction where securities are exchanged for cash or other securities.
Exchange Ratio	The ratio of the number of shares an acquirer will issue of its own stock for each share of the target.
Ex-Dividend Date	The first day of the ex-dividend period such that transactions may be completed before the record date.

F

Fair Market Value	The price that an interested buyer would be willing to pay and an interested seller would be willing to accept on the open market assuming a reasonable period of

	time for an agreement to arise, and assuming that neither party is desperate to make a transaction.
Fairness of Price	Fairness of price relates to the financial fairness of the transaction. From a financial perspective, a fair transaction is one where a rational buyer and seller would the buy or sell stock in the contemplated transaction given the same relevant facts of the situation.
Fairness Opinion	A letter written by an investment bank on behalf of a board of directors or other fiduciary, that states that a transaction is fair from a financial point of view.
Fair Price Provision	A fair price provision is a charter amendment that requires a potential acquirer that owns stock in a company to pay the remaining shareholders at least the maximum price that was paid for the initial holdings.
Fair Price Statute	Fair price statutes generally state that in the event an acquirer is able to purchase a significant stake in a company, the remaining shareholders are entitled to receive a "fair price" for their shares.
Fiduciary duty	A board of director's fiduciary duty to shareholders is his responsibility to shareholders.
FIFO	Inventory valuation methodology whereby inventory is priced on a first-in, first-out basis.
Financial Statement Analysis	The analysis of a company's or industry's financial health through the use of ratio and other analyses.
Firm Value	Market value is the value of the company's equity plus its net debt, i.e., total debt minus cash. It is also sometimes known as market capitalization, firm value, enterprise value or aggregate value.
Fixed Assets	A long-term, tangible asset held for business use.
Fixed Asset Turnover Ratio	Sales divided by average fixed assets.
Fixed Charge Coverage Ratio	Earnings before fixed charges divided by fixed charges.

Fixed Exchange Ratio	The ratio of seller shares per target share is fixed in the transaction, i.e., the number of shares to be issued is fixed. In a fixed exchange ratio transaction, the value of the transaction may fluctuate between signing and closing.
Fixed Price	The price the buyer pays for the seller is fixed. In a fixed price transaction, the number of shares the seller pays the target shareholders may fluctuate between signing and closing.
Fixed Price Tender Offer	A tender offer in which a company offers to purchase its stock at a fixed price per share.
Flip-In	A form of trigger in a poison pill whereby shareholders have the right to acquire stock in the target in the event an acquirer acquires over a certain percentage in the target.
Flip-Over	A form of poison pill trigger whereby shareholders have the right to acquire stock in the acquirer in the event the acquirer is successful in merging with the target.
Forecast Period	The period in the future for which the target company's cash flows are projected.
Form 10	The disclosure document that must be filed in connection with a spin-off transaction.
Forward Triangular Merger	In a forward triangular merger, the target merges with and into a subsidiary of the acquirer. The stock of the acquiring parent corporation is issued in the transaction. No stock of the subsidiary may be issued. The subsidiary must be at least 80% owned by the aquirer.
Free Cash Flow	The "un-levered" after tax cash flow of a company.
Freeze Out	See Squeeze Out.

G

Going Concern	To operate going forward in substantially the same way as the past.

Going Concern Value	The value of a company as a stand alone entity, independent of any merger or acquisition transaction (See Stand Alone Value.)
Going Private Transaction	A going private transaction is the acquisition of the equity securities of a corporation by the issuer or an affiliate of the issuer, in which, as a result of the transaction, less than 300 shareholders remain or the stock of the corporation is delisted from an exchange or is no longer quoted on the NASDAQ.
Good Faith	Presumes that a director has the best interests of shareholders and the company in mind when taking an action.
Goodwill	The difference between the fair market value of a company's assets and its book value.
Goodwill Impairment	The amount by which good will is reduced.
Gross Margin	Gross profit divided by sales.

H

High Yield Debt	Otherwise known as "Junk Bonds," the form of public debt that is issued by below investment grade issuers.

I

Information Memorandum	Otherwise known as a descriptive memorandum, it is the document used in a sale process to describe the operations and financial performance of a company, subsidiary business or other asset.
Initial Bid	The first, preliminary offer made by an acquirer when seeking to purchase an asset or business.
Internal Rate of Return (IRR)	The rate of return investors seek on an investment.
Internal Restructuring	A company evaluates its internal processes, capital allocation and strategic priorities, and refocuses its attentions on those areas that will maximize operating performance.

In-the-Money	Stock that is trading above the exercise or strike price.
Intrinsic Value	The value of a company's future dividend stream discounted to the present using a discount rate reflecting the risk inherent in the dividend stream.
Inventory Days	365 divided by inventory turnover ratio.
Inventory Turnover Ratio	Cost of goods sold divided by average inventory.
IPO Valuation	A valuation approach that benchmarks a private company's value against that of its publicly traded peers.

J

Joint Venture	A joint venture is an arrangement or partnership between two or more parties where an independent entity is formed by the parties with the purpose of undertaking a specific activity.
Junk Bonds	See High Yield Debt.

L

Last Twelve Months (LTM)	Also known as trailing 12 months (TTM), it applies to the financials for a company's most recent four quarters.
Letter of Intent (LOI)	A non-binding letter sent by a potential acquirer to the seller that indicates the preliminary financial and legal terms of a proposed transaction.
Letter of Transmittal	The letter that accompanies a document explaining the purpose of the document.
Letter Stock (also, Tracking Stock, Alphabet Stock or Targeted Stock)	Specially designated stock of a company where the stock that trades publicly reflects reflects the earnings and financial performance of a specific business.
Leverage	The amount of debt on a company's balance sheet.
Leveraged Buyout (LBO)	The acquisition of a company, division or subsidiary using a highly leveraged

	financial structure, whereby the cash flows of the acquired business are used to service and repay the borrowed debt.
Leveraged ESOP	An employee stock ownership plan that acquired the stock of the company using debt to finance the purchase of the stock.
Leveraged Recapitalization	Shareholders sell or exchange their stock for a package of cash, debt and/or other instruments, plus potentially a small amount of stock, for shares in the company.
Levered Beta	A form of Beta that is adjusted for the company's capital structure.
LIFO	Inventory valuation methodology whereby inventory is priced on a last-in, first-out basis.
LIFO Reserve	The difference between the LIFO value and the FIFO value of inventory, i.e., the difference between the carrying cost of the inventory and the current cost of the inventory.
Limited Liability Corporation	A form of corporate ownership where the shareholders receive limited liability protection of a typical corporation but the tax benefits of an S Corporation without having to conform to S Corporation restrictions.
Liquidity Discount	The discount placed on a company's valuation that results from its small size, private nature or other constraints that render the securities of the company illiquid.
Lock-Up Option	An option provided to a favored bidder that gives it the option to acquire stock (stock lock-up option) or assets (crown jewel option) in the target under certain circumstances.

M

Market Capitalization	Market value is the value of the company's equity plus its net debt, i.e., total debt minus cash. It is also sometimes known as market capitalization, firm value, enterprise value or aggregate value.
Market Value	Market value is the value of the company's equity plus its net debt, i.e., total debt minus

cash. It is also sometimes known as market capitalization, firm value, enterprise value or aggregate value.

Merger	The joining of two companies in a stock-for-stock transaction.
Merger Analysis	Evaluates the impact of a transaction on the surviving company and indicates an acquirer's ability to pay for a target.
Merger of Equals	The joining of two companies of similar size in a stock-for-stock transaction.
Mezzanine Debt	See Unsecured Debt.
Minority Squeeze Out	The purchase of the shares of a publicly traded company not owned by majority shareholder(s).

N

Negotiated Sale	The sale of a company, subsidiary, division or assets in a privately negotiated process between a seller and a single potential buyer.
Net Debt	Total debt minus cash.
Net Income Margin	Net income divided by sales.
Net Present Value	The present value of a project's future cash flows minus the initial investment to realize such cash flows.
Non-Disclosure Agreement	Otherwise known as a confidentiality agreement, it is a binding letter that outlines the restrictions and usage of confidential material provided to the parties to the non-disclosure agreement. It is designed to prevent the misuse of such information.

O

Open-Market Share Repurchase	A company acquires its stock over time in the open market.
Operating Cash Flow Ratio	Cash flow from operations divided by current liabilities.
Operating Margin	Operating profit divided by sales.

P

Payables Turnover	Purchases divided by average accounts payable.
P/E/G Ratio	The ratio of a company's price/earnings multiple to its projected near-term earnings growth rate.
Poison Pill (Shareholder Rights Plan)	An anti-takeover device that gives a target's shareholders the right to acquire stock in the target at a discount in the event an unwanted bidder acquires, or announces its intention to acquire, a certain percentage of the target.
Preferred Stock	Equity securities that rank ahead of common stock and behind debt in liquidation.
Preliminary Offer	See Initial Bid.
Premiums Paid Analysis	A transaction based valuation methodology for public target companies that uses the premiums paid from transactions comparable to the transaction under review and applies the premiums to the target's stock price.
Pre-tax Margin	Pre-tax profit divided by sales.
Pooling-of-Interests Accounting	A method for accounting for a stock-for-stock, control merger transaction. In a pooling-of-interests transaction, no goodwill is created.
Present Value	The value of a future stream of cash flows derived from discounting such cash flows to present at a pre-determined discount rate.
Price/Earnings Multiple (P/E)	The ratio of a company's stock price to its earnings.
Price/Volume Analysis	Analyzes the number of shares that have traded at various price ranges for a target company over a period of time, for example, six months, in order to help establish the recent basis of certain shareholders in the company's stock.
Procedural Fairness	Procedural fairness relates to the process that a board went through in evaluating a transaction and deciding on a course of action.

Pro-Forma

Financial results that reflect the combined operations of two companies subject to a transaction.

Pro-Forma Merger Analysis

An approach to analyzing a merger or acquisition transaction that evaluates the accretion or dilution to the acquirer or surviving corporation, and the contribution of each company to the combined entity.

Proxy Statement

A document which the Securities and Exchange Commission requires a company to send to its shareholders that provides material facts concerning matters on which the shareholders will vote.

Public Float

The shares of a public company that are freely traded in the market place.

Purchase Accounting

A method of accounting for a transaction that is either stock-for-stock, stock-for-cash or a combination of both. In a purchase transaction, goodwill is created.

Q

Queer

A condition whereby a pooling transaction becomes invalid because it does not meet one of the twelve conditions set out in APB No. 16. The condition that is not met is known to "queer" the pooling transaction.

Quick Ratio

Cash plus marketable securities plus accounts receivables divided by current liabilities.

R

Recapitalization

A recapitalization usually entails the assumption of incremental debt or the reduction in equity through a repurchase of shares. Recapitalizations are done to dramatically alter the capitalization or ownership of companies.

Receivables Turnover

Sales divided by average receivables.

Record Date

The date upon which eligible participants will receive stock, dividends or other distributions.

Redemption Period	The period during which a security may be reclaimed.
Registration Statement	A document that must be filed with the SEC prior to an intial public filing or other form of securities issuance.
Regulation 13D	Regulation 13D requires that any person, or group of persons acting together, who acquired directly or indirectly greater than 5% of the class of any equity security, must file a report on Schedule 13D within ten days disclosing that acquisition with the SEC, and send a copy of the report to the company.
Regulation 14A	Regulation 14A establishes the rules for the filing and dissemination of a proxy statement on Schedule 14A and the solicitation of proxies. The proxy statement is designed to ensure that shareholders are given the information they need to make a reasonably informed decision. It must be filed in preliminary form with the SEC at least ten days before the date definitive copies are sent to the shareholders.
Regulation 14C	Regulation 14C governs transactions that do not require shareholder approval.
Regulation 14D	Regulation 14D pertains to any tender offer by an affiliate of the issuer or a third party and governs the filing, disclosure and dissemination of information in tender offers commencement by a person other than the issuer.
Regulation 14E	Regulation 14E pertains to all tender offers, and governs the procedures and prohibitions of certain tender offer practices.
Relative Stock Price Performance	Compares a target's stock price performance to an index or indexes that may include its peers.
Relative Value	The value of a company based on applying financial multiples of comparable companies to the metrics of the target corporation.
Relative Walk-Away Provision	If the stock price of the acquirer declines by a pre-determined percentage relative to its peer group or similar index, the seller has

the right to walk away from the transaction without penalty.

Reorganization, A

In an A reorganization, also known as a statutory merger, two corporations combine subject to the procedures established by the corporate laws of the state(s) where the parties are incorporated. The parties merge via a merger agreement that is signed by both parties.

Reorganization, B

B reorganizations are stock acquisitions whereby the stock of one company is acquired using exclusively the voting stock of another company in a stock-for-stock exchange. After the exchange of stock, the acquirer must have control of the target, in this case, greater than 80% of the voting stock plus 80% of the total shares of the non-voting stock. No more than 20% of the consideration can be in the form of cash.

Reorganization, C

C Reorganizations are asset acquisitions whereby the assets of one company are acquired using exclusively the voting stock of another company. After the transaction is complete, the target typically liquidates and distributes the stock received in the transaction to its shareholders. As a result of the transaction, the shareholders of the target become shareholders of the acquirer.

Reorganization, D

A D reorganization is one in which one corporation transfers part or all of its assets to another corporation such that immediately after the transfer, the transferor or its shareholders are in control of the corporation to which the assets where transferred. In addition, the stock of the corporation to which the assets were transferred are distributed in a transaction that meets the requirements of Sections 354, 355 or 356 of the Internal Revenue Code.

Restructuring

A restructuring is the realignment of the ownership, operations, assets or capital structure of a company in order to improve operating performance, optimize a capital structure, and enhance public perception.

Return on Assets	EBIT divided by average total assets.
Return on Capital	EBIT divided by average debt plus stockholders equity.
Return on Equity	Pre-tax income divided by average stockholders equity.
Reverse Triangular Merger	In a reverse triangular merger, the subsidiary of the acquiring company merges with and into the target, and the target becomes the surviving entity. For this structure to be tax free, the subsidiary must acquire at least 80% of the voting stock of the target and 80% of all other classes of target stock in exchange for the voting stock of the subsidiary.
Rights Plans	See Shareholder Rights Plans.
Risk Free Rate	The rate on a theoretically "riskless" security.
Rule 13e-3	The rule that governs going private transactions.
Rule 13e-4	Rule 13e-4, *Tender Offers by Issuers*, governs tender offers by issuers, and outlines the filing, dissemination, and disclosure requirements for cash tender offers or exchange offers that are made by the issuer for its own securities.
Rule 14(d)-9	If the third party uses solicitations or recommendations of third parties, it must file a Schedule 14D-9, which is governed by Rule 14d-9. Schedule 14D-9 requires disclosure of the person making the solicitation or recommendation and the relationships between that party and the party making the offer.
Rule 14(d)-10	Rule 14d-10 is designed to ensure that all shareholders receive equal treatment in a tender offer. The rule mandates that a tender offer is open to all security holders of the class of securities that is subject to the tender offer (the "all holders" rule), and the consideration that is paid to any security holder is the highest consideration paid to any other security holder during the tender offer (the "best price" rule).

S

Sale	The divestiture of the stock or assets of a company, the divestiture of a business, subsidiary or division of a company, or the divestiture of certain individual assets, intellectual property or property, plant and equipment of a company.
Schedule TO	Schedule TO, *Tender Offer Statement*, must be filed in the case of tender offers.
Schedule 13D	If the third party acquires greater than 10% of the target's stock in the open market prior to the tender offer, it must file a Schedule 13D which is governed under Section 13(d) of theExchange Act. Schedule 13D is used to identify, among other things, who the acquirer is, which securities it has purchased, and the acquirer's interest with respect to its acquisition of those securities.
Schedule 13E-3	The schedule that must be filed in conjunction with a going private transaction.
Schedule 13E-4	The schedule that must be filed in conjunction with a tender offer by affiliates.
Schedule 14D-9	Schedule 14D-9 requires disclosure of the person making the solicitation or recommendation and the relationships between that party and the party making the offer.
S Corporation	A form of corporate ownership where shareholders have the protections of a typical C Corporation yet receive tax benefits associated with a partnership.
Section 14(e)	Prohibits insider trading, misstatements and certain other practices in connection with tender offers.
Section 338(h)10 election	An election under the Internal Revenue Code made in a transaction by the buyer and seller such that the purchase of the stock will be treated for tax purposes as the purchase of the subsidiary's assets.
Section 355	The provision in the Internal Revenue Service Tax Code that governs the tax-free nature of transactions.

Secured Debt	Senior debt is secured by the assets of the company, and will look to those assets as protection in a downside scenario.
Self-Tender	A company tenders for a defined percentage of its stock either at a fixed price, i.e., fixed-price self-tender, or at a range of prices, i.e., Dutch auction self-tender.
Senior Debt	A form of debt security that is senior to other forms of debt in a capital structure.
Shareholder Analysis	Analyzes the individual shareholders of a company and tries to determine their individual bases.
Shareholder Rights Plan	See Poison Pill.
Shareholder Value	As a concept, shareholder value is the value of a company that is attributed to its shareholders. For a public company, its stock price is the daily barometer of its shareholder value.
Share Repurchase	A company buys back its own shares through an open-market share repurchase, a targeted block repurchase or a self-tender.
Special Dividend	A company pays a one-time, non-recurring dividend, usually in cash, to shareholders.
Spin-Off	A spin-off is a distribution of stock in a subsidiary to shareholders in the form of a dividend. In most cases, the dividend is on a tax-free basis to shareholders and with no tax consequences to the parent.
Split-Off	A split-off is the separation of a subsidiary from the parent by segregating the shareholder base into two, one group owning stock in the parent and the other owning stock in the subsidiary. Like spin-offs, most split-offs are undertaken on a tax-free basis.
Squeeze Out (also, Minority Squeeze out)	The acquisition of the minority shareholders of a corporation.
Staggered Board	A staggered board varies the terms of each of a target company's board members such that only one or two directors may be re-elected in any given year. A staggered board prevents a hostile third party from removing a majority of the target's board of directors in any one year.

Stand Alone	A company on its own without the impact of any transaction.
Stand Alone Value	The value of a company as a going concern, independent of any merger or acquisition transaction. (See Going Concern Value.)
Stock Analysis	The analysis of a company's historical trading patterns as well as its shareholder base.
Stock Lock-Up Option	The target gives the favored bidder the right to acquire authorized but unissued shares of the target.
Stock Price Analysis	The analysis of the historical price performance of a company's stock for different periods prior to a transaction. Entails absolute price performance, relative price performance and price/volume analysis.
Subordinated Debt	A form of debt security that is subordinated to senior debt in the capital structure.
Substantially All Test	A condition in APB No. 16 that requires that at least 90% of the outstanding common stock of the target in a pooling transaction is exchanged for stock in the acquirer.
Supermajority Provision	An amendment to the charter that provides for a substantially higher threshold for shareholder approval. Generally, supermajority provisions range from 66% to 80%, with a few instances where supermajority thresholds have been seen as high as 95%.
Surviving Corporation	The legal entity that survives as the ongoing company once an acquisition or merger transaction is complete.
Synergies	The cost savings or revenue enhancements that may be achieved in a transaction.

T

Tainted Shares	Shares above a certain threshold in a pooling-of-interests transaction that are reacquired prior to, in conjunction with or post merger that result in queering—or tainting—the pooling accounting methodology of a pooling transaction and thus become known as tainted shares.

Takeover Premium	The premium paid to shareholders in an acquisition of their securities.
Target	The company that is acquired in or is the subject of the transaction.
Target Capital Structure	The proposed capital structure of a target entity in a discounted cash flow valuation analysis.
Targeted Share Repurchase	A share repurchase that is specific to a number of shares owned by a given entity.
Tax Basis	The basis shareholders have in a company's stock or assets.
Tender Offer	A public offer to acquire a company's securities.
Terminal Value	The value of a company attributed to the cash flows expected to be generated after the forecast period in perpetuity.
Termination Fee	Fees paid to one party in a transaction where the other party terminates the transaction.
Times Interest Earned	EBIT divided by interest expense.
Topping Fee	An agreement between the target and the acquirer designed to compensate the acquirer in the event its offer is exceeded by a third party.
Total Asset Turnover	Sales divided by average total assets.
Tracking Stock (also, Letter Stock, Alphabet Stock or Targeted Stock)	Specially designated stock of a company where the stock that trades publicly reflects the earnings and financial performance of a specific business.
Trailing Twelve Months (TTM)	Also known as last 12 months or LTM, it applies to a company's financial metrics for the most recent four quarters.
Transaction Equity Value	The value of a target company's equity that assumes an acquisition or other transaction takes place.
Transaction Premium	See Takeover Premium.
Transaction Value	The value of a target company that assumes an acquisition or other transaction takes place.

U

Unlevered Beta — A company's Beta adjusted to eliminate the effects of its capital structure.

Unsecured Debt — Unsecured debt is also known as subordinated debt. It has a claim on assets that is junior or subordinated to the secured debt. It is also known as mezzanine financing or mezzanine debt.

W

Walk-Away Provision — The seller has the right to walk away from a transaction without penalty if the acquirer's stock price declines below a certain level after the announcement of the transaction.

Weighted Average Cost of Capital (WACC) — The cost at which a target company can raise debt and equity capital at any given moment in time. (See Cost of Capital.)

White Knight — A white knight is a third party that the target merges with or sells to in a friendly transaction.

White Squire — A white squire is a third party to whom the target issues a large block of shares, sufficient to thwart the takeover efforts of the hostile party.

Working Capital — The short-term assets and liabilities used to generate the revenues of a company. Includes accounts receivable, inventories and accounts payable.

Working Capital Turnover — Sales divided by average working capital.

PART I

A SHAREHOLDER VALUE FRAMEWORK

Chapter 1

OVERVIEW OF SHAREHOLDER VALUE

§ 1.01 OVERVIEW

Shareholder value. Think about it. These are two simple words we hear quite often in the context of mergers and acquisitions, yet they are frequently forgotten or swept under the rug when it comes time to do a deal. People get caught up in the excitement of a transaction or, "deal heat," and forget what shareholder value creation is all about. Inherent in these words are the two most critical questions in mergers, acquisitions and restructurings: on whose behalf are we acting, and what are we trying to do for them?

In answer to the first question, regardless of whether the company is private or public, we all work for our shareholders, investors, or stockholders. And who are these shareholders? They include private individuals, mutual funds, corporations, arbitrageurs, money management firms, managers and employees. These investors acquired their stock either from the company itself in a public or private offering, from another investor on the stock market or in a private sale, as the result of a stock distribution in an M&A deal, or through stock or option incentive plans.

The answer to the second question is that these investors are expecting to realize a return on their investment. Management's mandate is to create and enhance value for shareholders by successfully operating the company, financing it prudently, and communicating the company's story well to shareholders. A sound M&A strategy is integral to each of these.

§ 1.02 WHAT IS SHAREHOLDER VALUE?

For a public company, its stock price is its daily barometer of shareholder value. Pick up the newspaper each day and you can quickly ascertain the changing shape of a company's value. Each time a company takes an action such as releasing earnings, selling a division, or raising capital, its stock price will change. Over time, if the positive actions outweigh the negative actions, a company's stock

3

price should increase. The same principles apply to a private company, as its stock value is central to its ability to buy competitors, raise capital, and build wealth for shareholders.

Mergers, acquisitions, and restructurings play a pivotal role in building value for shareholders. Three elements, as shown in Exhibit 1-1, form the foundation of shareholder value:

- a company's operating performance,
- its capital structure, and
- its public perception.

Operating Performance: A company's operating performance incorporates many benchmarks that are used in financial analysis; namely, earnings, gross margins, operating margins, working capital, leverage, growth rate, etc. A company has the ability to influence its operating performance through a number of internal and external means. These include selling more products via increased marketing, enhancing margins by lowering cost structure or raising prices, or entering into new markets or selling new product lines. Mergers, acquisitions, and restructurings can also play an important role in improving operating performance — for example, increasing profitability by selling a money-losing division.

Capital Structure: A company's balance sheet provides investors with a snap shot of its health at the end of any given month, quarter, or year. It tells us how a company finances its growth and how well — or poorly — it uses its working capital. It also provides a means to evaluate whether or not a company is delivering on its promises. In the context of mergers and acquisitions, a balance sheet

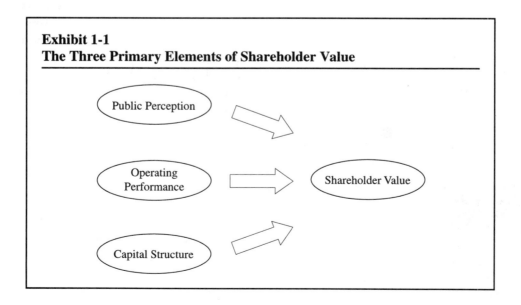

Exhibit 1-1
The Three Primary Elements of Shareholder Value

gives us information with which to analyze the impact of M&A activity on a capital structure. For example, the sale of an unprofitable division may help reduce debt and enhance equity.

Public Perception: Public perception is largely responsible for the day-to-day and intra-day movements in a company's stock price. It is influenced by a number of factors, including the track record of the company and management's credibility with Wall Street, the number and quality of equity research analysts that cover the stock, and the quality of the company's communication's program with Wall Street, institutions and the public. It can also be influenced by the liquidity in the company's stock. A sound mergers and acquisitions program can significantly enhance the perception of a company.

§ 1.03 HOW DO MERGERS, ACQUISITIONS, AND RESTRUCTURINGS RELATE TO SHAREHOLDER VALUE?

Shareholder value is profoundly influenced by all types of M&A activity, and the finest way to assess what type of transaction is right for a company is in this context. Each alternative should be evaluated in terms of how it either creates (or destroys) value today or positions a company to build value tomorrow. Only well-conceived and well-executed transactions will reward shareholders with an increase in stock price.

Companies continue to pursue mergers and acquisitions as well as other forms of corporate and financial restructurings as a way to boost long-term shareholder value. And, what attracts these companies to play in the M&A game? It is the irresistible attraction to the opportunity to capitalize on synergies that arise from the combination of two companies. Whether operational, financial, or managerial, these synergies are the overriding driver of M&A activity in today's market.

How do various merger and acquisition transactions help create shareholder value? What is their impact on operating performance, capital structure and public perception? The answer lies in the strategic and financial analysis performed to evaluate a proposed transaction. Each time you look at a transaction, you should ask yourself what the impact will be on the three basic elements of shareholder value: operating performance, capital structure and public perception. If the operating performance or capital structure of your company will suffer, or the public perception is not clear, you should think twice about commencing the deal. If you conclude that the overall impact will be positive, then it is likely you are undertaking a smart transaction.

Let's examine some of the more common merger, acquisition, and restructuring transactions to assess how each has the potential to enhance or destroy shareholder value. These are shown in Exhibit 1-2.

First, let's review why companies undertake these types of transactions. Exhibit 1-3 provides a list of some of the many reasons why companies undertake mergers, acquisitions, and restructurings.

Exhibit 1-2
Common Merger, Acquisition & Restructuring Transactions

M&A Transactions	*Restructuring Transactions*
Mergers	Spin-Offs
Acquisitions	Split-Offs
Divestitures	Equity Carve-Outs
Joint Ventures	Share Repurchases
Leveraged Buyouts	Recapitalizations

Exhibit 1-3
Reasons for Mergers, Acquisitions & Restructurings

M&A Transactions	*Restructuring Transactions*
Expand market share	Focus on core business
Eliminate a competitor	Enhance operating performance
Enter new markets	Clarify vision of company
Diversify product base	Highlight hidden assets
Build critical mass	Strengthen balance sheet
Lower supplier costs	Eliminate poorly performing subsidiary
Eliminate redundant overhead	Highlight strong subsidiary
Eliminate redundant manufacturing	Use excess cash
Capitalize on partner strengths	Shrink capitalization
Strengthen balance sheet	Shed assets
Redeploy excess capital	Redeploy excess capital
Forward or backward integration	

While not exhaustive, this list highlights the importance of mergers, acquisitions, and restructurings in supporting the fundamental tenets of shareholder value: operating performance, capital structure and public perception.

Now, let's look at how each of the principal types of transactions relates to the three tenets. Most transactions can influence just about every aspect of a company's value. Exhibit 1-4 diagrams the essential relationships between M&A and shareholder value creation.

To illustrate the importance of this shareholder value tree, let us look at two hypothetical companies. Tropical Products Corp. has been in business for 50 years. It has a strong market position and brand name, yet its success was built on a single product line. A number of new players have entered the market and are putting pressure on Tropical's market share, growth rates, and operating margins. Since its market share is eroding, Tropical's leverage with suppliers has been diminishing and consequently, its product sourcing costs have been increasing, squeezing margins.

Global Snacks, Inc. is a relatively new entrant into the market. It makes products that compete with Tropical, yet since Tropical is still the strongest player in

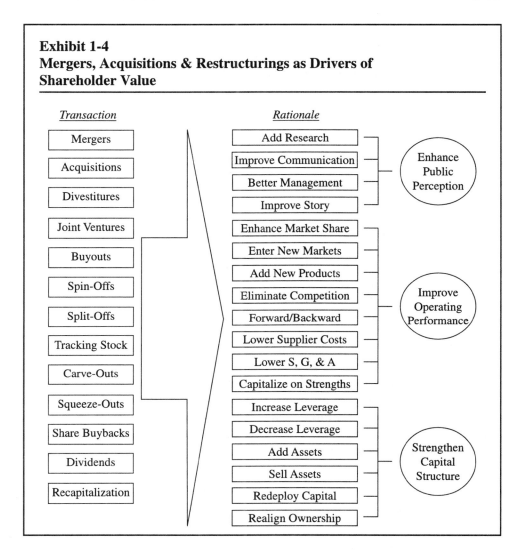

Exhibit 1-4
Mergers, Acquisitions & Restructurings as Drivers of Shareholder Value

Transaction

- Mergers
- Acquisitions
- Divestitures
- Joint Ventures
- Buyouts
- Spin-Offs
- Split-Offs
- Tracking Stock
- Carve-Outs
- Squeeze-Outs
- Share Buybacks
- Dividends
- Recapitalization

Rationale

- Add Research
- Improve Communication
- Better Management
- Improve Story

→ Enhance Public Perception

- Enhance Market Share
- Enter New Markets
- Add New Products
- Eliminate Competition
- Forward/Backward
- Lower Supplier Costs
- Lower S, G, & A
- Capitalize on Strengths

→ Improve Operating Performance

- Increase Leverage
- Decrease Leverage
- Add Assets
- Sell Assets
- Redeploy Capital
- Realign Ownership

→ Strengthen Capital Structure

the domestic market, Global Snacks has built its presence in Europe. In addition, to differentiate itself in the domestic market, Global Snacks has a broader product offering than Tropical. The company has focused on research and development, allowing it to introduce new products at a much faster rate than Tropical.

Under pressure because investors are starting to recognize its deteriorating market share, management at Tropical decides it needs to protect its position and shore up its operating performance. After evaluating a number of alternative acquisitions, Tropical decides to pursue a merger with Global Snacks.

What are the strategic reasons for the merger?

- Eliminate a competitor
- Expand the market share of both companies

- Broaden the combined company's product offering

- Use respective geographic distribution strengths to cross-sell products

- Leverage the technology of Tropical

- Lower supplier costs with combined purchasing power

- Eliminate redundant selling, general, administrative and other operating expenses

- Eliminate duplicate manufacturing costs

- Enhance the story of the combined company to investors

- Deepen management team

- Optimize capital structure by enhancing assets and debt mix

These potential benefits all need to be substantiated through sound valuation and financial analysis. If the analysis does not support the deal, regardless of how good it sounds, I would be very wary of proceeding. Using Tropical and Global Snacks as an example, even though the business and strategic merits of the proposed combination are compelling, the price that Tropical may have to pay for Global Snacks might be too high to warrant a good return on investment to Tropical's shareholders. The financial outcome of the proposed transaction would thus undermine the favorable strategic benefits of the merger. Chapters 2 through 11 review the different types of valuation analysis required to substantiate the various types of mergers, acquisitions, and restructurings, using the Tropical Products acquisition of Global Snacks as an example. Chapter 11 provides a comprehensive review of the financial and strategic analyses for the transaction.

§ 1.04   CARDINAL HEALTH: A CASE STUDY IN VALUE CREATION THROUGH MERGERS AND ACQUISITIONS

To demonstrate the possible value creation from mergers and acquisitions, let us look at one company that has executed its M&A strategy quite successfully: Cardinal Health. Cardinal is a pharmaceutical services company based in Ohio. The company's current in 1971 when Robert Walter acquired Cardinal in a leveraged buyout. Mr. Walter was 26 years old at the time and had recently graduated from Harvard University. The original company was in the food distribution business. Frustrated because this sector had already undergone substantial consolidation, Mr. Walter took the company in a different direction, moving into the pharmaceutical distribution sector in 1980 with the acquisition of Zanesville. The company soon went public, in 1983, and began its national campaign to expand its distribution business. In 1988 Cardinal sold its food business and narrowed its focus to pharmaceuticals.

During the 1990s Cardinal participated in the rapid consolidation of the drug distribution sector, acquiring numerous regional players, including Ohio

Valley-Clarksburg, Chapman Drug Co., PRN Services, Solomons Co., Humiston-Keeling and Behrens. A landmark acquisition of Whitmire Distribution in 1994 vaulted Cardinal to the number three position in the industry. With this acquisition, Cardinal changed its name to Cardinal Health.

1995 saw Cardinal Health make its largest acquisition to date when it purchased Medicine Shoppe International out of St. Louis, the United States' largest franchisor of independent retail pharmacies. This acquisition initiated Cardinal's foray into extending its reach out of pure drug distribution in order to continue to build its margins and capture more of the retail and manufacturer prescription dollar.

In 1996, the company acquired Pyxis, a company that provides hospitals with machines that automatically dispense pills to patients. Later that same year, Cardinal Health acquired PCI Services, a pharmaceutical packaging company. In 1997, the company acquired Owen Healthcare, a provider of pharmacy management services.

During the late 1990s, Cardinal Health attempted to acquire Bergen Brunswig, then one of the largest drug distribution companies in the United States. McKesson countered this acquisition with its own purchase of AmeriSource Health. The Federal Trade Commission ended up blocking both deals on antitrust grounds and the deals ultimately terminated.

Not deterred, Cardinal Health continued to make acquisitions including the 1999 acquisition of R.P. Scherer, the world's largest maker of softgels. This acquisition was quickly followed by an acquisition of Allegiance, the largest medical products distributor in the United States. In 2000, Cardinal Health acquired Bindley-Western Industries, a Indianapolis-based drug distributor, making it the largest drug distributor in the country. With the onset of the new Millenium, Cardinal continued its acquisition spree with the purchase of Syncor in 2002.

The company has grown from $1.2 billion in revenue in 1991 to over $38 billion in revenue in 2001. It generated earnings of over $1.6 billion, had a market capitalization of over $30 billion, and had 49,000 employees. From its start as a food distribution company, Cardinal Health is now in four primary lines of business related to the distribution of pharmaceuticals. Exhibit 1-5 provides an overview of Cardinal's lines of business, and shows the change in business mix from 1997 to 2001.

The overriding reason why Cardinal has been able to grow its product lines and business segments, and cater to a broad customer base, is its acquisitive strategy. Since 1980, Cardinal has merged with or acquired over 50 companies. As a result, today, Cardinal has a market capitalization greater than $30 billion, as of year-end 2001. Exhibit 1-6 provides a list of significant mergers and acquisitions completed by Cardinal since 1980.

From this list, it is apparent that Cardinal has used M&A as a way to extend its capabilities in the pharmaceutical value chain by integrating backward and forward in order to get closer to its customers and suppliers, extending its product lines to provide more products to existing customers, and leveraging its products into new customer segments.

Exhibit 1-5
Cardinal Health: Business Segments

	2001 Revenues (billions)	% of 1997 Operating Earnings	% of 2001 Operating Earnings
Pharmaceutical Distribution & Provider Services (Rx Distribution)	$31	81%	51%
Medical-Surgical Products & Services (Medical-Surgical)	$6	0%	26%
Pharmaceutical Technology & Services (PTS)	$1.2	5%	13%
Automation & Information Services (Automation)	$0.5	14%	10%

Exhibit 1-6
Cardinal Health: Significant Acquisitions[1]

Date	Target	Business Segment
05/12/80	The Bailey Drug Company	Rx Distribution
09/14/84	Ellicott Drug Company	Rx Distribution
01/20/86	John L. Thompson Sons & Company	Rx Distribution
04/30/86	James W. Daly, Inc.	Rx Distribution
01/20/88	Marmac Distributors, Inc.	Rx Distribution
06/18/90	Ohio Valley-Clarksburg, Inc.	Rx Distribution
10/15/91	Chapman Drug Company	Rx Distribution
04/01/92	Medical Strategies, Inc.	Rx Distribution
05/04/93	Solomons Company	Rx Distribution
12/17/93	PRN Services, Inc.	Rx Distribution
02/07/94	Whitmire Distribution Corp.	Rx Distribution
07/01/94	Humiston-Keeling, Inc.	Rx Distribution
07/18/94	Behrens Inc.	Rx Distribution
11/13/95	Medicine Shoppe International, Inc.	Rx Distribution
05/07/96	Pyxis Corporation	Automation
10/11/96	PCI Services, Inc.	PTS
03/18/97	Owen Healthcare, Inc.	Rx Distribution
02/18/98	MediQual Systems, Inc.	Automation
05/15/98	Comprehensive Reimbursement Consultants, Inc.	PTS
08/07/98	R.P. Scherer Corporation	PTS
02/03/99	Allegiance Corporation	Medical-Surgical
04/01/99	Surgical Instrument Repair Services, Inc.	Medical-Surgical

(Continued)

---

1. Public Company Documents.

Exhibit 1-6

(*Continued*)

Date	Target	Business Segment
05/20/99	PHARMACISTS: prn, Inc.	Rx Distribution
05/21/99	Pacific Surgical Innovations, Inc.	Medical-Surgical
06/04/99	The Enright Group, Inc.	Medical-Surgical
06/25/99	Pharmaceutical Packaging Specialties, Inc.	PTS
06/30/99	AutoValet Systems Int'l — Product line purchase	Automation
07/12/99	MedSurg Industries, Inc.	Medical-Surgical
08/25/99	Herd Mundy Richardson Holdings	Limited PTS
09/10/99	Automatic Liquid Packaging, Inc.	PTS
11/18/99	Trimaras Printing Company, Inc.	PTS
12/30/99	HelpMate Robotics, Inc.	Automation
01/21/00	Contract Health Professionals and Pharmacists — Ance, Inc.	Rx Distribution
07/19/00	Rexam Cartons, Inc.	PTS
07/26/00	Dermatology division from Advanced Polymer Systems, Inc. (Enhanced Derm Technologies, Inc.)	PTS
08/16/00	Bergen Brunswig Medical Corporation	Medical-Surgical
09/01/00	ENDOlap, Inc.	Medical-Surgical
11/01/00	Ni-Med kit manufacturing (from Oak Medical Industries LLC)	Medical-Surgical
11/01/00	CurranCare, LLC	Medical-Surgical
12/15/00	Manufacturing Facility in Humacao, Puerto Rico from Alcon (Puerto Rico), Inc.	PTS
12/22/00	VegiCaps Division from American Home Products Corporation	PTS
01/02/01	International Processing Corporation	PTS
02/14/01	Bindley Western Industries, Inc.	Rx Distribution
02/26/01	Astra-Zeneca Plant in Corby, UK	PTS
03/16/01	Critical Care Concepts	Medical-Surgical
03/23/01	American Threshold	Medical-Surgical
03/28/01	FutureCare	Medical-Surgical
06/29/01	SP Pharmaceuticals, LLC	PTS
10/23/01	Purchase of Manufacturing facility in Raleigh, NC from Schering-Plough Animal Health Corporation	PTS
11/15/01	Professional Health-Care Resources, Inc.	Medical Surgical
05/15/02	Boron LePore	PTS
06/14/02	Syncor	Rx Distribution

This M&A strategy has helped Cardinal create significant shareholder value. Through the years, Cardinal's stock price has grown from $1.24 per share in January 1988 on a split-adjusted basis to $66.40 per share on May 31, 2002. Exhibit 1-7 provides a graphic overview of the value creation of Cardinal Health since 1988.

Exhibit 1-7
Cardinal Health Stock Price Performance Versus S&P 500:
1988 – May 31, 2002

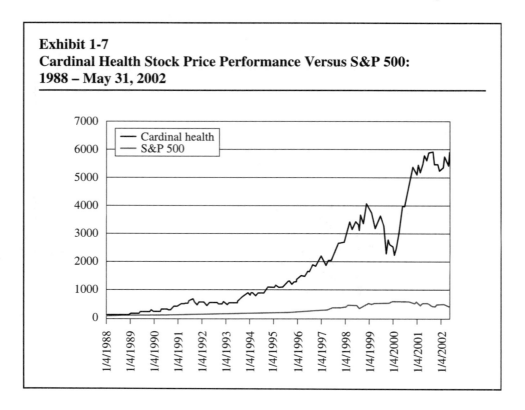

Exhibit 1-8
Cardinal Health Financial Metrics: 1991 and 2001[2]

	1991	*2001*
Revenues	$1.2 billion	$38 billion
Operating Earnings	$35 million	$1.6 billion
Market Capitalization	$3.4 billion	$30 billion
Total Assets	$354 million	$14.6 billion
Long-Term Debt	$124 million	$1.8 billion
Shareholders Equity	$193 million	$5.4 billion

As supporting evidence for the increase in shareholder value, Cardinal's balance sheet and income statement performance has consistently improved over time, as the synergies from each acquisition have been incorporated into the company. Exhibit 1-8 provides a comparison of key ratios for Cardinal in 1991 and 2001.

Cardinal is an excellent example of how a sound merger and acquisition strategy can consistently enhance shareholder value.

---

2. Public Company Documents.

§ 1.05 SUMMARY

The creation or destruction of shareholder value is what drives the fluctuation in a company's stock price. On a day-to-day basis, management is engaged in growing, operating and financing a company. Simply enhancing a company's operations or improving its balance sheet through internal means may often not be sufficient. Competitive pressures, changing markets, and other forces may put pressure on management to seek external means to improve shareholder value. Mergers, acquisitions, and restructurings can play a central role in enhancing shareholder value, and should be an integral part of every company's strategic development plans. A prudent merger and acquisition strategy can help the management team of a company enhance its public perception, improve operating performance, and optimize its capital structure.

Chapter 2

OVERVIEW OF VALUATION AND FINANCIAL ANALYSIS

§ 2.01   OVERVIEW

Valuing the financial implications of a transaction is fundamental to the merger and acquisition business. Without proper financial analysis, regardless of how attractive the strategic and business merits of a deal may be, it is impossible to quantify the potential shareholder value creation embodied in the deal. This chapter provides a general framework for thinking about valuation in the context of mergers and acquisitions.

§ 2.02   INTRINSIC VERSUS RELATIVE VALUE

Traditionally, both intrinsic value and relative value have been used as the principal methodologies for valuing publicly traded companies.

The intrinsic value of a company is derived by taking its projected future dividends, and discounting them by a discount rate that reflects the shareholders' return requirement on their investment and the growth rate of the company. Though this approach has theoretical appeal, it suffers from a number of problems, including a lack of agreement on the appropriate discount rate to use and a declining number of companies that pay dividends. Today, investors who use the intrinsic approach instead focus on the discounted cash flow methodology. Similar to the dividend discount approach, it takes future cash flows of a company and discounts these at a rate approximating the company's cost of capital.

The relative value approach is based on various metrics derived from comparison with a company's peers. For example, if the average price/earnings multiple for a group of similar companies is 20 times earnings, applying this

15

multiple to the target company's earnings yields a theoretical stock price. This can then be compared to the current price of the company's stock.

For day-to-day stock price analysis, investors lean more toward the relative value approach. However, as information on the performance of companies has become more widely and readily available, public investors have begun to use an additional approach that is based on expectations. For example, equity research analysts, as well as numerous agencies, publish estimated projected earnings and growth rates for companies. To the extent the company disappoints, meets, or exceeds those earnings projections, the public investor then bids the stock down or up.

One would think that with the alleged efficiency of the public markets, the valuation of securities would be an accurate science. In fact, it is not. Rather, it is an art that goes far beyond looking at the intrinsic and relative valuation of a company and assessing its performance based on expectation. Consequently, one will frequently see stocks that are either grossly undervalued or overvalued in the market. In addition, financial analysis alone will not enable you to make a decision to pursue a deal. Rather, a combination of strategic and business evaluation, valuation and financial analysis, and intuition all work together to help shape a good decision.

Why is this so important? Mergers and acquisitions would be simple if the market was an accurate reflection of value. An acquirer could use the public stock price of a target as its benchmark value. Unfortunately, life is not so easy. Valuation for mergers, acquisitions, and restructurings, while it does rely on the same concepts of intrinsic value, relative value and expectations, requires additional, more detailed analysis.

§ 2.03   DEAL VALUATION FOR MERGERS, ACQUISITIONS, AND RESTRUCTURINGS

Deal valuation requires several phases or steps. When considering a transaction, it is prudent to evaluate the target company from a variety of different standpoints to determine whether it is being acquired, merged or sold at a fair value.

- The first step is to look at the stand-alone value of each party to the transaction.

- The second step is to look at the transaction related values for the target company.

- The third step is to analyze the proposed transaction and assess its possible impact on the surviving corporation.

It doesn't matter whether the proposed deal is a merger, a divestiture, a joint venture, or a split-off, all deals should be thought of in this type of framework. While all deals won't necessitate every analysis, the principles of the framework still apply.

[A]   Stand Alone Value

The stand alone value of a company is its value today, absent any deal. For public companies, it is used to determine whether the company is fairly valued in the marketplace and serves as a preliminary indicator of whether a transaction is worth pursuing. For private companies, stand alone valuation establishes a benchmark value for a company that can be used as a basis for negotiation. This method uses a combination of the intrinsic value, relative value, and expectations approaches. The two most common stand alone valuation techniques are discounted cash flow analysis and comparable company analysis.

Discounted Cash Flow Analysis: This is a corporate finance approach that evaluates the projected cash flows of a target company using a discount rate that approximates the target's cost of financing. The cash flows for a defined projection period plus a terminal value approximating the cash flows beyond the projection period for the company are discounted back to the present, using a discount rate to determine a present value for the target. This represents the value of the target and can be compared to the company's public valuation. Discounted cash flow analysis is discussed in more detail in Chapter 4.

Comparable Company Analysis: This approach values the private or public target company in the context of its peer group. In other words, comparable company analysis applies the earnings multiple — as well as other multiples — of companies in the target's industry or sector to the operating metrics of the target company in order to assess its value. For example, an industry peer group may trade at an average multiple of 20 times projected earnings. Applying this multiple to the target company's earnings yields an implied price per share. Comparable company analysis is covered in more detail in Chapter 5.

[B]   Transaction Value

Transaction values help us to value a target company in the context of other deals done in the industry. There are two primary approaches to transaction valuation: comparable transaction multiples analysis and premiums paid analysis.

Comparable Transaction Multiples Analysis: Applying multiples from acquisitions that are comparable to the deal at hand gives an indication of how the company should be valued in the context of a deal. This approach uses the transaction multiples of comparable deals and applies those multiples to the target's operating metrics. For example, if the average multiple of sales for five comparable transactions is 1.5 times, the proposed target should probably also sell for a multiple of sales in this range. Comparable transaction multiples analysis is discussed at greater length in Chapter 6.

Premiums Paid Analysis: Premiums paid analysis also looks at comparable public transactions; however, it determines the average premiums over the stock prices of the comparable targets that were paid just prior to the announcement of the transaction and applies that stock price premium to the company under consideration. For example, if the average premium paid was 30%, then the target company could sell for roughly the same premium. Premiums paid analysis is reviewed in Chapter 6.

[C]   Pro Forma Merger Analysis

Merger analysis studies the impact of a transaction on the surviving company, and indicates an acquirer's ability to pay. It is another set of data points that validates or invalidates a transaction. It may be feasible to value a target company and find that even though its valuation may be attractive, the overall impact of the transaction on the surviving company may be negative, and thus, be cause to terminate the deal discussions.

There are two principal forms of transaction valuation: accretion/dilution analysis and contribution analysis.

Accretion/Dilution Analysis: This analysis looks at the impact of the transaction on the surviving company by evaluating its pro forma earnings post-transaction relative to the stand alone earnings of the predecessor acquiring company prior to the deal. For example, a company that has stand alone projected earnings of $1.25 per share may have pro forma earnings of $1.30 per share post transaction. In this case, the transaction would be accretive. Accretion/dilution analysis is covered in more detail in Chapter 7.

Contribution Analysis: This methodology analyzes the relative contribution of revenues, gross profits, operating profits, and earnings of each company that is party to the transaction. It benchmarks the contribution of each company against their relative ownership in the combined company post transaction. For example, if a company contributes 50% of revenues, gross profits and earnings to the combined company, yet its shareholders receive 40% of the ownership in the combined company, it may make sense to revisit the deal. Contribution analysis is covered in more detail in Chapter 7.

[D]   Other Analyses

The analyses just presented are the primary indicators of company value, deal value, and deal success. They are by no means the only approaches to valuing a transaction. The following chapters also discuss other useful techniques. Chapter 8 discusses leveraged buyout analysis, often used to value more mature companies that have strong cash flows. Chapter 9 explores price/volume relationships, which show the range of prices within which a public company has traded over a period of time. This analysis helps us understand when and at what price investors purchased stock in the target and whether the current trading price reflects any market sentiment supporting a sale of the company or some other form of event that could enhance shareholder value. Chapter 10 provides an overview of private company analysis and the key factors that differentiate it from public company analysis. Chapter 11 reviews the entire valuation framework in the context of a case study.

§2.04   SUMMARY

Valuation and financial analysis is a vital aspect of assessing the viability of a transaction. Armed with the right analyses, the principal negotiator in a deal should be well prepared to construct an agreement that makes sense for shareholders and creates value. The valuation methodologies presented here are some of the more common forms used by investment bankers. However, it is important to remember that valuation and financial analysis alone are not sufficient to substantiate a transaction. Rather, it is imperative to combine the analysis with strategic and business rationale to develop a complete picture of a transaction's likely success.

Chapter 3

FINANCIAL STATEMENT ANALYSIS

§ 3.01   OVERVIEW

Central to corporate finance valuation is the analysis and understanding of financial statements. Financial statement analysis (FSA) provides us with an approach to understanding a company's income statement, balance sheet and cash flow, assessing its growth, profitability and capital structure, and evaluating its utilization of assets and capital.

Why is financial statement analysis important? It offers a number of tools that help us determine whether or not a target company is an attractive acquisition or merger candidate, better understand a company's position within a sector, compare one industry sector with another, assess the impact of a transaction on the surviving entity, and determine the optimal approach to financing the transaction. It is also an important precursor to company and deal valuation. Without a sound understanding of financial statement analysis, it is difficult to assess the validity of valuation tools and analysis.

Financial statement analysis allows us to assess the profitability, efficiency, liquidity and leverage of a target company. The analysis evaluates gross and operating margins, the utilization of assets and capital in generating those margins, returns on capital and assets that margins provide, the resulting cash flow that is delivered, and the balance sheet that supports the company's profits. FSA provides a context within which to evaluate the overall financial success of the company, on a stand alone basis and compared to other industry competitors, and whether the management team has accomplished its mandate.

FSA provides a snapshot of a company's health at a given point in time and in the context of its historical performance. A company's ratios may indicate its absolute and relative performance, yet the ratios also provide a basis for comparing current with past financial health. Combined, FSA can provide a strong statement regarding a company's improving or deteriorating financial and operating performance within the context of its own financial statements, as well as in the context of its industry peer group.

Finally, financial statement analysis enables comparison between industry sectors to evaluate the relative shifts in profitability, returns on capital, leverage and industry position.

§3.02 PROBLEMS WITH FINANCIAL STATEMENT ANALYSIS

While financial statement analysis is an important tool, it has certain drawbacks that qualify its application. First, FSA often ignores company-specific issues. For example, it may not take into consideration recent significant capital expenditures that were expended to support new technology and fuel future growth. Thus, in the absence of understanding a company's particular situation, financial statement analysis by itself may not provide a complete picture of a company's past performance or future prospects.

Second, financial statement analysis is based on certain assumptions that may not be relevant in a given sector and must be adjusted for. For example, certain companies — or industries — may rely more heavily on capital or operating leases, while others may rely more on the ownership of assets. Comparing financial statements across companies and industries should take this thinking into consideration.

Third, FSA ignores size and therefore must be used in conjunction with an analysis of common size statements. Size is an important factor in establishing the strength and health of a company. Financial statement analysis tends to ignore size and therefore, companies should be compared on a common size and absolute basis in order to optimally assess a company's performance ratios or other metrics.

As an adjunct to the concern over size, efficiency and leverage may also skew the analysis in that ratios do not necessarily factor in growth and operating efficiencies. Therefore, evaluating ratios in the absence of a strong understanding of a company's story and particular situation may result in a less-than-perfect analysis.

Fourth, ratios are used for different purposes. For example, a lender may rely heavily on ratios that compare a company's leverage and interest expense to its cash flow, while an investment banker may not be as sensitive to these ratios and rely more on margins, profitability and return on capital.

Fifth, FSA is typically performed at quarter or year-end, and therefore ignores interim variances and issues such as seasonal or monthly working capital swings. This anomaly keeps open the possibility that companies may "dress up" their financial statements for quarter or year-end results. In addition, companies may have different fiscal years and thus comparing companies across periods should be done on the same basis.

Finally, companies utilize different accounting methodologies, for example, the valuation of inventory using LIFO or FIFO methods. These, and other, accounting differences should be taken into consideration as one employs financial statement analysis.

§3.03 ELEMENTS OF FINANCIAL STATEMENT ANALYSIS

Financial statement analysis is a broad approach to evaluating the financial health of a company. It entails not just a rote analysis of the financial ratios of a company, but rather, a comprehensive review of its financial statements, footnotes, management discussion and analysis and other public documents, in order to obtain a well-informed picture of the company's past performance and future prospects.

FSA involves independently analyzing the primary financials for a company, i.e., its income statement, balance sheet and cash flow, reviewing ancillary material such as the footnotes, management discussion and analysis, and auditor's opinion, and then factoring third party analysis, such as equity research reports, into the equation. Once this is complete, it is also important to place the company analysis in the context of its industry peer group and review common sized financial statements and ratios.

[A]   Income Statement Analysis

An annual income statement is typically produced at the end of a company's fiscal year, which in many cases may also be at calendar year-end. For public companies, the income statement is found as a public filing with the SEC in a 10-K or annual report. Interim income statements are also produced at the end of each quarter. These public filings are found in a company's 10-Q's. The income statement provides us with valuable information. First, one can evaluate the historical growth rates of a company at multiple levels in the income statement: revenues, gross profit, operating profit, EBITDA, pre-tax earnings, net income and earnings per share.

Second, the income statement — including detailed operating data — may provide us with a breakdown of revenue and operating profit or EBITDA by segment, product, geographic market or business unit. This is important information as it offers a window into how the company is performing at a granular level and whether any business units, markets or products are suffering or overwhelming other areas. It affords a view of concentration risk and how a company's core business makeup is changing. The income statement also reveals how margins at the gross and operating level are changing, and whether there are any noteworthy issues to consider.

Inasmuch as an income statement provides a good indicator of growth and profitability, it also offers incites into the relationship between debt and equity capital and net income growth, and the impact a company's financial strategy has on earnings. For example, if, during any given period, a company raised debt or equity capital, net income and consequent earnings per share may be materially affected. To the extent debt capital is raised, the company's net income would be impacted by the increase in interest expense. To the extent equity capital is raised in the interim period, the company's earnings per share are materially impacted. Thus, while a company's operating earnings may be increasing at an attractive rate, if the company has extended itself through the assumption of incremental debt or through raising incremental equity, its earning per share may be materially impacted, suggesting that shareholder value creation may not be in line with the increase in operating earnings.

Therefore, an income statement not only provides us with a means to measure the growth and profitability of a company, it also offers one measure on the efficacy of the company's financing strategy.

[B]   Balance Sheet Analysis

Like an income statement, a balance sheet is found in the 10-K, annual report or 10-Q. It articulates a company's capital structure and presents short-term and long-term assets and liabilities as well as a record of the company's shareholder equity account. While any individual balance sheet provides a snapshot of a company's capital structure at the end of any given period, it also provides a context for evaluating any inter-period changes in balance sheet accounts. In particular, by evaluating the trends in a company's balance sheet, we are better able to assess the quality of a company's revenues and cash flows.

The primary areas of focus in balance sheet analysis are: (1) working capital management, (2) asset management, (3) capital management and (4) return analysis. Each provides and indication of a company's current financial health and how it utilizes its assets and liabilities.

Working capital assets includes cash and short-term investments, accounts receivables, inventory, prepaid expenses and other current assets, while working capital liabilities includes accounts payable, accrued liabilities, notes payable, current maturity of long-term debt and other current liabilities. The utilization of these short-term items helps determine the level and quality of a company's cash flows, and the efficiency of its cash flow generation. For example, quarter-over-quarter increases in a company's receivables without a commensurate increase in payables may be symptomatic of a company's deteriorating cash flow position. Likewise, a buildup in inventory above levels of comparable companies or in relationship to a company's sales, may indicate a slowdown in its growth or, conversely, an expectation of near-term growth. The change in the net difference between working assets and working liabilities as a percentage of sales is a strong indicator of how a company is either investing in its working capital or draining its working capital. The most effective way to analyze this is to exclude cash and short-term investments as follows:

$$\text{Net working capital} = (\text{Accounts Receivable} + \text{Inventory} \\ + \text{Prepaid Expenses}) \\ - (\text{Accounts Payable} + \text{Accrued Liabilities})$$

Then, evaluate the net working capital for each period as a percentage of sales for the most recent four quarters. To the extent the percentage is increasing over time, a net investment in working capital was required to generate the increase in sales. On the surface, this may suggest that a company is having to be more aggressive in order to generate revenue than it had been in the past.

Analysis of working capital may also indicate how a company is financing its growth. Many companies have credit facilities in place to support working capital needs. While utilization of a working capital line is not a negative observation, it is prudent to understand why a company utilizes the line and what assets are used as collateral for the line. For example, a company in high-growth mode may be forced to draw down on its credit line to have sufficient cash to operate the business, while a more mature company may generate sufficient cash flow from operations in order to support inventory investment as well as other operating needs. To further clarify, it is prudent to ascertain whether a company has sufficient availability in its credit lines to support future growth. In other words, while today, a company may exhibit strong growth, its future growth may be impacted by its availability of short-term liquidity.

Long-term assets include property, plant and equipment (PP&E) while long-term liabilities include bank debt, public debt, subordinated debt and other forms of long-term financing. Evaluating a company's property, plant and equipment will give one a sense for what types of assets are used to support revenue generation and provides a measure of whether a company has a greater—or lesser—investment in PP&E than its peers. The PP&E account net of depreciation will also provide a window into the age of assets and whether the company may be subject to future capital expenditures to update its fixed assets.

Companies finance themselves with different forms of capital including short-term debt, long-term debt—senior and subordinated, preferred stock and equity. A company's decision to use one or more of these instruments to finance its operations will depend on the type of asset to be financed—working capital, machinery, real estate, etc., the life of the asset to be financed, and the cost of capital of the instrument to be used. For example, it would be typical to see working capital financed via a revolving credit facility that can be drawn down or paid back as needed, while a new office building is likely to be financed with long-term mortgage debt.

Analysis of a company's capital accounts will offer a gauge on how levered a company is stand alone and by comparison to its peer group. In addition, it helps us evaluate how a company has financed its assets and operations, and whether the financing strategy has resulted in attractive returns to shareholders. While it is true that returns to shareholders can be leveraged with the increasing use of debt, in that a company's overall cost of capital will decline with the increasing use of debt, it is also true that each industry and company has its own maximum level of debt above which the company's risk of default increases exponentially, eliminating the benefits of leverage and exposing shareholders to bankruptcy.[1]

In evaluating a company's capital structure, it is wise to assess the absolute amount of debt that the company is supporting and compare it to other companies in the sector. It is also prudent to evaluate the different forms of debt to ascertain whether the assets and operations have been prudently financed. Finally, by linking the company's earnings and cash flows to the company's capital structure and assets, one can determine whether the company is generating a return to providers of capital and on assets that is attractive by itself and relative to comparable companies.

---

1. For a broader discussion on cost of capital, please refer to *Chapter 4: Discounted Cash Flow Analysis.*

[C]   Cash Flow Statement Analysis

Much like the separate analysis of the income statement and balance sheet, cash flow statement analysis reveals a few additional pieces of information that are not as readily available in the other statements. The statement of cash flows supplements the information provided in the income statement and balance sheet, with a focus on the cash flows derived from operating, financing and investing sources. For example, distinct from EBITDA, operating profit and earnings before interest and taxes, the cash flow statement provides a measure of the company's operating cash flow. Operating cash flow is the cash flow that is derived from the business operations, distinct and apart from the cash flow derived from the company's investing and financing activities. Depending on the sector, operating cash flow can have multiple definitions, however, one common definition is as follows:

$$\text{Operating Cash Flow} = \text{Net Income} + \text{Depreciation \& Amortization} - \text{Capital Expenditures} - \text{Increase in Working Capital}$$

In addition to assessing the operating, financing and investing cash flow of a company, the statement of cash flows offers a concrete view of the changes in a company's working capital, which allows us to analyze how the company is either using its working capital as a source of cash or as a means to invest in growth.

[D]   Common Size Analysis

Common size analysis is a vehicle for comparing a company's financial statements across a given sector. This type of analysis eliminates the size difference between companies in a sector and allows one to standardize the financial statements as a percent of specified benchmark. For example, the income statement is usually spread as a percentage of sales or revenues, while the balance sheet is typically spread as a percentage of assets.

Common size analysis allows us to analyze financial statements of multiple companies in a sector to determine industry and company differences on a common scale. It also allows us to look at companies in different sectors to determine variability between sectors. Finally, the analysis evaluates trends over time on a common scale which simplifies the analysis considerably.

Exhibit 3-1 provides an illustration of common size analysis of the income statement and balance sheets for Tropical and Global.

[E]   Footnotes

The footnotes to a company's financial statements may reveal interesting insights into a company's financials. They qualify unusual items on the income statement, show changes in accounting methods for certain categories, highlight significant issues, and explain that which is not immediately obvious. Footnotes can appear at the bottom of each page in the financial statements or at the end of the entire presentation.

Exhibit 3-1
Common Size Comparison of Tropical Products and Global Snacks

	Tropical Products	Global Snacks
Common Size Income Statement[2]		
Revenues	100.0%	100.0%
Cost of Goods Sold	59.6%	53.5%
Gross Profit	40.4%	46.5%
EBITDA	21.2%	22.3%
EBIT	16.9%	17.6%
Net Income	8.6%	9.2%
Common Size Balance Sheet[3]		
Assets		
Cash and Cash Equivalents	0.1%	5.4%
Accounts Receivable	11.5%	8.2%
Inventory	16.6%	9.7%
Other Current Assets	0.8%	4.0%
Total Current Assets	29.0%	27.2%
Net Property, Plant & Equipment	29.9%	53.4%
Intangible Assets, Net of Amortization	27.8%	13.9%
Other Assets	13.3%	5.5%
Total Assets	100.00%	100.0%
Liabilities and Shareholders' Equity		
Accounts Payable	10.3%	7.3%
Notes Payable	4.0%	0.0%
Other Current Liabilities	11.4%	9.9%
Total Current Liabilities	26.1%	17.2%
Total Long-Term Debt	21.7%	32.2%
Non-pension Post Retirement Benefits and Other	11.4%	7.1%
Deferred Tax	4.9%	8.5%
Total Liabilities	64.1%	64.9%
Capital Stock	1.3%	0.4%
Capital Surplus	3.7%	7.3%
Retained Earnings	64.4%	27.4%
Treasury Stock	−33.5%	0.0%
Total Shareholders' Equity	35.9%	35.1%
Total Liabilities and Equity	100.00%	100.00%

2. Most recent 12 months ended third quarter 2001.
3. Most recent 12 months ended third quarter 2001.

The footnotes work in tandem with the financial statements, and provide further information on a number of topics including, accounting methodologies, assumptions made by management in preparing the financial statements, unusual charges and expenses, and hidden or off-balance sheet liabilities.

[F] Management Discussion and Analysis

The management discussion and analysis (MD&A) section of the financial statements provides color to the company's financial statements. Specifically, the MD&A offers testimonial behind the historical changes in the business, current trends, and how these trends may affect the future. The MD&A explains each major item in the financial statements and provides the reasoning and rationale behind substantive differences.

[G] Third Party Commentary

One valuable source of information for financial statement analysis is third party analysis. This can come in a variety of forms including equity research reports, rating agency analyses, credit reports, and the like. There are a multitude of third parties that offer analytical tools and corporate financial analysis for free or for a fee.

§ 3.04 CATEGORIES OF FINANCIAL STATEMENT ANALYSIS

There are four primary categories of financial statement analysis. Profitability analysis benchmarks a company's gross, operating and other margins in terms of their percentage of sales as well as their return on investment. Efficiency analysis explains how well a company utilizes its assets. Liquidity analysis assesses a company's liquid resources to fund operations. Leverage analysis evaluates a company's leverage in the context of its assets and equity, and provides evidence of its ability to service its debt and other fixed charges.

While there are standard definitions for each ratio in every category of analysis, there may be sector specific definitions that pertain to given companies and industries. Regardless of what ratio is evaluated, it is important to calculate a given ratio the same way for all companies in an entire analysis on the same basis.

[A] Profitability

A company's profitability can generally be defined as its sales minus cost of goods sold less all the expenses that are required generate the profits. Using this broad definition, profitability can be measured on a variety of bases, including at the gross margin level, i.e., sales minus cost of goods sold, at the operating profit level, i.e., sales minus cost of goods sold minus operating expenses, at the EBITDA level, i.e., earnings before interest, taxes, depreciation and amortization, and, among others, at the net income after tax level.

[1]   Analysis of Return on Sales

A number of ratios help define a company's profitability as measured by return on sales. As with all ratios, each of these should be considered in light of their industry-specific definition.

[a]   *Gross Margin.* Gross profit is the absolute dollar amount of profits generated from sales and after deducting the cost of such sales. For example, for a basic product manufacturer, the gross profit is the sales generated by the product minus the cost of the product that is sold. Gross profit does not include any of the operating expenses associated with selling or marketing the product or any of the selling, general or administrative expenses. The measure for assessing gross profits is gross margin, as defined below.

$$\text{Gross Margin} = \frac{\text{Gross Profit}}{\text{Sales}}$$

In certain industries, companies may have different measures of revenues, sometimes known as gross revenues or net revenues, and thus any definition of gross margin should reflect these differences.

[b]   *Operating Margin.* The operating profit of a company is defined by subtracting the direct operating expenses of a business from its gross profit. Operating margin as defined below, is the measure of profitability that articulates the company's operating return on sales.

$$\text{Operating Margin} = \frac{\text{Operating Profits}}{\text{Sales}}$$

Operating margin specifically ignores the effects of investment or asset sales, financing and taxes, and rather, focuses on the profitability of the company's core operations.

[c]   *EBIT Margin.*[4] EBIT margin is similar to operating margin yet may include investment income or income from asset sales. It does not include the effects of financing, i.e., interest expense, or taxes. EBIT margin is defined below.

$$\text{EBIT Margin} = \frac{\text{EBIT}}{\text{Sales}}$$

[d]   *EBITDA Margin.*[5] EBITDA margin excludes financing and tax effects as well as depreciation and amortization, and is defined as follows:

$$\text{EBITDA Margin} = \frac{\text{EBITDA}}{\text{Sales}}$$

---

4. EBIT = Earnings before interest and taxes.
5. EBITDA = Earnings before interest, taxes, depreciation and amortization.

Exhibit 3-2
Profitability Analysis for Tropical Products and Global Snacks[6]

	Tropical Products	Global Snacks
Gross Margin	40.4%	46.5%
EBIT Margin	16.9%	17.6%
EBITDA Margin	21.2%	22.3%
Pre-Tax Margin	13.2%	14.2%
Net Income Margin	8.6%	9.2%

[e]   Pre-Tax Margin. Pre-tax margin includes the effects of financing but excludes the impact of taxes. It is defined below.

$$\text{Pretax Margin} = \frac{\text{Pretax Profit}}{\text{Sales}}$$

[f]   Net Income Margin. Net income margin includes the effects of investment income and asset sales, financing and taxes. Net income margin excludes any impact of dividends.

$$\text{Net Income Margin} = \frac{\text{Net Income}}{\text{Sales}}$$

Exhibit 3-2 provides a comparative profitability analysis of Tropical Products and Global Snacks.

[2]   Analysis of Return on Investment

A company is only able to generate revenue and cash flow if there has been a certain amount of investment in the business. This investment can come in the form of equity or debt, and is spent on purchasing different types of assets ranging from real estate to machinery to inventory. Return on investment measures the level of profitability against the amount and type of investment. In other words, the analysis of return on investment tells us how well a company — and its peers — has invested in its assets to generate profitability.

Typically, return on investment is measured by using a pre-tax measure of profitability, such as earnings before interest and taxes (EBIT). EBIT provides a measure of profitability for all providers of capital, i.e., debt and equity capital providers. It also excludes any impact of taxes.

[a]   Return on Assets. A company's ability to generate revenue is dependent on investment in certain types of assets depending on its industry or sector. For example, a restaurant's revenues are dependent on

---

6. Most recent 12 months ended third quarter 2001.

a facility to house the restaurant and the raw ingredients required to prepare the food. There is a cost associated with utilizing assets as well as a cost of expensed items, such as personnel costs. Each type of asset will help generate a different level of revenue, and the consequent returns on investment for a given company.

A standard definition of return on assets is defined below. This measure looks at EBIT in relation to average total assets for a company. The average total assets is determined by taking the most recent year's EBIT and dividing it by the average of the most recent year's total assets and the prior year's total assets.

$$\text{Return on Assets} = \frac{\text{EBIT}}{\text{Average Total Assets}}$$

It is also common to perform this calculation utilizing Net Income adding back the after-tax cost of debt in order to obtain a pre-financing, post-tax earnings figure.

[b] *Return on Equity.* Return on equity analyzes the return to equity providers of capital, and therefore utilizes pre-tax income as the numerator in the equation. It is also common to use net income after taxes to measure return on taxes, as it takes into consideration the taxes paid by the company. The ratio for return on equity is shown below.

$$\text{Return on Equity} = \frac{\text{Pre-tax Income}}{\text{Average Stockholders Equity}}$$

[c] *Return on Capital.* Return on capital analyzes the return to all providers of capital, and therefore utilizes EBIT in the numerator in the equation. The denominator is calculated using the sum of the average total debt and stockholders' equity for the most recent year and prior year. Return on capital may also be calculated by substituting EBIT with net income after tax plus the after tax cost of debt financing in order to obtain an after-tax, pre-financing cost profitability figure. The ratio is shown below.

$$\text{Return on Capital} = \frac{\text{EBIT}}{\text{Average (Total Debt + Stockholders' Equity)}}$$

Exhibit 3-3 provides a comparative return on investment analysis for Tropical Products and Global Snacks.

[B] Efficiency

Efficiency explains how well a company utilizes its various assets, not necessary how profitably. In other words, instead of measuring the profitability of a company in terns of its asset classes or its capital, it measures, for example, how frequently a company "turns over" or sells and replaces its inventory, or how frequently its is able to bill and collect its receivables.

Exhibit 3-3
Return on Investment Analysis for Tropical Products and Global Snacks[7]

	Tropical Products	Global Snacks
Return on Assets	14.0%	11.9%
Return on Equity	49.8%	37.5%
Return on Capital	14.0%	11.9%

[1] Inventory Turnover Ratio

Inventory turnover measures how efficiently a company uses its inventory. The ratio measures the company's annual cost of goods sold against its average inventory balance for the period, as seen below.

$$\text{Inventory Turnover Ratio} = \frac{\text{Cost of Goods Sold}}{\text{Average Inventory}}$$

[2] Inventory Days

Inventory days converts the inventory turnover ratio into a measure on an annual basis, and tells us how may days of inventory a company had on hand for a given period.

$$\text{Inventory Days} = \frac{365}{\text{Inventory Turnover Ratio}}$$

[3] Receivables Turnover

Similar to inventory turnover, receivables turnover looks at how efficiently managed the company's receivables are. The ratio measures annual sales against average receivables.

$$\text{Receivables Turnover} = \frac{\text{Sales}}{\text{Average Receivables}}$$

[4] Days Sales Outstanding

Days sales outstanding further converts receivables turnover into a measure of how many days worth of inventory were outstanding for a given period.

$$\text{Days Sales Outstanding} = \frac{365}{\text{Receivables Turnover}}$$

---

7. Based on balance sheet data for year ended 1999 and 2000.

[5]   Payables Turnover

Payables turnover analyzes the company's payable cycle and measures its purchases against its average accounts payable for a given period.

$$\text{Payables Turnover} = \frac{\text{Purchases}}{\text{Average Accounts Payable}}$$

[6]   Days Payables Outstanding

Days payables outstanding converts payables turnover into a measure of how many days worth of payables were outstanding for a given period.

$$\text{Days Payables Outstanding} = \frac{365}{\text{Payables Turnover}}$$

[7]   Working Capital Turnover

Working capital turnover reviews all classes of working capital as it relates to sales. In other words, what is the turnover of working capital that supported sales for a given period.

$$\text{Working Capital Turnover} = \frac{\text{Sales}}{\text{Average Working Capital}}$$

[8]   Fixed Asset Turnover

Fixed asset turnover measures the turnover in fixed assets as it relates to sales for a given period.

$$\text{Fixed Asset Turnover} = \frac{\text{Sales}}{\text{Average Fixed Assets}}$$

[9]   Total Asset Turnover

Total asset turnover measures the turnover in total assets as it relates to sales for a given period.

$$\text{Total Asset Turnover} = \frac{\text{Sales}}{\text{Average Total Assets}}$$

Exhibit 3-4 provides a comparative efficiency analysis for Tropical Products and Global Snacks

[C]   Liquidity

Liquidity analysis offers a view of a company's liquid resources available to fund operations. These liquid resources include current assets such as cash,

Exhibit 3-4
Efficiency Analysis for Tropical Products and Global Snacks[8]

	Tropical Products	Global Snacks
Inventory Turnover Ratio	2.7×	3.5×
Inventory Days	137	103
Receivables Turnover	5.9×	7.8×
Days Sales Outstanding	62.3	46.6
Payables Turnover	4.4×	8.9×
Days Payables Outstanding	83.0	40.9
Working Capital Turnover	6.0×	8.9×
Fixed Asset Turnover	2.9×	1.3×
Total Asset Turnover	0.8×	0.7×

marketable securities and accounts receivable, adjusted for the impact of current liabilities. In addition, liquidity analysis reviews how a company's cash flow from operations is available to service near-term liabilities and commitments.

[1] Current Ratio

The current ratio is a common means for analyzing a company's short-term assets and liabilities, and measures all the company's current assets versus its current liabilities. The greater the current ratio, the greater the company's ability to service its current liabilities.

$$\text{Current Ratio} = \frac{\text{Current Assets}}{\text{Current Liabilities}}$$

[2] Quick Ratio

The quick ratio looks specifically at the company's most liquid assets including cash, marketable securities and accounts receivable, and measures the sum of these against current liabilities.

$$\text{Quick Ratio} = \frac{\text{Cash} + \text{Marketable Securities} + \text{Accounts Receivable}}{\text{Current Liabilities}}$$

[3] Cash Ratio

The company's cash ratio further details the company's liquidity by focusing exclusively on the cash and marketable securities current assets as they relate to current liabilities.

$$\text{Cash Ratio} = \frac{\text{Cash} + \text{Marketable Securities}}{\text{Current Liabilities}}$$

---

8. Based on balance sheet data for years ended 1999 and 2000.

Exhibit 3-5
Liquidity Analysis for Tropical Products and Global Snacks[9]

	Tropical Products	Global Snacks
Current Ratio	1.1×	1.6×
Quick Ratio	0.4×	0.8×
Cash Ratio	0.0×	0.3×
Operating Cash Flow Ratio	0.7×	0.5×

[4]   Operating Cash Flow Ratio

The operating cash flow evaluates a company's cash flow from operations (OCF) in the context of its outstanding current liabilities.[10]

$$\text{Operating Cash Flow Ratio} = \frac{\text{Cash Flow From Operations}}{\text{Current Liabilities}}$$

Exhibit 3-5 provides a comparative liquidity analysis for Tropical Products and Global Snacks

[D]   Leverage

Leverage ratios evaluate a company's leverage as it relates to total capital and equity, and in the context of a company's ability to service the interest expense and principal repayment.

[1]   Debt-to-Total-Capital Ratio

Debt-to-total-capital ratios provide a measure of how healthy a company's balance sheet is by itself and in relation to its peer group. Total debt is defined as current debt plus long-term debt, while total capital is defined as total debt plus total equity. Companies with high debt-to-total-capital ratios are considered leveraged and have less financial flexibility than those with lower debt-to-total-capital ratios.

$$\text{Debt-to-Total-Capital} = \frac{\text{Total Debt}}{\text{Total Capital}}$$

[2]   Debt-to-Equity Ratio

Debt-to-equity ratios evaluate a company's debt in the context of the total equity in the firm. High debt-to-equity ratios are indicative of high leverage and

---

9. Based on balance sheet for third quarter 2001.

10. OCF = Net income plus depreciation and amortization minus an increase in working capital.

less financial flexibility than those companies with low debt-to-equity ratios. For this ratio, it is appropriate to use the book value of the company's debt.

$$\text{Debt-to-Equity} = \frac{\text{Total Debt}}{\text{Total Equity}}$$

As an alternative, it is common to use market-based ratios for both debt and equity to further assess the leverage of a company. Thus, total debt and total equity can be substituted with their market-based equivalents.

$$\text{Market Debt-to-Equity Ratio} = \frac{\text{Market Value of Debt}}{\text{Market Value of Equity}}$$

There are a number of caveats to utilizing market-based ratios. First, market values of debt and equity can fluctuate dramatically over a short period of time and thus an analysis one day may not be relevant another. Second, while the debt on a company may trade at a discount to its book value, in the context of a transaction, the debt may need to be reacquired at its face value, and thus it may not provide an accurate portrayal of leverage in the context of a transaction.

[3] Times Interest Earned (TIE)

Also known as interest coverage ratio, times interest earned measures a company's ability to service its interest expense on its debt. It is typical to use earnings before interest and taxes (EBIT) as the unit of measure in calculating TIE.

$$\text{TIE} = \frac{\text{EBIT}}{\text{Interest Expense}}$$

[4] Fixed Charge Coverage Ratio

An alternate means for evaluating a company's ability to meat its obligations is to expand the definition of obligations to include other "fixed charges" not simply interest expense. Fixed charges may include items such as lease payments. In this case, the appropriate unit of measure to determine the fixed charge coverage ratio is earnings before fixed charges and taxes.

$$\text{Fixed Charge Coverage Ratio} = \frac{\text{Earnings Before Fixed Charges and Taxes}}{\text{Fixed Charges}}$$

Where, fixed charges include not only interest expenses but also principal payments on debt and leases.

Exhibit 3-6 provides a comparative leverage analysis for Tropical Products and Global Snacks.

Exhibit 3-6
Leverage Analysis for Tropical Products and Global Snacks[11]

	Tropical Products	*Global Snacks*
Debt-to-Total Capital Ratio	0.2×	0.3×
Debt-to-Equity Ratio	0.6×	0.6×
Times Interest Earned	4.9×	4.8×

§ 3.05　SOURCES OF INFORMATION

There are multiple sources of public and private information that can be drawn upon for financial statement analysis. Private information most likely comes directly from the target company and may include internal historical and projected financial information such as budgets, operating plans and forecasts.

Public information is available from a variety of sources and can be accessed through a number of online and other sources. Public companies are required to disclose certain information on their company. These documents can be found through the Edgar database and other similar sources. Documents that should be reviewed include an annual report, a document prepared by the company on an annual basis and distributed to shareholders; a 10-K, a disclosure document that provides annual information on the company and its finances; a 10-Q, a disclosure document that provides quarterly financial information on a company; a 8-K, a document that is periodically filed to provide periodic updates on significant events; a proxy statement, a document filed and mailed to shareholders on an annual basis in advance of a company's shareholder meeting, and registration statements, documents that are required to be filed when a company registers securities to raise capital or in the context of certain M&A transactions.

Other public information that can be accessed includes equity research reports, prepared by research analysts for dissemination to investors, credit analyst reports, that evaluate a company's credit worthiness and analyze its leverage.

§ 3.06　FINANCIAL STATEMENT ANALYSIS IMPLICATIONS FOR M&A AND SHAREHOLDER VALUE

Financial statement analysis often stands independent of shareholder value considerations and mergers and acquisitions. It is frequently used by analysts to determine the credit worthiness of a company. It is used by individual investors to analyze their equity investments. It is used by accountants to challenge certain assumptions with respect to a given company. Yet, FSA also plays an important role in M&A and shareholder value creation.

---

11. Based on balance sheet data for third quarter 2001.

FSA is used as a support feature to simple company analysis. First, it allows the analyst to assess historical financial statements and build credible forecasts based on historical trends and ratios. Second, it enables the comparison of a target company with its peer group in order to assess the target's growth, profitability, efficiency and leverage.

Financial statement analysis also supports other forms of valuation analysis such as comparable trading multiples, comparable transaction multiples and discounted cash flow analysis.[12] In trading multiples analysis, the operating and valuation multiples of comparable companies are applied to the target's ratios to determine a valuation based on the multiples of its peer group. FSA offers a means to check whether the operating performance and leverage of the peer group are reasonable in comparison to the target company, and whether there are unique considerations that should be taken into account when applying the multiples.

The same logic applies to transaction multiples analysis in which the multiples of transactions comparable to the one under consideration are applied to the target's parameters to derive a transaction-based value. FSA once again provides an objective view on the applicability of certain multiples to the metrics of the target company.

In discounted cash flow analysis, financial statement analysis assists the analyst in building forecasts that most accurately reflect the target company's financial performance. It allows comparison between historical and projected periods; evaluation of a target's performance relative to its peer group, and an objective assessment of the feasibility of its projections.

In building financial forecasts, FSA helps identify unique company-specific problems and how those issues may affect future performance. For example, a company's utilization of assets may have been poor historically — for a reason, yet its projected utilization may be dramatically different.

Outside of building forecasts and performing valuation analysis, financial statement analysis helps identify common industry problems that may impact the logic behind an acquisition.

Finally, FSA helps assess the impact of an acquisition on the surviving corporation in a transaction. It looks at the pro-forma profitability, efficiency, leverage and liquidity of the company post transaction.

§3.07 SUMMARY

Financial statement analysis allows us to evaluate a company stand alone, in relation to its peer group, and across industry sub-sectors. Much like comparable multiples, financial ratios provide a barometer of a company's performance. They help answer such questions as: Has the company grown at the expense of margins? Is it growing faster than its peers? Is it generating a return on capital and investment

---

12. Please refer to Chapters 4, 5 and 6 for a more detailed description of discounted cash flow analysis, trading multiples analysis and transaction multiples analysis.

that is commensurate with its earnings growth? Is it using its working capital wisely? Does its balance sheet afford enough financial flexibility to grow?

Potential buyers and investors don't only look at comparable multiples as a gauge of value. They also analyze other financial ratios to determine the overall health of a company and industry. These ratios include sales and earnings growth, gross margin, operating margin, changes in working capital, return on capital, return on investment, return on assets and capital investment.

Chapter 4

DISCOUNTED CASH FLOW ANALYSIS

§ 4.01 OVERVIEW

Discounted cash flow (DCF) analysis is one of the most widely used valuation methodologies. It forms the core of most undergraduate and graduate school corporate finance curricula and serves as the foundation for the mergers and acquisitions valuation tool kit. DCF analysis is used to value everything from small projects, such as an investment in machinery, to large acquisitions and joint ventures.

Discounted cash flow analysis is an intrinsic value approach that places a value today on the future cash flows of a target company. The cash flows are projected for a defined period, and then discounted back to the present using a discount rate that approximates the target company's cost of capital. An assumption is made about the value of the target company after the projection period. Known as the terminal value, this value is also discounted back to the present, and then added to the present value of the cash flows. This exercise produces a present value that represents the value today of all the cash flows that can be generated by the target in the future.

The entire analysis is based on two fundamental tenets. First, DCF analysis assumes that a dollar today is worth more than a dollar tomorrow. In other words, if $100 were invested in a savings account today earning 5%, it would be worth $105 one year from when it was invested. Likewise, $105 one year from today would be equal to $100 today at a 5% investment rate. Second, DCF analysis assumes that investments with different risk profiles command investment rates commensurate with their level of risk. For example, a corporation's public debt with a one-year maturity may bear an interest rate of 6%, while a U.S. Government security with the same maturity, backed by the credit of the United States, may bear an interest rate of only 5%. DCF analysis relies on the selection of an appropriate discount rate that reflects the risk profile of the cash flows being valued.

DCF analysis is integral to valuation in mergers and acquisitions. Take the case of two companies in the same industry that are for sale. Company A is mature, has $1.0 billion in sales, is growing at 5% per year, has 10% operating margins, and has a strong balance sheet with little debt. Company B is young, has $750 million in sales, is growing at 15% per year, has 9% operating margins, and has a highly leveraged balance sheet. Without substantial analysis, it is difficult to tell which company has a higher value: Company A might, because it is larger and has a stronger balance sheet; Company B may, because it is growing faster. Discounted cash flow analysis helps us understand the value of a company based on its stand alone financial performance and the risk of its business.

Fundamental to understanding the value differential between the two companies is the discount rate that is used to value the cash flows derived from each business. Company A, with its size, strength, and stability, is likely to have a relatively low discount rate, implying a relatively higher valuation. Company B, with its slim margins, small size, and weak balance sheet, is likely to have a relatively higher discount rate, indicating a lower value for its cash flows. Unfortunately, DCF analysis does not depend solely on a company's discount rate. It incorporates a variety of factors that influence value. These are each explained in more detail in the remainder of the chapter.

§ 4.02 THE ANATOMY OF DISCOUNTED CASH FLOW ANALYSIS

There are a few terms that need to be defined in order to gain a comprehensive understanding of discounted cash flow analysis. Each of these will be discussed further in this chapter.

Free Cash Flow: This is typically defined as the "unleveraged" after-tax cash flow of a company. It is calculated by taking the earnings before interest and goodwill amortization[1] and tax affecting those earnings. The following items are then

---

1. Note: Subsequent to the elimination of pooling accounting in 2002, goodwill amortization is no longer as relevant.

added back to this "after-tax" number known as EBIAT: depreciation and change in working capital. Capital expenditures, or investment in fixed assets, are then subtracted to yield the free cash flow of the company.

> Earnings Before Interest After Taxes (EBIAT)
> + Depreciation
> + Change in Working Capital[2]
> − Capital Expenditures
> _____
> = Free Cash Flow

Unleveraged free cash flows are typically used because these cash flows support all providers of capital. First, a company is usually financed with two primary sources of capital: equity and debt. The providers of those sources are entitled to returns on their capital commensurate with their level of risk. The free cash flows in theory are used to provide the return to both the debt and the equity providers. Since they are unleveraged, they do not include any impact of interest payments. In this sense then, free cash flows are "free" to be used for all providers of capital.

Discount Rate: This is the rate of return required by an investor, given the level of risk associated with the investment. In DCF analysis, the discount rate used for the target company is its cost of capital. The discount rate is used to derive a net present value for the business by discounting the free cash flows and terminal value of the target to the present. Because the free cash flows used are unleveraged, the discount rate is determined by analyzing the company's cost of debt and equity financing. The calculation yields a discount rate known as a "weighted average cost of capital" (WACC).

Forecast Period: This is the period in the future for which the target company's free cash flows are projected. Free cash flows are usually forecast for five, seven, or ten years, depending on the ability to accurately forecast them. Forecasts are typically based on specific assumptions regarding the operating performance of the target company.

Terminal Value: This is the value of a company attributed to the free cash flows that are expected to be generated after the forecast period in perpetuity. The terminal value is calculated in the first year after the forecast period, known as the "terminal value period." Since the terminal value incorporates the company's free cash flows in perpetuity, it can often represent a high percentage of a company's overall value.

---

2. Working capital is typically defined as current assets minus current liabilities. Debate can often center around whether or not cash and short-term investments are included in the definition. For DCF valuation purposes, it is advisable to separate restricted cash and cash necessary to operate the company on a daily basis from excess cash not utilized in current working capital.

§ 4.03   DCF METHODOLOGY

A number of steps are required to perform a DCF analysis. First, calculate the target's weighted average cost of capital or the rate that will be used to discount the free cash flows. Second, forecast the target's free cash flows by projecting its income statement, balance sheet, and cash flow statement. Third, calculate the target's terminal value. Fourth, perform the analysis.

[A]   Calculating an Appropriate Discount Rate

The discount rate used in DCF analysis varies with the type of business being valued. Businesses with greater risk profiles will command higher discount rates and vice versa. Factors contributing to a higher risk profile include: size of the business, stage of development, leverage, and industry sector. These risks are reflected in the discount rate as they are incorporated in the company's cost of equity and cost of debt financing.

As it is most common to perform a discounted cash flow analysis on free cash flows that are unleveraged, the discount rate used is calculated using the weighted average cost of capital methodology and incorporates the target's cost of debt and equity financing.

Alternatively, it is possible to use "levered" cash flows in a DCF analysis. These cash flows take into consideration the interest expense paid to debt holders of the company. In this case, the discount rate used is the target company's cost of equity, since the debt holders have already been paid their return via interest payments.

[1]   Cost of Equity

A company's cost of equity is the rate of return that investors demand in order to invest in its stock. It is calculated using a celebrated concept known as the Capital Asset Pricing Model (CAPM). This model prices a company's equity using three variables: a risk free rate, an equity market premium, and the target company's Beta. The CAPM formula is as follows:

$$\text{Cost of Equity } (k_e) = \text{Risk Free Rate } (R_f) + \text{Beta } (\beta) \times \text{Equity Market Premium } (R_m)$$

For example, given the following information, we can calculate the cost of equity for a company:

Beta $= 1.10$
Risk Free Rate $= 7\%$
Equity Market Premium $= 6\%$

$$
\begin{aligned}
K_e &= R_f + \beta(R_m) \\
    &= (7\%) + (1.10) \times (6\%) \\
    &= 13.6\%
\end{aligned}
$$

[a] *Beta.* Beta is a measure of risk determined by correlating the performance of a company's stock to the general performance of the market. Betas usually can be found in a wide range from 0.5 to 1.15, depending on the volatility of the target's stock compared to the overall market at the time of the analysis. To illustrate, if during a certain period, the overall market increased 7% and the company's stock increased 7%, its Beta would be 1.0. Likewise, if during the same period, its stock rose 9%, its Beta would be 1.29. The same logic applies if when the overall market falls by 7%, the company's stock falls 9%. Higher Betas suggest greater risk in the company's stock, since it is more volatile than the market. Exhibit 4-1 shows recent Betas for a broad range of public companies.

Betas are not something that you need to worry about deriving, they are readily available from a number of services, including Barra and Value Line. Each service may use a slightly different methodology; however, there are two conventional forms of Betas that are usually used in DCF analysis: historical Betas and predicted Betas. Historical Betas are derived by performing an historical correlation of a company's stock with the overall market. Predicted Betas are derived by performing a regression analysis on historical information to derive a projected Beta for the company.

When using Betas, it is common to use a levered Beta for the target company. This Beta assumes that the company's volatility will depend partly on the company's capital structure. To determine the levered Beta, calculate the average unlevered Beta for the target's peer group and then relever the Beta using a target capital structure for the company. The formula for unlevering a Beta is as follows:

$$\text{Beta(L)} = \text{Beta(U)} \times [1 + (D/E)(1 - T)]$$

Where,

$Beta(L)$ = Beta of company with leverage
$Beta(U)$ = Beta of company without leverage
D/E = Company's debt to market value of equity
T = Income tax rate of the company

Exhibit 4-1
Recent Betas for Public Companies

Company	Industry	Beta
Oracle	High Technology	1.81
Home	Depot Consumer	1.25
Ford Motor Company	Basic Industries	1.07
Bank of America	Financial Services	1.04
Pfizer	Health Care	0.60

As an example, assume that a peer group of companies has an average levered Beta of 1.25 and a debt to market equity ratio of .20. Also, assume that the target has an ideal debt to equity ratio of .15. Using the above formulas, if we first unlever the average peer group Beta, we get an unlevered Beta of 1.04. If we then relever the Beta using the target's debt to equity ratio, we get a target Beta of 1.19.

Companies in the same industry will tend to have Betas that are in a similar range, since a portion of a company's stock price performance compared to the over-all market is dependent on the sector in which it does business. Another means for validating a target company's Beta is to cross-check it with those of its peer group. In addition, as Betas are not calculated for privately held companies, it is feasible to use a composite Beta of an industry sector as a proxy for the Beta of a private company.

[b]   Risk-Free Rate. The risk-free rate is the interest rate ascribed to a theoretically "riskless" security. Typically, the yield on government bonds is used, most often in the ten–20 year maturity range. Current yields on gov-ernment bonds can be found in the Wall Street Journal, on Bloomberg terminals, and most sophisticated financial Web sites. For example, the yield on the 20-year Treasury Bond on March 22, 2002, was 6.02%.

[c]   Equity Market Premium. The equity market premium is the return that investors who invest in the stock market demand over the risk-free rate of return. Typically, the equity market premium ranges between 5% and 7%. Current estimates of the equity market premium can be obtained from a num-ber of sources, the most reliable of which is from, Ibbotson & Associates.

[2]   Cost of Debt

A company's cost of debt is the interest rate at which it could fund itself in the market at the time of the analysis. There are a number of ways to determine a com-pany's cost of debt. First, to the extent the company has public debt, it is possible to check the current yield on its debt in the Wall Street Journal or on various online sources. Second, if the company has bank debt, the interest rate on that debt often will be disclosed in the company's public information, such as its 10-K or 10-Q. Third, it is also possible to discuss current funding costs with a company's inter-nal treasury department or with the commercial lending arm of a bank. Finally, much like cross-checking Betas, it is possible to analyze the composite lending rates of comparable companies in the target's sector.

As the entire DCF analysis is performed on an after-tax basis, the cost of debt used in determining a discount rate is also calculated on an after-tax basis. Therefore, given the following information:

$$
\begin{aligned}
\text{Cost of Debt} &= 9\% \\
\text{Tax Rate} &= 34\% \\
\text{After Tax Cost of Debt } (k_d) &= (\text{Cost of Debt}) \times (1 - \text{Tax Rate}) \\
&= (9\%) \times (66\%) \\
&= 5.9\%
\end{aligned}
$$

[3]   Weighted Average Cost of Capital

The weighted average cost of capital (WACC) combines the cost of the target company's debt and equity, determined by analyzing the percentage of the company that is financed with debt and the portion financed with equity. It reflects the weighted average return required by a target company's debt and equity holders. To calculate a WACC, we first need to determine the company's target capital structure. This is a normalized capital structure that takes into consideration a number of factors including: the company's existing capital structure, its long-term ideal capital structure, and the overall capital structure for its industry peer group. The relative proportions of debt and equity used are calculated by estimating the total market capitalization of the target company by summing its equity market capitalization and its total debt outstanding. This is then evaluated in the context of the capital structure for its peer group, derived by looking at comparable public information. This information is then compared to a theoretical ideal capital structure for the target company.

Given the following information, we can derive the WACC for a company:

$$
\begin{aligned}
K_e &= 13.6\% \\
K_d &= 5.94\% \\
\text{Percent Debt} &= 30\% \\
\text{Percent Equity} &= 70\% \\
\text{WACC } (K) &= (\text{Percent Debt}) \times (K_d) + (\text{Percent Equity}) \times (K_e) \\
&= (30\%) \times (5.94\%) + (70\%) \times (13.6\%) \\
&= 11.3\%
\end{aligned}
$$

Based on the calculation, a discount rate of 11.3% would be used in the DCF analysis. However, given the number of variables in the WACC analysis, it is prudent to use a range of discount rates around the one derived from the analysis. For example, for the discount rate derived above, it would be typical to use a 1% range around the rate, i.e., 10.3% to 12.3%.

[B]   Preparing Financial Forecasts

There are a few points to make on financial projections that are specific to discounted cash flow analysis. The free cash flows from a company should be projected based on company-specific historical and projected financial information, as well as information regarding its industry and the economy as a whole. As you build the financial projections, it is important to cross-check your future results with past experience for the company. Unless there are some new assumptions regarding investment or a change in the business model, I would be careful not to deviate too dramatically from past growth rates, margins and investment.

When projecting financial statements, the most effective model is one that contains a separate income statement, cash flow and balance sheet, as well as other pertinent financial ratio and metric worksheets. For optimal usage, each worksheet in the financial projections should work together, so that changes to one assumption will flow through the entire model. For example, a decrease in sales should not only appear in the income statement, but on the balance sheet as well, through a possible reduction in working capital. Much like financial statements, the discounted cash flow analysis should work in tandem with the projections so that changes to the base projections are reflected immediately in the DCF analysis.

A note of caution: DCF analysis is usually performed on cash flows that are unleveraged. As you build the DCF portion of the model, make sure that your free cash flows exclude any impact of leverage on the company.

[C]   Calculating Terminal Value

For most companies, it is possible to create financial forecasts for a reasonable period, usually from three to ten years, although you should make your own assumptions about the predictability of the target business. Depending on the type of business, after the initial forecast period it becomes very difficult to predict future financial performance. A variety of factors will influence the unpredictability of financial performance, including the target company's sector, technology shifts, government regulation, and the economic climate as a whole. The terminal value is ordinarily calculated in the terminal value period, in the first year after the financial projections. Deciding when to calculate the terminal value will depend on the cyclicality of the business as well as the company's position within the industry.

Depending on when in the company's cycle the terminal value is derived, the overall valuation for the target can vary widely. For example, calculating terminal value at the top of a cycle instead of the bottom of the cycle could lead to an unrealistically high perception of value — the cycle high cannot last forever.

There are four different approaches to calculating a company's terminal value: the growth in perpetuity method, the multiples method, the sale method, and liquidation value. While the most common techniques are the perpetuity and multiples methods, each has a slightly different rationale.

Growth in Perpetuity Method: This approach assumes that the target company's free cash flows continue in perpetuity after the initial forecast period. The fundamental premise underlying this methodology is that during the terminal value period, i.e., after the financial projections, the target company's business model does not significantly change and the economic environment does not dramatically shift. Consequently, simplifying assumptions are made about key financial metrics, such as sales growth, operating margins, working capital usage and capital expenditures. These assumptions are encapsulated in a formula to derive the terminal value.

Multiples Method: Much like the perpetuity method, this approach assumes that the target company continues to grow in perpetuity. However, instead of calculating the terminal value based on internal growth rates, the terminal value is calculated using different multiples, e.g., price/sales, price/earning, price/EBIT or market/book value. The underlying premise is that the target company will continue to "trade" in the market place much like its peer group. Therefore, the multiples used are based on those of the target company's industry peers. By default, the multiples act as proxies for the company's perpetual growth rate.

Sale Method: The sale method is one that is rarely used, but nonetheless it merits discussion. Like the multiples approach, this methodology uses various multiples to derive the terminal value; the difference, however, is that the multiples are based on comparable sale transactions for companies in the target's industry. This is an aggressive approach since it may yield an abnormally high terminal value, and incorporates two levels of risk. First, it requires that the target be sold in the terminal period. Second, it assumes that the premiums in sale transactions will still be possible at the end of the forecast period.

Liquidation Value: Another rarely used approach is liquidation value. This methodology is typically used for projects or companies with a limited life or where the cash flows deteriorate over time. The terminal value is based on the liquidation value of the assets at the end of the initial forecast period.

[1] Growth in Perpetuity Method

This approach makes simplifying assumptions, known as "steady state assumptions," after the initial forecast period. These assumptions are based on the premise that the target company will not significantly change its business model in perpetuity and that the general economic environment will not change dramatically. There are five key assumptions about the future financial performance of the company that are made during the terminal value period to substantiate the terminal value. These assumptions are the sales growth rate, operating margin, tax rate, investment in capital, and change in working capital. The relationship between these metrics is assumed to remain constant during the terminal value period. Implicit in this assumption is that the target's free cash flow will "grow in perpetuity" at a constant or "steady state."

The growth in perpetuity model calculates the terminal value at the end of the terminal value period. This period lasts for one year, sufficient to derive a terminal free cash flow that is used in the calculation. The terminal value is based on a single formula that derives a present value of the perpetual cash flows resulting from the terminal free cash flow. Once the terminal value has been calculated, it is then discounted back to the present along with the cash flows from the initial forecast period to derive the overall present value for the company.

The formula that is typically used for calculating the growth in perpetuity terminal value can be attributed to Myron J. Gordon, a well-known mathematician who derived the formula known as the Gordon Growth Model. The long form growth in perpetuity formula is as follows:

$$\text{Terminal Value} = \frac{\text{FCF}}{(1 + \text{WACC})} + \frac{\text{FCF}(1 + g)}{(1 + \text{WACC})^2} + \frac{\text{FCF}(1 + g)^2}{(1 + \text{WACC})^3}$$

$$+ \cdots + \frac{\text{FCF}(1 + g)^{n-1}}{(1 + \text{WACC})^n}$$

This formula can be rearranged into a simplified form:

$$\text{Terminal Value} = \frac{FCF}{WACC - g}$$

Where,

> *Terminal Value* = The value of the total enterprise, i.e., the value of the debt and equity of the company, at the end of the first year of the terminal value period
> *FCF*   = Free cash flow for the terminal period
> *WACC*   = Weighted Average Cost of Capital
> *g*   = The expected growth rate in free cash flow

Each component of the formula requires an estimate. First, the weighted average cost of capital should be calculated based on the explanation in this chapter. Second, the free cash flow for the terminal period should be estimated. Third, an assumption should be made regarding the perpetual expected growth rate in the free cash flow.

>   *[a]   Terminal Free Cash Flow.* From above, we know that free cash flow is defined as the following:

> Earnings Before Interest After Taxes (EBIAT)
> + Depreciation
> + Change in Working Capital
> − Capital Expenditures
> ‾‾‾‾‾‾‾‾‾‾‾‾‾‾‾‾‾‾‾‾‾‾‾‾‾‾‾‾
> = Free Cash Flow

When calculating the free cash flow for the terminal period, each key metric in the financial projection is forecast for one incremental period to derive the terminal free cash flow. However, when forecasting this free cash flow in particular, it is typical to make normalizing adjustments that convert the theoretical perpetual stream of cash flows into a steady state. Do not simply extend the forecast period by one year. You should estimate an independent free cash flow amount using the steady state assumptions specific to the terminal period. Often, the terminal period will have different growth rates and margins than the initial forecast period. These differences can have a dramatic impact on value. For example, if the terminal value is calculated just after a period of heavy investment, the free cash flow in the year just prior to the terminal value calculation will be unusually low because of high capital expenditures.

Therefore, it would be appropriate to modify the level of capital expenditures relative to sales, allowing the terminal value free cash flow to "reap the benefit" of the investment. Conversely, if the initial forecast period ends at the end of a cycle, and new investment is required to sustain growth, the free cash flow in the last year of the initial forecast period will be overstated, and the free cash flow for the terminal value period will need to be adjusted to reflect required investment to sustain sales growth.

Following is a list of some of the more important relationships to analyze:

- Operating margin as a percent of sales

- Capital expenditures as a percent of sales

- Change in working capital as a percent of change in sales

HINT: It is important to understand that the growth in perpetuity model is highly variable. Therefore, you should thoroughly understand the impact that each assumption has on the terminal value. One way to assess the impact of changes in the assumptions is to create a ratio that looks at the percent of the total company or enterprise value that is represented by the terminal value. By simply changing one or two variables, you will see how easy it is to change both the overall company value and the amount that the terminal value represents. Terminal value as a percentage of total value will be a lot higher for high growth companies than it will be for more mature companies. Typically, the terminal value for mature companies will represent between 10% and 20% of the total value, while for high growth companies, it may represent as much as 70% or 80%. Given the magnitude of the terminal value, it is very sensitive to the assumptions made regarding the terminal year.

---

[b] Expected Growth Rate. The terminal value is sensitive to changes in the expected growth rate. In most DCF analyses, there is considerable debate over the right growth rate to use. Picking an appropriate growth rate will depend on your insight into the target company's business and the industry in which it operates. As guidance, there are four factors that generally influence a company's growth rate: the expected long-term real rate of growth of the economy and the industry, the expected long-term inflation rate, and the competitive position of the company within its industry.

Two commonly used approaches for estimating a company's long-term growth rate are inflation and nominal GNP growth.

Inflation: As a proxy for long-term growth, inflation assumes a company can pass along increases in its costs, but cannot necessarily increase its volume. Estimates of historical and expected inflation are available from a number of sources. Arguments in favor of using inflation as a measure of growth maintain that it is difficult, if not impossible, for companies to sustain real long-term growth rates that exceed inflation. Various explanations have been offered, including that companies lose their competitive edge over time, driving down sales growth. It could also be that as markets mature, demand for a product becomes less.

Nominal GNP Growth: Using Nominal GNP Growth as an expected growth target is a more aggressive approach than using inflation. It assumes that a company can pass along increases in its costs and increase its volume at a rate equaling real growth in the economy. Proponents of using GNP growth believe that if a company can maintain its competitive position, it can sustain a growth rate higher than inflation. While there are those who argue for GNP growth as a good proxy for long-term growth, there are people who don't believe that the growth rate should exceed GNP growth. Their argument is that if the company grows faster than GNP in perpetuity, it could become larger than the entire economy!

Terminal value can be highly sensitive to different growth rate assumptions. Adjusting the growth rate can often have a large impact on terminal value. However, as you make assumptions about the expected growth rate, it is wise to rethink your assumptions about the capital required to support that level of growth, the margins that can be obtained, and the fixed and working capital required to support the sales growth. Consequently, as you adjust all of your assumptions, there may be very little impact on terminal value.

Exhibit 4-2 demonstrates the impact of changes in the expected growth rate on terminal value.

While there is much debate regarding the most appropriate expected growth rate, you will need to make your own decision about what growth rate to assume for the terminal value period. Even though you may make a defensible argument for a certain growth rate, it is also possible that your counter party can make just as strong an argument regarding its own proposed growth rate — and other assumptions.

[2]   Multiples Method

A terminal value may be calculated using multiples such as EBIT or EBITDA multiples. This is a common approach to determining terminal value, as

---

Exhibit 4-2
Impact of Growth Rate on Terminal Value
(Assumes a five year forecast)

Free Cash Flow (FCF) = $75
WACC   = 11.3%

$$\text{Terminal Value} = \frac{FCF}{WACC - g}$$

Expected Rate of Growth (g)	*Terminal Value*	*Present Value*
0%	$ 664	$389
1%	$ 728	$426
2%	$ 806	$472
3%	$ 904	$529
4%	$1,027	$602
5%	$1,190	$697

Exhibit 4-3
Calculating Terminal Value Using Multiples
(Assumes a five year forecast)

Final Forecast Year EBIT	= $80
Average Industry EBIT Multiple	= 8.0×
Terminal Value	= $640
Present Value at 11.3%	= $375

---

it is simple to calculate and is based on the trading multiples of the company's peer group.

First, calculate the current trading multiples (see Chapter 5) for the company and its peer group. Second, apply the average multiple from the peer group to the relevant financial metric for the target at the end of the forecast period. The resulting terminal value is then discounted back to present along with the free cash flows of the company. Exhibit 4-3 provides an example of using the multiples approach.

Remember that discounted cash flow analysis typically uses unleveraged free cash flows, and that these cash flows are to all providers of capital. When calculating terminal value using multiples, be careful to use the multiple that is applicable to the source of the cash flow. For example, EBIT and EBITDA multiples are enterprise value multiples. Therefore, the present value of the terminal value will correspond to the present value of the unleveraged free cash flows. Conversely, using a price/earnings multiple for calculating terminal value will yield a value that is inconsistent with the present value of the free cash flows. To remedy this situation, you should add the net debt of the target in the year you calculate the terminal value, in order to yield a correct measure of value.

[3] Sale Method

The sale method assumes the target is sold at the end of the forecast period. Deriving this sale value is difficult as it may be impossible to predict what a company may sell for in five or ten years. It is possible, however, to use current sale multiples for a group of companies that are comparable to the target.

To use the sale method, first calculate the transaction multiples for companies in the same industry as the target (see Chapter 6). Second, much like the multiples approach above, apply the multiples to the relevant financial metrics of the target to obtain the terminal value. The same cautions apply in that it is important to use multiples that are consistent with the unleveraged nature of the free cash flows.

The sale method has a number of downsides, the most important of which is that it is counter to the "going concern" approach of discounted cash flow analysis. By default, using the sale method will include a transaction premium that is event specific, not driven by the going concern mentality.

[4]   Liquidation Value

Liquidation value assumes that the assets of the business will be disposed of or liquidated at the end of the forecast period. Situations that are most appropriate for using liquidation value are when the company or project have a limited life or will not generate cash flows in perpetuity.

[D]   Performing the DCF Analysis

In performing the entire analysis, there are a couple of things to be aware of. First, the projected free cash flows from the initial forecast period are discounted back to the present using the target company's weighted average cost of capital (WACC). Because the free cash flows are unleveraged, it is important to remember to use the WACC, not the cost of equity, as the discount rate. Second, as you may recall, the terminal value derived from the Gordon Growth Model is a discounted present value, only, it is discounted to the terminal year. This value still needs to be discounted back to the time of the overall analysis. This is done by applying the weighted average cost of capital to the discounted terminal value and further discounting this number back to the present. Third, since the free cash flows are unleveraged, the terminal value is that for the overall enterprise. In order to derive the equity value or stock price for the company, the debt outstanding at the company must be subtracted from the enterprise value.

§ 4.04   DISCOUNTED CASH FLOW EXAMPLE

Following is an illustration of a discounted cash flow analysis. Let's assume that our two hypothetical companies, Tropical Products and Global Snacks, have initiated discussions regarding an acquisition of Global by Tropical. Both companies are in the snack food business, yet Tropical is larger and more mature, while Global is smaller with higher growth rates. Tropical has begun to perform its valuation work on Global, and as a first step, performs a DCF analysis.

Step 1: Calculate Global's Weighted Average Cost of Capital.

The first step for Tropical is to calculate Global's weighted average cost of capital. To do so, it must determine each of the components of the WACC formula.

(i) Beta Calculation

To calculate Global's Beta, the first step is to obtain the Beta for Global and its peer group, and then determine the average unlevered Beta for the universe. The peer group's unlevered Beta is then relevered using Global's target capital structure.

Exhibit 4-4 provides the overview of Global's and its peer group's predicted levered and unlevered Betas. From this analysis, we derive a target Beta for Global of 0.68.

Exhibit 4-4
Beta Calculation for Global Snacks
($ in millions)

	Debt	Equity Value	Enterprise Value	Cost of Debt	Tax Rate	Beta (L)	Beta (U)
Crunch Corp	$ 867	$4,002	$4,869	7.3%	40.0%	0.55	0.48
Fried Food Hldgs	$1,003	$1,869	$2,872	7.2%	38.0%	0.66	0.49
Health Nut	$1,407	$1,836	$2,242	4.5%	38.0%	0.55	0.48
Salty Seasons	$1,592	$3,036	$3,628	10.1%	40.0%	0.59	0.52
Sweeties	$1,393	$2,592	$2,985	7.7%	40.0%	0.71	0.55
			Average	**8.0%**	**39.2%**	**0.61**	**0.52**
			Median	**7.5%**	**40.0%**	**0.59**	**0.49**
Global Snacks	$1,732	$3,780	$5,512	7.2%	35.0%	0.69	0.53

Remember that we use a levered Beta for Global in our DCF analysis. The calculation to derive an unlevered Beta from a levered Beta is:

$$Beta(U) = \beta_L / (1 + (D/E)(1 - T))^3$$

And,

Target Beta = Avg. Unlevered Beta × [1+(1 − tax rate) × (target debt to equity ratio)]

(ii) Cost of Equity
Using the following formula:

$$K_e = R_f + \beta \times R_m$$

We can derive Global's cost of equity.
Our assumptions are as follows:

R_f = Yield on the 10-Year Government Bond = 5.2%
R_m = 8.1%
β = 0.68

---

3. Please note that if a company has preferred stock in its capital structure, the equations all need to be modified to include preferred stock in addition to debt.

Therefore, substituting our assumptions into the equation, we derive the cost of equity for Global of 10.7%.

(iii) Cost of Debt

Looking at Global's public debt, as well as having discussions with bankers regarding Global's cost of debt financing, we have determined that its pre-tax financing cost is approximately 7.4%. Using the following formula:

$$K_d = 7.2\% \times (1 - \text{tax rate})$$

and assuming the tax rate is 35%, on an after-tax basis, Global's cost of debt is 4.6%.

(iv) Weighted Average Cost of Capital

To derive the WACC for Global, we need to assimilate all the information from steps (i) through (iii). First however, we need to determine a target capital structure for Global. Exhibit 4-5 shows the comparable capital structures for Global and its peer group.

To derive a target capital structure for Global, the first step is to determine the average debt to market capitalization ratios for the peer group. The second step is to compare Global's capital structure with that of the peer group and make a determination regarding the optimal capital structure for Global.

The formula for deriving Global's WACC is:

$$K = (\text{Percent Debt}) \times (K_d) + (\text{Percent Equity}) \times (K_e)$$

Substituting the information from above, we get the following:

$$\begin{aligned} K &= (20.0\% \times 4.6\%) + (80.0\% \times 10.7\%) \\ &= 9.5\% \end{aligned}$$

Therefore, Global's weighted average cost of capital is 9.3%.

Exhibit 4-5
Comparable Capital Structures

	Debt	Equity Value (mm)	Enterprise Value (mm)	Debt to Cap. Ratio	Debt to Equity Ratio
Global Snacks	$1,732	$3,780	$5,512	31.4%	45.8%
Crunch Corp	$ 867	$4,002	$4,869	17.8%	7.3%
Fried Food Hldgs	$1,003	$1,869	$2,872	34.9%	7.2%
Health Nut	$ 407	$1,836	$2,242	18.1%	7.5%
Salty Seasons	$ 592	$3,036	$3,628	16.3%	10.1%
Sweeties	$ 393	$2,592	$2,985	13.2%	7.7%

Step 2: Forecast Global's Free Cash Flows.

Global's free cash flows are derived from the detailed projected income statement, balance sheet and sources and uses that are prepared as a part of the overall analysis. Exhibit 4-6 illustrates the free cash flows as per our definition of free cash flow.

From the five-year projections, we can see that Global's unlevered free cash flows are growing at a compound growth rate through the projection period of 7.5%. This compares to compound average growth in revenue and EBIT of 4.0% and 5.9%, respectively.

Step 3: Calculate Global's Terminal Value.

The two primary methods for calculating terminal value are the multiples method and the growth in perpetuity method.

(i) Multiples Method

Using EBITDA from the last year of the projection period, we can calculate the terminal value by applying enterprise value/EBITDA multiples to the metric. Based on comparable company analysis, discussed in detail in Chapter 5, we can see that comparable companies trade at multiples of six–eight times EBITDA, with an average multiple of 7.7 times. This yields a terminal value in 2006 of $7.5 to $9.6 billion. Remember that this is the future terminal value, and will need to be discounted back to present at Global's weighted average cost of capital to yield a present value of the terminal value. Exhibit 4-7 shows the terminal value calculation using EBITDA multiples.

Exhibit 4-6
Projected Free Cash Flows for Global Snacks
($ in millions)

	Projected					
	2001	*2002*	*2003*	*2004*	*2005*	*2006*
Revenues	$3,632	$3,778	$3,929	$4,086	$4,249	$4,419
EBITDA	819	864	911	960	1,012	1,066
EBIT	647	686	726	769	814	862
Less: Cash Taxes @35%	(226)	(240)	(254)	(269)	(285)	(302)
Tax Effected EBIT	$ 421	$1,446	$1,472	$1,500	$1,529	$1,560
Plus: Depreciation	172	178	184	191	198	205
Less: Capital Expenditures	223	231	239	247	256	265
Less: Inc. in WC	29	10	10	10	11	11
Unlevered Free Cash Flow	**$ 341**	**$1,384**	**$1,408**	**$1,434**	**$1,460**	**$1,489**

Exhibit 4-7
Terminal Value Calculation Using EBITDA Multiples

	EBITDA Multiple		
	7.0×	*8.0×*	*9.0×*
2006 EBITDA	$1,066	$1,066	$1,066
2006 Terminal Value	**$7,463**	**$8,529**	**$9,596**

Exhibit 4-8
Terminal Value Calculation Using Growth in
Perpetuity Method

Terminal Value = (FCF/(WACC 2 g))
WACC = 9.5%

	Expected Growth Rate		
	2%	*3%*	*4%*
2006 FCF	$ 489	$ 489	$ 489
2007 FCF	$ 499	$ 503	$ 508
Terminal Value	**$6,677**	**$7,786**	**$9,299**

(ii) Growth in Perpetuity Method

The growth in perpetuity method involves a number of steps. First, the free cash flow for the terminal period must be forecast using an expected growth rate. Since there is often debate over what growth rate to use, it is often worthwhile using a range of growth rates to accommodate all mindsets. In this analysis, we use 2%–4% as the expected growth rate, yielding a terminal free cash flow of $499 to $508 million. This free cash flow range is then inserted into our growth in perpetuity formula to derive the terminal value. Exhibit 4-8 demonstrates this analysis. For this exhibit, we use the single WACC of 9.5%. However, as you will see below, it is prudent to use a range of discount rates when calculating terminal values using the growth in perpetuity method. These discount rates should correspond.

Step 4: Perform the DCF Analysis.

Now that we have calculated Global's weighted average cost of capital, projected out its free cash flows, and calculated its terminal value, we are ready to perform the overall DCF analysis. To do so, we put together each of the inputs from the above analysis and combine them into two spreadsheets, one showing the

Exhibit 4-9
Discounted Cash Flow Analysis Using Multiples for Terminal Value

Discount Rate		9.5%	
Terminal EBITDA Multiple	7.0×	8.0×	9.0×
2006 EBITDA	$1,066	$1,066	$1,066
Terminal Value	$7,463	$8,529	$9,596
PV of Terminal Value	$4,748	$5,426	$6,105
PV of Free Cash Flows	$1,556	$1,556	$1,556
Implied Enterprise Value	$6,304	$6,982	$7,660
Plus: Cash & Cash Equivalents	$1,292	$ 292	$ 292
Less: Total Debt	$1,732	$1,732	$1,732
Implied Equity Value	$4,864	$5,542	$6,221
Implied Value Per Share	**$23.16**	**$26.39**	**$29.62**

Exhibit 4-10
Discounted Cash Flow Analysis Using the Growth in Perpetuity Method for Terminal Value

Discount Rate		9.5%	
Perpetual Growth Rate	2.0%	3.0%	4.0%
2006 FCF	$ 489	$ 489	$ 489
Continuing FCF (2007)	$ 499	$ 503	$ 508
Terminal Value	$6,677	$7,786	$9,299
PV of Terminal Value	$4,248	$4,953	$5,916
PV of Free Cash Flows	$1,556	$1,556	$1,556
Implied Enterprise Value	$5,804	$6,509	$7,472
Plus: Cash & Cash Equivalents	$ 292	$ 292	$ 292
Less: Total Debt	$1,732	$1,732	$1,732
Implied Equity Value	$4,364	5,069	$6,032
Implied Value Per Share	**$20.78**	**$24.14**	**$28.72**

DCF with the terminal value calculated using multiples and the other using the growth in perpetuity method. Exhibits 4-9 and 4-10 provide these calculations.

We can see from the two methodologies that the range of enterprise values for Global is between $5.8 and $7.7 billion. Assuming we have chosen reasonable inputs and assumptions, the two terminal value approaches should yield values in roughly the same ballpark. If they are not, it would be wise to revisit your assumptions to determine which of the variables or inputs may need adjustment. From the

DCF analysis, we can then translate the market value into equity and per share values for Global. Based on the analysis, Global's per share value of $20.78 to $29.62 per share is at a 15%–65% premium to its current stock price, indicating that Global may be undervalued in the market place.

§ 4.05   SUMMARY

Discounted cash flow analysis provides a means for valuing a company on a stand alone, going concern basis. It assumes that the target's cash flows grow during the forecast period, and then an assumption is made about the growth of those cash flows after the forecast period. The value obtained from a DCF analysis provides a benchmark value for a company assuming it continues to operate substantially the same as it has in the past, and assuming the economy does not dramatically change.

The range of values obtained from a DCF analysis can be quite large, depending on the assumptions made in growth rates, margins and terminal value. It can also vary widely if the range of discount rates used is wide. The analysis does not usually include a transaction or takeover premium, unless a premium is included in the terminal value. However, it is not uncommon for a discounted cash flow value to be less than and/or greater than a takeover value for a company. Consequently, while DCF analysis is an excellent tool for valuing a business, it should be used in conjunction with other valuation methodologies to determine a narrower range of values for a target.

Chapter 5

COMPARABLE COMPANY ANALYSIS

§ 5.01   OVERVIEW

A quick and simple valuation methodology is "comparable company" or "comparable trading multiple" analysis, an approach that values a target company based on the operating multiples and financial ratios of its industry peer group. This analysis gives us a means to compare a company's current valuation to that of its peer group and determine if it is under- or overvalued in the market. In addition, it gives us a methodology for valuing a business based on the overall valuation parameters of a sector or industry. In comparable company analysis, potential buyers or investors look at a number of enterprise and equity value multiples as well as other financial ratios ranging from market share to sales growth, gross margins to operating margins, and earnings to earnings growth. In addition, it analyzes a company's leverage and how well it utilizes its working and fixed assets.

By way of example, a shorthand approach to determining whether a public company is under-, fairly- or overvalued on a stand alone basis, is to look at the ratio of its stock price to its earnings, its "price/earnings" or P/E multiple. If a company has earnings of a $1.00 per share, and its stock price is $20 per share, then its P/E multiple is 20×. Conventional wisdom dictates that a stand alone company with a multiple equal to its projected earnings growth rate is fairly valued. If a company's earnings are expected to grow at 25% next year, its stock should theoretically trade at a 25 times multiple of its projected earnings. Therefore, for the same company with a $20 stock price, it is reasonable to conclude that it may be undervalued relative to its growth rate.

The same approach can be used to value a company based on the multiples of its peer group. If the average P/E multiple for the company's peer group, excluding itself, is 24×, the implied value per share for the target is $24 per share. This indicates that the stock is potentially undervalued in the market. Combined with the

61

Exhibit 5-1
Common Comparable Company Multiples

Enterprise Value/Sales
Enterprise Value/EBITDA (earnings before interest, taxes, depreciation and amortization)
Enterprise Value/EBIT (earnings before interest and taxes)
Equity Value/Historical Net Income
Equity Value/Projected Net Income
Price/Historical Earnings Per Share
Price/Projected Earnings Per Share
Price Earnings/Estimated Growth Rate
Enterprise Value/Book Value

---

stand alone P/E multiple analysis, the target would most certainly be undervalued, supporting an acquisition price in excess of its current stock price.

Comparable company analysis does not only analyze price/earnings multiples. It also includes other multiples such as revenue, EBIT and book value multiples. Exhibit 5-1 provides a summary of the key multiples that are used in comparable company analysis.

§ 5.02   ENTERPRISE VALUE VERSUS EQUITY VALUE

There are two primary modes for viewing the value of a company: enterprise value and equity value. There is often confusion between the two, and under what circumstances each is used. Enterprise value is the value of the company's total market capitalization, i.e., its equity plus its net debt. It is sometimes known as firm value, market value or aggregate value. Equity value is simply the value of the company's equity, i.e., its shares outstanding multiplied by its stock price. It is also sometimes known as equity market capitalization.

While these definitions provide a methodology for calculating value, they do not shed light on the difference between the two and why they are used in comparable company multiples analysis. This distinction is important because different multiples relate to either enterprise value or equity value, and mixing up the two can give you a distorted view of a company's value.

One way to compare enterprise and equity value is to understand that a company is typically financed via a combination of equity and debt. When a company generates cash flows, earnings, and profits, the various financing constituents are entitled to different cash flows depending on their level of preference in the capital structure. Specifically, before equity shareholders are entitled to any dividends from a company, the debt holders are entitled to payment for lending the company money. Therefore, theoretically, the debt holders are paid their interest from the cash flows generated above the net income line and the equity holders are entitled to dividends only after the debt holders — and taxing authorities — have been paid.

Enterprise value based multiples yield a valuation of the company on behalf of all the providers of capital — the equity holders and the debt holders. Therefore, the metrics used in calculating market value multiples should be those that provide cash flow to all levels of the capital structure, i.e., revenue, EBIT and EBITDA. Likewise, equity value based multiples yield a valuation on behalf of the equity holders and uses metrics after the distribution of interest payments to the debt holders and payments to taxing authorities, i.e., net income or earnings.

§5.03 COMPARABLE COMPANY VALUATION METHODOLOGY

Determining the multiples for a universe of companies yields important information about the group that can be used to assess the overall financial health of a sector and analyze the relative valuation and other financial metrics for specific companies within an industry. Comparable company multiples can also be used to determine the value of a target company — public or private.

The approach includes a number of steps. First, spread the individual financial and operating ratios for each company in the peer group, including the target company. Second, calculate the various enterprise and equity value multiples for each company, and determine the mean and median including and excluding the target company. Third, apply the average multiples from the peer group to the target company to derive an implied range of values. For example, if a group of companies excluding the target has an average price/earnings multiples of $21.0\times$ and the target's earnings are $1.10, then the implied stand alone equity value for the target would be $23.10 per share.

§5.04 HISTORICAL VERSUS PROJECTED MULTIPLES

Comparable multiples can be calculated off historical or projected financial ratios. However, it is typical to use historical ratios for all enterprise value based multiples and a combination of historical and projected ratios for equity value based multiples. The reason for this is that public companies do not generally disclose to the public their detailed forecasts for the business, while equity research analysts do publish projected estimates of earnings.

The convention for historical multiples is to use the prior four quarters worth of public numbers. These are known as the "last twelve month" (LTM) or "trailing twelve month" (TTM) numbers. The method for calculating the LTM numbers are as follows. Using revenues as the example, first, gather the public information on the company. Second, from the most current 10-K, use the most recent fiscal year's revenues as the base revenue. Third, from the most recent 10-Q, add the most recent set of revenue numbers to the base year. If the revenue number is for six months, add in the six months revenue number. If it is for nine months, add in the nine-month revenue number. Fourth, from the 10-Q for the corresponding

Exhibit 5-2
Calculating Last 12 Month Numbers
($ in millions)

Period/Source	Revenues
December 31, 2000 10-K	$1,000.00
March 31, 2001 10-Q	+$ 225.00
March 31, 2000 10-Q	−$ 185.00
LTM Revenues	$1,040.00

period for the prior fiscal year, subtract the revenue number for the corresponding period. Exhibit 5-2 provides a numerical example.

In this example, the analysis is performed after the end of the third quarter 2001. While the revenues for the most recent fiscal year ended December 2000 are $1,000 million, the revenues for the most recent four quarters ended March 2001 are $1,040 million.

For equity value multiples, it is common to look at both historical and projected financial ratios. Projected net income ratios are based on estimates derived from research reports provided by equity analysts from brokerage firms and investment banks. These research estimates are available from multiple sources including First Call, I/B/E/S and Hoovers, in addition to individual reports from research analysts or brokerage houses. It is common to look at more than one estimate in order to obtain a "consensus" forecast for the target.

When calculating a target's projected earnings, it is common to evaluate the next four or eight quarters that follow the most recent publicly announced earnings. Since most analysts provide their estimates on a quarterly basis, it is simple to calculate the projected earnings for a company. It is important, however, to ensure that the earnings estimates are calculated on the same basis in order to derive an apples-to-apples comparison. Make sure you check the footnotes to the earnings estimates to see if there are any major outlying assumptions that are incorporated in an earnings estimate, for example, a large stock issuance or debt financing.

It is also common for analysts to provide earnings estimates on a comparable basis for all companies in a sector. In this case, you may be forced to use annual estimates for each company in the peer group that are based on the same time frame.

§ 5.05   PRICE/EARNINGS MULTIPLES

The most helpful multiple is the price/earnings multiple. It provides a wealth of information about a company and its peer group. The single most important factor influencing a company's earnings multiple is its projected growth rate. However, investors will adjust the multiple placed on a company's earnings depending on its size, market position, performance relative to its peers, and its leverage.

In addition to providing earnings estimates, the equity research community will also usually provide an estimated growth rate for a company. Using this information, it is possible to calculate a ratio known as a "P/E to Growth Rate" (P/E/G). This ratio gives us a view on whether a company or sector is trading in line with its growth estimates. For example, a company trading at 100% of its estimated growth rate is considered fairly valued. Companies that have superior market position or brand recognition or that demonstrate a strong track record of meeting or exceeding their earnings targets can often trade higher than 100% of their estimated growth rates.

§ 5.06   COMPARABLE COMPANY ANALYSIS EXAMPLE

Let's look once again at the companies from our snack food industry case study. These are all mostly well-established public companies with good records of growth and profitability. In *Chapter 4: Discounted Cash Flow Analysis*, we derived a stand alone market value for Global Snacks of $5.9 to $7.7 billion or $21.35 to $29.71 per share. Comparable company analysis will give us another valuation benchmark for Global Snacks on a stand alone basis.

There are a number of steps to performing the comparable company analysis. First, spread the most recent financial metrics for Global Snack's peer group. Second, derive the historical and projected enterprise and equity value multiples including and excluding Global Snacks. Third, apply the multiples derived for the peer group to the financial metrics for Global Snacks to yield an implied value range.

Exhibit 5-3
Snack Food Comparable Financial Metrics
($ in millions)

	Enterprise Value[1]	Equity Value	LTM Sales	LTM EBITDA	LTM EBIT	LTM Net Income	Proj. Net Income
Global Snacks	$ 5,220	$3,780	$3,561	$ 794	$ 628	$328	$344
Tropical Products	$11,115	$8,975	$7,005	$1,487	$1,186	$600	$637
Crunch Corp	$ 4,842	$4,002	$3,001	$ 541	$ 413	$198	$198
Fried Food Hldgs	$ 2,794	$1,869	$3,153	$ 629	$ 498	$165	$168
Health Nut, Inc.	$ 2,220	$1,836	$1,902	$ 254	$ 190	$123	$122
Salty Seasons	$ 3,609	$3,036	$2,509	$ 367	$ 283	$145	$151
Sweeties, Inc.	$ 2,927	$2,592	$2,452	$ 403	$ 381	$196	$202

---

1. Enterprise value = equity value plus total debt, minority interest and preferred stock, less cash & cash equivalents.

Step 1: Spread Most Recent Financial Metrics for Peer Group.

From the 10-Ks and 10-Qs of the public companies, calculate the trailing 12 months results as well as the projected earnings for the companies. Exhibit 5-3 shows the recent financial metrics for Global Snack's peer group.

Step 2: Calculate Enterprise and Equity Multiples.

Now that we have the key metrics for each company, we can apply them to enterprise value and equity value multiples, as seen in Exhibit 5-4. This exhibit shows the multiples including and excluding Global Snacks.

The comparable company analysis of Global Snacks yields a number of insights. First, it is the second largest company in the sector as measured by revenues and by enterprise value. Its EBITDA and EBIT margins are higher than the average in the industry and above those of Tropical Products. It trades at a premium to the comparable universe based on revenues but at a discount to the peer group based on EBITDA and EBIT. It has the second highest amount of debt on its balance sheet, almost double the next most highly levered company. This results in an equity value that drops it to third in terms of size. Its historical and

---

Exhibit 5-4
Snack Food Comparable Multiples

	Enterprise Value to:			Equity Value to:		
	LTM Revenues	*LTM EBITDA*	*LTM EBIT*	*LTM Net Income*	*Projected Net Income*	*P/E/G[2]*
Global Snacks	1.5×	6.6×	8.3×	11.5×	11.0×	130×
Tropical Products	1.6×	7.5×	9.4×	15.0×	14.1×	220×
Crunch Corp	1.6×	8.9×	11.7×	20.4×	20.4×	240×
Fried Food Hldgs	0.9×	4.4×	5.6×	11.3×	11.1×	120×
Health Nut, Inc.	1.2×	8.7×	11.7×	15.3×	15.1×	150×
Salty Seasons	1.4×	9.8×	12.7×	20.3×	20.0×	180×
Sweeties, Inc.	1.2×	7.3×	7.7×	13.7×	12.8×	180×
Excluding Global:						
Average	**1.3×**	**7.8×**	**9.8×**	**16.0×**	**15.6×**	**180×**
Median	**1.3×**	**8.1×**	**10.5×**	**15.1×**	**14.6×**	**180×**
Excluding Global and Tropical:						
Average	**1.3×**	**7.8×**	**9.9×**	**16.2×**	**15.9×**	**180×**
Median	**1.2×**	**8.7×**	**11.7×**	**15.3×**	**15.1×**	**180×**

---

2. P/E/G is the price earnings multiple as a percentage of the company's projected earnings growth rate. It provides a relative valuation of a company by comparing its earnings multiple to its growth rate.

Exhibit 5-5
Comparable Company Value for Global Snacks
($ in millions)

	Global Metric	*Comparable Multiple*[3]	*Implied Enterprise Value*	*Implied Equity Value*[4]
LTM Revenues	$3,561	1.3×	$4,680	$3,241
LTM EBITDA	$ 794	7.8×	$6,180	$4,740
LTM EBIT	$ 628	9.8×	$6,152	$4,713
LTM Net Income	$ 328	16.0×	$6,685	$5,246
Projected Net Income	$ 344	15.6×	$6,788	$5,348

projected earnings multiples trail those of the industry and its P/E to growth rate is the second lowest of its peer group.

Step 3: Apply Multiples to Global Snack's Metrics.

Apply the multiples from the analysis in step 3 to the metrics of Global Snacks to yield a comparable company value. Exhibit 5-5 shows a comparable company enterprise value for Global between $4.7 and $6.8 billion, an equity value range of $3.2 to $5.4 billion and a price per share range of $15.43 to $25.47.

Based on this analysis, a few conclusions can be drawn. First, based on the multiples of its peer group, Global is trading at the lower end of the range of implied values — $18.00 versus an implied range of values of $15.43 to $25.47 per share. This suggests that Global is undervalued in the marketplace and the market has not given it credit for its stronger margins and growth rate. Second, it suggests a range of values that could be used in formulating an offer for Global. The range suggests that an acquirer could pay more than the current stock price of Global and still have some value in the company to share with the acquirer's shareholders.

§5.07   COMPARABLE COMPANY ANALYSIS VERSUS DISCOUNTED CASH FLOW ANALYSIS

Both DCF and comparable company analysis are good valuation tools. Each yields a stand alone, going concern value. However, both methodologies have their pros and cons. DCF analysis forces us to use explicit assumptions in valuing the business, whereas multiples analysis has a tendency to lump numerous assumptions into a single multiple as a proxy for growth, margins, or capital investment.

---

3. Based on the average multiple for the peer group including Tropical Products but excluding Global Products.

4. When calculating the implied equity value, it is important to remember to subtract the debt outstanding at the target.

By contrast however, the assumptions made in DCF analysis can be easily manipulated, while multiples are based on concrete comparable data.

As a result, it is prudent to use both methods as a means to check the other and determine how reasonable a valuation is. If the two methods, performed independently, generate values that are in the same range, it would seem logical that the valuation range is reasonable. Likewise, if the two analyses yield results that are dramatically different, it would make sense to review the assumptions underlying the DCF as well as the companies in the comparable multiple peer group.

From our DCF example in Chapter 4, we derived a range of values for Global of $5.9 to $7.7 billion or $21.35 to $29.71 per share. This compares to a range of values resulting from our comparable company analysis of $4.6 to $6.8 billion or $15.43 to $25.47 per share.

§ 5.08   SUMMARY

Comparable company analysis is a simple and relatively quick means for determining the stand alone value of a company. It establishes a value for the target based on the trading values of the company's peer group. Therefore, the value range does not include any form of takeover premium or speculation regarding a transaction. In the context of a merger or acquisition, it is likely then that a potential buyer would need to pay in excess of the implied value resulting from this analysis in order to acquire a company. This having been said, comparable company analysis can often reveal that a target company is trading at a significant premium or discount to the market and therefore may already have takeover speculation built into its stock price, or may be languishing in the market, indicating an opportunity for it to be acquired.

On a spectrum of valuation ranges derived from different methodologies, the comparable company valuation range is typically at the lower end of the spectrum and should help you establish a minimum bidding range for the target. Used in conjunction with other valuation methodologies, it helps provide a comprehensive view of the target's value. One should be careful in using comparable company analysis by itself for valuing a company because multiples can hide assumptions that discounted cash flow analysis makes explicit. Multiples provide no explicit information regarding long term sales growth, margins or investment patterns, while discounted cash flow analysis forces us to determine each of these parameters.

Used in conjunction with other methodologies, comparable company analysis is a valuable tool. Valuations based upon comparable multiples are sometimes used to check the reasonableness of a discounted cash flow valuation. If the two methods generate results that are dramatically different, you should challenge both the DCF and the comparable company analysis. Check whether the multiples used are truly comparable to the target in question and discern why the target trades in its present range of prices. Reexamine the assumptions in the discounted cash flow analysis to ensure they are reasonable.

HINT: While comparable company analysis is an indispensable tool in valuing a company, it is also helpful in evaluating the impact of an acquisition on an acquirer. Bearing in mind that companies are valued in the marketplace based on their margins and growth rates, to the extent an acquisition has a negative impact on a acquirer, its own multiples may be adversely impacted.

HINT: To the extent an acquirer's own multiples are less attractive than those of the target, it would be wise to strongly think through the rationale for the acquisition. Low multiple companies acquiring higher multiple companies may indicate earnings dilution. Conversely, high multiple companies acquiring low multiple companies may indicate multiple contraction of the acquirer post closing.

Chapter 6

COMPARABLE TRANSACTIONS ANALYSIS

§ 6.01   OVERVIEW

The comparable transactions method of valuation entails an analysis of the prices paid in deals comparable to the transaction under review. The acquisition multiples and takeover premiums used in the analysis are applied to the target's metrics to yield a transaction-based value. The rationale behind this approach stems from the fact that a company in a certain industry will sell for a price dictated by the market, and that the price will vary depending on the state of the market and the competitive acquisitions environment.

For example, a high growth technology company may command a higher price relative to its net income than would a mature coal company. There are two types of comparable transaction analyses: comparable transaction multiples and premiums paid. Both analyses suggest a range of values that could be paid for a target based on prices paid in comparable transactions. In other words, if the target company was acquired based on the multiples or premiums paid in comparable transactions, an acquirer could reasonably expect to pay a price for the target in the range suggested by the valuation approach. Comparable transaction multiples can be used with public and private companies, whereas premiums paid analysis only be used with public companies.

These two methods are important as they provide an event specific range of values for the target that incorporates an expected transaction or takeover premium. For example, to the extent companies in a sector have sold in the past for an average enterprise value/sales multiple of $1.4\times$, an acquirer could expect to pay in the same ballpark for its present acquisition. Likewise, if the average acquisition premium was 30%, the acquirer could expect to pay a 30% premium for its proposed acquisition.

Because comparable transaction analysis includes a transaction or takeover premium, it may yield a range of values that is higher than that resulting from DCF or comparable company analysis. However, the analysis is based on the merger and acquisition environment at the time each comparable transaction took place. Therefore, even though the overall analysis provides an apple-to-apples comparison of transaction data, each individual multiple or premium may have been influenced by the takeover market at the time of the particular transaction. In order to apply this valuation approach in a deal, make sure you do not apply the multiples or takeover premiums in a vacuum. You should understand the takeover market at the time of each comparable transaction, as well as the current market for mergers and acquisitions.

§ 6.02　　COMPARABLE TRANSACTION MULTIPLES ANALYSIS

Much like comparable company analysis, this analysis uses enterprise and equity values to analyze the multiples from comparable transactions. Exhibit 6-1 provides common acquisition multiples.

[A]　Methodology

Many of the multiples used in comparable transaction analysis are the same as those used in comparable company analysis, and the approach to determining the multiple is conceptually the same. However, there are a number of substantial differences in the way the multiples are used and calculated. These differences take place in the numerator (enterprise or equity value) and the denominator (financial metric) of the transaction multiple.

First, transaction multiples are typically calculated on a historical basis. For the peer group of companies, calculate the financial information for the denominator using the last 12 month information, ending on the most recent quarter prior to the announcement of the transaction. For example, if the transaction was announced on November 25, 2001, use the LTM data ending on September 30, 2001.

Exhibit 6-1
Common Transaction Multiples

Enterprise Value/Sales
Enterprise Value/EBITDA
Enterprise Value/EBIT
Equity Value/Net Income
Price/Earnings Per Share
Enterprise Value/Book Value

The most common information calculated for the peer group includes: LTM sales or revenue, LTM EBITDA, LTM EBIT, LTM net income,[1] and LTM EPS.[2]

Second, to calculate the market and equity values of the comparable transactions, there is a distinct methodology. Following is the definition of transaction equity value:

$$\text{Transaction Equity Value} = (\text{Target Shares Outstanding} \times \text{Offer Price}) \\ + (\text{Offer Price} - \text{Avg. Option Exercise Price}) \\ \times (\text{No. of Options Outstanding})$$

Where,

Target shares outstanding	= The number of shares outstanding at the time of the transaction.
Offer price	= The price offered for the company. If the acquirer uses its stock as the acquisition currency, base the offer price on the acquirer's stock price the day before the announcement of the transaction.
Average option exercise price	= The average price at which option holders can exercise their options into common stock of the company. (This information can be found in the company's annual proxy statement.) For this portion of the analysis to be valid, the offer price must be greater than the exercise price.
Number of options outstanding	= The total number of options that have an exercise price greater than the offer price.[3] Be sure to include warrants, if any.

Quite important is determining if the transaction was cash or stock. If it involved stock, use the acquirer's stock price one day prior to the transaction announcement to determine the equity value. For example, if the transaction was announced on November 25, 2000, use the closing stock price for the acquirer on November 24, 2001. While this is a general rule, you should use your judgment as to whether it is appropriate in all cases. There are transactions where the news of

---

1. Sales data should exclude any non-recurring or one-time items. EBIT, EBITDA, and net income should exclude any unusual or extraordinary charges.

2. LTM EPS should be calculated using the company's primary shares outstanding assuming a weighted average number of shares for the period. Do not use the period end number of shares outstanding.

3. In the calculation, assume that the option proceeds are included in the cash of the target.

the transaction was leaked prior to the announcement or where the market speculated that the transaction would take place. In those cases, the stock price of the acquirer is likely to have been affected by the premature news of the deal.

There will also be circumstances where, between the transaction announcement and closing, the terms of the deal may change. In this case, if the target has released public financial results subsequent to the announcement, it is appropriate to revisit the range of values derived from the analysis. For example, if the company released its results for the December 2001 quarter and the terms of the deal were changed prior to closing on March 1, 2002, the implied values for the target would be adjusted based on the LTM financial results for December 31, 2001.

Once the equity value has been calculated, make sure you add in the amount of net debt from the target that is being assumed by the acquirer. This will yield the enterprise value of the transaction. Following is the definition of net debt:

$$
\begin{aligned}
\text{Net Debt} = \ & \text{Total Debt} + \text{Accrued Interest} + \text{Dividends Payable} \\
& + \text{Minority Interest} + \text{Preferred Stock} + \text{Restructuring Reserves} \\
& - \text{All Cash Items} - \text{Investments} \\
& - \text{Equity Investments in Unconsolidated Subsidiaries}^4
\end{aligned}
$$

Where,

$$
\textit{Total Debt} = \text{Long} - \text{Term Debt} + \text{Short} - \text{Term Debt} + \text{Notes Payable}
$$

Following is the definition of Enterprise Value:

$$
\text{Enterprise Value} = \text{Transaction Equity Value} + \text{Net Debt}
$$

Third, the multiples obtained from the analysis are applied to the acquisition target's financial metrics. This will yield an implied transaction value.

[B] Example

In Chapters 4 and 5, we valued Global Snacks on a stand alone, going concern basis, yielding a range of values of $5.8 to $7.7 billion and $4.6 to $6.8 billion using discounted cash flow and comparable company analysis respectively. Using comparable transactions analysis, we can now derive a value for Global that includes a takeover premium.

Step 1: Spread the Financial Information for the Comparable Companies.

As a first step, much like in comparable multiples analysis, we spread the financial metrics of each company based on the trailing 12 months' financials for each company at the time of the deal. Exhibit 6-2 shows these financial metrics.

---

4. Use market value where possible; otherwise, use book value.

Exhibit 6-2
Financial Metrics for Comparable Transactions

Acquirer/ Target	Ann Date	Ent Value[5]	Equity Value	LTM Sales	LTM EBITDA	LTM EBIT	LTM Net Income	Book Value
Grupo Nationale/ Euromix	Jun 1, '01	$1,470	$ 853	$ 942	$128	$114	$36	$371
Wholegrains/ Biscuit Basket	Mar 5, '01	$1,450	$1,250	$ 967	$137	$109	$67	$417
Stage Two/ MishMash	Dec 5, '00	$1,287	$ 881	$1,313	$238	$165	$71	$275
Global Snack/ Claus Baking	Nov 20, '00	$ 625	$ 425	$ 568	$ 56	$ 42	$18	$304
Argyle Foods/ Homey Bagels	Jul 10, '00	$ 265	$ 275	$ 203	$ 31	$ 21	$15	$145
Biscuit Basket/ JJJ Jellies	Jun 15, '00	$ 456	$ 320	$ 304	$ 45	$ 32	$15	$119
Sweeties/ Baking Bonanza	Feb 12, '00	$ 445	$ 313	$ 445	$ 62	$ 49	$21	$149
Tropical Products/ Nutsahoy	Nov 5 '99	$ 241	$ 228	$ 165	$ 20	$ 17	$10	$ 65
Global Snacks/ Lekkers	Jul 23, '99	$ 302	$ 330	$ 275	$ 31	$ 22	$14	$103
Fried Food Hldgs/ Munchies	Apr 5, '99	$ 505	$ 445	$ 297	$ 41	$ 50	$27	$144

Step 2: Derive the Acquisition Multiples.

Once the metrics have been spread, we derive the transaction multiples for the peer group, as seen in Exhibit 6-3.

Step 3: Calculate the Implied Value for Global.

The average acquisition multiples from the comparable group are then applied to the relevant financial metrics for Global to derive implied enterprise and equity values as seen in Exhibit 6-4.

The implied range of values for Global based on comparable transaction multiple analysis is $4.7 to $8.0 billion in terms of enterprise value, $3.3 billion to

---

5. Enterprise value = equity value plus total debt, minority interest, and preferred stock, less cash & cash equivalents.

Exhibit 6-3
Comparable Transaction Multiples

Acquirer/ Target	Enterprise Value to:			Equity Value to:	
	LTM Revenues	LTM EBITDA	LTM EBIT	LTM Net Income	Book Value
Grupo Nationale/ Euromix	1.56×	11.5×	12.9×	23.6×	2.3×
Wholegrains/ Biscuit Basket	1.5×	10.6×	13.3×	18.7×	3.0×
Stage Two/ MishMash	0.98×	5.4×	7.8×	12.5×	3.2×
Global Snack/ Claus Baking	1.1×	11.1×	15.0×	23.7×	1.4×
Argyle Foods/ Homey Bagels	1.3×	8.6×	12.5×	18.7×	1.9×
Biscuit Basket/ JJJ Jellies	1.5×	10.2×	14.3×	22.0×	2.7×
Sweeties/ Baking Bonanza	1.0×	7.2×	9.0×	14.7×	2.1×
Tropical Products/ Nutsahoy	1.46×	12.2×	14.2×	23.0×	3.5×
Global Snacks/ Lekkers	1.1×	9.7×	13.6×	23.8×	3.2×
Fried Food Hldgs/ Munchies	1.70×	12.3×	10.1×	16.8×	3.1×
Average	**1.32×**	**9.9×**	**12.3×**	**20.1×**	**2.6×**
Median	**1.38×**	**10.4×**	**13.1×**	**22.0×**	**2.9×**

Exhibit 6-4
Implied Valuation of Global
($ in millions)

	Global Metric	Comparable Multiple[6]	Implied Enterprise Value	Implied Equity Value[7]
LTM Revenues	$3,561	1.32×	$4,701	$3,261
LTM EBITDA	$ 794	9.9×	$7,851	$6,411
LTM EBIT	$ 628	12.3×	$7,704	$6,265
LTM Net Income	$ 328	20.1×	$8,031	$6,591
Book Value	$1,916	2.6×	$6,423	$4,983

---

6. Based on the average multiple for the peer group.

7. When calculating the implied equity value, it is important to remember to subtract the debt outstanding at the target.

$6.5 billion in equity value, or $15.53 to $31.39 per share. This analysis suggests that if Global Snacks was valued based on the multiples paid in comparable transactions, a feasible range of purchase prices would be between $15.53 and $31.39 per share. The range of values encompasses and exceeds that derived in the comparable company analysis which is to be expected, since the transaction multiples analysis includes a premium for control.

[C] Notes of Caution

As you begin the analysis, questions will start to arise regarding the treatment of various items on the income statement, balance sheet and sources and uses of funds. Following are a few common issues that arise and suggestions for how to treat them.

Fees and Expenses: In many transactions, the investment banker, accounting and legal fees can be quite large. Since this is typically money that is paid out predominantly by the acquirer, it needs to be financed and therefore, a question arises over whether it should be included in the comparable transaction analysis; i.e., in the offer price calculation. While there are analyses that include it in the calculation, it is not typical to do so. Fees can vary widely, and in some cases, an investment bank is not used. Also, for past transactions, it may be difficult to obtain the information. Thus, fees are not included in the offer price calculation for comparable transactions; however, they are included in the proposed transaction's sources and uses of funds. Extraordinary and One-Time Charges: Many companies will have non-recurring items in the revenue, EBIT, EBITDA, and net income lines. These gains or losses are usually not included in the financial metric since they are nonrecurring, and do not reflect the ongoing operating profile of the company.

Convertible Securities: Today, many companies finance themselves using convertible securities such as convertible debt or convertible preferred stock. These securities are convertible into the common stock of the company at a predetermined stock price, the strike price. If the offer price for a company is greater than the strike price, the securities are considered "in-the-money." In this case, they are treated as common stock equivalents (CSEs) on an "as converted" basis. For example, if the strike price is $15 per share, and the offer price is $25 per share, the convertible security is in-the-money. The target's shares outstanding should be increased to reflect the conversion of the security. The income statement should be adjusted to reflect the new net income line: the after-tax interest on a convertible debt instrument would be added back; the dividend on a convertible preferred would be added back. Likewise, book value should be increased by the amount of stock issued for the convertible security.

Partial Acquisitions: It is not uncommon to see transactions where less than 100% of a company is acquired, e.g., 80% or 90%. Likewise, there are often circumstances where only a small portion of a company is acquired, e.g., 10% or 20%. You should use your judgment regarding the applicability of these transactions to your analysis. For example, if you are contemplating a 100% acquisition, and there is a comparable transaction in the target's industry where the acquirer purchased 10% of the stock of a company, you should question whether the data that would result from including this transaction in your analysis would yield helpful information. In cases where a significant stake is acquired, it is usual to gross up the amount of the acquisition to 100%. For example, if an acquirer purchased 95% of a company for $95 million, it would be appropriate to gross up the acquisition price to $100 million to yield a 100% purchase price.

There are situations where a significant portion of a company is acquired, e.g., 15%–40%, and where the acquirer already owns a significant stake in the target. These deals are known as "minority squeeze-out transactions." In these cases, you should be wary of including the multiples in your analysis, since often, this type of transaction can command a much higher premium than pure 100% acquisitions. Discussed in detail in Chapter 16, minority squeeze-out transactions tend to play by their own set of acquisition premium rules.

Preferred Stock: A question often arises on whether preferred stock is treated as debt or equity in a transaction multiple. If it is convertible and the issue is in-the-money, it is treated on the as-converted basis explained above. If it is a non-convertible or straight preferred stock, the preferred stock should be treated as debt in calculating the transaction multiples. Since it is included as equity for reporting purposes, it should be removed from the shareholders' equity account on the balance sheet and added to net debt.

Equity and Other Investments: In our definition of net debt, we subtract minority interest, investments and equity investments in unconsolidated subsidiaries as if they were cash. While they are not cash, they are treated as such, since they represent value that could be realized in settling a debt obligation, much the same way as cash could be used. In addition, we do not see the value of these investments reflected in the unleveraged operating results of the company, i.e., sales, EBIT an EBITDA. They are reflected in the leveraged operating results such as net income and book value, through the inclusion of the company's proportionate share of after-tax earnings in the investment. While it is most helpful to use the market value of these investments in the net debt calculation, it may not be readily available, in which case, you should use the stated book value.

HINT: When in doubt regarding how to treat an item, use your best judgment; however, to be safe, always create a footnote that references the item, what the decision was, and why it was made. In fact, it makes sense to footnote any modification to an individual item, or if there is anything in particular that stands out about a certain company, multiple or metric. Often, there is no "correct" answer to a particular question. In addition, you will see the same question answered differently depending on which investment firm does the analysis. The key however, is to make sure that if the same question arises for multiple companies in the analysis, it is answered consistently across all companies. It is not uncommon to see one or two full pages of footnotes for an analysis.

---

§6.03 COMPARABLE TRANSACTION PREMIUMS ANALYSIS

Another form of comparable transactions analysis is premiums paid analysis. It focuses on public company acquisitions and the stock price premium that was paid in the transaction. For example, if a company paid $30.00 per share for a target company whose stock was trading at $25.00 per share, the acquisition premium would be 20%.

Acquisition premiums will vary by industry, sector, and transaction type. Premiums in control transactions will differ depending on when they are calculated relative to the transaction announcement date. The time frame used to determine the acquisition premium is the most important aspect of the analysis. First, the closer it is to the announcement date, the greater the risk that information has leaked into the market and therefore, the stock price of the target and acquirer may already show speculative signs of the impact of the deal. Second, as a result of market speculation, it is not prudent to look solely at one set of data points from a given time frame. Therefore, it is usual to look at three or more sets of data from different time frames. Common time periods are 1-day prior to announcement, 2-weeks prior to announcement, and 1-month prior to announcement. It is also not uncommon to see premiums from as far back as six months prior to announcement. Exhibit 6-5 shows cash and stock acquisition premiums since 1990.

Exhibit 6-5
Premiums* Paid in Cash and Stock Transaction: 1990–2003[8]

	Cash Tender Offer Premiums	Merger Premiums
1990	34.3%	30.7%
1991	34.3%	26.4%
1992	30.8%	22.2%
1993	92.8%	41.0%
1994	37.8%	17.3%
1995	39.0%	21.0%
1996	29.7%	18.3%
1997	25.8%	20.4%
1998	30.9%	31.2%
1999	39.5%	34.7%
2000	47.5%	40.4%
2001	50.0%	36.4%
2002	48.9%	39.1%
2003	86.7%	57.5%

*Average offer price to target stock price premium 1-day prior to announcement.

8. Thomson Financial.

[A]   Methodology

The most attractive aspect of this analysis is its ease of use. First, determine the universe of comparable transactions. These are often the same transactions that are used in the comparable transaction multiple analysis. Armed with this universe of companies, determine the trading stock prices for each target company at the chosen interval prior to announcement. Second, calculate the offer price in each transaction. Third, establish the premium that was paid in each transaction at the given time period. Fourth, apply the range of premiums paid to the transaction under consideration.

[B]   Example

Using comparable transactions analysis, we derived a range of values for Global of $4.7 to $8.0 billion. This compares to going concern values for Global of $4.4 to $7.7 billion using DCF and comparable company analysis. Premiums paid analysis of Global should yield another benchmark value for Global on a takeover basis that can be used to narrow our range of prices for Global and possible the offer price. In our comparable transaction analysis, each of the transactions that were analyzed was public and therefore, comparable stock market data is readily available.

Step 1: Calculate the Prior Stock Prices for the Comparable Companies.

The first step is to determine what each target company's stock price was on certain dates prior to the announcement of the transaction. Exhibit 6-6 shows these stock prices.

Exhibit 6-6
Stock Prices at Various Dates for Comparable Transactions

Acquirer/Target	Ann. Date	1-Month Prior	Stock Price 2-Weeks Prior	1-Day Prior
Grupo Nationale/*Euromix*	Jun 1, '01	$35.58	$43.88	$38.72
Wholegrains/*Biscuit Basket*	Mar 5, '01	$20.65	$28.50	$22.20
Stage Two/*MishMash*	Dec 5, '00	$12.15	$16.13	$13.25
Global Snack/*Claus Baking*	Nov 20, '00	$14.82	$22.5	$16.90
Argyle Foods/*Homey Bagels*	Jul 10, '00	$23.55	$31.25	$24.32
Biscuit Basket/*JJJ Jellies*	Jun 15, '00	$20.34	$33.75	$24.30
Sweeties/*Baking Bonanza*	Feb 12, '00	$15.97	$21.13	$17.80
Tropical Products/*Nutsahoy*	Nov 5, '99	$ 8.77	$11.13	$ 9.62
Global Snacks/*Lekkers*	Jul 23, '99	$10.26	$14.25	$11.46
Fried Food Hldgs/*Munchies*	Apr 5, '99	$ 9.96	$12.88	$10.74

Exhibit 6-7
Transaction Offer Prices

Acquirer/Target	Ann. Date	Offer Price Per Share
Grupo Nationale/*Euromix*	Jun 1, '01	$43.88
Wholegrains/*Biscuit Basket*	Mar 5, '01	$28.50
Stage Two/*MishMash*	Dec 5, '00	$16.13
Global Snack/*Claus Baking*	Nov 20, '00	$22.50
Argyle Foods/*Homey Bagels*	Jul 10, '00	$31.25
Biscuit Basket/*JJJ Jellies*	Jun 15, '00	$33.75
Sweeties/*Baking Bonanza*	Feb 12, '00	$21.13
Tropical Products/*Nutsahoy*	Nov 5, '99	$11.13
Global Snacks/*Lekkers*	Jul 23, '99	$14.25
Fried Food Hldgs/*Munchies*	Apr 5, '99	$12.88

Step 2: Calculate the Offer Price of the Transaction.

The second step is to calculate the offer price for each company at the time that the transaction was announced. This per share price is the same as the per share prices that were derived in the comparable transaction multiples analysis. Exhibit 6-7 shows these offer prices.

Step 3: Calculate the Premium in each Deal.

The third step is to compare the offer price in each transaction to the stock price of the target on each date prior to the announcement of the transaction. This will yield the acquisition premium in each situation. Exhibit 6-8 shows these premiums.

Based on this analysis, we can see that the average one-day, two-week and one-month premiums paid for the comparable universe are 12.9%, 24.2%, and 37.2%.

Step 4: Derive the Implied Value for Global Based on Comparable Acquisition Premiums.

Based on the premiums derived in step 3, a value is calculated for Global based on its current stock price. This analysis is shown in Exhibit 6-9.

Based on comparable transaction premiums, an implied value of Global Snacks is calculated at $5.6 to $6.7 billion in enterprise value, $4.1 to $5.2 billion in equity value, or $19.71 to $24.29 per share.

Exhibit 6-8
Comparable Acquisition Premiums

			Premium	
Acquirer/Target	Ann. Date	1-Month Prior	2-Weeks Prior	1-Day Prior
Grupo Nationale/*Euromix*	Jun 1, '01	23.3%	13.3%	9.0%
Wholegrains/*Biscuit Basket*	Mar 5, '01	38.0%	28.4%	15.6%
Stage Two/*MishMash*	Dec 5, '00	32.7%	21.7%	9.7%
Global Snack/*Claus Baking*	Nov 20, '00	51.8%	33.1%	11.5%
Argyle Foods/*Homey Bagels*	Jul 10, '00	32.7%	28.5%	19.9%
Biscuit Basket/*JJJ Jellies*	Jun 15, '00	65.9%	38.9%	15.7%
Sweeties/*Baking Bonanza*	Feb 12, '00	32.3%	18.7%	12.2%
Tropical Products/*Nutsahoy*	Nov 5, '99	26.9%	15.6%	11.1%
Global Snacks/*Lekkers*	Jul 23, '99	38.9%	24.3%	12.9%
Fried Food Hldgs/*Munchies*	Apr 5, '99	29.3%	19.9%	11.4%
	Average	**37.2%**	**24.2%**	**12.9%**
	Median	**32.7%**	**23.0%**	**11.9%**

Exhibit 6-9
Implied Value for Global Snacks

	Global Metric	Comparable Premium[9]	Implied Enterprise Value (mm)	Implied Equity Value (mm)[10]
1-Day Prior	$17.46	12.9%	$5,579	$4,140
2-Week Prior	$17.95	24.2%	$6,122	$4,682
1-Month Prior	$18.31	37.2%	$6,713	$5,274

§ 6.04   COMPARABLE TRANSACTIONS ANALYSIS VERSUS DCF AND COMPARABLE COMPANY ANALYSIS

The DCF, comparable company and comparable transactions analyses yielded value ranges as seen in Exhibit 6-10.

As can be seen from the analysis, the stand alone, going concern values tend to have values at the lower end of the range, while the transaction analyses yield values that have overall higher ranges of value, reflecting a premium for control.

---

9. The average transaction premium was used for this analysis.

10. When calculating the implied equity value, it is important to remember to subtract the debt outstanding at the target.

Exhibit 6-10
Comparison of DCF, Comparable Multiple and Comparable Transactions Analyses

Current Stock Price:	$18.00
Discounted Cash Flow Analysis:	$20.78–$29.62 per share
Comparable Trading Multiples Analysis:	$15.43–$25.47 per share
Comparable Transaction Multiples Analysis:	$15.53–$31.39 per share
Comparable Transaction Premiums Analysis:	$19.71–$24.29 per share

---

§ 6.05   SUMMARY

Comparable transaction analysis often yields convincing data that can provide a sound benchmark for valuing a target in the context of a transaction. The analysis includes a takeover or transaction premium and establishes the value of the target based on other comparable transactions. Even though the analysis is widely used, it should not be relied upon by itself, since the multiples and premiums obtained from the analysis do not reflect the current state of the merger and acquisition market.

Comparable transaction multiples are difficult to calculate and require thought and judgment. It is important to understand each transaction on its own, what the state of the M&A market was at the time of the transaction, and what the particular circumstances were surrounding the transaction. With careful analysis, you will find that each transaction by itself, and the transactions together as a whole, will tell a story, and provide you with sound rationale for supporting a given offer price in your own transaction.

Chapter 7

MERGER ANALYSIS

§ 7.01   OVERVIEW

Chapters 4 through 6 discuss different approaches to valuing a company from a going concern and transaction perspective. Discounted cash flow analysis yields an intrinsic value that assumes the company operates in fundamentally the same way going forward as it has in the past. Comparable trading multiples analysis results in a relative value that is based on the trading characteristics of companies in the same industry as the target. Both of these approaches assume the target continues as a going concern, with no takeover event, and thus neither of these two methods includes any form of acquisition premium. Comparable transactions analysis builds on the going concern values by including a premium for control. The premium is based on transactions similar to the one being analyzed, and will likely result in a value for the target that is higher than the values derived from comparable trading multiples analysis, yet may not be as high as the DCF value range.

While these methodologies provide a basis for determining a range of values for a target, they do not provide an absolute road map for what an acquirer should pay for an acquisition. This is more clearly illuminated in merger analysis, which translates the values obtained from the going concern and transaction analyses into an acquirer-specific examination that evaluates the impact of an acquisition on the acquirer at various prices, and hence suggests a range of prices an acquirer could pay.

There are two types of merger analyses: accretion/dilution analysis and contribution analysis. Accretion/dilution analysis studies the impact of a proposed transaction on the acquirer's earnings per share, and indicates what an acquirer could pay for the target. A transaction that is accretive is one where the acquirer's earnings per share increase as a result of the transaction, while a dilutive transaction is the opposite. For example, if an acquirer's stand alone earnings per share prior to a transaction are $1.10, and, as a result of the transaction, the pro forma earnings of the combined company increases to $1.15, the transaction is accretive by $0.05 per share. In this example, because the transaction is accretive, it suggests that the acquirer could pay more for the target if necessary. Each time the acquirer increases the purchase price, the accretion in the transaction erodes.

Contribution analysis compares the relative contribution of revenues, EBIT, EBITDA and net income by the acquirer and target to the combined entity, with the ownership of each entity's shareholders after the transaction is complete. It provides a measure of reason or fairness, in that a transaction where substantially more of the revenues and EBITDA, for example, are contributed by the target, but more of the combined company is owned by the acquirer's shareholders, would not seem reasonable and should be questioned. For example, if the target contributes 40% of the EBITDA but owns 25% of the combined company, one should question whether this transaction makes sense.

Prior to performing an accretion/dilution or contribution analyses, it is helpful to create a spreadsheet that outlines a range of offer prices for the target and the multiples that result from these prices. This analysis, known as an acquisition at various prices (AVP) analysis, is a useful reference tool that helps in establishing a range of values that, on the one hand, allows the acquirer to pay a competitive price, yet on the other hand, prevents the acquirer from paying too much.

To create the AVP analysis, first define a range of purchase prices for the target based on the values derived from the DCF, comparable multiple and comparable transaction analyses. Second, spread the most recent historical and projected financial metrics for the target, i.e., revenue, EBIT, EBITDA, net income, and projected net income. Third, apply the range of purchase prices to the financial metrics to derive the implied acquisition multiples that would result at various prices. As you then create the accretion/dilution and contribution analysis, the prices used in these analyses can then be quickly referred to in the AVP analysis as a way to substantiate the potential price for the target in relation to its stand alone values.

Exhibit 7-1 provides an illustrative AVP analysis based on the examples from Chapters 4 through 6.

Global Snacks is trading at a current stock price of $18.00. Its 52-week high and low are $27.04 and $14.97 respectively. We know from our valuation analysis that the company's per share valuation ranges from below its current stock price, based on comparable trading multiples, to $30.00 per share derived from the DCF and comparable transactions analyses. From the AVP analysis, we can see that at $20.00 to $30.00 per share, or $4.2 to $6.4 billion in enterprise value, the multiples range from, for example, 1.58 × to 2.19 × LTM Revenues, 7.1 × to 9.8 × LTM EBITDA, and 9.0 × to 12.4 × LTM EBIT. From an equity value perspective, at the $20.00–$30.00 range of values, the company's valuation range represents 12.6 ×–18.9 × LTM EPS and 12.2 ×–18.3 × projected EPS. From this analysis at various prices, we have obtained a broad range of values that can be used in our merger analysis. This should indicate a probable range of prices that could be paid for Global, subject to the acquirer's — Tropical's — ability to pay and current market conditions.

Exhibit 7-1
Acquisition at Various Prices for Global Snacks
($ in millions, except per share data)

Global Per Share Purchase Price		*$20.00*	*$22.00*	*$24.00*	*$26.00*	*$28.00*	*$30.00*
Premium/(Discount) to:							
Current Stock Price ($18.00)		11.1%	22.2%	33.3%	44.4%	55.6%	66.7%
52-Week High ($27.04)		(26.0%)	(18.6%)	(11.3%)	(3.9%)	(3.5%)	(10.9%)
52-Week Low ($14.97)		(33.6%)	(46.9%)	(60.3%)	(73.7%)	(87.0%)	(100.4%)
Total Equity Value[1]		$4,200	$4,620	$5,040	$5,460	$5,880	$6,354
Plus: Total Debt		1,732	1,732	1,732	1,732	1,732	1,732
Less: Cash & Equivalents		(292)	(292)	(292)	(292)	(292)	(292)
Total Enterprise Value		$5,640	$6,060	$6,480	$6,900	$7,320	$7,794
Enterprise Value Multiple of:							
LTM Revenues	$3,561	1.58×	1.7×	1.82×	1.94×	20.6×	2.19×
LTM EBITDA	$ 794	7.1×	7.6×	8.2×	8.7×	9.2×	9.8×
LTM EBIT	$ 628	9.0×	9.7×	10.3×	11.0×	11.7×	12.4×
Per Share Purchase Price Multiple of:							
LTM EPS	$ 1.59	12.6×	13.9×	15.1×	16.4×	17.6×	18.9×
Projected EPS	$ 1.64	12.2×	13.4×	14.7×	15.9×	17.1×	18.3×

§7.02 ACCRETION/DILUTION ANALYSIS

Accretion/dilution analysis assesses the impact of a transaction on an acquirer's earnings per share. In addition, it indicates a range of prices that an acquirer could pay in order to maintain or enhance its stand alone earnings. From the perspective of Wall Street, accretive transactions are typically well received, while dilutive transactions may not be, unless there is clear rationale for the dilution.

Market sentiment toward accretion and dilution changes occasionally; therefore, be aware of the current state of the market. During some periods, the market has forgiven dilutive transactions if it can be demonstrated that the surviving company can earn its way out of the dilution within a reasonable period of time, e.g., two years. During other periods, the market has no sympathy at all for a dilutive deal, and will deal punitively with the surviving corporation's stock post announcement.

To calculate the accretion or dilution in a transaction, the projected income statements of the target and acquirer are combined, and adjusted for the impact of the transaction. The accretion or dilution is dependant on a number of variables, in addition to purchase price. Clearly purchase price has the most significant impact on earnings. However, the structure and form of consideration mitigate or amplify the degree of change.

---

1. Based on option-adjusted shares outstanding of 210.0 million from $20.00–$28.00 per share, and 211.8 million shares outstanding at $30.00 per share.

> **Exhibit 7-2**
> **Basic Forms of Consideration**
> _____
>
> Stock-for-Stock
> Stock-for-Cash
> Stock-for-Cash and Stock

The structure of a transaction and form of consideration are independent of the going concern and takeover values of a target. They indicate how a transaction should be financed, and the impact that accounting rules will have on the transaction.

To illustrate, Exhibit 7-2 shows three basic forms of consideration that can be used in a transaction.

Purchase accounting can dramatically affect the earnings and earnings per share of the acquirer post transaction. The culprit is the goodwill created in a purchase accounting transaction. Goodwill is the difference between the purchase price of the target and its book value. It is evaluated annually for impairment, and any impaired goodwill is amortized through the income statement of the surviving company. The annual amortization is non-tax deductible and serves to reduce the earnings of the acquirer. Historically, pooling transactions did not suffer from the same constraint, since no goodwill was created in these transactions.

Financing a transaction with stock or cash can have a material affect on earnings. Stock-for-stock transactions require adjusting the surviving company's shares outstanding by the number of shares issued in the transaction. Stock-for-cash transactions require adjusting the acquirer's earnings by the interest expense associated with debt taken on in the transaction. However, if the acquirer uses existing cash, the interest income associated with that cash must be deducted from the combined income statement.

The decision to use stock and/or cash will depend largely on the acquirer's cost of financing. Theoretically, an acquirer should use its lowest cost source of capital to fund an acquisition. As we saw in DCF analysis, cost of financing relates to both equity and debt. To the extent a company's stock price is high relative to its debt financing cost, it is more advantageous to use equity than debt. Likewise, if a company's stock is languishing, it may make more sense to use debt to finance an acquisition. Accretion/dilution analysis can be used to determine whether or not to use stock and/or cash to finance a transaction.

From the above discussion, it should be evident that accretion/dilution analysis helps determine the price that an acquirer can pay in a transaction based on a range of purchase prices, the type of accounting methodology used and the form of consideration. It should be noted that in many circumstances, an acquirer's ability to pay, i.e., the price that results from the accretion/dilution analysis, may not necessarily coincide with the range of values from the DCF, comparable multiples, and comparable transactions analyses. The potential purchase price may be substantially higher than the target's stand alone value if the acquirer has a strong stock price or very low funding costs. Likewise, the potential purchase price may be lower than the target's stand alone values if it is a strong, high-growth successful company that is in an industry with strong takeover premiums.

All these factors should be evaluated prior to formulating an offer for a company. *Chapter 26: Formulating an Offer* discusses formulating an offer in much greater detail.

[A]   Methodology

To perform an accretion/dilution analysis, you will need to have the following information: projected income statements for the target and acquirer, a range of values for the target, the form of consideration, the accounting methodology for the transaction, and a sources and uses of funds for the transaction.

To begin, let us assume a 100% stock-for-stock transaction. The first step is to consolidate the income statements through the net income line to derive a pro forma income statement. Second, calculate the number of shares that are issued by the acquirer to the target's shareholders. Third, increase the acquirer's shares outstanding by the number of shares issued and calculate the revised earnings per share of the acquirer by dividing the consolidated net income by the pro forma number of shares outstanding. Fourth, compare the pro forma earnings per share with the stand alone EPS of the acquirer excluding the transaction. The difference between the two EPS numbers is the accretion or dilution in the transaction.

In a purchase accounting transaction, the income statement may need to be adjusted in the transaction for annual goodwill impairment if appropriate, and/or the interest expense (or loss of interest income) that is a consequence of the financing. In addition, to the extent part or all of the consideration is acquirer stock, the number of pro forma shares outstanding must be increased to reflect the number of shares issued in the transaction.

[B]   Example

From a valuation perspective, we derived values for Global ranging from $4.2 to $6.4 billion or approximately $20.00 to $30.00 per share. This range is quite wide and therefore does not provide us with all the information we need to develop a final valuation and offer price for Global. In addition, the valuation range does not take into consideration Tropical's ability to pay for Global. Using accretion/dilution analysis, we can evaluate the impact of the transaction on Tropical and determine at what point the transaction is accretive or dilutive to the company. Based on the valuation analysis, we pick a range of values for Global to use in our accretion/ dilution analysis. In the analysis, we have assumed a range of acquisition prices from the valuation analysis of $4.2 to $6.4 billion or $20.00 to $30.00 per share.

Step 1: Calculate Goodwill in Transaction.

For illustrative purposes, let's pick a purchase price of $25.50 to help determine the potential goodwill in the transaction. This purchase price represents a 42% premium to Global's current stock price and a 5.7% discount to its 52-week high.

Exhibit 7-3
Goodwill Calculation
($ in millions)

Equity Consideration[2]	$5,365	$5,365
Assumed Net Debt[3]	$1,443	
Total Consideration[4]	$6,807	
Global Shareholder's Equity	$1,864	
Existing Goodwill	$ 728	
Tangible Book Value	$1,136	$1,136
Goodwill Created		$4,229

From a multiple perspective, this is $16.0 \times$ trailing earnings per share and $15.6 \times$ projected earnings per share. The goodwill created is the amount by which the equity purchase price exceeds the tangible book value of the company. In the case of Global Snacks, the assumed equity consideration at $25.5 per share is $5.365 billion. The company's tangible book value is $1.136 billion. The difference between the two is $4.229 billion. Exhibit 7-3 illustrates the goodwill calculation for the acquisition of Global Snacks.

Step 2: Determine Financing for Transaction.

In the Tropical Products acquisition of Global Snacks, Tropical will acquire the stock of Global Snacks using its own equity, issuing shares of Tropical to the shareholders of Global in exchange for their stock. In addition, Tropical will need to assume or refinance Global's outstanding debt. In this calculation, Tropical will issue 141.2 million shares of its stock to Global's shareholders. This is calculated by dividing the equity consideration paid by Tropical's current stock price of $38.00 per share. In addition, Tropical will assumed approximately $1.4 billion in net debt. Exhibit 7-4 illustrates this calculation.

Step 3: Combine the Income Statements.

Once the amount of goodwill created in the transaction has been calculated, and you have determined the number of shares to be issued in the transaction, it is now time to combine the income statements for the two parties, in this case, Global Snacks and Tropical Products. This is illustrated in Exhibit 7-5. In performing this analysis, one must make an assumption regarding when the transaction closes. In this case, we assumed the transaction closed December 31, 2001.

---

2. Equity value.
3. Total debt less cash and cash equivalents.
4. Enterprise value.

Exhibit 7-4
Financing Calculation
($ in millions, except per share)

Equity Consideration[5]	$5,365	$5,365
Assumed Net Debt[6]	$1,443	
Total Consideration[7]	$6,807	
Tropical Current Stock Price		$38.00
No. of Tropical Shares Issued (mm)		141.2

Exhibit 7-5
Combined Calendar Year 2002 Income Statements for Global Snacks and Tropical Products
($ in millions)

	Tropical	Global	Adj.	Pro Forma
Revenue	$7,515.5	$3777.6	$ –	$11,293.1
Cost of Sales	4,471.7	2013.4	–	6,485.1
Gross Profit	3,043.8	1764.2	–	4,808.0
Operating Expenses	1,434.4	900.2	–	2,334.6
EBITDA	1,609.4	864.0	–	2,473.4
Depreciation Expense	205.1	158.3	–	363.4
Goodwill	89.1	20.0	(20.0)	89.1
Transaction Expense Amortization	0.0	0.0	8.5	8.5
Operating Income	1,315.2	685.7	11.5	2,012.4
Other Income (Net)	(23.1)	8.9	–	(14.2)
Interest Expense (Net)	228.3	122.4	6.8	357.5
Pre-Tax Income	1,063.8	572.2	4.7	1,640.7
Income Taxes	372.3	200.3	(2.4)	570.2
Net Income	$ 691.5	$ 371.9		$ 1,070.5

The accretion or dilution that the market will be observant of is the first and second years after the closing of the transaction. More particularly, they will be focused on the near term quarters post closing. For this example, we look at the annual accretion/dilution impact for the first year post closing.

In combining the income statements, it is important to recognize a few issues. First, the existing goodwill is eliminated at Global and replaced with the new

5. Equity value.
6. Total debt less cash and cash equivalents.
7. Enterprise value.

91

goodwill created in the transaction. This goodwill is expensed to the extent there is goodwill impairment at the end of the year. The impaired amount is expensed through the income statement and cannot be used to offset taxes. Second, M&A deals typically have significant transaction expenses associated with structuring, negotiating, and closing the deal. Third, it is important to take into consideration any debt financing costs that may result from the transaction. For example, in an acquisition, the acquirer may have to refinance the debt of the target that it assumes. It may have a positive or negative impact on the earnings of the combined company depending on current interest rates, the acquirer's cost of debt financing, and the terms of the debt to be assumed. Fourth, these adjustments need to be taxed to ensure that they accurately reflect their impact on the combined company's income statement.

Step 4: Calculate Pro Forma Shares Outstanding.

In order to calculate the pro forma earnings per share for the combined company, the new shares outstanding must be calculated to take into consideration the shares issued by the acquirer to the target's shareholders. The new shares outstanding at Tropical Products are simply the existing number of shares plus the shares issued to Global Snack's shareholders. The number of shares outstanding at Tropical Products pro forma the acquisition of Global Snacks is 377.4 million. Exhibit 7-6 illustrates this calculation.

Step 5: Determine Accretion or Dilution.

It is now possible to calculate the 2002 calendar year pro forma accretion or dilution in the transaction. The pro forma net income is divided by the pro forma shares outstanding to derive the pro forma earnings per share. Exhibit 7-7 illustrates this calculation.

From the accretion/dilution analysis, we can see that at a $25.50 per share purchase, the transaction is dilutive to Tropical Product's calendar year 2002 earnings per share by $0.09 per share. This indicates that while the $25.50 purchase price is well within the range of values for Global Snacks derived from the valuation analysis, because Tropical's stock price may not be high enough to warrant making the acquisition. The implication from this is that Tropical should consider

---

Exhibit 7-6
Pro Forma Shares Outstanding
(in millions)

Tropical Shares Outstanding	236.2
Tropical Shares Issued in Transaction	141.2
Pro Forma Shares Outstanding	377.4

Exhibit 7-7
2002 Accretion/Dilution Table
($ in millions, except per share data)

2002 Pro Forma Net Income	$1,070.5
Pro Forma Shares Outstanding	$ 377.4
2002 Pro Forma Earnings Per Share	$ 2.84
Stand Alone Earnings Per Share	$ 2.93
Accretion/(Dilution)	($ 0.09)
Percent Accretion/(Dilution)	(3.1%)

Exhibit 7-8
2002 Accretion/Dilution Sensitivity to Offer Price
(per share)

	Global's Purchase Price/Premium to Current Share Price						
Tropical	**$18.00**	**$20.00**	**$22.00**	**$24.00**	**$26.00**	**$28.00**	**$30.00**
Share Price	0.0%	11.1%	22.2%	33.3%	44.4%	55.6%	66.7%
$30.40	$0.03	($0.08)	($0.19)	($0.29)	($0.38)	($0.47)	($0.56)
$32.30	$0.10	($0.01)	($0.12)	($0.21)	($0.31)	($0.39)	($0.48)
$34.20	$0.16	$0.05	($0.05)	($0.15)	($0.24)	($0.32)	($0.41)
$36.10	$0.22	$0.11	$0.01	($0.08)	($0.17)	($0.26)	($0.34)
$38.00	$0.27	$0.17	$0.07	($0.02)	($0.11)	($0.20)	($0.28)
$39.90	$0.32	$0.22	$0.12	$0.03	($0.06)	($0.14)	($0.22)
$41.80	$0.36	$0.26	$0.17	$0.08	($0.01)	($0.09)	($0.17)
$43.70	$0.40	$0.31	$0.21	$0.13	$0.04	($0.04)	($0.12)
$45.60	$0.44	$0.35	$0.26	$0.17	$0.09	$0.01	($0.07)

---

a lower price or delay the transaction until its stock price is higher. A higher stock price would enable Tropical to issue fewer shares in the transaction, thus reducing the number of pro forma shares outstanding and thereby reducing the dilutive impact of the transaction. Alternatively, Tropical could determine the extent of synergies in the transaction to assess whether it is feasible to utilize some of those synergies in paying the $25.50 per share price for Global.

Exhibits 7-8 to 7-10 demonstrate the accretion or dilution in the transaction under different scenarios: a higher or lower offer price, a higher or lower Tropical stock price, different forms of consideration and various levels of synergies.

The accretion/dilution sensitivity to offer price shows that at an offer price of $18.00 per share for Global, the transaction in accretive to Tropical by $0.27 per share, assuming it acquires the company when its stock price is $38.00. The transaction becomes marginally dilutive to Tropical when the offer price for Global reaches $24.00 per share. If Tropical's stock price rises by 5% to $39.90 per share,

Exhibit 7-9
2002 Accretion/Dilution Sensitivity to Form of Consideration[8]

	Global's Purchase Price/Premium to Current Share Price						
% Stock	**$18.00**	**$20.00**	**$22.00**	**$24.00**	**$26.00**	**$28.00**	**$30.00**
Consideration	0.0%	11.1%	22.2%	33.3%	44.4%	55.6%	66.7%
0.0%	$0.85	$0.76	$0.67	$0.58	$0.48	$0.39	$0.29
12.5%	$0.75	$0.66	$0.56	$0.47	$0.37	$0.28	$0.18
25.0%	$0.67	$0.57	$0.47	$0.37	$0.28	$0.18	$0.09
37.5%	$0.59	$0.49	$0.39	$0.29	$0.19	$0.10	$0.01
50.0%	$0.52	$0.41	$0.31	$0.21	$0.12	$0.03	($0.06)
62.5%	$0.45	$0.34	$0.24	$0.15	$0.05	($0.04)	($0.13)
75.0%	$0.39	$0.28	$0.18	$0.09	($0.01)	($0.09)	($0.18)
87.5%	$0.33	$0.23	$0.13	$0.03	($0.06)	($0.15)	($0.23)
100.0%	$0.27	$0.17	$0.07	($0.02)	($0.11)	($0.20)	($0.28)

Exhibit 7-10
2002 Accretion/Dilution Sensitivity to Margins[9]

	Global's Purchase Price/Premium to Current Share Price						
Operating	**$18.00**	**$20.00**	**$22.00**	**$24.00**	**$26.00**	**$28.00**	**$30.00**
Synergies (mm)	0.0%	11.1%	22.2%	33.3%	44.4%	55.6%	66.7%
$ 0.0	$0.27	$0.17	$0.07	($0.02)	($0.11)	($0.20)	($0.28)
$ 75.0	$0.42	$0.31	$0.20	$0.11	$0.02	($0.07)	($0.16)
$150.0	$0.56	$0.45	$0.34	$0.24	$0.14	$0.05	($0.04)
$225.0	$0.71	$0.59	$0.48	$0.37	$0.27	$0.18	$0.08
$300.0	$0.85	$0.73	$0.61	$0.50	$0.40	$0.30	$0.20
$375.0	$1.00	$0.87	$0.75	$0.64	$0.53	$0.42	$0.33
$450.0	$1.14	$1.01	$0.89	$0.77	$0.66	$0.55	$0.45
$525.0	$1.29	$1.15	$1.02	$0.90	$0.78	$0.67	$0.57
$600.0	$1.43	$1.29	$1.16	$1.03	$0.91	$0.80	$0.69

the transaction is marginally accretive — $0.03 per share — if it offered $24.00 per share.

Another way to assess the accretion or dilution in a transaction is by measuring the impact of a change in the form of consideration. For example, in the Tropical acquisition of Global Snacks, Tropical is assumed to be acquiring Global by issuing stock for 100% of the equity. A sensitivity analysis should be performed

---

8. Assumes a $38.00 per share price for Tropical.
9. Assumes a $38.00 per share price for Tropical.

to determine the impact of paying part of the consideration in cash. In the sensitivity shown in Exhibit 7-9, one can see that at 100% stock consideration, the transaction becomes dilutive to Tropical at a $24.00 offer price. If cash is offered as a part of the consideration, for example, 25% cash, the transaction is not dilutive until Tropical offers approximately $26.00 per share. The implication from this analysis is that Tropical should consider financing a portion of the transaction with cash.

This sensitivity is illustrated in Exhibit 7-9.

Synergies can play an important role in structuring the consideration of an acquisition. To the extent there are immediate, tangible synergies that can be extracted from the deal, it may be feasible to share the value of those synergies with the target's shareholders in order to increase the purchase price of the transaction. It is wise to be cautious in this arena, because as you can see from the sensitivity analysis in Exhibit 7-10, the dollar amount of synergies realized in a transaction can have a significant impact on the accretion or dilution in a transaction.

In this sensitivity analysis, the way to model the synergies is to assume that it is possible to achieve a given level of synergies as a percent of sales. For example, if there is overhead that can be immediately eliminated in the transaction, this should be estimated as a percent of sales and then translated into a dollar margin impact. Exhibit 7-10 shows, for example, that if $75 million of synergies can be realized in the first year representing 0.6% of revenues, then approximately $0.13 cents per share can be added to the accretion in the transaction. Specifically, at a purchase price of $24.00 per share, with no synergies, the transaction is dilutive by $0.02 per share. If $75 million in synergies are realized, the transaction is accretive by $0.11 per share at the same purchase price of $24.00 per share. This suggests that the offer price could potentially be increased to $28.00 per share before the deal becomes dilutive again.

§ 7.03   CONTRIBUTION ANALYSIS

As a complement to accretion/dilution analysis, contribution analysis provides a means to check whether the price paid for a company is fair relative to the amount each company contributes to the surviving entity post transaction. It does this by translating the price paid for the target into an ownership position. In other words, if an acquirer issues its stock for the acquisition, the target's shareholders will own an amount of stock in the surviving company that is dependent on the price paid.

Using the Tropical acquisition of Global Snacks as an example, it is evident that as Tropical pays more for Global, its ownership in the combined company goes down proportionately. For example, using Tropical's stock price of $38.00 per share, it would own 70% of the combined company if it paid $18.00 per share, and 59% of the combined company if it paid $30.00 per share. Likewise, if Tropical's stock price was higher it would own a greater percentage of the combined company. For example, if Tropical's stock price rose from $38.00 to $42.00 per share, its ownership in the combined company, at an $18.00 per share purchase price, would rise from 70% to 73%. Exhibit 7-11 illustrates how pro forma ownership can change relative to the price paid and the price of the acquirer's stock.

Contribution analysis has most applicability in stock-for-stock transactions, since in cash transactions, the target's shareholders are no longer equity holders in the combined company. It analyzes each significant metric in the income statement, i.e., revenue, EBIT, EBITDA, and net income, and evaluates it in the context of its contribution to the surviving company. If each party's contribution to the surviving company is significantly different than its post closing ownership, then the transaction merits review. Exhibit 7-12 presents an example of a contribution analysis.

When performing this type of analysis, it is typical to review more than one metric as well as more than one year. Companies pursue acquisitions for multiple reasons: a target could have higher growth rates or margins than its own, it could

---

Exhibit 7-11
The Impact of Price on Tropical's Ownership of Pro Forma Combined Company

	Global's Purchase Price/Premium to Current Share Price						
Tropical	**$18.00**	**$20.00**	**$22.00**	**$24.00**	**$26.00**	**$28.00**	**$30.00**
Share Price	0.0%	11.1%	22.2%	33.3%	44.4%	55.6%	66.7%
$30.00	65%	63%	61%	58%	56%	55%	53%
$32.00	67%	64%	62%	60%	58%	56%	54%
$34.00	68%	66%	63%	61%	59%	58%	56%
$36.00	69%	67%	65%	63%	61%	59%	57%
$38.00	70%	68%	66%	64%	62%	60%	59%
$40.00	71%	69%	67%	65%	63%	62%	60%
$42.00	72%	70%	68%	66%	64%	63%	61%
$44.00	73%	71%	69%	67%	65%	64%	62%
$46.00	74%	72%	70%	68%	66%	65%	63%

Exhibit 7-12
Example Contribution Analysis
($ in millions)

				Contribution	
	A	*B*	*Pro Forma*	*A*	*B*
Revenue	$1,000	$500	$1,500	67%	33%
Cost of Sales	700	300	1,000	70%	30%
Gross Profit	300	200	500	60%	40%
Operating Expenses	150	100	250	60%	40%
EBITDA	$ 150	$100	$ 250	60%	40%

---

have better technology or products, or it could have a stronger sales force or distribution. Some of these reasons may or may not be overtly apparent in the target's financial statements today — or in the future. Therefore, reviewing multiple metrics and years assures both parties to the transaction that the greatest effort has been made to ensure the transaction is fair to both sides. For example, if a target's shareholders owns 30% of the pro forma company, yet contributes 20% of pro forma EBIT in 2001 and 40% in 2002, the transaction pricing would seen reasonable. However, if any one-year was reviewed by itself, the transaction may appear to warrant re-evaluation.

[A] Methodology

Contribution analysis entails a four-step process. First, spread the key income statement items for each company adjacent to each other by year. Second, calculate the pro forma income statement for the combined company. Third, determine the percentage contribution that each company makes to the combined organization. Fourth, compare the overall contribution of each metric to each company's pro forma ownership.

[B] Example

Much like the analysis performed to determine the accretion or dilution in a transaction, the income statements of the two parties to the transaction should be combined to form the pro forma statements.

Step 1: Spread Key Income Statement and Balance Sheet Data.

The income statements for the two parties to the transaction are spread much the same as they were for the accretion/dilution analysis.

Step 2: Calculate Pro Forma Income Statement of Combined Company.

As the income statements are combined, it is important not to forget to adjust the pro forma income statement for the new goodwill created in the transaction, any adjustments for impaired goodwill at the end of the year, the amortization of transaction expenses and any necessary adjustments to the financing costs associated with the assumption of the target's debt. Exhibit 7-13 shows the pro forma combined income statement or Tropical Products and Global Snacks for the 2002 calendar year, assuming a purchase price of $25.50 per share.

Step 3: Determine Percent Contribution of Each Company.

Once the income statements have been combined reflecting any necessary adjustments related to the transaction, it is then possible to determine the percent contributed by each company to the combined company. One can see from the Exhibit 7-14, that Tropical Products contributes 65.5% of Revenues, 65.1% of

Exhibit 7-13
2002 Pro Forma Combined Income Statement for Tropical and Global

	Tropical	Global	Adj.	Pro Forma
Revenue	$7,515.5	$3777.6	$ –	$11,293.1
Cost of Sales	4,471.7	2013.4	–	6,485.1
Gross Profit	3,043.8	1764.2	–	4,808.0
Operating Expenses	1,434.4	900.2	–	2,334.6
EBITDA	1,609.4	864.0	–	2,473.4
Depreciation Expense	205.1	158.3	–	363.4
Goodwill	89.1	20.0	(20.0)	89.1
Transaction Expense Amortization	0.0	0.0	8.5	8.5
Operating Income	1,315.2	685.7	11.5	2,012.4
Other Income (Net)	(23.1)	8.9	–	(14.2)
Interest Expense (Net)	228.3	122.4	6.8	357.5
Pre-Tax Income	1,063.8	572.2	4.7	1,640.7
Income Taxes	372.3	200.3	(2.4)	570.2
Net Income	$ 691.5	$ 371.9		$ 1,070.5

Exhibit 7-14
2002 Contribution Analysis

	Tropical	Global	Adj.	Pro Forma	% Contribution Tropical	Global
Revenue	$7,515.5	$3,777.6	$ –	$11,293.1	65.5%	33.5%
Cost of Sales	4,471.7	2,013.4	–	6,485.1		
Gross Profit	3,043.8	1,764.2	–	4,808.0		
Operating Expenses	1,434.4	900.2	–	2,334.6		
EBITDA	1,609.4	864.0	–	2,473.4	65.1%	34.9%
Depreciation Expense	205.1	158.3	–	363.4		
Goodwill	89.1	20.0	(20.0)	89.1		
Transaction Expense Amortization	0.0	0.0	8.5	8.5		
Operating Income	1,315.2	685.7	11.5	2,012.4	65.7%	34.3%
Other Income (Net)	(23.1)	8.9	–	(14.2)		
Interest Expense (Net)	228.3	122.4	6.8	357.5		
Pre-Tax Income	1,063.8	572.2	4.7	1,640.2	65.0%	35.0%
Income Taxes	372.3	200.3	(2.4)	570.2		
Net Income	$ 691.5	$ 371.9		$ 1,070.5	65.0%	35.0%

EBITDA and 65.7% of Operating Income to the combined company. It is important to remember that this analysis assumes a purchase price for Global Snacks of $25.50 per share, and that the contribution to Operating Income will change as the purchase price changes. Exhibit 7-14 shows this analysis.

Step 4: Compare Contribution to Pro Forma Ownership.

With the contribution analysis completed, it is possible to compare the contribution of each of the companies to the pro forma organization with their respective ownership in the company post closing. As you may recall from Exhibit 7-11, if Tropical acquired Global for $25.50 per share when its stock price was $38.00 per share, Tropical would own approximately 63% of the combined company. Comparing this to its percentage contribution of 65.5%, 65.1% and 65.7% or Revenues, EBITDA and Operating Income, one can ascertain that at the $25.50 per share offer price, Tropical would own less of the combined company than it is contributing to it. This suggests that Tropical should evaluate the proposed $25.50 per share offer price and potentially adjust it downwards accordingly. Assuming Tropical's stock price remained the same at $38.00 per share, it could lower the price to approximately $23.00 per share and its 65% contribution to the combined company would reflect its 65% ownership of the combined company.

§ 7.04   SUMMARY

Merger analyses helps bring together an entire valuation analysis. It takes the values derived from the going concern and takeover analysis and puts them in a framework specific to the acquirer. Accretion/dilution analysis establishes an acquirer's ability to pay while contribution analysis determines the relative fairness of the price paid versus how much each company contributes to the pro forma company.

As with all analyses, the two merger analyses cannot be looked at by themselves. They need to be reviewed in the context of the entire analysis, and they require your own business judgment. Specific situations and transactions require individual knowledge and a certain level of subjective input in order to determine the feasibility of the analysis. In addition, these analyses should be viewed in the context of the mergers and acquisitions environment at the time of the transaction, the acquirer's rationale for undertaking the transaction, and the target's negotiating strength.

Chapter 8

LEVERAGED BUYOUT ANALYSIS

§ 8.01   OVERVIEW

A leveraged buyout or LBO is the acquisition of a company, division, or subsidiary using a highly leveraged financial structure, whereby the cash flows of the acquired business are used to service and repay the borrowed debt. LBO analysis is often performed when valuing a company in order to determine whether a leveraged buyout is feasible and if the valuation of the target under a LBO scenario is competitive with that of a takeover valuation. In this chapter, the valuation methodology behind LBO's is discussed, while Chapter 16 provides a historical and structural overview of LBO's.

Generally, LBO's are sponsored by private investor groups such as Kohlberg Kravis Roberts & Co. and Forstmann Little & Co., and include the participation of management. Leveraged buyouts are undertaken for a variety of reasons, the most significant of which is the ability to acquire stable, cash flow generating assets using a limited amount of equity capital and a significant amount of borrowed capital. Using this financial structure, it is possible to generate attractive returns for equity investors by using the company's cash flows to repay the debt assumed to finance the acquisition. As the debt is repaid, value is transferred to equity holders.

Exhibit 8-1
Simple Leveraged Buyout Illustration

Assumptions:

Purchase Price:	$100
Equity:	$ 30
Debt:	$ 70
Debt Term:	5 years
Interest Rate on Debt:	8%
Sale Price:	$100

	Initial Investment	Debt Repayment	Interest	Debt Outstanding	Sale Price	IRR Cash Flows
Beginning Yr. 1	−$30					−$ 30
End Yr. 1		$14	$6	$56		$ 0
End Yr. 2		$14	$5	$42		$ 0
End Yr. 3		$14	$3	$28		$ 0
End Yr. 4		$14	$2	$14		$ 0
End Yr. 5		$14	$1	$ 0	$100	$100

IRR	27%

To illustrate the concept, assume that a company is acquired in a leveraged buyout for $100. The purchase price is financed with $30 in equity — or cash — and $70 in debt. The debt has a five-year term and an 8% interest rate. The company generates cash flow that is sufficient to pay the interest on the debt and repay the principal in five years. Finally, at the end of the fifth year, the company is sold for $100. Exhibit 8-1 shows the simple analysis.

There are a few points to be taken away from this example. First, the LBO sponsor that invested the equity was able to garner a 27% internal rate of return (IRR). This return was generated by investing $30 at the beginning of the first year and realizing $100 at the end of year five. Second, the transfer of wealth that took place accrued to the benefit of the equity holders. This was achieved by financing the bulk of the initial purchase price with the cash flows of the target company. The wealth transfer was in the form of converting the $70 in debt that was used to acquire the company into equity that was realized in the sale of the company in year five. The wealth transfer occurs because the lenders do not benefit from the increase in value of the target's assets. They simply are repaid the debt they lent to the target as well as the interest on that debt, while the equity investors retain the upside.

While the opportunity to realize attractive financial returns in LBO's is typically their driving force, there are other reasons for pursuing a leveraged buyout, some of which a summarized in Exhibit 8-2.

LBO's can take various forms. An LBO can be performed on public and private companies, as well as divisions and subsidiaries of public and private companies. In addition, LBO's can be used to create value for shareholders when other alternatives

---

Exhibit 8-2
Reasons to Pursue a Leveraged Buyout

The market does not recognize the value in the target's assets
The target is under takeover threat
Management believes they can operate more effectively as a private company
An alternative to going public
An alternative to a sale, spin-off, or split-off from a conglomerate

---

Exhibit 8-3
Characteristics of an Attractive LBO Candidate

Capable, experienced and committed management team
Industry leader with defensible market position
Stable business with little cyclicality
Little existing debt
Strong historical and projected cash flows with a reasonable degree of predictability
Minimal ongoing capital expenditure needs
Reasonable future working capital needs
Assets that can be sold to repay debt or used as collateral to support debt
Assets that can be written up and depreciated in order to reduce taxes
Attractive valuation

---

do not work. For example, if a private company cannot be taken public due to poor market conditions, the company can be sold in a leveraged buyout to management and a sponsor group, realizing value for current shareholders and keeping existing management in place.

§ 8.02   HOW TO EVALUATE A LBO CANDIDATE

Leveraged buyouts typically entail high levels of leverage, and therefore create significant financial and operating risk once completed. As a consequence, only certain types of businesses make good LBO candidates. Exhibit 8-3 summarizes key criteria for establishing whether a business would make a viable LBO candidate.

Based on these criteria, it is apparent that certain types of businesses make better LBO candidates than others. Generally, people intensive and technology-based businesses are difficult to acquire in a leveraged buyout, while more asset intensive businesses are more easily purchased using a LBO. Ultimately however, every LBO candidate has to survive an intense analytical screen to determine if it can generate returns that are commensurate with the risk in the transaction.

Successful leveraged buyouts are those that first meet the acquisition criteria in Exhibit 8-3 and second, accomplish a number of goals. Most important, they should be able to repay the debt assumed in the transaction in a reasonable time frame and be able to generate equity returns to investors that reward them for taking on the risk of the transaction. These equity returns historically have been in the 25% to 40% range.

In addition to retiring all the acquisition debt and providing a return to shareholders, the LBO candidate must generate enough cash flow to support continued reinvestment in the business in order to fund the working capital and capital expenditure needs of the company. Finally, the company needs to be sold or taken public at some point in the near future in order to realize the returns to equity investors.

§ 8.03   THE ANATOMY OF LBO ANALYSIS

There are a number of interrelated financial concepts that underlie LBO analysis, the two most important of which are capital structure and IRR analysis.

[A]   Capital Structure

Leveraged buyouts are financed based on the target's ability to repay a large amount of debt while coincidentally generating equity returns to investors sufficient to warrant undertaking the transaction. The capital structure used in a LBO is determined by a number of considerations. First, general guidelines dictated by current market conditions provide an initial framework for structuring a LBO. The amount of equity and debt in a LBO can fluctuate accordingly, but generally, the following mix of debt and equity can be used:

Equity:	10%–30%
Senior debt:	50%–60%
Subordinated debt:	20%–40%

Second, the target's assets will determine whether the loans will be collateralized or not. Generally, bank debt secured by quality assets will be relatively easy to obtain. As a benchmark, commercial banks will lend money up to the following percentages of certain assets. These percentages will vary depending on current conditions in the bank market.

Accounts receivable:	70%–85%
Inventories:	35%–55%
Property, plant, and equipment:	55%–75%

Debt secured by assets is considered quite attractive, since the lenders are "fully secured," and will not necessarily require participation in the equity in order to provide the debt.

Third, the capital structure will be determined by the excess cash flow that is generated by the target above and beyond its day-to-day operating needs. LBO's

---

Exhibit 8-4
Common Forms of Debt Financing in LBO's

Long-term senior debt: Banks, insurance companies, and pension funds
Medium-term debt: Banks
Revolving credit: Banks
Subordinated debt: Equity and mezzanine-debt sponsors, banks, and insurance companies

---

that are cash-flow based tend to be highly structured and more complex than asset based LBO's, in that the lender will require comfort that it's loan can be repaid if there are few assets to serve as collateral. Generally, cash-flow based LBO's will have multiple layers or types of debt that are used to finance the transaction. These levels of debt are provided by different financial institutions, each requiring returns on their portion of the financing commensurate with their priority in the capital structure and the commensurate level of risk. Exhibit 8-4 offers a summary of the common forms of LBO debt financing and the financial institutions that provide it.

The tiers of debt that are used in a cash-flow based leveraged buyout generally are dictated by the current lending environment, but more importantly by the magnitude, growth and predictability of the target's cash flows. As guidelines, following are benchmarks for tiering the debt in a cash-flow based LBO.

Long-term debt:	30%–50%
Medium-term debt:	10%–30%
Revolving credit:	10%–20%
Subordinated debt:	20%–40%

The debt portion of the capital structure will be based on the target's capacity to repay debt over a defined time frame. Known as its "debt capacity," it will help determine the purchase price of the target in the LBO, as well as the equity returns to investors. So, for example, if a company is to be sold for $100, and its debt capacity is $70, the required equity to meet the price hurdle is $30. Assuming the cash flows are sufficient to repay the debt and the company can be sold or taken public at a valuation that results in an IRR of 25%–40%, the LBO may be feasible.

The interest rate and term of debt will change depending on the priority in the capital structure and the risk in the transaction. They will also depend on current lending conditions. Generally, the more senior the debt is in the capital structure, the shorter the maturity and the lower the interest rate. Likewise, the more subordinated the debt is in the capital structure, the longer the maturity and the higher the interest rate.

When lending into leveraged buyouts, financial institutions will want to see enough cash flow to adequately pay or "cover" the interest. A ratio known as interest coverage is typically monitored in a LBO and a target ratio of 1.25–1.40 times EBIT to interest expense is typically a prerequisite for funding a LBO.

[B] IRR Analysis

Driving most leveraged buyouts is the ability for equity investors to generate attractive returns. Generally, investors will expect a return of between 25% and 40%. Returns can be generated in a variety of ways, but most commonly they are realized through the eventual sale or initial public offering of the target. Occasionally a company can be recapitalized or subject to another LBO to provide the return to equity investors.

There are various forms of equity used in a LBO including common stock and preferred stock. In addition, certain lenders will require participation in the equity in the form of warrants and/or options. Furthermore, lenders may require that various types of debt be convertible into equity upon the occurrence of certain events such as an initial public offering.

§ 8.04   LBO METHODOLOGY

Performing a leveraged buyout analysis typically entails a number of steps. First, establish a preliminary range of values for the target. Second, determine an initial capital structure for the buyout. Third, establish the target's debt capacity. Fourth, structure the equity component of the capital. Fifth, perform the LBO analysis.

[A] Establish a Preliminary Range of LBO Values

Traditional valuation analysis provides us with a range of values for a company that assume on the one hand a going concern framework, and on the other hand, a transaction-driven takeover valuation. While these valuation approaches can provide guidance in determining value under a LBO scenario, they may not be entirely applicable as well. Since a leveraged buyout is fundamentally determined by the target's debt capacity and the equity returns that can be generated in the transaction, the company's valuation will also be driven by these two criteria. Therefore, a simple approach to establishing a preliminary range of values for a target under a LBO is to start by evaluating cash flow multiples.

Cash flow multiples allow us to compare a LBO target's valuation to its capital structure. The multiple typically used for these purposes is Enterprise Value/Pre-Tax Cash Flow, defined as follows:

Enterprise Value   = Cost to acquire the outstanding equity (or the cost to acquire the assets), plus existing debt outstanding, less liquid assets such as cash

Pre-Tax Cash Flow = Pre-tax operating income plus depreciation and amortization and any other non-cash charges

Revisiting our earlier example where the company was acquired for $100, the debt assumed in that transaction was $70. If the pre-tax cash flows generated by the company were $15, the purchase price would have been 6.7 times pre-tax cash flow and the debt would have been 4.7 times pre-tax flow. LBO valuations will typically be in a range of 4.5 to 7.0 times pre-tax cash flow. These multiples will vary depending on current interest rates and lending conditions, as well as the current demand for LBO candidates. As interest rates increase, multiples will fall. As demand for LBO targets increases, multiples will increase.

It is also possible to look at other valuation multiples such as Price/Earnings, Enterprise Value/Book Value, and Enterprise Value/EBIT and EBITDA. LBO's do not work well in high multiple situations, since high multiples connote strong growth prospects or an overvalued market or company. While these companies may represent attractive acquisition candidates, they may not generate sufficient cash flows to support the level of debt required to finance the purchase price. In addition, high growth companies tend to require high levels of investment in capital and working assets.

When establishing a preliminary range of values for a LBO candidate, it is common to evaluate comparable recent leveraged buyout transactions to determine the overall range of multiples used in the current environment. In addition, it is possible to discuss valuation levels with the leveraged lending arm of commercial banks that lend into LBO's. They should be well versed in current valuation levels.

[B] Establish a Preliminary Capital Structure

Once the preliminary range of values has been established for the target, it is necessary to determine the initial capital structure for the transaction, i.e., how the transaction will be financed. As a first step, the existing debt obligations of the target should be established. It is important to recognize all debt-like instruments in the target's capital structure such as public debt, bank debt, convertible debt, and preferred stock. An assumption should be made regarding how each of these instruments will be treated in the transaction. Certain types of debt can be assumed while others require refinancing in the transaction. For example, bank debt will typically be refinanced in a LBO. Convertible debt and preferred stock could convert into common stock depending on the purchase price.

A second step is to look at the excess assets that result from the transaction. For example, proceeds from the exercise of stock options will generate cash. Additionally, excess cash and investments can be used to finance a portion of the purchase price.

Finally, LBO's can be expensive transactions to execute. It is important to include estimated transaction costs that can range from 3–5% of the transaction value.

Once you have clarified the liabilities to be assumed, any changes to the capital structure that result from the transaction, and estimated transaction fees, it is possible to build a preliminary sources and uses table that outlines the capital structure for the deal. To begin, the simplest approach is to use current market guidelines for the mix of debt and equity in the capital structure. For example, from our guidelines above, one could start with 15% equity (or common stock), 15% preferred stock, 50% bank debt, and 20% subordinated debt. Adding all these

Exhibit 8-5
Example LBO Sources and Uses Table

Sources of Funds	$mm	Uses of Funds	$mm
Debt	$1,000	Purchase Price for Equity	$1,150
Equity	300	Refinance Existing Debt	100
Total Sources	$1,300	Fees and Expenses	50
		Total Uses	$1,300

components should result in a total sources of funds equivalent to the total uses of funds. Exhibit 8-5 provides an example sources and uses of funds for a LBO.

The junk bond market has allowed companies to complete transactions with levels of debt that were not previously feasible. This is due in part to the relaxed principal repayment requirements and debt restrictions imposed by this market.

Neither the preliminary valuation range nor the capital structure is cast in stone at this stage. Both will most certainly change based on the overall LBO analysis. The missing ingredients are the target's debt capacity and the equity returns that may be generated by the transaction. If the company's cash flows are not strong enough to service and repay the debt, or the equity returns are not sufficient, then the purchase price and consequent capital structure will need to be revisited.

[C] Confirm Initial Debt Capacity

The preliminary capital structure is based on current market guidelines for levels of debt that can be raised to support a LBO purchase price. However, there are other benchmarks that are commonly used to help further clarify a target's debt capacity. There are two simple means commercial lenders have to establish debt capacity.

First, capitalize the target's earnings before interest and taxes (EBIT) at a rate that approximates the overall interest rate for the transaction. If the resulting level of debt is close to that derived earlier for the capital structure, then your estimate of debt is likely to be close to correct. For example, if the target's EBIT is $9, and the implied cost of the debt financing portion of the transaction is 10%, then the estimated debt capacity of the company is $90. To the extent the estimated debt capacity is greater or less than the chosen debt level in the capital structure, then you may need to adjust your assumed debt level up or down.

Second, based on the debt level chosen for the initial capital structure, calculate one year's worth of interest expense. Determine what the target's EBIT represents as a multiple of that interest expense. Known as the coverage ratio, if EBIT is between 1.25 and 1.40 times interest expense, then the debt level is probably in a feasible range.

A further means for determining the viability of the target's debt capacity is to check the asset collateral values that could be used to support the debt. Based on the percentages discussed earlier, accounts receivable of 70%–85%, inventories of

35%–55% and property, plant, and equipment of 55%–75%, check to see the how much debt can be supported by the assets of the company. In some cases, the asset coverage may be greater than the chosen level of debt, in which case the financing is plausible. In other cases, the asset values may not be sufficient to cover all the debt, in which case, the LBO has higher risk. This does not mean, however, that the LBO cannot be financed; it suggests that the financial institutions lending into the transaction will rely more on the strength of the cash flows of the company rather than on the company's assets for their downside protection.

When looking at ratios such as interest coverage or asset coverage, there is often a question over what period financials to use for the analysis. This will depend entirely on current market conditions and the commercial lender's view toward lending into LBO's in general. At times, the financial institutions will use the most recent four quarters financials for income statement driven ratios, while at other times, they will use the most recent quarter's financials on an annualized basis. It is wise to check with a leveraged lender to determine current market thinking.

[D] Structure the Equity

In a leveraged buyout, there are a number of constituents that will want to participate in the equity upside in the transaction. These participants range from the equity sponsor, to management, to subordinated debt lenders.

The initial equity capital infused into the transaction is the difference between the purchase price and the amount of debt raised to finance the purchase price. This capital is usually provided by the equity sponsor in the form of common and/or preferred stock. The mix of common and preferred stock is driven by the structural requirements of the equity sponsor's fund.

Most LBO's require the active support of management, and the equity sponsor usually provides for equity participation of management. This is accomplished by allowing management to earn their equity over a period of time. While there are various forms that this equity participation can take, the most common is to reserve 3% to 15% of the company's equity in the form of options that vest over a four-year time frame. The nature of the equity participation and the vesting period will vary on the current state of the market for LBO's.

Subordinated lenders will often require participation in the equity in order to lend into a transaction. Since their debt is of lower priority — or subordinated — in a downside scenario, the equity participation provides them with incremental upside to compensate for the additional risk they are assuming in the transaction. While the participation that subordinated lenders will require varies as lending conditions change, they will typically expect total returns on their debt and equity in the 20%–30% range. This additional return typically comes in the form of warrants.

[E] Perform the LBO Analysis

The first four phases in the analysis provide a framework for analyzing a leveraged buyout. They are by no means the final answer. Each of these should be overlayed onto the projection model built for the target company. There are a number of steps that should be followed in performing the LBO analysis.

First, prepare the projected financial statements. While the basis for the projections can often be those used for the acquisition scenarios, it is important to remember that a company subject to a LBO operates with a high degree of leverage, and must be managed for cash flow rather than earnings. This implies that the target company may not be in a position to grow as quickly or invest as much capital in its property, plant, and equipment or working capital as it would under an acquisition scenario. Therefore, it is wise to review and potentially revise the projections to be more suited to a LBO scenario.

Second, you should create a balance sheet — the opening balance sheet — that portrays the new capital structure of the target once the transaction is complete. This balance sheet is effectively the expected closing balance sheet for the company with respect to the working capital and long-term assets accounts, adjusted for the new debt and equity structure.

Third, input the debt paydown assumptions into the model. Each tier of debt will have a different maturity schedule that needs to be confirmed with the financial institution lending into the deal.

Once the model has been modified to reflect the LBO assumptions, it needs to be run to analyze the output. There are a number of criteria that then need to be met to ensure the LBO has the greatest potential for success. These criteria will change with current market conditions dictated by the lenders as well as the equity sponsors. In Exhibit 8-6 are some of the core criteria used to evaluate the viability of a LBO. These criteria are simple guidelines for analyzing a LBO. They will differ based on the type of company subject to the LBO as well as current lending conditions and the demands of equity investors.

Exhibit 8-6
Key Success Variables

Leverage Criteria
Ability to repay senior bank debt in 5–7 years
Ability to repay all debt in buyout in 10–12 years
EBIT interest coverage initially between 1.25 to 1.4 times, improving to 2.0 times within
    five years
Ability to reach industry level debt ratio by the end of the fifth year

Equity Criteria
25%–40% returns on common equity
3–6 times total dollar return on initial equity investment in under five years
Overall return to subordinated lenders of 20%–30%

---

§8.05 LBO EXAMPLE

In the valuation of Global Snacks, a range of $20.00 to $30.00 per share was derived from the stand alone and takeover analyses. As a first step in performing the leveraged buyout analysis of Global, let's use the low point of the valuation range, i.e., $20.00 per share, as the initial purchase price for Global. This is an 11% premium to its current stock price of $18.00 per share, and represents an equity value for the company of $4.2 billion. Assuming Global's existing $1.7 billion in debt is refinanced and there are approximately $140 million in fees, representing 2.5% of the aggregate consideration, the implied pro forma enterprise value for the LBO is $5.7 billion. This is more fully illustrated in Exhibit 8-7.

The overall purchase price represents enterprise value multiples of 7.1× EBITDA and 8.8× EBIT.

Exhibit 8-7
Transaction Assumptions for Global Snacks LBO
($ in millions, except for per share)

	$mm
Current Price Per Share	$18.00
Premium to Current Price Per Share	11.0%
Purchase Price Per Share	$20.00
Fully Diluted Shares Outstanding	210
Implied Equity Value	$4,158
Plus: Existing Debt	$1,732
Less: Cash	289
Implied Enterprise Value	$5,601
Fees and Expenses @ 2.5%	140
Implied Pro Forma Enterprise Value	$5,741

Exhibit 8-8
Global Snacks LBO Sources and Uses Table

Sources of Funds	$mm	Uses of Funds	$mm
Debt	$3,890	Purchase Price for Equity	$4,158
Equity	2,000	Refinance Existing Debt	1,732
Cash on Hand	140	Fees and Expenses	140
Total Sources	$6,030	Total Uses	$1,250

Based on the initial valuation range, then determine the sources and uses for the transaction and the corresponding debt capacity of the company. The sources and uses for the Global LBO are outlined in Exhibit 8-8.

As you can tell from the sources and uses table, the leveraged buyout effectively would replace the equity in the capital structure with debt, thereby substantially increasing the leverage in the company. Based on the sources and uses table, the pro forma capitalization would be approximately 65% debt and 35% equity.

The next step entails formulating the opening balance sheet for the company upon the closing of the transaction. This is illustrated in Exhibit 8-9 below.

Exhibit 8-9
Opening Balance Sheet for Global Snacks
($ in millions)

	At Closing	Adjustments		Closing
	12/31/01	*Debit*	*Credit*	*Closing*
Assets				
Cash	$ 289		$ 140	$ 149
Accounts Receivable	448			448
Inventory	532			532
Other Current Assets	218			218
Total Current Assets	$1,487			$1,347
Net P, P & E	2,925			2,925
Other Assets	295	140[1]		435
Intangibles	728	3,022[2]	728[3]	3,022
Total Assets	$5,435	$3,162	$ 728	$7,730
Liabilities and Owners Equity				
Accounts Payable	$ 399			399
Other Current Liabilities	545			545
Total Current Liabilities	$ 944			$ 944
Long-Term Debt	1,732	1,732[4]	3,890[5]	3,890
Other Liabilities	896			896
Stockholders Equity	1,864	1,864[6]	2,000[7]	2,000
Total Liabilities and Stockholders Equity	$5,435	$3,595	$5,890	$7,730

Notes:
(1) Fees and expenses of 2.5% of aggregate considerations
(2) New goodwill created in transaction
(3) Elimination of old goodwill at Global Snacks
(4) Elimination of existing debt at Global Snacks
(5) Addition of new debt to finance LBO
(6) Elimination of old stockholders equity
(7) Capital infusion from equity sponsors

The next step is to project the financial statements for the company using steady state assumptions. Exhibit 8-10 shows the base case assumptions for Global Snacks under a leveraged buyout scenario and the resulting income statement is shown in Exhibit 8-11.

Exhibit 8-10
Global Snacks Financial Assumptions

	Historical			Est.		Projected		
	1998	1999	2000	2001E	2002	2003	2004	2005
Growth Rate Analysis								
Revenue Growth		5.0%	1.0%	4.0%	4.0%	4.0%	4.0%	4.0%
S, G & A Growth		8.0%	3.7%	4.7%	3.5%	3.5%	3.5%	3.5%
Margin Analysis								
Gross Margin	45%	47%	47%	47%	46.7%	47.2%	47.7%	48.2%

Exhibit 8-11
Global Snacks Income Statement
($ in millions)

	Historical			Est.		Projected		
	1998	1999	2000	2001E	2002	2003	2004	2005
Revenue	$3,288	$3,439	$3,482	$3,632	$3,778	$3,929	$4,086	$4,249
Cost of Goods Sold	1,797	1,824	1,861	1,943	2,013	2,074	2,137	2,201
Gross Profit	1,492	1,615	1,621	1,689	1,764	1,854	1,949	2,048
S, G & A	742	801	830	870	900	932	964	998
EBITDA	750	814	790	819	864	923	985	1,050
Depreciation & Amortization	162	164	176	172	307	313	320	326
EBIT	588	650	614	647	557	609	665	724
Interest Income	1	1	5	12	6	6	6	6
Interest Expense	125	138	123	130	275	256	232	205
Pre-Tax Income	464	513	496	529	288	360	439	525
Income Taxes	162	180	174	185	136	161	189	219
Net Income	$ 302	$ 333	$ 322	$ 344	$ 152	$ 199	$ 250	$ 306

Exhibit 8-12
Global Snacks Projected Balance Sheet
($ in millions)

			Projected		
	Est.Closing	2002	2003	2004	2005
Assets					
Cash	$ 149	$ 149	$ 149	$ 149	$ 149
Accounts Receivable	448	466	484	504	524
Inventory	532	552	568	585	603
Other Current Assets	218	227	236	245	255
Total Current Assets	$1,347	$1,393	$1,438	$1,484	$1,531
P, P & E	2,925	3,156	3,394	3,641	3,897
Accumulated Depreciation	0	178	363	554	751
Net P, P & E	2,925	2,977	3,032	3,088	3,146
Other Assets	435	407	379	351	323
Intangibles	3,022	2,922	2,821	2,720	2,619
Total Assets	$7,730	$7,699	$7,669	$7,642	$7,619
Liabilities and Owners Equity					
Notes Payable	$ 0	$ 0	$ 0	$ 0	$ 0
Accounts Payable	399	414	426	439	452
Other Current Liabilities	545	567	589	613	637
Total Current Liabilities	$ 944	$ 980	$1,016	$1,052	$1,090
Long-Term Debt	3,890	3,671	3,407	3,094	2,727
Other Liabilities	896	896	896	896	896
Stockholders Equity	2,000	2,152	2,350	2,600	2,906
Total Liabilities and Stockholders Equity	$7,730	$7,699	$7,669	$7,642	$7,619

Exhibit 8-12 shows the projected balance sheet for Global Snacks resulting from the analysis.

The cash flow statement indicates that the company has the ability to pay down substantial debt in the first four years of the forecast period. The cash flow statement is shown in Exhibit 8-13.

In analyzing the LBO of Global Snacks, there are a number of factors to consider. First, what does the company's credit profile look like? Second, what is the potential internal rate of return to the equity sponsors?

At the $20.00 proposed purchase price and given the capital structure we have assumed, the company generates sufficient EBITDA to cover the interest expense on the debt. In fact, based on the analysis, the company may be able to withstand greater levels of leverage. Exhibit 8-14 illustrates the credit statistics for Global Snacks post transaction.

Exhibit 8-13
Global Snacks Cash Flow Statement
($ in millions)

	2002	Projected 2003	2004	2005
Sources				
Net Income	$152	$199	$250	$306
Depreciation and Amortization	307	313	320	326
Total Sources	$459	$512	$570	$632
Uses				
Change in Working Capital	$ 10	$ 9	$ 10	$ 10
Capital Expenditures	231	239	247	256
Total Uses Before Debt Repayment	$240	$248	$257	$266
Available for Dept Repayment	218	264	313	367
Repayment of Debt	218	264	313	367
Change in Cash	$ 0	$ 0	$ 0	$ 0

Exhibit 8-14
Global Snacks Pro Forma Credit Statistics
($ in millions)

	At Closing	Year 1 2002P	Year 3 2004P	Year 5 2006P
Debt	$3,890	$3,671	$3,094	$2,302
% Debt Repaid		6%	20%	41%
EBITDA/Interest		3.1×	3.6×	4.2×

The equity returns appear acceptable to the financial sponsor community. Based on an 8× EBITDA multiple, the internal rate of return to investors is approximately 30%, given the $20.00 per share purchase price and the capital structure presented. Exhibit 8-15 illustrates the internal rate of return analysis.

One can draw a number of conclusions from this preliminary LBO analysis of Global Snacks. First, the company has substantial debt capacity, indicated by its ability to pay down substantial debt in the first five years of the forecast as well as by the attractive EBITDA/Interest coverage ratios. The implication from this is that it may be possible to increase the purchase price for the company by increasing the leverage. Second, the equity returns are attractive to investors, indicating that there may be additional opportunity to increase the purchase price and not materially reduce the internal rate of return on the transaction.

Exhibit 8-15
Global Snacks Internal Rate of Return Analysis
($ in millions)

EBITDA Multiple	7×	8×	9×
2005 Projected EBITDA	$1,050	$1,050	$1,050
Implied Enterprise Value	$7,350	$8,400	$9,450
Net Debt Outstanding	$2,578	$2,578	$2,578
Implied Equity Value	$4,772	$5,822	$6,872
Initial Equity Investment December 31, 2001	$2,000	$2,000	$2,000
Internal Rate of Return	24.3%	30.6%	36.1%

To further refine the analysis requires a detailed review of the capital structure with the various lenders and financial institutions that will provide the debt capital for the transaction. Through the sophisticated structuring of the debt and equity components of the transaction, it is possible to enhance the internal rate of return to investors.

§ 8.06   SUMMARY

Leveraged buyout analysis provides a value for a company that is dependent on the cash flows the company can generate and its implied debt capacity. In addition, it depends on the equity return requirements of investors that sponsor LBO's. As a result, it is typical for LBO valuations to be lower than conventional stand alone and takeover valuation methodologies. LBO's can only be performed on companies with stable cash flows with the participation of management. High growth companies or companies with few assets are hard to acquire in a leveraged buyout and therefore lend themselves better to outright acquisition by a corporate acquirer. Because of the complex nature of LBO's, it is wise to engage the services of a banker knowledgeable in leveraged transactions.

Chapter 9

STOCK PRICE ANALYSIS

§ 9.01   OVERVIEW

Once a target's valuation range has been established, there are a number of additional factors that influence the price an acquirer might pay in an acquisition. Stand alone valuation provides a view of a company's value as a going concern, independent of a takeover proposal. Takeover valuation analysis yields a value that factors in a premium for control. Merger analysis helps establish what an acquirer is able to pay, and whether that price is reasonable given the pro forma financial performance of each company party to the transaction. While these analyses help establish a price for the target from the acquirer's perspective, they do not address what the target's shareholders may accept.

There is yet another factor that comes into play at the time the acquirer chooses to make an offer — where a target's stock presently trades and where it has traded in the past. Coinciding with this is the basis that various shareholders have in the company. This may influence what it may be forced to pay in order to "get the deal done."

Let's take a hypothetical situation to illustrate the problem. A company's stock is temporarily depressed due to a poorly performing market, and is trading at $12 per share. In the months prior to its stock price decline, an institutional shareholder built up a 15% stake in the company. Its average basis in the stock is $16 per share. Other significant shareholders that recently acquired the stock own another 15% of the company and have an average basis of $14 per share. While the acquirer has determined a range of values for the target of $14–$20 per share, based on current market conditions, its ability to pay is $15 per share. In addition, the target's stock traded as high as $18 per share in the last six months.

What price does the acquirer offer? If it offers $15 per share, the transaction would be break even from an accretion/dilution standpoint, there would be no premium to one set of 15% shareholders and a small premium to the second group of 15% shareholders. Therefore, these shareholders would be unlikely to vote in favor of the deal. If the acquirer offers $16 or $17 per share, the 30% shareholders may accept the offer, but the market is likely to look negatively on the deal since the acquirer is "paying too much" for the company, causing dilution to the company's earnings. This very well could be a case where the parties table their discussions until the equity markets recover and the two parties' stock prices are more favorably disposed to a deal.

This type of understanding cannot be achieved with valuation and merger analysis alone. It requires analysis of a company's stock price over time as well as its shareholder base. This is called stock analysis.

There are two primary components of stock analysis: stock price analysis and shareholder analysis.

§ 9.02   STOCK PRICE ANALYSIS

Stock price analysis entails analyzing the historical price performance of a company's stock for different periods prior to presenting an offer. There are three aspects of stock price analysis: absolute price performance, relative price performance, and price/volume analysis.

[A]   Absolute Price Performance

This analysis evaluates a company's stock price by itself for a period of time prior to presenting the offer. It allows an acquirer to visualize a range of prices at which the target's stock has traded. Common time periods are six months, 12 months, and two years. It also allows one to determine if there has been any run-up or deterioration in recent history based on certain events.

As an adjunct to this analysis, it is helpful to review press releases and other public statements for the target company, and plot significant dates and events on the absolute stock price chart. This makes it simple to see the impact of certain events on a company's stock price and provides a further framework to support an offer. Exhibit 9-1 provides an example of an absolute price chart for Cardinal Health.

[B]   Relative Price Performance

This analysis builds on absolute price performance by comparing the target's stock price performance to an index or indexes. It is common to use broad indexes such as the S&P 500, or targeted indexes such as one made up of the company's peer group.

Relative stock price analysis allows an acquirer to visualize how a company's stock has performed relative to the market and its peer group, and whether it has performed in line with the two groups over time. It also helps distinguish what changes in a target's stock price have been influenced by the market and have impacted all the companies in the sector or market, and what events have been company specific. Exhibit 9-2 illustrates a relative price chart for Cardinal Health versus the S&P 500.

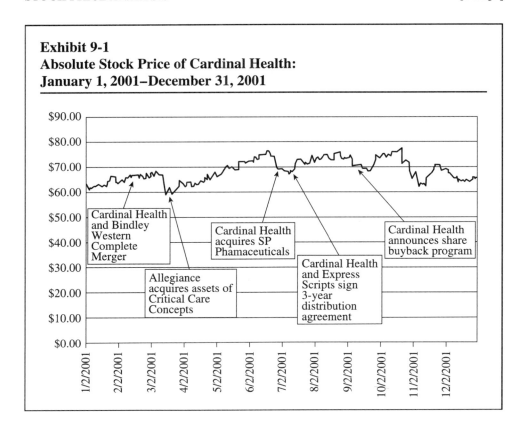

Exhibit 9-1
Absolute Stock Price of Cardinal Health:
January 1, 2001–December 31, 2001

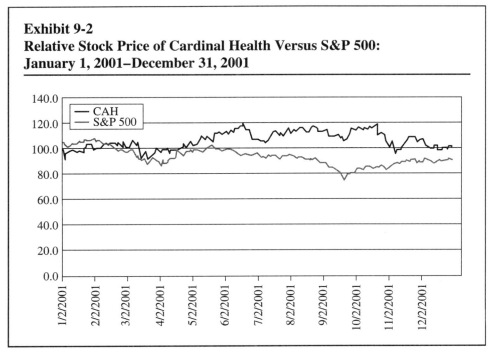

Exhibit 9-2
Relative Stock Price of Cardinal Health Versus S&P 500:
January 1, 2001–December 31, 2001

Exhibit 9-3
Price/Volume Analysis for Cardinal Health:
June 1, 2001–December 31, 2001

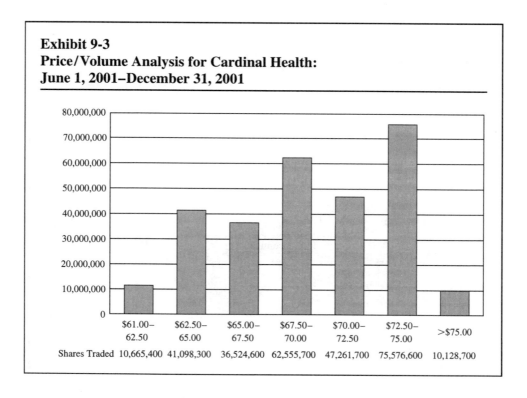

	$61.00–62.50	$62.50–65.00	$65.00–67.50	$67.50–70.00	$70.00–72.50	$72.50–75.00	>$75.00
Shares Traded	10,665,400	41,098,300	36,524,600	62,555,700	47,261,700	75,576,600	10,128,700

[C]   Price/Volume Analysis

This analysis is quite helpful in determining the overall basis that recent share-holders in the company's stock have. For example, it is typical to perform a price/volume analysis on a company for a six-month time frame. During this period, a defined number of shares will have traded at certain prices. Based on this analysis, it is possible to determine at what prices those shares traded and thus conclude that a large portion of the shareholders have a basis in the company's stock at a given level. Exhibit 9-3 provides an example of price/volume analysis for Cardinal Health.

During the six months from June 1, 2001, to December 31, 2001, approximately 283 million shares traded for Cardinal Health. The company has approximately 450 million shares outstanding. This would suggest that during that period, a significant portion of Cardinal Health's shares traded hands. All the shares traded at a price of between $61.00 and $78.00 per share. The greatest amount of stock traded at prices of between $67.50 and $70.00 per share and $72.50 and $75.00 per share, implying shareholders that purchased the stock have a relatively high basis in the stock.

§ 9.03   SHAREHOLDER ANALYSIS

Shareholder analysis drills further into the stock price analysis by looking into the individual shareholders of a company and trying to determine their individual

```
┌─────────────────────────────────────────┐
│                                           │
│  Exhibit 9-4                              │
│  Public Shareholder Types                 │
│  ─────────────────────────────           │
│                                           │
│  Institutions                             │
│  Hedge Funds                              │
│  Management                               │
│  ESOPs                                    │
│  Employees                                │
│  Individuals                              │
│                                           │
└─────────────────────────────────────────┘
```

bases. There are multiple categories of shareholders that can be analyzed. Exhibit 9-4 provides an overview of the significant shareholder categories for a company.

It is possible to find information on each shareholder type and determine their basis in the target. Significant shareholders will generally be described in the proxy or 10-K. Start by looking at the most recent few proxies and build a chart that describes the shareholders and their ownership. Next, turn to significant public filings, most often found in 13(f) and 13(g) filings. 13(f) filings are made by institutional shareholders that acquire stock for investment purposes and 13(g) filings are made by all investors owning less than 20% of a class of securities for investment purposes only. 13(d) filings are made by those shareholders that have intentions other than investment. Management shareholder information can typically be found in the registration statement and sales can be tracked in filings made by the manager. Exhibit 9-5 shows the current share ownership for Cardinal Health.

Once the analysis has been performed, the question becomes what to do with it. First, for significant shareholders — institutions, management or other significant shareholders — determine at what price they acquired their stock. This information will generally be disclosed in the public filing or the proxy or 10-K. Second, determine what stock has been acquired or sold since the initial purchase, and at what price. Third, add up the significant shareholders to determine how much of the stock is held by large shareholders and how much is owned by the public or individual shareholders (public float).

For Cardinal Health, we can draw the conclusion that a large portion — approximately 53% — of the company is owned by institutions, mutual funds, insiders, and management. If one were to check each of the filings made by the institutions and mutual funds, it is possible to determine what their approximate basis in Cardinal Health's stock is. Based on this, it is possible to determine their receptivity to a transaction at a given price range.

§9.04   SUMMARY

Stock price analysis is not necessarily a valuation tool. It initially provides an overall range of values at which a company's stock has traded over a given time frame. However, in addition to this, it offers a subjective view of why a stock has

Exhibit 9-5
Shareholder Ownership of Cardinal Health

	Shares Held	*% Outstanding*
Top Institutional Fund Holders[1]		
FMR Corporation	55,201,090	12.24%
AXA Financial, Inc.	26,675,635	5.91%
Capital Research and Management Company	13,874,000	3.07%
Barclays Bank Plc	12,719,851	2.82%
Janus Capital Corporation	10,934,377	2.42%
State Street Corporation	10,298,771	2.28%
American Express Financial Corp.	8,909,298	1.97%
Rittenhouse Financial Services	8,454,488	1.87%
Vanguard Group	7,812,503	1.73%
TIAA Cref Investment Management, LLC	6,982,820	1.54%
Total	161,862,833	35.85%
Top Mutual Fund Holders[2]		
Fidelity Dividend Growth Fund	13,607,620	3.01%
Fidelity Magellan Fund Inc.	13,429,336	2.97%
AXP New Dimensions Fund	7,000,000	1.55%
Vanguard Specialized Health Care Fund	5,851,608	1.29%
Fidelity Asset Manager	5,307,830	1.17%
Investment Company of America	5,171,500	1.14%
College Retirement Equities Fund	5,159,944	1.14%
Washington Mutual Investors	4,700,000	1.04%
Vanguard Index 500 Fund	3,678,089	0.81%
Vanguard U.S Growth Fund	2,938,470	0.65%
Total	66,844,397	14.77%
Insiders and Management[3]		
Robert D. Walter	6,694,792	1.50%
William E. Bindley	3,835,296	NMF
Melburn G. Whitmire	2,244,224	NMF
George L. Fotiades	391,785	NMF
James F. Millar	334,123	NMF
John B. McCoy	120,144	NMF
Richard J. Miller NMF	78,328	NMF
Robert L. Gerbig NMF	76,963	NMF
John F. Havens NMF	54,726	NMF
John F. Finn NMF	46,464	NMF
Anthony J. Rucci NMF	37,815	NMF
Richard C. Notebaert NMF	22,379	NMF
J. Michael Losh NMF	19,964	NMF
Regina E. Herzlinger NMF	18,101	NMF

(*Continued*)

1. Source: SEC Filings.
2. *Id.*
3. Source: Cardinal Health, Inc. public documents.

Exhibit 9-5
(*Continued*)

	Shares Held	*% Outstanding*
Michael D. O'Halleran NMF	13,528	NMF
Dave Bing NMF	10,595	NMF
George H. Conrades NMF	7,964	NMF
All Executive Officers and Directors as a Group	14,861,806	3.30%

traded historically the way it has, and whether stock price moves have been market driven, sector driven or company specific. Furthermore, the analysis shows at what prices freely tradable stock has traded during the recent past, indicating the basis that public shareholders have in the stock. Finally, it allows us to analyze the basis of large shareholders to determine if a potential offer price would be attractive to these shareholders.

Stock price analysis goes beyond company valuation and attempts to provide guidance on what range of prices may be acceptable to shareholders independent of value.

Chapter 10

PRIVATE COMPANY VALUATION

§ 10.01   OVERVIEW

Private companies come in a variety of flavors, from small family owned enterprises, to divisions or subsidiaries of publicly traded conglomerates, to large corporations operating alongside their public counterparts. Private companies suffer from their own issues when subject to valuation, resulting in a marked difference between valuing a privately held company, subsidiary, or division, and a publicly traded corporation. Using financial tools, valuation analysis places a discount on these differences, usually resulting in a lower value for a private company than for its public counterpart.

The lower value attributed to private companies comes primarily from the fact that there is no liquid market for the company's stock. Thus, a liquidity — or lack of liquidity — discount is applied to the valuation to reflect this problem. Other factors that influence a private company's valuation are its size, lack of operating history, management and operational control, difficulty in quantifying earnings and cash flow, capital structure and risk in the business.

Many of the same valuation methodologies used to value public companies can be used to value private companies, with the caveat that each approach must be utilized incorporating specific modifications for the fact that the company is private. For example, in determining the cost of capital for a private company, it is necessary to estimate the cost of debt and equity as the private company does not have publicly traded securities.

While valuing a private company, there are numerous issues that may affect the cash flows and hence the financial analysis. Each of these issues should be examined in due diligence to elucidate their true impact on value. For example, many private companies are structured as S Corporations where the earnings of the company are treated no differently than a limited partnership. The implication of this is that the owners — or shareholders — are required to report the earnings of the company on their personal income statements, suggesting first, that the manager owners are not likely to draw a salary, and second, the after-tax net income of the company is not a true reflection of the company's earnings. In valuing a private company, it is wise to try and "normalize" as many of these types of issues as possible prior to attempting the analysis.

In some instances, private companies are valued as public companies. When a company is expected to go public, or it is sold to a public company, or it is large enough where it is in effect no different than a public company but for the fact that it is not publicly traded, the usual liquidity discount does not necessarily apply. Much like valuing a public company, no one methodology can be relied upon; rather, multiple methods should be used in order to converge on a likely range of values for the company. In addition, one should bear in mind the reason why the valuation is being performed. Is it for a sale, divorce proceeding, estate valuation, option pricing, or something else? As this is a text on mergers and acquisitions, the valuation approaches will be focused in that arena.

§ 10.02 FACTORS THAT INFLUENCE THE VALUATION OF PRIVATE COMPANIES

There are a number of distinctions between private and public companies, each of these having an impact on a private company's value.

[A] Lack of Market Liquidity

Private company equity by its very nature is illiquid. Many private companies are owned by families, venture capitalists, or other investors, where there is no active market for buying and selling shares. As a result, there are no benchmarks for valuing these companies' stock on a daily basis, unlike public companies whose securities trade each day on a stock exchange. This lack of liquidity gives rise to a discount, often estimated to be as high as 50%. This discount is applied by valuing the company as if it were public, and then reducing that value by the liquidity discount. For example, if a $50 million revenue business is valued at $75 million, based on a public company valuation methodology, the private company value could very well be half of that value, or $37.5 million.

As there are no hard and fast rules on how to apply the discount or how much it should be, your best judgment should be used in determining the appropriate percentage discount. While in theory, the liquidity discount relates to the fact that the private company's equity is not public, in practice, the size of the discount is also determined by other factors. Features that will increase the size of the discount include lack of size, lack of operating history, quality of earnings and cash flow, quality of the management team, profile of the industry, and inherent risks in the business.

[B] Size

Generally, privately held companies are a lot smaller than their publicly traded counterparts. Start-up, pre-public, and even some mature private companies sometimes rarely reach $100 million in revenues, and may not be candidates to go public. However, they may be appropriate roll-up or acquisition candidates for public companies. In addition, many privately held companies might simply be bought or sold as ongoing privately held businesses.

Size is an issue for two reasons and will contribute to the magnitude of the liquidity discount. First, a private company's size may be a reflection of the industry or sector within which it operates. The industry may be small or it may not be growing at attractive rates. In these situations, the company does not warrant the same multiple or premium as one in a larger, more attractive industry. Second, size is an indication of stage of growth. The smaller the size, the less likely it is that the company has a long track record, in which case, the risk inherent in the business is higher than one that is large in size.

[C]   Operating History

Companies that have not been in business a long time are difficult to value as there is no real track record of revenue growth, profitability, or earnings growth. Therefore, the less operating history a company has, the higher the risk in its earnings and cash flow, and consequently, the greater the discount that should be applied to the valuation.

[D]   Business Mix

In many cases, private companies may be niche oriented, concentrating business risk in a single or handful of product lines. Conversely, the private company may have a broad product mix yet little critical mass in any single business line. Each scenario may add to increased risk in the business, and therefore contribute to a higher liquidity discount.

[E]   Management Control

Private companies are often closely held, where the shareholders are also the managers. Invariably, control is concentrated among a few individuals. This profile may add to the risk of the company from a variety of perspectives. First, there may not be a pool of talent upon which to draw in order to build the business. Second, there may be no succession plan in place, exposing the company to significant risk if the principal manager or managers die, or are no longer able to work in the business. Third, many family-controlled firms are filled with family members, creating a level of internal conflict over operational control. Divergent objectives may cloud the decision-making capacity of the management team. Each of these concerns may lead to greater risk in the company itself and consequently cause a higher discount on the value.

[F]   Earnings Measurement

Public companies are generally managed for earnings on a quarter-to-quarter basis, as earnings and earnings growth are the most visible benchmarks by which a public company is valued. On the other hand, private companies may be managed for completely different reasons: tax minimization, cash flow, long-term growth, etc. Family-held businesses may be managed to provide enough operating earnings to pay salaries to the on-staff family members. Each of these scenarios makes it difficult to measure true earnings and cash flows of the company. In building financial models to value a private company, it is important to normalize, recast, or restate the financials of the company to determine what the true earnings would be if the company were operated on an arm's-length basis or like a public company.

[G]   Capital Structure

Much like earnings, a private company's capital structure is difficult to assess, as capital planning for a private company may differ dramatically from that of a public company. Public companies have access to both public equity and debt markets, and therefore may finance themselves using their lowest cost source of capital. In fact, public companies should be maintaining an optimal capital structure that leads to their lowest cost of capital, i.e., picking that debt/equity ratio that gives them the lowest cost of capital without causing the company to suffer from the risk of default.

Conversely, private companies may not have access to the public debt or equity markets, and consequently their sources of capital may be limited. A prime source of funding for a private company is bank debt, which can be quite expensive. As a result, private companies may rely on internally generated funds to support capital expansion, in which case the company will have little debt. Alternatively, the company may be a heavy user of bank debt, in which case the company may have a relatively weak balance sheet.

[H]   Risk

The overall risk in a private company is generally higher than that of a public firm. A lack of size and earnings history, coupled with the industry and business concentration risk, make for a potentially risky profile.

§ 10.03   PRIVATE COMPANY VALUATION METHODOLOGIES

There are a number of implications arising from the valuation issues that are endemic to private companies. First, because private companies manage their balance sheet and earnings for different end goals than public companies, using discounted cash flow or comparable valuation techniques requires additional insight. The earnings may need to be reconstructed in order to create financials comparable to that of public counterparts. The capital structure may need to be normalized for the same reason. Second, because of the lack of liquidity and increased risk in the business, the discount rates used in discounted cash flow analysis need to be modified accordingly. Third, because of issues with earnings and capital structure, the multiples used to value private companies may need to be limited to "above the line," i.e., operating earnings and above, because the net income of a private company may not be comparable to that of a public company.

In addition to the nuances that are imposed on public valuation techniques when valuing private companies, there are additional approaches that make sense in the case of private companies, namely, analyzing total invested capital, estimating replacement cost, asset appraisal, and capitalization of earnings.

[A]   Public Company Approaches to Valuing Private Companies

[1]   Discounted Cash Flow Analysis

DCF analysis places a present value on the future cash flows of a company by discounting those cash flows using a discount rate commensurate with the risk inherent in those cash flows. The discount rate most commonly used is known as a weighted average cost of capital (WACC). In using DCF analysis with public companies, the WACC is determined by estimating the company's cost of debt and cost of equity. Each element is fairly easy to determine, as a public company's equity is traded publicly and it is likely that public benchmarks exist to help estimate the cost of debt.

DCF analysis for private companies must be modified as there are no public estimates for the components used to derive a WACC. For example, a private company has no Beta. In addition, its cost of debt may not be easy to determine, as it is unlikely that it has public debt. Therefore, each aspect of the WACC derivation must be adapted to account for these deficiencies.

[a] *Estimating Beta.* Beta is a historical measure of a stock's trading volatility versus the market as a whole. By its very nature, a private company does not have public equity securities and therefore has no basis for determining a Beta for its equity. This applies not only to independent private companies, but also to divisions and subsidiaries of public companies. In this case, the Beta for the public parent is not necessarily a fair representation of estimated equity risk in the division or subsidiary. Estimating Betas for private companies is therefore based on an approach that extrapolates from the trading volatility of public companies comparable to that of the private company or target under investigation.

The methodology for estimating a private company Beta is quite simple. First, gather a group of publicly traded companies that are generally in the same line of business as the target company. To the extent the target company operates in more than one line of business, collect companies that are in each line of business.

Second, obtain the Betas and leverage ratios for each company in the comparable universe. Calculate the unlevered Betas for each company, deriving the average unlevered Beta for the universe of comparable companies. As you may recall, the formula for unlevering a Beta is as follows:

$$\beta_{(\text{unlevered})} = \beta_{(\text{levered})} / (1 + \text{Debt}/\text{Equity})(1 - \text{T}))$$

Third, estimate the optimal debt ratio for the private company, either by assuming its existing capital structure or using the debt ratio for the industry as a whole. In your analysis, you will have to use your judgment as to which approach to take. For example, as a division or subsidiary, it is unlikely that the parent company will have capitalized the business separately from the rest of the company. In this case, it is not unreasonable to assume the debt ratio for the industry as the private firm's optimal debt ratio. Likewise, for a large independent private company with a long operating history, it may have its own capital structure that reflects its optimal debt ratio. Once the debt ratio has been determined, relever the average Beta for the industry using the private company's optimal debt ratio to derive a levered Beta for the private firm. The formula for relevering a Beta is as follows:

$$\beta_{(\text{levered})} = \beta_{(\text{unlevered})} \times (1 + (\text{Optimal Debt}/\text{Equity})(1 - \text{T}))$$

Exhibit 10-1
Comparable Levered and Unlevered Betas for
Public Coffee Chains

Company	Levered Beta	Debt /Equity Ratio	Unlevered Beta
Starbucks Corporation	1.11	0.01	1.103
Krispy Kreme Doughnuts	1.52	0.04	1.481
Diedrich Coffee	1.70	0.29	1.427
Average:		0.113	1.337

Exhibit 10-2
Calculating Levered Beta for a Private Company: Joe's Coffee Shops

$$\beta(\text{levered}) = \beta(\text{unlevered}) \times (1 + (\text{Debt /Equity})(1 - T))$$
$$= 1.337 \times (1 + 0.00)$$
$$= 1.337$$

Let's look at an example to illustrate the concept. Assume that you are valuing Joe's Coffee Shops, a $50 million revenue private chain of coffee shops. As there are a few public coffee companies, it is possible to gather Betas and debt ratios for public comparables.

Once the information has been gathered, determine the average unlevered Beta for the industry. Exhibit 10-1 details this analysis.

Once the unlevered Beta for the comparable universe has been calculated, determine the optimal debt ratio for Joe's Coffee Shops. Since Joe's has financed itself via internally generated funds, it has no debt in its capital structure. However, going forward, it is likely that for the company to continue to expand, it will need to secure outside funding to grow. Consequently, it would not be unreasonable to use the industry leverage ratio as the optimal or target debt /equity ratio for Joe's Coffee Shops in determining a levered Beta for the company. Exhibit 10-2 provides the details of this analysis.

Based on the analysis, Joe's Coffee Shops would have a levered Beta of 1.337.

[b] Problems with the Equity Risk Premium. A second component required to estimate a company's cost of equity is the equity risk premium (R_m). This is the return that investors who invest in the stock market demand over the risk-free rate of return. Typically, the equity market premium for large publicly traded companies ranges from 5% to 7%, while the equity market premium for small capitalization stocks can be 6%–8% higher. The equity risk premium for private companies should be adjusted to reflect a higher return requirement that investors would need in order to invest in private companies.

Using an example, venture capitalists have historically required a return on their equity investments of 35% to 40%, and in some cases higher.

[c]   *Estimating Cost of Equity.* From Chapter 4, we know that a company's cost of equity (K_e) is a function of the risk-free rate plus an equity market premium adjusted for the specific volatility of the company's stock, i.e., its Beta. Following is that equation:

$$\text{Cost of Equity } (K_e) = R_f + \beta(R_m)$$

We know that the risk free rate (R_f) is the interest rate ascribed to a theoretically "riskless" security, and that typically, the yield on government bonds is used, most often in the 10–20 year maturity range. Regardless of whether the valuation analysis is performed on a public or private company, the risk-free rate remains the same. Therefore, using our earlier example, Joe's Coffee Shops has a cost of equity of 14.76%, as derived as follows:

$$
\begin{aligned}
\text{Cost of Equity } (K_e) &= R_f + \beta(R_m) \\
&= 7\% + 1.337(R_m) \\
&= 7\% + 1.337 \times 8\% \\
&= 17.70\%
\end{aligned}
$$

[d]   *Estimating Cost of Debt.* From Chapter 4, we know that the cost of debt used in a WACC analysis is the target company's after-tax cost of debt (K_d). The formula for calculating K_d is as follows:

$$\text{After-Tax Cost of Debt } (K_d) = (\text{Cost of Debt}) \times (1 - \text{Tax Rate})$$

There are a number of problems in estimating the cost of debt for a private company. First, many small companies rely on bank debt as their source of debt capital. Bank agreements may be long-term in nature, with interest rates that reflect outdated funding costs. Consequently, a private company's bank agreement may not be indicative of its current debt cost of capital. Second, bank debt is typically priced at a premium to public debt, and therefore its cost of capital may be higher than that of a public peer company. For these reasons, there are two approaches to estimating the cost of debt for a private company. The first is to estimate the company's current bank debt funding cost as if it were to secure new financing. The second approach is to estimate the company's cost of debt using comparable funding costs for companies with similar credit profiles. The credit profile should be that of the optimal debt ratio that was used in the Beta calculation. Public information is available for companies that have public debt. This information will show the rating and ratios for the company's public debt. It is feasible therefore to use this comparables approach to determine a pre-tax cost of debt for the private company.

[e]   *Estimating Cost of Capital.* Calculating a WACC for a private company requires putting together each of the adjusted components

of the formula, reflecting each of the modifications made to it because of the private nature of the target company. The formula for calculating WACC is as follows:

$$\text{WACC } (K) = (\text{Percent Debt}) \times (K_d) + (\text{Percent Equity}) \times (K_e)$$

One additional item to discuss is the need to weight the cost of debt and cost of equity using the targeted capital structure for the private company. Make sure that the debt ratio used in the WACC analysis is consistent with the ratio used in determining the relevered Beta and the cost of debt.

[f] *Special Problems with Private Company Cash Flows.* Once the discount rate for the private company has been estimated, it is necessary to focus on the cash flows of the target company. Most important is the need to ensure that the cash flows are stated on a basis that reflects an arm's-length approach to managing the organization. For example, family controlled organizations may be managed for tax efficiency rather than earnings or cash flow. Likewise, these companies may have many family members on the payroll, as the company may be the extended family's primary source of income. Other items to watch for in recasting cash flows are shown in Exhibit 10-3.

The goal of recasting the cash flows for the company is to determine the true value of the company based on "real" cash flows. In particular, in the context of an acquisition, a purchaser will want to acquire a private company on the basis upon which it will be operated going forward, including only those expenses that are necessary to run the organization.

[g] *Issues with Calculating Terminal Value.* There are two primary methods for calculating terminal values for a company: growth-in-perpetuity and comparable multiples. Using the growth-in-perpetuity method, the main consideration for a private company is to ensure that the appropriate recast cash flows are used and the growth rates are commensurate with the company's growth opportunity.

The more difficult approach for a private company is using comparable multiples to determine terminal value. First, it is important to ensure that the financial statements of the private company are recast along the same lines as its public

---

Exhibit 10-3
Items to Consider in Recasting Cash Flows

Insurance	Personal items such as laundry
Benefits	Capitalized versus expensed items
Car allowances	Depreciation periods
Travel and Entertainment	Personal loans
Dues and subscriptions	

---

counterparts. Second, since many private companies are either S Corporations, limited liability corporations, divisions, or subsidiaries, their net earnings and capital structure may not provide a realistic view of net income against which to use an earnings multiple. Therefore, it is feasible to use a comparable multiple at the revenue and operating levels, excluding net income.

    [h] Final Observations on DCF Analysis. The most important aspects of private company DCF analysis are recasting the financial statements for the private company and adjusting the components of the WACC analysis and terminal value for issues specific to private companies. However, once the analysis is complete, it is always prudent to step away from the analysis and judge it in the context of (a) the transaction that is under contemplation, (b) the potential acquirer or merger partner, and (c) the universe of comparable public companies. In addition, it is wise to reassess the valuation in light of the company's lack of liquidity and other risks.

[2]   Comparable Company Trading Multiples Analysis

Comparable company trading multiples analysis uses the multiples of publicly traded companies to value a target business, public or private. Using this approach to value a private company requires a few modifications. First, as in DCF analysis, the financial statements of the company must be restated or recast to eliminate unnecessary non-arm's-length expenses. Second, the multiples derived from public companies should be used against benchmarks for the private company that allow comparison between public and private company. In other words, it is likely that such multiples as price/earnings multiples may not be appropriate when valuing private companies. Third, an applicable discount for liquidity should be applied to the company that reflects its private company risk.

One exception to this is for companies that are under valuation for an initial public offering. In such cases, the liquidity discount is usually eliminated and in its place an "IPO discount" is inserted. The IPO discount takes into consideration the market discount that institutional investors require in order for them to invest in an initial public offering. The IPO discount historically has ranged between 7% and 15%.

[3]   Comparable Transactions Analysis

Comparable transactions analysis uses multiples and premiums paid in comparable transactions to value target companies. When using this approach to value private companies, only one perspective can be used — comparable transactions multiples. Premiums paid analysis only applies to public valuations, as the premiums paid in comparable public transactions are applied to the public security of the target. As there are no public securities for private companies, the analysis is meaningless.

When using comparable transactions multiples, the same modifications that were made in comparable trading multiples should be applied: (1) restate the target's financial statements, (2) use multiples that are appropriate to the company and comparable with public company benchmarks, and (3) apply an appropriate liquidity discount.

[B]   Other Valuation Methodologies

[1]   Total Invested Capital

Many small private companies may be valued on the basis of the capital invested in the company. For example, in Joe's Coffee Shops, the owner invested $1 million in real estate, $500,000 in fixtures and furnishings, $250,000 in inventory, and $5 million in operating costs. In selling his company, Joe will want to recoup his investment in the business. When evaluating a private company, evaluate the sources and uses of capital since inception, and use this as a benchmark for value.

[2]   Replacement Cost

Much like the total invested capital approach, replacement cost analysis evaluates the cost of reproducing the business in today's environment. This may entail start-up expenses, real estate acquisitions, expenditures for property, plant, and equipment, inventory costs, and other miscellaneous expenses. This benchmark should be used in combination with the total invested capital approach to establish a baseline valuation for a company.

[3]   Asset Appraisal

In some businesses that are asset intensive, it may be appropriate to get an independent appraisal of the assets of the firm. Some assets, such as software, depreciate fairly rapidly, while others, such as real estate, may not depreciate at all. Depending on the company, an asset appraisal may yield a valuation that is higher or lower than a discounted cash flow or other stand alone valuation methodologies.

[4]   Internal Rate of Return

As a buyer of a private company, the purchaser is faced with the question of how to finance the acquisition. In most cases, two conventional forms of acquisition financing will be used: debt and equity. In order for the acquirer to make the acquisition, it must be comfortable that the returns it will garner from using equity to make the acquisition will be commensurate with the risk it is taking in the deal, and that it is better off making the investment than simply investing the capital in the stock market or public debt markets.

By way of comparison, venture capitalists historically have demanded 35% to 50% equity returns on their investments. Likewise, leveraged buyout funds have demanded 25% to 40% equity returns. At the other end of the spectrum, investors in treasury securities can expect to receive returns in the 4%–8% range, subject to current market rates.

As a result, an investor or acquirer evaluating a potential acquisition can value the acquisition of a private company based on two factors: (1) the sources of financing for the acquisition and (2) the return required on the equity investment. For example, Joe's Coffee Shops has recast operating cash flow available to service debt of $5 million. In addition, banks are currently willing to lend approximately 2.0 × operating cash flow, indicating total debt that can be placed on Joe's

Exhibit 10-4
IRR Acquisition Analysis for Joe's Coffee Shops

Purchase Price	$20					
Equity	$10					
Debt	$10					
Interest Rate on Debt	8%					
Term on Debt	5					
Sale Price	$36					

	Initial Investment	Cash Flow	Debt Repayment	Debt Outstanding	Interest Expense	Sale Price	IRR Cash Flows
Beginning Year 1	($10)						$(10)
Year 1		$5	$2	$8	$1		0
Year 2		$6	$2	$6	$0.64		0
Year 3		$7	$2	$4	$0.48		0
Year 4		$8	$2	$2	$0.32		0
Year 5		$9	$2	$0	$0.16	$36	$36
						IRR	**29%**

of $10 million. The acquirer has made a number of acquisitions in the past and determined that its internal rate of return requirement is 25%–30%. The acquirer has made an assumption that it can resell the business after five years at the same multiple that it acquires the business for. As a result, the amount of equity that the acquirer can afford to invest in the transaction is approximately $10 million. This indicates a purchase price of approximately $20 million for Joe's Coffee Shops, based on an acquirer specific analysis. Given these parameters, the acquisition of Joe's would generate an IRR of 29%. This analysis is quite similar to a leveraged buyout analysis. Exhibit 10-4 shows the IRR acquisition analysis for Joe's Coffee Shops in more detail.

§ 10.04 SPECIAL ISSUES IN VALUING PRIVATE COMPANIES

There are a number of specific items that should be considered whenever valuing a private company. Mostly, these issues will impact the way the financial statements of the company are recast or restated.

[A] Corporate Structure

Private companies can be owned using a number of legal structures, S Corporations, limited liability corporations, sole proprietorships, and C Corporations, as well as divisions or subsidiaries of public companies. Each of these ownership structures will impact the way a company is managed from an accounting and tax perspective. Private companies often are managed for tax efficiency, and consequently will be structured as S Corporations or limited liability corporations, where the earnings of the company will flow through to the individual income tax statements of the shareholders. In addition, private C Corporations may pay salaries as well as dividends to managers and shareholders. Consequently, it is prudent to look at the salary and benefit level of manager shareholders versus the level of dividends extracted from the company.

[B]   Intermingling of Personal and Business Expenses

Often, private companies are owned and operated by the same people. Inasmuch as these owners may not be breaking any laws, there may be differences in the amount and type of expenses that a given private company may have in relation to a public counterpart. For example, there may be excessive entertainment expenses or car allowance that might not exist in a public company.

[C]   Accounting Standards

The type of ownership structure may also impact the accounting standards used by the company. While public companies typically adhere to accounting regulations promulgated by the Financial Accounting Standards Board, commonly known as Generally Accepted Accounting Principles (GAAP), many private companies may not adhere to the same standard. It is wise, therefore, to understand completely the method of accounting used by a private company and the impact of that accounting methodology on the financial statements of the company.

§ 10.05   VALUING A PRIVATE COMPANY AS A PUBLIC COMPANY

[A]   IPO Valuation

The valuation of a private company for an initial public offering typically involves using the comparable trading multiples approach. Most likely, the private company is of a size where it would make an attractive public company and it is operated on the same basis as its public counterparts, e.g., it has audited financial statements that adhere to GAAP. In these cases, the company is valued the same way as a public company yet it is subjected to a market IPO discount that reduces the value by the amount required by institutional investors to make an investment in the company.

[B]   Stand Alone Public/Private Valuation

At a certain size threshold, a private company no longer becomes subject to the constraints of private company valuation. For example, a $500 million in revenue manufacturer that has been in operation for ten years is unlikely to suffer from many of the risks of start-up or pre-public private companies. In these cases, there is little distinction between a public or private company valuation approach, but for the need to ensure that the financial statements for the company are stated appropriately.

[C]   Private Company Sale to Public Company

In circumstances where the private company is being valued by a public acquirer, it is entirely appropriate to use additional methodologies to confirm the valuation. In particular, the public company acquirer may want to look at pro forma merger analysis, including dilution and contribution analysis.

§ 10.06   SUMMARY

Private company valuation analysis is fraught with vagaries that are particular to private companies. Most significant are the need to restate financial statements on an arm's-length basis, apply an appropriate liquidity discount, and adjust each of the public valuation methodologies to account for private company variances. In addition, private company valuation will include methodologies that are not often used in public company valuation, including total invested capital analysis, replacement cost analysis and IRR acquisition analysis.

Each valuation approach has its own particular use and should be used in that light. It is doubtful that any one analysis by itself will yield a pinpoint number that can be relied upon. Rather, it is likely that one will need to use multiple approaches to yield a range of values for a private company. It is also possible that certain analyses, such as total invested capital and replacement cost analysis, will yield valuation ranges at the lower end of the range. This is because these valuation approaches do not place high value on the ongoing operation of the business; rather, they look at a pinpoint estimate of value based on capital required to build the company. Discounted cash flow and comparable trading and transaction multiples analysis will yield valuations at the higher end of the range, as they assume a going concern approach. However, it is possible that these values may be low if the liquidity discount placed on the business is high. Sitting somewhere in the middle of the valuation range is IRR analysis, which is dependent on an acquirer's personal equity return requirements, rather than on a true measure of value for the company.

Chapter 11

VALUATION CASE STUDY: TROPICAL PRODUCTS CORP. ACQUISITION OF GLOBAL SNACKS, INC.

§ 11.01 OVERVIEW

This chapter provides a consolidated view of the strategic and financial analysis of Global Snacks, Inc., the hypothetical company that was analyzed and valued for illustrative purposes in Chapters 2 through 10. In addition, it summarizes the overall approach to analyzing the merger of two companies, Global Snacks, Inc. and Tropical Products Corp. In the foregoing chapters, each of the analyses was performed in a vacuum, absent any real strategic or business logic and without the benefit of any industry or competitive review. This case study brings the entire valuation analysis together, quite similar to that which would be produced by an investment bank.

§ 11.02   TRANSACTION BACKGROUND

Tropical Products Corp. is a publicly traded company that has been in business for over 50 years. The leader in the domestic snack food business, it has a strong market position and brand name, yet its success was built on a handful of related product lines. A number of smaller, more aggressive players have been putting pressure on Tropical's market share, growth rates, and operating margins. Since its market share is eroding, Tropical's leverage with suppliers has been diminishing and consequently, its product sourcing costs have been increasing, squeezing margins. Global Snacks, Inc. is a publicly traded company that has also been in the snack food business for many years. It makes products that compete with Tropical, yet since Tropical has a stronghold in the domestic market, Global has built its presence predominantly in Europe. In addition, to differentiate itself further, Global has a broader product offering than Tropical. The company has focused on research and development, allowing it to introduce new products at a much faster rate than Tropical.

Under pressure because investors have begun to recognize its deteriorating market share, Tropical's board of directors has decided it needs to protect its market position and shore up its operating performance. After evaluating a number of alternative acquisitions, Tropical has decided to pursue a merger with Global Snacks.

Tropical has been asked by Global and its investment banker to submit a preliminary offer for Global proposing terms upon which Tropical would acquire the company. The challenge for Tropical is to determine a purchase price that will be attractive enough to Global and its shareholders to warrant their selling the company, yet not so high that it destroys shareholder value for Tropical's shareholders by overpaying for Global. The following case study presents the overall valuation framework and analysis used in determining the initial offer price for Global Snacks, and demonstrates the mindset behind creating value through mergers and acquisitions.

§ 11.03   OVERVIEW OF TROPICAL PRODUCTS CORP.

Tropical Products Corp. is a Delaware Corporation that was founded in 1946. Moving home to Florida after World War II, Tropical Products' founder, Eli Scharf, went into business making cookies out of his mother's kitchen. Very quickly his famous recipe for macadamia nut chocolate cookies caught on and before he knew it, he had opened manufacturing plants across the Southeast and was distributing products across the United States. Tropical expanded beyond cookies and began offering other snack foods as well. Numerous products that Tropical developed became synonymous with the snack food industry.

Eli Scharf died in 1997 at the age of 76 with no heirs. His company was left in the hands of a board of directors made up of many of his old friends from his War days. Slowly but surely, without Eli's watchful eye, the company began to show signs of slowing growth. Product innovation came to a standstill and the company began to rely on the strength of its existing brands to carry its financial performance. In 2000, Tropical's principal products were cookies, potato chips,

---

Exhibit 11-1
Summary Data on Tropical Products Corp.
($ in millions, except per share data)

LTM1[1] Revenues	$7,005	Employees	15,000
LTM EBITDA	$1,487	Public Float	50%
LTM EBIT	$1,186	Institutional Ownership	29%
LTM EPS	$ 2.54	Percent Owned by Insiders	6%
Proj. EPS	$ 2.70	Fully Diluted Shares Outstanding (mm)	236
		Top Five Shareholders	
		Growth Advisors	6.7%
		Clearview Fund	5.3%
		Asset Advisors	4.2%
		Prophet Capital	2.3%
		Fortune Investors	1.1%

---

crackers, condiments, sauces, and pre-mixed ingredients for home baking. The company manufactures all its own products in modern kitchens around the United States. Its products are sold directly to institutions and food service companies and to consumers through a retail distribution network of convenience stores, grocery stores, and supermarkets. Over 90% of its sales are in the United States.

In 2000, the company generated $6.9 billion in revenue, an increase of 1.2% from 1999. Its gross margin in 2000 was 39.9%, a decrease of 0.4% from 1999. Earnings per share grew at a paltry 0.6% in 1999. The company's stock price has languished in the past year, settling at $38.00 per share. The company has generated less than 5% stock price growth in the past two years. It trades at 15.6× 2001 earnings per share, a discount to the industry, yet still surprisingly strong given it has the lowest five-year growth rate in earnings of the peer group.

Exhibit 11-1 provides summary information on Tropical Products Corp.

Tropical Products has shown relatively modest sales growth in the past few years, growing 1.0% in 1999 and 1.2% in 2000. While its EBITDA is strong, at approximately 21%–22% of sales, its margin is showing signs of decline. Its EBIT margin is also declining, having dropped from 17.8% in 1999 to 16.9% for the last 12 months. Exhibit 11-2 provides Tropical Products' historical income statement.

Tropical Products has a strong balance sheet with approximately $5.4 billion in total capital including $3.0 billion in shareholders equity. However, the company has recently begun to increase its leverage, rising to $2.1 billion at year-end December 31, 2001. Exhibit 11-3 shows Tropical Products' historical balance sheet. For the most recent fiscal year, Tropical generated $597 million in earnings from operations, yet its working capital and capital expenditures soaked up $484 million of that cash. In addition, the company repaid approximately $304 million

---

1. Last 12 months as of September 30, 2001.

Exhibit 11-2
Tropical Products Corp. Summary Historical Income Statement
($ in millions, except per share data)

	1998	*1999*	*2000*	*LTM*[2]
Revenues	$ 6,723	$ 6,789	$ 6,868	$ 7,005
% Growth	–	1.0%	1.2%	–
EBITDA	$ 1,414	$ 1,509	$ 1,494	$ 1,487
% Revenues	21.0%	22.2%	21.7%	21.2%
EBIT	$ 1,101	$ 1,207	$ 1,186	$ 1,186
% Revenues	16.4%	17.8%	17.3%	16.9%
Net Income	$ 554	$ 620	$ 597	$ 600
% Revenues	8.2%	9.1%	8.7%	8.6%
EPS	$ 2.37	$ 2.72	$ 2.74	$ 2.54
% Growth	–	15.0%	0.7%	–

Exhibit 11-3
Tropical Products Corp. Summary Historical Balance Sheet
($ in millions)

	As of Sept. 30, 2001	*Proj. Dec. 31, 2001*
Cash & Equivalents	$ 5.0	$ 5.0
Short-Term Debt	332.2	332.2
Long-Term Debt	1,812.4	2,061.8
Total Debt	$2,144.6	$2,393.9
Shareholders Equity	3,001.2	3,038.0
Total Capitalization	$5,145.7	$5,431.9

in debt resulting in a net reduction in its cash of $304 million. Exhibit 11-4 shows Tropical Products' historical cash flow statement.

§ 11.04 OVERVIEW OF GLOBAL SNACKS, INC.

Global Snacks, Inc. is a Delaware Corporation that was founded in 1974 by two college dropouts. Ernest Henry and Frank Stellar started the company based

---

2. Last 12 months as of September 30, 2001.

Exhibit 11-4
Tropical Products Corp. Summary Historical Cash Flow Statement
($ in millions)

	December 31, 2000
Cash Flows From Operating Activities:	
Earnings from Operations	$ 597
Non-Cash Items	71
Net Change in Working Capital	(276)
Cash From Operations	$ 392
Cash Flows From Investing Activities:	
Capital Expenditures	(206)
Net Proceeds, Other	0
Net Cash From Investing Activities	($206)
Cash Flows From Financing Activities:	
Change in Borrowings	(304)
Dividends Paid	0
Net Cash From Financing Activities	($304)
Exchange Rate Effect	0
Net Change in Cash	($118)
Beginning Cash	$ 123
Ending Cash	$ 5

on Ernest's penchant for junk food and Frank's fondness for travel. As best friends, they took their junior year abroad in Europe, only to quickly become disenchanted because of the lack of availability of simple snack food. After receiving a care package from home, they shared their spoils with their new-found friends abroad, and realized the opportunity to import the American-style love for snack food to Europe. They returned home without completing college and incorporated Global Snacks. Based on the tastes of their friends abroad, they developed a line of chips and cookies that were geared to the European market. From those humble beginnings, they grew the company to $3.5 billion by 2000, based on continued research and development in Europe and the United States.

Today, Global Snacks derives most of its revenue from Europe. Its principal products include chips and cookies as well as jams, jellies, condiments, and sauces. Its products are sold across Europe and the United States to institutions and food service companies and to consumers through a retail distribution network of convenience stores, grocery chains, and supermarkets.

Exhibits 11-5 and 11-6 provide summary information on Global Snacks.

Global Snacks showed strong 4.6% revenue growth in 1999 and has shown signs of increased growth for the last four quarters. Its EBITDA margin has varied

Exhibit 11-5
Summary Data on Global Snacks, Inc.
($ in millions)

LTM[3] Revenues	$3,561	Employees	8,500
LTM EBITDA	$ 794	Public Float	58%
LTM EBIT	$ 628	Institutional Ownership	44%
LTM EPS	$ 1.59	Percent Owned by Insiders	9%
Proj. EPS	$ 1.64	Fully Diluted Shares Outstanding (mm)	210
		Top Five Shareholders	
		Food Fund	5.6%
		Starfish Holdings	3.9%
		Asset Advisors	3.1%
		New Age	2.2%
		Van Peak Funds	1.5%

Exhibit 11-6
Global Snacks, Inc. Summary Historical Income Statement
($ in millions, except per share data)

	1998	1999	2000	LTM[4]
Revenues	$ 3,288	$ 3,439	$ 3,482	$ 3,561
% Growth	–	4.6%	1.2%	2.3%
EBITDA	$ 750	$ 814	$ 790	$ 794
% Revenues	22.8%	23.7%	22.7%	22.3%
EBIT	$ 588	$ 650	$ 614	$ 628
% Revenues	17.9%	18.9%	17.6%	17.6%
Net Income	$ 302	$ 333	$ 322	$ 328
% Revenues	9.2%	9.7%	9.3%	9.2%
EPS	$ 1.36	$ 1.59	$ 1.57	$ 1.59
% Growth	–	16.4%	−1.3%	–

from 22.7% in 2000 to 23.7% in 1999. For the most recent four quarters, its EBITDA margin was down to 22.3%. At the EBIT line, its margins have stabilized in 2000 and the last 12 months at 17.6%. The company has shown relatively flat earnings per share for the past few years.

Global Snacks has a strong balance sheet with $3.6 billion in total capital including $2.0 billion in shareholders equity. For the year ended December 31, 2001, the company had long-term debt of $1.6 billion, a decrease of $100 million from the prior year. Exhibit 11-7 shows Global Snacks' historical balance sheet. For the year ended December 31, 2000, Global Snacks generated cash flow from operations of $486 million. After capital expenditures of $208 million and dividends

---

3. Last 12 months as of September 30, 2001.
4. Last 12 months as of September 30, 2001.

Exhibit 11-7
Global Snacks, Inc. Summary Historical Balance Sheet
($ in millions)

	As of Sept. 30, 2001	*Proj. Dec. 31, 2001*
Cash & Equivalents	$ 292	$ 223
Short-Term Debt	0	0
Long-Term Debt	1,732	1,632
Total Debt	$1,732	$1,632
Shareholders Equity	1,887	1,960
Total Capitalization	$3,619	$3,591

Exhibit 11-8
Global Snacks, Inc. Summary Historical Cash Flow Statement
($ in millions)

	December 31, 2000
Cash Flows From Operating Activities:	
Earnings from Operations	$ 322
Non-Cash Items	179
Net Change in Working Capital	(16)
Cash From Operations	$ 486
Cash Flows From Investing Activities:	
Capital Expenditures	(208)
Net Proceeds, Other	17
Net Cash From Investing Activities	$(191)
Cash Flows From Financing Activities:	
Change in Borrowings	51
Dividends Paid	(170)
Net Cash From Financing Activities	$ 119
Exchange Rate Effect	6
Net Change in Cash	$ 182
Beginning Cash	$ 83
Ending Cash	$ 265

---

of $179 million, it increased its cash balance to $265 million. Exhibit 11-8 shows Global Snacks' historical cash flow statement.

§ 11.05 INDUSTRY OVERVIEW

The snack food industry, defined as cookies, crackers, and salty snacks, is a $25 billion industry in the United States. It is dominated by large, diversified manufacturers and a few strong regional/niche players, who together comprise over 70% of the market share in the United States. Most of these conglomerates have expanded globally in the last ten–20 years. Market shares of the conglomerates are typically lower outside of the United States, but they are not insignificant, and many brands continue to gain market share abroad. Growth in the United States is moderate at 4%–6%, driven mostly by a shift in product mix to more premium priced and convenience-oriented products. Producers of snack foods must balance their need to introduce new products to meet consumer demand with maintaining their market shares in their current brands. To that end, marketing as well as research and development dollars must be carefully allocated. Other issues facing producers include upgrading and fully optimizing their distribution channels through state-of-the-art technology and the addition of non-snack items.

§ 11.06   COMPETITIVE OVERVIEW

In addition to Tropical and Global, there are five main competitors in the United States. They are all public corporations.

Fried Food Holdings distributes its chips, pretzels, and related items in both ready-to-eat and frozen food formats. It is the sole snack food producer with distribution capabilities in the frozen arena. Distribution is primarily through grocery stores and convenience outlets, with about 30% going to restaurants, schools, and hospitals. The company began as a regional player in the South in the 1980s, and expanded to the Midwest in the 1990s. Fried Food Holdings has announced plans to continue its growth in the West but will not expand internationally for several years.

Crunch Corporation is a major conglomerate with half of its business coming from snack foods and the other half from cereals. Distribution is throughout the United States and Europe. Crunch is primarily focused on cereals in Europe, where it has gained a solid reputation. A joint venture with an Asian partner was recently dissolved after only two years of operations. Internal strife has left management less focused on the business than it should be, but once these issues are resolved, Crunch has the potential to become a major competitor in snack foods.

Salty Seasons has a focused product offering including the number two chip brand behind Tropical. Over 30% of its sales are through a well-known U.S. discount chain. Salty was born through the successful merger of two regional players who strategically aligned their brands and product lines to focus on their top sellers. Continued innovations and improvements in taste and packaging have kept consumers clamoring for more. Salty does not currently operate outside of the United States but has stated that it has hired both a major strategy consultancy and an investment bank to help Salty formulate its growth strategy.

Sweeties, Inc. is all about sugar. Founded in 1955 with the introduction of their first product, the Cookie Monster, they have remained focused on this niche of the snack food industry. Their main products are cookies and sweet glazed popcorn, around which they have built a solid reputation with a suite of strong brand names. Distribution is through U.S. and Canadian retailers and vending

Exhibit 11-9
Comparable Company Financial Overview
($ in millions)

	Enterprise[5] Value	Equity Value	LTM Sales	LTM EBITDA	LTM EBIT	LTM Net Income	Proj. Net Income
Global Snacks	$ 5,220	$3,780	$3,561	$ 794	$ 628	$328	$344
Tropical Products	$11,115	$8,975	$7,005	$1,487	$1,186	$600	$637
Crunch Corp	$ 4,842	$4,002	$3,001	$ 541	$ 413	$198	$198
Fried Food Hldgs	$ 2,794	$1,869	$3,153	$ 629	$ 498	$165	$168
Health Nut, Inc.	$ 2,220	$1,836	$1,902	$ 254	$ 190	$123	$122
Salty Seasons	$ 3,609	$3,036	$2,509	$ 367	$ 283	$145	$151
Sweeties, Inc.	$ 2,927	$2,592	$2,452	$ 403	$ 381	$196	$202

channels. They are rumored to be close to signing a major distribution deal with a European partner.

Health Nut, Inc. was founded in the early 1970s, at a time when the trend toward natural foods was emerging. Their products included mainly granola, dried fruits and nuts, and were distributed through independent health food stores. They expanded quickly across the United States by buying up the independent operators and opening several stores in key metropolitan markets. The quick growth and additional product lines brought financial problems in the mid 1980s, which caused them to restructure. While they still operate their own stores under the Health Nut name, they now also distribute through grocery stores and other retail outlets.

Exhibit 11-9 provides summary financial information on the significant companies in the snack food industry.

§ 11.07 STRATEGIC AND BUSINESS ANALYSIS

From the information provided, we can ascertain the strategic reasons for a potential acquisition of Global Snacks by Tropical Products.

- *Eliminate a competitor:* Tropical could shrink the number of players in the industry helping to shore up its price advantage with customers and suppliers.

- *Expand the market share of both companies:* The combined company would be the largest company in the U.S. and European markets.

- *Broaden the combined company's product offering:* While both companies have a number of products that overlap, they also have products such as jams and jellies that are complementary.

---

5. Enterprise value = equity value plus total debt, minority interest and preferred stock, less cash & cash equivalents.

- *Use respective geographic distribution strengths to cross-sell products:* While both companies offer many similar products, their geographic distribution is quite dissimilar, allowing the companies to cross-sell products in each others' markets.

- *Leverage Global's technology:* Global has a strong orientation to research, development, and product innovation. Tropical would be able to capitalize on Global's strong R&D to introduce new products in the United States.

- *Lower supplier costs with combined purchasing power:* The combined company would have greater economies-of-scale to secure better prices from suppliers.

- *Eliminate redundant selling, general, administrative, and other operating expenses:* Because the companies both have significant corporate staffs, they could eliminate redundant overhead and generate substantial cost savings.

- *Eliminate duplicate manufacturing costs:* Both companies have substantial manufacturing facilities in the United States, and in certain facilities they have excess capacity. A combination would allow the companies to consolidate manufacturing and take advantage of excess capacity.

- *Enhance the story of the combined company to investors:* The combination serves to create a strong global organization with leading market shares in the United States and Europe.

- *Deepen management team:* Both companies would benefit from the depth of expertise at each company.

- *Optimize capital structure by enhancing assets and debt mix:* The combined company would be in a position to optimize their capital structures and lower borrowing costs.

These potential benefits all need to be substantiated by sound valuation and financial analysis. If the analysis does not support the deal, regardless of how good it sounds, one should be very wary of proceeding. Even though the business and strategic merits of the proposed combination are compelling, the price that Tropical would have to pay for Global Snacks may be too high to warrant a good return on investment to Tropical's shareholders. The financial outcome of the proposed transaction would thus undermine the favorable strategic benefits of the merger.

§ 11.08 FINANCIAL STATEMENT ANALYSIS

In order to initiate the analysis of Tropical and Global, we start by looking at simple financial statement analysis. First, we compare the income statements and balance sheets for the two companies on a common size basis in order to form a comparable basic view of their financial metrics.

Exhibit 11-10
Common Size Comparison of Tropical Products and Global Snacks
Common Size Income Statement[6]

	Tropical Products	*Global Snacks*
Revenues	100.0%	100.0%
Cost of Goods Sold	59.6%	53.5%
Gross Profit	40.4%	46.5%
EBITDA	21.2%	22.3%
EBIT	16.9%	17.6%
Net Income	8.6%	9.2%

Common Size Balance Sheet[7]

	Tropical Products	*Global Snacks*
Assets		
Cash and Cash Equivalents	0.1%	5.4%
Accounts Receivable	11.5%	8.2%
Inventory	16.6%	9.7%
Other Current Assets	0.8%	4.0%
Total Current Assets	29.0%	27.2%
Net Property, Plant & Equipment	29.9%	53.4%
Intangible Assets, Net of Amortization	27.8%	13.9%
Other Assets	13.3%	5.5%
Total Assets	100.00%	100.0%
Liabilities and Shareholders' Equity		
Accounts Payable	10.3%	7.3%
Notes Payable	4.0%	0.0%
Other Current Liabilities	11.4%	9.9%
Total Current Liabilities	26.1%	17.2%
Total Long-Term Debt	21.7%	32.2%
Non-pension Post Retirement Benefits and Other	11.4%	7.1%
Deferred Tax	4.9%	8.5%
Total Liabilities	64.1%	64.9%
Capital Stock	1.3%	0.4%
Capital Surplus	3.7%	7.3%
Retained Earnings	64.4%	27.4%
Treasury Stock	−33.5%	0.0%
Total Shareholders' Equity	35.9%	35.1%
Total Liabilities and Equity	100.00%	100.00%

[A]   Common Size Analysis

Exhibit 11-10 shows the common size comparison of the income statements and balance sheets for Tropical Products and Global Snacks. As you can see from the comparison, for the last 12 months ended September 30, 2001, Global Snacks has

---

6. Most recent 12 months ended third quarter 2001.
7. Most recent 12 months ended third quarter 2001.

gross margin, EBITDA margin, EBIT margin and net income margin that are higher than those of Tropical Products. Comparing the two companies' balance sheets, there are significant differences. Global has a higher cash and cash equivalent balance as a percent of total assets, yet lower inventory and accounts receivable as a percent of total assets. Global also has substantially higher net property, plant and equipment than Tropical on a percentage of total assets basis. From a liability perspective, Global has lower accounts payable, notes payable and other current liabilities as a percent of total assets, yet substantially higher debt on a percentage basis. Interestingly, the two companies have comparable equity as a percent of total assets.

[B] Profitability Analysis

Much like the common size analysis of a company's income statement, profitability analysis, as shown in Exhibit 11-11, provides a comparison of various companies' margins.

The return on investment analysis, as shown in Exhibit 11-12, provides a gauge for measuring a company's profitability as a return on assets, equity and capital. As shown for the year ended 2000, and based on balance sheet data for December 31, 2000, Tropical Products showed more attractive returns on assets, equity and capital than Global Snacks.

Exhibit 11-11
Profitability Analysis for Tropical Products and Global Snacks[8]

	Tropical Products	Global Snacks
Gross Margin	40.4%	46.5%
EBIT Margin	16.9%	17.6%
EBITDA Margin	21.2%	22.3%
Pre-Tax Margin	13.2%	14.2%
Net Income Margin	8.6%	9.2%

Exhibit 11-12
Return on Investment Analysis for Tropical Products and Global Snacks[9]

	Tropical Products	Global Snacks
Return on Assets	14.0%	11.9%
Return on Equity	49.8%	37.5%
Return on Capital	14.0%	11.9%

---

8. Most recent 12 months ended third quarter 2001.
9. Based on balance sheet data for year ended 1999 and 2000.

[C]   Efficiency Analysis

Efficiency analysis shows us how well a company utilizes its assets, not necessarily in the context of its profitability. Exhibit 11-13 provides this overview of Tropical Products and Global Snacks based on their December 31, 2000 balance sheet and year-end income statement for 2000.

Exhibit 11-13
Efficiency Analysis for Tropical Products and Global Snacks[10]

	Tropical Products	Global Snacks
Inventory Turnover Ratio	2.7×	3.5×
Inventory Days	137	103
Receivables Turnover	5.9×	7.8×
Days Sales Outstanding	62.3	46.6
Payables Turnover	4.4×	8.9×
Days Payables Outstanding	83.0	40.9
Working Capital Turnover	6.0×	8.9×
Fixes Asset Turnover	2.9×	1.3×
Total Asset Turnover	0.8×	0.7×

[D]   Liquidity Analysis

Liquidity analysis provides a comparative measure of various companies' liquidity. The definition of liquidity depends on the ratio under scrutiny, but can vary from all current assets to cash plus marketable securities plus accounts receivables. Exhibit 11-14 illustrates the liquidity analysis for Tropical Products and Global Snacks.

Exhibit 11-14
Liquidity Analysis for Tropical Products and Global Snacks[11]

	Tropical Products	Global Snacks
Current Ratio	1.1×	1.6×
Quick Ratio	0.4×	0.8×
Cash Ratio	0.0×	0.3×
Operating Cash Flow Ratio	0.7×	0.5×

[E]   Leverage Analysis

Leverage analysis evaluates a company's leverage as it relates to total capital and equity, and in the context of a company's ability to service the interest expense

10. Based on balance sheet data for years ended 1999 and 2000.
11. Based on balance sheet for third quarter 2001.

and principal repayment. Exhibit 11-15 illustrates the leverage analysis for Tropical Products and Global Snacks.

Exhibit 11-15
Leverage Analysis for Tropical Products and Global Snacks[12]

	Tropical Products	*Global Snacks*
Debt-to-Total Capital Ratio	0.2×	0.3×
Debt-to-Equity Ratio	0.6×	0.6×
Times Interest Earned	4.9×	4.8×

---

§ 11.09   GLOBAL SNACKS VALUATION ANALYSIS

In order to value Global Snacks, we look at the three principle valuation methodologies: comparable trading multiples analysis, comparable transactions analysis, and discounted cash flow analysis.

[A]   Comparable Trading Multiples Analysis

Exhibit 11-16 shows comparable financial metrics for Global Snacks, Tropical Products, and its peer group. As can be seen from the exhibit, Global is the second largest company in the industry by most measures.

Exhibit 11-17 provides the comparable trading multiples for the snack food peer group based on the financial metrics in Exhibit 11-16.

Based on comparable trading multiples, Global Snacks trades at 1.5× LTM Revenues, 6.6× LTM EBITDA, and 11.0× Projected Net Income. This is a substantial discount to the average of the peer group excluding Global Snacks of 1.3× LTM Revenues, 7.8× LTM EBITDA, and 15.6× Projected Net Income. In addition, its Price Earnings to Growth rate is 130%, a discount to the 180% Price Earnings to Growth Rate for the peer group.

Based on the average comparable trading multiples for Global Snacks shown in Exhibit 11-17, the company has an implied enterprise value of $4.5–$6.8 billion, implying an equity value of $3.2–$5.4 billion. This translates into a price per share range of $15.43–$25.93 per share. Exhibit 11-18 illustrates the application of the trading multiples derived in Exhibit 11-17, to the financial metrics of Global Snacks to yield the implied value range of $15.43–$25.93 per share.

[B]   Comparable Transactions Analysis

[1]   Comparable Transaction Multiples Analysis

Exhibit 11-19 shows the ten most comparable transactions to that of the Tropical Products acquisition of Global Snacks.

---

12. Based on balance sheet data for third quarter 2001.

Exhibit 11-16
Comparable Company Financial Information
($ in millions)

	Enterprise[13] Value	Equity Value	LTM Sales	LTM EBITDA	LTM EBIT	LTM Net Income	Proj. Net Income
Global Snacks	$ 5,220	$3,780	$3,561	$ 794	$ 628	$328	$344
Tropical Products	$11,115	$8,975	$7,005	$1,487	$1,186	$600	$637
Crunch Corp.	$ 4,842	$4,002	$3,001	$ 541	$ 413	$198	$198
Fried Food Hldgs	$ 2,794	$1,869	$3,153	$ 629	$ 498	$165	$168
Health Nut, Inc.	$ 2,220	$1,836	$1,902	$ 254	$ 190	$123	$122
Salty Seasons	$ 3,609	$3,036	$2,509	$ 367	$ 283	$145	$151
Sweeties, Inc.	$ 2,927	$2,592	$2,452	$ 403	$ 381	$196	$202

Exhibit 11-17
Comparable Multiples

	Enterprise Value to:			Equity Value to: Projected		
	LTM Revenues	LTM EBITDA	LTM EBIT	LTM Net Income	Net Income	P/E/G[14]
Global Snacks	1.5×	6.6×	8.3×	11.5×	11.0×	130%
Tropical Products	1.6×	7.5×	9.4×	15.0×	14.1×	220%
Crunch Corp.	1.6×	8.9×	11.7×	20.4×	20.4×	240%
Fried Food Hldgs	0.9×	4.4×	5.6×	11.3×	11.1×	120%
Health Nut, Inc.	1.2×	8.7×	11.7×	15.3×	15.1×	150%
Salty Seasons	1.4×	9.8×	12.7×	20.3×	20.0×	180%
Sweeties, Inc.	1.2×	7.3×	7.7×	13.7×	12.8×	180%
Excluding Global:						
Average	1.3×	7.8×	9.8×	16.0×	15.6×	180%
Median	1.3×	8.1×	10.5×	15.1×	14.6×	180%
Excluding Global and Tropical:						
Average	1.3×	7.8×	9.9×	16.2×	15.9×	180%
Median	1.2×	8.7×	11.7×	15.3×	15.1×	180%

13. Enterprise value = equity value plus total debt, minority interest and preferred stock, less cash & cash equivalents.

14. P/E/G is the price earnings multiple as a percentage of the company's projected earnings growth rate. It provides a relative valuation of a company by comparing its earnings multiple to its growth rate.

Exhibit 11-18
Comparable Multiples Valuation for Global Snacks
($ in millions)

	Global Metric	Comparable Multiple[15]	Implied Enterprise Value	Implied Equity Value[16]
LTM Revenues	$3,561	1.3×	$4,680	$3,241
LTM EBITDA	$ 794	7.8×	$6,180	$4,740
LTM EBIT	$ 628	9.8×	$6,152	$4,713
LTM Net Income	$ 328	16.0×	$6,685	$5,246
Projected Net Income	$ 344	15.6×	$6,788	$5,348

Exhibit 11-20 shows the transaction multiples arising from the comparable transactions. Based on the transactions, the average multiples are 1.32× LTM Revenues, 9.9× LTM EBITDA, and 20.1× LTM Net Income.

Exhibit 11-21 shows the comparable transaction multiples analysis for Global Snacks. Based on the average transaction multiples, Global Snacks would have an implied enterprise value range of $4.7–$8.0 billion, suggesting equity value range of $3.2–$6.5 billion. This translates into a per share price of $15.53–$30.53 per share.

[2]   Comparable Transaction Premiums Analysis

Exhibit 11-22 shows the comparable premiums for transactions comparable to that of the Tropical Products acquisition of Global Snacks. The average premiums for this universe of companies were 37.2%, 24.2%, and 12.9% for the one-month, two-weeks, and one-day prior to stock price on the announcement date.

Exhibit 11-23 shows the valuation of Global Snacks based on the premiums paid in comparable acquisitions. Based on the one-day, two-week, and one-month prior premiums, the implied enterprise value range for Global Snacks would be $5.6–$6.7 billion, suggesting an equity value range of $4.1–$5.3 billion. The implied per share valuation range is $19.71–$25.11.

[C]   Discounted Cash Flow Analysis

To perform the DCF analysis of Global Snacks, the first step is to determine the company's weighted average cost of capital. To do this, we look at the comparable Betas for the company's peer group and unlever them to determine the average unlevered Beta. Exhibit 11-24 presents the information required to unlever the Betas of comparable companies.

---

15. Based on the average multiple for the peer group including Tropical Products but excluding Global Products.

16. When calculating the implied equity value, it is important to remember to subtract the net debt outstanding at the target.

Exhibit 11-19
Comparable Transactions Financial Data

Acquirer/ Target	Ann. Date	Ent. Value[17]	Equity Value	LTM Sales	LTM EBITDA	LTM EBIT	LTM Net Income	Book Value
Grupo Nationale/ Euromix	Jun 1, '01	$1,470	$ 853	$ 942	$128	$114	$36	$371
Wholegrains/ Biscuit Basket	Mar 5, '01	$1,450	$1,250	$ 967	$137	$109	$67	$417
Stage Two/ MishMash	Dec 5, '00	$1,287	$ 881	$1,313	$238	$165	$71	$275
Global Snack/ Claus Baking	Nov 20, '00	$ 625	$ 425	$ 568	$ 56	$ 42	$18	$304
Argyle Foods/ Homey Bagels	Jul 10, '00	$ 265	$ 275	$ 203	$ 31	$ 21	$15	$145
Biscuit Basket/ JJJ Jellies	Jun 15, '00	$ 456	$ 320	$ 304	$ 45	$ 32	$15	$119
Sweeties/ Baking Bonanza	Feb 12, '00	$ 445	$ 313	$ 445	$ 62	$ 49	$21	$149
Tropical/Products Nutsahoy	Nov 5, '99	$ 241	$ 228	$ 165	$ 20	$ 17	$10	$ 65
Global Snacks/ Lekkers	Jul 23, '99	$ 302	$ 330	$ 275	$ 31	$ 22	$14	$103
Fried Food Hldgs/ Munchies	Apr 5, '99	$ 505	$ 445	$ 297	$ 41	$ 50	$27	$144

Exhibit 11-20
Comparable Transaction Multiples

Acquirer/Target	Enterprise Value to:			Equity Value to:	
	LTM Revenues	LTM EBITDA	LTM EBIT	LTM Net Income	Book Value
Grupo Nationale/Euromix	1.56×	11.5×	12.9×	23.6×	2.3×
Wholegrains/Biscuit Basket	1.5×	10.6×	13.3×	18.7×	3.0×
Stage Two/MishMash	0.98×	5.4×	7.8×	12.5×	3.2×
Global Snack/Claus Baking	1.1×	11.1×	15.0×	23.7×	1.4×
Argyle Foods/Homey Bagels	1.3×	8.6×	12.5×	18.7×	1.9×
Biscuit Basket /JJJ Jellies	1.5×	10.2×	14.3×	22.0×	2.7×
Sweeties /Baking Bonanza	1.0×	7.2×	9.0×	14.7×	2.1×
Tropical Products/Nutsahoy	1.46×	12.2×	14.2×	23.0×	3.5×
Global Snacks/Lekkers	1.1×	9.7×	13.6×	23.8×	3.2×
Fried Food Hldgs/Munchies	1.70×	12.3×	10.1×	16.8×	3.1×
Average	**1.32×**	**9.9×**	**12.3×**	**20.1×**	**2.6×**
Median	**1.38×**	**10.4×**	**13.1×**	**22.0×**	**2.9×**

17. Enterprise value = equity value plus total debt, minority interest and preferred stock, less cash & cash equivalents.

Exhibit 11-21
Comparable Transaction Multiples Valuation Analysis
($ in millions)

	Global Metric	Comparable Multiple[18]	Implied Enterprise Value	Implied Equity Value[19]
LTM Revenues	$3,561	1.32×	$4,701	$3,261
LTM EBITDA	$ 794	9.9×	$7,851	$6,411
LTM EBIT	$ 628	12.3×	$7,704	$6,265
LTM Net Income	$ 328	20.1×	$8,031	$6,591
Book Value	$1,916	2.6×	$6,423	$4,983

Exhibit 11-22
Comparable Transaction Premiums

Acquirer/Target	Ann. Date	Premium 1-Month Prior	1-Day 2-Weeks Prior	Prior
Grupo Nationale/*Euromix*	Jun 1, '01	23.3%	13.3%	9.0%
Wholegrains/*Biscuit Basket*	Mar 5, '01	38.0%	28.4%	15.6%
Stage Two/*MishMash*	Dec 5, '00	32.7%	21.7%	9.7%
Global Snack/*Claus Baking*	Nov 20, '00	51.8%	33.1%	11.5%
Argyle Foods/*Homey Bagels*	Jul 10, '00	32.7%	28.5%	19.9%
Biscuit Basket /*JJJ Jellies*	Jun 15, '00	65.9%	38.9%	15.7%
Sweeties /*Baking Bonanza*	Feb 12, '00	32.3%	18.7%	12.2%
Tropical Products/*Nutsahoy*	Nov 5, '99	26.9%	15.6%	11.1%
Global Snacks/*Lekkers*	Jul 23, '99	38.9%	24.3%	12.9%
Fried Food Hldgs/*Munchies*	Apr 5, '99	29.3%	19.9%	11.4%
	Average	**37.2%**	**24.2%**	**12.9%**
	Median	**32.7%**	**23.0%**	**11.9%**

Exhibit 11-23
Premiums Paid Valuation for Global Snacks

	Global Metric	Comparable Premium[20]	Implied Enterprise Value (mm)	Implied Equity Value (mm)[21]
1-Day Prior	$ 17.46	12.9%	$ 5,579	$ 4,140
2-Week Prior	$ 17.95	24.2%	$ 6,122	$ 4,682
1-Month Prior	$ 18.31	37.2%	$ 6,713	$ 5,274

18. Based on the average multiple for the peer group.

19. When calculating the implied equity value, it is important to remember to subtract the debt outstanding at the target.

20. The average transaction premium was used for this analysis.

21. When calculating the implied equity value, it is important to remember to subtract the debt outstanding at the target.

Exhibit 11-24
Comparable Betas and Leverage Ratios
($ in millions)

	Debt	Equity Value	Enterprise Value	Cost of Debt	Tax Rate	Beta (L)	Beta (U)
Crunch Corp	$ 867	$4,002	$4,869	7.3%	40.0%	0.55	0.48
Fried Food Hldgs	$1,003	$1,869	$2,872	7.2%	38.0%	0.66	0.49
Health Nut	$ 407	$1,836	$2,242	4.5%	38.0%	0.55	0.48
Salty Seasons	$ 592	$3,036	$3,628	10.1%	40.0%	0.59	0.52
Sweeties	$ 393	$2,592	$2,985	7.7%	40.0%	0.71	0.55
		Average		**8.0%**	**39.2%**	**0.61**	**0.52**
		Median		**7.5%**	**40.0%**	**0.59**	**0.49**
Global Snacks	$1,732	$3,780	$5,512	7.2%	35.0%	0.69	0.53

Exhibit 11-25
Global Snacks Weighted Average Cost of Capital Calculation

WACC = $K_d \times (D/(D + E)) + K_e \times (E/(E + E))$

Where:

K_d = After Tax Cost of Debt
K_e = Cost of Equity
D = Book Value of Debt
E = Market Value of Equity

I. K_d = Pre-Tax Cost of Debt $\times$ (1 − Tax Rate)
Pre-Tax Cost of Debt   = 7.2%
Tax Rate   = 35.0%
K_d = 7.2% X (1 − 35%) = 4.6%

II. $K_e = R_f + \beta \times R_m$

Where:

R_f = Risk Free Rate (10-Year Note) = 5.2%
β = Target Beta   = 0.68
R_m = Market Risk Premium   = 8.1%
K_e = 5.2% + 0.68 X 8.1%   = 10.7%

III. WACC = $K_d \times (D/(D + E)) + K_e \times (E/(E + E))$

Where:

Target Debt to Capital Ratio   = 20.0%
Implicit Equity to Capital Ratio   = 80%
K = ((4.6% $\times$ 20.0%) + 10.7% = 80.0%) = 9.5%

Exhibit 11-25 illustrates the weighted average cost of capital calculation for Global Snacks.

Exhibit 11-26
Projected Free Cash Flows for Global Snacks
($ in millions)

	Projected					
	2001	*2002*	*2003*	*2004*	*2005*	*2006*
Revenues	$3,632	$3,778	$3,929	$4,086	$4,249	$4,419
EBITDA	819	864	911	960	1,012	1,066
EBIT	647	686	726	769	814	862
Less: Cash Taxes @35%	(226)	(240)	(254)	(269)	(285)	(302)
Tax Effected EBIT	$ 421	$ 446	$ 472	$ 500	$ 529	$ 560
Plus: Depreciation	172	178	184	191	198	205
Less: Capital Expenditures	223	231	239	247	256	265
Less: Inc. in Working Capital	29	10	10	10	11	11
Unlevered Free Cash Flow	**$ 341**	**$ 384**	**$ 408**	**$ 434**	**$ 460**	**$ 489**

Exhibit 11-26 illustrates the projected free cash flows for Global Snacks. Remember that for the discounted cash flow analysis, the cash flows that are discounted are the unlevered after-tax-free cash flows of the company defined as:

Earnings Before Interest After Taxes
Plus: Depreciation
Less: Capital Expenditures
Less: Increase in Working Capital

= Free Cash Flow

In calculating the discounted cash flow value for Global Snacks, we perform the analysis by calculating terminal value using the multiples method and the growth in perpetuity model. Exhibit 11-27 illustrates the discounted cash flow valuation using the multiples method. Based on this analysis, the DCF enterprise value range for Global Snacks is $6.3–$7.6 billion, implying an equity range of $4.8–$6.3 billion or $23.16–$29.62 per share.

Exhibit 11-28 shows the DCF analysis for Global Snacks using the growth in perpetuity method for terminal value. Based on this analysis, Global has an enterprise value range of $5.8–$7.5 billion, implying an equity value range of $4.4–$6.2 billion or $21.35–$29.71 per share.

[D] Stock Price Analysis

For the prior 12 months, Global Snacks has traded between $18.00 and $32.00 per share, with 55% of the cumulative volume trading below $26.00 per share. Of this amount, a total of 15% traded between $24.00 and $26.00 per share. Exhibit 11-29 shows the absolute stock price for Global Snacks for the past year.

Exhibit 11-27
DCF Analysis of Global Snacks Using Multiples Method
for Terminal Value
($ in millions)

	9.5%		
Discount Rate			
Termined EBITDA Multiple	7.0×	8.0×	9.0×
2006 EBITDA	$1,066	$1,066	$1,066
Terminal Value	$7,463	$8,529	$9,596
PV of Terminal Value	$4,748	$5,426	$6,105
PV of Free Cash Flows	$1,556	$1,556	$1,556
Implied Enterprise Value	$6,304	$6,982	$7,660
Plus: Cash & Cash Equivalents	$ 292	$ 292	$ 292
Less: Total Debt	$1,732	$1,732	$1,732
Implied Equity Value	$4,864	$5,542	$6,221
Implied Value Per Share	**$23.16**	**$26.39**	**$29.62**

Exhibit 11-28
DCF Analysis for Global Snacks Using Growth in
Perpetuity Method for Terminal Value

	9.5%		
Discount Rate			
Perpetual Growth Rate	2.0%	3.0%	4.0%
2006 FCF	489	489	489
Continuing FCF (2007)	499	503	508
Terminal Value	$6,677	$7,786	$9,299
PV of Terminal Value	$4,248	$4,953	$5,916
PV of Free Cash Flows	$1,556	$1,556	$1,556
Implied Enterprise Value	$5,804	$6,509	$7,472
Plus: Cash & Cash Equivalents	$ 292	$ 292	$ 292
Less: Total Debt	$1,732	$1,732	$1,732
Implied Equity Value	$4,483	$5,223	$6,240
Implied Value Per Share	**$21.35**	**$24.87**	**$29.71**

Exhibit 11-30 shows the relative stock price performance of Global Snacks versus the S&P 500. As can be seen from the analysis, Global Snacks has dramatically underperformed the market.

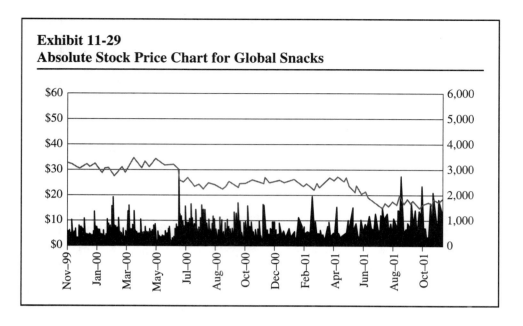

Exhibit 11-29
Absolute Stock Price Chart for Global Snacks

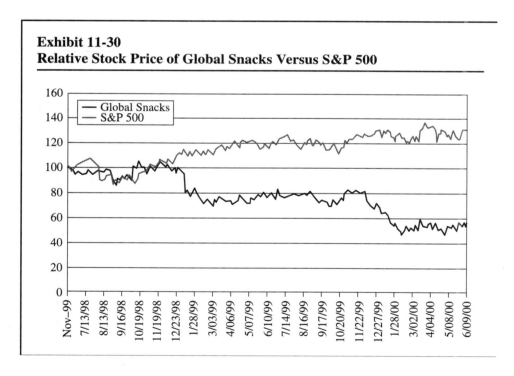

Exhibit 11-30
Relative Stock Price of Global Snacks Versus S&P 500

Exhibit 11-31 shows the trading in Global stock at various prices for the past 12 months. Approximately 197 million shares traded at or below $27.04 per share, with 32% trading between $14.97 and $17.50 per share. Exhibit 11-32 provides an overview of the significant shareholders of Global Snacks. Approximately 15% of

Exhibit 11-31
Price/Volume Analysis for Global Snacks

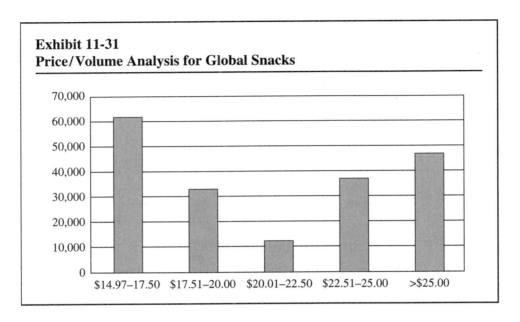

Exhibit 11-32
Significant Shareholder Analysis
for Global Snacks

Top Shareholders	
Food Fund	5.6%
Starfish Holdings	3.9%
Asset Advisors	3.1%
New Age	2.2%
Insiders	
The Ernest Henry Family Trust	5.4%
The Frank Stellar Family Trust	4.9%
Management	2.5%

Global's stock is owned by major institutions, 12.8% by management and insiders, with approximately 72% freely traded. Based on the stock price and shareholder analysis, a few observations and conclusions can be drawn. First, Global is traded at or close to its low price for the past year, $18.00 per share. Second, the stock has shown a downward trend over the past year, with approximately 55% of the stock having traded at or below $26.00 per share. This suggests that a significant number of shares have traded above the $26.00 per share price. Third, based on the large amount of stock owned by institutions and the downward trend in the company's stock price, it is reasonable to assume that their basis in the stock is higher than its current stock price.

Exhibit 11-33	
Global Snacks Summary Valuation Analysis	
Current Stock Price:	$18.00
Stock Price Range for Last Twelve	
Months:	$18.00–$32.00
Trading Multiples Valuation Range:	$15.43–$25.93
Discounted Cash Flow Valuation Range:	$21.35–$29.71
Transaction Multiples Valuation Range:	$15.53–$30.53
Transaction Premiums Valuation Range:	$19.71–$25.11

[E]   Summary Valuation Analysis

Exhibit 11-33 illustrates the overall summary valuation for Global Snacks. Based on the above analyses, we can make a number of observations regarding the valuation of Global Snacks. The stand alone, going concern valuation range is between $15.43 and $30.00 per share. This wide range however, reflects the different operating performance of companies in Global's peer group, as well as specific issues with the discounted cash flow analysis. For example, a 1% change in the long-term growth rate used in the DCF analysis can change the overall valuation for Global by $800 million!

The transaction values range from $15.53 per share to $30.53 per share, reflecting the different types of transactions that have been executed in the industry. The transaction multiples differ because transaction pricing will vary depending on what the target's stock price is, the state of the current M&A market, and the size premium offered in the deal. The premium, as reflected in the transaction premiums analysis, will depend on the same factors, but will also depend on the whether the transaction is perceived as a "merger-of-equals" or a sale of control.

While the overall valuation analysis yields a wide range of values, encompassing prices below and way above the current stock price, the range falls short of the company's 12 month high of approximately $32.00 per share. The going concern valuations suggest the long-term value of the company assuming it continues to grow according to expectation. The transaction ranges suggest what price should be paid for the company if it were acquired today. Therefore, to refine the valuation analysis further in order to determine a feasible purchase price in a sale or merger, additional analysis must be performed.

§ 11.10   MERGER ANALYSIS

Merger analysis entails assessing the ability of an acquirer to pay for a target based on the accretion or dilution inherent in a deal at an assumed purchase price. A second component to the analysis, contribution analysis, compares the relative

Exhibit 11-34
Acquisition at Various Prices

Global Per Share Purchase Price		$20.00	$22.00	$24.00	$26.00	$28.00	$30.00
Premium /(Discount) to:							
Current Stock Price ($18.00)		11.1%	22.2%	33.3%	44.4%	55.6%	66.7%
52-Week High ($27.04)		(26.0%)	(18.6%)	(11.3%)	(3.9%)	(3.5%)	(10.9%)
52-Week Low ($14.97)		(33.6%)	(46.9%)	(60.3%)	(73.7%)	(87.0%)	(100.4%)
Total Equity Value[22]		$4,200	$4,620	$5,040	$5,460	$5,880	$6,354
Plus: Total Debt		1,732	1,732	1,732	1,732	1,732	1,732
Less: Cash & Equivalents		(292)	(292)	(292)	(292)	(292)	(292)
Total Enterprise Value		$5,640	$6,060	$6,480	$6,900	$7,320	$7,794
Enterprise Value Multiple of:							
LTM Revenues	$3,561	1.58×	1.7×	1.82×	1.94×	20.6×	2.19×
LTM EBITDA	$ 794	7.1×	7.6×	8.2×	8.7×	9.2×	9.8×
LTM EBIT	$ 628	9.0×	9.7×	10.3×	11.0×	11.7×	12.4×
Per Share Purchase Price Multiple of:							
LTM EPS	$ 1.59	12.6×	13.9×	15.1×	16.4×	17.6×	18.9×
Projected EPS	$ 1.64	12.2×	13.4×	14.7×	15.9×	17.1×	18.3×

contribution of the parties in terms of revenues, EBITDA, and operating earnings, to the respective ownership of each company in the combined organization post transaction.

As a first step in understanding the implications of the analyses, it is helpful to look at the multiples implied in an acquisition at various assumed prices. Exhibit 11-34 illustrates this analysis.

For example, a purchase price of $22.00 per share represents a 22% premium to the company's current stock price. This compares to a comparable one-day prior to announcement acquisition premium of 12.9%. In addition, the purchase price represents an enterprise value multiple of LTM revenues and LTM EBITDA of 1.58× and 7.1×, compared to comparable transaction multiples of 1.32× LTM revenues and 9.9× LTM EBITDA.

[A] Accretion/Dilution Analysis

As a start, the accretion dilution analysis was performed at an assumed purchase price of $25.00 per share, the top end of the comparable transaction

---

22. Based on option-adjusted shares outstanding of 210.0 million from $20.00–$28.00 per share, and 211.8 million shares outstanding at $30.00 per share.

Exhibit 11-35
Accretion/Dilution Analysis

2002 Pro Forma Net Income	$ 1,070.5
Pro Forma Shares Oustanding	$ 377.4
2002 Pro Forma Earnings Per Share	$ 2.84
Stand Alone Earnings Per Share	$ 2.93
Accretion/(Dilution)	($ 0.09)
Percent Accretion/(Dilution)	(3.1%)

Exhibit 11-36
Accretion/Dilution Sensitivity to Offer Price

	Global's Purchase Price/Premium to Current Share Price						
Tropical Share Price	**$18.00** 0.0%	**$20.00** 11.1%	**$22.00** 22.2%	**$24.00** 33.3%	**$26.00** 44.4%	**$28.00** 55.6%	**$30.00** 66.7%
$30.40	$0.03	($0.08)	($0.19)	($0.29)	($0.38)	($0.47)	($0.56)
$32.30	$0.10	($0.01)	($0.12)	($0.21)	($0.31)	($0.39)	($0.48)
$34.20	$0.16	$0.05	($0.05)	($0.15)	($0.24)	($0.32)	($0.41)
$36.10	$0.22	$0.11	$0.01	($0.08)	($0.17)	($0.26)	($0.34)
$38.00	$0.27	$0.17	$0.07	($0.02)	($0.11)	($0.20)	($0.28)
$39.90	$0.32	$0.22	$0.12	$0.03	($0.06)	($0.14)	($0.22)
$41.80	$0.36	$0.26	$0.17	$0.08	($0.01)	($0.09)	($0.17)
$43.70	$0.40	$0.31	$0.21	$0.13	$0.04	($0.04)	($0.12)
$45.60	$0.44	$0.35	$0.26	$0.17	$0.09	$0.01	($0.07)

premiums valuation range. Based on this analysis, as evidenced in Exhibit 11-35 the transaction is dilutive to Tropical Products by $0.09 per share in 2002. This suggests that an offer would need to be significantly below $25.00 per share for the transaction to be attractive to Tropical's shareholders. This analysis assumes the current stock price of Tropical of $38.00 per share.

In order to further narrow the valuation range down to a level that is feasible for Tropical to pay, we look at a sensitivity to the overall purchase price that could be paid by Tropical. Exhibit 11-36 shows that the transaction is marginally dilutive in 2002 at a purchase price of $24.00 per share. Revisiting our acquisition at various prices analysis in Exhibit 11-34, we can see that this represents a premium of 33% to Global's current stock price. This may suggest that a $24.00 per share offer price is not only feasible for Tropical, but can also be substantiated for Global's shareholders by the transaction premiums analysis.

In order to give additional comfort to Tropical's board, it is advisable to assess the impact of any synergies in the transaction. For example, cost savings of

Exhibit 11-37
Accretion/Dilution Sensitivity to Margins

Operating Synergies (mm)	Global's Purchase Price/Premium to Current Share Price						
	$18.00 *0.0%*	**$20.00** *11.1%*	**$22.00** *22.2%*	**$24.00** *33.3%*	**$26.00** *44.4%*	**$28.00** *55.6%*	**$30.00** *66.7%*
$ 0.0	$0.27	$0.17	$0.07	($0.02)	($0.11)	($0.20)	($0.28)
$ 75.0	$0.42	$0.31	$0.20	$0.11	$0.02	($0.07)	($0.16)
$150.0	$0.56	$0.45	$0.34	$0.24	$0.14	$0.05	($0.04)
$225.0	$0.71	$0.59	$0.48	$0.37	$0.27	$0.18	$0.08
$300.0	$0.85	$0.73	$0.61	$0.50	$0.40	$0.30	$0.20
$375.0	$1.00	$0.87	$0.75	$0.64	$0.53	$0.42	$0.33
$450.0	$1.14	$1.01	$0.89	$0.77	$0.66	$0.55	$0.45
$525.0	$1.29	$1.15	$1.02	$0.90	$0.78	$0.67	$0.57
$600.0	$1.43	$1.29	$1.16	$1.03	$0.91	$0.80	$0.69

Exhibit 11-38
Accretion/Dilution Sensitivity to Form of Consideration

% Stock Consideration	Global's Purchase Price/Premium to Current Share Price						
	$18.00 *0.0%*	**$20.00** *11.1%*	**$22.00** *22.2%*	**$24.00** *33.3%*	**$26.00** *44.4%*	**$28.00** *55.6%*	**$30.00** *66.7%*
0.0%	$0.85	$0.76	$0.67	$0.58	$0.48	$0.39	$0.29
12.5%	$0.75	$0.66	$0.56	$0.47	$0.37	$0.28	$0.18
25.0%	$0.67	$0.57	$0.47	$0.37	$0.28	$0.18	$0.09
37.5%	$0.59	$0.49	$0.39	$0.29	$0.19	$0.10	$0.01
50.0%	$0.52	$0.41	$0.31	$0.21	$0.12	$0.03	($0.06)
62.5%	$0.45	$0.34	$0.24	$0.15	$0.05	($0.04)	($0.13)
75.0%	$0.39	$0.28	$0.18	$0.09	($0.01)	($0.09)	($0.18)
87.5%	$0.33	$0.23	$0.13	$0.03	($0.06)	($0.15)	($0.23)
100.0%	$0.27	$0.17	$0.07	($0.02)	($0.11)	($0.20)	($0.28)

$75 million, representing approximately 2%–3% of the combined company's operating earnings, yields an increase in accretion of $0.13 per share. For example, at the $24.00 proposed purchase price, the 2002 accretion would be $0.11 per share, including $75 million in cost savings, rather than the $0.02 dilution excluding any synergies. This is illustrated in Exhibit 11-37.

An additional approach to evaluating the potential acquisition is to assess the impact of the form of consideration on the overall accretion or dilution in the transaction. As shown in Exhibit 11-38 at the $24.00 per share purchase price, if the consideration paid were 50% stock and 50% cash instead of all stock, the

Exhibit 11-39
Contribution Analysis

	Tropical	Global	Adj.	Pro Forma	% Contribution Tropical	Global
Revenue	$7,515.5	$3777.6	$ –	$11,293.1	65.5%	33.5%
Cost of Sales	4,471.7	2013.4	–	6,485.1		
Gross Profit	3,043.8	1764.2	–	4,808.0		
Operating Expenses	1,434.4	900.2	–	2,334.6		
EBITDA	1,609.4	864.0	–	2,473.4	65.1%	34.9%
Depreciation Expense	205.1	158.3	–	363.4		
Goodwill	89.1	20.0	(20.0)	89.1		
Transaction Expense Amortization	0.0	0.0	8.5	8.5		
Operating Income	1,315.2	685.7	11.5	2,012.4	65.4%	34.1%
Other Income (Net)	(23.1)	8.9	–	(14.2)		
Interest Expense (Net)	228.3	122.4	6.8	357.5		
Pre-Tax Income	1,063.8	572.2	4.7	1,640.7	64.8%	34.9%
Income Taxes	372.3	200.3	(2.4)	570.2		
Net Income	$ 691.5	$ 371.9		$ 1,070.5	64.6%	34.7%

transaction would be accretive by $0.21 per share in 2002 instead of dilutive by $0.02 per share. This analysis may cause Tropical to consider altering the mix of consideration if it needs to increase its purchase price to remain competitive with other bidders.

[B] Contribution Analysis

As an adjunct to the accretion/dilution analysis, the contribution analysis shows the relative contribution of the parties to the combined organization. It then compares the contribution to the proposed ownership of each shareholder group post transaction. For example, Exhibit 11-39 shows the contribution of the parties in a stock-for-stock transaction. As we can see from the analysis, Tropical contributes approximately 65.5%, 65.1%, and 65.7% of revenues, EBITDA, and operating income respectively.

Comparing this to the post-transaction ownership, at a purchase price of $20.00, Tropical would own approximately 68% of the combined company. At a $22.00 per share purchase price, it would own approximately 66% of the combined company. This is illustrated in Exhibit 11-40.

Exhibit 11-40
The Impact of Price on Tropical's Ownership of Pro Forma
Combined Company

	Global's Purchase Price/Premium to Current Share Price				
	$18.00	**$20.00**	**$22.00**	**$24.00**	**$26.00**
Tropical Share Price	0.0%	11.1%	22.2%	33.3%	44.4%
$34.00	68%	66%	63%	61%	59%
$36.00	69%	67%	65%	63%	61%
$38.00	70%	68%	66%	64%	62%
$40.00	71%	69%	67%	65%	63%
$42.00	72%	70%	68%	66%	64%

§ 11.11 SUMMARY

The analysis of the acquisition of Global Snacks by Tropical Products illustrates a few interesting points. First, the stand alone valuation analysis should be viewed separately from the transaction analysis and the merger analysis. The stand alone analysis yields a range of values for Global that would stand true if the company continued to grow and perform based on its current assumptions. The range of values reflects the multiples inherent in the companies in Global's peer group. These multiples reflect the performance and growth characteristics of each of these companies and therefore values Global based on the average of these multiples. The methodology values Global based on the average multiple — and thus performance — of the industry, rather than Global's own performance. The discounted cash flow analysis yields a more theoretically pure valuation range for Global. It values the company based on its own performance metrics including long-term growth rates, margins and capital structure. This methodology however is also fraught with its own concerns, most significantly, that there are a number of assumptions that are made to implement this methodology. Forecasts need to be made, a capital structure must be assumed, and a discount rate must be derived. As we have seen, marginal shifts in even one of these assumptions can have a material impact on the overall value for the company.

Second, the transaction driven valuation methodologies have issues unique to them. Transaction multiples and premiums can vary based on the type of transaction — stock or cash, or control sale versus merger-of-equals. A cash deal may present a higher premium, as would a sale of control, whereas a stock merger-of-equals may present a smaller premium. They can also differ depending on where the target company's stock is trading at the time of the announcement of the transaction. A more fully valued stock price may yield a lower premium than a stock that is temporarily depressed. In addition, the state of the M&A environment may influence the premium or multiple paid in a transaction — if M&A is currently out of favor, the premium in a deal may be lower than when M&A as a strategy is in favor.

Third, the valuation analyses must be viewed in the context of their use. For example, if the valuation is to be used to determine if a company's stock price is undervalued relative to its projected performance, it may not be relevant to include the transaction-driven approaches. Likewise, if a company is looking to sell for cash in a sale of control, it may be more appropriate to focus on premiums paid in cash acquisitions. In the case of the Tropical Products acquisition of Global Snacks however, it is appropriate to analyze both the stand alone and transaction-driven methodologies first to determine what the overall stand alone value for the company is, and second, to determine what its takeover value is.

In addition to the primary valuation methodologies, merger analysis yields a refined value for a target company based not just on its worth as a going concern, but as a measure of what an acquirer is able to pay. Contribution analysis provides a yardstick for assessing the relative fairness of a transaction to each party's share-holders. Yet like discounted cash flow, and trading and transaction multiple and premiums analyses, merger analysis cannot stand by itself. It must be viewed in the context of the overall stand alone and takeover value of a company.

HINT: This case study illustrates how to evaluate a potential acquisition of Global Snacks by Tropical Products. The merger analysis assesses Tropical's ability to pay for Global and therefore places the valuation of Global in that context. It does not, however, address the valuation of Global in the context of other potential acquirers. In other words, while Tropical may be in a position to pay approximately $24.00 per share in stock consideration, which is well within the stand alone and takeover valuation ranges for Global, other potential acquirers may be able to pay more for Global than Tropical. In order to further assess an acquirer's likely success in making an acquisition at a given price, it is suggested that you consider performing the same merger analysis between Global and other potential acquirers. The stand alone valuation of Global will remain the same, yet the feasible prices that other acquirers can pay will differ depending on the strength of each acquirer's stock and/or the cost of each acquirer's capital.

PART II

M&A
ACCOUNTING

Chapter 12

M&A ACCOUNTING

§ 12.01 OVERVIEW OF M&A ACCOUNTING

Accounting principles and techniques form the basis of every transaction under-taken and influence the impact that each deal has on shareholder value. By gaining a sound understanding of the fundamentals of M&A accounting, you will be able to assess a transaction not just on its strategic merits, but also on its impact on the balance sheet and operating performance of the company. M&A practitioners with a solid grasp of accounting tend to have a competitive advantage in deal negotiations, as they can anticipate the impact of changes on shareholder value.

M&A accounting changed quite dramatically in 2001, as the Financial Accounting Standards Board (FASB) issued new accounting regulations that govern accounting for business combinations and the recognition of goodwill and intan-gible assets. Statement of Financial Accounting Standards (SFAS) 141, "Business Combinations," and 142, "Goodwill and Intangible Assets," radically alter the way transactions are accounted for. Prior to the adoption of these standards, mergers and acquisitions fell into four general categories: pooling-of-interests, purchase, cost, and equity methods of accounting. Approved for issuance on June 29, 2001, SFAS 141 and 142 eliminated the pooling-of- interests method entirely, except for transactions initiated before July 1, 2001, and restructured the way goodwill is accounted for under purchase accounting.

In order to fully understand the importance of SFAS 141 and 142, it is worth-while revisiting pooling-of-interests accounting, as well as the other general types of M&A accounting. These methods fall into two broad categories: (1) acquisition of control and (2) acquisition of less than control.

[A] Accounting for Acquisition of Control

By definition, control of a company takes place once the 50% ownership threshold has been reached. In other words, a company acquiring 50.1% of a target corporation has acquired control of that company. These deals are com-monly known as "control transactions." However, even within control transac-tions, there are degrees of control. Control transactions less than 100% usually conform to consolidated accounting principles. Under consolidated accounting, the target's balance sheet is consolidated with that of the acquirer for accounting purposes, but the net income that is "not-acquired" is backed out of the acquirer's income statement as minority interest. Historically, accounting for a 100% acqui-sition of a company was generally treated under either pooling-of-interests or pur-chase accounting. With the inception of SFAS 141 and 142, pooling-of-interests accounting was done away with and all control transactions are accounted for using purchase accounting.

Pooling-of-Interests Accounting: For transactions that were initiated up to July 1, 2001, pooling accounting was used in stock-for-stock, tax-free transactions where at least 90% of the target's stock was exchanged for stock in the acquirer. Also known simply as "pooling" transactions, the income statements and balance sheets of the target and acquirer were combined and no goodwill was created. With pooling now eliminated, these same transactions are accounted for using purchase accounting.

Purchase Accounting: Historically, purchase accounting was used in stock-for-stock or cash transactions where greater than 50% of the target was acquired or where the proposed combination did not meet the requirements for pooling accounting treatment. All control transactions initiated after June 30, 2001, are required to use purchase accounting. Most often, purchase accounting transactions are taxable. In a purchase transaction, the acquirer is required to book the difference between the fair market value of the target's assets and the target's book value as goodwill on its balance sheet.

[B] Accounting for Acquisition of Less than Control

Transactions where less than 50.1% of a target company is acquired are usually accounted for using equity or cost accounting.

Equity Accounting: Equity accounting is used when more than 20% but less than 50% of the voting stock of the target is acquired. In equity accounting, the acquirer reflects its percentage ownership of the target on its income statement and balance sheet.

Cost Accounting: Cost accounting is used when less than 20% of the voting stock of the target is acquired. In cost accounting, the acquirer simply records the investment on its balance sheet at cost. If the target company pays a dividend, the acquirer recognizes a portion of the dividend income on its income statement. Otherwise, the acquirer does not recognize any income.

Accounting has often formed the center of debate in a transaction. For control transactions, the greatest discussion usually concerned goodwill. Goodwill is created in purchase transactions, but also in those pooling-of-interests deals that failed to meet certain conditions. There are innumerable cases where the expected goodwill has terminated the deal, so historically, it was always prudent to ensure that a contemplated pooling transaction met all the requirements. As the regulations regarding pooling and purchase accounting have changed, despite the requirement for all transactions to be accounted for using purchase accounting, the debate over goodwill shall remain, as companies continue to question how to calculate impairment of goodwill as defined in SFAS 142.

For transactions less than control, numerous questions arise regarding the financial, accounting, and control effects of a deal. The remainder of this chapter discusses the mechanics and importance of each of these accounting methodologies to a given transaction type.

§ 12.02   SUMMARY OF SFAS 141 AND SFAS 142

SFAS 141, "Business Combinations," and SFAS 142, "Goodwill and Intangible Assets," were approved for issuance by the FASB on June 29, 2001. The statements eliminate pooling accounting and the annual amortization of goodwill, and no longer recognize goodwill as an intangible asset. The statements require that companies separate out goodwill from other intangible assets and perform an annual "impairment" test on goodwill and indefinite lived intangible assets, and amortize that impairment through the income statement. While there has been a long running debate over the use of pooling-of- interests accounting in business combinations, the controversy is sure to continue as proponents and opponents of SFAS 141 and 142 discuss the elimination of goodwill amortization.

Advocates of eliminating pooling accounting felt that certain companies that could pool were at a competitive advantage over those companies that could not pool, because in pooling accounting, there is no amortization of goodwill. The effect of this is that on a comparable basis, a bidder who could use pooling accounting could "afford" to pay more than a bidder who could only use purchase accounting.

Opponents of the new statements believe that they will encourage bidders to pay high premiums in acquisitions, while proponents will be likely to continue to believe that analysts ignore the goodwill created in acquisitions. One area of common belief is that the new requirements for annual testing on impairment of goodwill will be difficult to implement.

The significant provisions of these statements are as follows:

- As of June 30, 2001, all business combinations initiated after that date must use the purchase method of accounting, effectively eliminating the pooling-of-interests method of accounting for all transactions except for those initiated before July 1, 2001.

- Goodwill and intangible assets with indefinite lives are not amortized but are tested annually for impairment.

[A]   SFAS 141: Business Combinations

SFAS 141 applies to business combinations whereby the net assets of a business or an equity interest of the business is acquired, giving the acquirer control of the enterprise. It does not apply to not-for-profit entities, transactions between entities that have common control, or transactions whereby control was obtained via another means.

SFAS 141 supersedes Accounting Principles Board (APB) Opinion 16, "Business Combinations." However, the statement does not alter the principles for accounting for asset acquisitions, determining the cost of acquired enterprises, and allocating the cost of acquisition to assets acquired and liabilities assumed. Specifically, SFAS 141 mandates that all business combinations initiated after

June 30, 2001, must be accounted for using the purchase method of accounting. The definition of when the transaction was initiated includes the public announcement of the transaction or when the offer is made known to its shareholders, or when the company notifies its stockholders in writing of the transaction. To the extent the terms of the transaction change after the transaction is initiated, this requires a change in the date of initiation. Therefore, a transaction that may have been considered a pooling-of-interests transaction at the outset, may very well be accounted for using the purchase method, if the terms of the transaction change after June 30, 2001.

Importantly, SFAS 141 requires that intangible assets acquired in a business combination be recognized separately from goodwill under two principle scenarios: (1) when the intangible asset arises from contractual or other legal rights, and (2) when the intangible asset does not arise from contractual or other legal rights but is separable from the acquired entity and can be sold, transferred, rented, or exchanged, either individually or as part of a related contract, asset, or liability.

Negative goodwill, will reduce the carrying value of certain acquired assets. Any negative goodwill remaining after reducing such assets to zero will be recognized as an extraordinary gain. This approach also applies to equity method investments.

The scope of SFAS 141 does not include joint ventures and not-for-profit organizations.

[B] SFAS 142: Goodwill and Intangible Assets

SFAS 142 outlines how goodwill and intangible assets are treated in business combinations. It supersedes APB Opinion 17, "Intangible Assets." The goodwill created in a business combination is not amortized; rather, it is tested for impairment annually. To test the impairment, the assets and liabilities of an acquired company should be allocated to the specific reporting unit, as defined in SFAS 131, where the asset or liability is employed. In addition, the associated goodwill created in a transaction is allocated at the unit level. The impairment of goodwill is tested at the unit level. The unit where the reporting takes place could be one level lower than the reporting unit if the operating unit below has separate financial statements, economic characteristics that are different than the reporting unit, or if the goodwill benefits are realized at the operating unit.

[1] Goodwill Impairment Testing

The testing for goodwill impairment requires that the reporting unit being valued and the fair market value should be compared to the carrying value of the unit. If the carrying value is greater than the fair market value, the goodwill "impairment" should be reported in the income statement of the reporting unit as a separate line item. The fair market value of the reporting unit should be calculated the same way that goodwill is calculated in business combinations, i.e., the fair market value is the reporting unit's purchase price. If the fair market value test indicates that the value of the goodwill has increased, there is no step-up in the basis of the assets of the reporting unit.

The goodwill impairment test must be done annually, however, the test for each reporting unit need not be done at the same time; each reporting unit may perform its own text at a different time of the year than other operating units, as long as for the individual unit, it is completed at the same time each year. The goodwill impairment test does not need to be conducted if the following conditions are met:

- The prior fair market value of the operating unit far exceeded its carrying value.

- There have been no indications that the goodwill has been impaired since the last valuation.

- There have been no significant changes in the reporting unit since the prior assessment.

A significant event is deemed to have occurred under the following circumstances:

- A change in the business climate for the reporting unit
- An adverse action by a regulator
- A loss of key personnel
- Unanticipated competition
- A likely sale of part or all of the reporting unit
- Recognition of goodwill impairment of a subsidiary that is a subset of a reporting unit

For equity investments, accounted for using the equity method, the goodwill associated with that transaction should not be amortized, but rather, is tested for impairment under APB Opinion 18, "The Equity Method of Accounting for Investments in Common Stock."

[2] Accounting for Intangible Assets Excluding Goodwill

Intangible assets, other than goodwill, acquired in a business combination should be amortized over the useful life of the asset. Intangible assets that have indefinite lives should not be amortized until their life is determined to be finite. Intangible assets that are amortized should be tested for impairment in accordance with SFAS 121, "Accounting for the Impairment of Long-Lived Assets and for Long-Lived Assets to be Disposed Of." Intangible assets that are not amortized should be tested for impairment annually or whenever there is reason to believe the asset has been impaired. The approach to assessing the impairment is no different than that for calculating goodwill impairment — the fair market value of the asset is compared to its carrying cost.

Separately identifiable intangible assets include the following:

- Marketing Related Intangible Assets
  - — Trademarks and trade names
  - — Internet domain names
  - — Non-competition agreements
- Customer Related Intangible Assets
  - — Customer lists
  - — Customer contracts
- Artistic Related Intangible Assets
  - — Books, magazines, literary works
  - — Plays, operas, ballets
  - — Musical works
  - — Pictures and photographs
- Contract Based Intangible Assets
  - — Licensing, royalty, and standstill agreements
  - — Advertising and service contracts
  - — Lease agreements
  - — Permits
- Technology Based Intangible Assets
  - — Patented and unpatented technology
  - — Computer software and mask works
  - — Databases
  - — Trade secrets

[C] Pros and Cons of SFAS 141 and SFAS 142

There are numerous proponents and opponents of the new releases by FASB. Opponents believe that the new accounting statements will encourage bidders to overpay in transactions because the elimination of amortization will artificially inflate pro forma earnings of the combined company, indicating an increased ability for the acquirer to pay a premium price. The focus on earning accretion may overshadow the underlying economic benefits of the transaction. Other disadvantages of the new statements is the difficulty in identifying intangible assets versus goodwill and the difficulty that companies are going to have in valuing goodwill and intangible impairment on an annual basis.

The advocates of the accounting changes claim that the equity markets and research analysts ignore the goodwill amortization when analyzing the financial merits of a transaction. In addition, there are individuals that believe that pooling accounting gave certain acquirers an unfair bidding advantage in transactions because there is no need to amortize goodwill generated in the transaction. Furthermore, numerous proponents agree that pooling accounting was too restrictive in that it prohibited deal structuring, for example, limiting an acquirer's ability to create strong incentive programs for target company employees, selling non-core assets soon after a merger is closed, or buying stock back post merger. Many of these types of programs would have violated pooling requirements.

While there are a number of advantages and disadvantages of the new statements, it appears that they will at least level the playing field between acquirers in mergers and acquisitions.

[D] Timing of Introduction of SFAS 141 and SFAS 142

SFAS 141 and 142 were issued on June 29, 2001. Business combinations initiated prior to that date may still use pooling accounting; however, business combinations initiated after July 1, 2001, must use purchase accounting. Companies that were subjects of a business combination prior to June 30, 2001, must adopt the requirements of SFAS 142 effective for fiscal years beginning after December 15, 2001. Companies may adopt the requirements prior to this fiscal year-end, but only beginning after March 15, 2001, and only if the first quarter financial statements have not been issued. Companies that have a calendar year end may not adopt the statement early.

Companies that used purchase accounting for a business combination prior to July 1, 2001, should continue to amortize goodwill as they have in the past, until they adopt SFAS 142. However, by the end of the first quarter after adoption, the company should have separated acquisition goodwill from other intangible assets. In addition, amortization of intangible assets with indefinite lives should stop and then be tested for impairment from the point of adoption.

Upon adoption of SFAS 142, the goodwill should be allocated to respective reporting units along with the assets and liabilities of those reporting units. Within six months of adoption, the goodwill should be valued for impairment, and the impairment amount, if any, should be reflected in the income statement of the operating unit. For this initial period of evaluation, any impairment of goodwill should be recognized as "transitional" impairment, not a change in accounting principles.

[E] Disclosure Requirements

There are significant disclosure requirements surrounding SFAS 141 and 142. Companies should disclose all information pertaining to a transactions, including the fair market values assigned to each significant asset and liability. In addition, the company should provide pro forma information on the operations of the combined entity, and the amount of goodwill expected to be deducted for tax purposes.

There should be significant disclosure on any impairment losses including the facts and circumstances leading to the loss.

§ 12.03   POOLING OF INTERESTS METHOD OF ACCOUNTING

Even though pooling-of-interests accounting has been eliminated, it is worth-while understanding how pooling accounting worked, as there were innumerable transactions completed using this accounting approach. A pooling-of-interests transaction was a control transaction that entailed the merger of two companies in a stock-for-stock tax-free transaction. At least 90% of the target must be acquired using the acquirer's stock as the consideration in the deal. In a pooling transaction, no goodwill is created; rather, the balance sheets and income statements of the acquirer and target are simply added together. A pooling transaction assumes that the two companies continue on as one single entity with no adjustments to their capital structure or income statement as a result of the deal.

[A]   The 12 Conditions for a Pooling Transaction

In order to qualify for pooling-of-interests accounting treatment, the target and acquirer must meet certain conditions. In the case where those conditions cannot be met, purchase accounting must be employed. There are 12 conditions that are set forth in Accounting Principles Board Opinion No. 16, "Accounting for Business Combinations." Following is a summary of those conditions.

(a)   *The Target and Acquirer Must Be Autonomous.* For the two-year period prior to the inception of the transaction, both the target and the acquirer must have been separate and autonomous companies. In addition, the target cannot have been a subsidiary or division of the acquirer. One exception to this condition is a company newly incorporated within the prior two years, unless however, the newly incorporated company was a successor to part or all of a company that was not autonomous.

(b)   *The Target and Acquirer Must Be Independent.* On the inception and completion dates of the merger, neither the target nor the acquirer can own more than 10% of the outstanding voting stock of the other. One exception to this condition is if the shares were exchanged in order to affect the merger.

(c)   *The Merger Transaction Must Be Concluded Within a Year of Inception.* The merger must be consummated in a single transaction, or as a part of a plan to consummate the transaction, within one year of inception.

(d)   *The Acquirer Can Only Issue Common Stock with Rights Identical to Those of the Majority of Its Outstanding Voting Common Stock.* The stock must be exchanged for substantially all of the voting common stock of the target.

(e) *The Target and Acquirer Must Keep Substantially the Same Voting Common Stock Interest.* Neither of the companies may change the voting interests of their common stock in contemplation of the transaction.

(f) *The Combined Company Is Limited in Its Ability to Reacquire Shares of Voting Stock Prior to or Post Transaction.* The combined company may only repurchase shares of voting common stock for purposes other than merger and acquisition transactions, and in any event, no more than a "normal" number of shares.

(g) *An Individual Stockholder's Interest in the Target or Acquirer Relative to Other Stockholders May Not Change as a Result of the Merger.* This condition is to ensure that certain stockholders are not given preferential treatment in the transaction.

(h) *The Common Stockholders Must Be Able to Exercise Their Voting Rights.* No structures such as voting trusts can be used to inhibit the ability of the common stockholders to exercise their voting rights.

(i) *The Merger Transaction Must Be Concluded on the Date the Plan Is Consummated.* There can be no plan to issue additional securities or other consideration such as contingent payments.

(j) *The Combined Company May Not Reacquire or Retire All or Part of the Common Stock Issued in the Transaction as Consideration.* The repurchase can neither be a direct purchase, nor an agreement to reacquire or retire the common stock.

(k) *The Target and/or Acquirer May Not Enter into a Financial Arrangement for the Benefit of the Certain Former Stockholders of Either Company.* The purpose of this condition is to ensure that there is no differential consideration that accrues to certain shareholders to the detriment of other stockholders.

(l) *The Combined Company May Not Intend to Divest a Significant Portion of the Assets of the Merged Entity Within Two Years After the Merger.* The only exceptions to this condition are the divestiture of duplicate or excess operations, and those assets that would have been disposed of in the ordinary course of business of the Target and Acquirer acting separately.

[B]   Mechanics of Accounting for a Pooling Transaction

The mechanics of accounting for a pooling transaction are quite simple. The balance sheets and income statements of the target and acquirer are added together to form one combined balance sheet and one combined income statement. The financial statements are then restated retroactively for the five-year period prior to the merger. The pro forma shares outstanding are calculated by adding the acquirer's shares outstanding to the number of shares that are issued to the target's shareholders in the transaction. The earnings per share (E.P.S.) of the combined company are then calculated on the pro forma number of shares of the combined company.

[C] Pooling-of-Interests Accounting Example

Company A — the acquirer — has decided to purchase a smaller competitor, Company B — the target. Both companies are publicly traded. To simplify matters, let us assume that Company A has agreed to acquire Company B by issuing Company B's shareholders one-and-a-half shares of Company A's common stock for each share of Company B common stock outstanding. This is typically known as the exchange ratio in the deal, i.e., a 1.5:1 exchange ratio.

Step 1: Combine the Balance Sheets.

(millions)

	Stand Alone		Combined
	Company A	Company B	A + B
Assets			
Current Assets	$100	$ 50	$150
Net Plant & Equipment	100	50	150
Goodwill	50	25	75
Total Assets	$250	$125	$375
Liabilities & Shareholders Equity			
Current Liabilities	$ 25	$ 25	$ 50
Long-Term Debt	100	25	125
Other Liabilities	40	10	50
Total Liabilities	$165	$ 60	$225
Shareholders Equity	$ 85	$ 65	$150
Total Liabilities & Shareholders Equity	$250	$125	$375

Step 2: Combine the Income Statements.

(millions)

	Stand Alone		Combined
	Company A	Company B	A + B
Sales	$500	$200	$700
Cost of Goods Sold	350	150	500
Selling, General & Administrative Expense	75	20	95
Interest Expense	10	5	15
Income Before Taxes	$ 65	$ 25	$ 90
Income Taxes	22	9	31
Net Income	$ 43	$ 16	$ 59

Step 3: Calculate Pro Forma Earnings Per Share.

In the transaction, Company A issues three shares for each Company B share outstanding. Therefore, a total of 15 million shares are issued.

(millions)

| | Stand Alone | | Combined |
	Company A	Company B	A + B
Shares Outstanding	30	10	35
Earnings Per Share	$ 1.43	$ 1.6	$ 1.69
Accretion/Dilution	–	–	$ 0.26

Step 4: Restate Combined Financials for Prior Five Years.

As a final step, repeat steps 1 through 3 for the financial statements of the combined company on a pro forma historical basis for the preceding five years.

§ 12.04   PURCHASE METHOD OF ACCOUNTING

A purchase transaction is a control transaction that entails the acquisition of greater than 50% of a target's voting stock, and is held as a long-term investment. The acquisition of the target's voting stock can be for stock of the acquirer, cash, or a combination of both. The assets and liabilities of the target are adjusted to fair market value. In a purchase transaction, goodwill is recorded by taking the difference between the purchase price and the net value of the assets as adjusted to fair market value. The goodwill is then evaluated for impairment annually.

[A]   Mechanics of Accounting for a Purchase Transaction

The mechanics of accounting for a purchase transaction are not quite as simple as those of a pooling-of-interests transaction. First, the balance sheet of the target must be adjusted to reflect the fair market value of the assets and the liabilities. Second, the net asset value of the adjusted balance sheet should be calculated by deducting the adjusted fair market value of the liabilities from the adjusted fair market value of the assets. Third, the goodwill amount should be calculated by subtracting the adjusted net asset value from the purchase price. The goodwill is then recorded on the combined balance sheet. If the purchase price is below the net asset value, then the long-term assets are written down proportionately to reflect the purchase price. Any negative goodwill created in the transaction is ordinarily not recorded. Fourth, the adjusted balance sheet of the target is then added to the acquirer's balance sheet. The goodwill created in the transaction and the financing for the transaction are assumed on the combined balance sheet as well. The pro forma earnings of the combined company should reflect the incremental

182

earnings of the target and the impact of the financing of the transaction. Finally, for acquisitions of greater than 50% of the target, the results of the two companies are generally consolidated. The portion of the target's earnings that is not owned by the acquirer is reflected as minority interest on the income statement.

[B] The Purchase Accounting Adjustments in More Detail

A number of adjustments are made to the target's balance sheet in the transaction. Generally, the detailed adjustments will be made by the acquirer's accounting firm; however, any adjustments will also be blessed by the accounting firm of the target. In evaluating a purchase accounting transaction, it is usually safe to assume that for preliminary analysis, the balance sheet of the acquirer is close to the fair market value of the assets and liabilities. Special circumstances will exist however, where there are undervalued assets or where the debt of the target has a fair market value that is lower than the recorded value. Nevertheless, following is a partial list of the balance sheet items that warrant attention in assessing whether or not to adjust to fair market value.

1. Current assets: inventory (LIFO reserve), receivables
2. Long-term assets: customer lists, hidden assets
3. Current liabilities: payables
4. Record liabilities for underfunded pension and other unrecognized liabilities
5. Long-term liabilities: public debt

In addition to these adjustments to fair market value, a few additional modifications are made to the target's balance sheet.

1. Eliminate the target's existing goodwill.
2. Calculate the target's new deferred tax balance.
3. Record the new goodwill as a result of the transaction.
4. Record transaction financing.

In addition to adjustments to the balance sheet, there are income statement adjustments that need to be made to appropriately record the impact of the acquisition on the combined company.

1. Financing: The acquisition could be financed using a number of means, including the target's cash, new debt, or shares issued by the acquirer. The cost of these financing sources should be reflected in the income statement as interest expense (or a reduction in interest income), if the financing source is debt or cash, or, as an increase in the number of shares outstanding, if the financing source is shares of the acquirer.

2. Depreciation: In the transaction, certain long-term assets may have been written up. These assets are then depreciated over the appropriate lives of the asset, resulting in an adjustment to the target's depreciation schedule.

3. Goodwill: Goodwill is evaluated annually for impairment. Any reduction in the value of the goodwill is run through the income statement.

HINT: By this point you may be thinking that there is a great opportunity to adjust the target's financials to enhance the perceived impact of the transaction. Don't be fooled. It is easy to confuse the transaction-related impact of a deal with the true business logic for a transaction. What may look like an outstanding deal on paper may in fact be a loser. Wall Street is well-versed in analyzing different transaction types and will quickly ferret out transactions that are driven by accounting adjustments versus those that are driven by sound business sense. A transaction that appears "too good to be true" may well be just that!

[C] Purchase Method of Accounting Example

Company A — the acquirer — has decided to purchase 85% of Company B — the target. Company A is public and Company B is private. Company A will use a combination of cash and stock to acquire Company B. To facilitate the accounting exercise, following are a few assumptions:

1. The purchase price for the 85% of Company B is $100 million.

2. The purchase price consideration is $50 million in cash and $50 million in Company A stock. Company A borrows the cash at a 10% interest rate. With a $10 per share stock price, Company A will issue 5 million shares to Company B's shareholders.

Step 1: Adjust the Assets and Liabilities to Fair Market Value and Calculate the Adjusted Net Asset Value.

(millions)

	(i) Company B	Adjustments	Restated
Assets			
Current Assets	$ 50	$7 (1)	$ 57
Net Plant & Equipment	50		50
Goodwill	25	(25) (2)	0
Total Assets	$125		$107
Liabilities & Shareholders Equity			
Current Liabilities	$ 25		$ 25
Long-Term Debt	25		25
Other Liabilities	10		10
Total Liabilities	$ 60		$ 60
Net Asset Value	$ 65		$ 47

184

Adjustments:

1. The adjustment to inventory is calculated as follows:

(millions)	
Beginning Inventory	$50
LIFO Reserve	10
Tax Rate	34%
Inventory Write-Up	$ 7

2. The existing goodwill of the target is eliminated.

Step 2: Calculate the Goodwill Created in the Transaction and Reflect on the Balance Sheet.

(millions)	
Purchase Price:	
Cash	$ 50
Stock	50
Total Purchase Price	$100
Adjusted Net Asset Value	47
Goodwill	$ 53

Step 3: Combine the Adjusted Balance Sheet with the Acquirer.

(millions)

	Stand Alone			Combined
	Company A	Restated Company B	Transaction Adjustments	Pro Forma
Assets				
Current Assets	$100	$ 57		$157
Net Property & Equipment	150	50		200
Goodwill	0	0	$53 (1)	53
Total Assets	$250	$107		$410
Liabilities & Shareholders Equity				
Current Liabilities	$ 25	$ 25		$ 50
Long-Term Debt	100	25	$50 (2)	175
Other Liabilities	40	10		50
Total Liabilities	$165	$ 60		$275
Shareholders Equity	$ 85	$ 47		$135
Total Liabilities & Shareholders Equity	$250	$107		$410

Transaction Adjustments:

(1) When combining the balance sheets of the two companies, the new goodwill is added.

(2) Company A assumed $50 million in new debt to finance the acquisition.

Step 4: Combine the Income Statements of the Target and Acquirer.

(millions)

	Company A	Company B	Transaction Adjustments	Pro Forma
	Stand Alone			*Combined*
Sales	$500	$200		$700
Cost of Goods Sold	350	150		500
S, G & A	75	20		95
Interest Expense	10	5	5 (1)	20
Income Before Taxes	$ 65	$ 25		$ 85
Income Taxes	18	7		24
Net Income	$ 47	$ 18		$ 61
Minority Interest				95
			(2)	
Adjusted Net Income				$519

Transaction Adjustments:

(1) Company A assumed $50 million in new debt to finance the acquisition. At 10% interest, the annual interest charge is $5 million.

(2) Company A must pay out 15% of the net income of Company B to the 15% shareholders other than Company A.

Step 5: Calculate Pro Forma Earnings Per Share.

In the transaction, Company A issues 5 million shares to Company B shareholders for 85% of the company.

(millions)

	Stand Alone Company A
Shares Outstanding	30
Shares Issued in Transaction	5
Total Shares Outstanding	35
Pro Forma Net Income	$51.9
Pro Forma Earnings Per Share	$ 1.48
Company A Stand Alone Earnings Per Share	$ 1.57
Accretion/Dilution	($ 0.09)

HINT: Unlike a pooling transaction, the historical financial statements of the target and acquirer combined are not restated. Thus, a purchase accounting acquisition may distort the growth rates and operating performance of the acquirer. While on the surface, this may appear as a positive result of purchase accounting, be wary of relying on purchase accounting acquisitions to show growth in your company.

HINT: As you evaluate the financial impact of the merger, one preliminary — but extremely important — measure of the viability of the transaction is the accretion or dilution in the transaction. Accretion (or dilution) is the amount by which the combined earnings per share of the merged companies exceeds (accretion) or does not meet (dilution) the earnings per share of the acquirer stand alone. Accretive transactions are typically received well by Wall Street, whereas dilutive transactions should be heavily scrutinized before proceeding.

HINT: Despite the need to evaluate the financial effects of a transaction based on the combined forward looking financial results, it is important to point out that Wall Street — institutions, equity research analysts, investors — will also assess the combined historical financial performance of the company on a pro forma basis. In addition, combined future growth rates, margins, and other operating and financial ratios will be evaluated based on the prior combined operating performance of the merged company on a pro forma basis.

HINT: Purchase accounting gives the acquirer the flexibility to look at various financing structures or combinations of stock and cash that a pooling transaction could not. Depending on the current interest rate environment and the stock price of the acquirer, it is prudent to look at different capital structures when financing the acquisition of the target. A higher stock price would result in less shares issued to the target's shareholders and consequently greater accretion in the deal. Likewise, a lower interest rate environment would result in less interest expense in the deal. Therefore, it may be prudent to review a case where more debt is assumed in place of issuing stock.

§ 12.05   SPECIAL TOPICS IN PURCHASE ACCOUNTING

[A]   LIFO Reserve Adjustment

As you evaluate a target in a purchase accounting transaction, one asset class that often comes under scrutiny is inventory. Companies can typically follow two types of inventory valuation methodologies: LIFO or last-in, first-out and FIFO or first-in, first-out. As a generalization, companies that use the LIFO method will tend to overstate cost of goods sold, understate net income, and understate inventory. In a purchase accounting transaction, an amount is calculated, the "LIFO Reserve," that is, the difference between the LIFO and FIFO inventory amounts. This amount reflects the excess of the current cost of the inventory over the carrying cost of the inventory. In a purchase accounting transaction, adjustments are made to assets and liabilities to adjust them to fair market value. The LIFO inventory account must be adjusted to market value. This is accomplished by writing up the inventory by the after-tax amount of the LIFO Reserve.

[B]   Writing Up Assets

In a purchase accounting transaction, assets are adjusted to fair market value. Under current accounting regulations, only the book value of the assets acquired is "written up." In the write-up, the book basis of the assets is increased. The tax basis of the assets is rarely "stepped up." One situation where it is still possible to step up the tax basis of the assets is where the target is an S Corporation. When the assets are written up, the increased book basis serves to increase the amount of the book depreciation recognized on the income statement. Because there is rarely any step-up in the tax basis of the assets, the increase in depreciation helps to reduce the tax burden.

§ 12.06   EQUITY METHOD OF ACCOUNTING

Equity accounting is used in transactions where less than control is acquired and where greater than 20% but less than 50% of the voting stock of a target company is acquired as a long-term investment. The acquirer's balance sheet and income statement should reflect the proportionate equity interest in the target. Below a 50% interest, there is no requirement to use consolidated accounting since the acquirer does not exercise full control over the target. An exception to this rule is when it can be established that the acquirer has de facto control of the target even though it owned less than 50%.

[A]   Mechanics of Accounting for an Equity
Transaction

When making the investment or acquiring the stake in the target, the acquirer records the original investment at cost. As the target earns income, the acquirer increases its investment in it by the proportionate interest in its net income. Additionally, the acquirer records its proportionate interest in the target's net income in its own net income.

To the extent the purchase price paid for the investment is greater than the pro rata portion of the target's book value, the acquirer must calculate the implied goodwill that results from the investment. While the goodwill does not need to be recorded on the acquirer's balance sheet, the amortization of the goodwill must flow through the income statement and cannot be used to offset taxes. The goodwill that results from this type of transaction is known as "shadow goodwill." If the acquirer receives cash dividends from the target, the dividends have no direct impact on the amount of net income recorded on the acquirer's income statement. However, the amount of the cash dividend reduces the acquirer's investment in the target.

[B]   Equity Method Accounting Example

Company A acquires 25% of the voting common stock of Company B for cash. The purchase price paid is $25 million.

Step 1: Calculate Shadow Goodwill.

(millions)

	Company B
Assets	
Current Assets	$ 50
Net Plant & Equipment	50
Goodwill	25
Total Assets	$125
Liabilities & Shareholders Equity	
Current Liabilities	$ 25
Long-Term Debt	25
Other Liabilities	10
Total Liabilities	$ 60
Shareholders Equity	$ 65
Total Liabilities & Shareholders Equity	$125
Company A Book Value	$ 65
Percent Acquired	× 25%
Share of Company B Book Value	$ 16
Purchase Price	$ 25
Share of Company B Book Value	−$ 16
Shadow Goodwill	$ 9

Step 2: Reflect Investment in Company A on Company B's Balance Sheet at Cost.

(millions)

	Company A	*Adjustments*	*Pro Forma*
Assets			
Current Assets	$100	($25) (2)	$ 75
Net Plant & Equipment	100		100
Investment in Company A	–	$25 (1)	25
Goodwill	50		50
Total Assets	$250		$250
Liabilities & Shareholders Equity			
Current Liabilities	$ 25		$ 25
Long-Term Debt	100		100
Other Liabilities	40		40
Total Liabilities	$165		$165
Shareholders Equity	$ 85		$ 85
Total Liabilities & Shareholders Equity	$250		$250

Adjustments:

(1)   Investment in Company B's voting common stock at cost.

(2)   Reduction in cash for purchase of voting common stock in Company B.

Step 3: Calculate Pro Forma Impact on Earnings.

(millions)

	Stand Alone Company B
Sales	$200
Cost of Goods Sold	150
S, G & A	20
Interest Expense	5
Income Before Taxes	$ 25
Income Taxes	7
Net Income	$ 18
Company B Net Income	$ 18
Company A Share	25%
Company A Reporting Share	$ 4.5

(millions)

	Company A	Transaction Adjustments	Pro Forma
Sales	$500		$ 500
Cost of Goods Sold	350		350
S, G & A	75		75
Interest Expense	10	1.3 (1)	11.3
Income Before Taxes	$ 65		$63.7
Investment in Company B	–	4.5 (2)	4.5
Income Taxes	18		18.0
Net Income	$ 47		$50.2

Adjustments:

(1)   Loss of interest income from cash on balance sheet. 5% interest on $25 million in cash.

(2)   Company A share of Company B's net income. (This is not taxed twice.)

Step 4: Increase Company A's Investment in Company B.

At the end of each reporting year, Company A must increase its investment in the Company B account by the amount of net income Company A reports from Company B. In addition, to the extent Company A receives dividends from Company B, it should reduce its investment in the Company B account by the amount of the dividend.

HINT: Making an investment in another company can be a good way to test the waters on whether a full acquisition makes sense. It can be temping to structure an investment of less than 50% ownership with other non-investment related agreements, such as operating or management agreements, board seats or voting provisions, that give the acquirer significant control over the target. In these situations, the Securities and Exchange Commission as well as your accountants may force you to use consolidated accounting, in which case, the benefits of the minority investment may disappear.

HINT: When evaluating an investment in a company, don't look solely at making the investment on a plain vanilla basis by buying the voting common stock. You should experiment with other structures and investment vehicles such as preferred stock, subordinated debt, convertible debt, or combinations thereof. It very well may be possible to enhance the financial impact of the investment through good financial engineering and tax planning.

---

§ 12.07   COST METHOD OF ACCOUNTING

Cost accounting is used in transactions where less than 20% of the voting stock of the target is acquired as a long-term investment. The investment is reported on the acquirer's balance sheet at cost and no adjustments are made on the financial statements of the target company. Because the investment is significantly below control and there are generally no governing concerns, the acquiring or investing company usually recognizes income only upon the receipt of dividends from the target company.

[A]   Mechanics of Accounting for a Cost Accounting Transaction

The acquiring or investing company records the investment in the target on its balance sheet at cost, and the investment is then carried on the balance sheet at the lower of the cost of the investment or the market value of the investment. As the acquiring company receives dividends from the target company, it recognizes income from the investment. In the United States, where U.S. corporations own stakes in U.S. targets, 70% of the dividends received are excluded from taxes.

[B]   Cost Method Accounting Example

Company A acquires a 10% interest in the voting common stock of Company B for $5 million. At year-end, Company B pays a $5 million dividend on its common stock, of which Company A receives $500,000.

Step 1: Reflect the Investment on Company A's Balance Sheet.

(millions)

	Company A	Adjustments	Pro Forma
Assets			
Current Assets	$100	($5) (2)	$ 95
Net Plant & Equipment	100		100
Investment in Company A	–	$5 (1)	5
Goodwill	50		50
Total Assets	$250		$250
Liabilities & Shareholders Equity			
Current Liabilities	$ 25		$ 25
Long-Term Debt	100		100
Other Liabilities	40		40
Total Liabilities	$165		$165
Shareholders Equity	$ 85		$ 85
Total Liabilities & Shareholders Equity	$250		$250

Adjustments:

(1)   Company A records the $5 million investment at cost.

(2)   Company A reduces its cash account by $5 million to reflect the purchase of Company B common stock.

As a result of the investment, if Company A acquires the stock of Company B in the open market, there is no reporting requirement on the financial statements of Company B. If Company A acquires the stock of Company B directly from the company as a primary issuance, then Company B would need to increase its cash account by the amount of cash received, increase its equity account by the amount of the investment, and adjust its shares outstanding to reflect the number of shares issued to Company A.

Step 2: Record the Dividend on Company A's Income Statement.

Company B subsequently declares and pays a $5 million dividend on its common stock. Company A records its 10% share of the dividend by increasing its cash balance by $500,000 = (10% × $10,000,000) and recognizing $500,000 in investment income, of which 70% is excluded from income tax.

(millions)

	Company A	Adjustments	Pro Forma
Sales	$500		$500
Cost of Goods Sold	350		350
S, G & A	75		75
Interest Expense	10		10
Income Before Taxes	$ 65		$ 65
Investment Income	–	$0.5 (1)	0.5
Taxable Income	$ 65	$0.15 (2)	$ 65.15
Income Taxes	22		22
Net Income	$ 43		$ 43

Adjustments:

(1)   Company A records the $500,000 as investment income.

(2)   Only 30% of the dividend is taxed. Therefore, the taxable portion of the dividend is $150,000 or ($500,000 × 30%). Income taxes increase marginally since only 30% of the dividend is taxed.

§ 12.08   SPECIAL TOPIC IN ACCOUNTING

[A]   Dividend Received Deduction

Generally, when a company receives a dividend from another corporation in which it owns stock, the investing company is allowed to deduct a portion of the dividend. The amount of the deduction or dividend received deduction (DRD) depends on the amount of stock the investing company owns. With less than 20% ownership, the investing company is allowed a DRD of 70%. With between 20% and 80%, the investing company is allowed a DRD of 80%. As an aside, a corporation is allowed a DRD of 100% if the target corporation is a member of the same group of companies affiliated with the investing or acquiring company. These dividend received deduction guidelines are specific to U.S. corporations owning stock in other U.S. corporations. The rules are modified to the extent dividends are received by a foreign corporation.

§ 12.09 SPECIAL TOPICS IN M&A ACCOUNTING

[A] Synergies and Joint Opportunities

A key driver in most transactions is the synergies that are attainable as the result of the transaction. In fact, an argument could be made that if there are no synergies in the proposed deal, it probably shouldn't be done. As you evaluate the financial outcome of the transaction, it is prudent to build a case — or cases — to analyze the synergies in the transaction.

Synergies come in many forms and are specific to each industry. However, there are a number of synergies that are common to each transaction. One suggestion would be to go through each item on your and the counter party's income statement and balance sheet, and assess whether there are any individual or joint revenue or cost savings opportunities. Synergies can be found in the most obvious and obscure places, ranging from duplicate personnel to lower interest costs from enhancing the combined company's credit. Exhibit 12-1 provides a partial list of some of the more obvious places to look for synergies.

Don't be fooled; however, synergies are never guaranteed in a deal and should not be relied upon to make the deal work from a financing or structural perspective. For example, commercial bankers tend not to look at the vast majority of synergies when it comes to assessing the cash-flow dynamics of a deal. In addition, using paper synergies to rationalize a purchase price or financing structure can be quite dangerous.

HINT: Synergies should be taken into account as transaction adjustments to the income statement and balance sheet. When building the rationale for or against a transaction, it is always good practice to build a base case that does not include any synergies as well as one that includes the synergies. If the deal makes sense without synergies, any realized synergies only serve to enhance the success of the deal. Often however, companies look to synergies to "make" the deal, or they pay the value of the synergies to the seller. Be wary of these approaches, since realizing synergies is a lot harder than penciling them on paper.

Exhibit 12-1
Common Synergies

Revenue Enhancements:

- Push the products of one party through the distribution of the other party
- Introduce one party's products into the markets of the other
- Gain greater market share by offering the combined product suite of the parties to the transaction

Cost Savings:

- Reduce cost of goods sold due to greater purchasing power of the combined company
- Eliminate duplicate or excess warehouses and reduce inventory
- Eliminate redundant corporate personnel
- Eliminate overlapping sales force
- Eliminate redundant auditing, legal, accounting, and other third party fees
- Eliminate duplicate public company expenses

Financing Savings:

- Evaluate credit of the combined company and target a capital structure that optimizes credit and financing costs

---

[B] Common Investment Vehicles

There are a number of ways to make an investment in another entity. The simplest approach is to buy the securities that are already outstanding, most often voting common stock. However, there are drawbacks to acquiring voting common stock. Acquiring a significant stake in the voting common stock does not necessarily give the acquirer the control or preferential treatment that it may deserve or require to make the investment. Additionally, there are numerous other structures that can be used to optimize not only the financial impact of the investment, but also operational control of the investment. Each type of investment vehicle solves a slightly different problem.

[1] Preferred Stock

Preferred stock is a class of ownership in a corporation that has preferential rights over other shareholders. The rights can be in the form of a stated dividend that must be paid before dividends are paid to common stockholders or in the form of a preferred claim over common stockholders in liquidation. Preferred stock is often used when raising capital, as common shareholders can retain voting control while providing the preferred shareholders preferential financial treatment.

There are no hard and fast rules that require all preferred stocks to look alike. In fact, one of the advantages of preferred stock is the ability to shape the terms of the preferred stock to fit a deal. To that end, there are a number of features that can be applied to preferred stock in order to meet the requirements of the investor and the investee. For example, the company can have the right to buy-out the preferred stockholders at a given price or on a given date. Preferred stock can be convertible into common stock on certain conditions. Preferred stock can have different classes, with each class having different financial and voting preferences.

In structuring investments, one key benefit of preferred stock is the ability to use it to realize a financial return for the investment that is not dissimilar to common stock. Used wisely in combination with other securities, a preferred stock investment also can realize attractive financial and voting preference without forcing consolidation.

Preferred stock usually has a perpetual life. However, issuers tend to attach features to the preferred stock that either force conversion or trigger a buy-back prior to the end of a ten-year period.

One drawback of preferred stock for the issuing company is that the dividends on the preferred stock are not usually tax deductible. Conversely, corporate shareholders participating in the convertible preferred stock receive a 70% dividend received deduction from taxation of dividend income. An advantage for the investor is that by using a conversion feature (see below), the investor can reap the benefits of current income through the dividend and preserve the benefits of future equity appreciation.

A note of caution: Subchapter S Corporations cannot have preferred stock, so when investing in private companies, make sure they are not Subchapter S Corporations.

[2] Subordinated Debt

Subordinated debt is a form of loan that ranks below other loans in the case of a liquidation. It has a claim on assets and earnings that is subordinated to other debt on the balance sheet but is senior to the preferred and common equity holders. Much like preferred stock, subordinated debt can be structured to meet the different objectives of the investor and the investee. The interest on the subordinated debt can be paid in cash or in kind. The subordinated debt can be convertible into common stock upon certain events or at a given time. It can be bought back by the company at a given price or time or upon certain events.

Much like preferred stock, careful use of subordinated debt can yield attractive financial returns for the investor while preserving voting control for the investee corporation and minimizing the accounting constraints that can inhibit a future pooling transaction or force consolidated accounting. Unlike preferred stock, subordinated debt typically has a defined life or maturity, for example, ten years.

An advantage of subordinated debt for the issuer is that the interest payments are tax deductible. However, interest received from convertible debt by the investor is not deductible and fully taxable. An advantage for the investor is that by using a conversion feature (see below), the subordinated debt can give the investor current income with equity upside.

[3]   Bells, Whistles, and Other Features

[a]   Conversion Features. A conversion feature enables the holder to convert a given security into another form of security in the target company. Conversion features can be applied to many types of securities; however, they are most often used with preferred stock and subordinated debt that is convertible into common stock of the target. The preferred stock or subordinated debt is converted into common stock at a conversion ratio. This ratio is the number of shares of common stock that are issued for each share of preferred stock or for the par value of each bond of subordinated debt.

In addition to the conversion ratio, the security would state the price of the common stock at which the preferred stock or subordinated debt would be converted. For example, in the case of convertible subordinated debt with a par value of $1,000 and a conversion price of $25, there would be 40 shares of common stock issued for each bond converted into common stock.

A nuance of the conversion feature is to have the conversion price change — increase — over time. This is done to encourage the holder of the convertible security to convert as soon as possible. The sooner the holder converts, the greater the number of common shares he/she will own in the target.

[b]   Exchangeable Features. An exchangeable feature enables the issuer to swap a given security for another form of security. For example, an issuer may exchange preferred stock for convertible debt with identical pre-tax cash flows. The motivation for the issuer to exchange the securities is to swap the non-tax-deductible expense of the preferred stock for the tax-deductible expense of the subordinated debt.

[c]   Call Provisions. Many preferred stock and subordinated debt issues have what are called "call provisions" which give the issuer the right to buy back the security under certain circumstances. For example, if the common stock of the issuer reaches a specific price, the issuer may "call" or buy back the issue from the issuer. However, to protect the investor, the security will also likely have a period — the "call period" — during which the issuer may not call the security.

[d]   Warrants. Warrants are securities that give the holder the right to acquire other securities of the issuer or target at a specified price. Warrants can be issued along with other securities, such as preferred stock or subordinated debt, in order to increase the upside or return to the investor. They are typically viewed as long-term investments with expiration dates a number of years out in the future. In many ways, warrants function much the same way as options. However, options usually have a limited or short life, whereas warrants have a long life.

The different investment vehicles and their respective features all help to facilitate the structuring of a transaction. Invariably, buyers and sellers have different objectives and incentives and often expectations in a deal can differ to the point where a deal becomes unfeasible. Creative structuring can serve to bridge these gaps in expectations so that the buyer's and seller's objectives can be better met.

HINT: Before you finalize any investment vehicle, make sure you consult with your accountants. Even though an investment vehicle may make financial sense, and appear that you do not have to consolidate financials with the target, other nonfinancial constraints and agreements may suggest "deemed control" and force consolidation.

HINT: When evaluating synergies, solicit input from key areas or functional managers. You'll be surprised to learn where costs can be cut or additional revenue can be gained. Also, after the transaction is completed, make sure those same managers are accountable for delivering on the synergies.

PART III
TRANSACTION TYPES

Chapter 13

MERGERS & ACQUISITIONS

§ 13.01   OVERVIEW

Mergers and acquisitions are arguably the most prolific form of M&A transactions. A merger is the combination of two companies in a stock-for-stock transaction. An acquisition is the purchase of the stock or assets of a business using the stock of the acquirer, cash or other securities. In many cases, a merger or acquisition are not mutually exclusive, i.e., an acquisition may be structured as a stock-for-stock transaction and hence can be viewed as a merger. Most often however, a merger is thought of in the context of two companies of relatively equal size combining, while an acquisition is thought of in the context of a purchase of a smaller target by a larger acquirer.

Domestic M&A activity increased in 2003, with 7,928 transactions announced in 2003 representing $574 billion up from 7,395 transactions representing $457 billion in 2002.[1] Exhibit 13-1 provides an overview of the market for U.S. mergers and acquisitions since 1990.

Mergers and acquisitions range in scale from the $72 billion merger between AT&T Broadband and Comcast, to the small, private acquisition of a family-owned company. Exhibit 13-2 shows the top ten completed U.S. mergers and acquisitions in 2003.

---

1. Thomson Financial.

Exhibit 13-1
Announced Mergers & Acquisitions: 1990–2003[2]
(*$ in billions*)

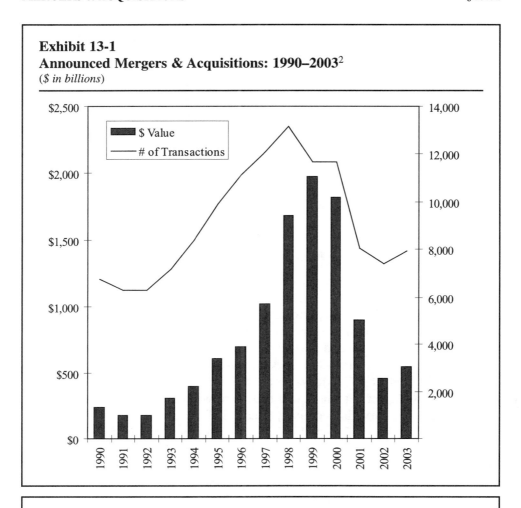

Exhibit 13-2
Top Ten Completed U.S. Mergers & Acquisitions: 2001–2003[3]
(*$ in millions*)

Ann. Date	Target	Acquirer	Deal Value
07/08/2001	AT&T Broadband & Internet Services	Comcast Corp	$72,041
07/15/2002	Pharmacia Corp	Pfizer Inc	$59,515
09/04/2001	Compaq Computer Corp	Hewlett-Packard Co	$25,263
12/17/2001	Immunex Corp	Amgen Inc	$16,900
04/09/2003	General Motors Corp	General Motors Corp	$15,432
11/18/2001	Conoco Inc	Phillips Petroleum Co Inc	$15,349
11/14/2002	Household International Inc	HSBC Holdings PLC	$15,294
12/19/2001	Travelers Property Casualty	Shareholders	$12,213
12/14/2001	USA Networks Inc-Ent Assets	Vivendi Universal SA	$10,749
09/05/2000	Niagara Mohawk Holdings Inc	National Grid Group PLC	$ 8,048

2. Thomson Financial.
3. Mergerstat, Dealogic.

§ 13.02   EVIDENCE BEHIND MERGERS & ACQUISITIONS

Over the last 100 years, mergers and acquisitions have received mixed reviews in terms of their success. Much has been written about the failure of mergers and acquisitions, likewise, there have been many instances of highly successful mergers and acquisitions, both on a discrete, one-off basis, or when used in conjunction with an overall long-term M&A strategy.

As a result of the controversy surrounding the long-term benefits of M&A, there has been significant academic research on the subject. Research has focused on a broad range of subjects including, among others, the success of bidders in mergers and acquisitions, the long-range returns to shareholders, why target companies become subject to takeover, and why companies undertake mergers in the first place.

[A]   General Evidence Behind Mergers & Acquisitions

Most of the general research on M&A involves the long-term benefits of mergers and acquisitions to shareholders. In this context, the analyses have focused on the pre-transaction performance of a target in relationship to the post-transaction performance of the surviving corporation. A variety of measures have been used to quantify pre- and post-transaction performance, including operating measures such as profitability and market measures such as equity value.

In a 1977 study by G. Meeks titled "Disappointing Marriage: A Study of the Gains from Merger," it was found that there was no consistent evidence that performance of the surviving company changed after an acquisition or merger.[4]

A comprehensive 1987 study by David J. Ravenscraft and F.M. Scherer titled "Mergers, Sell-Offs, and Economic Efficiency," examined 6,000 mergers from 1950 to 1977.[5] One of their fundamental questions was how acquirers fared after an acquisition, the answer to which was, quite poorly. They distinguished between pooling and purchase accounting transactions, finding that pooling transactions did not perform above the control group, and in fact performed worse than the target's pre-merger return. Purchase transactions also performed poorly, evidencing returns below that of the control group. However, they did find that mergers-of-equals out-performed their control group and their pre-merger returns.

At the other end of the spectrum, certain studies have found positive performance for companies post takeover. A 1992 study by Paul M. Healy, Krishna G. Palepu, and Richard S. Ruback titled "Does Corporate Performance Improve After Mergers," examined the post-acquisition performance of the largest 50 mergers in the United States between 1979 and mid-1984.[6] Recognizing that an acquirer's

---

4. Meeks, G., *Disappointing Marriage: A Study of the Gains from Merger*, Cambridge University Press, Cambridge, 1977.

5. Ravenscraft, David J., and F.M. Scherer, *Mergers, Sell-Offs, and Economic Efficiency*, The Brookings Institution, Washington, D.C., 1987.

6. Healy, Paul M., Krishna G. Palepu, and Richard S. Ruback, "Does Corporate Performance Improve After Mergers?" *Journal of Financial Economics* 31, 135–175 (1992).

stock price can be influenced by numerous factors, they focused on the measurement of cash flow generated by the companies post transaction. In addition, the cash flow measurement did away with any impact of the accounting for the transaction, as the cash flow was prior to any goodwill amortization. Therefore, the measurement neutralized the impact of pooling versus purchase accounting. The study produced a number of findings. First, it evaluated the cash flow returns for the merged companies pre and post merger. The cash flow returns were defined as operating cash flow divided by the market value of the firm's assets at the beginning of the period. They found that there was an increase in the cash flow returns for the merged companies, resulting primarily from the increase in asset productivity relative to the company's industry. Second, they compared the increases in cash flows to the announcement returns in the merger, and found that there was a correlation between the two. The expectation of an improvement in cash flows led to abnormal stock returns.

In a similar study by Jeannette Switzer titled "Evidence on Real Gains in Corporate Acquisitions," Switzer studied 324 combinations between 1967 and 1987.[7] Like the Healy study, Switzer looked at the changes in operating performance of the merged companies post transaction. The findings were that the operating cash flow returns for the post-merger companies were larger than would have been expected if the two firms had not merged. There was both an improvement in the operating cash flow margin and the asset utilization of the merged companies. The study also maintained that investors' reactions to the transaction announcement reflect the belief in the synergistic benefits of the transaction.

Much of the research that has been performed in the past has taken a macro view of mergers and acquisitions, looking at a significant number of transactions over various time periods and drawing broad conclusions from the data. Given the lack of conclusive evidence resulting from this approach, other academics have approached the issue from different perspectives. For example, various academics have looked at the relationship between the buyer and seller. This research too, seems to provide inconclusive evidence as to the benefits of mergers and acquisitions. Some empirical studies showed that related buyers and sellers show decreased shareholder returns post transaction,[8] while others have shown de minimus returns[9] or positive returns.

Similarly, there have been numerous studies that look at hostile versus friendly transactions to determine whether there is a difference in the performance of companies post transaction. These analyses also seem to produce mixed results,

---

7. Switzer, Jeannette A., "Evidence on Real Gains in Corporate Acquisitions," *Journal of Economics and Business* 48, 443–460 (1996).

8. Argawal, Anup., Jeffrey F. Jaffe, and Gershon N. Mandelker, "The Post-Merger Performance of Acquiring Firms: A Reexamination of an Anomaly," *Journal of Finance* 47(4), 1605–1660 (1992).

9. Fowler, Karen L., and Dennis R. Schmidt, "Determinants of Tender Offer Post-Acquisition Financial Performance," *Strategic Management Journal* 10, 339–350 (1989).

suggesting both positive and negative post-merger performance.[10] Kennedy and Limmack in their 1996 study showed there was little difference in the performance of companies pre-and post-hostile takeover.[11]

In 1997, Ronan Powell performed an analysis of 411 targets and 532 firms not subject to takeover between 1984 and 1991 in order to model the likelihood of takeover based on a number of factors.[12] Powell reviews multiple different studies that conclude there are a variety of factors that determine whether a company is a likely takeover target, including size, growth, leverage, and poor stock price performance. Powell's model focuses more on an examination of specific firm and industry characteristics as determinants of takeover likelihood. Powell found that factors such as size, liquidity, and free cash flow were significant determinants of takeover likelihood, i.e., the smaller the firm and the larger the free cash flow, the greater the likelihood of takeover. Powell also found that hostile and friendly targets were viewed differently. Specifically, firms subject to hostile takeover were more likely to be larger, have low liquidity, and have low profitability. Firms subject to friendly takeover were more likely to be small in size and have high leverage. A recent study conducted in the United Kingdom by Paul Barnes titled "Why Do Bidders Do Badly Out of Mergers? Some UK Evidence," looked at how the stockholders in acquiring corporations fare in mergers and acquisitions.[13] In the study he showed that target stock prices increased by 31.5% on average during the period surrounding the announcement of a transaction, while the stock price of the acquirer typically only increased 1% on average. The reasons for this he finds can generally be explained by the eagerness of the acquiring management team to make the acquisition rather than the desire to enhance shareholder value.

[B] What Types of Companies Are Taken Over?

There are a number of factors that play a role in why certain companies are taken over and others are not. The evidence is somewhat mixed and provides certain compelling and less compelling reasons as to which companies are more vulnerable than others and why. Some literature has argued that more profitable firms are more subject to takeover than less profitable companies,[14] while others have

---

10. Cannella, A.A. Jr., and D.C. Hambrick, "Effects of Executive Departures on the Performance of Acquired Firms," *Strategic Management Journal* 14, 137–152 (1993).

11. Kennedy, V.A., and R.J. Limmack, "Takeover Activity, CEO Turnover, and the Market for Corporate Control," *Journal of Business Finance and Accounting* 23(2), 267–285 (1996).

12. Powell, Ronan G., "Modeling Takeover Likelihood," *Journal of Business Finance and Accounting* 24(7/8), 1009–1030 (1997).

13. Barnes, Paul, "Why Do Bidders Do Badly Out of Mergers? Some UK Evidence," *Journal of Business Finance and Accounting* 25(5) & (6), 571–594 (1998).

14. Ravenscraft, David J., and F.M. Scherer, *Mergers, Sell-Offs, and Economic Efficiency*, Brookings Institution, Washington, D.C.: 1987.

argued that they are equally as profitable[15] or less profitable.[16] In contrast to looking at measures of profitability as a determinant of the likelihood of being taken over, market value has been looked at as a proxy for performance. Here again, the research results are mixed, with some analyses suggesting that targets' performance is little different than that of companies not subject to takeover,[17,18,19] while others suggest that target firms tend to have lower valuations than firms not taken over.[20, 21]

A recent 2001 study conducted by Susan Trimbath, Halina Frydman, and Roman Frydman titled "Cost Inefficiency, Size of Firms and Takeovers," analyzed companies in the Fortune 500 for at least a year between the years 1980 and 1997.[22] They looked at the determinants and effects of takeovers. Their analysis suggests that a corporation "faces a higher risk of takeover if it is relatively inefficient." They also demonstrated a significant improvement in efficiency post transaction.

In 2001, Mary Zey and Tami Swenson of Texas A&M University analyzed the acquisition history of public companies that were in the Fortune 500 in 1976 between the time period 1981 and 1995.[23] Their research drew a number of interesting conclusions. First, they established that in periods where there are shifts in the capital markets, i.e., in periods of high interest rates or when capital accumulation is difficult through external means, companies pursue mergers and acquisitions using internal capital, i.e., their own stock. Second, significant M&A activity is driven by external forces such as the change in tax laws like the Tax Reform Act of 1986,

---

15. Billiet, Matthew T., "Targeting Capital Structure: The Relationship Between Risky Debt and The Firm's Likelihood of Being Acquired," *Journal of Business* 69(2), 173–192 (1996).

16. Cheh, John J., Randy S. Weinberg, and Ken C. Yook, "An Application of an Artificial Neural Network Investment System to Predict Takeover Targets," *Journal of Applied Business Research* 15, 33–45 (1999).

17. Palepu, Krishna G., "Predicting Takeover Targets: A Methodological and Empirical Analysis," *Journal of Accounting and Economics* 8, 3–35 (1986).

18. Powell, Ronan G., "Modeling Takeover Likelihood," *Journal of Business Finance and Accounting* 24(7/8), 1009–1030 (1997).

19. Ambrose, Brent W., and William L. Megginson, "The Role of Asset Structure, Ownership Structure, and Takeover Defenses in Determining Acquisition Likelihood," *Journal of Financial and Quantitative Analysis* 27(4), 575–589 (1992).

20. Morck, Randall, Andrei Shleifer, and Robert W. Vishny, "Alternative Mechanisms for Corporate Control," *American Economic Review* 79(4), 842–852 (1989).

21. Davis, G.F., and S.K. Stout, "Organization Theory and The Market for Corporate Control: A Dynamic Analysis of the Characteristics of Large Takeover Targets, 1980–1990," *Administrative Science Quarterly* 17, 605–633 (1992).

22. Trimbath, S., H. Frydman, and R. Frydman, "Cost Inefficiency, Size of Firms and Takeovers," *Review of Quantitative Finance and Accounting* 17, 397–420 (2001).

23. Zey, Mary, and T. Swenson, "The Transformation and Survival of Fortune 500 Industrial Corporations Through Merges and Acquisitions, 1981–1995," *The Sociological Quarterly* 42(3), 461–486 (2001).

which facilitated a significant amount of restructuring activity. Third, corporations undergo significant M&A activity when they can no longer accumulate capital internally at an adequate rate.

[C] Mergers Versus Tender Offers

Negotiations in mergers and acquisitions tend to be conducted privately as a one-to-one dialogue between the management of two companies, or publicly between the acquirer and the target's board and shareholders. Privately negotiated transactions tend to be executed as mergers whereas public transactions tend to be executed as tender offers.

Because of this distinction between mergers and tender offers, there is a difference between the information that is disseminated to the public under the two scenarios. Tender offers, by their nature, tend to make available vast amounts of information regarding the overall transaction, as target shareholders must decide for themselves whether or not to pursue a transaction. In contrast, a negotiated merger reveals little information until the transaction is agreed to by the companies.

The information made available and the form of consideration in the transaction can have numerous effects. First, a public tender offer usually results in multiple bidders for a target, pushing the price of a transaction up as competition between the parties heats up. The impact of this is that the cost to the bidder goes up, driving down the shareholder value creation opportunity for the acquirer's shareholders. Conversely, the value of the offer goes up to the target's shareholders, increasing the shareholder value return for those stockholders. Second, the information made available as well as the competition encourages bidders to explore the synergies that are available in the transaction. These synergies offer a bidder who can take advantage of them the opportunity to increase its bid, "paying" some of those synergies to the target's shareholders.

In privately negotiated mergers, because the transaction is conducted between the management teams of the two parties, the public-market scrutiny of the transaction may be less. Consequently, the likely competition in the deal is less, allowing the acquirer to possibly pay less for the target. This may mean that the target's shareholders get less value in the transaction and the acquirer pays less in value. However, it may also mean that as a stock-for-stock transaction, the capital structure of the surviving organization is not compromised, allowing remaining shareholders to capitalize on the combined opportunity.

Much of these observations have been confirmed in the literature. Michael Jensen and R. Ruback, in their 1983 study titled "The Market for Corporate Control — The Scientific Evidence," came to the following conclusions.[24] First, target shareholders do better under tender offers than under mergers. Target shareholder returns surrounding the tender range from 16.9% to 34.1%, while target

---

24. Jensen, Michael C., and Richard S. Ruback, "The Market for Corporate Control— The Scientific Evidence," *Journal of Financial Economics* 11, 5–50 (1983).

returns in a merger range from 6.2% to 13.4%. For bidders in tender offers, the range of returns for the group studied was from 2.4% to 6.7%, while the evidence for bidders in mergers was mixed, essentially zero.

In a similar study, Michael Bradley, Anand Desai, and E. Han Kim in their 1988 study titled "Synergistic Gains from Corporate Acquisitions and Their Division Between the Stockholders of Targets and Acquiring Firms," found that bidders in tender offers do progressively worse as competition drives up prices, and target shareholders do progressively better.[25] They looked at successful tender offers from 1963 to 1984. The overall value of target and acquiring firm in the group studied increased an average of 7.4%. However, they found that target shareholders garnered the bulk of the gain in these transactions. They also found that the gains to the acquiring firm declined proportionately as the number of bidders in the tender offer increased. Targets that were subject to multiple bids averaged a zero percent gain for the acquiring firm.

In related research, Elazar Berkovitch and Naveen Khanna looked at a theoretical model of mergers versus tender offers in their 1991 paper titled "A Theory of Acquisition Markets: Mergers Versus Tender Offers, and Golden Parachutes."[26] In their study, they posited that an acquirer has the choice between making a tender offer and negotiating a merger. They concluded that a bidder will pursue a merger up to the point that it can justify a purchase price that includes the value if synergies obtained in the transaction. It will likely not pursue a tender offer if others can achieve synergies greater than it can, as it would expect to lose in the tender offer competition. Berkovitch and Khanna, like Jensen and Ruback, observe that acquirer's are better off in mergers while target shareholders are better off in tender offers.

[D] Cross-Border Mergers & Acquisitions

International mergers and acquisitions began to gather steam in the 1980s as companies looked to external markets for growth. In particular, mature U.S. companies increasingly went abroad to enhance shareholder value. There have been many studies that have looked at why firms acquire abroad. Specifically, these studies have suggested that companies pursue acquisitions outside of their core market in order to capitalize on internal strengths in foreign markets, i.e., financial, organizational, technological, etc. In a study by Pedro Gonzales et al. titled "Cross-Border Mergers and Acquisitions: Maximizing the Value of the Firm," they found, among other things, that companies with significant assets and mature cash flows are more likely to pursue an international M&A strategy than those less mature and

---

25. Bradley, Michael, Anand Desai, and E. Han Kim, "Synergistic Gains from Corporate Acquisitions and Their Division Between the Stockholders of Targets and Acquiring Firms," *Journal of Financial Economics* 21, 3–40 (1988).

26. Berkovitch, E., and N. Khanna, "A Theory of Acquisition Markets: Mergers Versus Tender Offers, and Golden Parachutes," *The Review of Financial Studies*, Vol. 4-1, 149–174 (1991).

with fewer assets.[27] Slower growth is a prime motivator in going abroad. They suggest that the international move is a signal to the market that an increase in global diversification is a risk reduction event as well as a growth opportunity.

§ 13.03   RATIONALE BEHIND MERGERS & ACQUISITIONS

Mergers and acquisitions take place for a variety of reasons. The academic literature has focused on the macro, theoretical reasons why takeovers occur including, disciplining management teams who operate inefficient organizations, exploiting synergies between firms, and managers pursuing their own self interest in hopes of building an empire, sometimes at the expense of shareholders. Putting the literature aside, companies pursue mergers and acquisitions for a number of financial and operating reasons. Companies may wish to grow, diversify, broaden a product line, access new markets, or acquire a new technology. Companies may wish to leverage joint synergies or simply acquire a competitor. Exhibit 13-3 offers a list of some of the more common reasons behind mergers and acquisitions.

[A]   Gain Scale

One of the most common reasons for mergers and acquisitions is to gain scale. Whether it is gaining economies of scale or economies of scope, a sound M&A strategy can accelerate a company's position in the industry at a pace that exceeds what is achievable via organic growth. Gaining scale through merger or acquisition has a number of benefits. First, it eliminates certain

---

Exhibit 13-3
Common Rationale Behind Mergers & Acquisitions

Gain Scale:	Acquire complimentary and overlapping products and services
Growth:	Acquire new products
	Access new markets
	Leverage existing products and services into new customer base
	Leverage existing customers with new products
	Capture additional market share
Diversification:	Enter new markets
	Add on new products
	Access new customers
Capitalize on Synergies:	Financial synergies
	Operating synergies
Enhance R&D:	Acquire new technology
Integrate:	Vertical integration
	Horizontal integration

---

27. Gonzalez, P., G.M. Vasconcellos, R.D.J. Kish, and J.K. Kramer, "Cross-Border Mergers and Acquisitions: Maximizing the Value of the Firm," *Applied Financial Economics* 7, 295–305 (1997).

execution risks associated with trying to amass scale through organic means. A company may not have the management in place or the financial resources immediately available to pursue a rapid internal growth process. M&A allows a company to grow in size quickly while at the same time adding management and potentially strengthening its balance sheet. Second, M&A allows one to gain scale by accessing new markets, new customers, new geographic regions, or new products and services. Likewise, it allows a company to leverage a merger partner's assets with those of its own and vice versa. Third, gaining scale through M&A allows a company to leap frog the competition and gain a stronger foothold in an industry than it might have been able to do if internal growth was pursued instead of an acquisition.

[B]   Growth

Internal or organic growth is often difficult to achieve, in particular in competitive or mature industries. In addition, as industries mature, overall growth rates may decline, forcing companies to look beyond internal strategies to realize growth. Growth through M&A can come from a number of sources including acquiring businesses that are in the same or similar industries or sectors as the purchaser, or acquiring companies in new industries or sectors. By consolidating players with similar products and services, or markets and customers, the growth of a company can be enhanced through gaining economies of scale and scope. The top line, or revenue growth rate can be enhanced as well as the bottom line, net income. Most important in this strategy is the ability to add revenue while at the same time shedding some of the costs associated with producing that revenue, resulting in enhanced earnings growth.

By acquiring or merging with companies in industries dissimilar to that of the acquirer, a purchaser is able to enter markets or offer products and services that are in industries with higher growth opportunities than its current business. While the industries may be different, the acquirer is still able to capitalize on certain financial synergies thus accelerating the company's revenue and earnings growth.

[C]   Diversification

Diversification can come in many forms, and like growth and gaining scale, can always be pursued through internal means. However, diversification through internal means has certain problems. First, diversification may be a distraction from the core business. Second, it may require capital to fund, which could strain the balance sheet and inhibit the growth opportunity of the remaining business. Third, building a de novo effort may dilute earnings while the business grows to scale. Fourth, the right management may not be in place to appropriately capitalize on the opportunity. Fifth, a diversification strategy may take significant time, during which the company's competitors may gain market share.

Various studies on diversification have shown mixed results from this strategy. A 1995 study by Philip Berger and Eli Ofek titled "Diversification's Effect on Firm Value," looked at the effects of diversification on firm value.[28] They concluded that diversification reduces value. In particular, they showed that the value loss averaged 13% to 15% over the time period of the analysis and was consistent across all industry sectors. The study did show, however, that diversification within an industry mitigated the value loss. Loss in value stems from over investment of firms in multiple segments versus firms in one business line. In addition, it evidenced that value loss could be attributed to subsidization of poorly performing subsidiaries. They were able to establish marginal benefits to diversification in the form of increased interest tax shields and the ability to use losses of one subsidiary to offset taxable earnings of another subsidiary.

One company that has pursued acquisitions as a core part of its strategy is General Electric Company. General Electric Company is a diversified industrial company with revenues of over $125 billion and a market capitalization of over $400 billion. The company is engaged in developing, manufacturing, and marketing a wide variety of products for the generation, transmission, distribution, control, and utilization of electricity. Its products include major appliances, lighting products, industrial automation products, medical diagnostic imaging equipment, motors, electrical distribution and control equipment, locomotives, power generation and delivery products, nuclear power support services and fuel assemblies, commercial and military aircraft jet engines, and engineered materials such as plastics, silicones, and super-abrasive industrial diamonds. Through its affiliate, the National Broadcasting Company, Inc., the company delivers network television services, operates television stations and provides cable, Internet and multimedia programming and distribution services. Through another affiliate, General Electric Capital Services, Inc., the company offers a broad array of financial and other services.

General Electric is one of the more acquisitive companies in the world. In 2001 alone, it announced or completed approximately 49 mergers or acquisitions, that span all divisions and subsidiaries, ranging from the $5.3 billion acquisition of Heller Financial, a financial services firm, to the acquisition of certain assets of Enron in the power generation business. Exhibit 13-4 details the company's recent acquisition history.

Despite the varied results of diversification through mergers and acquisitions, the strategy does have a number of benefits. First, it accomplishes in one step what may otherwise take a company years to achieve through internal means. Second, it potentially eliminates the dilution associated with building a new business in house. Third, it has the potential to add management to the company that already has expertise in the sector or industry being pursued. Fourth, M&A driven diversification can take less time to execute than one driven by internal

---

28. Berger, P.G., and E. Ofek, "Diversification's Effect on Firm Value," *Journal of Financial Economics* 37, 39–65 (1995).

Exhibit 13-4
General Electric Recent Acquisition History

Date	Target	Business Description
03/04/02	iPath	Surgery management software
02/21/02	Interlogix, Inc.	Electronic security
02/20/02	Enron Wind Corp (Certain Assets)	Power generation
02/13/02	Visualization Technologies, Inc.	Electromagnetic based image guided surgery systems
02/13/02	KVB-Enertec	Air emissions monitoring and data acquisition
02/12/02	Betz Dearborn (Water Treatment Business)	Water treatment
01/24/02	Bentley Nevada Corp	Machinery monitoring and diagnostics
01/24/02	Daimler Chrysler Capital Services Commercial Real Estate and Asset Based Lending Portfolio	Loan portfolio
01/16/02	PII Group Ltd	Pipeline I-line inspections
01/09/02	Danica Biomedical	Telemetry systems for health care
01/08/02	Unison Industries Inc.	Sells products and services to aerospace and power generation industries
12/20/01	Kawasaki Steel Corporation's LNP Engineering Plastics Business	Plastics
12/19/01	Imatron Inc.	Electron beam tomography scanners
12/07/01	Honeywell's Fuel Cell and Microturbine Assets	Measuring tools, surveying equipment
11/02/01	Wabtec Corporation (Locomotive services assets and long-term services contracts)	Products and services to locomotive industry
10/25/01	Heller Financial, Inc.	Financial services
10/11/01	Telemundo	Hispanic television network
10/08/01	Bals Electrical Engineering Ltd.	Substation engineering solutions and services provider
10/04/01	Coincidence Technologies	PET radiopharmaceuticals
09/21/01	Sofion, AG	IT services provider

means. Finally, a sound acquisition strategy can help strengthen an acquirer's balance sheet.

[D] Synergies

Synergies should result from just about every M&A transaction, regardless of rationale. The word synergy can be defined in a number of ways. A synergy can be thought of as leveraging the combined strengths of two parties to a transaction such that by adding the individual capabilities of the two companies, their sum is greater than their parts. The best way to understand synergies is to explore a few examples. Synergies come in many forms, including financial and operating synergies.

[1]   Operating Synergies

Operating synergies are those synergies that come from capitalizing on the consolidation of two companies' operations. There are numerous examples of operating synergies including:

Revenues: Revenue synergies come from a variety of places including leveraging one company's products through another's sales force, cross-selling one company's products with another company's customer base, or selling products of one company into geographies of another company. Revenue synergies can also come from gaining pricing power in a given market.

Cost of Goods Sold: Through gaining economies of scale and consolidating purchasing power, cost synergies can be had by gaining bargaining power with suppliers.

Operating Expenses: There are usually many opportunities to reduce operating expenses in a merger or acquisition. For example, if the two parties to a transaction are public, by virtue of the deal, one public company is eliminated, in the process doing away with its public company costs which can often be significant. There is no need for both companies to have separate investor relations departments and separate auditors. In addition, the basic costs of maintaining the public filings can be eliminated. As another example, there may be redundant sales forces or marketing departments, as well as duplicate corporate staff. All these may be areas for potential cost savings.

[2]   Financial Synergies

While operating synergies can often result in enhancing the financial performance of a company, financial synergies are more commonly thought of as those that enhance the company's capital structure or improve its ability to obtain financing on favorable terms. First, when a company's assets and cash flows are increased through acquisition, banks and other lending institutions may be willing to provide the combined company with capital on more favorable terms because of the increased security provided by the assets and cash flow. Second, transactions that provide a measure of diversification may lower the risk inherent in the company's cash flows and offer greater predictability. These financial synergies all serve to lower a company's cost of capital and provide it with greater access to the capital markets.

[E]   Enhance Research & Development

Many industries pursue mergers and acquisitions as a means to further research and development efforts. For example, both the pharmaceutical and technology industries make frequent acquisitions in order to acquire technology. Research and development acquisitions may be for companies that have technology that does not exist in-house or would be costly to develop. These acquisitions may also be undertaken at a point where the up-front investment has been made and what remains is the commercialization, production, and marketing of the product. In many cases, the acquirer may not wish to fund certain research and development because of the potential cost and consequent earnings dilution involved in developing the technology. Acquiring a company that has already spent the money to develop technology allows the acquirer to capture the earnings upside without the prior earnings dilution associated with the development costs.

In industries where the pace of change in technology is swift, it may make sense for companies to acquire technologies one the technology has been validated by the market. For example, in the pharmaceutical industry, the cost of developing a new drug can exceed $500 million — some estimates reach as high as $800 million. Developing a new drug in house can be cost-prohibitive and may be dilutive to earnings. Acquiring the rights to a drug or acquiring a company once the drug has been approved lowers the risk of execution and reduces the earnings impact to the acquirer of commercializing the drug.

[F]   Integrate

Mergers and acquisitions may also take place in an effort to integrate a company throughout its value chain. In other words, an acquirer may purchase or merge with a target in order to capture a greater share of the overall dollar spent in a category. For example, a distributor may acquire a manufacturer of a product to capture the margin inherent in the manufacturing of the products that are distributed.

Even though these reasons may provide a rationale for a certain merger or acquisition, they do not by themselves provide a rationale for "buying" or merging instead of building the capability oneself. There are a number of reasons why a company might choose to purchase or merge with another company to acquire a capability. The decision to acquire or merge is often based on the cost of acquiring versus building the capability, the availability of management, the time to completion, and the risk of execution.

There are a number of factors to consider when comparing the cost of building versus acquiring a capability. First, it will depend on the type of business. For example, a manufacturing plant may be cost-prohibitive, as could be building a sales force from scratch. Second, it may be easy to build a business but it's harder to build a brand. Even if a sales force can be built, it may still be necessary to invest in significant advertising and brand building in order to realize any value from the sales force. Third, additional infrastructure such as technology and office space, may be necessary to build the business. Acquiring capabilities, facilities and infrastructure may be a lot less expensive than building them from scratch.

Often a company's success is dependent on its management team. Therefore, regardless of a company's ability to build a capability, its success may be undermined by not having the right management in place to execute the strategy. A company may have strong management talent in the business where it currently focuses, while it may lack expertise in products, markets or sectors where it does not have direct exposure. Acquiring a company with management may be cheaper and more efficient than building in-house.

Building a new capability may take a significant amount of time, whether it entails constructing a new facility, entering a new market, introducing a competing product, or the like. The time to build may give competitors a further edge while you build the capability, further distancing yourself from the competition. Acquiring the desired business eliminates the risks associated with building the business and reduces the time required to gain the capability.

As with any new business, building a capability has significant execution risk, whereas in an acquisition or merger, much of the initial execution risk has been eliminated. However, once the acquisition has been made, there is a risk that the businesses are not integrated well.

§ 13.04   VALUATION OF MERGERS & ACQUISITIONS

The valuation of mergers and acquisitions entails utilization of many of the classic valuation methodologies used in corporate finance valuation: comparable trading multiples, comparable transaction multiples, discounted cash flow analysis, and pro forma merger analysis. In addition, other analyses are performed to confirm the financial merits of a transaction and whether it has the potential to create shareholder value. The following discussion should be read in conjunction with Chapters 2–9, which include detailed discussions on each of the foregoing valuation methodologies.

The approach to valuing either a merger or acquisition candidate is essentially the same. First, the target — or merger candidate — should be valued on a stand alone basis using discounted cash flow and comparable trading analysis. Second, the value of the target on a takeover basis should be determined using comparable transactions analysis. Third, the pro forma financial statements of the combined company should be created to determine the accretion or dilution arising from the transaction, as well as the relative contribution of each company to the combined organization. Once the preliminary valuation and pro forma merger analysis have been performed, the stock price and shareholders of the target should be analyzed.

[A]   Stand Alone Analysis

The first step is to determine the stand alone value of the target. Using comparable trading multiples analysis, determine the universe of peer companies comparable to the target. Then calculate the pertinent trading multiples for that universe including aggregate value to revenues, EBIT and EBITDA, and equity value to net income and projected earnings. In this analysis, it is typical to use the most recent four quarters of financial results for all metrics, plus the projected earnings of the companies for P/E multiples. Once the ratios have been calculated, determine the mean and median of those multiples for the universe. Apply the mean and median to the metrics of the target to derive an implied value for the target. This value represents the stand alone, going concern value for the target company. It can be used to establish an independent value for a business based on the multiples of its peer group, and can be used to compare the target's current market value to its implied value to establish whether it is over- or under-valued in the marketplace.[29]

The second approach to stand alone valuation is discounted cash flow analysis. In this analysis, the free cash flows of the target are forecasted and then discounted back to the present using a discount rate that approximates the target's weighted average cost of capital. In addition, a terminal value is calculated at the end of the forecast period. This terminal value is discounted to the present using the company's WACC and is added to the present value of the future free cash flows. A discounted cash flow analysis yields an implied going concern value for the target company as if it were to continue to be operated on the same basis going forward is it has in the past.[30]

[B]   Takeover Analysis

The second step is to establish the target's takeover value. The two principal means for valuing a company from a takeover perspective are comparable transaction multiples analysis and comparable transaction premiums analysis.

The magnitude of the transaction multiples and the size of the premiums will vary depending on the size of the target relative to that of the acquirer. In merger-of-equal transactions, where the target and acquirer are roughly the same size, it is not uncommon to see very little premium paid to the target corporation. Conversely, in "control" transactions where a company is acquired and the management and shareholders give up control of the target, it is not uncommon to see transaction premiums in excess of 30% of the target's stock price just prior to the announcement of the transaction. Known as a "control" premium, this premium is paid to compensate shareholders for the fact that they are giving up control of the company. Like acquisition premiums, transaction multiples will reflect the degree to which the transaction is a merger-of-equals or a control transaction.[31] Both of these analyses will provide an indication of a range of values that would be paid for the target based on comparable transactions.

[1]   Cash Tender Offer Premiums

Cash tender offers have historically ranged on average between 25% and 45% in any given year since 1994. Cash tender premiums for 2003 were approximately 86.7%.[32] Exhibit 13-5 provides the trend in cash premiums since 1990.

[2]   Merger Premiums

Merger premiums depend on the size of the target relative to the acquirer and the degree to which the selling management and shareholders are giving up

---

29. For a more detailed discussion of comparable trading multiples analysis, please refer to *Chapter 5: Comparable Company Analysis.*

30. For a more detailed discussion of discounted cash flow analysis, please refer to *Chapter 4: Discounted Cash Flow Analysis.*

31. For a more detailed description of comparable transactions analysis, please refer to *Chapter 6: Comparable Transactions Analysis.*

32. Mergerstat.

control in the transaction. Historically, merger premiums have ranged on average from 17.3% in 1994 to 57.5% in 2003. Exhibit 13-6 provides a list of recent mergers and their associated acquisition premiums.

[C]   Pro Forma Merger Analysis[33]

The third step in the valuation analysis is to perform pro forma merger analysis. The two principal approaches hereunder are accretion/dilution analysis and contribution analysis. Accretion/dilution analysis studies the impact of a proposed transaction on the acquirer's earnings per share, and indicates what an acquirer could pay for the target. A transaction that is accretive is one where the earnings per share increase as a result of the transaction, while a dilutive transaction is the opposite. For example, if an acquirer's stand alone earnings per share prior to a transaction are $1.10, and, as a result of the transaction, the combined earnings of the company increases to $1.15, the transaction is accretive by $0.05 per share. In this example, because the transaction is accretive, it suggests that the acquirer could pay more for the target if necessary. Each time the acquirer increases the purchase price, the accretion in the transaction erodes. From the perspective of Wall Street, accretive transactions are typically well received, while dilutive transactions may not be, unless there is clear rationale for the dilution.

Contribution analysis compares the relative contribution of revenues, EBIT, EBITDA, and net income by the acquirer and target to the combined entity, with

Exhibit 13-5
Cash Tender Offer Premiums:*
1990–2003[34]

1990	34.3%
1991	34.3%
1992	30.8%
1993	92.8%
1994	37.8%
1995	39.0%
1996	29.7%
1997	25.8%
1998	30.9%
1999	39.5%
2000	47.5%
2001	50.0%
2002	48.9%
2003	86.7%

*Average offer price to target stock price premium 1-day prior to announcement.

33. For a more detailed description of accretion/dilution analysis and contribution analysis, please refer to *Chapter 7: Merger Analysis*.

34. Thomson Financial.

**Exhibit 13-6
Merger Premiums:* 1990–2003**[35]

1990	30.7%
1991	26.4%
1992	22.2%
1993	41.0%
1994	17.3%
1995	21.0%
1996	18.3%
1997	20.4%
1998	31.2%
1999	34.7%
2000	40.4%
2001	36.4%
2002	39.1%
2003	57.5%

*Average offer price to target stock price premium 1-day prior to announcement.

the shareholder ownership after the transaction is complete. It provides a measure of reason or fairness, in that, a transaction where substantially more of the revenues and EBITDA, for example, are contributed by the target, but more of the combined company is owned by the acquirer's shareholders, would not seem reasonable and should be questioned. For example, if the target contributes 40% of the EBITDA but owns 25% of the combined company, one should question whether this transaction is fair to the target's shareholders.

Based on these two methodologies, it is possible to determine a range of feasible prices that could be paid by an acquirer, and independently, if that price is reasonable by comparison with the target's contribution of revenues, EBIT and EBITDA to the combined company. However, it should be noted that in many circumstances, an acquirer's ability to pay, i.e., the price that results from the accretion/dilution analysis, may not necessarily coincide with the range of values from the DCF, comparable multiples and comparable transactions analyses. The potential purchase price may be substantially higher than the target's stand alone value, if the acquirer has a strong stock price or very low funding costs.

[D] Stock Price and Shareholder Analysis[36]

Once a possible valuation range for a target has been established, there are a number of other factors that influence the price an acquirer should pay. Merger analysis

---

35. *Id.*

36. For a more detailed description of stock price and shareholder analysis, please refer to *Chapter 9: Stock Price Analysis.*

helps establish what an acquirer is able to pay, and whether that price is reasonable given the pro forma financial contribution of each company party to the transaction. There is yet another factor that comes into play at the time the acquirer chooses to make an offer—where a target's stock presently trades and where it has traded in the past. Coinciding with this is the basis that various shareholders have in the company. This may influence what it may be forced to pay in order to "get the deal done."

Stock price analysis entails analyzing the historical price performance of a company's stock for different periods prior to presenting an offer. There are three aspects of stock price analysis: absolute price performance, relative price performance, and price/volume analysis. Absolute stock price performance evaluates a company's stock price on its own for a period of time prior to presenting the offer. It visually presents the range of prices at which the target's stock has traded. Common time periods are six months, 12 months, and two years. It allows one to determine if there has been any stock price run-up or deterioration in recent history based on certain events.

Relative stock price performance builds on absolute price performance by comparing the target's trading history to an index or indexes. It is common to use broad indexes such as the S&P 500, or targeted indexes such as one made up of the company's peer group. Relative stock price analysis allows an acquirer to visualize how a company's stock has performed in relation to the market and its peer group, and whether it has performed in line with the two groups over time. It also helps distinguish what changes in a target's stock price have been influenced by the market and have impacted all the companies in the sector or market, and what events have been company specific.

Price/volume analysis is quite helpful in determining the overall basis that recent shareholders in the company's stock have. For example, it is typical to perform a price/volume analysis on a company for a six-month time frame. During that six-month time frame, a defined number of shares will have traded at certain prices. Based on the analysis, it is possible to determine at what prices those shares traded and thus conclude that a large portion of the shareholders have a basis in the company's stock at a given level.

Shareholder analysis drills further into the stock price analysis by looking into the individual shareholders of a company and trying to determine their individual bases. There are multiple categories of shareholders that can be analyzed, including mutual funds, hedge funds and other institutional investors, individuals, and strategic investors.

Once the analysis has been done, the question becomes what to do with it. First, for significant shareholders — institutional, management, or other significant shareholders — determine at what price they acquired their stock. Second, determine what stock has been acquired or sold since the initial purchase, and at what price. Third, add up the significant shareholders to determine how much of the stock is held by large shareholders and how much is owned by the public or individual shareholders (public float).

Stock price analysis is not necessarily a valuation tool. It initially provides an overall range of values at which a company's stock has traded over a given time frame. However, in addition to this, it offers a subjective view of why a stock has traded the way it has historically, and whether stock price moves have been market driven, sector driven or company specific. Furthermore, the analysis shows at what prices freely tradable stock has traded during the recent past, indicating the basis that public shareholders have in the stock. Finally, it allows us to analyze the basis of large shareholders to determine if a potential offer price would be attractive to these shareholders.

Based on the valuation and financial analysis of the target and the transaction, it is possible to determine whether the anticipated benefits of the transaction are supported by the projected financial performance, and whether the transaction creates value for shareholders.

§ 13.05   VALUE CREATION IN MERGERS & ACQUISITIONS

Creating value through mergers and acquisitions appears simple. For example, it is easy to draw the conclusion that an accretive transaction creates value. Much like the P/E game of the 1960s, it is easy to fall into this trap. The acquirer — or surviving company's — earnings are greater than they were prior to the transaction and therefore if you apply the same multiple of earnings that the acquirer has prior to the deal to the pro forma earnings of the combined company post transaction, its stock price should rise. Seems simple enough. This is arguably one of the more common mistakes in mergers and acquisitions, i.e., to assume that because a transaction is accretive, it creates value.

To shed some light on how mergers and acquisitions create value, let us revisit Exhibit 1-4: Mergers, Acquisitions, and Restructurings as Drivers of Shareholder Value, and recall the three fundamental tenets of shareholder value: public perception, capital structure, and operating performance. Each of these must be evaluated in every transaction to determine if it creates value; financial analysis alone is not sufficient. For example, it may be possible to acquire a company at an attractive price, and the transaction may be accretive, but the target company may have had its own public perception problems that carry over to the acquirer. These perception issues may override the financial merits of the transaction and result in destroying shareholder value for the acquirer or surviving corporation.

Within the framework for creating shareholder value, let us look at the various components that may determine whether value is being created in a given transaction. First, thoroughly understand and evaluate the strategic merits of the transaction. Second, assess the financial merits of the transaction and whether the financial analysis supports the strategic merits. Third, understand the implications of the transaction on the surviving company's capital structure and operating performance. Fourth, appraise the public market's response to the proposed transaction.

[A]   Strategic Analysis

Prior to undertaking any financial analysis, a thorough assessment should be done of the strategic merits of the transaction. One should ask a few fundamental questions such as: What is the objective of the transaction? What is driving the transaction? What core competencies are you trying to leverage? Are there synergies in the transaction? Can you leverage the target's products or services through your distribution to your customers? Can you leverage your products or services through the target's distribution to their customers? What is the quality of the target's management? How does the transaction alter your competitive position? Will the merger or acquisition serve to enhance earnings and earnings growth of the surviving company? Would a combination of the two companies result enhance both companies' ability to grow and compete, i.e., does one plus one equal three?

To the extent the answers to these questions are positive, it would make sense to try and support the strategic assessment with financial analysis.

[B]   Financial Analysis

The financial analysis includes stand alone and takeover analysis as well as the pro forma merger analysis and stock price and shareholder analysis discussed earlier. The stand alone analysis provides one with a benchmark value for the target to determine what its implied value is based on the valuation of its industry peers, and also offers a means to determine if the stock is over or under valued in the market. The takeover analysis yields a value for the target that incorporates a takeover premium. The takeover analysis suggests a price that could be paid for the target based on prior comparable transactions. Based on these two approaches, it is possible to come up with a range of potential prices to be paid for the target company. Typically, in an acquisition, the price would be at a premium to the target's current stock price, while in a merger-of-equals, the price could have little or no premium.

Pro forma merger analysis shows us what the potential accretion or dilution in the transaction may be based on the range of prices determined in the stand alone and takeover analysis. Assuming the strategic merits of the transaction are sound and the transaction is accretive, there is a good chance that the transaction may enhance shareholder value. The contribution analysis serves as a check on the proposed range of purchase prices, and forces one to rethink the basis of the financial terms. It compares the pro forma ownership of the two parties to the combined organization with respect to their contribution of revenues, cash flow, and earnings. For example, two companies with different growth rates and margins may result in the smaller company owning more of the combined company than the acquiring company relative to its near term contribution to earnings. While this may suggest that the target is being paid too much, it may also suggest that the target is going to contribute more to the combined company in the future and therefore should command a greater share of the upside.

While the stock price and shareholder analysis do not necessarily give us a view as to whether a transaction will create value or not, it provides us with a real time snapshot of the opportunity to create value. For example, if a company has been trading at a depressed stock price for a prolonged period of time and the market has not recognized the inherent value in the stock, whereas the implied stand alone and takeover value of the company are substantially higher than the current stock price, it may be possible to pay a premium to the current stock price yet a discount to the takeover value, allowing the acquiring shareholders to capture the arbitrage.

Analyzing the shareholder base of the target also provides valuable information on the receptivity of shareholders to a transaction. Based on public filings, it is possible to determine at what prices certain large shareholders acquired stock in the target. Based on analyzing the trading volume of the target at various prices, it is feasible to approximate the average basis of current shareholders. This analysis may reveal the lowest price that may be acceptable to shareholders, once again indicating an opportunity for acquiring shareholders to capture the arbitrage between the stand alone and takeover value of the target and the price that may win the deal.

[C]   Financial Impact on Surviving Company

Independent of the valuation and pro forma merger analysis, it is important to separately assess the transaction's impact on the surviving company's capital structure and operating performance. We do this because a company's value in the marketplace is very quickly assessed by its earnings growth rate and its capital structure. Therefore, first assess how the proposed transaction will impact the surviving company's earnings growth. While the transaction may be accretive, it is possible that the pro forma earnings growth of the combined company may decline, resulting in a contraction in the surviving company's multiple, and effectively eliminating any value enhancing benefits of the transaction. Wall Street will assess not just the accretion in the deal, but the pro forma historical and projected earnings growth of the combined company. Therefore, accretive transactions where the earnings growth of a surviving company declines should be critically assessed to confirm whether the transaction should proceed. Likewise, dilutive transactions that on the surface look like they should be terminated, should be further studied if the earnings growth of the surviving corporation increases. In this instance, one way to further assess the transaction is to determine how long it takes for the pro forma earnings to become accretive to the stand alone earnings of the acquirer.

The second component of the impact analysis is to determine the pro forma capital structure of the combined company. To the extent the surviving corporation's capital structure is materially worse than that of the acquirer stand alone, it may result in a contraction in the company's multiple due to the risk that the leverage in the transaction may impact the financial and operating performance of the company.

While these are the two most important elements on which to focus when assessing the impact of the transaction, it is important not to overlook the many other operating and financial ratios of the combined company. For example, what is the impact of the transaction on the gross margins, operating margins, working capital requirements, and cash flows of the surviving corporation?

[D]   Public Market Response

The final step is to appraise the public market's response to the proposed transaction. Assuming the financial analysis supports the strategic merits of the transaction, and the earnings growth, operating performance and/or capital structure of the surviving corporation are enhanced, it is feasible to assume that the stock market may react favorably to the transaction. However, it is important to communicate the rationale and benefits of the transaction to the public so that the key messages and assumptions can be evaluated by the market. A well-crafted communications strategy can be worth the investment. In many cases, the parties to the transaction may issue a joint press release and host a conference call with investors to answer questions.

§ 13.06 STRUCTURAL ALTERNATIVES

Mergers and/or acquisitions may be structured to be taxable or tax free. In taxable transactions, the consideration paid by the acquirer is taxable to the party that receives the consideration, e.g., if assets are acquired from a target, it must pay a gain on the difference between the purchase price and its tax basis in the assets. In tax-free transactions, the consideration paid is not taxed upon receipt; rather, it is taxed when there is a later taxable transaction. For example, if a shareholder received stock in an acquirer in exchange for its stock in the target, the exchange would not be taxable. Instead, the shareholder would pay taxes when it ultimately sells the stock.

The choice of a certain structure to use in a merger or acquisition will depend on the objectives of the buyer and seller including a number of factors: form of currency used by the acquirer, whether the stock or assets of the target are being acquired, the desired tax treatment of the transaction, the tax basis of the target in its assets, and the desire to complete the transaction expeditiously. Generally, most merger and acquisition transactions use the stock of the acquirer or cash as the currency to acquire the stock or assets of the target.

[A] Tax-Free Transactions

Many mergers and acquisitions are structured as tax-free transactions in order to provide the shareholders of the target the opportunity to defer taxes. In addition, tax-free transactions are undertaken to limit the amount of capital that is lost in the transaction due to taxes. The tax-free nature of corporate mergers and acquisitions is governed by Section 368 of the Internal Revenue Code. Section 368 specifies that transactions that are essentially a corporate reorganization are treated as tax-free or partially tax free. For a transaction to qualify as tax free under Section 368, it has to meet certain requirements:

1. *There must be a continuity of interest*: Continuity of interest means that the target's shareholders maintain an ongoing interest in the combined company post transaction. For the IRS to provide assurance that the transaction will be tax-free, at least 50% of the consideration must be in the form of stock.

2. *There must be a continuity of business enterprise*: There must be a continuation of the target's business. In other words, the acquirer must continue to use the target's historical business, or a substantial portion thereof, in its ongoing operations.

3. *There must be a valid business purpose*: The transaction must have valid business reasons underlying the transaction. A valid business purpose may not be the avoidance of taxes.

4. *It must be conducted using one of seven forms of transaction*: There are even types of reorganizations proscribed by Section 368, known as A, B, C, D, E, F, and G reorganizations. The most frequent of theses transactions, types A, B, C, and D, are discussed below.

If a transaction qualifies, the party transferring stock or assets in the transaction does not recognize any gain or loss on the transaction, as long as there is stock in the counter party received as consideration. Underlying the entire principle is the notion that the stock issued in the transaction allows the old investment to "continue" and thus any gains should be deferred until the stock, or investment, is sold.

As a target corporation or target corporation shareholder, there are a number of benefits to tax-free transactions. First, the target corporation recognizes no gain or loss on the transfer of assets or liabilities to the acquirer. Second, the target corporation's shareholders recognize no gain or loss on the exchange of their stock for stock in the acquirer. However, if a portion of the consideration is cash, debt or other securities, it is taxable to the extent that the value of the consideration exceeds the shareholder's basis in the stock. Third, the target's shareholders carry over their basis into the new stock they receive in the transaction. However, if cash, debt, or other securities are received in the transaction, the basis is adjusted downward by the amount of the cash or debt received, and adjusted upwards for any gain. Fourth, the target shareholders' holding period on their investment includes the period they owned the target's stock.

There are also benefits of a tax-free transaction to the acquiring corporation. First, the acquirer assumes the target's tax basis and holding period in the stock or assets of the target. Second, the acquirer recognizes no gain or loss on the stock that it issues in the transaction.

The three most common structures used in tax-free merger and acquisition transactions are A reorganizations or statutory mergers, B reorganizations, and C reorganizations. In addition, D reorganization are sometimes used, both in acquisitive and divisive transactions.

[1]   A Reorganizations

In an A reorganization, also known as a statutory merger, two corporations combine subject to the procedures established by the corporate laws of the state(s) where the parties are incorporated. The parties merge via a merger agreement that is signed by both parties. A certificate of merger is filed with the respective state agencies and the one corporation then ceases to exist, leaving the other corporation as the surviving entity. Legally, the two entities become one, with the surviving corporation assuming all the assets and liabilities of the corporation that ceases to exist. In an A reorganization, the shareholders of the target exchange their stock for stock of the acquiring corporation.

There are a number of benefits to a statutory merger. First, the transfer of title to the assets of the seller is simple. Upon the filing of the certificate of merger, the title to the assets automatically transfers. In other words, all the titles to the various assets of the target do not need to be individually transferred to the acquirer. Second, a statutory merger is effective in eliminating minority shareholders. While dissident minority shareholders may have the ability to dissent and have their shares valued independently, they are none the less bound by the vote in the transaction, thereby assuring the acquirer that it will gain 100% ownership of the target. Third, a statutory merger gives the target and acquirer flexibility to structure either party as the surviving corporation. Thus, in cases where title to certain assets may not transfer, the transaction may be structured such that the target is the surviving corporation, thereby sidestepping the issue. Fourth, statutory mergers allow flexibility in the types of securities that may be offered. For example, in a tax-free statutory merger, preferred stock may be issued tax free, whereas in cash and stock acquisitions, only voting stock may be issued for the transaction to be tax free.

There are however, a number of downsides to statutory mergers. First, by virtue of the merger, the surviving corporation is liable for the liabilities of the party that ceases to exist, regardless of whether they are known or unknown, disclosed, or undisclosed. Second, statutory mergers can take a long time to complete, as it is likely that both parties to the transactions will require shareholder approval. This can introduce significant market and other risks that may affect the outcome of the transaction. Third, in a statutory merger, while the overall vote of the transaction will determine whether 100% of the seller is acquired, dissident minority shareholders may be able to have their shares independently valued, and may be able to receive cash for those shares. This could produce a cash drain on the parties to the transaction, altering the financial implications of the deal.

There are generally three forms of A reorganizations: a direct merger, a forward triangular merger, and a reverse triangular merger.

  [a]   Direct Merger. In a direct merger, the target merges directly into the acquirer, or vice versa. In this scenario, the target's shareholders are generally not taxed, as long as they receive stock in the surviving corporation for their stock in the target, and that stock of the acquirer comprises at least 50% of the total consideration. While the 50% threshold is not a hard and fast rule, it is prudent to seek advice of tax counsel on the amount of cash that can be issued in a direct merger and continue to be tax free to the target's shareholders. In the case where cash or debt—known as "boot"—is a portion of the consideration, that portion will be taxable to the target's shareholders based on the gain they have in the stock over their basis in the stock. Exhibit 13-7 illustrates a direct merger.

Exhibit 13-7
Direct Merger Structure

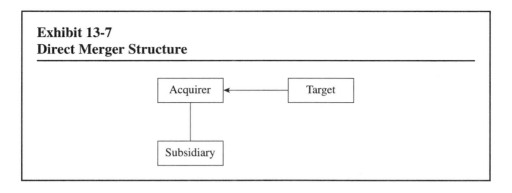

Exhibit 13-8
Forward Triangular Merger Structure

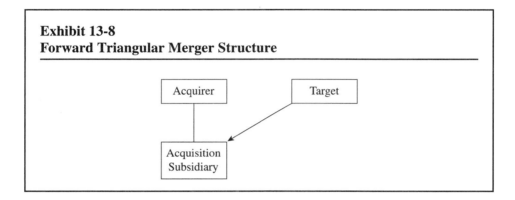

[b]   Forward Triangular Merger. In a forward triangular merger, the target merges with and into a subsidiary of the acquirer. The stock of the acquiring parent corporation is issued in the transaction. No stock of the subsidiary may be issued. The subsidiary must be at least 80% owned by the aquirer. Like a direct merger, at least 50% of the total consideration must be stock of the aquirer, implying that a certain amount of cash or debt may be issued in lieu of stock. The boot consideration is taxable. Furthermore, the subsidiary of the acquiring company that is merging with the target, must acquire "substantially all" of the assets of the target. In general, this means at least 90% of the net assets and 70% of the gross assets of the target. Exhibit 13-8 illustrates a forward triangular merger.

[c]   Reverse Triangular Merger. In a reverse triangular merger, the subsidiary of the acquiring company merges with and into the target, and the target becomes the surviving entity. For this structure to be tax free, the subsidiary must acquire at least 80% of the voting stock of the target and 80% of all other classes of target stock in exchange for the voting stock of the subsidiary. For example, preferred stock of the target must be exchanged for voting stock of the subsidiary. In addition to the prior requirements, the target must retain substantially all of its assets after the merger. In a reverse triangular merger, the boot

Exhibit 13-9
Reverse Triangular Merger Structure

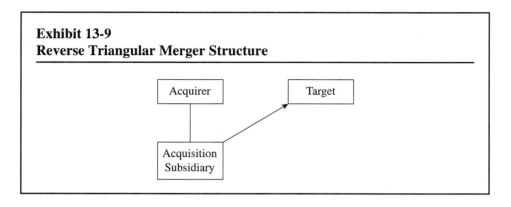

Exhibit 13-10
B Reorganization

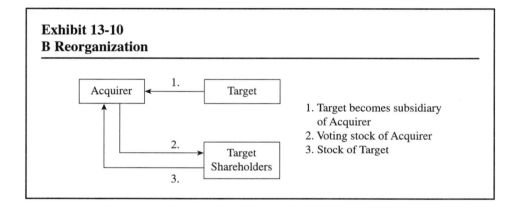

consideration is limited to 20% of the value of the target's stock. Exhibit 13-9 illustrates a reverse triangular merger.

[2]   B Reorganizations

B reorganizations are stock acquisitions whereby the stock of one company is acquired using exclusively the voting stock of another company in a stock-for-stock exchange. After the exchange of stock, the acquirer must have control of the target, in this case, greater than 80% of the voting stock plus 80% of the total shares of the non-voting stock. No more than 20% of the consideration can be in the form of cash. In a B reorganization, the target becomes a subsidiary of the acquirer, and thus, like the A reorganization, the shareholder's financial interest "continues" in the acquirer, making the transaction tax free at the time of the deal. One drawback of a B reorganization is that consideration other than voting common stock may disqualify the transaction, with one exception — voting preferred stock. Exhibit 13-10 outlines the basic structure of a B reorganization.

[3]   C Reorganizations

C reorganizations are asset acquisitions whereby the assets of one company are acquired using exclusively the voting stock of another company. After the

---

Exhibit 13-11
C Reorganization

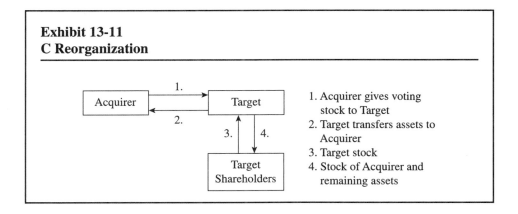

1. Acquirer gives voting stock to Target
2. Target transfers assets to Acquirer
3. Target stock
4. Stock of Acquirer and remaining assets

---

transaction is complete, the target typically liquidates and distributes the stock received in the transaction to its shareholders. As a result of the transaction, the shareholders of the target become shareholders of the acquirer. Any remaining assets are distributed to shareholders as well. A primary benefit for the acquirer is that it may not require shareholder approval to undertake the transaction. Exhibit 13-11 outlines the basic structure of a C reorganization.

For a C reorganization to qualify as tax free, at least 90% of the net assets and 70% of the gross assets of the target must be acquired in the transaction. It is possible for a certain amount of the consideration, usually 20%, to be issued as taxable consideration, i.e., cash. These guidelines are typically relied upon if the parties to the transaction wish to obtain an advance ruling from the IRS regarding the tax status of the transaction. There have, however, been cases where the IRS has proclaimed a transaction to be tax free where these thresholds have not been met.

[4]   D Reorganizations

A D reorganization is one in which a corporation transfers part or all of its assets to another corporation such that immediately after the transfer, the transferor or its shareholders are in control of the corporation to which the assets where transferred. In addition, the stock of the corporation to which the assets were transferred are distributed in a transaction that meets the requirements of Sections 354, 355, or 356 of the Internal Revenue Code. Exhibit 13-12 outlines the basic structure of an acquisitive D reorganization.

[B]   Taxable Transactions

Taxable transactions are those that do not qualify for tax free treatment under Section 368 of the Internal Revenue Code. In addition, the consideration can include both stock and cash and can be for the stock or assets of the target.

[1]   Stock-for-Cash Transactions

In the case of a stock acquisition for cash, the acquirer simply acquires all the outstanding voting stock as well as other stock of the target. Shareholders are

Exhibit 13-12
D Reorganization

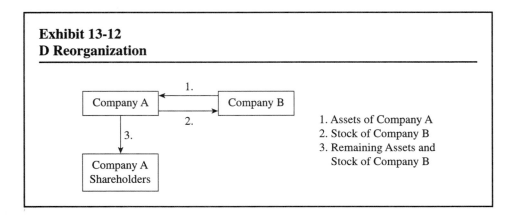

1. Assets of Company A
2. Stock of Company B
3. Remaining Assets and
   Stock of Company B

taxed based on the difference between the cash price paid and their basis in the stock. The acquirer's basis in the target's stock is its cost basis upon the acquisition. In the event the seller is a corporation that is selling the stock of a subsidiary, it will have a capital gain or loss on the sale of the subsidiary's stock. If more than 80% of the subsidiary is owned by the target's parent, the parent will not be able to recognize any tax benefit if there is a loss in the sale.

    [a] Section 338(h)(10). In certain circumstances, an acquirer may purchase the stock of a subsidiary from the selling parent in a taxable transaction and the buyer and seller may make an election under Section 338(h)(10) of the Internal Revenue Code such that the purchase of the stock will be treated for tax purposes as the purchase of the subsidiary's assets. This may only be applied if the acquirer purchases at least 80% of the target's stock. From the perspective of the seller, the transaction is viewed as the sale of the assets in a taxable transaction for an amount that equates to the consideration received for the stock plus the liabilities assumed. The proceeds are then distributed to shareholders. From the perspective of the buyer, the transaction is viewed as if the acquirer created a new subsidiary which purchased the assets of the target for the consideration amount plus the assumed liabilities. The acquirer will have a basis in the assets equal to the taxable purchase price.

    This election makes sense if the seller has a higher tax basis in the subsidiary's stock than the subsidiary has in its net assets. The Section 338(h)(10) election substitutes the gain on the sale of assets for the gain the seller would have recognized on the sale of the subsidiary's stock.

[2] Asset Transactions

    In the case of an asset acquisition, the acquirer purchases assets of or from the target. The target is then taxed at the parent level based on the gain over its tax basis in the assets. The acquirer's basis in the assets is equal to the purchase price plus any liabilities that are assumed in the transaction.

    In an asset acquisition, the purchase price is allocated to each of the assets purchased, and the gain or loss is calculated separately. If the target liquidates after selling the assets, the distributed proceeds are taxable to the shareholders. If the target is an 80% or more owned subsidiary of another company, there is no additional tax.

§ 13.07   FORM OF MERGER OR ACQUISITION

Mergers and/or acquisitions can be executed using multiple methods, depending on the structure used, the tax-free nature of the transaction, the need to seek shareholder approval and the form of consideration. Stock-for-stock transactions are usually executed under the following scenarios: the target and/or acquirer need shareholder approval; the parties desire a tax free transaction for their shareholders; and the time to close the transaction is not a material consideration. However, stock-for-stock mergers have certain downsides. There is significant market risk due to the time it takes for a stock-for-stock transaction to close. Typically, between signing and closing of a stock-for-stock transaction, there is at least a 90-day lag, during which time the stock prices of both parties to the transaction can fluctuate wildly, causing the transaction to potentially terminate.

Cash transactions will typically take the form of a cash tender offer. In a cash tender offer, the shareholders will usually receive their money before a stock-for-stock merger that requires shareholder approval. The tender offer documents are not reviewed by the SEC prior to the tender offer, unlike a transaction that requires shareholder approval where the proxy statement must be reviewed by the SEC prior to mailing it to shareholders. If the transaction is a cash tender offer, one consideration is whether it is possible to obtain 90% of the target's shares in order to use a short-form merger to squeeze out the remaining shareholders? Second, will the acquirer require or seek shareholder approval. Specifically, will the acquirer seek to get a majority of the minority shareholders to vote in favor of the deal? Seeking shareholder approval, in particular, a majority of the minority, will provide additional protection to the board of directors and special committee; however, it introduces significant delay into the transaction.

[A]   Stock-for-Stock Mergers

Stock-for-stock transactions are usually executed as a merger, whereby shareholder approval is usually sought. The acquirer will typically need shareholder approval if it issues greater than 20% of its shares outstanding. The target will usually require shareholder approval for the sale. In these situations, the company seeking shareholder approval will have to file a proxy and information statement with the Securities and Exchange Commission, schedule a shareholder meeting, mail the proxy statement to shareholders and have the shareholders vote on the transaction at the shareholder meeting. Only once the transaction has received shareholder approval may the transaction close.

[1]   Timeline for Stock-for-Stock Mergers

The overall process for a one-step merger can take upwards of 16 weeks. Exhibit 13-13 outlines the time required for each step of the process.

Exhibit 13-13
Time Line for a One-Step Merger Transaction

Time Required	Event
1 Week	Process begins.
2–4 Weeks	Acquirer and target negotiate terms of transaction. Transaction announced, after considerable review by board of directors of both companies and their respective legal and financial advisors.
2–4 Weeks	Documents are prepared including merger proxy and information statement and are filed with the SEC.
4–5 Weeks	The SEC reviews the documents, and after they are approved, are mailed to shareholders.
4–6 Weeks	Shareholders receive the documents and the solicitation process begins. At the end of this period, the shareholders vote on the transaction, and if approved, the transaction is consummated.

[2]   Disclosure Requirements[37]

In a one-step merger, shareholders vote on the transaction by virtue of a proxy that is mailed to shareholders in advance of the transaction. In transactions where shareholder approval is required, a proxy statement must be filed and sent to shareholders. Proxy statements are disclosure documents that provide information to shareholders in cases that require shareholder approval, and are governed by Regulations 14A. The proxy statement provides sufficient information for shareholders that they can make a well-informed decision with respect to voting in favor or against the transaction. The statement must be filed with the SEC at least ten business days prior to it being mailed to shareholders.

In the event the transaction has enough votes and shareholder approval is not required, then it is governed by Regulation 14C and an information statement must be filed. An information statement must be filed if the issuer chooses not to solicit proxies. The information statement requires essentially the same information as the proxy statement. In addition, it requires an item that states that proxies are not being solicited and that security holders are asked not to send in a proxy.

[B]   Cash Transactions

In cash acquisitions, it is common for the aquirer to launch a tender offer for the target's shares. Cash transactions are most often executed under the following scenarios: the target is small relative to the acquirer; the acquirer has a strong cash position and does not wish to issue stock; the parties wish to bring the

---

37. The detailed requirements of Regulation 14A and 14C are detailed in *Chapter 22: Legal Aspects of Mergers and Acquisitions*.

Exhibit 13-14
Time Line for a Cash Tender Offer Followed by a Short-Form Merger

Time Required	Event
1 Week	Process begins. Financial advisors begin their valuation work.
2–4 Weeks	Negotiation takes place between the parties. At the end of the negotiation, the transaction is announced. During this time, the tender offer documents are prepared — Schedule TO, Offer to Purchase, Letter of Transmittal, Notice of Guaranteed Delivery. The board of directors then approves the transaction and the tender offer documents are filed with the SEC.
1–2 Weeks	The SEC approves the tender offer documents and the materials are mailed to shareholders and the tender documents are published in the newspaper. At the end of this period, the tender offer commences.
20 Business Days	The tender offer remains open for 20 business days, at the end of which, the tender offer expires. The issuer issues a press release announcing the expiration.
1 Day	If the acquirer is successful in tendering for greater than 90% of the shares, then the transaction is completed through a short-form merger.

---

transaction to conclusion quickly; or the target's shareholders do not want stock in the transaction.

[1] Timeline for Cash Tender Offers

Cash tender offers can take upwards of 12 weeks to complete, with the tender offer portion of the process lasting at least 20 business days. Exhibit 13-14 outlines the time required to complete each step of a cash tender offer followed by a short form merger.

[2] Disclosure Requirements

In a cash tender offer, the public shares of the target company are acquired for cash. If the cash tender offer results in 90% ownership by the acquirer, a second-step merger "short-form" can be performed, which can be accomplished quite rapidly. A short-form merger is accomplished by filing a certificate with the secretary of state or corporation commission. The shares held by the remaining minority shareholders are cancelled without the need for a shareholder meeting or to solicit proxies.

The transaction is subject to the tender offer rules. The tender offer rules require various filings depending on who is actually making the tender offer, and what that person's relationship is to the issuer.

[a] Third Party Tender Offers. A third party tender offer is one where a person, other than the issuer, seeks to acquire, directly or indirectly, greater than 5% of the equity securities of the company. These types of tender offers

are governed by Regulations 14D and 14E,[38] which cover the filing, dissemination, disclosure and other requirements of third party tender offers. Specifically, third party tender offers must remain open for 20 business days. Any time there is a change in the terms of the offer, the offer must remain open for an additional ten business days. Shares tendered may be withdrawn at any time up till the closing of the tender offer. In addition, deposited shares may be withdrawn up to 60 days after the commencement of the offer. If more shares are tendered than called for, the shares are to be accepted on a pro rata basis, based on the number of shares tendered by the shareholders during the first ten business days of the tender offer.

Schedule TO, Tender Offer Statement, must be filed with the SEC upon the commencement of the tender offer. A copy of the Tender Offer Statement must be hand-delivered to the target company and must be sent to the exchange where the company is listed or to the NASDQ to the extent the shares are quoted there.[39]

If the third party acquires greater than 10% of the target's stock in the open market prior to the tender offer, it must file a Schedule 13D, which is governed under Section 13(d) of the Exchange Act.[40] This section requires that any person who directly or indirectly acquires greater than 5% of a Section 12 company's securities, must file Schedule 13D within ten business days of the purchase, and send a copy of the filing to the target. Schedule 13D is used to identify, among other things, who the acquirer is, which securities it has purchased, and the acquirer's interest with respect to its acquisition of those securities.

[b] Tender Offers Requiring Shareholder Approval. In transactions where shareholder approval is required, a proxy statement must be filed and sent to shareholders. Proxy statements are disclosure documents that provide information to shareholders in cases that require shareholder approval, and are governed by Regulations 14A. The proxy statement provides sufficient information for shareholders that they can make a well-informed decision with respect to voting in favor or against the transaction. The statement must be filed with the SEC at least ten business days prior to it being mailed to shareholders.

[c] Regulation 14D. Regulation 14D pertains to any tender offer by an affiliate of the issuer or a third party and governs the filing, disclosure, and dissemination of information in tender offers commencement by a person other than the issuer. Following are some of the more significant provisions of Regulation 14D.

- A tender offer is deemed to have commenced at 12:01 a.m. on the date on which the bidder first publishes, sends, or gives the tender offer material to

---

38. The specific provisions of Regulations 14D and 14E are covered in *Chapter 22: Legal Aspects of Mergers and Acquisitions.*

39. The details behind Schedule TO are covered in *Chapter 22: Legal Aspects of Mergers and Acquisitions.*

40. The requirements of Schedule 13D are provided in *Chapter 22: Legal Aspects of Mergers and Acquisitions.*

security holders. Specifically, the tender offer material must include the means for the security holder to tender their shares. In addition, the bidder will have filed Schedule TO with the SEC no later than the date of the communication to shareholders, and the bidder must have delivered to the target company the communications related to the transaction.

- A bidder may not tender for the shares of a company unless it has filed a Schedule TO with the SEC as soon as practicable on the date of the commencement of the tender offer, and delivered copies to the target company and to any other bidders that have filed Schedule TO. The bidder must also inform by telephone and send copies of Schedue TO to each exchange where the target company's securities are listed or quoted.

- The bidder must also promptly file any amendments to Schedule TO and then file a final amendment to the schedule that reports the final results of the tender offer.

- The bidder must publish, send or give disclosure of the tender offer as soon as practicable on the date of commencement of the tender offer. For cash tender offers and exempt securities offers, the bidder must publish a long-form publication in a newspaper. If the tender offer is not a going private transaction, the biddder may publish the tender offer in summary form and mail the tender offer materials to security holders who request the material. For tender offers where the consideration is securities registered under the Securities and Exchange Act of 1933, a registration statement must be filed and a preliminary prospectus must be prepared.

[d]   *Rule 14d-9 and Schedule 14D-9.* If the third party uses solicitations or recommendations of third parties, it must file a Schedule 14D-9, which is governed by Rule 14D-9. Schedule 14D-9 requires disclosure of the person making the solicitation or recommendation and the relationships between that party and the party making the offer. In addition, the schedule requires disclosure of a transaction in the target's stock within the prior 60 days.[41]

[e]   *Rule 14d-10.* Rule 14d-10 is designed to ensure that all shareholders receive equal treatment in a tender offer. The rule mandates that a tender offer is open to all security holders of the class of securities that is subject to the tender offer (the "all holders" rule), and the consideration that is paid to any security holder is the highest consideration paid to any other security holder during the tender offer (the "best price" rule). Therefore, if during the tender offer, the bidder increase the consideration that is offered to shareholders, the increased consideration must be paid to all tendering shareholders, irrespective of whether they have previously tendered their shares or not.

---

41. The detailed requirements of Schedule 14D-9 are found in *Chapter 22: Legal Aspects of Mergers and Acquisitions.*

[f]   Regulation 14E. Regulation 14E pertains to all tender offers, and governs the procedures and prohibitions of certain tender offer practices. Some of the material provisions of Regulation 14E are as follows:

- The tender offer must remain open for no less than twenty business days from the date the tender offer is first published or sent to security holders;

- If there is an increase or decrease in the percentage of the class of securities being sought, or the consideration offered, the tender offer must remain open for at least ten days from the time the notice of the increase or decrease is given to security holders;

- The person making the tender offer must promptly pay for the securities or return the securities deposited after the termination or withdrawal of a tender offer;

- The length of the tender offer may not be extended without issuing a notice of the extension; and,

- Within ten days of the commencement of the tender offer, the subject company must publish or send to security holders a statement disclosing whether the company recommends acceptance or rejection of the bidder's tender offer, expresses no opinion as to the tender offer, or is unable to take a position with respect to the tender offer.

[g]   Regulations 13D and 13G. Regulation 13D requires that any person, or group of persons acting together, who acquired directly or indirectly greater than 5 % of the class of any equity security,[42] must file a report on Schedule 13D within ten days disclosing that acquisition with the SEC, and send a copy of the report to the company. Certain entities or persons may file a 13G in lieu of the 13D if, among other things, the person acquired the securities in the ordinary course of his business and not with the purpose of changing or influencing control in the company. At any point that there is a material change in the facts set forth in the 13D, or the intent of the party filing the 13G changes, the party must file an amendment to the original filing, in the case of the 13D, or the party becomes subject to the rules of Regulation 13D, and must file a 13D.[43]

Schedule 13G includes much of the same information required in Schedule 13D, however in summary form.

---

42. As per the SEC, an equity security is "any equity security of a class which is registered pursuant to section 12 of the Act, or any equity security of any insurance company which would have been required to be registered except for the exemption contained in section 12(g)(2)(G) of the Act or any equity security issued by a closed-end investment company registered under the Investment Company Act of 1940: provided, such term shall not include securities of a class of non-voting securities."

43. The detailed disclosure requirements of Schedule 13D can be found in *Chapter 22: Legal Aspects of Mergers and Acquisitions.*

§ 13.08 ACCOUNTING FOR MERGERS & ACQUISITIONS[44]

Until 2001, merger and acquisition transactions could be accounting for under two general approaches: pooling-of-interests accounting and purchase accounting. In 2001, the Financial Accounting Standards Board did away with pooling accounting and now all transactions are accounted for using the purchase method. Generally, accounting for mergers and acquisitions falls into two broad categories: acquisition of control and acquisition of less than control. A "control" transaction is one where an acquirer purchases greater than 50.1% of a target. Control transactions typically use consolidated accounting which means that the target's balance sheet and income statement are consolidated with that of the acquirer. If the acquirer purchases greater than 50.1% but less than 100% of the target, the net income that is "not acquired" by the acquirer is backed out of the acquirer's income statement as minority interest. Control transactions typically use purchase accounting to account for the acquisition. In a purchase accounting transaction, the acquirer must book the difference between the fair market value of the assets and the target's book value as goodwill on its balance sheet. Each year this goodwill is evaluated for impairment. Any impairment is then expensed through the income statement.

For transactions where the acquirer purchases less than control of the target, there are two forms of accounting: equity accounting and cost accounting. Equity accounting is used when more than 20% but less than 50% of the voting stock of the target is acquired. In equity accounting, the acquirer reflects its percentage ownership of the target on its income statement and balance sheet.

When less than 20% of the voting stock of the target is acquired, the acquirer must use cost accounting. In cost accounting, the acquirer simply records the investment on its balance sheet at cost. If the target pays a dividend, the acquirer recognizes a portion of the dividend income on its income statement. Otherwise, the acquirer does not recognize any income.

§ 13.09 CASE STUDY

[A] Cardinal Health Acquisition of Boron LePore

On May 25, 2002, Cardinal Health, Inc. announced an agreement to acquire Boron LePore & Associates, Inc. in a cash tender offer of $16.00 per share. The transaction was valued at approximately $190 million. The transaction closed on June 27, 2002.

Founded in 1981, Boron LePore provides integrated medical education to the health care industry. The company's services include strategic consultation, content development, accredited and non-accredited program development and execution, logistics management, and a variety of internet-based solutions related to these

---

44. For a more detailed discussion of accounting for mergers and acquisitions, please refer to *Chapter 12: M&A Accounting.*

services. The company's customers are primarily large pharmaceutical companies seeking to educate physicians and other health care professionals. Core services include accredited and non-accredited symposia, advisory boards, satellite symposia, teleconferences, sales force education meeting support, large-scale video-conferences, advocacy development, patient-based services (such as support groups and community awareness programs), publication planning, and web conferencing. Services are integrated along the "pre" and "post" launch periods of the pharmaceutical product life cycle. Boron LePore generated revenues of approximately $210 million in 2001.

Cardinal Health is the leading provider of products and services supporting the health care industry. Cardinal Health companies develop, manufacture, package and market products for patient care; develop drug-delivery technologies; distribute pharmaceuticals, medical surgical and laboratory supplies; and offer consulting and other services that improve quality and efficiency in health care. Cardinal Health generates annual revenues of more than $40 billion.

There was strong rationale for the transaction. The Boron LePore medical education services platform complements Cardinal Health's existing businesses and the needs of its customers. Through its pharmaceutical and technologies services segment, Cardinal Health has traditionally accessed its customers in the R&D and manufacturing areas, and with Boron LePore, the company now has access to their customers' marketing groups who are in control of the product life cycle and product line extensions that can utilize Cardinal's delivery systems and other capabilities. Boron LePore has 60 customers served by 650 employees. The company reaches over 250,000 physicians. The transaction has significant value to both companies in their efforts to provide effective marketing solutions to their common customer, the pharmaceutical manufacturer. By expanding the knowledge along the spectrum of the product life cycle, Boron LePore and Cardinal Health offer greater breadth and depth of services and become a total outsourced pharmaceutical development, manufacturing, sales and marketing alternative.

A core competence of Boron LePore is content development, which entails significant product and market knowledge. Boron LePore employs scientific writers and researchers for the purpose of content development, and possesses significant industry experience in pharmaceutical marketing. This expertise benefits Cardinal Health upstream in its efforts to provide more specific and informed product development solutions to customers. In addition, this expanded market and product knowledge base greatly benefits the pharmaceutical and technologies services segment in its evaluation of a product's regulatory and commercial viability. Boron LePore enhances cross-selling of other Cardinal Health services while broadening the pharmaceutical and technologies services segment's exposure to customers. Cardinal Health now is able to provide the full spectrum of product services at launch and beyond, particularly for biotech and smaller pharmaceutical companies, covering medical education, specialty distribution needs, and physician detailing.

The transaction was structured as a merger of a Cardinal Health subsidiary into Boron LePore. The cash acquisition was structured as a tender offer. The tender offer began on May 28, 2002, and expired at midnight on June 24, 2002. In the tender offer, Cardinal Health obtained 94.64% stock; the remaining stock was converted into the right to receive the $16.00 per share in consideration. The transaction had been approved by the board of directors of Boron LePore and was subject to Cardinal Health obtaining 50.1% of the shares in the tender offer. Upon announcement of the transaction, Boron Lepore' stock rose from $13.31 per share to $15.91 per share, an increase of 19%. Cardinal Health's stock rose 2.4% on the announcement to $68.69 per share.

§ 13.10   SUMMARY

Mergers and acquisitions are the most prolific form of M&A transaction. Mergers are typically thought of as stock-for-stock transactions where parties of roughly equal size combine, while acquisitions are more often thought of as a larger company acquiring a smaller company. Both forms of transaction may be structured to resemble a merger however, for example, in the case of the Cardinal Health acquisition of Boron LePore. Here, the transaction was structured as a cash tender offer, yet a subsidiary of Cardinal Health was merged into Boron LePore.

There are two fundamental means for executing a merger or acquisition — a stock-for-stock transaction or a cash transaction. Stock-for-stock transactions are often tax free. For these transactions to receive tax free status, they must meet the requirements of Section 368 of the Internal Revenue Code. Cash transactions are typically taxable to the stockholders of the target corporation.

Transactions that require shareholder approval require the filing and dissemination of a proxy, designed to provide shareholders with sufficient information to make an educated decision regarding the transaction. Transactions that do not require shareholder approval, may still require the filing of an information statement that includes much the same information that is found in the proxy statement. Cash transactions that are executed as a tender offer, must comply with the filing and disclosure requirements pertaining to tender offers. In general, a tender offer must remain open for 20 business days prior to the tender offer expiring.

Mergers and acquisitions have a stormy history of failure and success. Many transactions fail while there are numerous cases where sound acquisitions have succeeded. Evidence suggests that target shareholders reap the bulk of the benefits of the negotiated merger or tender offer, while the acquiring shareholders may receive certain benefits depending on the form of transaction and the nature of the bidding for the target.

Given the mixed success of mergers and acquisitions, it is imperative to evaluate a target and the transaction from a strategic and financial perspective and ensure that the financial analysis supports the strategic rationale for the transaction. Likewise, it is prudent to plan for the integration of the two companies to ensure that the synergies and merger benefits of the transaction are realized.

Chapter 14

DIVESTITURES AND ASSET SALES

§ 14.01 OVERVIEW

Divestitures and asset sales are an approach to corporate restructuring that create value by eliminating underperforming assets, capitalizing on the value of a strong performing asset, or simply divesting a business to repay debt. Most often, divestitures are thought of in the context of the sale of a company, the primary topic of this chapter. However, technically, divestitures can take many forms ranging from a private market sale to a third party, to a 100% initial public offering, to a leveraged buyout of a division, subsidiary or a public company, to the restructuring of a company through a spin-off, split-off, or letter stock. The other divestiture alternatives are discussed in Chapters 18 and 20. For purposes of this chapter, the term "divestiture" applies to the sale of the stock or assets of a company, the sale of a business, subsidiary, division of a company, or the sale of certain individual assets, intellectual property or property, plant, or equipment.

The sale of a business has certain benefits over other forms of divestiture. These benefits include the ability to negotiate with multiple parties in order to obtain maximum value; the flexibility to take different forms of currency in consideration for the stock or assets of the business; and the ability to affect the transaction in a relatively short period of time without necessarily obtaining share-holder approval or making onerous disclosure filings with the SEC.

The sale of the stock or assets of a business can also have a number of drawbacks, most significantly, the tax inefficiency of the transaction. For example, in a subsidiary sale, to the extent there is a gain on the sale, the parent company pays taxes on the difference between its basis in the stock and the fair market value of the stock.

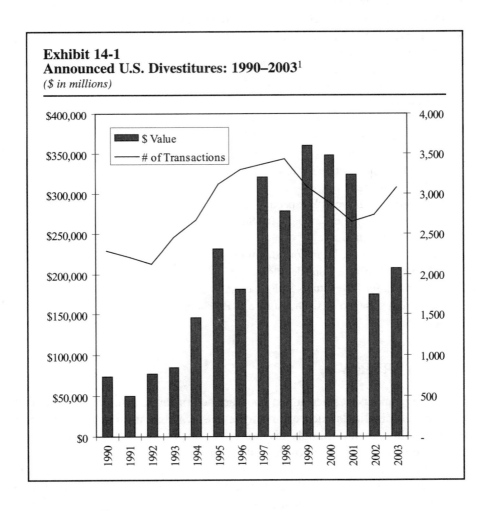

Exhibit 14-1
Announced U.S. Divestitures: 1990–2003[1]
($ in millions)

---

1. Thomson Financial.

Exhibit 14-2
Top Ten Divestiture Transactions in 2002–2003
($ in millions)

Ann. Date	Target	Acquirer	Deal Value
07/08/2001	AT&T Broadband & Internet Services	Comcast Corp	$72,041
12/19/2001	Travelers Property Casualty	Shareholders	$12,213
12/14/2001	USA Networks Inc-Ent Assets	Vivendi Universal SA	$10,749
07/03/2003	QVC Inc	Liberty Media Corp	$ 7,903
07/15/2003	Sears Roebuck & Co-Credit Card	Citigroup	$ 7,100
04/22/2003	Medco Health Solutions Inc	Shareholders	$ 6,809
05/30/2002	Miller Brewing(Philip Morris)	South African Breweries PLC	$ 5,574
01/14/2002	Rodamco-Real Estate Assets	Investor Group	$ 5,338
11/17/2002	TRW Inc-Automotive Parts	Blackstone Group LP	$ 4,725
09/04/2003	Ondeo Nalco Co	Investor Group	$ 4,350

Proceeds, if any, that are then paid out to shareholders are taxed again, effectively reducing the distribution to shareholders twice. In the event of a sale of the stock of the parent, i.e., the sale of a public or private company, the shareholders are taxed on the gain. There are certain tax-free transactions that can be executed, most notably, the sale of the stock of a parent corporation in a stock-for-stock transaction. The taxation of this type of merger is more fully discussed in Chapter 13.

The sale form of divestiture ranges from the sale of an entire company, whether public or private, to the sale of a subsidiary or division, to the sale of assets, facilities, or intellectual property. These types of divestitures have become quite prolific as a form of restructuring or realizing value for a company. Since 1990, there have been approximately 39,406 sales, with approximately 3,072 transactions announced in 2003, representing approximately $207 billion in value. Exhibit 14-1 illustrates this trend.

There were a number of significant divestiture transactions in 2002 and 2003. Exhibit 14-2 provides a summary of the top ten transactions.

§14.02 EVIDENCE BEHIND DIVESTITURES AND ASSET SALES

The evidence surrounding divestitures and assets sales has focused on why companies divest businesses, the resulting increase in shareholder value associated with the divestiture, and the stock market response to different types of corporate divestiture programs.

In March 1994, John Kose and Elif Ofek completed a study on asset sales and the increase in focus of divesting firms, and the consequent improvement in operating performance and stock return.[2] The study, titled "Asset Sales and Increase in

---

2. Kose, John, and Eli Ofek, "Asset Sales and Increase in Focus," *Journal of Financial Economics* 37,105–126 (1995).

Focus," found that asset sales resulted in an improvement in the operating performance of the selling company in the three years following the sale. In addition, they found that an increase in focus as a result of the divestiture resulted in an increase in the seller's stock price upon announcement. Their study evaluated 187 companies that made a total of 261 divestiture announcements.

The study showed that there was an increase in cash flow performance of the seller after the divestiture. The median EBITDA to sales ratio showed a significant increase between years 0 and 1 and 2. In addition, the study showed that there was an average cumulative excess return to the seller of 1.5% surrounding the announcement of the divestiture.

A similar study by Robert Comment and Gregg A. Jarrell in 1995 showed that there was a positive relation between stock returns and increase in focus.[3] In addition, large focused firms were seen to be less susceptible to takeover than other firms. They studied firms between June 1978 and October 1989. They showed that 55.7% of the firms in 1988 had a single business line while 38.1% of the firms had a single business line in 1979. They also showed that the trend toward focus was associated with enhanced shareholder wealth. The best stock price return performance was seen in companies experiencing an increase in focus, while the worst performance was seen in firms that decreased their focus. The net difference in return over the 34-month period evaluated was 7.4%.

A 1994 study by Myron Slovin, Marie Sushka, and Steven Ferraro, titled "A Comparison of the Information Conveyed by Equity Carve-Outs, Spin-Offs, and Asset Sell-Offs," looked at the difference in valuation effects of sell-offs in relation to other forms of divestiture.[4] They showed that the different forms of divestiture result in positive returns to the parent. In asset sell-offs, these improvements were the result of the parent company transferring ownership of the asset to an acquirer that can better utilize the assets. The sample period was from 1980 through 1991. Based on the study, it was shown that parent firms announcing a divestiture saw a 0.72% median return compared to 1.51% and 1.57% median returns for equity carve-outs and spin-offs respectively. The rivals of the parent firm showed negative returns in all cases during the same time period: −0.01% for sell-offs, −0.12% for equity carve-outs, and −0.04% for spin-offs.

§ 14.03 RATIONALE BEHIND DIVESTITURES AND ASSET SALES

The motivation behind divestitures and asset sales ranges from simply maximizing the value of an asset, to the divestiture of an under-performing business.

---

3. Comment, Robert, and Gregg A. Jarrell, "Corporate Focus and Stock Returns," *Journal of Financial Economics* 37, 67–87 (1995).

4. Slovin, M.B., M.E. Sushka and S.R. Ferraro, "A Comparison of the Information Conveyed by Equity Carve-Outs, Spin-offs, and Asset Sell-Offs," *Journal of Financial Economics*, Vol. 37, No. 1, 89–104 (January 1995).

Exhibit 14-3
Rationale Behind Divestitures[5]
($ in millions)

Effective Date	Target/ Parent	Acquirer	Deal Size	Rationale
12/11/00	Nabisco Holdings/ Nabisco	Philip Morris Cos. Inc.	$19,275	Result of contested battle for Nabisco.
06/30/00	E-Tek Dynamics/ Summit Partners	JDS Uniphase Corp.	$15,394	Discrete sale by financial investors.
05/23/00	Consulting Business/Ernst & Young	Cap Gemini SA	$11,774	Separate consulting from auditing business.
10/31/01	Pillsbury Co./ Diageo PLC	General Mills Inc.	$10,528	Focus on core liquor business and reduce debt.
5/07/02	Entertainment Assets/USA Networks	Vivendi Universal SA	$10,750	Focus on interactive commerce.

The rationale will depend on the type of asset or business sold, i.e., whether the target is the entire company or a division or subsidiary thereof, and whether the target is an operating business or a discrete asset. In addition, it will depend on the operating performance of the parent company and its underlying corporate strategy. Exhibit 14-3 provides an overview of five recent divestitures and the rationale behind each.

[A] Enhance Operating Performance

A divestiture may enhance a company's operating performance by rationalizing a company's operating businesses, selling under-performing assets, or capitalizing on the value of strongly performing businesses. A poorly performing business may drag down the financial performance of the parent, negatively impacting margins and growth rates, and possibly requiring capital investment that outweighs its required return on capital. Operating this type of business may also have a detrimental impact on employee morale and require a significant amount of management's time. Selling the business can serve to improve the long-term financial performance of the remaining company, free up capital to invest in more attractive businesses, boost employee morale, and give management the opportunity to refocus its attention on higher return businesses.

---

5. Thomson Financial.

In some cases, the strategic direction of a company may change, as supplier and customer trends may shift. While the business may not be performing badly, it may not fit the long-term strategy of the company, it could make sense to preempt any potential deterioration in the financial performance of the business by selling it. Under each of these scenarios, it is possible to create value for shareholders by divesting the subject business or asset, either by capitalizing on the private market valuation of the business in a leveraged buyout, or selling the business to a strategic acquirer that can create even greater value with the asset. Clearly, other divestiture alternatives besides a sale should be included in the analysis.

[B]   Enhance Capital Structure

In an effort to enhance its capital structure, a parent company may wish to divest certain businesses or assets. The proceeds may be used to repay debt if its balance sheet is over leveraged, or paid out to shareholders in the form of a dividend if its balance sheet is not optimized. The dividend also serves as means, albeit tax inefficient, to deliver the value of a divestiture directly to shareholders. Different businesses require varying levels of capital investment to build the business, whether through investment in working capital or property, plant and equipment. High levels of debt attributed to individual businesses may serve to drag down the earnings of a company and have a negative impact on its trading multiples. If the capital requirements outweigh the required returns to continue to be held under the corporate umbrella, divesting the guilty business and using the proceeds to pay down debt could serve to enhance the capital structure of a company. Additionally, the proceeds of the sale may be used to fund growth or capital expenditures in an alternate sector with better return profiles.

[C]   Capitalize on Strength of Private Market
Value Versus IPO Value

During various business and economic cycles, there may be a disparity between the private market and public market valuation of a business or sector. In addition, companies with operating businesses in different segments may be valued based on the operating performance of the whole company or a single overriding business, and the company's public market valuation may not reflect the true growth rate and financial performance of the company. In other words, the market may not be iving credit to the company's business segments. The lack of recognition may be due to the business being hidden within the parent's operations and financial performance. Alternatively, the public market may not understand how to value the different growth rates and financial performance of disparate assets in the company.

In these situations, it is common to seek an alternative to deliver value to shareholders. At the one extreme is the case of the under-appreciated company where the market value does not reflect the company's growth rates and financial performance. In this case, the company may be a suitable candidate for an overall sale or leveraged buyout in order to boost shareholder value. Another example is the situation where a subsidiary's growth rate and financial performance far exceed that of the overall company, and where the market has not recognized the subsidiary's value in the parent's stock price. The public pure play comparables to the subsidiary may be trading at multiples substantially higher than that of the parent company. In this case, it could make sense to take advantage of the public market valuation of the assets by either selling the company to a public competitor, or pursuing another form of public market divestiture approach such as an initial public offering, spin-off, or split-off.

[D]   Thwart Takeover

Much like other restructuring alternatives, divestitures have been used in the past as a means to thwart a takeover. Essentially, the sale is undertaken to deliver value to shareholders by either improving the operating performance of the remaining company, enhancing the capital structure of the parent, or paying out a cash dividend to shareholders with the proceeds of the sale. In addition, divestitures may be undertaken in order to divest an asset that is sought after by the unwanted acquirer.

§14.04   DIVESTITURES VERSUS OTHER FORMS OF RESTRUCTURING

The sale of an asset, subsidiary, or division is a simple means of divesture and an effective method of restructuring a company. Nevertheless, there are numerous pros and cons of a pure sale versus other forms of divestitures including spinoffs, letter stock, and 100% initial public offerings. Exhibit 14-4 summarizes the primary differences between a sale and other divestiture approaches.

Exhibit 14-4
Comparison Between Divestiture Approaches

	Sale	100% IPO	Spin-Off	Letter Stock
Taxable/tax free	Taxable	Taxable/Tax free[6]	Tax free	Tax free
Requires shareholder approval	Not usually	Not usually	Yes	Yes
Requires other SEC filings as precondition to deal	Not usually	Yes	Yes	Yes

Note: For this exhibit, a sale is the sale of the stock or assets of a subsidiary or division of a company. It does not apply to the sale of a company in a stock-for-stock, tax-free transaction.

---

6. If the sale is parent stock in the subsidiary, the transaction is taxable to the parent to the extent the sale price is in excess on the parent's basis in the stock. If the sale is primary stock in the subsidiary, by the subsidiary, the sale is tax free to the parent and subsidiary.

The most important distinction between the various approaches is the tax effectiveness of the transaction. Spin-offs and letter stock can be executed as tax free to the parent corporation and to shareholders. The subsidiary or division is distributed as a tax-free dividend to shareholders. However, to the extent the parent initiates the transaction with an initial public offering, selling a portion of its stock in the business, the proceeds of that sale are taxable to the parent company. The sale of stock in a subsidiary in a 100% initial public offering is taxable to the parent corporation if the parent sells its stock in the subsidiary in a secondary sale. No taxes are paid if the stock is sold in a primary sale by the subsidiary. The sale of a subsidiary, division, or assets is typically taxable to the parent company to the extent the market value of the transaction exceeds the parent's basis in the stock or assets in the business sold.

A sale may be preferable over other alternatives from a tax perspective, if the company's tax basis in the stock and/or assets its high relative to the fair market value of the business, suggesting minimal tax leakage in the sale. A second differentiating characteristic between the methods is the regulatory and disclosure requirements inherent in each transaction. In a sale of the stock or assets of a division or subsidiary, the parent company does not usually have to make any filings with the SEC prior to disposition, and the effectiveness of such filings are not a precondition to the transaction. This is not the case in other forms of divestiture such as an initial public offering, spin-off, or letter stock, where multiple filings such as a registration statement for the initial public offering or Form 10 filings for spin-offs are required.

A third feature of a sale is that it usually does not require shareholder approval, most particularly in the sale of a subsidiary or division of a business. This is not necessarily the case in the sale of a company where shareholder approval may be required. In the case of a spin-off or letter stock, it is very typical for the parent company to seek shareholder approval. This approval process usually requires the preparation, filing, and dissemination of a proxy statement that, once it becomes effective with the SEC, is mailed to shareholders. The process of seeking shareholder approval can be quite time consuming.

§ 14.05 VALUATION OF DIVESTITURES AND ASSET SALES

Valuation of companies, businesses, or assets in the context of a divestiture is not too different than the valuation of a company in a merger or acquisition. The discrete asset or business is valued using stand alone, going concern, and takeover valuation analyses. In addition, from the perspective of the acquirer, the impact of the acquisition must be taken into consideration in order to determine the accretion/dilution resulting from the deal. Furthermore, from the perspective of the seller, the impact of the sale must be assessed to determine the accretion or dilution resulting from the divestiture.

[A]   Stand Alone Value

The valuation of a sale candidate follows along the same lines as that of an acquisition or merger candidate. In other words, the business is valued using comparable trading multiples analysis and discounted cash flow analysis. To the extent the candidate is an asset or facility, it is likely that other stand alone methodologies would be used, i.e., asset valuation, cost approach, or liquidation value.

Using trading multiples analysis, one should recognize the differences between valuing a public company that is for sale, a division or subsidiary of a public company, or a privately held business. In each case, as more fully described in Chapters 2–10, the business will be valued according to its own set of circumstances. The public companies, large private companies and the larger divisions of public companies will be valued using the multiples of the candidate's peer group. In the case of smaller divisions or subsidiaries and private companies, it is important to remember that an appropriate discount be applied for the risk or lack of liquidity inherent in the stock.

The same mindset is valuable when valuing the sale candidate using DCF analysis. The smaller divisions, subsidiaries, or private companies should include a discount for liquidity, and the weighted average cost of capital used to discount the cash flows should reflect an appropriate capital structure and cost of equity for the target business.

[B]   Takeover Value

Takeover valuation includes analyzing comparable transaction multiples and transaction premiums, and applying the results from this analysis to the target. If the company that is being valued is public, it is feasible to use the transaction premiums as the target company has a public stock price against which to apply the premium. The transaction multiples can be applied to companies both public and private, yet must be used with caution with smaller businesses, recognizing the risk or liquidity discount associated with small operations.

[C]   Accretion/Dilution Analysis

Accretion/dilution analysis used in the context of a sale candidate is slightly different than that performed in acquisition or merger analysis. First, if the candidate is a stand alone company, there is no reason to perform the analysis from the perspective of the seller since there will be no remaining earnings after the sale. However, it may be important to perform the analysis from the perspective of the acquirer to determine the acquirer's ability to pay for the business.

Second, if the business to be divested is a division or subsidiary, it should be deconsolidated from the seller's income statement and balance sheet. The deconsolidation should take into consideration the currency to be received by the seller, i.e., stock, cash, note, or the like, and the impact of this should be reflected in the seller's earnings. The resulting earnings should provide an indication of the accretion or dilution in the transaction. When evaluating the pro forma earnings, it is likely that a sale transaction will be dilutive to the seller — revenues, operating earnings, and cash flows are deducted from the income statement. This does not necessarily mean that the sale is a poor idea. The remaining company could have a higher growth rate, better margins, or a stronger capital structure. The consideration received in the transaction can be used to reinvest in existing businesses or redeployed to acquire or build new businesses. These assumptions should be included in any financial projections.

With a sale, the seller should develop an effective communications strategy with the market. The reasons for the sale as well as the use of proceeds from the sale should be outlined for equity research analysts and investors, otherwise the market may not have a good understanding of the dilution resulting from the sale.

§ 14.06   THE DIVESTITURE PROCESS

Investment banks are known for their approach to divesting businesses. These methods are tried and true, and serve to maximize value for a company, business, or asset. Generally, there are three principal approaches to selling a company: the negotiated sale, the controlled competitive sale, and the auction. While these are the main approaches, each process must be tailored to the specific circumstances of the situation under consideration.

[A]   The Negotiated Sale

In a negotiated sale, the seller typically will enter into discussions with one likely party. This type of approach is used in a number of situations, namely, when a business or asset cannot be sold in a competitive process because of unique issues; if there is a limited universe of buyers that may be interested in the business, if the seller is approached on a one-off basis by a potential acquirer; or, if the demands for confidentiality are extremely high. This type of approach has numerous advantages and disadvantages as outlined in Exhibit 14-5.

The negotiated sale process affords the seller the maximum control over the process and the information utilized in the process, and consequently, this process

---

Exhibit 14-5
Advantages and Disadvantages of the Negotiated Sale Process

Advantages	*Disadvantages*
Limits risk of disclosure	May not realize maximum value
Maximizes control of process	Risk of failure
Minimizes disruption to business	

Exhibit 14-6
Advantages and Disadvantages of the Controlled
Competitive Sale Process

Advantages	*Disadvantages*
Control over process	Moderate risk of disclosure
Flexibility to change process	May taint asset if unsuccessful
Ability to maximize value	Moderate disruption to business

---

results in the least possible risk of disclosure. On the other hand, this process has a high risk of failure in that the seller is typically negotiating with only one counterparty at a time and may have little negotiating leverage. In addition, the negotiated sale process is not necessarily the most effective means to maximize the value of an asset.

[B]   The Controlled Competitive Sale

The controlled competitive sale is used if the asset or business is attractive but does not necessarily lend itself to a full auction. In this approach, a very limited number of parties are contacted to solicit their interest in the business to be sold. The parties may be contacted at the same time or sequentially depending on the circumstances. There are a number of advantages and disadvantages to this process as outlined in Exhibit 14-6.

The controlled competitive sale allows the seller to maintain good control over the process, yet because there are more buyers looking at the information, there is a modest risk of disclosure. The seller is able to modify the process; however, there is a risk that the asset is tainted if no real buyer materializes. Because there is more than one potential buyer in the process, there is a greater opportunity to maximize value for the company; however, along with this comes the increased disruption to the business, as the seller must now entertain discussions with more than one party.

[C]   The Auction

An auction is an investment banker's favored approach to selling a business. It establishes a firm timeline and framework for selling the company; it forces discipline on the process and helps maximize the value of the business. The greatest drawback of the auction process is the risk that confidentiality is not maintained. Exhibit 14-7 provides and overview of the advantages and disadvantages of the auction process.

The auction process gives the seller the greatest opportunity to maximize value for a business if the asset lends itself to this type of approach. The most significant downsides to this format are the increased risk of disclosure that accompanies the multiple conversations, and the increase in the disruption to the seller's business.

Exhibit 14-7
Advantages and Disadvantages of the Auction Process

Advantages	Disadvantages
Ability to maximize value	High risk of disclosure
Flexibility to alter process	Maximum disruption to business
Maximum control over process	

Exhibit 14-8
Key Topics in an Information Memorandum

I. Executive Summary
II. Investment Considerations
III. Industry Overview
IV. Company Overview
 • Business Description
 • Technology
 • Customers
 • Suppliers
 • Sales and Marketing
 • Environmental
 • Legal
 • Management and Employees
V. Financial Overview

---

[1]   The Auction Process

An auction generally follows a four-phase process: preparation of the information memorandum, first round bids, second round bids, and negotiation and closing. The first phase entails preparing the memorandum that is used to market the business. During this phase, information is gathered on the target business, and due diligence is performed by the banker undertaking the sale. The memorandum is then prepared. Included in the memorandum is a detailed set of financial projections that outline the potential for the business. Exhibit 14-8 provides an outline of the key topics that are included in the information memorandum.

During this phase, the seller and its banker will also agree on which buyers will be approached, the timing of the process, and the desired valuation range. Prior to sending the information memorandum to potential bidders, they will be asked to sign a non-disclosure or confidentiality agreement. This agreement will limit the potential buyers' ability to misuse the information provided in the information memorandum.

The second phase entails obtaining preliminary indications of interest from prospective buyers. The buyers are typically sent a letter, known as a "procedure

---

Exhibit 14-9
Bidding Requirements in a Sales Process

---

1. The dollar amount attributed to the value of the business.
2. The form of consideration to be used in the acquisition.
3. The sources of financing for the acquisition and the status of such financing.
4. The necessary approvals required to complete the transaction, i.e., shareholder approval, regulatory, etc.
5. The nature of due diligence required to complete the investigation of the business.

---

letter," in which they are given a deadline when they must submit their first round bids. Additionally, they are told what information they should submit in their indication of interest. For example, the buyer will usually be asked to indicate a range of values for the business based on the material provided in the memorandum, the form of consideration to be used to acquire the business, the type of due diligence required to complete and evaluation of the business, any approvals necessary to complete the transaction, and any financing or other contingencies that may impede the timing of closing of a transaction. Exhibit 14-9 provides example items required for a first round bid in a sale process.

Based on the bids received in the first round, the seller will determine which of the potential buyers, if any, it would like to continue to include in the sales process. It is typical to include more than one buyer in the second round, preferably two or three buyers, in order to maintain a competitive process.

In the third phase, the potential buyers invited to continue to evaluate the business for sale are asked to submit a final bid. They are provided with additional detailed financial and other information and are given an opportunity to meet with management, tour the operations of the company and perform due diligence on the business. In addition, they may be given a contract that outlines the legal terms of a deal. Prospective buyers will then be asked to submit their revised, final bid based on the due diligence they have performed in the third phase. Additionally, they may be asked to submit a markup of the contract. In this way, the seller can assess the merits of the transaction from a financial and legal perspective.

Based on the final round bids, the seller may choose one or two of the prospective buyers with whom to negotiate a definitive transaction. In certain cases, the seller may negotiate on an exclusive basis with one of the parties, yet in other cases, it may continue to maintain a competitive process with multiple parties during the negotiation and closing phase. At the end of the final phase, the seller and prospective buyer will enter into a definitive contract that is binding on the parties.

An auction process can be conducted under a very short time frame, say two–four weeks, yet it is more typical for the auction process to run three to six months, with the first three phases running four to six weeks each, and the final phase lasting two to four weeks. The closing of the transaction will then be subject to market driven closing concerns such as antitrust clearance, board of directors, shareholder, regulatory, and other approvals.

§ 14.07   SELLER CONSIDERATIONS

There are a number of factors for the seller to consider when evaluating the prospects of a potential sale. The seller needs to approach the process from a variety of viewpoints. First, the seller should consider the perspective to be taken by each possible buyer. Second, the target should position itself to address each particular buyer's concerns as well as to highlight its strengths and speak to its weaknesses. Third, managers or agents acting on behalf of selling shareholders should approach the negotiating strategy to maximize the pricing, structure, post-deal relationship and other objectives of the company and shareholders. Finally, the company should prepare itself for sale by addressing employee and confidentiality concerns, as well as the ongoing relationship between the parties post closing.

[A]   Strategic Buyer's Perspective

It is important to understand a strategic buyer's approach to making an acquisition. Knowledge of an acquirer's own strategic and financial objectives as well as of its products, markets, customers, technology and industry position, are helpful in enabling a seller to position itself or sale. It allows the target to present itself in a light that most favorably addresses a buyer's particular concerns.

From a market perspective, a buyer will evaluate a number of factors. Industry size, industry dynamics and the target's market share or position within the industry are of critical importance. The larger the market, the more unique the barriers to entry, and the greater degree of fragmentation of the market, the greater the possibility that the acquirer will place a high value on the asset. An acquirer will also analyze its defensive or offensive need to own the target. For example, if the target company has state-of-the-art technology, it may give the acquirer a competitive advantage in its industry. Likewise, the acquirer may simply wish to purchase the target in order to keep its technology out of the hands of another competitor.

Companies make acquisitions for a variety of reasons, whether to access new products, markets or technologies, or to gain market share, increase economies of scale, or eliminate a competitor. Irrespective of the reason for the acquisition, the acquirer will evaluate the pros and cons of the acquisition in light of its opportunity grow its own business and leverage the target's assets with its own operations. To the extent the risks of execution outweigh the perceived benefits, the likelihood of the acquirer undertaking the acquisition is quite low. Acquirer's will also evaluate geographic reach and product breadth, as well as the reputation of the firm and its management.

It is important for a seller to bear in mind each of these considerations as it prepares itself for sale, in order to maximize its opportunity set with each buyer. Each buyer will have a slightly different approach to making the acquisition. As a seller, it is crucial to assess the approach that each buyer will take in the deal and try and address each buyer's issues in the sale process.

The tactic a strategic buyer will take to valuation of the target will depend not only on its assessment of each of the above considerations, but also on the perceived competition for the target company. A strategic acquirer bidding for a seller alone, without perceived competition, is less likely to pay a full price than if it is bidding in competition with another buyer. In fact, a buyer may be willing to exceed its own purchase price hurdles if it believes the business is highly sought after, and if it's inability to purchase the business may hurt its own operations.

[B]   Positioning the Company for Sale

In light of how a buyer approaches an acquisition, a seller must tailor its own sale process and mindset in order to meet its objectives in the sale. The target company should critically examine its own business and evaluate its strengths and weaknesses. It should emphasize those strengths that are most appealing to a particular buyer. Strengths to emphasize might include intellectual property, competitive advantage, customer and supplier relationships, market opportunity and platform. In addition, it should be prepared to address weaknesses in order to minimize their impact on valuation.

Critical to correctly positioning a company for sale is anticipating the acquirer's concerns and interests. For example, a buyer may be pre-occupied with its lack of technological superiority, in which case, the seller should demonstrate how its technology solves the buyer's issues.

Of significant importance in the sale of a company is for the seller to establish a sense of real competition for its business. Competition may range from a third party bidder to the company having other alternatives to the sale such as continuing to go it alone.

Prior to embarking on a sale, the selling company should anticipate how it will perform during the process. A seller should recognize that the typical sale process can take four to six months to conclude, if not longer, during which, a company will generate another quarter of financial performance which may or may not substantiate its projections. How the company performs in this period will either help support a higher purchase price or give the buyer reason to lower its price.

[C]   Negotiation Strategy

Negotiation in mergers and acquisitions is an art. Chapter 25 further outlines an approach to overall negotiation strategy that should be applied to selling a company. Nevertheless, there are a few basic rules that should be adhered to when attempting to sell a company. First, negotiate openly, and focus on what the buyer and seller can achieve together. The more you can focus on joint objectives and how the two companies combined can create value, the greater the chance to achieve a premium purchase price.

Second, a seller should understate its future financial performance and then over-deliver on its promises. Frequently, selling companies attempt to capture a premium value by presenting aggressive projections, yet are unable to meet the projections during the sale process. This strategy often results in unmet expectations on the behalf of seller and buyer, and frequently results in a failed sale process.

Underpromising and then exceeding performance during the process often helps a buyer justify a high price and leads to a seller's expectations being met.

Third, establish trust with the buyer and maintain credibility during the sale process. Once credibility is lost, it is difficult to regain, and may cause a transaction to fail. Remember that the people working on the transaction during the sale process are likely to be the same people the seller will have to work with post transaction.

Fourth, consider using an agent as a means to act as a buffer between buyer and seller. Agents are able to remain unemotional during a transaction and may have the difficult, unpleasant conversations that are trying for the principals to have person to person.

[D]   Pre- and Post-Deal Considerations

In addition to anticipating the concerns of buyers and preparing to position the company for sale, selling management should consider the people involved in the process. Identify management and key employees and decide who needs to be retained in the transaction process, who is critical to keep motivated during the process, and who will be likely casualties of the deal. In order to effectively manage the sale process, the company should have a small coterie of people that are charged with various aspects of the transaction, for example, managers from human resources, finance, business development, operations, etc. Each of these people will be called on at various points in the process to assist in preparing material, offering answers to buyer's questions, and managing the process. One word of advice is to include these managers early on in the process. First, there is always the possibility that information on the transaction leaks internally, and it is better to bring key managers into the process rather than to have them learn the information second or third hand. Second, any prudent buyer is likely to want to meet with these people during the course of due diligence, and thus, it is better to have them educated on the deal early on. Third, it is difficult to operate a company and conduct a sales process at the same time. Including a broader group of personnel shifts some of the burden from the senior-most managers and enables the company to continue to operate during the sale process.

Selling management should also be concerned with the ongoing operation of the company during the sale process, and therefore should consider putting in place mechanisms for ensuring certain employees remain motivated and stay during the process. Many a transaction has failed during the sales process because key salespeople or area managers have left. Financial and other incentives may be issued in a deal. The financial cost of stay bonuses and other incentive compensation should be reserved for in the transaction and taken into consideration in the post-closing operating performance of the company.

Confidentiality is always paramount in any transaction. In the sale of a company, there is always concern that customers, suppliers and competitors learn of the potential sale. Customers may shift to a competitor or reconsider signing a new contract, suppliers may become concerned over being paid, and competitors may take advantage of the prospective sale to tarnish the company's name in the market. One should prepare a communication strategy to manage the information regarding the sale process in order to minimize the damage caused by a leak.

During the deal process, one should determine what the roles of management will be post transaction and whether there are employees that will be subject to employment agreements. As the deal negotiation progresses, it is important to have these roles, responsibilities and employment arrangements agreed to and in place prior to the completion of the transaction.

[E] Deal Structure Considerations

From a structural standpoint, selling shareholders need to consider a number of factors in a transaction. First is the form of consideration to be received. Cash provides certain compensation, yet it is subject to immediate taxation and provides no direct upside in the combined company. Taking stock in the acquiring company potentially allows selling shareholders to time their exit and thus better manage their tax exposure, and it also allows selling shareholders to benefit from the upside in the combined company. However, accepting stock subjects selling shareholders to risk in the transaction, not only between signing and closing, but after the transaction is closed. Swings in the stock price of the acquirer, resulting from market or company specific events, can adversely affect the value that was paid to the seller.

In a stock transaction, selling shareholders may liquidate their holdings subject to certain constraints. First, an acquirer may issue stock that has been registered with the SEC; conversely, it may issue stock that is not registered. The prime benefit of an acquirer issuing unregistered stock to selling shareholders is that the transaction may close sooner than if the stock has to be registered prior to closing. However, if the stock is not registered prior to closing, selling shareholders taking stock are subject to the uncertainty that the acquirer will register the stock.

In the event stock is issued to selling shareholders, the stock may be subject to lock-up provisions or the limitations of Rule 145. Lock-up provisions are a contractual obligation of target shareholders not to sell their shares in the acquirer for a given period of time after the transaction closes. Rule 145 affects management, directors and other insiders of the selling company, and limits the sale of their stock at any given time to the [greater of [1]% of the company's shares outstanding or the average of the prior four weeks trading volume.]

In stock transactions, there are mechanisms for a selling shareholder to protect the value of the consideration they are receiving in the deal. In addition, it may be necessary for the acquirer to protect itself in the transaction. This price protection comes in the form of a fixed-price or fixed-share structure in which either the price of the deal is protected, whereby the number of shares paid to selling shareholders fluctuates in order to keep the price the same, or the number of shares issued by the seller is fixed and the price fluctuates accordingly. These fixed price or fixed share exchange ratios are often collared such that there is a range of prices within which the transaction may fluctuate or there is a range of shares issued within which the transaction may fluctuate. Outside the range, the parties to the transaction often have the ability to walk away from the transaction.

§ 14.08   ACCOUNTING FOR DIVESTITURES AND ASSET SALES

The accounting for the sale of a company, subsidiary, division, or asset will depend on a number of factors. If the sale is for 100% of a parent company, the transaction may be structured tax free for shareholders in a merger of the two companies, to the extent the transaction is performed as a stock-for-stock transaction. In this case, neither the parent nor the shareholders are taxed, and the income statements and balance sheets of the two parties are combined. Goodwill is often created in the transaction that is recorded on the balance sheet of the acquirer. To the extent there is any impairment of the goodwill in the future, the impaired amount is expensed in the income statement as a non-cash charge. For a more detailed discussion of accounting for this type of transaction, please refer to Chapter 12.

In the sale of the stock in a subsidiary, the parent is taxed based on the difference between its basis in the stock and the sales price of the stock. If the consideration paid is stock in the acquirer, the parent will account for the stock in the acquirer based on how much of the acquirer it owns post transaction. Below 20% ownership, and the seller accounts for its stock using the cost method. Between 20% and 50% ownership, the seller accounts for its ownership using the equity method. Above 50% and the company must use consolidated accounting.

§ 14.09   CASE STUDY: DIAGEO PLC DIVESTITURE OF PILLSBURY CO.

On July 17, 2000, Diageo PLC announced a strategic restructuring of its global business which entailed the integration of its spirits, wine and beer businesses, and the sale of The Pillsbury Company to General Mills in a transaction valued at $10.5 billion.

Diageo is an international company that owns a portfolio of brands including a restaurant chain — Burger King, and multiple wine and spirits brands including Guiness, Johnnie Walker Scotch whiskies, Smirnoff vodka, J&B Scotch whisky, Baileys Original Irish Cream liqueur, Tanqueray gin, and Malibu specialty spirit. At the time of the announcement, Diageo also owned The Pillsbury Company, one of the largest food companies in the world, with recognized brand names in biscuits and cookies, frozen foods, and other snacks.

General Mills is a leading manufacturer and marketer of consumer food products that had worldwide sales in 2000 of $7.5 billion. Some of its brand names include: Betty Crocker dessert, Big G ready-to-eat cereals, and Yoplait and Colombo yoghurt. Driving the divestiture of The Pillsbury Company was the desire of Diageo to enhance shareholder value. Integrating its spirits, wine, and beer businesses would create a platform of products that cater to consumers' different drinking tastes. In addition, the integration of these operations would generate substantial revenue benefits and cost savings. The cost savings were estimated at 130 million pounds annually.

The sale of Pillsbury to General Mills would create the fifth largest food company in the world. The combined company would have $13 billion in world-wide revenue. In the initial transaction, Diageo was to be issued 141 million newly issued General Mills shares comprising 33% of General Mills issued capital. In addition, General Mills would assume $5.1 billion in Pillsbury debt.

The transaction was completed on November 1, 2001. The overall terms of the transaction upon closing were as follows:

- 134 million newly issued shares of General Mills, representing 32% of the company's capital;

- assumption of $3,830 million of net debt; and

- $670 million in the form of a contingent value right under which Diageo would receive some or all of the right at the 18-month anniversary of the completion of the transaction to the extent the average General Mills stock price is lower than $49 per share over the 20-day trading period prior to the anniversary.

As a part of the transaction, Diageo negotiated the option to sell back 55 million shares that it received in the transaction to General Mills at $42.14 per share.

§ 14.10 SUMMARY

Divestitures and asset sales have become quite popular, as evidenced by the trends over the last decade. They are a quick and efficient means for restructuring a company's business lines. However, unlike other forms of divestiture such as spin-offs and letter stock, they are not tax free to the seller, and any proceeds that are distributed are taxable to shareholders. Their primary benefits are the ability to maximize the value of the business or asset to be sold by negotiating with multiple parties in a competitive process, and the ability to manage a controlled process to completion in a short length of time without necessarily having to seek share-holder approval or make onerous regulatory filings.

Chapter 15

JOINT VENTURES AND ALLIANCES

§ 15.01 OVERVIEW

A joint venture is an arrangement or partnership between two or more parties where an independent entity is formed by the parties with the purpose of undertaking a specific activity. The joint venture usually takes the form of a new enterprise jointly owned by the parties. Generally, the parties to the joint venture will each take on an active role in it, contributing either intellectual capital, financial resources, assets or all of the above. An alliance is a simple form of joint venture that may not involve the creation of a new entity to undertake the enterprise and may not involve equity ownership or a contribution of capital by either party. Therefore, joint ventures and alliances can range in magnitude from simple arrangements to complicated relationships where each party has significant capital at stake. Because many issues pertaining to joint ventures and alliances are common to both, in this chapter, we often refer to joint ventures and alliances as a single category; however, where necessary, we make the appropriate distinction between the two.

Joint ventures are entered into for a variety of reasons, among them, growth, exploitation of synergies, and to share costs or risks in a project. They are often used as an alternative to mergers or acquisitions, where the parties to the joint venture may not wish to cede autonomy of their business or company that may result from an outright sale or merger, yet are eager to capitalize on opportunities presented by the counter party. Alliances and joint ventures are popular as a means to seek growth, and in many cases, are viewed as a better solution than mergers and acquisitions.

Since 1990, there have been approximately 40,554 disclosed joint ventures and 55,416 disclosed alliances. Exhibit 15-1 shows the trend in both since 1990.

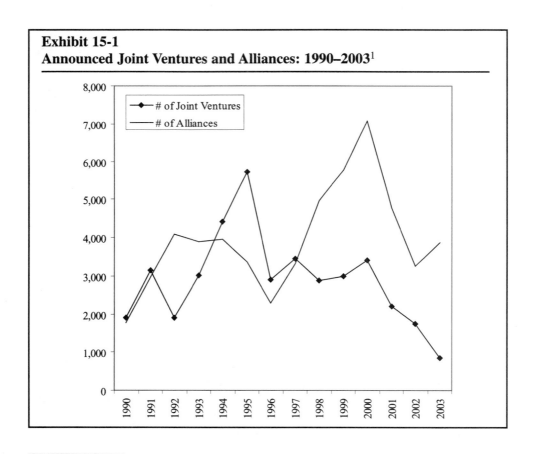

Exhibit 15-1
Announced Joint Ventures and Alliances: 1990–2003[1]

---

1. Thomson Financial

Joint ventures have been used in many industries ranging from health care to technology to aerospace and defense to basic manufacturing. They have involved some of the largest and most recognized companies in the world including AOL, Coke, Genentech, Boeing, and Hewlett-Packard. One of the more recent joint ventures of note is the joint venture between Renault and Nissan, two of the largest manufacturers of automobiles in the world. The alliance brought the two companies together to cut costs and develop new technology. The details of the alliance are outlined more fully in the case study at the end of the chapter. Exhibit 15-2 provides an overview of recent significant joint ventures and alliances.

Exhibit 15-2
Recent Significant Completed Joint Ventures and Alliances[2]

Announce. Date	Participants in Venture/Alliance	Est. Value (millions)	Overview
03/23/98	Royal Dutch/Shell Group; Undisclosed Chinese Partner	$4,460	Royal Dutch/Shell (RDS) and 3 undisclosed Chinese (UP) partners formed a joint venture named the South China Sea Offshore Petrochemical Complex (SCS), in Huizhou, Guangdong province in China to manufacture petrochemicals. SCS was to be capitalized at $4.46 billion U.S. and to begin operations in the 4th quarter of 2003. RDS held a 25% stake and UP held a 75% interest in SCS.
10/07/99	Toshiba Corp.; Sandisk Corp.	$ 700	Toshiba Corp. and Sandisk Corp. formed a joint venture named FlashVision LLC (FV) to manufacture higher capacity flash memory cards for digital cameras, music players, and other consumer electronics in Virginia, United States. FV was capitalized at $700 million and its production was to begin in 2001. FV had estimated sales for 2002 of $100 million.
12/17/99	Duke Energy Corp.; Phillips Petroleum Co. Inc.	$6,000	Duke Energy Corp. (DEC) and Phillips Petroleum Co. Inc. (PPC) formed a joint venture named Dukes Energy Field Services (DEFS) to gather and Process

(Continued)

---

2. Thomson Financial

Exhibit 15-2
(*Continued*)

Announce. Date	Participants in Venture/Alliance	Est. Value (millions)	Overview
			natural gas and chemicals, such as propane and butane, which are extracted from natural gas. The joint venture pooled assets valued at $5.5 billion to $6 billion to fund DEFS. DEC retained a 70% interest and PPC retained a 30% stake. Debt financing was used in the amount of $2.4 billion.
03/09/00	Hutchison Whampoa Ltd; Internet Capital Li Ka Shing Foundation	$1,556	Hutchison Whampoa Ltd (HW), based in Hong Kong, Internet Capital Group Inc. Group Inc.; in the U.S., and Li Ka Shing Foundation (LKS), based in Hong Kong, formed a joint venture named ICG AsiaWorks Ltd. (IAW) to provide e-commerce incubation investment services. Under the joint venture, ICG was to hold a 55% interest, HW was to hold a 15% stake, and LKS was to hold a 5% stake IAW, and the remaining 25% was to be the public float.
03/13/00	Microsoft Corp.; Andersen Consulting	$1,000	Microsoft Corp (MS) and Accenture (AC), a unit of Andersen Worldwide, formed a joint venture named Avenade (AV) to provide e-commerce services in the United States. AV started a 5,000 employee technology services company as part of a broad alliance to help build internet businesses running Microsoft software. AV was capitalized at $1 billion, of which AC as to contribute $600 million in resources such as employee training, specialized services, and intellectual property, and MS was to cotribute $385 million in cash. MS and AC held a 50% interest each in AV.

(*Continued*)

Exhibit 15-2
(Continued)

Announce. Date	Participants in Venture/Alliance	Est. Value (millions)	Overview
4/06/00	Ticketmaster Online-CitySearch; Kadokawa Shoten Publishing;	$3,143	Ticketmaster Online-Citysearch (TOC), based in the United States, Kadokawa Shoten Publishing Co Ltd (KSP), Sumitomo Corp (SM), Sumitomo Corp JCB Co (JCB), Shufunotomo Co JCB Co Ltd; (SF), and Trans Cosmos Inc. (TC), Shufunotomo Co; all based in Japan, formed a joint Trans Cosmos Inc. venture named Walkerplus.com Inc. to provide online domestic regional information and be linked with a magazine series. The joint venture was owned 10% by TOC, 66% by KSP, 7% by SM, 10% by JCB, 2% by SF, and 5% by TC. The joint venture was capitalized at $30 million.
06/08/00	Telefonos de Mexico SA de CV; Bell Canada International Inc.; SBC Communications Inc.	$3,500	In November 1999, Telefonos de Mexico SA de CV(TM), Bell Canada International (BC), a unit of BCE Inc and SBC Communications completed their joint venture agreement to form Telecom Americas LLC(TA) to provide a wide range of telecommunications services in Brazil. TA links the operations of all three telecommunications companies. The joint venture was originally announced in June 2000, between TM and BC, with SBC being offered an option to acquire a stake of up to 25%. The joint venture is owned 44.3% by TM and BC, with SBC owning 11.4%. The joint venture was expected to be capitalized at $3.5 billion.
03/09/01	BP Co. PLC; SINOPEC Corp.; SINOPEC Shanghai Petro	$2,700	BP Co. PLC; (BP), a unit of British Petroleum Co. PLC. a joint venture between BPPLC

(Continued)

Exhibit 15-2

(*Continued*)

Announce. Date	Participants in Venture/Alliance	Est. Value (millions)	Overview
			and its subsidiary BP Amoco PLC, China Petroleum Chemical Corp (SINOPEC), a unit of state owned China Petrochemical Corp, and SINOPEC Shanghai Petrochemical Co (SSP), a unit of Shanghai Petrochemical Co. Ltd., planned to form a joint venture named Shanghai Shevcheko Co (SSC) to manufacture and market Announce. Participants in Est. Value Date Venture/Alliance (millions) Overview petrochemical products in China. Under terms of the agreement, SSC was to build a petrochemical manufacturing facility. BP was to hold 50% interest in SSC, SINOPEC was to hold 30% stake, and the remaining 20% stake was to be held by SSP. SSC was capitalized at $2.7 billion.
03/14/01	Level 3 Communications Inc.; Yulon Group	$ 800	Level 3 Communications Inc. (L3C) and Yulon Group (YG) formed a joint venture named Level 3 Communications (Taiwan) Ltd. (LC) to provide submarine cable leasing services in Taiwan. Level 3 Communications (Taiwan) Ltd. was capitalized at $800 million. L3C invested $9.8 million and held a 60% interest in LC, and the remaining 40% was held by YG.
06/21/01	DaimlerChrysler AG; Hyundai Motor Co.	$1,000	DaimlerChrysler AG and Hyundai Motor Co., a unit of Hyundai Group, formed a joint venture named Daimler Hyundai Truck Corp to manufacture truck engines in South Korea. The two firms would invest $100 million in the joint venture which would initially be capitalized at 100 billion Korean won ($76.74 million).

[A]   Joint Ventures Versus Alliances

A joint venture usually entails a new, separate entity created to entertain the business of the parties to the venture. A joint venture often involves a capital contribution from the parties as well as contributions of intellectual assets and other tangible assets. They are time consuming to structure and require governance much the same as a corporation. Because they are more time consuming to structure and require more complex legal structuring, they are often difficult to unwind and therefore can be viewed with more skepticism by the market. Alliances are usually simpler transactions to structure. They do not necessarily require a separate entity to operate the business of the alliance. Most often, the alliance is not independently capitalized.

§ 15.02   EVIDENCE BEHIND JOINT VENTURES AND ALLIANCES

Alliances and joint ventures have become quite commonplace, and have become the subject of numerous academic and other studies. Research has suggested that shareholder value is often created in the formation and operation of joint ventures and alliances, and in may instances, are better received than mergers and acquisitions. They have been established as a preferred means to access new markets, acquire technologies and diversify product lines. They are also an efficient means for minimizing risk in a new venture.

A recent study by McKinsey & Company examined the effect of alliance announcements on the share prices of over 2,100 companies.[3] This was an event study that looked at the abnormal return to shareholders on the days surrounding the announcement. It covered all types of structures including joint ventures, contractual alliances, and equity stakes. The analysis concluded that the announcement of an alliance can have a dramatic effect on share price. In particular, significant alliances can "move market capitalization." More than 50% of the large alliances — created a top ten player or over $500 million in assets — caused a significant increase or decrease in share price for the parent announcing the alliance. Of these, 70% of the price changes were positive. For alliances overall, they found that 29% caused a share price movement, with half of those showing a price increase.

They also found that alliances are better received than mergers and acquisitions in "fast-moving, highly uncertain industries such as electronics, mass media, and software." With high technology companies, 64% of all alliances were seen as "winners,"[4] while only 33% of mergers and acquisitions were seen as "winners." For deals involving media companies, 73% of alliances were seen as "winners,"

---

3. Ernest, David, and Tammy Haley, "When to Think Alliance," The McKinsey Quarterly Number 4, 48–55 (2000).

4. Winners were defined as having a share price increase than 1 standard deviation.

while 53% of mergers and acquisitions were seen as "winners." McKinsey cites a few concrete examples where there was significant shareholder value creation in alliances. For example, when Displaytech and Hewlett-Packard announced an alliance to develop and manufacture display systems, Hewlett-Packard's stock increased nearly 6% percent and Displaytech's increased more than 17%. This announcement created more than $4 billion in value.

Alliances were also found to be the preferred choice for companies trying to build new businesses, enter new geographies, or access new distribution channels. Of the 236 companies McKinsey studied that used alliances to build new businesses, 54% were "rated successes by the market, compared with only 40% for acquirers in compararble M&A transactions." Of the 54 companies that aimed to enter new channels through an alliance, 60% were "deemed to be successful by the market."

Between the different types of structures, they found that "contractual alliances were better received by the market than more complicated equity joint ventures." Finally, the study observed that multipartner alliances were well received. Conclusions from their analysis suggest that the market responds favorably to those alliances where risk is reduced and businesses are built in "turbulent" environments, as well as those that unite partners. The market was seen to react more favorably to simpler structures rather than complicated structures.

§ 15.03   CREATING VALUE THROUGH JOINT VENTURES AND ALLIANCES

Joint ventures can be an effective way to create shareholder value. There are a number of reasons for this. First, joint ventures spread risk among multiple parties. In a joint venture, it is typical for the parties to contribute certain expertise, capital and resources to the entity. Therefore, joint ventures can often serve as a vehicle to initiate higher risk projects that may not suit the appetite of each company's existing shareholders if it were accomplished within the company.

Second, there may be less of a direct earnings impact on each of the companies party to the joint venture. Because the alliance is not necessarily consolidated on the financial statements of either company, there is potentially less of a dilutive impact of any losses from the joint venture on the earnings of either partner. This is particularly important in research and develop or start-up alliances.

Third, they allow a company to undertake a project that they may not ordinarily pursue. Alliances spread the risk and dilution inherent in a project among the participants.

§ 15.04   MOTIVATION AND RATIONALE BEHIND JOINT VENTURES AND ALLIANCES

Alliances and joint ventures are excellent vehicles for generating growth for a company. Growth can mean a number of things, including new products, new customers, and new technologies. It is difficult to pursue many of these at once and in some cases, it is difficult to pursue any one growth strategy internally. At issue are the capital to pursue the project, the management required to execute the vision, the risk involved in building the new business, and the time required to build it. Joint ventures provide companies with a means to generate growth by leveraging off the intellectual capital and other resources of partners. In addition, they can be executed with less internal capital and with less exposure to risk. As a result, alliances, joint ventures, and equity stake structures have proven to be an efficient means for pursuing new businesses.

[A]   Access New Technology

With rapid advances in technology, keeping pace with competitors can be a challenging problem. Companies focusing on maximizing the value of existing technologies may very quickly find themselves leapfrogged by the competition. Capital required to keep apace with technological shifts may be prohibitive for small companies. Likewise, new companies with cutting edge technology may supersede existing technologies. Joint ventures allow companies to capitalize on the relative strengths of different parties. One may have capital while another may have technology. The venture allows the companies to jointly develop a technology to minimize cost and risk to the parties while providing both with the upside of the venture.

[B]   Diversification

A joint venture allows the participants to potentially diversify their revenue sources, markets and customers by providing each other with access to their respective assets, capital, and human resources. For example, a car manufacturer might enter into an alliance with an airplane manufacturer to develop a light aircraft using the car manufacturer's engine manufacturing efficiencies and the aircraft manufacturer's aerodynamic expertise. In this way the car manufacturer is diversifying its revenue base while capitalizing on its, and its partners, expertise.

[C]   Leverage Partner's Competencies

Using the prior example as an illustration, companies may exploit another's core competencies for its own benefit. There are numerous competencies that can be leverage across multiple sectors. For example, manufacturing, research and development, commercialization, and sales and distribution. These competencies inherent in one company can be brought to bear for the benefit of a partner. One good example is in the pharmaceutical industry, where companies that develop and commercialize pharmaceuticals may enter into an alliance with a company that has a sales force.

[D]   Exploit Synergies

Synergies can be exploited in joint ventures and alliances, it is not necessary for two companies to merge outright to take advantage of them. Companies can utilize common resources for the benefit of both parties, for example, manufacturing capacity or sales and distribution capability. The synergies may accrue to the party providing the common resource or it may accrue to the joint venture established to capitalize on the opportunity.

[E]   Enter New Markets or Develop New Products

A common reason for joint ventures and alliances is for the parties to jointly develop new products or enter into new markets. For example, one company may have a product with a strong domestic presence and use the marketing skills of a partner with a strong foreign presence to introduce the product in those markets. Likewise, one company with strong intellectual property may use the commercialization expertise of a partner to develop the product.

[F]   Gain Competitive Advantage

A primary goal of joint ventures and alliances is for the participants to gain competitive advantage over other companies in the sector. Joint ventures allow the companies to expeditiously gain advantage, as it may be easier to gear up a joint venture to compete than merging two companies to achieve the same objective. The parties to the joint venture may wish to maintain their autonomy yet also may need the resources of another party to gain competitive advantage.

[G]   Share Risk or Costs

Accessing new markets, developing new products, diversifying a revenue stream, or building new capacity can be quite prohibitive to a company, in particular, if the company wishes to do so in a short period of time. By entering into a joint venture, the companies can minimize their risk inherent in the project and spread the cost of the project among the participants.

[H]   Maximize Efficiencies

Joint ventures often allow parties with particular expertise to contribute such capability to a venture. By combining the complimentary expertise of multiple parties to a venture, it is possible to maximize the strategic and financial efficiency of the relationship. Companies that might not ordinarily be able to undertake a given project because they lack capital or other resources, are now able to contribute their area of expertise to a joint venture and participate in the upside of the venture.

[I]   Attract and Retain Employees

Joint ventures often require human capital with specific expertise. Given the typically targeted mandate of a joint venture allows the parties to recruit and retain employees with the required skill set. In addition, a joint venture makes it simpler to compensate employees as there is a defined objective with clearly delineated outcomes against which the employee's performance can be benchmarked.

§ 15.05   VALUATION OF JOINT VENTURES AND ALLIANCES

Joint ventures typically entail a new enterprise taken on by two parties who own equity in the entity undertaking the activity and to which the parties contribute financial or other resources. In order to value the joint venture, there are a number of components that must be valued. First, the capital or other resources that the parties contribute to the venture must be valued. Second, an estimate should be made of the cash flows that can be generated from the joint venture. Third, an assumption should be made regarding the long-term outcome of the joint venture, whether it simply continues in perpetuity, is shut down, acquired by either one of the parties, or is sold.

Joint ventures are valued for a number of reasons. First, a decision must be made over how much of the venture each party will own. Second, the overall value of the joint venture must be established to determine whether the return is worth the investment. Third, an assessment should be made if the venture will have value to each of the parties long-term or whether it should be sold, shut down, or left standing by itself.

The valuation of joint ventures, alliances and partnerships is not an exact science. The process is quite dissimilar to that of valuing a publicly traded company as most often, the joint venture entails the creation of a new entity to pursue a new enterprise. This is a generalization, however, as it is possible for two companies to contribute discrete businesses to a joint venture, in which case, the valuation of the joint venture is based on the valuation of the individual businesses as well as the joint potential arising from their combination.

For most joint ventures, two valuation approaches are commonly used: discounted cash flow analysis and internal rate of return analysis. Discounted cash flow analysis values the project by itself on a stand alone basis. It values the discrete cash flows of the project using a discount rate that is based on the funding cost of the joint venture. The discounted cash flow analysis can also be used by the parties to the joint venture to determine whether their return from the joint venture justifies the investment. For example, if one party invests $100 million and the discounted cash flow value of its interest in the venture is $200 million, then the undertaking has a net present value to the partner of $100 million.

The internal rate of return analysis looks at the pro rata return from the joint venture to the partner based on its investment in the partnership. For example,

```
┌─────────────────────────────────────────────────────────┐
│                                                           │
│   Exhibit 15-3                                            │
│   Internal Rate of Return/NPV Example                     │
│   ─────────────────────────────────────────────────      │
│   Initial Investment:                     $ 100          │
│   Annual Cash Flow:                       $  20          │
│   Term:                                   10 years       │
│   IRR:                                    15%            │
│   Net Present Value at IRR:               $   0          │
│                                                           │
└─────────────────────────────────────────────────────────┘
```

if one party invests $100 million, and each year over the life of the ten-year venture, the party receives $20 million, at the end of which the venture dissolves, the internal rate of return to the partner is 15%. By definition, there is a relationship between the internal rate of return analysis and the present value of the project. The present value of a project is zero using a discount rate equal to the internal rate of return. If the present value of a project is greater than zero at the internal rate of return, then the project has a positive net present value. For example, in the foregoing example, the net present value of the project at an IRR of 15% is $0. This analysis is shown in Exhibit 15-3.

[A]   Value the Initial Contributions of the Parties

When establishing an alliance, the parties to the venture may contribute certain tangible and intangible assets. At one extreme, one party may contribute solely intellectual capital in the form of a management team, while the other party may contribute all the financial capital to fund the venture. At the other extreme, both parties to the venture may contribute financial capital, assets such as manufacturing facilities and human resources. Additionally, in many joint ventures, there may be intellectual property assets that are contributed by one or both parties.

Clearly the easiest asset to value is the financial capital. For simplification, it is usually given a dollar value equal to its face value. For example, if $100 million is contributed, it is given a value of $100 million. The other tangible and intangible assets will be valued according to the method most applicable to that type of asset. For example, real estate would be valued according to widely accepted real estate valuation methodologies. This logic applies to most other tangible assets as well.

Intangible assets such as human capital and intellectual property are more difficult to value and should be based obtained with the assistance of qualified experts in their respective fields.

Ultimately, the valuation of the individual contributions of the parties to the joint venture will determine their pro rata ownership in the venture. This is a negotiation by itself.

[B] Value the Potential Cash Flows of the Venture

The joint venture will typically have a purpose. For example, the purpose may be to develop new products or distribute existing products through one of the party's sales forces. The joint venture could simply be to pool purchasing power. Under any scenario, the cash flows that result from the enterprise should be valued. In so doing, it is typical to use the discounted cash flow methodology or an internal rate of return analysis.

As a first step, a forecast should be prepared for the enterprise, no different than one would for a stand alone company or business. Project the revenues, material costs, and operating expenses. You will also have to project the balance sheet required to support the operation. Working capital and well as other long-term debt and equity capital will need to be forecast. Finally, the capital expenditures required to support the project should be forecast.

Once the forecasts have been prepared, the after-tax, unlevered free cash flows for the project should be determined using the following definition from *Chapter 4: Discounted Cash Flow Analysis.*

Earnings Before Interest After Taxes
+ Depreciation
− Capital Expenditures
− Increase in Working Capital
= Free Cash Flow

The forecast period will vary depending on the type of venture and the nature of the business. For example, if the venture has a defined life, for example, ten years, then the cash flows should be projected for the ten-year period. If the joint venture has no predetermined life or may continue in perpetuity, then it is more typical to project the project for three to ten years as one would in a conventional DCF analysis.

The cash flows from the project may be used in DCF analysis or in calculating the internal rate of return on the project. If used for DCF analysis, it is important to estimate a discount rate for the enterprise that reflects its overall funding cost. Since many joint ventures may not have direct public comparables, it may be difficult to estimate the discount rate. However, the discount rate should take into consideration a number of factors. First, the discount rate will reflect its stand alone debt funding cost on an after-tax basis. Second, the discount rate should reflect the cost of the equity that is used to fund the venture.

It may be possible to use comparable public companies to determine the cost equity and the appropriate capital structure for the venture. If not, it may require some creative thinking to determine the WACC.

If the cash flows are used to calculate an internal rate of return, an estimate should be made by the party performing the analysis of what cash flow is paid back to the party and when. These cash flows are then benchmarked against the capital invested to determine the IRR.

[C]   Estimate the Long-Term "Outcome" of the Venture

As in most discounted cash flow valuations, a terminal value must be calculated. The terminal value will depend on the type and purpose of the joint venture as well as the "outcome." The outcome very much depends on the objectives of the parties and whether or not the alliance is subject to a term. For example a partnership to undertake joint purchasing may be for a period of ten years, and the cost savings may be valued by themselves. At the end of the ten-year period, the venture is over and has no remaining value. Therefore, there is no terminal value for the partnership. In fact, there may be a cost to dissolving the partnership. Another example may be a joint venture to develop a mine or oil field or other natural resource. While the cash flows during the life of the operation may be valued independently, the natural resource may be depleted by the end of the venture, in which case there is no value left in the venture. Conversely, there may be a cost to shutting down the operation.

At the other extreme, a joint venture to create a new business or develop a new product may spawn a new company that has lasting value above and beyond the forecast period or the initial term, if any, of the partnership. In this type of situation, there is clearly value beyond the forecast period. For perpetual life ventures, the growth-in-perpetuity method or multiples method discussed in *Chapter 4: Discounted Cash Flow Analysis* can be used.

[D]   Calculate the Overall Value of the Venture

Based on the cash flows and the terminal value of the project, if any, the overall value of the venture should be determined. The discounted cash flow valuation can be benchmarked against the initial capital contributed to the venture. The difference between the DCF value and the capital contributed is the value created in the joint venture.

§ 15.06   KEY SUCCESS VARIABLES

[A]   Plan Ahead

Joint ventures and alliances range from the simple and mundane to highly complex, multi-party equity ventures with substantial at stake for all the parties. Successful joint ventures require tremendous planning and forethought. Objectives must be clearly established, responsibilities of the parties should be delineated, and the outcome, dissolution or other end-game should be discussed and agreed upon by the parties.

Without prior planning, joint ventures can quickly become lost inside the organizations of the respective parties to the venture. Instead of creating a vehicle for building value for the parties, the joint venture becomes a burden to them and ultimately may fail. Planning does not only entail the creation and management of the venture, it also should account for potential downside scenarios. In other words, how is the joint venture to be dissolved in the event the objectives are not met or the planned end-game cannot be realized? How can the individual parties to the venture back away from the project or sell their respective interests such that the other parties to the transaction are not materially damaged?

Good planning for the creation, management, and potential dissolution of the venture will ensure that all parties to the project are treated fairly and that their downside is adequately protected in the event of an uneventful negative experience.

[B] Simplicity

While research indicates that in many cases alliances or joint ventures are preferable to mergers and acquisitions, there is also a distinction between types of structures used in alliances and joint ventures. It is wise to keep the structure used as simple as possible in order for the market to digest it more easily. In addition, the simpler and more clear-cut the project, the easier it will be for the parties to manage. Expectations will be clear, goals will be well-defined, and employees will be easier to motivate.

[C] Align Incentives

One crucial area that can often lead to the dissolution of a joint venture is the expectation placed on the parties to the venture. Each party's contribution to the project should be recognized and valued appropriately. Their incentive to perform and ensure their contribution to the venture is living up to expectation should be recognized. Each party should be duly incentivized to maximize their own contribution yet should be treated equitably in the process. No one party should receive an outsized return relative to that of the other parties. Returns should be proportional to invested and contributed resources.

[D] Learn as You Go and Make Adjustments

Joint ventures can fail for a variety of reasons. The initial mandate may not have been clearly delineated. The right management and other human resources may not have been put in place. The joint venture may not have been given sufficient autonomy to succeed. Irrespective of these reasons, the parties to the joint venture, as well as its management, should monitor the joint venture and track its progress. They should evaluate mistakes and make adjustments accordingly, in order to continually revise the business model for success.

§ 15.07 CASE STUDIES

[A] Renault SA Alliance with Nissan Motor Corp.

Renault SA is a French automobile manufacturer with 2001 revenues of $41.3 billion and a market capitalization $11.8 billion. Nissan Motor Corp. is a Japanese automobile manufacturer with 2001 revenues of $47.2 billion and a market capitalization of $28.5 billion. Renault acquired 44% of Nissan in 1999, and Nissan has announced its intention to acquire 13.5% of Renault.

In October 2001, the two companies announced they were forming an alliance to be based in the Netherlands where each company will have equal representation. The alliance was formed to allow both companies to cut costs by joining forces in purchasing and to develop new technology. Specifically, the alliance would undertake the following initiatives:

- Find savings in purchasing, production, and other areas. The alliance would form 11 teams to find the savings. This is expected to generate cost savings of more than $500 million.

- Jointly develop ten vehicle platforms. These would be the basic components for new lines of Renault and Nissan vehicles. This is expected to generate cost savings through higher-volume production of key components.

- Combine parts-purchasing. This is expected to generate savings of $1.7 billion.

- between 1999 and 2002 with the assistance of simplified designs and volume discounts.

- Combine back-office functions.

- Link sales and distribution activities in Europe.

[B]   Vodafone Airtouch Wireless Operations/Bell Atlantic Wireless Operations

On September 21, 1999, Vodafone AirTouch PLC and Bell Atlantic Corp. announced the formation of a joint venture named Verizon Wireless valued at approximately $15 billion. Upon completion, Bell Atlantic would own 55% and Vodafone the remaining 45% of the joint venture. The wireless assets included in the transaction were from Bell Atlantic Mobile, AirTouch Cellular, PrimeCo Personal Communications, and AirTouch Paging. The value was based on 45% of the total assets being contributed in the joint venture. Verizon would be further strengthened by the addition of the cellular and PCS assets of GTE Corp., which expected to complete its merger with Bell Atlantic in the first quarter of 2000. The transaction closed on April 3, 2000.

§ 15.08   SUMMARY

Joint ventures and alliances are popular transactions, and can be structured to accomplish a number of objectives including entering a new market, diversifying revenues, accessing technology, or leveraging a partner's competencies. They have significant advantages over other forms of mergers and acquisitions in that they allow the participants in the venture to spread the risk and cost of the venture among multiple parties. In addition, they allow companies to achieve a desired end-goal without giving up control of their business and maintaining their autonomy.

Critical to the success of a joint venture is prior planning, matching the structure to the desired objective, aligning the incentives of the parties, and continually making adjustments to the venture as it progresses. Without these goals, a joint venture is likely to be lost within the organizations of the respective parties to the venture and will ultimately fail. The venture will not be able to attract and retain the management talent required to build the business.

Joint ventures are valued no differently than any other project taken on by a company. The initial contributions of the parties are valued to establish the overall initial value of the venture. Then, the cash flows that can be derived from the project are valued along with the terminal value, if any. The initial contributions of the parties are then deducted from the cash flow and terminal value to derive the net present value of the project. The same approach can be taken to derive the internal rate of return for the project which can then be used to compare to each company's own return criteria.

Chapter 16

GOING PRIVATE TRANSACTIONS

§ 16.01 OVERVIEW

A going private transaction is the acquisition of the equity securities of a corporation by the issuer[1] or an affiliate of the issuer, in which, as a result of the transaction, less than 300 shareholders remain or the stock of the corporation is delisted from an exchange or is no longer quoted on the NASDAQ. The equity securities include securities that are convertible into common or preferred stock of the issuer.[2] Most often, going private transactions are thought of in the context of minority squeeze-out transactions where a public company acquires the shares it does not own in a publicly traded subsidiary. Another type of deal that usually qualifies as a going private transaction is a leveraged buyout in which a group of equity sponsors acquires an existing business usually in partnership with management. A leveraged buyout is financed with debt and equity capital, and uses the cash flows of the acquired company to repay the debt.

There have been numerous going private transactions in the past decade. Since 1990, there have been approximately 750 announced going private transactions[3] representing $94 billion in dollar value. There were 93 in 2003 alone, representing $8 billion in transaction value.[4] Exhibit 16-1 illustrates the trend in going private transactions since 1990.

Exhibit 16-2 shows the top ten largest going private transactions in the past two years.

Regardless of whether the going private transaction is a squeeze-out or a leveraged buyout, there are a number of potential benefits of going private transactions. First, public shareholders who relinquish their shares in the company typically receive a premium valuation for their shares. Second, as the company is no longer public, it can save substantial costs associated with the requirements of SEC filings and disclosure, accounting and public relations. Third, management has the opportunity to focus on the long-term future of the business, rather than the quarter-to-quarter earnings demanded by the public equity markets. Fourth, the parent company is able to eliminate any conflicts that may exist between different shareholder groups and the boards of directors of the parent and the subsidiary.

Likewise, there are a number of pitfalls of going private transactions, most importantly, the conflict of interest created as the directors in the company may have an ongoing financial interest in the company going private. For example, in

---

1. As defined by the SEC, an issuer is "any issuer which has a class of equity security registered pursuant to section 12 of the Act, or which is required to file periodic reports pursuant to section 15(d) of the Act, or which is a closed-end investment company registered under the Investment Company Act of 1940."

2. Section 3(a)(11) of the Exchange Act of 1934.

3. Thomson Financial Defines "going private transactions" a private acquirer ('private' meaning that none of the acquirer's ultimate parentage is public either) is acquiring a public target and upon completion, it will become a private company.

4. Thomson Financial.

Exhibit 16-1
Announced Going Private Transactions: 1990–2003[5]
($ in millions)

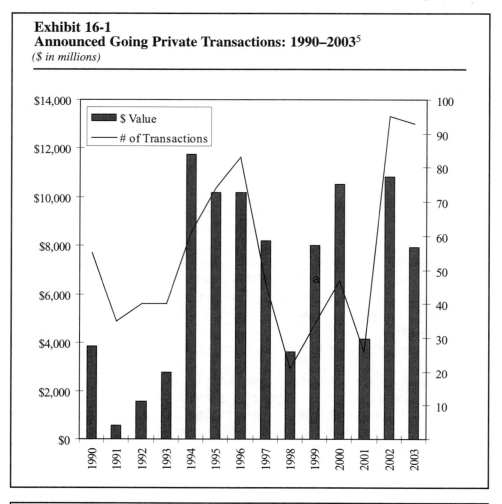

Exhibit 16-2
Top Ten Recent Closed Going Private Transactions
($ in millions)

Ann. Date	Target	Acquiror	Deal Value
03/15/2002	Anchor Glass Container Corp	Cerberus Capital Management LP	$ 393
03/17/2002	Associated Materials Inc	Harvest/AMI Holdings Inc	$ 436
04/11/2002	Herbalife International Inc	Investor Group	$ 718
04/13/2002	Nortek Inc	Investor Group	$ 526
09/23/2002	Dole Food Co Inc	David H Murdock	$1,464
10/01/2002	BWAY Corp	Kelso & Co	$ 342
10/11/2002	Quintiles Transnational Corp	Pharma Services Co	$1,721
12/09/2002	AmeriPath Inc	Amy Acquisition Corp	$ 808
02/18/2003	Insignia Financial Group Inc	CB Richard Ellis Inc	$ 430
07/08/2003	Prime Retail Inc	Lightstone Group LLC	$ 637

---

5. Thomson Financial.

a leveraged buyout, the conflict arises because the board of directors and officers, who have a fiduciary duty to shareholders, are equity participants in the acquisition and may not be interested in seeking the highest value transaction for shareholders. As a result of this type of conflict, going private transactions often attract litigation.

Because of the numerous issues surrounding going private transactions, they have come under intense scrutiny from the legal community and are subject to extensive disclosure requirements by the Securities and Exchange Commission. The disclosure requirements go beyond those of conventional tender offers and merger proxy statements.

§ 16.02 DEFINITION OF GOING PRIVATE TRANSACTIONS

Going private transactions are subject to extensive disclosure requirements set forth by Rule 13e-3 of the Exchange Act, and hence also are known as "Rule 13e-3 transactions." The SEC adopted Rule 13e-3 in 1979 as a way to use disclosure techniques to address transactions where the interests of public shareholders may conflict with those of management, a controlling shareholder or the board of directors. Under Rule 13e-3, a transaction qualifies as a going private transaction if it meets the following criteria:

1. The equity securities of the target are acquired by the issuer (the target) or an affiliate of the issuer;

2. The equity securities of the target are acquired through a tender offer by the issuer or an affiliate of the issuer; or,

3. The equity securities of the target are acquired through a proxy or consent solicitation, or the mailing of an information statement by the issuer or an affiliate of the issuer in connection with a merger, recapitalization, sale of assets to an affiliate of the issuer, or a reverse stock split in which the issuer acquires fractional shares.

In addition, the transaction qualifies as a going private transaction if, as a result of the previous criteria, the target is no longer subject to Section 12(g) or Section 15(d) of the Exchange Act of 1934. Companies are no longer subject to these provisions if there are less than 300 shareholders of the target remaining after the transaction, or the target is delisted from an exchange or no longer quoted on the NASDAQ.[6]

§ 16.03 SPECIAL ISSUES IN GOING PRIVATE TRANSACTIONS

In going private transactions, public shares of a company are either acquired by a controlling shareholder, by the issuer, or by a third party typically in concert with management which renders the acquirer an affiliate of the issuer. These situations give rise to some unique issues and problems that are somewhat different than those in a third party, unaffiliated acquisition.

---

6. Section 12(g) or Section 15(d) of the Exchange Act of 1934.

[A]   Acquirer Conflict

Whether the acquirer is a large, controlling shareholder, or an affiliate by virtue of a relationship with the target or its management, the acquirer has a conflict in acquiring the public shares of the company. As a controlling shareholder, it often will have representation on the target's board of directors. As a board member, its fiduciary duty is to the shareholders of the company whose public shares it seeks to acquire. Consequently, it has a conflict of interest in that it wishes to acquire the public shares at as low a price as possible, while its duty is to ensure the shareholders receive as high a price as possible.

[B]   Higher Standard of Fairness

Going private transactions that involve an acquisition by a controlling shareholder are typically held to a higher standard than third party acquisitions. In merger situations, the going private transaction is subject to an entire fairness test rather than the standard business judgment rule. In going private mergers, the board has to establish that the transaction was conducted using a fair process, and the consideration that was paid was fair.

[C]   Litigation

Going private transactions often lead to litigation because of the inherent conflicts of interest in the deal. The litigation usually surrounds the price that was paid by the acquirer in the transaction. Depending on the type of going private transaction, the public shareholders have varying ability to block or prevent a going private transaction. In tender offers, the shareholders have the ability to accept or reject the transaction; however, if the acquirer is successful in purchasing greater than 90% of the target's shares, it can then pursue a short-form merger and "squeeze-out" the remaining shareholders. In a merger, the shareholders have the ability to vote in favor or against a transaction, and, dissenting shareholders have appraisal rights. These appraisal rights allow the dissenting shareholders to receive a third party appraisal of their shares as a means to potentially increase the price paid by the company.

[D]   Enhanced Disclosure Requirements

Going private transactions are subject to intense scrutiny as a result of the inherent conflicts in the transaction. The SEC has imposed strict disclosure requirements that articulate not only what information must be disclosed to the SEC and shareholders, but also on how the information is disseminated. Rule 13e-3 governs the overall disclosure requirements of going private transactions; however, the transaction will also be subject to the other rules and regulations as promulgated by the Securities and Exchange Commission. Section 16.06 of this chapter addresses the filing and disclosure requirements of 13e-3 transactions in more detail.

[E]   Need for Objective Validation

Because of the unique issues surrounding going private transactions, it is typical for the board of directors of the target to appoint a special committee to represent the public shareholders. In addition, it is common for the special committee to obtain the advice of a third party financial advisor who will provide it with a fairness opinion that opines on the fairness of the consideration to be received by the public shareholders.

§ 16.04   COMMON FORMS OF GOING PRIVATE TRANSACTIONS

There are two common forms of going private transactions: minority squeeze-outs and leveraged buyouts.

[A]   Squeeze-Outs

[1]   Overview

A squeeze-out is the acquisition of the minority, or unaffiliated, shares of a public, or private, company by the remaining shareholders. Squeeze-outs typically relate to the acquisition by the majority shareholder of the shares of a publicly traded subsidiary that are not owned by the majority owner.

Since 1990, there have been approximately 1,736 minority squeeze-outs, representing approximately $161 billion in dollar volume. In 2003 alone, there were 127 minority squeeze-out transactions representing $8 billion in dollar volume. Exhibit 16-3 shows the trend in minority squeeze-out transactions since 1990.

As an example of a recent squeeze-out, one recent squeeze-out transaction is Tyco's acquisition of the public shares it did not own in TyCom. Tyco is a leading multi-national manufacturing and services conglomerate. TyCom is one of the world's largest providers of advanced broadband communications capacity, systems and services. In the Tyco situation, the company sold 14% of TyCom's stock to the public in July 2000 for $32 per share, raising $2.1 billion in the process. After the stock of TyCom slid below $10 per share in late 2001, Tyco offered to buy out the public minority shareholders at $14.00 per share. After a few weeks of negotiation, the independent directors agreed to a higher price, and Tyco agreed to purchase the public shares at $15.42 per share. From initial public offering to squeeze-out, the transaction took less than 15 months.

Exhibit 16-4 provides a list of recent squeeze-out transactions.

The acquisition of minority shares in a squeeze-out transaction usually entails paying a premium to shareholders. This premium can range depending on the circumstances of the transaction and whether the transaction is a cash tender offer or a stock merger. In the transactions shown above, cash tender offer premiums in minority squeeze-outs were an average of 61.5%.

For a squeeze-out transaction to take place, it is not necessary for the largest stockholder to own greater than 50% of the target. For transactions referenced in Exhibit 16-4, the average ownership by a parent just prior to the squeeze-out was approximately 69%, with average ownership in stock-for-stock squeeze-outs of

Exhibit 16-3
Minority Squeeze-Out Transactions: 1990–2003[7]
($ in millions)

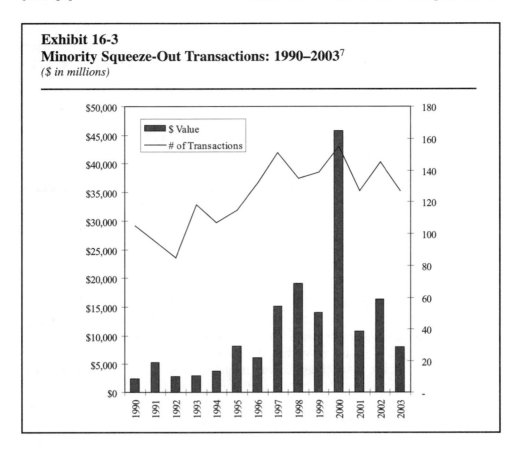

70.8% and the average ownership in cash squeeze-outs of 68.8%. The highest ownership pre buy-in was 98.9% and the lowest was 15%.

Often, squeeze-outs occur between a parent and subsidiary where the subsidiary was previously taken public. Examples of these would include Hertz, Intimate Brands and Infinity Broadcasting. It is common for the parent to acquire the unaffiliated minority shares at a discount to the price at which the subsidiary was taken public. As an example, the recent squeeze-out of TyCom by Tyo occurred at a discount to its IPO price.

Often, squeeze-outs occur between a parent and subsidiary where the subsidiary was previously taken public. It is common for the parent to acquire the unaffiliated minority shares at a discount to the price at which the subsidiary was taken public. Exhibit 16-5 shows a few recent instances where companies were taken private in a squeeze out transaction at a price below their IPO price.

Squeeze-outs come about as a result of a number of situations. Most often, they arise after a corporate parent has taken a subsidiary public and then desires to

---

7. Thomson Financial.

Exhibit 16-4
Recent Squeeze-Out Transactions[8]
($ in millions)

Date Effective	Target	Acquirer	Value	Synopsis
11/26/2002	Zomba Group	Bertelsmann Music Group Inc	$2,740	Bertelsmann Music Group Inc (BMG), a unit of Bertelsmann AG, acquired the remaining 80% interest, which it did not already own in Zomba Group (ZG), a provider of music publishing services, for $2.74 billion. The transaction was achieved through the exercise of a put option held by ZG which was to expire by the end of 2002. Previously, BMG acquired a 20% stake in ZG's Zomba Records Ltd unit.
06/06/2003	CC VIII LLC	Charter Communications Inc	$728	Charter Communications Inc acquired the remaining stake which it did not already own in CC VII LLC, a provider of cable television services, from its joint venture partner Comcast Corp, for an estimated $728 million in cash.
	Motiva Enterprises LLC	Investor Group	$3,860	An investor group, comprised of Shell Oil Co (SO), a unit of Royal Dutch/Shell Group (RDS), and Saudi Refining Inc (SR), acquired the remaining 35% stake, which it did not already own, in Motiva Enterprises LLC (ME), an oil and gas exploration and production company, from joint

(Continued)

---

8. Thomson Financial.

Exhibit 16-4

(*Continued*)

Date Effective	Target	Acquirer	Value	Synopsis
				venture partner Texaco Inc (TI). Prior to the acquisition, SO held a 30% stake in Motiva and SR held a 35% stake in ME. Upon completion, SO and SR were to each hold a 50% interest in ME. Concurrently, SO acquired the remaining 44% stake, which it did not already own, in Equilon Enterprises LLC (EE), an oil and gas exploration and production company, from TI. The two transactions had a combined value of $3.86 bil. The consideration consisted of $2.26 billion in cash and the assumption of $1.6 billion in liabilities. Originally in December 2000, TI announced that it was seeking a buyer for its 44% interest in EE and 35% stake in ME. These transactions were necessary for regulatory approval of Chevron Corp's acquisition of TI.
03/21/2002	Intimate Brands Inc	Limited Inc	$1,645	US — Limited Inc (LTD) acquired the remaining 16% stake, or 78.645 mil common shares, which it did not already own, in Intimate Brands Inc (IBI), an owner and operator of women's accessory stores, for $1.645 bil. LTD offered a sweetened 1.1 common shares per IBI share. Based on LTD's closing stock price of $17.93 on March 6, the

(*Continued*)

Exhibit 16-4
(*Continued*)

Date Effective	Target	Acquirer	Value	Synopsis
				last full trading day prior to the announcement of amended terms, each IBI was valued at $19.723. Earlier LTD completed an tender offer to acquire the remaining stake by accepting 72.6 mil common shares, or 14.77% of IBI's shares outstanding. Originally, LTD offered 1.046 common shares per IBI share. Based on LTD's closing stock price of $18.45 on February 1, the last full trading day prior to the announcement, each IBI share was valued at $19.299. The offer was conditioned upon at least 90% of IBI's shares being exchanged.
06/03/2002	NRG Energy Inc	Xcel Energy Inc	$673	Xcel Energy Inc (XE) acquired the remaining 25.65% stake, or 54.689 mil common shares, which it did not already own in NRG Energy Inc (NRG), a provider of electric & gas utility services, in a stock swap transaction valued at $672.556 million. Earlier; XE completed its unsolicited tender offer for NRG, by accepting 42.990 million shares, or 21.654% of NRG's common shares outstanding, equivalent to 84.41% of NRG's shares not owned by XE. XE offered a sweetened .5 common shares per NRG share. Based on XE's closing stock price of $25.72

(*Continued*)

Exhibit 16-4

(*Continued*)

Date Effective	Target	Acquirer	Value	Synopsis
				on April 3, the last full trading day prior to the announcement of amended terms, each NRG share was valued at $12.86. Originally, XE offered .4846 shares per NRG share. Based on XE's closing stock price of $23.73 on February 14, the last full trading day prior to the announcement, each NRG share was valued at $11.50. The offer was conditioned upon at least 90% of the total NRG shares outstanding being tendered or 60% of NRG shares not owned by XE.
08/08/2003	Expedia Inc	USA Interactive	$3,636	InterActiveCorp, formerly known as USA Interactive (UI), acquired the remaining 38.811% stake, or 83.311 million common shares, which it did not already own, in Expedia Inc (EI), a provider of online travel services for leisure and small businesses, in a stock swap transaction valued at a sweetened $3.636 bil. UI offered 1.93875 common shares per EI share held. Based on UI's closing stock price of $26.49 on March 18, the last full trading day prior to the announcement of the amended terms, each EI share was valued at $51.357 on a post-split basis. Previously, on

(*Continued*)

Exhibit 16-4

(*Continued*)

Date Effective	Target	Acquirer	Value	Synopsis
				March 10, 2003, EI recorded a 2-for-1 stock split. Previously, UI withdrew its unsolicited bid to acquire the remaining 22.973% stake in EI. UI had offered 2.6969 common shares per EI share. Concurrently, UI withdrew its plans to acquire the remaining 32% stake, which it did not already own, in Hotels.com. Moreover, UI acquired the remaining 32.985% stake, which it did not already own, in Ticketmaster.
01/17/2003	Ticketmaster	USA Interactive	$841	USA Interactive (UI) acquired the remaining 32.985% stake, or 55.739 million common shares, on a fully-diluted basis, which it did not already own, in Ticketmaster (TM), a provider of online city guide services, in a stock swap transaction valued at $841.051 mil. UI offered an amended .935 common shares per TM share. Based on UI's closing stock price of $16.95 on October 8, the last full trading day prior to the amendment, each TM share was valued at $15.85. The transaction was accounted for as a pooling of interests. Originally, in May 2002, UI planned to make an unsolicited offer of .8068 common shares per TM share. Concurrently, UI

(*Continued*)

Exhibit 16-4

(*Continued*)

Date Effective	Target	Acquirer	Value	Synopsis
				withdrew its plans to acquire the remaining 22.973% stake, which it did not already own, in Expedia Inc. Also, UI withdrew its plans to acquire the remaining 32% stake, which it did not already own, in Hotels.com.
03/31/2003	Time Warner Entertainment Co	AOL Time Warner Inc	$3,600	AOL Time Warner Inc (AOL) acquired the remaining 27.64% stake, which it did not already own, in Time Warner Entertainment Co LP, an owner and operator of cable television stations and a producer of motion pictures, from AT&T Corp's AT&T Broadband & Internet Services (ABI) subsidiary, for an estimated $3.6 billion in a restructuring transaction. The consideration consisted of $2.1 bil in cash, an estimated $1.5 billion in AOL common stock and a 21% stake in the newly restructured company, to be named Time Warner Cable Inc (TWC). Previously, Comcast Corp (CC) merged with ABI to form AT&T Comcast Corp in a reverse takeover stock swap transaction. As a result of this transaction, CC was to inherit the consideration offered in this deal. Moreover, CC had considered offering an undisclosed number of common shares in the new TWC to the public, with an estimated value of $5.5 billion.

(*Continued*)

Exhibit 16-4
(*Continued*)

Date Effective	Target	Acquirer	Value	Synopsis
06/23/2003	Hotels.com	USA Interactive	$1,237	USA Interactive (UI) acquired the remaining 32% stake, or 18.193 million shares, which it did not already own, in Hotels.com (HC), a provider of discount hotel accommodations services, in a stock swap transaction valued at $1.237 billion. UI offered 2.4 common shares per HC share. Based on UI's closing stock price of $25.1 on April 9, the last full trading day prior to the announcement, each HC share was valued at $60.24. The transaction was subject to approval by regulatory authorities. Upon completion, UI changed its name to InterActiveCorp.
12/10/2003	Emigrant Bancorp, New York, NY	Paul Milstein Family	$811	The Paul Milstein Family acquired the remaining 45.4% stake, which it did not already own, in Emigrant Bancorp, New York, NY, from Max Fisher, Oded Aboodi, David Wallace and members of the Seymour Milstein Family, for $811 million.

Exhibit 16-5
Minority Squeeze Out Transactions Below IPO Price

Date	Parent	Subsidiary	IPO Price	Buy-In Price
12/13/01	Tyco	TyCom	$32.00	$15.42
08/21/01	Credit Suisse First Boston	CSFB Direct	$20.00	$ 6.00

reacquire the public stock at a later stage. In these situations, squeeze-outs occur for three primary reasons: poor market performance, conflicts with the parent company, and desire to better capitalize on synergies.

[2]   Motivation Behind Squeeze-Outs

Squeeze-outs come about as a result of a number of situations. Most often, they arise after a corporate parent has taken a subsidiary public and then desires to reacquire the public stock at a later stage, as in the Tyco squeeze-out of TyCom. Another situation that gives rise to squeeze-outs, is when an acquirer purchases a large stake in a company but not 100% of the shares.

In these situations, squeeze-outs occur for three primary reasons: poor market performance, conflicts with the parent company, and desire to better capitalize on synergies.

[a]   Poor Market Performance. Often, a subsidiary is taken public because it may be valued higher as a public company than it is as a subsidiary of a public company. Alternatively, a parent company may decide to take a company public to raise capital or realize value from a high growth asset. These reasons may bode well for an equity carve-out, yet over time, this rationale may longer hold true, and the subsidiary may no longer be trading well. The stock may be languishing in the market as a result of limited liquidity, poor analyst research coverage, or poor financial performance. In these situations, the parent may wish to reabsorb the subsidiary in order to eliminate any negative perceptions in the market surrounding the subsidiary.

[b]   Conflicts with Parent Company. Partly owned subsidiaries may often have divergent interests with those of the parent company. For example, the subsidiary may wish to raise additional equity capital while the parent may wish to continue to consolidate for tax purposes. Over time, these conflicts may become intolerable, and the parent may wish to reacquire the public shares of the subsidiary to gain greater control.

[c]   Capitalize on Synergies. As an independent company, the subsidiary may well develop capabilities that are attractive to the parent. In addition, the parent and subsidiary could also build cost structures that are independent yet redundant. Furthermore, the parent and subsidiary may not be able to realize financing savings as independent companies. As a result, the parent may wish to absorb 100% of the subsidiary in order to take advantage of these potential operating and financial synergies.

[3]   Valuation of Squeeze-Outs

Squeeze-out valuation entails the stand alone, going concern and takeover analysis of the subsidiary as if it were an independent company. It also requires an analysis of the impact of the transaction on the parent company. First, a stand alone, going concern analysis should be performed on the subsidiary, using discounted cash flow and comparable trading multiples analysis. These analyses will reveal whether the subsidiary's stock is under or over-valued in the market. Second, using comparable transactions, both in control situations and squeeze-out transactions, the transaction value of the subsidiary stock should be analyzed. The comparable acquisition premiums and multiples will reveal what a third party may be willing to pay for the company in a sale of the company. The squeeze-out premiums will show a likely range of values the parent will have to pay in order to affect the transaction. Third, an analysis of the impact of the squeeze-out acquisition should be performed to determine the accretion or dilution in the transaction to the parent.

As an adjunct to these analyses, it is also helpful to look at the historical prices paid by shareholders, including the parent, for stock in the subsidiary. For example, if the subsidiary was taken public recently, say in the past 18 months, at a certain price, say $20 per share, and the proposed offer price is below that amount, yet the financial performance of the company has not deteriorated, the shareholders may question whether the offer price is reflective of the company's value. As another example, in the case where a company acquired its stake in the subsidiary over time, it may have paid different prices in the past. To the extent the proposed offer price is less than the most recent offer price, there may be significant issues in completing the offer. The "best price" rule — Rule 14d-10 of the Exchange Act — mandates that an affiliated acquirer has to offer the same price to all shareholders in a tender offer. One should be cognizant of the rules governing the pricing in going private transactions.

One final item to evaluate in a squeeze-out transaction is the historical basis of unaffiliated shareholders in the company. This will indicate the likelihood that a given shareholder will tender their stock or vote in favor of a merger.

[4] Squeeze-Out Case Study: Ford Motor Acquisition of Hertz Public Shares

On January 16, 2001, Ford Motor Co. announced that it had reached a decision to acquire the public shares of Hertz Corporation it did not own. Ford owned approximately 81.5% of Hertz prior to the acquisition. The $35.50 offer was a 46% premium, over the pre-offer share price for Hertz. This price was an increase over the original price of $30.00 per share. The transaction had an aggregate value of approximately $734 million. The offer was structured as a cash tender offer for the approximately 20 million shares that were publicly traded. Ford was represented by J.P. Morgan while the special committee to the board of directors of Hertz was advised by Lazard Freres. The transaction closed on March 19, 2001.

[B] Leveraged Buyouts

[1] Overview

A leveraged buyout is the acquisition of the existing private or public stock of a company by a group of equity sponsors that typically is financed with debt and equity, and uses the cash flows of the acquired company to repay the debt. The equity sponsors may include the management team of the company. The assets of the company are pledged as collateral behind the assumed debt in the transaction.

A typical leveraged buyout entails the acquisition of a public company in an under-appreciated sector or where the stock is out-of-favor relative to its peers. The goal of the LBO is to reinvigorate the management team, pay down the acquisition debt using the company's cash flows, and then sell or take the company public again at a later date and at a higher valuation, allowing the benefits of reduced debt and the increase in valuation to accrue to the equity investors.

Equity sponsors use debt as the primary source of capital to finance LBO's, in order to enhance their returns and limit the amount of equity required to finance the transaction. The amount of debt that can be financed in a leveraged buyout is heavily dependent on market conditions, and will fluctuate anywhere from two-three times EBITDA (earnings before interest and taxes) in bad times to six-seven times EBTIDA in good markets.

Leveraged buyouts have numerous benefits. First, as a private company, the target can lower its legal, accounting and public relations costs, which can often run upwards of $1 million per year, and can include costs associated with SEC disclosure, securities filings, auditing and annual reports, and additional costs associated with interfacing with the public. Second, the LBO allows management to focus on the long-term rather than quarter-to-quarter earnings. Management can focus on the business not necessarily Wall Street expectations. Third, the management team no longer has to worry about the threat of takeover.

There are a number of risks inherent in leveraged buyouts that begin with the execution of the transaction itself, and continue through the gestation of the LBO through its exit. These risks include those inherent in other going private transactions, the risk of bankruptcy, the need for a well-defined exit strategy, board control, forced sale, and management equity and vesting.

There are a number of ways to mitigate this type of risk in a management buyout. First, the board of directors of the company should elect an independent — or special — committee to represent the interests of the minority, or public, shareholders. Second, the special committee should have the ability to act independently of the board of directors and (i) negotiate on behalf of shareholders, (ii) hire a financial advisor to represent it, and (iii) obtain a fairness opinion from a qualified third party supporting their decision and the fairness of the transaction. Other steps that can be taken include (i) obtaining the vote of a majority of the minority investors in support of the transaction, (ii) making all the required disclosures and filings required by the SEC, and (iii) following a well-thought out process that demonstrates the special committee was well-informed in its decision making.

Since 1990, there have been over 2,992 leveraged buyouts, representing over $231 billion in transaction value.[9] In 2003 alone, there were 159 leveraged buyouts representing $20 billion in transaction value. Exhibit 16-6 shows the history in announced transactions.

Leveraged buyouts have included some of the largest transactions completed in mergers and acquisitions, including the 1988 LBO of RJR Nabisco, the tobacco and food conglomerate, in a $24.6 billion transaction. RJR was acquired by

---

9. Thomson Financial.

Kohlberg Kravis and Roberts, one of the leading equity sponsors of leveraged buyouts. Following in Exhibit 16-7 is a list of recent leveraged buyouts.

Exhibit 16-6
Leveraged Buyout Transactions: 1990–2003[10]
($ in millions)

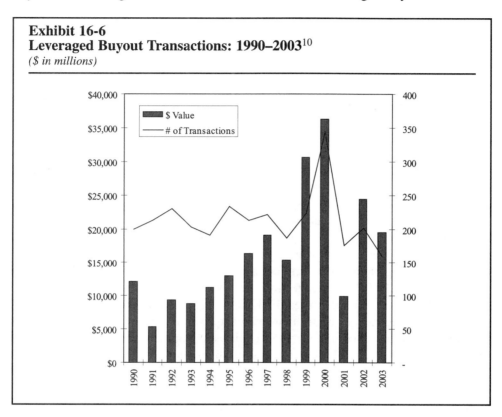

Exhibit 16-7
Recent Significant Leveraged Buyouts: 2002–2003[11]
($ in millions)

Ann. Date	Target	Acquirer	Deal Value
09/04/2003	Ondeo Nalco Co	Investor Group	$4,350
08/20/2002	Qwest Commun Intl Inc-QwestDex	Investor Group	$4,300
08/20/2002	Qwest Comm Intl-QwestDex	Investor Group	$2,750
10/11/2002	Quintiles Transnational Corp	Pharma Services Co	$1,721
11/07/2002	Houghton Mifflin Co	Investor Group	$1,660
02/21/2003	DB Capital Partners-Private Eq	MidOcean Partners LP	$1,617
07/25/2002	Burger King Corp	Investor Group	$1,499
09/23/2002	Dole Food Co Inc	David H Murdock	$1,464
06/06/2003	Transdigm Inc	Investor Group	$1,174
11/17/2003	Simmons Co(Fenway Partners)	Investor Group	$1,100

10. Thomson Financial.
11. Thomson Financial.

[2]   The History of Leveraged Buyouts and the Current
      State of the Market

Leveraged buyouts have been quite popular, but received their notoriety in the 1980s when Michael Milken, a notorious investment banker, built the high yield bond or "junk debt" business of Drexel Burnham Lambert into the premier financing vehicle behind leveraged buyouts. The number of leveraged buyouts increased quite dramatically in the 1980s thanks to the freely available debt capital, with 340 deals announced in 1988.[12] Yet, as the bull market of the 1990s took hold, and stock prices became more fully valued, LBO's became less frequent, with only 186 deals announced in 1998.[13] The late 1990s saw a resurgence in LBO activity, although not to 1988 levels, with 223 deals announced in 1999, and 344 deals announced in 2000.[14] 2001 saw a decline in LBO activity, with 176 announced deals, as the debt markets began to tighten and the economy soured.[15] 2002 and 2003 saw an uptick in activity with 202 and 159 transactions announced respectively, as interest rates declined and the economy began to recover.

The decline in LBO activity, while strongly associated with the overall decline in the economy, has been driven in part by the bank debt market's increasingly restrictive lending practices. Where companies could be acquired in the late 1980s with six times EBITDA leverage, in recent years, leveraged buyouts have seen leverage of about 2.5–3.5 times EBITDA. As a consequence, the historical approach of using cash flows to finance an acquisition and enhance equity returns no longer could be relied upon; rather, equity sponsors have been forced to invest more up-front equity, and look to better growth dynamics of the target company to generate desired equity returns.

Another associated factor that has evolved out of the tightening of credit markets, is the conditions placed on the closing of a transaction by the acquirer. Financing outs and material adverse change clauses have become de rigueur in leveraged buyout transactions, as equity sponsors have become more concerned about their ability to finance transactions and the target's ability to maintain financial performance in a tough economic climate. Complicating the market for LBO's has been the decline in the equity markets, and the perception that companies can attain their old valuation levels that were seen prior to the March 2000 decline in the NASDAQ.

Typical leveraged buyout candidates have been companies that have been generally overlooked by the market: limited trading volume and liquidity, poor research coverage, and low market capitalizations. However, these companies also had the distinction of having strong cash flows and in certain cases, strong cash balances.

---

12. Thomson Financial.
13. Thomson Financial.
14. Thomson Financial.
15. Thomson Financial.

[3] Overview of Financial Sponsors

The leveraged buyout financial sponsor community is quite vast, and includes notable companies such as Kholberg, Kravis and Roberts, Thomas H. Lee and Forstmann Little & Co. These funds came into prominence in the late 1970s and 1980s when they were established principally to fund leveraged buyouts. The funds invest in a broad array of leveraged buyouts, and thus spread the risk inherent in each transaction among a number of different deals, thereby mitigating the overall risk to the fund's investors while maintaining attractive financial returns. As recently as late 2001, there was over $120 billion in capital available from north of 250 firms focusing on leveraged buyouts. Exhibit 16-8 provides an overview of some of the largest sponsors of leveraged buyout groups and some of their representative investments.

LBO funds obtain their capital from a variety of different sources, including pension funds such as CALPERS, who account for over a third of the funds invested in these equity sponsors.

[4] Management Buyouts

Management buyouts are leveraged buyouts where the management group participates in the buying group. Equity sponsors usually want the participation of management because of their inside knowledge of the company and its industry. This same insider knowledge can cause a management led leveraged buyout to be

---

Exhibit 16-8
Overview of Leading Leveraged Buyout Sponsors

Sponsor	Fund Size ($ millions)	Representative Investments
Blackstone Group	$8,000	Allied Waste, American Axle, Centennial Communications, Graham Packaging
Kohlberg Kravis & Roberts		Primedia Inc., Accuride Company, Alliance Imaging, Borden, Inc. Evenflo Company
Forstmann Little & Co.	$2,300	XO Communications, Yankee Candle, General Instrument, Gulfstream Aerospace, Community Health Systems
Thomas H. Lee	$6,100	Snapple, Friendly Ice Cream, Conseco, Fisher Scientific
Clayton, Dubilier & Rice	$3,500	Covansys, Kinko's, Riverwood International, Remington Arms Company
Texas Pacific Group		Oxford Health Plans, Magellan Health Services, Del Monte, Ducati
Kicks, Muse, Tate & Furst	$3,000	AMFM, ICG Communications, Regal Cinemas, CableVision SA, Vlassic Foods, LIN Holdings

---

fraught with conflicts. Because the management team is an equity participant in the LBO, it has a self-interest in ensuring the company is acquired at a price that enables the equity group to realize attractive financial terms. Likewise, with a fiduciary duty to shareholders, it must be in a position to recommend the same transaction as fair to shareholders. This perceived conflict can result in allegations of self-dealing by shareholders, resulting in substantial litigation.

There are a number of ways to mitigate this type of risk in a management buyout. First, the board of directors of the company should elect an independent — or special — committee to represent the interests of the minority, or public, shareholders. Second, the special committee should have the ability to act independently of the board of directors and (i) negotiate on behalf of shareholders, (ii) hire a financial advisor to represent it, and (iii) obtain a fairness opinion from a qualified third party supporting their decision and the fairness of the transaction. Other steps that can be taken include (i) obtaining the vote of a majority of the minority investors in support of the transaction, (ii) making all the required disclosures and filings required by the SEC, and (iii) following a well-thought out process that demonstrates the special committee was well-informed in its decision making.

[5]   ESOP Leveraged Buyouts

[a] Overview of ESOPs. An ESOP is an employee stock ownership plan. It is a corporate vehicle that allows a corporation to make tax-deductible donations of stock or cash into a trust on behalf of employees. The assets of the trust are allocated to employees over time on a pre-determined basis. The employees are not taxed on the contributions to the trust; rather, they are only taxed as they withdraw their assets from the ESOP. Contributions on behalf of the employee are made to the ESOP based on the employee's compensation. Each employee usually receives the same percentage of his compensation. ESOPs are allowable under the Employee Retirement Income Security Act of 1974 (ERISA), laws that govern the administration of corporate pension plans.

The use of ESOPs has grown substantially in the last two decades, with over 11,500 plans in existence in 2000.[16] ESOPs have existed since the early 1900s, but went through a period of dramatic growth after the 1974 tax laws that allowed qualified retirement plans to borrow for the purposes of acquiring stock. Other factors contributed to the growth in ESOPs, in particular, the leveraged ESOP. These included improved tax incentives as a result of the 1984 Tax Reform Act, and the increase in the use of ESOPs as a means for defending against takeover threat. In particular, the enactment of the Delaware anti-takeover statute, discussed in Chapter 23, prevented a bidder who has acquired greater than 15% of a company's stock, from completing the acquisition unless the purchaser obtained over 85% of the target's shares, or two-third of the shareholders — excluding the bidder — approved the transaction, or the board of directors and shareholders opted to exclude themselves from the law.

---

16. National Center for Employee Ownership.

The way ESOPs aid in defense is by having enough stock in the ESOP and other friendly hands to prevent the acquirer from completing the transaction under the Delaware statute.

There are two types of ESOP plans: defined benefit and defined contribution plans. Defined benefit plans provide a specific benefit to the employee upon retirement. In a defined contribution plan, employers make a "defined" contribution to the plan on a recurring basis. The employee can withdraw a benefit when they retire, yet the benefit is determined by the funds performance. ESOP can also come in two forms: unleveraged and leveraged. Unleveraged ESOPs do not borrow to finance the plan while leveraged ESOPs borrow money to finance the plan. Under a leveraged ESOP, the corporation borrows to finance the acquisition of its own stock which is contributed to the ESOP. The ESOP pays the principal and interest on the loan.

[b] Use of ESOPs in Leveraged Buyouts. ESOPs have been widely used as in leveraged buyouts as a means to acquire a company. This is in part because the acquirer can get stock of the corporation into the hands of employees, providing them with a vested interest in ensuring the company succeeds. ESOPs have also been frequently used as a means to finance LBOs because of the significant financial benefits of using an ESOP.

Borrowing through an ESOP is far more attractive than a corporation borrowing directly from a bank or other financial institution. In a corporate loan, only the interest may be tax deductible, while in an ESOP loan, the interest and principal may be tax deductible. This difference makes the cost of financing the LBO much cheaper with the use of an ESOP.

There are additional financial and other benefits of ESOPs in the context of a buyout. First, shareholders who tender their shares into an acquiring leveraged ESOP may defer the gain on the sale of their stock, as long as the ESOP holds greater than 30% of the value of the shares of the target after the transaction. In addition, in the event the ESOP purchases greater than 50% of the target's stock, the corporation may continue to carry forward losses after a change of control.

[6] Attributes of Attractive Buyout Candidates

For a company to be acquired on a leveraged basis, it must have a number of positive characteristics.

[a] Stable Cash Flows. First, it must have stable cash flows. The greater the stability and predictability of cash flows, the less risk there is in the transaction. Lenders will look to the stability of cash flows to determine how much they will lend to the company. Historical measures of cash flows may indicate likely future stability; however, it is important to evaluate the future cash flows in the context of the leveraged buyout, and evaluate the company's overall financial performance and ability to generate cash with a significantly altered capital structure. Increased leverage may have an impact on the ability of the company to invest in capital and working assets and consequently, the future financial and operating profile of the firm may change.

[b]   Strong Management Team. Second, while stable cash flows are a pre-requisite for a successful leveraged buyout, they cannot be relied upon as the sole basis on which to proceed. The quality of the management team is equally as important. The equity sponsor and lenders will want to have comfort that the management team has been in place for an extended period and that the management team has the requisite experience to manage the company under a leveraged scenario.

[c]   Undervalued Assets. Third, an attractive buyout candidate may be a company that has undervalued assets or businesses that can be divested to help reduce leverage once the transaction has closed. While lenders may not depend on asset sales to repay debt, they can be an effective means to quickly reducing the leverage of a buyout.

[d]   Strong Balance Sheet. Fourth, other factors that an equity sponsor will look for in evaluating a buyout candidate are (i) the company's ability to reduce costs and (ii) the target's existing capital structure. The greater the ability to reduce expenses and the less leverage at the company, the greater the opportunity to realize value in the leveraged buyout.

[e]   Ability to Reduce Costs. Lenders into the leveraged buyout will also be concerned with the amount of equity the sponsors and management will inject into the transaction in support of the deal. The greater the amount of equity, the less perceived risk in the transaction. However, the greater the equity, the less potential return there is for the equity sponsors. Typically, the amount of equity in a leveraged buyout will be determined by the current state of the lending markets and the required return of the equity sponsors. To the extent the financing environment is tough, as it was in 2001, the amount of debt lenders are prepared to provide for an LBO will be small, forcing equity sponsors to supply larger amounts of equity capital to finance a transaction.

[7]   Issues and Risks in Leveraged Buyouts

There are a number of risks inherent in leveraged buyouts that begin with the execution of the transaction itself, and continue through the gestation of the LBO through its exit.

[a]   Conflicts of Going Private. As leveraged buyouts most often qualify as going private transactions, they bear many of the same risks as other forms of 13e-3 transactions. For example, in many cases, an equity group with the participation of management sponsors the LBO. In fact, most equity sponsors will not undertake an LBO unless the management team has significant equity at stake in the transaction. Management's participation in the transaction creates a potential conflict in that they have no incentive to help maximize the value of the company for shareholders; rather, they have every incentive to ensure the business is acquired for as low a price as possible. In addition, the management members must determine that the proposed transaction—on the terms that they are offering—is in the best interests of the minority shareholders. Finally, as

members of the buying group, the management team is using the assets and cash flows of the company—owned by the shareholders—to finance their acquisition. This view may conflict with the board's responsibility to shareholders, which is to maximize value. In addition, there may be third party bidders that are able to pay more for the company than the equity sponsor and management group. Finally, shareholders may view the management as self-dealing, which can give rise to substantial litigation.

Because of these issues, the equity sponsor, management group and board of directors must be acutely aware of the process that is undertaken to affect the leveraged buyout. The board of directors must be certain to retain a financial advisor and create a special committee with its own financial advisor to represent the public shareholders. In addition, the special committee should obtain a fairness opinion that states that the financial terms of the transaction are fair to the shareholders. The board must be sure to undergo a process that ensures it has served its fiduciary duty to shareholders.

[b] Bankruptcy. Numerous leveraged buyouts have resulted in bankruptcy, including some of the more famous transactions including Carter Hawley Hale, a department store chain acquired in 1987 that filed for bankruptcy in 1991, and Revco, a drug store chain acquired in 1986 that filed for bankruptcy in 1988. By their very nature, leveraged buyouts entail the use of a high level of debt. Management teams undergoing LBOs may have little experience managing for cash flow to service debt because usually, they are focused on managing for earnings. It is important to make sure the management team understands the difference between running a company for cash flow and running one for earnings, otherwise the transaction runs the risk of heading into bankruptcy.

This is not an ongoing management issue exclusively; rather, it is also a matter of ensure that the company is appropriately leveraged at the onset of the deal. While it may be possible to acquire a company using excessive leverage, it may not be prudent to over-lever the company at the outset because of the high risk of financial distress.

[c] Exit Strategy. In order for a leveraged buyout to be successful, the acquirer must feel comfortable that a viable exit strategy will exist in a few years. These exit strategies can range from a recapitalization of the company to a sale to an initial public offering. Therefore, while one of the principal goals of an LBO is to generate strong cash flows to repay debt, it is important not to forget that reinvestment in capital equipment and research and development, as well as marketing, is important to ensure the viability of future growth of the company.

[d] Board Control. In leveraged buyouts, a board of directors is usually put in place to represent the different shareholder groups. Buyouts sponsored by an institutional sponsor will usually have board representation from the equity sponsor. It is common to have representatives of management on the board, as well as outside third parties. The equity sponsor will wish to ensure they have effective control of the board as they are likely to have provided

the majority of the equity required to finance the transaction. Management however, should not forget that their expertise is required to ensure the viability of the transaction, and therefore should have adequate voice or representation on the board.

Board control can become an issue in leveraged buyouts under different scenarios when significant decisions are at hand. Numerous decisions will be made at the board level including significant capital expenditures, mergers and acquisitions, divestitures, financing decisions and the timing and form of the exit. These decisions will often need to balance the equity sponsor's desire to realize a return on their investment, management's desire to grow the business, and the company's need to repay debt.

[e]   Forced Sale. One area where board control becomes significant is in the company's potential exit strategy. To the extent the board is controlled by any one group, they may be in a position to force a sale of the company which may or may not be a preferred alternative of the other board members and management.

[f]   Management Equity and Vesting. Most leveraged buyouts are undertaken in concert with management, whereby the management team both invests their own equity in the transaction, and is granted additional equity in the company over time as they meet various performance objectives. In structuring the equity participation of management, one should be mindful of a number of issues. First, a percentage of the company's equity should be reserved for current and future management and employees. It is typical to see anywhere from 5% to 25% of the company's equity reserved for management and employees between the time the company goes private and the time it is taken public or sold. Of that amount, a significant portion — 2%–10% — is usually reserved for the chief executive officer and additional 5–10% is reserved for the rest of the senior management team. The remaining equity is held for employees.

While the equity provided to management can come in many forms, more often than not, it is awarded as options that vest over a period of time, for example, four years. These options may vest monthly, quarterly or annually, however, it is not unusual to see an initial period of time, for example, one year, before which any options may vest. This initial period is known as the cliff period.

[8]   Structuring a Leveraged Buyout

[a]   Sources of Financing in Leveraged Buyouts. Leveraged buyouts are typically financed with two primary forms of debt: secured and unsecured. Secured debt is typically collateralized with the assets of the company, and is often sub-categorized into senior secured debt and intermediate secured debt. Unsecured debt is not secured by the assets of the corporation, yet offers a higher return to lenders to counter balance the additional risk of the debt. Unsecured debt is also known as subordinated or junior-subordinated debt.

[i]   Secured Debt. Secured debt can come in the form of senior debt and intermediate term debt. Typically, senior debt is secured

by the assets of the company, and will look to those assets as protection in a downside scenario. Types of assets that can be used to secure debt include everything from the company's plant and equipment to its receivable and inventories. Lenders will provide funds that represent a percentage of the value of the assets. Theses percentages will vary depending on current market conditions. For example, lenders will loan up to 50% of the inventories of a company plus from 40–80% of a company's projected receivables.

Intermediate term debt is also usually secured with certain assets of the company, yet the claim on the assets is subordinated to the claim of the senior debt lenders. Assets that will typically support intermediate term debt include real estate.

Secured debt is most often obtained from banks or other asset-based lending institutions. The cost of secured debt will depend on the current state of the lending environment as well as the structure of the interest rate environment.

[ii] Unsecured Debt. Unsecured debt is also known as subordinated debt. It has a claim on assets that is junior or subordinated to the secured debt. It is also known as mezzanine financing or mezzanine debt. This type of debt comes with a higher interest rate than that of secured debt, and may also call for warrants to be provided to the lender to compensate them for the incremental risk in this layer of capital.

On occasion, leveraged buyouts are financed completely through unsecured debt, and are hence known as cash flow LBOs. This occurs in cases where there are few assets to secure the debt but where there are predictable cash flows. The interest rate structure on these types of buyouts call for higher interest rates as well as warrants or other equity participation to the lenders to compensate for the increased risk in the deal.

[iii] High Yield Debt. One form of unsecured debt is high yield debt, otherwise known as "junk bonds," which have become an integral part of the corporate financing of acquisitions, in particular, leveraged buyouts. While inferior grade bonds have been in use for decades, they rose to prominence in the 1980s when Drexel Burnham Lambert, the now defunct investment bank, began to underwrite high yield debt on a large scale, beginning with a transaction for Texas International in 1977. Drexel was critical to development of the junk bond market in that it served not only as underwriter for the bonds, but as market maker as well.

The high yield market reached a peak in 1998 with over $120 billion in bonds underwritten in the market. The growth in the market has been as a result of strong institutional demand from investors. Typical investors in junk bonds include insurance companies, mutual funds, pension funds and foreign investors.

High yield debt commands a higher interest rate than other forms of debt financing, as a result of the higher embedded risk in the product. The premium rate compensates investors for both the default risk on the high yield debt as well as the liquidity risk, or lack of liquidity in the secondary markets. In a study by Marshall Blume, Donald Keim and Sandeep Patel, they found that high yield bonds commanded a significantly higher return over high-grade bonds, but a lower

Exhibit 16-9
Capital Structure for a Leveraged Buyout

Type of Capital	Percent of Capitalization	Source of Capital
Common stock	5–20%	Equity sponsors, insurance companies
Preferred Stock	10–15%	Equity sponsors, insurance companies
Subordinated Debt	10–20%	Life insurance companies, commercial banks, public markets, LBO-specific funds
Senior Unsecured Debt	20–40%	Commercial banks, life insurance companies
Senior Secured Debt	40–50%	Commercial banks, life insurance companies, asset-based lenders
Short Term Debt	5–15%	Commercial banks; asset-based lenders

return over the S&P 500.[17] As an example, for the period 1977 through 1989, they found that high yield bonds had an average annual return of 10.2% while high grade bonds and the S&P 500 had returns of 9.7% and 14.6% respectively.

[b]   LBO Capital Structure. The capital structure of a typical LBO includes different forms of debt and equity, and will depend on the state of the financing market, the return requirements of the equity sponsors, and the cash flow and asset characteristics of the target company. Exhibit 16-9 provides an illustrative capital structure for a leveraged buyout.

[9]   Creating Value with Leveraged Buyouts

Leveraged buyouts have been used as a means to create value for shareholders from multiple perspectives. First, some public companies may face periods in their life cycle where the stock is underappreciated by the market. The research community may have dropped coverage; institutional investors may have lost interest, and the company's trading volume may have tailed off. As a consequence, the company's stock price may be languishing. Management and the board of directors may feel that the company is undervalued by the market and that the benefits of being a public company have eroded. Under these circumstances, a leveraged buyout may be used to take the company private in a manner that delivers a premium purchase price to public shareholders that may not be achievable if the company were left to trade publicly.

Second, an LBO may be used by a company wishing to divest a subsidiary or division. The parent company may retain equity in the subsidiary in addition to realizing value from the sale of the business to management and the equity sponsor. The benefit of this approach is the ability to generate cash proceeds from the sale yet also garner significant upside from the leveraged buyout equity returns.

---

17. Blume, Marshall E., Donald E. Keim, and Sandeep A. Patel, "Returns and Volatility of Low Grade Bonds: 1977–1989," *Journal of Finance* 46, 49–74, (March 1991).

As a private company, a business that has undergone a leveraged buyout is no longer subject to the scrutiny of the public markets and can focus on building value over the longer term. In addition, it is no longer subject to the cost of maintaining a public company, having to pay for listing fees and investor relations. These expenses can be reallocated to areas of productive investment that can create value for the company long term. Additionally, as the company is taken private, the equity of the firm can be redistributed to management and other employees, providing attractive incentives to deliver attractive financial and operating results.

[10] Leveraged Buyouts Versus Leveraged Recapitalizations

Leveraged buyouts and recapitalizations share a number of similarities. They both rely on companies that share the same attributes in terms of cash flows, balance sheet strength, management expertise and company and industry dynamics. In addition, they both achieve a similar endgame, i.e., concentrating the equity of the target company in the hands of a small group of shareholders and creating value for those shareholders by using the cash flows of the company to repay excess quantities of debt assumed in the transaction. Once the debt is repaid, as the equity is owned by the same small group of shareholders, it is worth considerably more than when the transaction took place — the value of the debt is effectively transferred to shareholders by virtue of the debt being repaid down using the company's cash flows.

One of the more significant advantages of both transaction types is the shelter from taxes the debt provides the operating earnings. The interest expense assumed in the transaction is tax deductible and thereby preserves some of the cash flows that are available to repay debt.

As a defensive tactic, recapitalizations have certain benefits over recapitalizations. For example, if a company attempts a leveraged buyout at a given price, it is difficult for it to turn away a third party offer at a higher price. A recapitalization, on the other hand, gives current shareholders value at the time of the deal as well as an ongoing stake in the company post transaction. The recapitalization serves to sidestep the company's Revlon duties, i.e., the need to put the company up for sale to the highest bidder.

[11] Case Study: Citadel Communications

On January 16, 2001, Citadel Communications announced that it would be acquired by Forstmann Little & Co. for $26 per share or approximately $2.0 billion in cash. Citadel Communications is the sixth largest radio broadcasting company in the United States. It owns or operates 140 FM and 65 AM stations concentrated in 42 mid-sized markets. The company generated approximately $285 million in revenues.

The board of directors of Citadel was advised by Credit Suisse First Boston who provided a fairness opinion opining that the consideration to be received by Citadel shareholders was fair from a financial point of view.

The transaction was structured as a merger between Citadel and a subsidiary of Forstmann Little, and as such, Citadel sought shareholder approval for the transaction. Citadel and Forstmann Little entered into a non-solicitation agreement that prevented Citadel from seeking other acquisition proposals, and required it to terminate any ongoing acquisition discussions. Citadel also agreed to pay to Forstmann Little a termination fee of a minimum of $10 million in the event that the company entered into an acquisition agreement with a third party prior to the completion of the Forstmann Little acquisition, or if within 12 months of terminating the agreement with Forstmann Little, it entered into an agreement to be acquired by a third party.

The transaction was approved by shareholders of the company on April 26, 2001. The transaction closed in June 2001. The $26 per share purchase price represented a 49% premium over Citadel's stock price prior to the announcement. Forstmann Little provided $1.5 billion in equity financing while the remaining $500 million was provided by a consortium of banks including J.P. Morgan Chase.

§ 16.05   TECHNIQUES FOR GOING PRIVATE

The structure of a going private transaction can vary depending on the specific circumstances of each deal. It will depend on whether the transaction is undertaken by a controlling shareholder, the issuer or a third party, needs shareholder approval, or is for stock or cash. The most common techniques for undertaking a going private transaction are a cash tender offer and a one-step, or long-form, merger.

[A]   Cash Tender Offer Followed by Clean-Up Merger

In a cash tender offer, the public shares of the target company are acquired for cash. If the cash tender offer results in 90% ownership by the acquirer, a second-step merger "short-form" can be performed, which can be accomplished quite rapidly. A short-form merger is accomplished by filing a certificate with the secretary of state or corporation commission. The shares held by the remaining minority shareholders are cancelled without the need for a shareholder meeting or to solicit proxies.

The transaction is subject to the tender offer rules as well as the going private rules. The tender offer rules require various filings depending on who is actually making the tender offer, and what that person's relationship is to the issuer.

[1]   Issuer Tender Offers

A cash tender offer by the issuer is governed by Rule 13e-4, and a Schedule 13E-4, *Issuer Tender Offer Statement* must be filed. Rule 13e-4 governs the filing, dissemination, disclosure and other requirements of issuer tender offers, regardless of whether or not the transaction qualifies as a going private transaction. Schedule 13E-4 must be filed prior to the commencement of the tender offer. Rule 13e-3 articulates a number of rules that govern issuer tender offers. Specifically, an issuer tender offer must remain open for 20 business days. Any time there is a change in the terms of the cash tender offer, the tender period is extended for ten business days. A change in the terms can mean a greater than 2% change in the amount of securities to be purchased, a change in the consideration to be given in the transaction, or a change in the dealer's solicitation fee. In addition, a shareholder who has tendered shares into the tender offer, can withdraw those shares at any time up to the closing of the tender offer, and, if the shares have not been accepted for payment, for up to 40 days post commencement of the tender offer.

The information included in the 13E-4 must be included in the tender offer document. The information disseminated depends on the type of cash tender offer. If the cash tender offer will result in a going private transaction, the information must be published. If the transaction does not result in a going private transaction, the information may be published in summary form. The offering must be distributed to those who request it. The issuer may always mail the tender documents to shareholders. The specific requirements of Rule 13e-4 and Schedule 13E-4 are detailed in Section 16.06.

If an issuer tender offer results in a going private transaction, the 13e-3 disclosure and filing requirements must also be met. Schedule 13E-3 must be filed at the same time, along with the tender offer documents, and must be sent to shareholders as well.

If the issuer makes any solicitations or recommendations, it must file a Schedule 14D-9 which must detail any negotiations the issuer has had with respect to alternative merger or other transactions, any material change in financial performance, or any change or sale in assets that would be material to the transaction.

[2] Third Party Tender Offers

A third party tender offer is one where a person, other than the issuer, seeks to acquire, directly or indirectly, greater than 5% of the equity securities of the company. These types of tender offers are governed by Regulations 14D and 14E. These regulations cover the filing, dissemination, disclosure and other requirements of third party tender offers. Specifically, third party tender offers must remain open for 20 business days. Any time there is a change in the terms of the offer, the offer must remain open for an additional ten business days. Shares tendered may be withdrawn at any time up till the closing of the tender offer. In addition, deposited shares may be withdrawn up to 60 days after the commencement of the offer. If more shares are tendered than called for, the shares are to be accepted on a pro rata basis, based on the number of shares tendered by the shareholders during the first ten business days of the tender offer.

Schedule TO, *Tender Offer Statement*, must be filed with the SEC upon the commencement of the tender offer. A copy of the Tender Offer Statement must be hand-delivered to the target company and must be sent to the exchange where the company is listed or to the NASDQ to the extent the shares are quoted there.

If the third party uses solicitations or recommendations of third parties, it must file a Schedule 14D-9, which is governed by Rule 14d-9. Schedule 14D-9 requires disclosure of the person making the solicitation or recommendation and the relationships between that party and the party making the offer. In addition, the schedule requires disclosure of a transaction in the target's stock within the prior 60 days.

The specific requirements of Regulations 14D and 14E are detailed in Section 16.06.

If a third party tender offer qualifies for a going private transaction, Rule 13e-3 must be complied with and Schedule 13E-3 must be filed.

If the third party acquires greater than 10% of the target's stock in the open market prior to the tender offer, it must file a Schedule 13D which is governed under Section 13(d) of the Exchange Act. This section requires that any person who directly or indirectly acquires greater than 5% of a Section 12 company's securities, must file Schedule 13D within ten business days of the purchase, and send a copy of the filing to the target. Schedule 13D is used to identify, among other things, who the acquirer is, which securities it has purchased, and the acquirer's interest with respect to its acquisition of those securities. The requirements of Schedule 13D are provided in section G.

[3] Affiliate Tender Offers

An affiliate tender offer is one that is made by an affiliate of the issuer. An affiliate is defined by the SEC as "a person that directly or indirectly through one or more intermediaries controls, is controlled by, or is under common control with the issuer." Affiliate tender offers fall under Regulations 14D and 14E, where the requirements are the same as those for third party tender offers. In addition, if the transaction qualifies as a going private transaction, the requirements and filings of Rule 13e-3 must be met. Furthermore, if the affiliate uses third party solicitations or recommendations, Schedule 14D-9 must be filed.

[4] Tender Offers Requiring Shareholder Approval

In transactions where shareholder approval is required, a proxy statement must be filed and sent to shareholders. Proxy statements are disclosure documents that provide information to shareholders in cases that require shareholder approval, and are governed by Regulation 14A. The proxy statement provides sufficient information for shareholders that they can make a well-informed decision with respect to voting in favor or against the transaction. The statement must be filed with the SEC at least ten business days prior to it being mailed to shareholders. The requirements of Regulation 14A are detailed in Section 16.06.

In tender offer situations, shareholders do not necessarily have the ability to take issue with the financial fairness of the transaction, as they don't have to accept the offer. They may reject it.

[5] Key Timing Events

Cash tender offers can take upwards of 12 weeks to complete. Exhibit 16-10 outlines the time required to complete each step of a cash tender offer followed by a short-form merger.

Exhibit 16-10
Time Line for a Cash Tender Offer Followed by a Short-Form Merger

Time Required	Event
Week1	Process begins. Special committee is formed and the financial advisors to the special committee begin their valuation work.
Weeks 2–4	Negotiation takes place between the special committee and the parent. At the end of the negotiation, the transaction is announced. During this time, the tender offer documents as well as the 13E-3 disclosure documents are prepared. The board of directors then approves the transaction and the tender offer and 13-E3 documents are filed with the SEC.
1–2 Weeks	The SEC approves the tender offer and 13E-3 documents and other materials are mailed to shareholders and the tender documents are published in the newspaper.
20 Business Days	The tender offer remains open for 20 business days, at the end of which, the tender closes.
1 Day	If the acquirer is successful in tendering for greater than 90% of the shares, the transaction is completed through a short-form merger.

[B] One-Step Merger Voted on by Shareholders

In a one-step merger, shareholders vote on the transaction by virtue of a proxy that is mailed to shareholders in advance of the transaction. In this case, it may be desirable to ask for a majority of the minority shareholders to vote in favor of the transaction, in which case it can provide further protection to the board of directors of the subsidiary as well as any special committee to the board of directors that they have served their fiduciary duties to shareholders.

In these situations, shareholders may still have dissenter's rights; however, by virtue of the vote, it implies that the minority shareholders are informed regarding the transaction, and therefore it shifts the burden of proving the fairness of the transaction to any plaintiffs in litigation. In fact, instead of simply establishing that the transaction was not fair, the plaintiffs must prove that the transaction was not fair.

[1] Key Timing Events

The overall process for a one-step merger can take upwards of 16 weeks. Exhibit 16-11 outlines the time required for each step of the process.

[C] Structural Considerations in Going Private Transactions

Despite the many techniques available to affect a going private transaction, there are a number of issues to consider prior to pursuing a given course. First, will the transaction be affected using cash or stock? Cash transactions will typically take

Exhibit 16-11
Time Line for a One-Step Merger Transaction

Time Required	Event
1 Week	Process begins. Special committee is put in place and evaluation work is performed by the financial advisors to the special committee of the board of directors.
2–4 Weeks	Transaction Announced. After considerable review by parent, subsidiary, the board of directors of both companies, including the special committee representing the minority shareholders, and their respective legal and financial advisors.
2–4 Weeks	Filing documents are prepared including merger proxy and 13E-3 and are filed with the SEC.
4–5 Weeks	The SEC reviews the documents, and after they are approved, are mailed to shareholders.
4–6 Weeks	Shareholders receive the documents and the solicitation process begins. At the end of this period, the shareholders vote on the transaction, and if approved, the transaction is consummated.

the form of a cash tender offer whereas stock transactions will take the form of an exchange offer or merger. In a cash tender offer, the shareholders will usually receive their money before a long-form merger that requires shareholder approval. The tender offer documents are not reviewed by the SEC prior to the tender offer, unlike a transaction that requires shareholder approval where the proxy statement must be reviewed by the SEC prior to mailing it to shareholders. If the transaction is a cash tender offer, a follow-up question is whether it is possible to obtain 90% of the target's shares in order to use a short-form merger to squeeze-out the remaining shareholders? Second, will the acquirer require or seek shareholder approval? Specifically, will the acquirer seek to get a majority of the minority shareholders to vote in favor of the deal? Seeking shareholder approval, in particular, a majority of the minority, will provide additional protection to the board of directors and special committee; however, it introduces significant delay into the transaction. In merger situations, the shareholder approval will cause the transaction to be subject to the entire fairness standard not just the standards of the normal business judgment rule.

§ 16.06   GOING PRIVATE FILING AND DISCLOSURE REQUIREMENTS

Going private transactions are governed by the disclosure requirements of the Securities and Exchange Commission, while the matters of fairness of the transaction are governed by the corporate laws of individual states. In many states, well-established precedents make it clear that minority shareholders cannot block going private transactions, except in cases where fraud can be demonstrated. The sole and exclusive remedy for dissenting stockholders is appraisal proceedings, whereby stockholders can seek a court determination of the fair value of their shares. Shareholders that tender their shares into a transaction forego their appraisal rights. Under the concept of "fair dealing," however, there is an obligation on the part of the majority stockholder to provide full and accurate disclosure. The adequacy of disclosure is thus the subject of almost all litigation that arises in a going private transaction. Courts generally inquire into the fairness of the process pursuant to which the public shares were acquired. Thus, "procedural fairness" becomes a key focus. Certain procedural devices have been recognized by the courts as helpful in assuring procedural fairness: establishment of an independent process and the creation of an independent board or special committee to review the transaction, and receipt of a fairness opinion by an independent investment banker.

The role of the SEC is to ensure that the going private transactions provide adequate disclosure of the transaction in order to allow shareholders to make an informed decision regarding the transaction. Going private transactions are subject to a great deal more disclosure than other transactions. These requirements relate not just to the going private transaction, but also to the form of going private transaction, whether through tender offer or merger, or whether the transaction is by an affiliate or a third party. Exhibit 16-12 provides an overview of the rules and

Exhibit 16-12
Rules, Regulations and Schedules Under Going Private Transactions

| | Rule 13e-3 Schedule 13E-3[18] | Rule 13e-4 Schedule 13E-4 | Regulations | | | | Forms & Schedules | |
			14A[19]	14C	14D Schedule 14D-9	14E	Schedule 14D-1	Schedule 13D
Issuer Tender Offer	X	X	X	X[20]	X			
Third Party Tender Offer	X		X		X	X	X	X[21]
Affiliate Tender Offer	X		X		X	X		
Long-Form Merger	X		X					

---

18. Any transaction that qualifies as a going private transaction must comply with Rule 13e-3.

19. Any transaction that seeks or requires shareholder approval is subject to Regulation 14A and must file and disseminate a Proxy Statement.

20. In the event the issuer does not seek solicit proxies, it must file an information statement.

21. Filed if third party acquires greater than 5% of the target.

regulations as well as the filings required under each type of going private transaction.

[A]   Rule 13e-3 and Schedule 13E-3

The disclosure requirements for going private transactions are governed by Rule 13e-3, *Going Private Transactions*, of the Securities and Exchange Act of 1934, which requires detailed disclosure about the going private transaction, including:

- Whether the company believes the transaction is fair to stockholders and the basis for that belief.

- Whether the transaction is structured to require the approval of a majority of disinterested shares.

- Whether the independent directors have retained an independent representative to negotiate on behalf of the public stockholders.

- Whether the transaction was approved by a majority of disinterested directors.

- Whether the company has received any report, opinion or appraisal from an outside party related to the 13e-3 transaction.

SEC disclosure requirements are particularly strict about disclosure of third party valuations that have been prepared within the last two years. In essence, the SEC seeks to force the party seeking to go private to disclose all information that might be relevant to a determination of whether the price being offered is "fair" to the stockholders.

The goal of Rule 13e-3 and the companion Schedule 13E-3 is to provide enough information to public shareholders that they can make an informed decision over whether the board of directors, management and/or the controlling shareholder are performing their fiduciary obligations to public shareholders in the going private transaction. The rule does not require that the board of directors establish an independent committee to review the going private transaction or other third party offers. In addition, it does not require that the board obtain a fairness opinion to support the transaction. Rather, it mandates disclosure of the process the board took in evaluating the transaction and in establishing the fairness of the price paid. This would suggest, that even though a board is not required to take the aforementioned steps, it behooves them to do so, because if they cannot establish the fairness of process and price, they may be exposed to litigation.

The approach to regulating going private transactions is to use federal securities laws to enforce appropriate disclosure of the transaction, yet rely on state law to evaluate the merits of fairness in the transaction. Under Delaware law, going private transactions are subject to the entire fairness standard, which incorporates fair dealing and fair price. Fair dealing deals with the overall timing, process and structure of the transaction, and incorporates the disclosure of such. Fair price relates to the amount and terms of consideration paid in the transaction.

The case, *Weinberger v. UOP* made significant progress in protecting the rights of minority shareholders. First, the case made appraisal rights the exclusive remedy of the minority shareholders in merger situations, when the only issue under contention is price. In addition, Weinberger shifted to the plaintiff the burden of establishing that a transaction is not fair, if the transaction is approved by a majority of the minority shareholders. The implications of these two points is that, in contrast to many other types of transactions where shareholders rely on class action litigation, the minority shareholders must rely on appraisal rights. Consequently, in the absence of fraud or breach of fiduciary duty by the board of directors, shareholders' ability to block going private transactions has been dramatically reduced.

In going private transactions where there is a tender offer by a controlling shareholder, the shareholders have the ability to freely accept or reject the offer. Consequently, the Weinberger fair price issues do not necessarily apply. In tender offers, in contrast to mergers, shareholders do not have appraisal rights or the option of dissent. Disclosure therefore in mergers are far more extensive than in tender offers, and require disclosure of appraisals, projections and other information that enables the shareholder to make an informed decision.

Some going private transactions are not subject to Rule 13e-3. These include the second step of a transaction where the going private transaction occurs within one year of a tender offer by or on behalf of a third party bidder that then becomes an affiliate of the issuer.[22] The bidder may only be exempt however if it previously made the requisite disclosures of Rule 13e-3. The rule also does not apply to situations where the stock of the minority shareholders is exchanged for stock having essentially the same rights as those exchanged.[23]

The entity engaged in a going private transaction must file Schedule 13E-3 with the SEC, including any ongoing amendments as well as the final amendment that includes the results of the going private transaction.

If the going private transaction involves a solicitation of proxies subject to Regulation 14A, if there are securities to be issued in the transaction, or the going private transaction is the result of a third party tender offer, the material disclosures required of Rule 13e-3 must be combined with the proxy statement, information statement, prospectus or tender offer material sent to shareholders.

If the going private transaction involves a purchase of securities by the issuer or an affiliate, or through a vote, consent, authorization, or distribution of information statements, the issuer or affiliate must disseminate the relevant 13e-3 disclosure information no later than 20 days prior to any purchase, vote, consent or authorization, or prior to any meeting date with respect to the distribution of information statements, or prior to the earliest date on which a corporate action is taken by means of a written authorization or written consent of shareholders. However, if the purchase of securities in the going private transaction is subject to a tender offer, the disclosure information must be disseminated subject to Rule 13e-4, *Tender Offers by Issuers*, no later than ten business days prior to any purchase

---

22. Exchange Act Rule 13e-3(g)(1).
23. Exchange Act Rule 13e-3(g)(2).

under the tender offer. This information must be disseminated to shareholders who are record holders of the securities on a date not more than 20 days prior to the dissemination of the information.

If the going private transaction is subject to a tender offer subject to Regulation 14D or Rule 13e-4, the tender offer containing the Rule 13e-3 disclosure information must be published or disseminated subject to Regulation 14D or Rule 13e-4 to shareholders.

Rule 13e-3 requires the filing of Schedule 13E-3 in conjunction with a going private transaction. The document contains the required disclosures regarding the transaction. The schedule must be filed with the SEC at the times that correspond below to the type of going private transaction that is undertaken.

- *Regulation 14A or 14C solicitations or information statements*: Schedule 13E-3 must be filed at the same time as the filing is made for the preliminary or definitive soliciting materials or information statement.

- *Registration Statement under Securities Act of 1933*: Schedule 13E-3 must be filed at the same time as the registration statement is filed.

- *Tender Offer*: Schedule 13E-3 must be filed as soon as practicable on the date the tender offer is published, sent or given to shareholders.

- *Purchase of Securities*: Schedule 13E-3 must be filed at least 30 days prior to the purchase of any securities subject to the going private transactions, if the transaction does not involve a solicitation, information statement, registration of securities or a tender offer.

- *Series of Transactions*: If the going private transaction involves a series of transactions, Schedule 13E-3 must be filed at the initiation of each of the prior transactions, and then updated upon the occurrence of each subsequent transaction.

If the going private transaction involves a tender offer, then a combined statement on Schedule 13E-3 and Schedule TO may be filed.

The material information that must be disclosed in Schedule 13E-3 includes the following:

- Summary term sheet describing the material terms of the proposed transaction;

- Information on the target subject to the going private transaction;

- The identity of the person filing the Schedule;

- The material terms of the transaction;

- Any past contacts, transactions, negotiations or agreements between the parties;

- The purpose of and reasons for the transaction;

- The fairness of the transaction including any reports, opinions and appraisals;

- Source and amounts of funds for the transaction;

- The number and percentage of securities owned by the filing person;

- Any recommendations of others;

- Disclosure of all persons that are directly or indirectly employed, retained or to be compensated to make solicitations or recommendations.

[B]   Rule 13e-4

Rule 13e-4, *Tender Offers by Issuers*, governs tender offers by issuers, and outlines the filing, dissemination, and disclosure requirements for cash tender offers or exchange offers that are made by the issuer for its own securities. Per the SEC, an issuer tender offer refers to a tender offer for, or a request or invitation for tenders of, any class of equity security, made by the issuer of such class of equity security or by an affiliate of such issuer. Rule 13e-4 applies not just to going private transactions, but also in cases that are irrespective of the intent to go private.

Rule 13e-4 requires that the issuer or the affiliate making the tender offer file with the SEC, Schedule TO, *Tender Offer Statement*, all written communications by the issuer or affiliate relating to the issuer tender offer, any amendments Schedule TO, and the final amendment to Schedule TO reporting the results of the issuer tender offer.

The issuer or affiliate making the tender offer must disclose a summary term sheet for the transaction, as well as the other information in Schedule TO, except Item 12. If there are any material changes in the information previously disclosed, the changes must be promptly disclosed to security holders.

The information to be disclosed should be disseminated to security holders in the following ways. If the consideration in the issuer tender offer is exclusively cash and/or securities exempt from registration, then the information is disseminated by (i) long-form publication in a newspaper or newspapers on the date of commencement of the tender offer; (ii) mailing or furnishing a statement containing the information to each security holder, by contacting each participant on the most recent security position listing of any clearing agency who represents the security holders, by furnishing to the participant enough copies of the information to make it available to the beneficial owners, and by agreeing to reimburse each participant for forwarding the information to beneficial owners. If the transaction is not a going private transaction, then the information can be disseminated by summary publication and by mailing or furnishing the statement and transmittal letter to any security holder who requests a copy of such.

If the tender offer consideration consists solely or partially of securities registered under the Securities Act of 1933, a registration statement containing all the required information, a prospectus and a letter of transmittal is delivered to shareholders.

Under Rule 13e-4, the issuer tender offer must remain open for at least 20 business days from commencement, and at least ten business days from the date of an increase or decrease in the percentage of the class of securities being sought or the consideration offered. In addition, securities that are tendered pursuant to the issuer tender offer may be withdrawn at any time during which the tender offer is open, and if not yet accepted for payment, after the expiration of forty business days from the commencement of the tender offer.

If the issuer or affiliate tenders for less than all of the securities of a class, and a number of shares is tendered that exceeds the amount sought, the issuer or affiliate will accept and pay for those securities on a pro rata basis. Much like the requirements under Rule 13d-10, if the issuer or affiliate increases the amount of consideration to be paid pursuant to the tender offer, the issuer or affiliate shall pay the increased amount to all security holders who have tendered their shares. The issuer or affiliate making the tender offer shall either pay for the securities or return the tendered securities promptly after the termination or withdrawal of the tender offer. In addition, the issuer or affiliate may not make any purchases of securities subject to the tender offer until at least ten business days after the date of termination of the issuer tender offer.

[C]   Schedule TO

Schedule TO, *Tender Offer Statement,* must be filed in the case of tender offers, whether in the context of a going private transaction or not. Schedule TO applies to third party tender offers subject to Rule 14d-1, issuer tender offers subject to Rule 13e-4, going private transactions subject to Rule 13e-3, and to amendments to Schedule 13D under Rule 13d-2.

Schedule TO requires the disclosure of the following information, much of which are the same items as Schedule 13E-3.

- Summary term sheet;
- Information on the target company;
- Identity of the filing person;
- Terms of the transaction;
- Past contacts, transactions, negotiations and agreements between the parties;
- Purpose of and plans for the transaction;
- Source and amounts of funds for the transaction;
- The number and percentage shares owned in the target by the filer;
- Persons directly or indirectly retained, employed or compensated to make solicitations or recommendations;
- Information required by Schedule 13E-3.

[D] Regulation 14D

[1] Regulation 14D

Regulation 14D pertains to any tender offer by an affiliate of the issuer or a third party and governs the filing, disclosure and dissemination of information in tender offers commenced by a person other than the issuer. Following are some of the more significant provisions of Regulation 14D.

- A tender offer is deemed to have commenced at 12:01 am on the date on which the bidder first publishes, sends or gives the tender offer material to security holders. Specifically, the tender offer material must include the means for the security holder to tender their shares. In addition, the bidder will have filed Schedule TO with the SEC no later than the date of the communication to shareholders, and the bidder must have delivered to the target company the communications related to the transaction.

- A bidder may not tender for the shares of a company unless it has filed a Schedule TO with the SEC as soon as practicable on the date of the commencement of the tender offer, and delivered copies to the target company and to any other bidders that have filed Schedule TO. The bidder must also inform by telephone, and send copies of Schedule TO, to each exchange where the target company's securities are listed or quoted.

- The bidder must also promptly file any amendments to Schedule TO and then file a final amendment to the schedule that reports the final results of the tender offer.

- The bidder must publish, send or give disclosure of the tender offer as soon as practicable on the date of commencement of the tender offer. For cash tender offers and exempt securities offers, the bidder must publish a long-form publication in a newspaper. If the tender offer is not a going private transaction, the bidder may publish the tender offer in summary form and mail the tender offer materials to security holders who request the material. For tender offers where the consideration is securities registered under the Securities Act of 1933, a registration statement must be filed and a preliminary.

[2] Rule 14d-9 and Schedule 14D-9

If the third party uses solicitations or recommendations of third parties, it must file a Schedule 14D-9, which is governed by Rule 14D-9. Schedule 14D-9 requires disclosure of the person making the solicitation or recommendation and the relationships between that party and the party making the offer. In addition, the schedule requires disclosure of a transaction in the target's stock within the prior 60 days.

Schedule 14D-9 requires disclosure of the following items:

- Information on the target company including the number of shares outstanding and the principal market in which the securities trade;

- The identity and background of the filing person;

- Any past contacts, transaction, negotiations and agreements between the parties;

- The recommendation of persons involved in the transaction as well as the reasons for the recommendations;

- Persons retained, employed or compensated in making the solicitation or recommendation;

- The interest of the filing person in the securities of the target company;

- The purpose of the transaction and plans or proposals.

[E]   Regulations 14A and 14C

[1]   Regulation 14A

In the event the transaction does not have enough votes to carry shareholder approval, and/or shareholder approval is required, it is governed by Regulation 14A which establishes the rules for the filing and dissemination of a proxy statement on Schedule 14A and the solicitation of proxies. The proxy statement is designed to ensure that shareholders are given the information they need to make a reasonably informed decision. It must be filed in preliminary form with the SEC at least ten days before the date definitive copies are sent to the shareholders. The final proxy must be filed or mailed for filing with the SEC no later than the date it is first distributed to the shareholders. Copies of the proxy must be sent to each of the national exchanges where the company is listed or quoted.

In the context of Regulation 14A, a solicitation of proxies includes "any request for a proxy whether or not accompanied by or included in a form of proxy; any request to execute or not to execute, or to evoke, a proxy; or the furnishing of a form of proxy or other communication to security holders under circumstances reasonably calculated to result in the procurement, withholding or revocation of a proxy."[24] While there are certain exceptions, Rule 14A applies to every solicitation of securities of a registered company subject to Section 12 of the Act.

[2]   Schedule 14A

The proxy must disclose the material features of the proposed merger/acquisition, a description of the businesses of the purchaser and the target, and detailed financial information on each. Schedule 14A requires disclosure of the following material items:

- Date, time and place of the shareholder meeting;

---

24. Securities and Exchange Commission.

- Any rights there are to revoke the proxy or any limitations on the security holder's ability to exercise the proxy;

- Whether or not there are any dissenter's rights;

- Disclosure of the parties making the solicitation;

- The interest of persons that own securities in the target;

- Who the principal holders of the voting securities are;

- Whether or not securities are to be issued and the amount and title of such securities;

- State the vote required for approval.

[3]   Regulation 14C and Schedule 14C

In the event the transaction does have enough votes and shareholder approval is not required, then it is governed by Regulation 14C and an information statement must be filed. An information statement must be filed if the issuer chooses not to solicit proxies. The information statement requires essentially the same information as the proxy statement. In addition, it requires an item that states that proxies are not being solicited and that security holders are asked not to send in a proxy.

[F]   Regulations 13D and 13G

[1]   Regulation 13D

Regulation 13D requires that any person, or group of persons acting together, who acquired directly or indirectly greater than 5% of the class of any equity security,[25] must file a report on Schedule 13D within ten days disclosing that acquisition with the SEC, and send a copy of the report to the company. Certain entities or persons may file a 13G in lieu of the 13D if, among other things, the person acquired the securities in the ordinary course of his business and not with the purpose of changing or influencing control in the company. At any point that there is a material change in the facts set forth in the 13D, or the intent of the party filing the 13G changes, the party must file an amendment to the original filing, in the case of the 13D, or the party becomes subject to the rules of Regulation 13D, and must file a 13D.

---

25. As per the SEC, an equity security is "any equity security of a class which is registered pursuant to section 12 of the Act, or any equity security of any insurance company which would have been required to be registered except for the exemption contained in section 12(g)(2)(G) of the Act or any equity security issued by a closed-end investment company registered under the Investment Company Act of 1940: provided, such term shall not include securities of a class of non-voting securities."

[2]   Schedules 13D and 13G

Schedule 13D requires a number of disclosures, the material ones as follows:

- The title and class of the equities that have been acquired;
- The identity and background of the filing person;
- The source and amount of funds used in making the acquisition;
- The purpose of the transaction;
- The aggregate number and percentage of the class of securities owned by the filing person;
- All arrangements, contracts, understandings or relationships between the persons named in the filing.

Schedule 13G includes much of the same information required in Schedule 13D, however in summary form.

§ 16.07   TAX ISSUES IN GOING PRIVATE TRANSACTIONS

There are numerous tax considerations in going private transactions, in particular in leveraged buyouts. In the case of issuer tender offers, the issuer, or target, makes a tender offer for its public shares, with the goal of obtaining sufficient shares in the company to take it private. The issuer typically incurs substantial debt to finance the tender offer. In this case, the target will incur no tax unless assets are distributed to accomplish the redemption, or acquisition, of stock. If the target sells assets to raise cash, it may incur a tax liability if there is a gain on the sale of the assets. There is no step-up in the tax basis of the target's assets.

In a cash tender offer, the tendering shareholders will pay a tax if there is a gain on the sale of their stock. Management and/or other owners, who continue as shareholders of the company after the tender offer, will incur no tax. Their basis will continue in the company, and will only incur a tax at the point at which they sell their stock.

One common form of structure used in leveraged buyouts is a newly created company ("Newco") that is formed for the specific purpose of allowing management to exchange their stock in the target for shares in Newco tax free. This structure takes advantage of Section 351 of the Internal Revenue Code. This structure entails the formation of a new holding company to which the management shareholders exchange their shares. Other equity investors in the transaction invest cash in exchange for stock in Newco. Newco then goes out and obtains additional funding with which it will acquire the public shares of the target. The provisions of Section 351 state that this type of structure will recognize the acquisition of the stock of the target for cash and/or notes as an acquisition of stock, and therefore Newco will not incur any tax liability, and will assume the tax attributes of the target company. For this treatment to qualify under Section 351, management and investors must own 80% or more of Newco once the transaction is complete.

§ 16.08   THE ROLE OF THE SPECIAL COMMITTEE AND ITS FINANCIAL ADVISOR

Going private transactions are subject to intense scrutiny and often are held to a higher standard than other transactions. In addition, going private transactions are rife with conflicts, in particular if the transaction involves a controlling shareholder or if the management is working with a third party to acquire the company in a leveraged buyout. Consequently, it is common for the board of directors to put in place a process that ensures it is mindful of its fiduciary duties to shareholders.

The special committee to the board of directors is set up as an independent entity to ensure the transaction is conducted in a fashion that is mindful of the public shareholders' interests. It is important to establish a committee that is as independent as possible with as few ties, financial or otherwise, to the target company, its board of directors or the controlling or affiliated shareholders. The special committee should be given a charter that is broad enough to enable it to retain its own financial advisor and negotiate the terms of the transaction with the acquirer without the influence of the board of directors.

Establishing a fully independent special committee is material to shifting the burden of fairness from the board of directors to the plaintiff having to establish instead that the transaction was unfair to shareholders. In order to establish the arm's-length nature of the committee, it is important to document the process that the special committee and its advisors go through in negotiating the transaction. This information will help establish that the special committee was well informed and took care in making its decision on behalf of the public shareholders.

The special committee will usually retain the services of a financial advisor to advise it with respect to the transaction and provide it with a fairness opinion. The advisor should be selected based on its competence in providing fairness opinions, and it should be determine whether there is any relationship between the advisor or its affiliates and the target, controlling shareholder or affiliates. To the extent there are current or prior relationships between the advisor and the parties involved in the transaction, there may be a real or perceived conflict of interest on the part of the advisor. Another item that can often come under question is the manner in which the advisor is paid for its work on the transaction. To the extent the fee is all contingent on the success of the transaction, a perceived conflict may exist as the advisor is incented to provide an opinion in order to get paid.

The advisor will usually provide a fairness opinion for the special committee that opines on the fairness of the transaction. The opinion should state what due diligence the advisor did in coming to its conclusions, what information it relied upon, and what limitations, if any, were placed on its work. It should be remembered that the financial advisor's opinion as well as the analysis that is presented to the special committee would have to be disclosed.

§ 16.09   SUMMARY

Going private transactions occur quite frequently and are not viewed as particularly difficult transactions to implement. In the absence of fraud, stockholders may have no right in many states to block a going private transaction. The sole and exclusive remedy for minority shareholders may be an appraisal of the "fair value" of their shares. However, generally "frivolous" litigation is relatively common due to the presence of "strike suit" lawyers. Litigation will focus on adequacy of disclosure and compliance with state law and securities law issues. In recent transactions, agreements with "strike suit" lawyers have been reached in coordination with the final recommendation of the independent committee. Agreement with "strike suit" lawyers typically results in a modest incremental cost per share. Procedural "safeguards" such as an independent process and committee and the fairness opinion greatly enhance the view of the transaction by the Delaware courts and the SEC.

For a successful going private transaction, it is important to remember a few points. First, it is important to have an independent special committee representing the public shareholders. Second, a financial advisor should be appointed by the special committee to represent it in the negotiations with the acquirer. Third, the special committee should be in a position to negotiate with the acquirer on an arm's-length basis, without the influence of the board of directors. Fourth, the special committee and its advisors should establish an accurate record of the process that it went through in evaluating the transaction. Fifth, the parties should take care to ensure that the required disclosure documents pertaining to the going private transaction as well as the form of transaction are filed and disseminated to shareholders. Finally, the parties should ensure that the individual requirements of going private transactions as well as the other rules and regulations of the SEC are followed closely.

Minority squeeze-out transactions are a common going private means for reacquiring the public shares of a corporation that is controlled by another parent company. Often, the company taken private was previously the beneficiary of an initial public offering. For a variety of reasons, including poor subsidiary market performance, conflicts between the parent and subsidiary, and the desire to capitalize on synergies between the parent and subsidiary, the parent may wish to take the company private by acquiring the public shares it does not own.

Often, minority squeeze-out transactions can result in litigation, as a result of a conflict that the parent company has in bidding for the minority shares, i.e., it is motivated on the one hand to acquire the shares at as low a price as possible, yet on the other hand, it has a fiduciary obligation to maximize shareholder value on behalf of shareholders. Because of this, minority squeeze-outs, as well as other going private transactions, are subject to intense scrutiny from the legal community, and are subject to extensive disclosure requirements by the Securities and Exchange Commission.

Leveraged buyouts have become quite commonplace as a means to realizing value for shareholders. Typically, shareholders will garner a premium as the stock of the target company is acquired. Targets of leveraged buyouts are usually purchased by a financial sponsor in tandem with management, with the financial sponsor contributing equity to the transaction. The remainder of the purchase price is typically financed with debt that is paid down using the cash flows of the company. In a leveraged buyout, the value created in the pay down of debt transfers to the equity investors, generating an attractive return on investment.

Leveraged buyouts have taken their place as one of the predominant forms of going private transactions. The deals have become increasingly complex over the years, as various financing techniques have proliferated. ESOPs have found a place as a prime vehicle for financing LBOs in that they provide attractive tax benefits to the company and result in a lower cost of overall debt financing to the acquirer. The high yield or junk bond market has proliferated, and now financing a highly leveraged transaction using high yield debt is commonplace. Dedicated LBO funds have raised significant capital for the express purpose of investing in leveraged buyouts.

While leveraged buyouts have generated attractive returns to many investors, they have also had their fair share of failures, and have generated significant controversy. There have been numerous noteworthy bankruptcy filings, including those of Carter Hawley Hale and Revco, and there has been significant litigation in the context of companies going private through a leverage buyout. As a going private transaction, leveraged buyouts are fraught with conflicts and perceived risks of self-dealing by the management team and board of directors. Nevertheless, LBO's are commonplace, and processes and procedures can be put in place to protect the company, board and management from litigation by shareholders.

Chapter 17

FAIRNESS OPINIONS

§ 17.01 OVERVIEW

A fairness opinion is a letter issued by an investment bank that provides the bank's view of the financial terms of a transaction. It is rendered in many types of transactions, including mergers, acquisitions, divestitures, spin-offs, split-offs, joint ventures, minority squeeze outs, and management buyouts. It will state, in the judgment of the investment bank, whether or not the transaction, or the considerations to be issued or received in the transaction is fair to shareholders from a financial point of view.

A fairness opinion is often prepared for the fiduciaries acting on behalf of those individuals with a financial stake in the transaction. Most commonly, it is delivered to the board of directors of a company in order to assist the board in making a decision with respect to the transaction and to help discharge the board's fiduciary duties to shareholders.

Since 1990, there have been approximately 3,790 disclosed fairness opinions written, with 184 written in 2003 alone. Exhibit 17-1 illustrates the trend in the delivery of fairness opinions per year.

§ 17.02 WHY GET A FAIRNESS OPINION?

In the context of mergers and acquisitions, a board of directors has a fiduciary duty to ensure that a transaction is fair to shareholders. Under the business

Exhibit 17-1
Delivered Fairness Opinions: 1990–2003[1]
($ in millions)

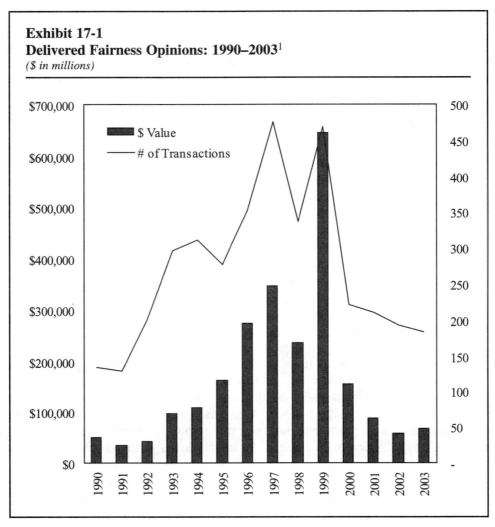

judgment rule,[2] board members are presumed to have acted with due care, in good faith, and with loyalty to shareholders, and thus are protected from liability unless shareholders can prove that in making a business decision, a director acted otherwise. A fairness opinion, along with other expert analyses and presentations by management, legal counsel, and accounting firms, helps the board to discharge its duty to shareholders, and establish that it has acted in good faith, with care and with loyalty to shareholders. First, the fairness opinion provides assistance to the board in making a decision regarding a transaction. Second, it offers objective justification that can be used to persuade shareholders to vote in favor of a transaction. Third, it provides legal protection to a board of directors.

1. Thomson Financial.

2. The Business Judgment Rule is discussed more fully in *Chapter 21: Business Judgment Rule*.

A director's duty of care means that he should make decisions on behalf of shareholders after taking into consideration all available information and after deliberate consideration of all the information at his disposal. In other words, the director needs to act responsibly when making a decision on behalf of stockholders.

A director's duty of loyalty means that he should act in the best interests of the shareholders and/or the entity for which he is a fiduciary. Implicit in this duty is the assumption that the director will act in good faith.

In tandem with the board's duty to shareholders, is its obligation to scrutinize and facilitate the work of the investment bank rendering the opinion. In particular, the board should select an investment banker with care, disclose accurate information to the investment banker, determine whether the investment banker followed accepted valuation procedures, and examine the investment banker's conclusions.

Boards of directors, as well as other fiduciaries, have become increasingly reliant on fairness opinions, as their legal exposure has increased significantly in the last 20 years. In the event a director is found to have breached his duty to shareholders, he can become personally liable for his actions. Several well-known court cases have helped establish the responsibility of a board of directors in certain transactions, most significantly in change of control and merger transactions. Essentially, these cases establish that a board has a responsibility to shareholders to ensure that a transaction is fair to shareholders.

In the case of *Weinberger v. UOP* in 1983, the Delaware court established that even though the board of directors had obtained a fairness opinion in the squeeze out transaction, it had not been prepared with due care and with adequate diligence, and therefore, they found that the directors had not been well informed of the transaction, nor had they proven to follow a process that established good faith consideration of the transaction.

In the case of *Smith v. Van Gorkom* in 1985, shareholders brought a class action suit against the board of directors of Trans-Union Corporation. In the suit, they alleged that the board was negligent in its duty of care to the shareholders for recommending that shareholders approve a merger at $55 per share. Even though the price was well above current market levels, the shareholders alleged the price was inadequate. Through the course of the litigation, the Delaware courts heavily scrutinized the transaction and the process by which the board reached its decision. The outcome of the case was that the court stated that, consistent with the business judgment rule, directors would receive no protection if they made uninformed decisions or poorly advised judgments. Leading up to the board meeting at which the board approved the transaction, Van Gorkom had not included its investment bankers in the negotiations; rather, it was relying on the substantial premium that was paid in the transaction. The courts, however, found that the premium by itself was not sufficient. Rather, they focused on the process the board went through to approve the transaction and found the board to have been inadequately prepared and ill-informed.

In the context of mergers and acquisitions, fairness has a very well articulated meaning. Two tenets form the basis of fairness in this framework: procedural fairness and fairness of price. Procedural fairness relates to the process that a board goes through in evaluating a transaction and deciding on a course of action. Fairness of price relates to the financial fairness of the transaction. From a financial perspective, a fair transaction is one where a rational buyer and seller would the buy or sell stock in the contemplated transaction given the same relevant facts of the situation.

In summary, a fairness opinion can be relied upon by a board of directors or other fiduciary in discharging their duties to shareholders under the business judgment rule. For shareholders to establish a breach of duty, the shareholders must establish that the board of directors knowingly misrepresented the facts in a fairness opinion or did not conduct the transaction with adequate care, even though the board received a fairness opinion.

§ 17.03 FINANCIAL ANALYSIS SUPPORTING THE FAIRNESS OPINION

When preparing a fairness opinion, the investment banker performs significant financial analysis, no different than it would in evaluating the transaction as an advisor. These valuation approaches include DCF analysis, comparable company, and comparable transaction analysis, leveraged buyout analysis, accretion dilution analysis, contribution analysis, AVP analysis, and stock price analysis. These methodologies are summarized briefly below.

Discounted cash flow analysis: This is an intrinsic value methodology that places a value today on the future cash flows of a target company. The cash flows are projected for a defined period, and then discounted back to the present using a discount rate that approximates the target company's cost of capital. An assumption is made about the value of the target company after the projection period. Known as the terminal value, this value is also discounted back to the present, and then added to the present value of the cash flows. This exercise produces a net present value that represents the value today of all the cash flows that can be generated by the target in the future. The DCF analysis yields a going concern value, assuming the company continues to operate going forward the same way it has in the past.

Comparable company analysis: This valuation approach values a company based on the operating multiples and financial ratios of its industry peer group. The multiples of the peer group are applied to the metrics of the target company to yield an implied valuation for the target. This analysis results in a going concern value that does not include any form of takeover or acquisition premium.

Comparable transaction analysis: The comparable transactions method of valuation entails an analysis of the prices paid in deals comparable to the transaction under review. There are two types of comparable transaction analyses: comparable transaction multiples and premiums paid. The acquisition multiples and takeover premiums derived from the analysis are applied to the target's metrics to yield a transaction-based value. Both analyses suggest a range of values that could be paid for a target based on prices paid in comparable transactions. In other words, if the target company was acquired based on the multiples or premiums paid in comparable transactions, an acquirer could expect to pay a price for the target in the range suggested by the valuation approach. Comparable transaction multiples can be used with public and private companies, whereas premiums paid only can be used with public companies.

Leveraged buyout analysis: A leveraged buyout or LBO is the acquisition of a company, division, or subsidiary using a highly leveraged financial structure, whereby the cash flow of the acquired business is used to service and repay the borrowed debt. LBO analysis is often performed when valuing a company in order to determine whether a leveraged buyout is feasible, and if the valuation of the target under an LBO scenario is competitive with that of a takeover valuation. This type of valuation is not often performed for fairness opinions unless the circumstances arise, i.e., a leveraged buyout is a feasible option.

Acquisition at various prices analysis: Prior to performing the accretion/ dilution or contribution analyses, it is helpful to create a spreadsheet that outlines a range of offer prices for the target and the multiples that result from these prices. This analysis, known as an acquisition at various prices or AVP analysis, is a useful reference tool that helps in establishing a range of values that, on the one hand, allows the acquirer to pay a competitive price, yet on the other hand, prevents the acquirer from paying too much.

Accretion/dilution analysis: Accretion/dilution analysis studies the impact of a proposed transaction on the acquirer's earnings per share, and indicates what an acquirer could pay for the target. A transaction that is accretive is one where the earnings per share increase as a result of the transaction, while a dilutive transaction is the opposite.

Contribution analysis: Contribution analysis compares the relative contribution of revenues, EBIT, EBITDA, and net income by the acquirer and target to the combined entity, to the shareholder ownership after the transaction is complete. It provides a measure of reason or fairness, in that, a transaction where substantially more of the revenues and EBITDA, for example, are contributed by the target, but more of the combined company is owned by the acquirer's shareholders, would not seem reasonable and should be questioned.

Stock price analysis: This type of analysis evaluates where a stock has traded in the past and what the basis is that shareholders have in a stock. All of the analyses are taken together. No one analysis is relied upon by itself; rather, it is the totality of all the analyses that substantiates the fairness of the transaction.

§17.04 OTHER ANALYSES PERFORMED

In addition to extensive financial analysis, the investment banker must also review other terms of the proposed transaction in rendering a fairness opinion. Some of these provisions are outlined below.

Terms of the transaction: Beyond the basic financial terms of the transaction, the banker must scrutinize the other provisions in the deal including, employment contracts, non-competition agreements, voting and shareholder agreements, representations, warranties and covenants, termination provisions, no-shop and lock-up provisions, and break-up fees. Each of these provisions, while taken alone may not have a material impact on the value of a transaction, taken together very well could alter the attractiveness of the deal to shareholders from a financial point of view.

Rationale for the transaction: Why a transaction is undertaken is quite important. For example, is the target for sale because of financial difficulties? Will a merger-of-equals create a stronger company, or will customers of one or the other company respond negatively to the deal? What are the merits of the transaction? These types of questions will help assess whether the qualitative merits of the deal support the financial analysis.

Timing of the transaction: All transactions are subject to a timing delay between signing and closing, and it would not be uncommon to find a collar with walk-away provisions structured as a part of the financial terms. The banker should assess the impact of the time to closing on the transaction, and have a view on how the stock market, employees, and customers, as well as other constituents will react to the announcement of the transaction.

Any outside appraisals: Investment bankers should be careful to question whether the company that is the subject of the opinion has received any outside appraisals in recent history. It could be quite damaging if a third party firm had supplied the company with an appraisal that supports a purchase price substantially higher than that considered in the fairness opinion.

Other offers: Much like outside appraisals, the investment banker should ensure that all other outside offers for the company have been disclosed. To the extent there are other offers, the validity of these offers should be explored and either pursued or disqualified for legitimate reasons.

While each of these terms taken by themselves may not be sufficient to raise concern regarding the fairness of the transaction, both the banker and the board of directors should be well informed of the details of each in order to discharge their duty of care and loyalty to shareholders.

§ 17.05   THE INVESTMENT BANKER'S PERSPECTIVE

Investment banks and bankers do not necessarily have a duty to their client's shareholders in delivering a fairness opinion; however, the investment bank does have certain responsibilities and duties of its own to ensure that the fairness opinion will stand up to the scrutiny of the courts. In most situations, the fairness opinion is rendered to the board of directors for its use and is not to be relied upon by shareholders. In this case, in the event a transaction goes sour, the shareholders do not have a direct claim against the investment bank, rather, they have a derivative claim against the bank. However, in the event the fairness opinion is relied upon by shareholders to make a decision with respect to voting in favor of a transaction, the shareholders may have direct claims against the investment bank in the event the transaction does not go well.

The investment banker's liability can come from a number of directions, yet all fairness opinions must survive two primary tests. First, did the investment banker use reasonable care and due diligence in reaching its conclusions? Second, are there any limitations on the investment banker's ability to impartially render the opinion, i.e., conflict of interest, limitation on ability to perform due diligence?

To this end, there are a number of disclosures the investment bank should make in order to establish that they have no conflicts and are in a position to deliver an objective fairness opinion. The disclosures are also meant to enable the board of directors to understand to the greatest extent possible, the issues that may affect the investment banker's ability to render the opinion.

Relationship of the investment bank to the parties in the transaction: In many cases, the investment bank engaged to render the opinion may have a significant relationship with the parties, in which case, it may have a conflict in rendering an objective opinion. For example, if the investment bank has provided equity under-writing services for one of the parties, its objectives may be clouded because of the fees paid it in prior transactions. Another example would be if the investment bank writes research on and/or trades the stock of one or both of the parties.

Significant issues that may affect the investment banker's ability to render the opinion: Other issues may arise that could create a conflict with the investment bank rendering the opinion. For example, bankers are typically paid fees for advising on a transaction as well as for rendering the fairness opinion. In the event the advisory fee is only paid upon completion of the transaction, the investment bank has a potential conflict, since in most cases, the transaction cannot close without the fairness opinion having been rendered.

Scope and limitation of the investment banker's due diligence: Bankers are expected to perform comprehensive due diligence, not only to ensure the financial and other analysis is performed with care, but also to give the board comfort that they are relying on an opinion that has been well prepared. In some cases, a company may not provide all the information that a banker requests, the banker may be told to ignore certain types of information, or the banker may be asked to limit its investigation to certain aspects of the transaction. In all cases, it is prudent for the investment bank to disclose the scope of its due diligence as well as the limitations that were placed on its ability to perform due diligence.

Blue book analysis: As opinions have come under increased scrutiny, the SEC has become more aggressive in ensuring that shareholders receive adequate disclosure regarding the analysis performed by investment banks in fairness opinions. One item the SEC now requires to be disclosed is the presentation prepared for the board of directors by the investment bank in support of its opinion. These presentations are known as "blue books."

In addition to making substantial disclosures, investment bankers can limit or reduce their liability by adhering to a simple set of rules and procedures. First, the investment banker should consider all relevant economic and financial factors in determining the fair price of the transaction. Second, the banker's due diligence should be extensive and should include an examination of all relevant information, on-site inspection of plants, facilities and assets, and interviews with key management. Third, the banker should spend sufficient time in preparing the analysis to establish that the opinion was done with care. Fourth, all assertions should be supported with adequate documentation. Fifth, the banker should use all information available to it, both public and confidential, making sure that it does not rely solely on public information if possible.

§ 17.06   BRING DOWN OPINIONS

A fairness opinion is written as of the date that it is rendered. Typically, it is delivered to the board of directors at the board meeting where the transaction is approved and the merger, acquisition, or other contract is signed. The opinion is written and drafted as of that date, based on information known at the time. The significance of this is that, to the extent the stock price of one or both of the parties changes dramatically after the announcement of the transaction, or some other event occurs that could change the fundamental financial fairness of the transaction, the fairness opinion may no longer support the transaction. This is why it is not uncommon to see investment banks provide a second opinion just prior to the closing of a transaction in order to reaffirm the fairness of the transaction. This opinion is known as a "bring down" opinion.

§ 17.07   FAIRNESS OPINION METHODOLOGY

The fairness opinion letter itself generally follows a fairly standard format, yet it is tailored to the transaction at hand.

First, the letter is typically addressed to the entire board of directors of the company requesting the opinion. Therefore, in the case of an acquirer requesting a fairness opinion regarding the financial fairness of an acquisition, the letter would be addressed to the board of directors of the acquirer.

The initial paragraph provides a summary description of the transaction under contemplation, with reference to the full description of the transaction in the merger agreement. As we can see from the illustration below, Company A is merging with Company B. The investment bank rendering this opinion is representing the acquirer, Company B.

> We understand that Company A, a Delaware corporation (the "Company"), and Company B, a Delaware corporation ("Acquirer"), have entered in a Merger Agreement dated December 31, 2001 (the "Merger Agreement"), pursuant to which the Company will be merged with and into Acquirer, which will be the surviving entity ("Merger"). Pursuant to the Merger, as more fully described in the Merger Agreement and as further described to us by management of Acquirer, we understand that each outstanding share of the common stock, $0.01 par value per share, of the Company (the "Common Stock") will be converted into 0.8534 shares of the common stock, $0.01 par value per share, of Acquirer, subject to certain adjustments (the "Consideration").

In this case, we can see that in the merger, each share of Company A will be converted into 0.8534 shares of Company B common stock, subject to adjustments. These adjustments referenced in the opinion will typically relate to the collar and walk-away, if any, that are outlined in greater detail in the merger agreement.

Once the significant terms of the transaction have been outlined, the letter expresses specifically what the investment bank has been retained to do. In the case of Company A, the investment bank has been asked to render an opinion as to the fairness of the consideration to be paid in the transaction.

> You have asked for our opinion as investment bankers as to whether the Consideration to be paid by Acquirer pursuant to the Merger is fair to Acquirer from a financial point of view, as of the date hereof.

In the event the opinion was being written for the target, the above wording would be changed such that the investment bank is opining on the fairness of the consideration to be received in the merger.

> You have asked for our opinion as investment bankers as to whether the Consideration to be received by the shareholders of the Company pursuant to the Merger is fair to the shareholders of the Company from a financial point of view, as of the date hereof.

Often, the investment bank rendering the opinion will not have been retained to advise the board on the transaction or alternatives to the deal. In addition, there may be specific limitations that the board has placed on the investment bank in the given situation. In these cases, at this point in the opinion, it is appropriate for the investment bank to make its first in a series of disclosures regarding what it has and has not been retained to do. Following is an example of such language.

> As you are aware, we were not retained to, nor did we, advise Acquirer with respect to alternatives to the Merger or Acquirer's underlying decision to proceed with or effect the Merger.

In the case of a fairness opinion written on behalf of a seller, it could be that the investment bank writing the opinion was not asked to seek other buyers for the company, in which case it should also make a disclosure.

> Further, we were not requested to nor did we solicit or assist the Company in soliciting offers for the Company from other potential acquirers.

Once the preliminary description of the transaction and the investment banker's disclosures have been written, the opinion then proceeds with a description of the information that the banker used in preparing its analysis in support of the opinion. Typically, this will include public and private information on the target company, and in the case of a stock-for-stock merger, the target and acquirer, and all contracts and agreements related to the transaction including the merger or acquisition agreement and proxy statement if shareholder approval is required.

> In connection with our opinion, we have, among other things: (i) reviewed certain publicly available financial and other data with respect to the Company and Acquirer, including the consolidated financial statements for recent years and interim periods to September 30, 2001, and certain other relevant financial and operating data relating to the Company and Acquirer made available to us from published sources and from the internal records of the Company and Acquirer; (ii) reviewed the Merger Agreement; (iii) reviewed certain publicly available information concerning the trading of, and the trading market for, the Common Stock; (iv) compared the Company and Acquirer from a financial point of view with certain other companies in the snack food industry which we deemed to be relevant; (v) considered the financial terms, to the extent publicly available, of selected recent business combinations of companies in the snack food industry which we deemed to be comparable, in whole or in part, to the Merger; (vi) reviewed and discussed with representatives of the management of the Company and Acquirer certain information of a business and financial nature regarding the Company and Acquirer, furnished to us by them, including financial forecasts and related assumptions of the Company and Acquirer; (vii) made inquiries regarding and discussed the Merger and the Merger Agreement and other matters related thereto with the Company's counsel; and (viii) performed such other analyses and examinations as we have deemed appropriate.

In the event the transaction requires shareholder approval, the investment bank would also review the proxy statement or prospectus used to seek shareholder approval. In addition, in the case of stock-for-stock transactions, the investment bank would review information regarding trading of both company's common stock.

The investment bank will also make certain disclosures with respect to any limitations on its analysis placed on it by its client, assumptions it has made that are material to the opinion, and other conditions on its rendering the opinion.

> In connection with our review, we have not assumed any obligation independently to verify the foregoing information and have relied on its being accurate and complete in all material respects. With respect to the financial forecasts for the Company and Acquirer provided to us by their respective management's, with your consent we have assumed for purposes of our opinion that the forecasts have been reasonably prepared on bases reflecting the best available estimates and judgments of their respective management's at the time of preparation as to the future financial performance of the Company and Acquirer and that they provide a

reasonable basis upon which we can form our opinion. We have also assumed that there have been no material changes in the Company's or Acquirer's assets, financial condition, results of operations, business or prospects since the respective dates of their last financial statements made available to us. We have relied on advice of counsel and independent accountants to the Company as to all legal and financial reporting matters with respect to the Company, the Merger and the Merger Agreement. In addition, we have not assumed responsibility for making an independent evaluation, appraisal or physical inspection of any of the assets or liabilities (contingent or otherwise) of the Company or Acquirer, nor have we been furnished with any such appraisals. Finally, our opinion is based on economic, monetary and market and other conditions as in effect on, and the information made available to us as of, the date hereof. It should be understood that, although subsequent developments may affect this opinion, we do not have any obligation to update, revise or reaffirm this opinion.

We have further assumed, with your consent, that the Merger will be consummated in accordance with the terms described in the Merger Agreement, without any further amendments thereto, and without waiver by the Company of any of the conditions to its obligations thereunder.

The final set of disclosures made by the investment bank relate to its relationship with the parties and the potential conflicts it may have in rendering the opinion.

We have acted as financial advisor to the Company in connection with the Merger and will receive a fee for our services, including rendering this opinion, a significant portion of which is contingent upon the consummation of the Merger. In the ordinary course of our business, we actively trade the equity securities of the Company and Acquirer for our own account and for the accounts of customers and, accordingly, may at any time hold a long or short position in such securities. We have also acted as an underwriter in connection with offerings of securities of the Company and Acquirer and performed various investment banking services for the Company and Acquirer.

In concluding the letter, the banker delivers the "opinion" itself, stating that the transaction is fair from a financial point of view. It is important to note that the opinion is rendered as of the date of the merger or acquisition agreement and is fair on that date.

Based upon the foregoing and in reliance thereon, it is our opinion as investment bankers that the Consideration to be paid by Acquirer pursuant to the Merger was fair to Acquirer from a financial point of view, as of the date of the Merger Agreement, and is fair to Acquirer from a financial point of view, as of the date hereof.

In addition, it is typical for the fairness opinion to state the terms upon which the opinion can be relied. For example, in many cases, the opinion is for the exclusive benefit of the board of directors, while in others, the opinion may be included in a proxy statement or prospectus seeking the vote of shareholders.

> This opinion is furnished pursuant to our engagement letter, dated September 15, 2001, and is solely for the benefit of the Board of Directors of Acquirer in its consideration of the Merger. This opinion is not a recommendation to any shareholder as to how such shareholder should vote with respect to the Merger. This opinion may not be used or referred to by the Company, or quoted or disclosed to any person in any manner, without our prior written consent. In furnishing this opinion, we do not admit that we are experts within the meaning of the term "experts" as used in the Securities Act of 1933 and the rules and regulations promulgated thereunder, nor do we admit that this opinion constitutes a report or valuation within the meaning of Section 11 of the Securities Act of 1933.

Finally, the letter is usually signed by the investment bank rendering the opinion, not by the individual responsible for the transaction.

Exhibit 17-2 provides a complete fairness opinion for the 1998 acquisition of Gulf South Medical Supply, Inc. by Physician Sales and Service, Inc. in a stock-for-stock transaction.

Exhibit 17-2
Fairness Opinion for Physician Sales and Service, Inc. Acquisition of Gulf South Medical Supply, Inc.[3]

December 14, 1997

Board of Directors
Gulf South Medical Supply, Inc.
One Woodgreen Place
Madison, Mississippi 39110

Ladies and Gentlemen:

We understand that Physician Sales & Service, Inc., a Florida corporation ("PSS"), PSS Merger Corp., a Delaware corporation and a wholly-owned subsidiary of PSS ("Merger Corp."), and Gulf South Medical Supply, Inc., a Delaware corporation ("GSMS"), have entered into an Agreement and Plan of Merger dated December 14, 1997 (the "Merger Agreement"), pursuant to which Merger Corp. will be merged with and into GSMS, which will be the surviving corporation and will become a wholly owned subsidiary of PSS (the "Merger"). Pursuant to the Merger, as more fully described in the Merger Agreement, we understand that each issued and outstanding share of the common stock, $0.01 par value per

(Continued)

---

3. Public Company Documents.

Exhibit 17-2

(*continued*)

share ("GSMS Common Stock"), of GSMS will be converted into and exchanged for the right to receive 1.75 shares of the common stock, $0.01 par value per share ("PSS Common Stock"), of PSS, subject to certain adjustments (the "Consideration"). The terms and conditions of the Merger are set forth in more detail in the Merger Agreement.

You have asked for our opinion as investment bankers as to whether the Consideration to be received by the stockholders of Seller pursuant to the Merger is fair to such stockholders from a financial point of view, as of the date hereof.

In connection with our opinion, we have, among other things: (i) reviewed certain publicly available financial and other data with respect to GSMS and PSS, including the consolidated financial statements for recent years and interim periods to September 30, 1997 and certain other relevant financial and operating data relating to GSMS and PSS made available to us from published sources and from the internal records of GSMS and PSS; (ii) reviewed the financial terms and conditions of the Merger Agreement; (iii) reviewed certain publicly available information concerning the trading of; and the trading market for, GSMS Common Stock and PSS Common Stock; (iv) compared GSMS and PSS from a financial point of view with certain other companies in the medical products distribution industry which we deemed to be relevant; (v) considered the financial terms, to the extent publicly available, of selected recent business combinations of companies in the medical products distribution industry which we deemed to be comparable, in whole or in part, to the Merger; (vi) reviewed and discussed with representatives of the management of GSMS and PSS certain information of a business and financial nature regarding GSMS and PSS, furnished to us by them, including financial forecasts and related assumptions of GSMS and PSS; (vii) made inquiries regarding and discussed the Merger and the Merger Agreement and other matters related thereto with GSMS's counsel; and (viii) performed such other analyses and examinations as we have deemed appropriate.

In connection with our review, we have not assumed any obligation independently to verify the foregoing information and have relied on its being accurate and complete in all material respects. With respect to the financial forecasts for GSMS and PSS provided to us by their respective managements, upon their advice and with your consent we have assumed for purposes of our opinion that the forecasts, including the assumptions G-1 regarding synergies, have been reasonably prepared on bases reflecting the best available estimates and judgments of their respective managements at the time of preparation as to the future financial performance of GSMS and PSS and that they provide a reasonable basis upon which we can form our opinion. We have also assumed that there have been no material changes in GSMS's or PSS's assets, financial condition, results of operations, business or prospects since the respective dates of their last financial statements made available to us. We have assumed that the Merger will be consummated in a manner that complies in all respects with the applicable provisions of the Securities Act of 1933, as amended (the "Securities Act"), the Securities Exchange Act of 1934 and all other applicable federal and state statutes, rules and regulations. In addition, we have not assumed responsibility for making an independent evaluation, appraisal or physical inspection of any of the assets or liabilities (contingent or otherwise) of GSMS or PSS, nor have we been furnished with any such appraisals. You have informed us, and we have assumed, that the Merger will be recorded as a pooling of interests under generally accepted accounting principles. Finally, our opinion is based on economic, monetary and market and other conditions as in effect on, and the information made available to us as of, the date hereof. Accordingly, although subsequent developments may affect this opinion, we have not assumed any obligation to update, revise or reaffirm this opinion.

(*Continued*)

Exhibit 17-2
(Continued)

We have further assumed with your consent that the Merger will be consummated in accordance with the terms described in the Merger Agreement, without any further amendments thereto, and without waiver by GSMS of any of the conditions to its obligations thereunder.

We have acted as financial advisor to GSMS in connection with the Merger and will receive a fee for our services, including rendering this opinion, a significant portion of which is contingent upon the consummation of the Merger. In the ordinary course of our business, we actively trade the equity securities of GSMS for our own account and for the accounts of customers and, accordingly, may at any time hold a long or short position in such securities. We have also acted as an underwriter in connection with offerings of securities of GSMS and PSS and performed various other investment banking services for GSMS.

Based upon the foregoing and in reliance thereon, it is our opinion as investment bankers that the Consideration to be received by the stockholders of GSMS pursuant to the Merger is fair to such stockholders from a financial point of view, as of the date hereof.

We are not expressing an opinion regarding the price at which the PSS Common Stock may trade at any future time. The Consideration to be received by the stockholders of GSMS pursuant to the Merger is based upon a fixed exchange ratio and, accordingly, the market value of the Consideration may vary significantly.

This opinion is directed to the Board of Directors of GSMS in its consideration of the Merger and is not a recommendation to any stockholder as to how such stockholder should vote with respect to the Merger. Further, this opinion addresses only the financial fairness of the Exchange Ratio to the stockholders and does not address the relative merits of the Merger and any alternatives to the Merger, GSMS's underlying decision to proceed with or effect the Merger, or any other aspect of the Merger. This opinion may not be used or referred to by GSMS, or quoted or disclosed to any person in any manner, without our prior written consent, which consent is hereby given to the inclusion of this opinion in any proxy statement or registration statement to be filed with the Securities and Exchange Commission in connection with the Merger. In furnishing this opinion, we do not admit that we are experts within the meaning of the term "experts" as used in the Securities Act and the rules and regulations promulgated thereunder, nor do we admit that this opinion constitutes a report or valuation within the meaning of Section 11 of the Securities Act.

Very truly yours,

NATIONSBANC MONTGOMERY SECURITIES, INC.

§ 17.08 INCLUSION OF THE FAIRNESS OPINION IN THE PROXY STATEMENT

In transactions that require shareholder approval, the fairness opinion is often included in the proxy statement or prospectus that is sent to shareholders seeking their vote in favor of the deal. In this case, there are a number of other items that are included with the fairness opinion that are directly related to it. Each of these items helps support the analysis performed in the opinion and help discharge the board of director's duty of care and loyalty to shareholders.

First, the financial analysis that supports the opinion is provided in summary form. Exhibit 17-3 provides that portion of the proxy statement in the Physician Sales & Service, Inc. acquisition of Gulf South Medical Supply, Inc.

Exhibit 17-3
Fairness Opinion Analysis Included in Proxy Statement[4]

In connection with its opinion, NationsBanc Montgomery, among other things: (i) reviewed certain publicly available financial and other data with respect to Gulf South and PSS, including the consolidated financial statements for recent years and interim periods to September 30, 1997 and certain other relevant financial and operating data relating to Gulf South and PSS made available to NationsBanc Montgomery from published sources and from the internal records of Gulf South and PSS; (ii) reviewed the financial terms and conditions of the Merger Agreement; (iii) reviewed certain publicly available information concerning the trading of, and the trading market for, Gulf South Common Stock and PSS Common Stock; (iv) compared Gulf South and PSS from a financial point of view with certain other companies in the medical products distribution industry which NationsBanc Montgomery deemed to be relevant; (v) considered the financial terms, to the extent publicly available, of selected recent business combinations of companies in the medical products distribution industry which NationsBanc Montgomery deemed to be comparable, in whole or in part, to the Merger; (vi) reviewed and discussed with representatives of the management of Gulf South and PSS certain information of a business and financial nature regarding Gulf South and PSS, furnished to NationsBanc Montgomery by them, including financial forecasts and related assumptions of Gulf South and PSS; (vii) made inquiries regarding and discussed the Merger and the Merger Agreement and other matters related thereto with Gulf South's counsel; and (viii) performed such other analyses and examinations as NationsBanc Montgomery deemed appropriate.

In connection with its review, NationsBanc Montgomery did not assume any obligation independently to verify the foregoing information and relied on such information being accurate and complete in all material respects. With respect to the financial forecasts for Gulf South and PSS provided to NationsBanc Montgomery by their respective managements, upon their advice and with Gulf South's consent, NationsBanc Montgomery assumed for purposes of its opinion that the forecasts, including the assumptions regarding synergies, were reasonably prepared on bases reflecting the best available estimates and judgments of their respective managements at the time of preparation as to the future financial performance of Gulf South and PSS and that they provided a reasonable basis upon which NationsBanc Montgomery could form its opinion. NationsBanc Montgomery also assumed that there were no material changes in Gulf South's or PSS' assets, financial condition, results of operations, business or prospects since the respective dates of their last financial statements made available to NationsBanc Montgomery.

NationsBanc Montgomery assumed that the Merger would be consummated in a manner that complies in all respects with the applicable provisions of the Securities Act, the Exchange Act and all other applicable federal and state statutes, rules and regulations. In addition, NationsBanc Montgomery did not assume responsibility for making an independent evaluation, appraisal or physical inspection of any of the assets or liabilities (contingent or otherwise) of Gulf South or PSS, nor was NationsBanc Montgomery furnished with any such appraisals. Gulf South informed NationsBanc Montgomery, and NationsBanc Montgomery assumed, that

(Continued)

---

4. Public Company Documents.

Exhibit 17-3

(Continued)

---

the Merger would be recorded as a pooling of interests under generally accepted accounting principles. Finally, NationsBanc Montgomery's opinion was based on economic, monetary and market and other conditions as in effect on, and the information made available to it as of, December 14, 1997. Accordingly, although subsequent developments may affect NationsBanc Montgomery's opinion, NationsBanc Montgomery has not assumed any obligation to update, revise or reaffirm its opinion. 4. Public Company Documents.

The following is a summary of the material analyses and factors considered by NationsBanc Montgomery in connection with its opinion to the Gulf South Board of Directors dated December 14, 1997.

Selected Comparable Public Company Analysis

NationsBanc Montgomery compared the implied value of the consideration to be received by the stockholders of Gulf South in the Merger to certain financial and stock market information of sixteen publicly-traded companies engaged in the medical products distribution business that NationsBanc Montgomery believed were comparable in certain respects to Gulf South (the "Comparable Companies"). The Comparable Companies included: Allegiance Corporation, Amerisource Health Corporation, Bergen Brunswig Corporation, Bindley Western Industries Inc., Cardinal Health Inc., Graham-Field Health Products Inc., Henry Schein Inc., McKesson Corporation, NCS Healthcare Inc., Omnicare Inc., Owens & Minor Inc., Patterson Dental Company, PharMerica Inc., PSS, Suburban Ostomy Supply Company Inc., and Vitalink Pharmacy Services Inc. The Comparable Companies were chosen by NationsBanc Montgomery as companies that, based on publicly available data, possess general business, operating and financial characteristics representative of companies in the industry in which Gulf South operates, although NationsBanc Montgomery recognizes that each of the Comparable Companies is distinguishable from Gulf South in certain respects. For each of the Comparable Companies and Gulf South, NationsBanc Montgomery obtained certain publicly available financial and stock market data, including last twelve months ("LTM") revenue, projected calendar year 1998 earnings per share, recently reported total debt and cash and cash equivalents, closing stock price as of December 12, 1997, and the projected secular growth rate of earnings. Calendar year 1998 and 1999 EPS estimates for the Comparable Companies were based on analysts' estimates as reported by First Call, a market research database, and EPS estimates for Gulf South and PSS were based on both analysts' estimates as reported by First Calland internal estimates of the managements of Gulf South and PSS, respectively. Projected secular growth rates for the Comparable Companies and Gulf South were obtained from I/B/E/S International, Inc. and Zacks Investment Research, Inc., market research databases, and from NationsBanc Montgomery research. NationsBanc Montgomery also compiled "aggregate value" for each of the Comparable Companies and for Gulf South implied in the Merger. Aggregate value is the total current equity value plus total debt less cash and cash equivalents. Based on this data, NationsBanc Montgomery calculated the following ratios for each of the Comparable Companies, for PSS, and for Gulf South implied in the Merger: current stock price to projected 1998 earnings per share ("1998 price/earnings ratio"); 1998 price/earnings ratio to secular growth rate; and aggregate value to LTM revenue. The 1998 price/earnings ratio for the Comparable Companies ranged from 17.1× to 28.1×, and averaged 21.8× compared to 26.4× for PSS and 29.2× for Gulf South implied in the Merger. The 1998 price/earnings ratio to secular growth rate for the Comparable Companies ranged from 70.6% to 143.4% and averaged 106.4%, compared to 145.8% for Gulf South implied in the Merger. The aggregate

(Continued)

Exhibit 17-3
(*Continued*)

value to LTMrevenue for the Comparable Companies ranged from 0.1× to 3.0× and averaged 1.1× compared to 1.0× for PSS and 2.6× for Gulf South implied in the Merger.

Selected Comparable Mergers and Acquisitions Analysis

NationsBanc Montgomery reviewed certain financial data for recently announced mergers and acquisitions in the medical products distribution industry that were deemed to be comparable to the Merger and in which the consideration paid was greater than $100 million (the "Comparable Acquisitions"). The Comparable Acquisitions included McKesson Corp.'s acquisition of General Medical Inc., Henry Schein Inc.'s acquisitions of Micro Bio-Medics and Sullivan Dental Products, Inc. and Graham-Field Health Products' acquisition of Fuqua Enterprises. For each such transaction NationsBanc Montgomery calculated, among other things, the ratio of aggregate value to LTM revenues, the ratio of aggregate value to LTM earnings before interest and taxes ("EBIT"), and the ratio of equity value to LTM earnings. All multiples were based on publicly available information at the time of announcement of the Comparable Acquisitions. These calculations yielded a range of aggregate values to LTM revenues of 0.5× to 1.2× with an average of 0.9×, a range of aggregate values to LTM EBIT of 15.8× to 31.1× with an average of 20.7×, and a range of equity values to LTM earnings of 22.8× to 51.8× with an average of 35.8×. NationsBanc Montgomery then calculated, among other things, the same ratios implied in the Merger. The calculations yielded, among other things, an aggregate value to LTM revenues of 2.6×, an aggregate value to LTM EBIT of 27.8×, and an equity value to LTM earnings of 43.7×. Premiums Paid Analysis. NationsBanc Montgomery reviewed the premiums paid in ten transactions that were deemed to be comparable to the Merger with transaction values between $100 million and $1 billion involving health care services companies in the past two years. NationsBanc Montgomery analyzed the following transactions: United HealthCare Corp./HealthWise of America, Cardinal Health Inc./Pyxis Corp., FPA Medical Management/Sterling Healthcare, Cardinal Health Inc./PCI Services Inc., Cardinal Health Inc./Owen Healthcare Inc., Sun Healthcare Group Inc. /Retirement Care Associates, Henry Schein Inc./Micro Bio-Medics Inc., CRA Managed Care Inc./Occusystems, Alternative Living Services/Sterling House Corp., and Henry Schein Inc./Sullivan Dental Products. In each of these transactions, NationsBanc Montgomery calculated the premiums of the price paid by acquirors over the target company's stock price one day, one week and four weeks prior to public announcement of the transaction. These calculations yielded average premiums paid based on the target company's stock price one day, one week and four weeks prior to public announcement of the transaction of 32.0%, 37.7% and 37.3%, respectively. NationsBanc Montgomery then calculated the premium to be paid in the Merger based on the Exchange Ratio and the closing stock price of PSS Common Stock as of December 12, 1997 of $23.00 to Gulf South's stock prices one day, one week and four weeks prior to public announcement of the Merger. These calculations yielded premiums paid of 38.5%, 23.6% and 18.4%, respectively.

Contribution Analysis

NationsBanc Montgomery analyzed and compared the respective contributions of Gulf South and PSS to the pro forma combined company net income for calendar years 1998 and 1999 and to the pro forma ownership of the respective stockholders in the combined company upon consummation of the Merger. Based on publicly available analyst estimates for Gulf South and PSS for calendar years 1998 and 1999, Gulf South would contribute approximately 39.2% and 35.7%, respectively, of the projected net income of the pro forma combined company. Based on internal estimates for Gulf South and PSS for calendar years 1998 and 1999,

(*Continued*)

Exhibit 17-3
(*Continued*)

Gulf South would contribute approximately 40.6% and 38.3%, respectively, of the projected net income of the pro forma combined company. Based on the Exchange Ratio, Gulf South's existing stockholders would own approximately 42.4% of the pro forma combined company, on a fully diluted basis, upon consummation of the Merger.

Pro Forma Merger Analysis

NationsBanc Montgomery analyzed the impact of the Merger on PSS stockholders on a pro forma fully diluted EPS basis for calendar years 1998 and 1999. NationsBanc Montgomery used publicly available analyst estimates for calendar years 1998 and 1999 for PSS and Gulf South and performed the analysis with and without giving effect to the synergies anticipated by the managements of PSS and Gulf South to result from the Merger (excluding nonrecurring costs resulting from the Merger) in each year. The analysis indicated that, for PSS stockholders, the Merger could be accretive in each of the years analyzed with the realization of the synergies and the Merger could be dilutive in each year without the realization of such synergies. The actual results achieved by the combined company may vary from projected results and the variations may be material.

Discounted Cash Flow Analysis

NationsBanc Montgomery performed a discounted cash flow analysis on certain projected financial statements that were provided to NationsBanc Montgomery by the management of Gulf South. In performing this analysis, NationsBanc Montgomery calculated the projected stand-alone unlevered after-tax cash flows of Gulf South for the calendar years 1998 through 2004. NationsBanc Montgomery calculated Gulf South's terminal values in calendar year 2004 based on aggregate value/EBIT multiples ranging from 20.0× to 23.0×. The unlevered aftertax cash flows and the terminal values were discounted to the present using discount rates ranging from 10.0% to 15.0%. This analysis yielded an equity value range for Gulf South of $28.53 to $41.50 per fully diluted share.

The summary set forth above does not purport to be a complete description of the presentation by NationsBanc Montgomery to the Gulf South Board of Directors or the analyses performed by NationsBanc Montgomery. The preparation of a fairness opinion is not necessarily susceptible to partial analysis or summary description. NationsBanc Montgomery believes that its analyses and the summary set forth above must be considered as a whole and that selecting portions of its analyses and of the factors considered, without considering all analyses and factors, would create an incomplete view of the process underlying the analyses set forth in its presentation to the Gulf South Board of Directors. In addition, NationsBanc Montgomery may have given various analyses more or less weight than other analyses, and may have deemed various assumptions more or less probable than other assumptions so that the ranges of valuations resulting from any particular analysis described above should not be taken to be NationsBanc Montgomery's view of the actual value of Gulf South. The fact that any specific analysis has been referred to in the summary above is not meant to indicate that such analysis was given greater weight than any other analysis.

In arriving at its opinion, NationsBanc Montgomery did not ascribe a specific range of values to Gulf South, but rather made its determination as to the fairness, from a financial point of view, of the consideration to be received by the holders of the Gulf South Common Stock in the Merger on the basis of the financial and comparative analyses described above. In performing its analyses, NationsBanc Montgomery made numerous assumptions with

(*Continued*)

Exhibit 17-3

(*Continued*)

respect to industry performance, general business and economic conditions and other matters, many of which are beyond the control of Gulf South. The analyses performed by NationsBanc Montgomery are not necessarily indicative of actual values or actual future results, which may be significantly more or less favorable than suggested by such analyses. Such analyses were prepared solely as part of NationsBanc Montgomery's analysis of the fairness of the transaction contemplated by the Merger Agreement to the Gulf South stockholders and were provided to the Gulf South Board of Directors in connection with the delivery of NationsBanc Montgomery's opinion. The analyses do not purport to be appraisals or to reflect the prices at which a company might actually be sold or the prices at which any securities may trade at the present time or at any time in the future. NationsBanc Montgomery used in its analyses various projections of future performance prepared by the management of Gulf South and by research analysts. The projections are based on numerous variables and assumptions which are inherently unpredictable and must be considered not certain of occurrence as projected. Accordingly, actual results could vary significantly from those set forth in such projections.

Pursuant to the terms of NationsBanc Montgomery's engagement, Gulf South has agreed to pay NationsBanc Montgomery a fee equal to $3.5 million. Gulf South paid NationsBanc Montgomery $150,000 upon rendering its opinion to the Gulf South Board and will be obligated to pay NationsBanc Montgomery the remainder of the fee upon the closing of the Merger. Accordingly, a significant portion of NationsBanc Montgomery's fee is contingent upon the closing of the Merger. Gulf South has also agreed to reimburse NationsBanc Montgomery for its reasonable out-of-pocket expenses, including counsel fees, up to a maximum of $50,000. Pursuant to a separate letter agreement, Gulf South has agreed to indemnify NationsBanc Montgomery, its affiliates, and their respective partners, directors, officers, agents, consultants, employees and controlling persons against certain liabilities, including liabilities under federal securities laws.

In the ordinary course of business, NationsBanc Montgomery actively trades Gulf South Common Stock and PSS Common Stock for its own account and for the accounts of customers and accordingly, may a0t any time hold a long or short position in such securities. NationsBanc Montgomery also has in the past performed certain investment banking services for Gulf South, which included participation as an underwriter in Gulf South's initial public offering in March 1994 and Gulf South's follow-on equity offerings in October 1994 and May 1996. NationsBanc Montgomery also has performed certain investment banking services for PSS, which included participation as an underwriter in a debt offering in October 1997.

From this real example, one can draw a few conclusions. First, the financial analysis supporting a fairness opinion is extensive, and one should assume that all the analysis will have to be disclosed, either to the board of directors, shareholders or the SEC. The analysis included in the proxy statement is a summary of the analysis prepared for the board of directors. In this particular case, the financial analysis included:

- Comparable company analysis
- Comparable transaction analysis

Exhibit 17-4
Investment Banker Consent to Include Fairness Opinion in Proxy Statement[5]

NATIONSBANC MONTGOMERY SECURITIES, INC.

January 13, 1998

We hereby consent to the inclusion of our opinion letter dated December 14, 1997 to the Board of Directors of Gulf South Medical Supply regarding the merger between Gulf South Medical Supply and Physician Sales & Service, in Physician Sales and Service's Registration Statement on Form S-4 (the "Registration Statement") and to the references therein to our firm and to our opinion under the headings "Summary—The Merger," "The Merger—Background of the Merger," "The Merger—Reasons for the Merger," "The Merger—Opinions of Financial Advisors," and "Annex G—Opinion of NationsBanc Montgomery Securities LLC." In giving the foregoing consent, we do not admit (i) that we come within the category of persons whose consent is required under Section 7 of the Securities Act of 1933, as amended (the "Securities Act"), or the rules and regulations of the Securities and Exchange Commission promulgated thereunder, and (ii) that we are experts with respect to any part of the Registration Statement within the meaning of the term "experts" as used in the Securities Act and the rules and regulations of the Securities and Exchange Commission promulgated there under.

Very truly yours,

NATIONSBANC MONTGOMERY SECURITIES LLC

- Contribution analysis
- Pro forma merger analysis
- Discounted cash flow analysis

Second, the disclosures made by the investment bank regarding the limitations on their analysis, the scope of its review, the potential conflicts it may have, and the fees it may earn, are exhaustive.

In the event the fairness opinion is included in the proxy statement or prospectus, the investment bank must provide its consent for it to be included. The banker's consent for the inclusion of the Gulf South Medical Supply fairness opinion in the Physician Sales and Services, Inc. proxy statement can be found in Exhibit 17-4.

§ 17.09   SUMMARY

Fairness opinions are a necessary aspect of just about every transaction, from merger or acquisition, to joint venture or spin-off. They accomplish a number of

---

5. Public Company Documents.

objectives, including assisting the board of directors of a company or the fiduciary acting on behalf of shareholders or constituents, in getting sufficiently informed that they can make a responsible decision with respect to a given transaction. In this way, the fairness opinion can help a board discharge its duty of care and loyalty to shareholders, and potentially avoid litigation.

The investment banker providing the opinion, while it does not have the same duty to the shareholders of a client as its board does, is responsible for performing due diligence with care, and ensuring that it has examined all information available to it under the circumstances. Even though the investment bank does not have a direct duty to its client's shareholders, if the investment bank does not perform its services with care, shareholders may have a derivative claim against the investment bank.

The preparation of a fairness opinion requires extensive financial and other analysis in order to arrive at an opinion that a given transaction is fair to shareholders from a financial point of view. The analysis is no different than that performed if the investment bank advises on the transaction; however, the documentation required for disclosure mandates that the banker prepare the analysis with extreme care.

While fairness opinions are letters issued by investment banks to fiduciaries, it is wise for the investment bank to work hand-in-hand with a lawyer qualified in drafting fairness opinions. This is done not only to ensure the investment bank makes the right disclosures and is adequately protected from a legal standpoint, but also because the board of directors relying on the opinion requires the same, if not greater, level of protection.

PART IV

RESTRUCTURING ALTERNATIVES

Chapter 18

OVERVIEW OF CORPORATE RESTRUCTURINGS

§ 18.01 OVERVIEW OF RESTRUCTURINGS

Since the late 1970s and early 1980s, restructurings have changed the landscape of corporate America. Between 1990 and 2003, there were over 673 spinoffs, 14 splitoffs, 66 equity carve-outs, and 22 tracking stocks, representing over $624 billion in transaction value.[1] In addition, there were approximately 7,129 share repurchases representing $1.359 billion in value.[2] Notable corporate restructurings in the last few decades include AT&T's breakup, Marriott International's

---

1. Thomson Financial.
2. *Id.*

spin-off of its management services business, and ITT's break-up into three businesses.

Common to all of these restructurings is one primary goal — create shareholder value. An example that symbolizes the wealth creation opportunity from restructurings, is the 1996 restructuring of AT&T. Prior to its announcement of its spin-off of NCR and Lucent Technologies, its market capitalization was approximately $75 billion. Just a year later, the combined market capitalization of AT&T, Lucent, and NCR was over $175 billion. The act of breaking up AT&T into its three components created over $100 billion.

What is a corporate restructuring? The simplest answer is that a restructuring is the realignment of the ownership, operations, assets, or capital structure of a company in order to improve operating performance, optimize a capital structure, and enhance public perception. The definition of a restructuring has evolved over the years from a simple balance sheet reconfiguration to a range of financial and transaction driven alternatives that include everything from simply enhancing internal operating performance to an outright sale or merger of a company, and from a sale of assets to a special dividend or share repurchase in the face of a takeover threat. Restructurings have been used in the past for a number of reasons, including, to lever and delever a balance sheet, concentrate equity ownership, realize value of a subsidiary, and appease vocal investors. When all is said and done, however, restructurings are usually designed to enhance shareholder value.

§ 18.02   THE EVIDENCE BEHIND RESTRUCTURINGS

Historically, there have been a number of factors that have led to an increase in the number of corporate restructurings. Over the past 20 years, we have witnessed a tremendous rise in the awareness and activity of institutional shareholders. They have become much more vocal, forcing issues by making proposals at shareholder meetings, waging proxy battles and going head-to-head with management and the board if their demands for increasing shareholder value are not met. At the same time, the equity markets have strengthened quite dramatically with a coincident emergence of the high yield and leveraged finance market, coupled with historically low interest rates. These three factors have bode well for aggressive takeover behavior such as hostile acquisitions and leveraged buyouts. In addition, while the equity markets have risen dramatically, and corporate America has become more acquisitive, the values of acquired businesses have not necessarily been reflected in companies' stock prices. As a result, restructurings have become de rigueur, with companies focusing or core businesses, divesting poor performers and highlighting strong performers. These transactions in turn have led to massive value creation for those companies that successfully have been able to restructure.

There have been innumerable studies in the past that cite the benefits of restructurings to shareholders. In a 1995 study titled "Corporate Focus and Stock Returns," Robert Comment and Gregg Jarrell observed that "greater corporate focus is consistent with shareholder wealth maximization."[3] Their study showed that in the 1980s, there was a trend toward deconglomeratization, with firms focusing on their core businesses. And, with this trend came increased shareholder wealth. They found a large difference in wealth creation between firms that were focused during the analysis period and firms that were not focused, with a net return difference of 7.4%. They found that increased focus results in additional stock return. In addition, divestitures typically evidenced an increase in stock price, while acquisitions only exhibited average positive returns, "not reliably greater than zero." Another interesting observation was that large, focused firms were less susceptible to takeover than diversified conglomerates.

Comment and Jarrell attribute the return behavior and susceptibility to takeover to inefficiencies created in conglomerates, and the inability of these companies to take advantage of internal synergies. In particular, these companies appeared unable to take advantage of economies of scale created by diversification, and were unable to enhance their capital structure through diversification.

In a separate study by John Kose and Eli Ofek in 1994, titled "Asset Sales and Increase in Focus," they found that asset sales "lead to an improvement in the operating performance of the seller's remaining assets in each of the three years following the asset sale."[4] They found that shareholder value was created in situations where companies divested assets and increased focus. The consequent improvement in operating performance of the seller was positively correlated with an improvement in its stock price.

§ 18.03   CREATING VALUE WITH RESTRUCTURINGS

Most of the studies performed in the past attempt to explain why value is created from a given type of restructuring, and provide evidence that the value was created in the form of stock price returns. To understand how value is created in a restructuring, let's review the relationship between type of transaction, overall rationale and shareholder value creation. You may recall Exhibit 1-4 from Chapter 1 that outlines the relationships between the three tenets of shareholder value creation, and mergers, acquisitions, and restructurings. For ease of reference, this exhibit is reproduced below as Exhibit 18-1.

As shown in Exhibit 18-1, corporate restructurings come in many forms, including financial and transaction driven methods. Financial restructurings include reengineering a balance sheet through means such as special dividends, share repurchases, and outright recapitalizations. Typically, these restructurings are designed to make a capital structure more efficient or to thwart a takeover threat. Transaction driven methods include approaches that reconfigure the assets,

---

3. Comment, Robert, and Gregg A. Jarrell, "Corporate Focus and Stock Returns," *Journal of Financial Economics* 37, 67–87 (1995).

4. Kose, John, and Eli Ofek, "Asset Sales and Increase in Focus," *Journal of Financial Economics* 37, 105–126 (1994).

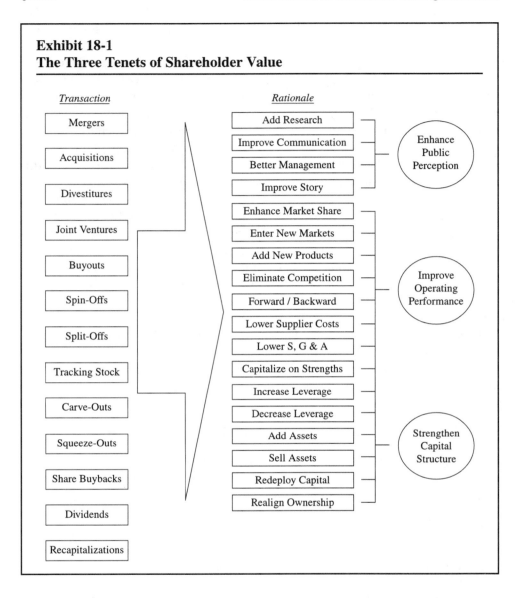

Exhibit 18-1
The Three Tenets of Shareholder Value

Transaction

- Mergers
- Acquisitions
- Divestitures
- Joint Ventures
- Buyouts
- Spin-Offs
- Split-Offs
- Tracking Stock
- Carve-Outs
- Squeeze-Outs
- Share Buybacks
- Dividends
- Recapitalizations

Rationale

- Add Research
- Improve Communication
- Better Management
- Improve Story

Enhance Public Perception

- Enhance Market Share
- Enter New Markets
- Add New Products
- Eliminate Competition
- Forward / Backward
- Lower Supplier Costs
- Lower S, G & A
- Capitalize on Strengths
- Increase Leverage

Improve Operating Performance

- Decrease Leverage
- Add Assets
- Sell Assets
- Redeploy Capital
- Realign Ownership

Strengthen Capital Structure

operations, and operating performance of a company. These methods include, among others, divestitures, spin-offs, split-offs, and equity carve-outs. Other less common transaction approaches include tracking stock, leveraged buyouts, leveraged ESOPs, and liquidations.

As an overview, following are brief descriptions of the primary forms of restructurings that will be the subject of Chapters 19 and 20.

Internal Restructuring: In an internal restructuring, a company evaluates its internal processes, capital allocation, and strategic priorities, and refocuses its attentions on those areas that will maximize operating performance. For example, new management incentives may be put in place, capital may be redeployed to accelerate the growth of particular assets, or the company may enter new markets.

Another simple form of restructuring may be to change the way the company communicates with Wall Street.

Special Dividend: A special dividend is a taxable distribution to shareholders. While many companies pay dividends on a regular basis, special or one-time dividends have been used to reconfigure a company's balance sheet and alter the company's leverage ratio. Companies may pay out excess cash or take on new debt in order to pay the proceeds to shareholders.

Share Repurchase: A share repurchase is the acquisition of a company's own shares by the corporation. Executed as an open market share repurchase or a tender offer, the acquisition of shares serves to shrink the equity capitalization of the company and expend excess cash, thereby altering the company's debt to equity ratio and potentially increasing the company's earnings per share. Share repurchases also concentrate ownership in the hands of the remaining shareholders.

Recapitalization: A recapitalization usually entails the assumption of incremental debt or the reduction in equity through a repurchase of shares. Recapitalizations are done to dramatically alter the capitalization or ownership of companies. In some cases, recapitalizations are undertaken by cash-rich public companies that are under takeover threat. The recapitalization serves to deter a potentially hostile acquirer from using the cash of the target to finance the bid.

Leveraged ESOP: While fairly uncommon, leveraged ESOPs have been used to concentrate the equity holdings of a company in the hands of employees and potentially thwart a takeover. An ESOP is an employee stock ownership plan, through which, employees own a portion of a company's equity. The creation of a leveraged ESOP allows a company to borrow money to leverage an ESOP plan and acquire a large portion of the company's equity at one time, allowing the shares to vest to individual employees over time. Leveraged ESOPs work by altering the debt and equity mix as well as the ownership of a company, significantly enhancing the debt on a company and concentrating the ownership of the company's stock in the hands of the ESOP.

Sale: A sale is the divestiture of a division or subsidiary through the taxable private sale of its stock or assets. In a sale, the proceeds can be redeployed in the company, used to pay down debt, or in some cases, paid out to shareholders in the form of a special dividend.

Spin-Off: A spin-off is a distribution of stock in a subsidiary to shareholders in the form of a dividend. In most cases, the dividend is on a tax-free basis to shareholders, with no tax consequences to the parent.

Split-Off: A split-off is the separation of a subsidiary from the parent by segregating the shareholder base into two, one group owning stock in the parent and the other owning stock in the subsidiary. Like spin-offs, most split-offs are undertaken on a tax-free basis. The effect of a split-off is to use subsidiary stock to repurchase parent stock.

Equity Carve-Out: An equity carve-out is the sale of a stake in a subsidiary to the public in an initial public offering (IPO). In most cases, the parent company retains a significant stake in the subsidiary company, usually greater than 80%. If the parent retains greater than 80%, it may preserve its ability to undertake a spinoff or split-off on a tax-free basis in the future. Arguably the most recognized equity carve-outs are those that have been undertaken by Thermo Electron. This company has successfully carved out multiple companies, including Thermolase and Thermo Instrument. In some cases, an equity carve-out has been used as a precursor to a spin-off or split-off. Most notable, are the AT&T IPO and subsequent spin-off of Lucent and the Sears IPO and subsequent spin-off of Allstate.

Tracking Stock: Tracking stock is a special class of common or preferred stock with earnings and/or dividends that are tied to a specific segment, division, or subsidiary of a company's business. Tracking stocks are a way for companies to separate certain divisions of its business, allowing investors to receive dividends and capital appreciation based on the performance of that division, yet without the parent giving up control of the assets.

Leveraged Buyout: A leveraged buyout or LBO is the acquisition of a company, division or subsidiary using a highly leveraged financial structure, whereby the cash flow of the acquired business is used to service and repay the borrowed debt. LBO's may be used as a means to enhance shareholder value in the face of a languishing stock price, counter a perceived takeover threat, or realize value of underappreciated assets.

§ 18.04   REASONS BEHIND CORPORATE RESTRUCTURINGS

While the goal of a restructuring is to enhance shareholder value, the specific motivation behind each form of restructuring is different, and will depend on the particular circumstances of each restructuring candidate. Exhibit 18-2 provides an overview of various reasons for a restructuring.

The value creation exercise comes from structuring a transaction, financial, or otherwise, that results in enhancing a company's operating performance and capital structure, and translates into enhanced public perception. Let's examine each of the reasons behind corporate restructurings, and look at how solving the problem creates shareholder value.

[A]   Focus on Core Business

Shareholder groups can often apply significant pressure on management and the board to shore up shareholder value by focusing on a company's core business or businesses. This pressure can lead management to devise a restructuring plan to focus on the primary business of the company. One good example of this is when Bally Entertainment, a gambling and casino operator, split the company in two in 1994 by spinning off Bally Health, the largest operator of health clubs in the nation.

[B]   Eliminate Poor Performers

It is not uncommon for a subsidiary to go through periods of prolonged downturn, a result of changing industry dynamics, poor management or shifting — or

---

Exhibit 18-2
Reasons for Corporate Restructurings

Improve Operating Performance:

- Focus on core business
- Certain subsidiaries and/or divisions may not be performing well, constraining the growth of the rest of the company or hurting financial performance
- Highlight the value of strong performers and underappreciated assets
- Various subsidiaries and/or divisions may have dramatically different capital needs
- Provide management incentives
- Lower borrowing costs and improve credit rating

Improve Capital Structure:

- Various subsidiaries and/or divisions may have dramatically different capital needs
- Company may be overlevered or underlevered, indicating a need to adjust capital structure
- Lower borrowing costs and improve credit rating

Enhance Public Perception:

- Release value of hidden or underappreciated assets — high growth subsidiaries and/or divisions are not recognized by equity markets
- Parent company trades at a discount to comparable companies
- Shareholders may be encouraging the company to focus of core business or businesses

Other Reasons:

- Avoid takeover threat
- Enhance corporate culture

---

divergent — corporate strategies. Consequently, a businesses' poor performance can drag down the financial results of the overall company, thereby having a negative impact on its stock price. Divesting a poorly performing business can have a significant impact on the company. First, it may immediately improve the company's operating performance by not including the target businesses' financials on the consolidated financials of the company. Second, it may eliminate the ongoing capital need to fund the business. Third, it may realize proceeds that can be deployed elsewhere to enhance the performance or capital structure of the company. Fourth, it may have a positive impact on the morale of the remaining employees and management. Finally, if communicated correctly, it may have an immediate positive impact on shareholder and public perception that should translate into an increase in stock price.

There have been numerous instances where companies have divested poorly performing businesses. One of the most notable cases of a company spinning off a poorly performing business, is AT&T's divestiture of NCR in 1995, a company it had acquired five years earlier and failed to turn into a thriving business.

Primary transaction types that accomplish this objective are, among others, divestitures, spin-offs, and split-offs.

[C]   Highlight Undervalued Assets

Some companies may have businesses that are strong performers, or assets that are underappreciated by the market. For example, a large conglomerate may have a small, high-growth subsidiary whose performance is masked by that of the parent because of its size. Consequently, the subsidiary's financials may not be disclosed separately. In this case, it may make sense to highlight the subsidiary and realize value for shareholders by divesting part or all of the company in a sale, spinoff, split-off, or equity carve-out.

Highlighting the undervalued business independently of that of the parent results in a number of benefits to shareholders, the company and employees. First, it allows the equity markets to value the business separately from that of the parent, enabling the market to apply valuation multiples to the separate businesses commensurate with their growth and operating performance. Second, it allows the independent company to raise debt and equity capital using its own cost of capital and not that of the parent. This eliminates any internal debate at the parent over capital allocation. Third, it enhances the capital structure of the parent by potentially raising proceeds from the sale or IPO of the unit. Fourth, it provides strong management incentives for the newly independent company's management team. Finally, it should enhance shareholder value for both companies.

A recent example of this is the 1996 spin-off of Viad from Dial Corp. Dial was in the skin care, laundry, household products, and food business, while Viad was in the airline catering and services, convention and leisure businesses. In this case, it was quite apparent that the markets were not valuing the different businesses appropriately, and the goal of the restructuring was to enhance value by allowing the market to value the discrete businesses independently.

[D]   Realize Value from Strong Businesses

In some cases, a strong performing business may not be valued by the market, and there is an opportunity for the company to realize value from a sale or divestiture. Proceeds from the divestiture can be used to pay down debt or fund the growth of remaining businesses. A good example of this is the 1995 spin-off of National Medical Enterprises from W.R. Grace. National Medical was an operator of dialysis clinics while W.R. Grace was a specialty chemicals company. In this transaction, National Medical paid a dividend to W.R. Grace which was used by Grace to delever its balance sheet.

[E]   Realign Funding Approach of Different Businesses

In companies with multiple business units, funding and capital allocation often takes place at the parent level. Often, this leads to internal conflicts between management teams as to which business should be entitled to parent capital.

Consequently, certain business units may starve for capital while others may have excess capital. In addition, companies that are strong operating performers and have little need for additional capital, may be providing capital to their less well performing counterparts. As a result, each of these potential problems may lead to internal capital conflicts.

One way to solve the problem is to separate the different businesses and allow them to raise capital independently at their own cost of capital. An example where this conflict was partly responsible for a restructuring was the 1993 Marriott International spin-off of its management services business. In this transaction, the conflicting capital requirements of the two primary businesses had resulted in a highly inefficient capital structure that was creating conflicts internally and constraining the growth of the company.

[F] Lower Borrowing Costs and Optimize Capital Structure

Corporations with multiple operating units often finance themselves at the parent level, attempting to take advantage of the critical mass of the entire organization. In some situations, however, the financial risks of one unit may overshadow the stability of another business unit, or the capital needs of one business may dominate the capital structure. In addition, a company may find itself in a position where it is over leveraged and consequently, its borrowing costs are too high. One prime motivation in a restructuring, financial or otherwise, may be to enhance the capital structure of the company and possibly lower borrowing costs. Debt can be repaid from the proceeds of an asset sale or a dividend from a subsidiary that is spun off. In 1996, PepsiCo spun off its restaurant business as a way not only to focus on its core bottling business but also to reduce debt.

A company's capital structure should be driven off its optimal funding costs, balancing the tradeoffs between a relatively higher cost of equity and a lower cost of debt. In some cases, a strong credit rating is required to secure discounts with suppliers. In other cases, a strong credit rating is not required. The trick is thus to balance the need for a strong credit rating with the desire to fund the company at the lowest possible cost. Many companies strive to seek the lowest funding cost without putting the company at risk of financial distress. Divesting a business and raising capital through a restructuring may be an efficient way to enhance the capital position of a company. Likewise, through dividends to shareholders or a recapitalization, it is possible to increase leverage and potentially lower the overall cost of capital for a company.

[G] Provide Management Incentives

Divisions or subsidiaries often have management whose incentives are driven off the performance of the parent company's financial results and stock price performance. This can often be a poor means to incent management. For example, the value of options issued to a subsidiary president that are based on the parent's stock price performance may not be appealing to the option holder since his contribution to the company through the subsidiary may not be visible to the market. By separating the subsidiary from the parent, it is possible to create attractive incentive packages for senior management and other employees. This is often a primary motivating factor in certain types of restructurings such as spin-offs, split-offs, and equity carve-outs.

[H]   Enhance Public Perception

A company's public perception is driven on the one hand by the communications that are made by the company to the public and Wall Street, and on the other hand, by the equity research analysts and investors that follow the stock. Public perception is as important to enhancing shareholder value as optimizing capital structure and improving operating performance. A company's perception can deteriorate for a variety of reasons, and investors, in particular large institutions, can be quite vocal in their relationships with the companies in which they invest. Consequently, with or without pressure from the investment community, companies may be forced to restructure in order to enhance their public perception. Perceptions can be changed by divesting poorly performing businesses, highlighting strong performers, improving operating performance and a balance sheet, or simply by communicating more effectively with Wall Street.

[I]   Avoid Takeover

Restructurings have been used by companies to avoid a takeover. Selling or spinning off a key business can serve as an effective poison pill. For example, in the event a tax-free spin-off is successful in the face of a takeover threat, if the acquirer is successful in acquiring the spun-off company soon after the spin-off date, it will have to pay capital gains taxes on the sale. Another approach is to increase leverage in the face of a takeover threat; however, one must consider the impact the increased leverage will have on the company's operating flexibility.

§ 18.05   HOW TO CHOOSE BETWEEN FORMS
OF RESTRUCTURING

Restructurings come in a two basic forms: financial and transactional. A financial restructuring usually takes place when the operating performance of a company is generally sound, yet the capital structure of a company is not optimal. For example, a company that makes money at the operating level, yet due to high leverage is unable to turn a profit after taxes. In this case, if the company is not restructured, the leverage may in fact begin to impact the company's operating performance. In addition, a financial restructuring may take place as a means to stave off a takeover offer. Transaction-driven restructurings are driven by a need to alter both the operating performance of the company and the balance sheet structure. In addition, transaction-motivated restructurings may be unrelated to operating performance or capital structure; rather, they may simply serve to enhance shareholder value. In many cases, financial and transaction-driven restructurings can work together, for example, a spin-off with a coincident dividend from the subsidiary to the parent that is used to pay down debt.

Deciding what type of restructuring to pursue will depend on a number of factors including the following:

- *Tax Basis in Different Businesses:* One of the most important determinants of a transaction-driven restructuring is the tax basis the parent company has in the asset under question. Those assets where the tax basis is high, may lend themselves to outright sale in a taxable transaction, whereas those assets where the tax basis is low, may lend themselves to tax-free alternatives such as spin-offs and split-offs.

- *Break-Up Valuation:* Prior to deciding on a particular type of divestiture alternative, the parent company should perform a break-up valuation that will highlight the degree to which the company is under- or overvalued, as well as the values of the different subsidiaries and divisions. The break-up valuation will indicate whether a given method of divestiture, such as IPO or sale, or sale versus spin-off is appropriate given market conditions. Break-up valuation works hand-in-hand with the tax basis the parent company has in the individual businesses.

- *Leverage:* If a company is over leveraged, it may force the company to divest assets to pay off debt. Alternatively, if a company is under leveraged, it may be reason to pay out excess cash or assume new debt and pay a special dividend to shareholders.

- *Operating Performance:* The operating performance of a parent may be symptomatic of the performance of the company's individual businesses. In each case, the company may either wish to divest a poorly performing business to enhance the operating performance of the parent, or divest the operations of a strong performer in order to highlight the financial attributes of that business. In either case, the alternative chosen will depend on the objective of the restructuring and the most appropriate method to divest the business.

- *Public Perception/Shareholder Pressure:* Institutional investors have become increasingly vocal about their views of how managements operate corporations, and in many cases, will put pressure on management to pursue a particular course of action.

- *Company Makeup:* A company's makeup may often be the result of historical strategies that may have made sense in the past. As a result, divisions or subsidiaries may no longer fit with a parent company's strategy or may present management with conflicting strategic priorities.

- *Threat of Takeover:* A proposed takeover may give a company reason to restructure. The form of restructuring however, will depend on the specific threat. For example, if an acquirer is interested in using the excess cash or debt capacity of a target to help it finance the purchase of the company, the target may wish to pay out the cash to shareholders as a special dividend, or take on incremental debt and repurchase stock. Alternatively, if the acquirer is after specific assets, it may make sense to undertake an IPO or spin-off of those assets to separate them from the parent and highlight their attractiveness to the market.

§ 18.06   RESTRUCTURING FINANCIAL ANALYSIS

Understanding the financial implications of a restructuring entails performing a number of types of analyses. For both financial and divestiture-driven restructurings, this is not a simple analytical exercise, and mandates that one look at the impact of the restructuring on the parent company, any new businesses that are divested, the ownership of the entities, and the value that is created for shareholders. In addition, prior to undertaking a divestiture-driven transaction, there is significant valuation analysis that must be performed on the parent and target businesses.

[A]   Break-Up Valuation Analysis

Break-up valuation is central to all transaction-driven restructurings, in particular all alternatives that involve the divestiture of part or all of a subsidiary or division. Let's begin our discussion by looking at a hypothetical company, All Mixed Up Co. with three distinct operating businesses: snack foods, personal care products, and pharmaceuticals. Each business has different growth rates, margin structures, and capital requirements.

The break-up valuation of All Mixed Up Co. will allow us to compare the value of the company on a break-up basis, to the overall value of the company as represented by its stock price. In addition, it will allow us to analyze the separate values of each of the businesses under various alternatives, for example, IPO, sale, spinoff, or split-off.

[1]   Break-Up Valuation Methodology

A typical break-up valuation follows four steps. First, each business, division, or subsidiary is valued independently on a stand alone basis. Typically, these businesses are valued on a firm or aggregate value basis, as the debt used to finance each company is usually held at the parent level. Second, the range of values for each business is then added together to come up with a composite firm value for the company. Third, a range of values — or deductions — is placed on the corporate overhead. Fourth, the "value" of the corporate overhead and the debt outstanding at the parent level is deducted from the combined aggregate value of the independent businesses. The resulting equity value represents the implied overall break-up valuation of the equity value of the company.

Exhibit 18-3
All Mixed Up Co. Financial Metrics
($ in millions, except share price data)

Business Unit	LTM EBIT	LTM Net Income	Debt Outstanding
Snack Foods	$15	–	–
Personal Care	$20	–	–
Pharmaceuticals	$25	–	–
Corporate	−$10	–	$100
Total	$50	$35	$100

Shares Outstanding: 25,000,000
Current Stock Price: $21.00 per share

[2] Break-Up Valuation Example

Using All Mixed Up Co. as an example, let's calculate the break-up value for the company. Exhibit 18-3 provides basic financial data on All Mixed Up Co.

Step 1: Value Each Business on a Stand Alone Basis.

Each business should be valued using two primary stand alone valuation methodologies: comparable multiples analysis and discounted cash flow analysis. In addition, to the extent one objective is to maximize the proceeds from the sale of a subsidiary or division, the analysis should include comparable transactions analysis.

Comparable Multiples Analysis: Since each company has the size and operating characteristics of comparable public companies, it would be appropriate to apply the average multiples of each subsidiary's peer group to the financial metrics of the subsidiary. Based on an analysis of companies comparable to the subsidiaries of All Mixed Up Co., the average LTM EBIT multiples for the peer groups of each subsidiary are as follows:

Snack Food Peers: 8.0–10.0 × LTM EBIT
Personal Care Products Peers: 12.0–14.0 × LTM EBIT
Pharmaceutical Peers: 14.0–16.0 × LTM EBIT

Based on these multiples, each subsidiary would have the following implied aggregate values.

Snack Foods: $120–$150 million
Personal Care Products: $240–$280 million
Pharmaceuticals: $350–$400 million

These imply a combined aggregate value, prior to eliminating the cost of corporate overhead, of $710–$830 million.

Discounted Cash Flow Analysis: Each subsidiary in the company should be valued based on the weighted average cost of capital of each business. From Chapter 10, we know that the components for the weighted cost of capital for each subsidiary — Beta, cost of debt, leverage ratio — should be determined based on estimates for comparable companies in each peer group. To shortcut the process a little, let's assume DCF values for each business of the following:

> Snack Foods: $130–$160 million
> Personal Care Products: $250–$300 million
> Pharmaceuticals: $375–$425 million

The implied value of All Mixed Up Co. prior to deducting the value of corporate overhead, is $755–$885 million.

Comparable Transactions Analysis: Comparable transactions analysis may not be appropriate in all situations; however, it should be calculated in the context of a break-up valuation as it may give an indication of which alternative to pursue. For example, transaction values for a given subsidiary may be sufficiently high enough to warrant pursuing a taxable sale over a tax-free spin-off.

Since the subsidiaries are not public, it is not possible to use comparable premiums analysis to value the subsidiaries. Rather, you should focus on comparable transaction multiples to value the businesses. Let's assume the following comparable transactions LTM EBIT multiples:

> Snack Food Comparable Transactions: 9.5–11.0 × LTM EBIT
> Personal Care Products Comparable Transactions: 14.0–15.0 × LTM EBIT
> Pharmaceutical Comparable Transactions: 17.0–18.5 × LTM EBIT

These multiples imply transaction-based values for each of the subsidiaries of:

> Snack Foods: $143–$165 million
> Personal Care Products: $280–$300 million
> Pharmaceuticals: $425–$463 million

In a transaction-based valuation, even though the premise would be to sell each of the businesses in a taxable transaction, the value of the corporate overhead would still need to be deducted to derive a net aggregate value number for the company. Based on this methodology, the implied aggregate value of the company, prior to corporate deductions, is $848–$928 million.

Step 2: Determine the Combined Aggregate Value of the Firm.

Each of the valuation components derived in Step 1 are then added together to derive a gross aggregate value for the company. Remember, this value represents the value of the combined businesses; however, it does not reflect the cost of the

Exhibit 18-4
Gross Aggregate Break-Up Value for All Mixed Up Co.
($ in millions)

Business Unit	Comparable Company Value	DCF Value	Comparable Transaction Value
Snack Foods	$120–150	$130–160	$143–165
Personal Care	$240–280	$250–300	$280–300
Pharmaceuticals	$350–400	$375–425	$425–463
Total	$710–830	$755–885	$848–928

corporate overhead. Exhibit 18-4 summarizes the combined value of each of the businesses of All Mixed Up Co.

Step 3: Calculate the Value of Corporate Overhead.

Corporate overhead typically does not grow at the same rate as revenues and operating profits of businesses. Economies of scale can be achieved through leveraging corporate overhead across multiple businesses. Consequently, overhead is usually valued at a much lower multiple than the operating profits of revenue generating businesses. For example, the operating profit of a subsidiary that is growing at 20% per year may be valued at 15.0–16.0×, whereas, the corporate overhead may be growing at only 3–5% per year, and consequently, may be valued at 2–4×. In the case of All Mixed Up Co., the corporate overhead is growing at approximately 4% per year. We could apply a valuation multiple of 2–4× to it, implying a value of $20–$40 million.

Step 4: Derive the Implied Equity Value for the Parent Company.

Once the different value components have been derived for the company, the next step is to calculate its implied equity value. Based on Steps 1 through 3, we know the discrete values for each business, the gross aggregate value for the company, and the value of the corporate overhead. The last remaining item needed to calculate the implied equity value for All Mixed Up Co. is the debt outstanding.

While in our example, there is only parent level debt, it is important to remember to include debt outstanding at each of the subsidiaries when calculating equity value.

Exhibit 18-5 provides a summary break-up valuation for All Mixed Up Co. On a stand alone basis, the break-up value of the company is approximately $590–$745 million, or, based on 25 million shares outstanding, $23.60–$29.80 per share. On a transaction basis, the value of the company is $728–$788 million, or, $29.12–$31.25 per share.

Exhibit 18-5
Break-Up Valuation of All Mixed Up Co.
($ in millions)

Business Unit	Comparable Company Value	DCF Value	Comparable Transaction Value
Snack Foods	$120–150	$130–160	$143–165
Personal Care	$240–280	$250–300	$280–300
Pharmaceuticals	$350–400	$375–425	$425–463
Total	$710–830	$755–885	$848–928
Corporate Overhead	–$ 20– 40	–$ 20– 40	–$ 20– 40
Debt Outstanding	–$ 100	–$ 100	–$ 100
Implied Equity Value	$590–690	$635–745	$728–788

Comparing this to the company's current stock price of $21.00 per share, it is easy to see that the company is grossly undervalued in the market place, both on an ongoing basis and a transaction basis, thereby suggesting that a corporate restructuring may possibly enhance value for shareholders.

[B] Capital Structure Analysis

Leverage plays a significant role in all types of restructurings. In financial restructurings, leverage may be increased in order to thwart a takeover offer or to repurchase shares, pay a special dividend, or simply optimize a company's capital structure by lowering its cost of capital. In divestiture-driven restructurings such as a spin-off, leverage needs to be analyzed for both the parent and the subsidiary to be spun-off. Common to all approaches however, is the notion that company's generally regress over time to their optimal capital structures.

Each industry will have an overall leverage ratio that is appropriate for that industry, and companies in an industry will exhibit leverage characteristics that are determined by their own growth opportunity, capital requirements and cash flow dynamics. As you approach analyzing the capital structure for a proposed restructuring, it is important to gather the comparable financial ratios for companies in the same sector as the company under question. For example, for all companies in a particular sector, one should review their credit ratings, evaluate their capital structure to understand the types of debt and equity each has, and look at their leverage ratios. In addition, it may be helpful to calculate each company's weighted average cost of capital to determine if they are using their capital structures wisely.

Once these comparable evaluations have been performed, it gives one a framework for understanding how a proposed restructuring may impact a given company. For example, a company in an industry that requires a strong balance sheet and high credit rating, may be at risk to a downgrade and subsequent earnings dilution if too much leverage is assumed.

In the case of divestitures, it is important to analyze the capital structures for the parent and the business to be divested. For example, a subsidiary to be spun-off or sold can assume debt and pay a dividend to the parent prior to the transaction. The parent can then use the cash proceeds to reduce debt, repurchase stock or pay out as a special dividend to its shareholders. In this case, it is important to ensure the divested business has a capital structure that is appropriate for its size, growth rates, industry sector and capital requirements.

[C] Accretion/Dilution Analysis

You may recall from Chapter 7: Merger Analysis, that accretion/dilution analysis assesses the impact of a transaction on parent company's earnings per share; however, in Chapter 7, the accretion/dilution analysis was performed in the context of a merger or acquisition, and the impact either of those transactions had on the acquirer. In the context of restructurings, accretion/dilution analysis evaluates the impact of the proposed divestiture or financial restructuring on the parent undertaking the transaction.

Using essentially the same methodology as outlined in Chapter 7, first project the income statement for the parent company prior to the restructuring. Then, separately, project the financial results for the parent company after the proposed transaction, and compare the resulting earnings per share with that of the company pre-transaction. To the extent the earnings per share have increased, the transaction is accretive; to the extent the earnings per share have declined, the transaction is dilutive.

As a cautionary note, while accretion/dilution analysis in mergers and acquisitions can indicate that an acquisition or merger is too expensive for the parent, if there is too much dilution, the same does not necessarily apply in a restructuring. For example, in a divestiture of a high-growth subsidiary that is undertaken to highlight the business, the earnings per share of the parent are likely to decline post transaction. However, the overall value to shareholders may increase. Therefore, it is important to go beyond simply looking at the dilution or accretion of a transaction, and analyze the results in the context of shareholder value creation.

[D] Shareholder Value Creation Analysis

Clearly restructurings are designed to enhance shareholder value. However, shareholder value creation evidences itself in a number of ways. In the eyes of the public equity markets, companies are typically valued based on their earnings per share and the estimated growth rate on their earnings. This evidences itself in the multiple that the market places on those earnings, known as a price/earnings (P/E) multiple. Two principle factors contribute to the magnitude of a P/E multiple: growth rate and leverage.

The growth rate of a company's earnings can be altered in a number of ways. In restructurings, growth can be slowed by increasing leverage, eliminating high growth businesses, or paying out cash as a special dividend to shareholders. Likewise, growth can be accelerated by shrinking a company's equity base, reducing leverage, or eliminating a slow growing business. All these actions translate into a shrinking or expanding of a company's P/E multiple.

As a result of this thinking, any restructuring, financial, or otherwise, should be translated not only into an impact on a company's capital structure and earnings, but also into an impact on shareholder value. For example, in a spin-off, a parent company's earnings per share are likely to decline as the results of the subsidiary are deconsolidated. However, the earnings growth rate of the parent may increase because the subsidiary that was spun-off may not be growing as fast as the parent. Therefore, the likely result is that the P/E multiple for the parent should expand. The multiple on the subsidiary's stock should then be appropriate for its own growth rate.

[E]   Ownership Analysis

Certain types of restructurings may result in a significant change in the equity ownership of a company post restructuring. For example, in a share repurchase, shares acquired by the company in the market are placed into the treasury, thus concentrating the ownership of the company among the remaining shareholders. Changing the ownership of a company can have a direct impact on the value of a company. For example, in a share repurchase, the earnings of the company will expand, suggesting that the implied earnings growth may accelerate. Consequently, the P/E multiple of the company may increase and the overall earnings of the company may do the same.

§ 18.07   THE ROLE OF TAXES IN DETERMINING A DIVESTITURE APPROACH

At the point that a decision has been made to maximize the value of certain assets in affecting a corporate restructuring, the question becomes which approach to pursue. One primary consideration will be the tax basis that the parent company has in each subsidiary or business. Those with a higher tax basis, may lend themselves to a taxable sale transaction, while those with a lower tax basis may lend themselves to a tax-free alternative.

For example, assume that All Mixed Up Co. has the following tax basis in each of its primary business units:

- Snack Foods: $100 million

- Personal Care Products: $50 million

- Pharmaceuticals: $75 million

The question becomes which form of divestiture to pursue to maximize value. Based on tax basis alone, the subsidiary most likely to be sold in a taxable sale would be the snack food business, while the pharmaceuticals business would be the least likely to be sold in a taxable sale.

Of course, taxes are not the only consideration that will impact the decision to pursue a taxable or tax-free alternative, they are, however, one of the most important determinants of transaction structure.

§ 18.08 SUMMARY

Corporate restructurings have evolved over time from a means to improve a poorly operating company or over levered balance sheet, to a number of different approaches to maximizing shareholder value or preventing a takeover. As a result, the shape of corporate America has changed dramatically over the past 30 years. Companies have divested assets to monetize their value, broken themselves up to harness the value contained in various subsidiaries, paid dividends to increase leverage, or taken a subsidiary public in an IPO to highlight the value of that business. Corporate restructurings, along with other plain vanilla mergers and acquisitions, are now a staple in a board's arsenal to improve shareholder value. When analyzing a restructuring, it is important to analyze its impact on the company's balance sheet, income statement and ownership. In addition, one must translate these changes into their impact on shareholder value. As a caution, it is not immediately intuitive that a given transaction creates value. One must understand how each change impacts the public market's view of valuation, for example, the impact of the changes on a company's P/E multiple.

Chapter 19

RECAPITALIZATIONS AND SHARE REPURCHASES

§ 19.01 OVERVIEW

A recapitalization is a form of restructuring designed to alter a company's capital structure and equity ownership. It involves a modification in the relative levels of a company's debt and equity in order to change its cost of capital and thus impact its valuation.

While recapitalizations are often undertaken to enhance shareholder value, they have also been implemented as a means to thwart an unwanted takeover threat, realign the equity ownership of a company's securities, and as a structural approach to effectively taking a company private. Recapitalizations can take a variety of forms, ranging from a modest share repurchase program designed to shrink a company's equity base and incrementally enhance leverage, to a leveraged recapitalization where the entire capital structure and ownership of the company is reconfigured. In a leveraged recapitalization, the existing equity securities of the company are replaced with cash, debt, preferred stock, or other equity securities that have different voting and economic interests. Companies undertaking recapitalizations usually increase the amount of debt on the balance sheet and/or reduce the amount of equity; however, technically, a recapitalization can also involve the issuance of additional equity.

The principal forms of recapitalization are shown in Exhibit 19-1.

Recapitalization plans, while they vary in form and structure, are recognized by many database companies as a discrete transaction. Between 1990 and 2003, there were approximately 233 announcements of recapitalization plans.[1] In 2003 alone, there were eight announced recapitalization plans. Exhibit 19-2 shows the trend in recapitalization announcements since 1990.

Exhibit 19-3 provides an overview of significant recapitalizations in the past few decades.

Share repurchases have become a common means to altering the capital structure of a company. They are generally executed in one of three forms: open-market share repurchases, targeted block purchases, or self-tender offers.

Between 1994 and 2003, there were approximately 7,129 share repurchase announcements representing a total of $1.4 trillion in dollar value. In 2003 alone, there were 378 share repurchase announcements representing $151 billion in

---

1. Thomson Financial defines a recapitalization plan as one in which the company issues a special one-time dividend in the form of cash, debt securities, preferred stock, or assets, while allowing shareholders to retain an equity interest in the company.

Exhibit 19-1
Principal Forms of Recapitalizations

Form of Recapitalization	Summary Description
Share Repurchase	A company buys back its own shares through an open-market share repurchase, a targeted block repurchase or a self-tender.
Special Dividend	A company pays a one-time, non-recurring dividend, usually in cash, to shareholders.
Leveraged Recapitalization	Shareholders sell or exchange their stock for a package of cash, debt, and/or other instruments, plus potentially a small amount of stock, for shares in the company.

Exhibit 19-2
Announced Recapitalization Plans: 1990–2003[2]

($ in millions)

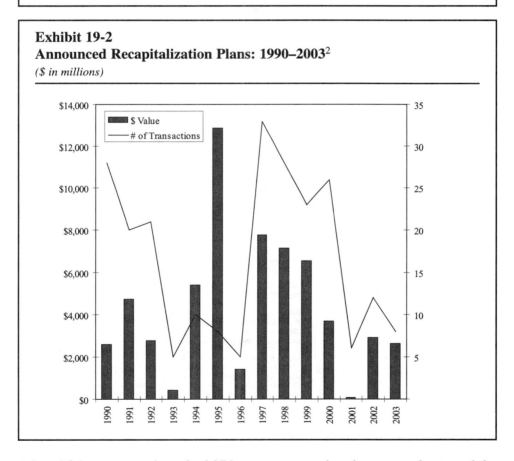

value. Of these, approximately 6,274 were open-market share repurchases and the remainder were self-tender offers and block repurchases. Exhibit 19-4 illustrates the increase in the number of share repurchases since 1994.

2. Thomson Financial.

Exhibit 19-3
Recent Significant Recapitalizations[3]

Date Effective	Target Name	Value	Synopsis
02/20/2002	MACTEC Inc	$ 80	A management-led investor group, comprised of Nautic Partners LLC (NP) and Wachovia Capital Partners (WC), acquired all the outstanding stock of MACTEC Inc, a provider of environmental management services, for $80 mil. Upon completion, NP was to hold a majority interest, while WC was to hold a minority stake.
01/10/2003	NTL Inc	$1,513	NTL Inc (OLDNTL), an owner and operator of cable TV systems and radio stations, completed its debt restructuring with bondholders (BH) in a transaction valued at an estimated $1.513 billion. BH received an estimated $322 million in cash, 50 mil new NTL Inc (NEWNTL) common shares valued at $1.18 billion, 17.3 mil new NTL Europe Inc (NE) common shares valued at $11.245 million, and 7.364 mil NE 10% fixed coupon redeemable preferred shares. The shares were valued based on NEWNTL's closing stock price of $23.60 and NE's closing stock price of $.65 on January 13, the first full trading day post-restructuring. Pursuant to the plan, OLDNTL was reorganized into two companies. OLDNTL changed its name to NE and was the holding company for all assets and business in continental Europe. NTL Communications Corp changed its name to NEWNTL and was the holding company for all assets and businesses in the UK and Ireland. Upon completion, BH held 100% of NEWNTL and an 86.5% interest in NE.
07/31/2002	APW Ltd	$ 100	APW Ltd (APW), a designer and manufacturer of a comprehensive portfolio of electronic products, including enclosures, power supplies, thermal management systems, backplanes, and cabling, completed its debt restructuring with creditors (CR) in a transaction valued at $100 million. CR's received 1 mil new common shares and $100 million in debt. Upon completion, CR's held a 99% interest in the restructured APW. New common APW shares did not trade on a public market, and were therfore unvalued.
10/29/2002	ITC Deltacom Inc	$ 130	ITC Deltacom Inc (ITC), a provider of telecommunications services, completed its debt restructuring with bondholders, who recieved 43.25 million common shares, valued at $129.75 million. The shares were valued based on ITC's closing stock price of $3, on October 30, the first full trading day post-restructuring. Upon completion, bondholders held a 96.65% interest in the restructured ITC.
03/07/2003	Sirius Satellite Radio Inc	$ 267	Sirius Satellite Radio Inc (SSR), an owner and operator of radio stations, completed its debt restructuring with creditors (CR), who received 545.012 million new common shares valued at $267.056 million. The shares were valued based on SSR's closing stock price of $.49 on March 10, the first full trading day post-restructuring. Upon completion, CR held an 87.622% interest in the restructured SSR. Concurrently, an investor group, comprised of Oppenheimer & Co Inc, Apollo Management LP and Blackstone Group LP, acquired an undisclosed stake in the restructured SSR.
03/07/2003	Sirius Satellite Radio Inc	$ 200	An investor group, comprised of Oppenheimer & Co Inc, Apollo Management LP and Blackstone Group LP, acquired an undisclosed minority stake, in Sirius Satellite Radio Inc (SSR), an owner and operator of radio stations, for $200 milionl. Concurrently, SSR completed its debt restructuring with creditors (CR) who received 545.012 million new common shares in SSR, in exchange for the reduction of $700 million in debt. Upon completion, CR held an 87.622% interest in the restructured SSR.
06/02/2003	Inland Resources Inc	$ 85	Inland Resources Inc (IRI), an oil and gas exploration and production company, completed its debt restructuring with creditors (CR) in a transaction valued $85.437 million. CR received 22.053 million common shares valued at $15.437 million and 1million Series F preferred shares convertible into additional common shares on a 1-for-100 basis, valued at $70 million. The shares were valued based on IRI's closing stock price of $.70 on June 3, the first full trading day post-restructuring. Upon completion, CR held all the outstanding common stock of IRI.
04/17/2003	American Media Inc	$ 508	An investor group comprised of Thomas H Lee Partners LP (TL), a unit of Thomas H Lee Co, and Evercore Capital Partners LP (EC) acquired all the outstanding stock of American Media Inc, a publisher of tabloid newspaper, for $508 million. Upon completion, TL and EC were to each own 50% of the recapitalized AM company. Investors in EC's first fund were to cash out and was to be replaced by new investors of EC and TL.
07/31/2003	Samsonite Corp	$ 777	Samsonite Corp (SSC), a manufacturer of luggage, completed its debt restructuring with creditors (CR). Upon completion, CR were to hold a 97% interest in the restructured SSC.

Like share repurchases, special dividends have become a popular form of recapitalizing a company and distributing cash to shareholders. A number of highly regarded companies have issued special dividends, most particularly as a part of

---

3. Thomson Financial.

Exhibit 19-4
Announced Share Repurchases: 1994–2003[4]

($ in millions)

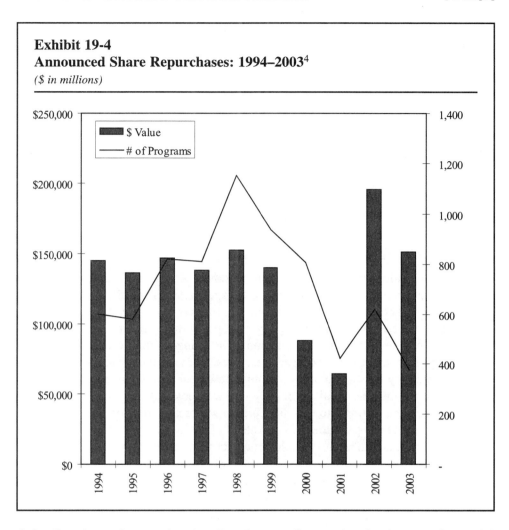

defending themselves against hostile takeover. Companies that have made special dividends include Holiday Corp, Harcourt Brace Jovanovich, Newmont Mining, USG, Interco, Caesar's World, Kroger and Texaco.

§ 19.02   MOTIVATION BEHIND RECAPITALIZATIONS AND SHARE REPURCHASES

[A]   Enhance Shareholder Value

A recapitalization plan often is considered when a company's stock is perceived to be undervalued. Share repurchases in particular, have been used to signal the market regarding management's view of the value of the company's stock. Special dividends and leveraged recapitalizations have been used to

---

4. Thomson Financial.

enhance shareholder value by increasing the company's debt in order to lower its cost of capital. Recapitalizations have also been used to enhance value out of fear of a potential takeover threat.

[B]   Distribute Excess Cash

A second reason why companies undertake a recapitalization is to distribute excess cash that the company may have accumulated as a result of asset sales or because the firm has generated excess profits. Special dividends and share repurchases are an effective means to distribute this cash to shareholders. With a special dividend, shareholders are able to receive the dividend while continuing to retain their stock, while in a share repurchase, the shareholder must decide whether it prefers to receive cash for its shares or forego the cash and retain its stock in the company.

[C]   Thwart Unwanted Takeover Threat

Recapitalizations became a prime anti-takeover defense tactic during the height of the hostile acquisition frenzy in the 1980s. A recapitalization allows the company subject to the takeover proposal to take control of its own destiny. Instead of selling the company to the highest bidder, as might happen if the company is put in play, the company can undertake the recapitalization. In so doing, it significantly increases the debt outstanding, making the company less attractive to potential acquirers. In addition, the company has the ability to reconfigure its equity ownership in the process and concentrate the stock of the company in fewer, possibly, friendlier hands.

The precedent setting Multimedia Corporation recapitalization transpired when the company had received numerous unwanted offers. Multimedia had been founded by a family who, in 1985, initiated a leveraged buyout of the company. In response to the LBO offer, the company received a number of unsolicited bids. As a consequence, Multimedia undertook a recapitalization that paid its shareholders a significant cash dividend as well as a stub payment of stock in the company post recapitalization.

Another example is the 1985 attempted hostile takeover of Union Carbide Corporation by GAF Corporation. To thwart the offer, Union Carbide offered its shareholders $20 per share in cash plus $65 in debt securities. The entire package was valued at $85 per share and represented approximately 35% of the company's shares outstanding.

[D]   Concentrate Equity Ownership

Recapitalizations most commonly serve to shrink the equity base of a company and in the process, consolidate the ownership of the equity in the hands of the remaining shareholders. In a share repurchase, the stockholders that forfeit their ownership in the company do so to the benefit of the remaining stockholders who own more of the remaining company post buyback. In a leveraged recapitalization, it is typical to see the inside shareholders such as management increase their stakes in companies quite significantly. By example, in the Multimedia transaction in 1985, insiders increased their ownership in the company from 13.0% to 43.0% post recapitalization.

A 1990 study by Michael Brennan and Anjan Thakor derived a model that showed that recapitalizations redistribute wealth from small, uninformed investors to large, informed investors.[5] In a share repurchase for example, it is common to see an "odd-lot" offer, where the company seeks to repurchase shares from those shareholders that own less than 100 shares. These investors are typically individual shareholders whose time horizon may be dramatically different than that of large institutions owning 1% or 2% of a company's equity.

[E]   Alternative to a Leveraged Buyout

Leveraged recapitalizations have been used as an alternative to a leveraged buyout. In a leveraged recapitalization, shareholders relinquish a substantial portion of their shares in the company in exchange for a package of securities that may contain cash, debt and/or other instruments, plus potentially a small amount of stock in the surviving corporation. In the process, it is typical to see management and other insiders increase their relative stake in the company during the process. A leveraged recapitalization, like a leveraged buyout, relies on the company's cash flows to repay debt. As the debt is paid down, the value created in the process is transferred to equity holders.

Unlike a leveraged buyout, the company is not actually "sold." This is significant in that a company undertaking a leveraged buyout that becomes faced with a higher offer from a third party, has a difficult time succeeding with the LBO since the company's board of directors and management must entertain the higher offer. A leveraged recapitalization is not typically viewed in the same light as a leveraged buyout as the company's shareholders will likely continue to own a predetermined amount of equity in the ongoing company.

§ 19.03   ADVANTAGES AND DISADVANTAGES OF RECAPITALIZATIONS AND SHARE REPURCHASES

There are significant advantages to a recapitalization over other forms of restructuring. Most importantly, a recapitalization allows the target company to remain independent while restructuring the company, which can be an effective deterrent to a takeover. It concentrates the ownership in the hands of a few loyal shareholders, as disloyal or uninformed shareholders sell their stock. It can lower the company's cost of capital, as incremental debt itself usually has a lower cost of capital than a company's equity. It may provide current shareholders with a return on their investment in the form of a purchase of their stock at a premium, plus give them ongoing participation in the upside of the company. A final benefit of certain types of recapitalizations, such as share repurchases, is that they can serve to

---

5. Brennan, Michael, and Anjan Thakor, "Shareholder Preferences and Dividend Policy," Journal of Finance 45, 993–1018 (1990).

enhance a company's financial ratios. For example, a share repurchase shrinks the number of shares outstanding and thus increases the earnings per share.

Despite the clear benefits of a recapitalization, there can also be a number of drawbacks. The demonstrable increase in leverage resulting from a recapitalization can result in severe financial distress and even bankruptcy. A good example is the infamous recapitalization of Interco in 1988, in which the conglomerate, in the face of a takeover threat from the Rales Brothers, undertook a leveraged restructuring that ultimately overwhelmed the company's ability to service its debt, resulting in the company defaulting on its obligations in 1990. The holders of the company's debt ultimately were forced to accept equity in exchange for the debt in order to prevent further value loss from the deal. If the recapitalization is successful, it can actually serve to make the target company more vulnerable to takeover, as the equity base of the company has shrunken considerably.

Another drawback of recapitalizations, in particular share repurchases and special dividends, is the potential negative signal they send to the market. Companies who announce these types of transactions may be perceived as having limited investment and growth opportunities, and that the company has no other use for the cash. In addition, certain studies have shown that companies that announce repurchases tend to have poorer financial performance than those companies with strong financial performance.

Exhibit 19-5 provides a summary of the advantages and disadvantages of recapitalizations.

Exhibit 19-5
Advantages and Disadvantages of Recapitalizations

Advantages	*Disadvantages*
• Lowers company's cost of capital	• May result in over-leverage and consequently severe financial distress and bankruptcy
• Enhances shareholder value	• Increase in leverage may constrain operating and financial flexibility
• Concentrates equity in hands of loyal shareholders	
• Potential to thwart takeover threat	• May send negative signal, in that the market may perceive the recapitalization as a sign the company has few other investment or growth opportunities
• Provides current return plus future upside	
• Effective means to distribute cash	• Masking financial ratios may cloud true financial performance
• May signal stock is undervalued	
• Can enhance financial ratios	

---

§ 19.04 EVIDENCE BEHIND RECAPITALIZATIONS AND SHARE REPURCHASES

There has been significant research into certain aspects of recapitalizations, most particularly share repurchases and special dividends, which evidence strong stock market responses upon the announcement of the program as well as long term. Numerous studies have shown that there is a strong positive response to the announcement of a stock repurchase, whether as an open-market repurchase or a self-tender offer (Asquith and Mullins,[6] 1983; Dann et al.,[7] 1981; and Masulis,[8] 1980). Theo Vermaelen, in a 1981 study, showed that there was a two-day positive return around the announcement of self-tender offers and open-market share repurchases of 1.3% and 3.0%, respectively.[9] A recent 2000 study by Erik Lie at the College of William and Mary studied 207 self-tender offers. He found that, consistent with other studies, there was a significant positive market reaction to the announcement of a share repurchase. He showed a mean announcement return for self-tenders of 8.0%.[10] Studies by Comment and Jarrell[11] in 1991 and Howe, He, and Kao[12] in 1992 showed comparable mean announcement returns of 8.4% and 7.5%, respectively. The Comment and Jarrell study reported that fixed-price tender offers showed abnormal returns of 8.3%, while Dutch auctions and open market repurchases showed abnormal announcement returns of 7.5% and 2.3%, respectively.

Looking at long-term returns to shareholders, a 1985 study by C.J. Loomis analyzed extended stock repurchases over a period from 1974 to 1983. He saw a compounded annual return to shareholders in the companies who undertook share repurchases of 22.6% versus a return of 14.1% for the S&P 500 over the same period.[13]

---

6. Asquith, P., and D. Mullins, Jr., "The Impact of Initiating Dividend Payments on Shareholder's Wealth," Journal of Business 56, 77–96 (1983).

7. Dann, L.Y., R.W. Masulis, and D. Mayers, "Repurchase Tender Offers and Earnings Information," Journal of Accounting and Economics 9, 217–251 (1981).

8. Masulis, R.W., "Stock Repurchase by Tender Offer: An Analysis of the Causes of Common Stock Price Changes," Journal of Finance 35, 305–319 (1980).

9. Vermaelen, T., "Common Stock Repurchases and Market Signaling: An Empirical Study," Journal of Financial Economics 9, 139–183 (1981).

10. Lie, Erik, "Excess Funds and Agency Problems: An Empirical Study of Incremental Cash Disbursements," The Review of Financial Studies Vol. 13, No. 1, 219–248 (2000).

11. Comment, R., and G.A. Jarrell, "The Relative Signaling Power of Dutch-Auction and Fixed-Price Self-Tender Offers and Open-Market Share Repurchases," Journal of Finance 46, 1243–1271 (1991).

12. Howe, K.M., J. He, and G.W. Kao, "One-Time Cash Flow Announcements and Free Cash-Cash Flow Theory: Share Repurchases and Special Dividends," Journal of Finance 47, 1963–1975 (1992).

13. Loomis, C.J., "Beating the Market by Buying Back Stock," Fortune, April 29, 1985, 42–48.

Despite significant data showing a positive stock price response to share repurchase announcements, there have also been a fair number of papers that have portrayed share repurchases in a negative light, not necessarily because the company's stock price does not rise, but rather because the share repurchase announcement is an indication of poor operating and financial performance and a signal that the company has few alternatives to pursue with its cash. In 1974, R. Norgaard and C. Norgaard showed that firms repurchasing their stock had poor expectations of their company's future earnings prospects.[14]

Special dividends have also been the subject of academic research and have shown a positive stock price reaction to special dividend announcements. Lie analyzed 570 special dividends and found that there was a mean announcement return of 3.5% for special dividends.[15] In 1983, James Brickley examined 165 special dividends and found a positive announcement effect of 2.1%.[16] Another study by Howe, He, and Kao in 1992 showed similar results with a 3.4% announcement effect.[17] Harry DeAngelo, Linda DeAngelo, and Douglas Skinner showed in a February 2000 paper that special dividend announcements yield a 1% average stock market response.[18]

Beyond the announcement effect of share repurchases and special dividends, there has also been analysis of the financial attributes of companies announcing these programs. For example, Lie showed that firms announcing special dividends and share repurchases tend to have higher levels of cash balances prior to the event than their industry peers.[19] He also found that firms paying one-time dividends and announcing share repurchases generated less cash flow before and after the announcement than their peer group.

Research on leveraged recapitalizations has been less prolific, as the evidence behind shareholder value creation is not quite as clear. The evidence certainly establishes that the target company's leverage increases substantially, but it does not necessarily establish that there are broad-based shareholder gains. Rather, there is research indicating that public companies which undertake leveraged

---

14. Norgaard, R., and C. Norgaard, "A Critical Examination of Share Repurchasing," Financial Management, Spring 1974, 44–51.

15. Lie, Erik, "Excess Funds and Agency Problems: An Empirical Study of Incremental Cash Disbursements," The Review of Financial Studies Vol. 13, No. 1, 219–248 (2000).

16. Brickley, James A., "Shareholder Wealth, Information Signaling and the Specially Designated Dividend," Journal of Financial Economics 12, 187–209 (1983).

17. Howe, K.M., J. He, and G.W. Kao, "One-Time Cash Flow Announcements and Free Cash-Cash Flow Theory: Share Repurchases and Special Dividends," Journal of Finance 47, 1963–1975 (1992).

18. DeAngelo, Harry, Linda DeAngelo, and Douglas J. Skinner, "Special Dividends and the Evolution of Dividend Signaling," Marshall School of Business, USC and University of Michigan School of Business (February 2000).

19. Lie, Erik, "Excess Funds and Agency Problems: An Empirical Study of Incremental Cash Disbursements," The Review of Financial Studies Vol. 13, No. 1, 219–248 (2000).

Exhibit 19-6
Comparison Between Recapitalizations[20]
($ in millions)

Company	Metric	Before Recapitalization	After Recapitalization*
Multimedia Corporation	Long-Term Debt	$0073.2	$ 0,877.7
	Net Worth	$0248.7	d$ 0,576.4
	Book Value/Share	$0014.9	d$ 00,52.4
FMC Coporation	Long-Term Debt	$0303.2	$ 1,787.3
	Net Worth	$1123.1	d$ 0,506.6
	Book Value/Share	$0007.54	d$0,011.25
Colt Industries	Long-Term Debt	$0342.4	$ 1,643.1
	Net Worth	$0414.3	d$ 1,078.0
	Book Value/Share	$0002.55	d$0,036.91
Owens-Corning	Long-Term Debt	$0543.0	$ 1,645.2
	Net Worth	$0944.7	d$ 1,025.0
	Book Value/Share	$0031.7	d$0,025.94
Holiday Corporation	Long-Term Debt	$0992.5	$ 2,500.0
	Net Worth	$0638.7	d$ 0,850.0
	Book Value/Share	$0027.1	d$ 0,031.2
Harcourt Brace Jovanovich	Long-Term Debt	$0790.3	$ 2,550.0
	Net Worth	$0531.5	d$ 1,050.0
	Book Value/Share	$0013.5	d$ 0,021.0

*d denotes deficit.

recapitalizations show a broad stock price decline after the restructuring. Larry Dann and Harry DeAngelo in a study in 1988, showed that share prices declined an average of 2%–3% upon the announcement of a restructuring.[21] Their study looked at a sample of 39 restructurings from 1963 to 1983.

Leveraged recapitalizations will increase the debt on a company to extreme levels, in many cases, completely wiping out a company's book value, as seen in a study by Robert Kleinman who analyzed the effects of leveraged recapitalizations.[22] Some of this data is reflected in Exhibit 19-6.

---

20. Kleinman, Robert, "The Shareholder Gain from Leveraged Cash Outs: Preliminary Evidence," Journal of Applied Corporate Finance 1, No. 1, 50 (Spring 1988).

21. Dann, Larry Y., and Harry DeAngelo, "Corporate Financial Policy and Corporate Control: A Study in Defensive Adjustments in Asset and Ownership Structure," Journal of Financial Economics 20, No. 1/2, 87–128 (1988).

22. Kleinman, *supra* n.20.

§ 19.05 CREATING VALUE THROUGH RECAPITALIZATIONS AND SHARE REPURCHASES

Shareholder value creation in recapitalizations and share repurchases is dependent on the type of recapitalization program and the particular circumstances behind the transaction. From a theoretical perspective, value creation or destruction in a recapitalization is dependent on three factors: the announcement or signaling effect, the investment effect, and the transaction effect. Each of these is most easily explained in the context of a share repurchase program.

Let us say for example, that a company has 10 million shares outstanding. It has earnings per share of $1.00 and it has a stock price of $15.00 per share. Therefore, its implied price/earnings multiple is 15 times earnings and its equity market value is $150 million. If the company announces a self-tender offer at $18.00 per share for 20% of its stock, it is expecting to acquire 2 million shares. Think about what the share repurchase announcement is telling shareholders and the market. First, management is suggesting that the company's stock price is undervalued. By offering to repurchase the stock at $18.00 per share, it is clearly suggesting that someone, in this case the company, should be willing to pay that price for the stock. This notion has been observed in numerous academic studies (Asquith and Mullins,[23] 1983).

The premise behind this idea is that management possesses inside information regarding the future prospects of the business and perceives the stock to be undervalued by the market. Therefore, the first impact of the share repurchase announcement, as substantiated by numerous studies, is that the company's stock price rises. Studies have shown the stock price rise due to the announcement effect is anywhere from 1.3% (Lie,[24] 2000) to 8.4% (Howe, He, and Kao,[25] 1992).

A second observation in the example is that the firm repurchasing its own stock does so rather than investing its excess cash in alternate growth opportunities, suggesting that the repurchase is a better investment than other available opportunities. This further provides a bullish statement to the market that the stock is undervalued, and in theory, encourages investors to bid up the stock price. However, there are academics who do not agree with this view, and certain studies suggest that companies announcing share repurchases do so not necessarily because the company's own stock is a good investment, but because the company has no other growth or investment alternatives. Further, some would suggest that

---

23. Asquith, P., and D. Mullins, Jr., "The Impact of Initiating Dividend Payments on Shareholder's Wealth," Journal of Business 56, 77–96 (1983).

24. Lie, Erik, "Excess Funds and Agency Problems: An Empirical Study of Incremental Cash Disbursements," The Review of Financial Studies Vol. 13, No. 1, 219–248 (2000).

25. Howe, K.M., J. He, and G.W. Kao, "One-Time Cash Flow Announcements and Free Cash-Cash Flow Theory: Share Repurchases and Special Dividends," Journal of Finance 47, 1963–1975 (1992).

share repurchases are announced by companies that have poor historical perform-ance and future prospects (Norgaard and Norgaard,[26] 1974).

The third impact of a share repurchase is the practical financial shift that occurs in the company's statements. By repurchasing 20% of the company's stock, it shrinks its shares outstanding to 8 million shares from 10 million shares. The company's net income stays the same, yet its earnings per share increases to $1.25 per share. Applying the company's historical 15 times price/earnings multiple yields a stock price of $18.75. In essence, even though the company has offered to repurchase stock at $18.00 per share, the company's stock should trade up to the $18.75 per share level.

A second set of logic surrounding the creation of value with recapitalizations revolves around how the market values a company with respect to its balance sheet leverage. In general, a company's multiple is determined by two primary factors, its growth rate and its leverage. Moderate increases in leverage tend to increase a company's multiple as a result of the tax shelter on operating earnings provided by the interest expense on debt. The market therefore, may tend to penalize compa-nies that are underleveraged and reward companies with more aggressive capital structures. This having been said, the market will also penalize companies that are too overleveraged, the idea being that those companies have a higher degree of risk associated with financial distress. In theory, a company's cost of debt is much less than its cost of equity. The more debt a company has in its capital structure, the lower its cost of capital. However, this only remains true up to the point where the company's operating cash flows are able to comfortably service the debt. Once the company reaches a point of financial distress, the cost of its debt increases dramatically, and the company's cost of capital may increase as well. This notion is explained in Exhibit 19-7.

In this exhibit, it is plain to see that a company's cost of debt increases as the amount of leverage in the capital structure increases. The same is true for the com-pany's cost of equity. However, as the percentage of debt in the company increases, the lower cost of capital attributed to the debt outweighs the cost of equity capital, and lowers the company's overall cost of capital. Only when the company increases leverage to the point where it goes beyond its optimal capital structure and begins to impinge on the company's financial flexibility, does the overall cost of capital begin to rise again, because the cost of financial distress begins to overly burden the company's debt cost of capital and consequently the company's overall weighted average cost of capital.

In an underleveraged scenario, undertaking a recapitalization through a share repurchase or paying a special dividend, can enhance shareholder value by opti-mizing the company's capital structure. The share repurchase or dividend can be financed with excess cash or through assuming new debt, both of which serve to increase the company's debt-to-equity ratio.

---

26. Norgaard, R., and C. Norgaard, "A Critical Examination of Share Repurchasing," Financial Management, Spring 1974, 44–51.

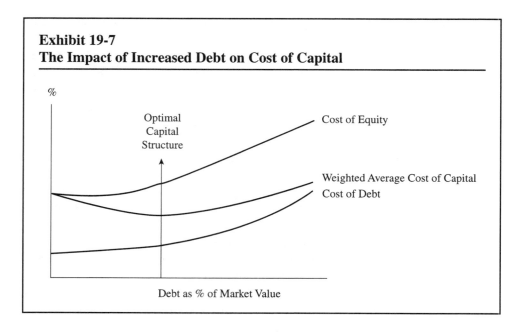

Exhibit 19-7
The Impact of Increased Debt on Cost of Capital

In a leveraged recapitalization, where a company is completely restructured, i.e., existing shareholders sell or exchange their stock for cash, debt, or other securities plus a "stub" share that represents their remaining interest in the company, the rationale behind shareholder value creation is far more difficult. First, the likely outcome of the transaction is that the equity base in the company shrinks quite dramatically and the debt increases significantly as well. In fact, in many cases, the company ends up having a negative book value. Second, it is important to remember that many leveraged recapitalizations are undertaken to fend off an unwanted takeover threat, and therefore, the goal is actually to temporarily "destroy" shareholder value by making the target company unattractive as an acquisition candidate. Third, in the leveraged recapitalization, shareholders are often paid cash plus other securities for their shares at a premium to the current stock price. Therefore, they receive a return on their investment to the extent they acquired the stock at a price below the value of the securities offered in the deal. Plus, they receive a small interest in the surviving company. Fourth, this type of transaction often results in the management and/or insiders consolidating and increasing their equity position in the company. While the public shareholders sell or exchange their stock for a new package of securities including cash and/or debt, management often forgoes the cash or debt securities and instead awards themselves additional equity securities in the transaction.

The premise behind value creation in a leveraged recapitalization is three-fold. First, the public shareholders receive a premium valuation for their shares at the time of the deal in the form of cash, debt, or other securities, plus an ongoing interest in the company. Second, the equity of the company is reconfigured such that management and insiders end up owning a disproportionate interest in the company relative to their pre-transaction ownership. Third, the leverage on the company renders the company unattractive as an acquisition candidate, and the potential unwanted suitor backs away from the transaction. The value creation occurs when the debt is paid down and the value is transferred to equity holders.

§ 19.06 STRUCTURING A RECAPITALIZATION

The structure of a recapitalization depends on a number of factors surrounding the specifics of the situation at hand. Most significantly, it is important to question how the company is valued in the market place relative to its peer group, and whether the company is undervalued. Second, the form of recapitalization will depend on whether the company is under immediate takeover threat or whether there is only the potential for a takeover offer. Third, the company should assess what its objectives are in undertaking a recapitalization. For example, is it attempting to distribute excess cash to shareholders, signal the market regarding its perceived undervaluation, or reconfigure the entire capital structure in order to make the company less attractive to a potential unwanted suitor. Fourth, the company will need to assess its current capital structure and its ongoing capital needs. Fifth, the structure will depend on the perceived risk inherent in the company's business, its cash flows, and the industry. Finally, the structure chosen will depend heavily on the state of the debt financing market and the availability and terms of capital.

[A]   Attributes of an Attractive Recapitalization Candidate

Companies that undertake recapitalizations, whether a special dividend, share repurchase, or leveraged recapitalization, share a number of common attributes to varying degrees, depending on the form of recapitalization. In addition, recapitalization candidates have many of the same characteristics as companies that undertake leveraged buyouts, i.e, stable cash flows, low levels of debt, strong industry and company dynamics, low capital intensity, experienced management, and assets that may be sold to repay debt.

[1]   Stable Cash Flows

The greater the stability and predictability of cash flows, the less risk there is in the transaction. Lenders will look to the stability of cash flows to determine how much they will lend to the company. Historical measures of cash flows may indicate likely future stability; however, it is important to evaluate the future cash flows in the context of the recapitalization, and evaluate the company's overall financial performance and ability to generate cash with a significantly altered capital structure. Increased leverage may have an impact on the ability of the company to invest in capital and working assets and consequently, the future financial and operating profile of the firm may change.

[2]   Low Levels of Debt

Recapitalizations most often entail assuming significant amounts of debt, regardless of whether the form of recapitalization is a share repurchase, a leveraged recapitalization or a special dividend. In some cases, the company may use excess cash as a means of payment of the transaction. Nevertheless, the company should have sufficient debt capacity to assume the incremental debt or absorb the loss of excess cash. The ultimate ability of the transaction to be financed will depend on the current state of the debt financing market which will be a primary driver of the level of debt the company can borrow.

[3]   Strong Company and Industry Dynamics

The target company should have a strong position in an industry with attractive dynamics. There should be little regulatory risk or other third party extraneous factors that could unexpectedly alter the cash flow dynamics of the company. The company should operate in an industry where there is minimal technology obsolescence risk and where the company is not necessarily dependent on product innovation. It is preferable for the company to operate in an industry that does not require extensive capital expenditures or significant levels of research and development.

[4]   Experienced Management

While stable cash flows and a strong balance sheet are pre-requisites for a successful recapitalization, they cannot be relied upon as the sole basis on which to proceed. The quality of the management team is equally as important. Lenders will want to have comfort that the management team has been in place for an extended period and that the management team has the requisite experience to manage the company under a leveraged scenario.

[5]   Undervalued Assets

An attractive recapitalization candidate may be a company that has undervalued assets or businesses that can be divested to help reduce leverage once the transaction has closed. While lenders may not depend on asset sales to repay debt, they can be an effective means to quickly reducing the leverage of a recapitalized company.

[B]   Forms of Recapitalization

The type of recapitalization pursued will depend on the objectives of the company and the specific opportunity or threat faced by the company. Some of the factors that will influence the decision to pursue a certain type of structure include, the threat faced by the company, the timing required to complete the recapitalization plan, the need for a shareholder vote, the restrictions on any recapitalization placed on the company by existing debt instruments, charter and by-law considerations, state corporate law considerations, and tax implications to the company and to shareholders.

The structure used may be as simple as a special dividend or as complicated as an exchange of a package of cash and/or debt plus new shares for the existing stock in the company. The more complicated the transaction, the more likely it will require shareholder approval.

Exhibit 19-8 provides examples of specific recapitalization strategies.

Exhibit 19-8
Examples of Recapitalizations[27]

Strategy	Example Companies
Special Dividend	Holiday Corp., Harcourt Brace Jovanovich, Newmont Mining, USG, Interco, Caesar's World, Kroger, Texaco
Open-Market Share Repurchase	Exxon, Celanese, Ralston Purina
Self-Tender Offer	Tektronix, GenCorp, Goodyear, Gelco, Burlington Industries, Polaroid
Self-Exchange Offer	FMC Corp., Owens-Corning, Holiday Corp, Santa Fe Southern, CBS, Unocal, Litton Industries, Phillips, Wickes, GAF Corp, Cluett, Gelco, Revlon
Targeted Block Repurchase	Kellogg, Scott Paper, W.R. Grace, Anderson, Clayton, Diamond Shamrock, Gencorp, Harcourt Brace Jovanocich, Lucky Stores, Pennwalt, Standard Brands, Polaroid
Leveraged Recapitalization	FMC, Owens Corning, Colt Industries, Harcourt Brace Jovanovich
ESOP	Phillips Petroleum, Polaroid

[1]   Assume Incremental Debt

The simplest means to recapitalize a company is to assume incremental debt. This is often the case where a company is vulnerable to takeover because it has very little leverage. The acquirer may use the debt capacity of the target to finance its own bid, thereby optimizing the use of the balance sheet to its, not the current shareholders', benefit. Increasing leverage can make the company less attractive to potential acquirers.

Adding incremental debt can also be used in other situations. Often, a company may not be using its capital efficiently, and may have a credit rating that is in excess of its requirements. For some companies that require continuous funding and refunding such as banks and financial institutions, a strong credit rating is very important, while for others that are less frequent users of capital or who operate in sectors that are less dependent on credit rating, a high credit rating is not as necessary. In these situations, it may make sense to increase the amount of leverage on the company in order to lower the company's cost of capital.

One of the distinct positives regarding assuming additional debt is that it does not typically require shareholder approval. However, a company may still be restricted in the amount of incremental debt it may assume because of restrictions in existing debt covenants.

---

27. Thomson Financial, Public Company Documents.

Exhibit 19-9
Recent Share Repurchase Announcements[28]

($ in millions)

Date	Company	Size	Type of Repurchase
01/04/2001	Bear Stearns Cos Inc	$1,000	Open Market
08/07/2002	Cardinal Health Inc	$ 500	Open market
04/28/2003	Rent-A-Center Inc	$ 129	Dutch Auction
07/01/2003	Zale Corp	$ 226	Dutch Auction
11/15/2002	BayCorp Holdings Ltd	$ 123	Fixed Price
02/24/2003	Digitas Inc	$ 25	Fixed Price
09/03/2003	Kelly Services Inc	$ 25	Targeted Block
09/05/2003	UnionBanCal Corp, CA	$ 300	Targeted Block

---

[2] Share Repurchase

A share repurchase is the buy back of stock by the company. Share repurchases are voluntary and tend to separate loyal from disloyal, short from long-term shareholders. Repurchases are an alternative to distributing cash. Share repurchases have distinct benefits. The announcement of a share repurchase can signal to the market that the company's stock is undervalued. As discussed earlier, studies have shown that the market responds positively to share repurchase announcements. Additional benefits are that they reduce the number of outstanding shares of the company and therefore serve to enhance the earnings per share of the company. In addition, the share repurchase can reduce the number of shares that may be available for a potentially unwanted acquirer. The share repurchase serves to concentrate the stock of the company in the hands of longer term and possibly friendly shareholders. If structured appropriately, a share repurchase does not obligate the company to buy back stock. For example, in an open-market share repurchase, the company can buy back stock at its convenience.

Drawbacks of share repurchases, in particular self-tenders, are that the company may signal a price to the market at which it could be acquired. And, in the event a tender offer is dramatically over subscribed, it may signal that a company is vulnerable to takeover.

Companies that have recently announced significant share repurchase programs include Bear Stearns, Cardinal Health, Kelly Services and Zale Corp. Exhibit 19-9 shows the terms of some recent share repurchases.

Of the three most common forms of share repurchases — open-market, tender offer, and targeted block repurchases, tender offers tend to be for the largest amount of stock while open-market share repurchases are for the least amount of stock.[29]

---

28. Thomson Financial.

29. Comment, R., and G.A. Jarrell, "The Relative Signaling Power of Dutch-Auction and Fixed-Price Self-Tender Offers and Open-Market Share Repurchases," Journal of Finance 46, 1243–1271 (1991).

Based on prior research, firms typically reacquire approximately 15% of their stock in a tender offer. According to a study done by Dann, approximately 14.6% of shares outstanding were acquired in the sample that was looked at.[30]

Different share repurchase approaches are used at varying times. For example, open-market share repurchases tend to be used when a company is trying to signal the market regarding the undervaluation of its stock or the future prospects for its business. For example, in the weeks after the September 11, 2001 attacks on the World Trade Center, roughly 240 companies announced open-market stock repurchases in an attempt to reassure the market regarding the companies' future financial performance.[31] Likewise, self-tender offers are used to distribute excess cash and help dramatically change the capital structure of a company. Exhibit 19-10 shows the relationship by dollar volume of Dutch auction, fixed-price, and open-market share repurchases since 1994.

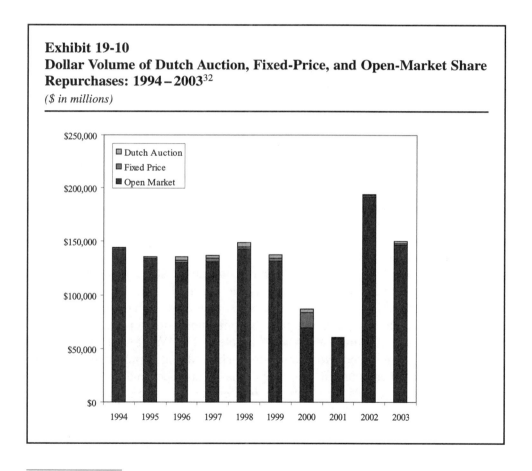

Exhibit 19-10
Dollar Volume of Dutch Auction, Fixed-Price, and Open-Market Share Repurchases: 1994 – 2003[32]

($ in millions)

---

30. Dann, L.Y., R.W. Masulis, and D. Mayers, "Repurchase Tender Offers and Earnings Information," Journal of Accounting and Economics 9, 217–251 (1991).

31. Herhold, Scott, "Buyback-O-Rama," Business 2.0 (November 2001).

32. Thomson Financial.

[a] Open-Market Share Repurchase. In an open-market share repurchase, a company simply announces its intention to acquire up to a given number of shares of the company's stock over a predetermined time period. It puts out a press release to that effect, and thereafter makes periodic, opportunistic purchases of its stock as the circumstances warrant.

The company has the flexibility to purchase the stock at any time, subject to a few Securities and Exchange rules. Shares may only be purchased at a price that is not higher than the published bid or the last independent sales price, whichever is higher. No more than 25% of any given day's daily volume may be repurchased at any one time. In addition, the company undertaking the repurchase should be cognizant of the timing of its repurchase in relation to material inside information and the dissemination of public information. Also, open-market share repurchases may not occur in conjunction with an equity offering or in conjunction with a block repurchase in a private negotiation. The specific rules surrounding a repurchase program are set out in Rule 10b-18 of the Securities and Exchange Act.

Generally open market share repurchases result in the least amount of shares being acquired by the issuer. This type of program typically results in 5%–10% of a company's shares being repurchased. A study by Kai Li and William McNally in June 1999 showed that on average, companies seek 6.9% of their shares in an open-market share repurchase.[33]

The most attractive aspects of open-market share repurchases are (1) the signaling effect of the announcement, (2) the impact the share buy back has on the company's financial ratios, (3) the flexibility the company has in terms of timing of the repurchase and the price at which it acquires the stock, and (4) no need to obtain shareholder approval. In addition to these benefits, an open-market share repurchase program allows a company to buy back the stock as its finances enable it to, rather than imposing on the company's financial flexibility the way a large, one-time purchase might.

The most significant drawback of an open-market share repurchase is the potential that it conveys a negative message to the market, in that, the company may be perceived to have few alternative investment or growth opportunities.

Open-market share repurchases have become increasingly popular relative to other forms of share repurchases. A 1995 article in The Wall Street Journal titled "Most Buybacks are Stated, Not Completed," showed that approximately 90% of the dollar value of announced share repurchases are open-market share repurchases,[34] despite the relatively low announcement return compared to Dutch Auction and fixed-price self-tender offers.

Since 1994, there have been approximately 6,274 announced open-market share repurchases, representing approximately $1.3 trillion in value. In 2003

---

33. Li, Kai, and William McNally, "Open Market Versus Tender Offer Share Repurchases: A Conditional Event Study," June 1999.

34. Power, William, "Heard on the Street: Most Buybacks are Stated Not Completed," The Wall Street Journal, March 7, 1995, c1–c2.

Exhibit 19-11
Announced Open-Market Share Repurchases: 1994–2003[35]

($ in millions)

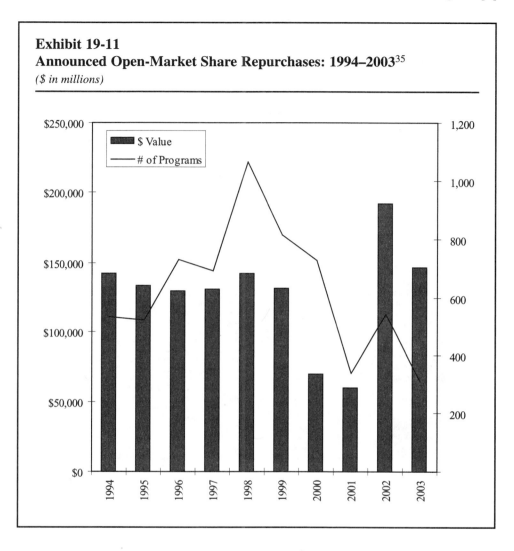

alone, there were 307 open-market share repurchase announcements representing $147 billion in value. Exhibit 19-11 illustrates the trend in open-market share repurchase announcements since 1994.

Exhibit 19-12 shows recent significant open-market share repurchase announcements.

In open-market share repurchases, firms generally do not acquire all of the stock they intend to or state they will acquire. A 1988 study by Clifford Stephens and Michael Weisbach titled "Actual Share Reacquisitions Programs in Open-Market Repurchase Programs," showed that of 450 programs from 1981 to 1990, firms acquired on average 74%–82% of the shares they announced they would

---

35. Thomson Financial.

Exhibit 19-12
Recent Significant Open-Market Share Repurchases[36]

($ in millions)

Auth. Date	Ending Date	Company	Amount	Synopsis
01/28/2003	03/31/2003	Cardinal Health Inc	$ 500	In March 2003, Cardinal Health completed its repurchase program by acquiring 8.6 mil common shares at a total cost of $500 million. On Jan 28, 2003, the board of Cardinal Health Inc authorized the repurchase of up to $500 mil worth of its common shares outstanding.
01/09/2003	03/31/2003 06/30/2003	SPX Corp	$ 143	SPX Corp completed its repurchase program by purchasing 3.9 mil common shares for a total cost of $143.4 mil. On January 9, 2003, the board of SPX Corp authorized the repurchase of up to $250 mil of its common stock outstanding, in open market transactions.
07/30/2003	08/24/2003	National Semiconductor Corp	$ 400	On July 30, 2003, the board of National Semiconductor Corp authorized the repurchase of up to $400 mil of its common stock outstanding, in open market transactions. As of August 24, 2003, the company repurchased 7.5 mil shares for a total cost of $202.2 mil.
01/28/2003	06/30/2003 09/30/2003	Becton Dickinson & Co	$ 243	On Jan 28, 2003, the board of Becton Dickinson and Co authorized the repurchase of 10 mil common shares outstanding in open market transactions. As of September 30, 2003, the company repurchased 6.4 mil common shares at a total cost of $243.2 million.
07/15/2003	09/30/2003	Washington Mutual	$ 455	On July 15, 2003, the board of Washington Mutual Inc, authorized the repurchase of up to 100 mil common shares. As of September 30, 2003, the company repurchased 11.6 mil common shares at a total cost of $455.3 million.
08/01/2003	09/30/2003	Cardinal Health Inc	$1,000	The program has been complete. As of September 30, 2003, the company repurchase 17 mil common shares at a total price of $1 billion. On August 1, 2003, the board of Cardinal Health Inc authorized the repurchase of up to $1 bil of its common shares outstanding in open market transactions.
04/29/2003	06/30/2003 09/30/2003	HCA Inc	$1,500	In April 2003, the board of HCA Inc authorized the repurchase of up to $1.5 billion of its common stock outstanding, in open market transactions. As of September 30, 2003, the company repurchased 16.2 mil common shares for a total cost of $5.38 million.
01/08/2003	03/31/2003 09/30/2003	Dean Foods Co	$ 150	In January 2003, the board of Dean Food Co authorized the repurchase of up to $150 mil of its common stock outstanding in open market transactions. In February 2003, the board authorized the repurchase of an additional $150 mil. As of September 30, 2003, Dean Food repurchased 5.2 mil shares at a total cost of $138 million.
09/04/2003	12/02/2003	PeopleSoft Inc	$ 350	PeopleSoft Inc completed its repurchase program, originally authorized in September 2003, by purchasing 16.515 mil common shares for a total cost of $350 million. On September 04, 2003, the board of PeopleSoft Inc authorized the repurchase of up to $350 mil of its common stock outstanding in open market transactions.
01/29/2003	02/15/2003 05/10/2003 08/30/2003 11/22/2003	AutoZone Inc	$ 500	On January 29, 2003, the board of Autozone Inc authorized the repurchase of up to $500 mil of its common shares outstanding in open market transactions. In June 2003, the board authorized an additional $500 mil to the program. As of November 2003, the company had repurchased $554.013 mil of its common stock.

---

36. Thomson Financial.

acquire within three years of the announcement.[37] Their study also showed that three years after the announcement, more than 57% of the firms had bought back "at least the number of shares targeted in the original repurchase announcement, 10% of the firms had bought less than 5% of the number of shares announced, and a substantial number of firms reacquired no shares at all."

[b] *Self-Tender.* In a self-tender share repurchase, the company typically offers shareholders a premium over the current stock price to buy back shares. Tender offer premiums historically have been in a wide range, from 15% to 25%. A study by Lie showed mean self-tender premiums of 16.1%,[38] while studies by Dann and DeAngelo and Comment and Jarrell showed self-tender premiums of 22.5%[39] and 16.8%[40] respectively. A study by Li and McNally showed that self-tender premiums averaged 18%.[41]

In a self-tender offer, the company typically seeks a large percentage of the company's shares. Absent a complete recapitalization, self-tenders typically garner less than 25% of the company's shares. Lie showed that on average, approximately 20.7% of a company's shares were sought in a self-tender offer.[42] Li and McNally showed that on average 19.78% of a company's securities are sought in tender offers.[43]

Since 1994, there have been approximately 465 self-tender share repurchases, representing $50 billion in value. In 2003 alone, there were 57 self-tenders representing $3.3 billion in value. Exhibit 19-13 illustrates the overall trend in self tender repurchases since 1994.

Self-tenders must comply with certain rules set forth by the Securities and Exchange Commission, most notably, Rule 13e-4. Exhibit 19-14 provides a summary of Rule 13e-4 as it relates to issuer tender offers.

In the event that an issuer tender offer results in a "going private" transaction, subject to the stringent conditions set forth in Rule 13e-3, the company must

---

37. Stephens, Clifford P., and Michael S. Weisbach, "Actual Share Reacquisition Programs in Open-Market Repurchase Programs," The Journal of Finance Vol. LII, No. 1, 313–333 (February 1998).

38. Lie, Erik, "Excess Funds and Agency Problems: An Empirical Study of Incremental Cash Disbursements," The Review of Financial Studies Vol. 13, No. 1, 219–248 (2000).

39. Dann, Larry Y., and Harry DeAngelo, "Corporate Financial Policy and Corporate Control: A Study in Defensive Adjustments in Asset and Ownership Structure," Journal of Financial Economics 20, No. 1/2, 87–128 (1988).

40. Comment, R., and G.A. Jarrell, "The Relative Signaling Power of Dutch-Auction and Fixed-Price Self-Tender Offers and Open-Market Share Repurchases," Journal of Finance 46, 1243–1271 (1991).

41. Li, Kai, and William McNally, "Open Market Versus Tender Offer Share Repurchases: A Conditional Event Study," June 1999.

42. Lie, Erik, "Excess Funds and Agency Problems: An Empirical Study of Incremental Cash Disbursements," The Review of Financial Studies Vol. 13, No. 1, 219–248 (2000).

43. Li, Kai, and William McNally, "Open Market Versus Tender Offer Share Repurchases: A Conditional Event Study," June 1999.

Exhibit 19-13
Announced Self-Tenders: 1994–2003[44]
($ in millions)

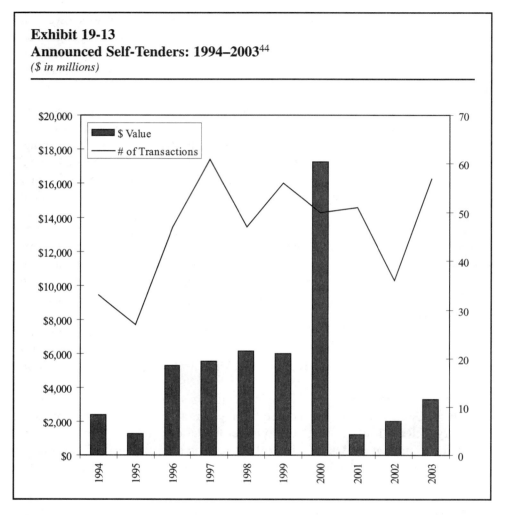

comply with the rules of Rule 13e-3 and file a Schedule 13E-3.[45] Generally, a transaction qualifies as a going private transaction if, after the repurchase, the class of stock remaining is held by less than 300 shareholders, or the class of stock repurchased is no longer listed on the exchange on which it was quoted or is no longer authorized to be quoted on an inter-dealer quotation system of any registered national securities association.

In a self-tender offer, the company has two primary choices in order to execute the repurchase: fixed-price tender offer or Dutch auction tender offer. The primary difference between the two approaches is that a Dutch auction offers to acquire shares at a range of possible prices while a fixed-price tender-offer announces a fixed price at which the company will repurchase shares. The Dutch

44. Thomson Financial.

45. Going private transactions are discussed more fully in *Chapter 16: Going Private Transactions.*

Exhibit 19-14
Rule 13e-4 and Issuer Tender Offers

---

1. The issuer must file a Schedule TO with the Securities and Exchange Commission prior to or as soon as practicable on the date of the commencement of the tender offer.

2. The tender offer must be open for at least 20 business days.

3. The consideration paid to a stockholder pursuant to the tender offer must be the highest consideration paid to any other stockholder (the "best price" rule).

4. If the tender offer is over-subscribed, the issuer must purchase the tendered shares on a pro rata basis.

5. If the issuer chooses to purchase greater than 2% more than the shares originally sought, it must extend the tender offer for at least ten business days. Shareholders who have previously tendered their shares are free to withdraw their shares during this time period.

6. The tender offer must be open to all holders of the class of securities that are subject to the tender offer.

7. Securities tendered during the tender offer period may be withdrawn any time while the tender offer remains open and, if not yet accepted for payment, after 40 business days from the commencement of the tender offer.

8. The issuer must pay for or return the tendered securities promptly after termination or withdrawal of the tender offer.

9. The issuer must publish, send or give stockholders a statement of information that details the pertinent information regarding the tender offer. This criteria is often satisfied by mailing the tender offer statement to shareholders.

---

auction forces the shareholder to make a decision regarding what price they are prepared to sell their stock.

         [i]   **Fixed-Price Self-Tender.** In a fixed price tender offer, the company acquires up to a predetermined number of shares at a specific stock price. If more shares are tendered than the maximum number specified, the company purchases the stock on a pro rata basis, although in certain cases, the company may purchase all the shares that are tendered.

Fixed-price self-tender offers have become quite common. Since 1994, there have been 259 fixed-price self-tender share repurchases, representing $28 billion in value. In 2003, there were 37 fixed-price self-tenders representing $1.3 billion in value. Exhibit 19-15 illustrates the trend in fixed-price self-tenders since 1994.

Exhibit 19-16 provides an overview of the terms of recent fixed-price self-tender offers.

Premiums paid in fixed-price tender offers are higher than those for Dutch auction tender offers, but generally are in the 20%–25% range. Exhibit 19-17 provides premiums in recent fixed-price self-tender offers.

         [ii]   **Dutch Auction.** In a Dutch auction, a range of prices is set by the company, within which shareholders may tender their shares. The tender offer, like other tender offers, is open for 20 business days. The

Exhibit 19-15
Announced Fixed-Price Tender Offer Share Repurchases:
1994–2003[46]

($ in millions)

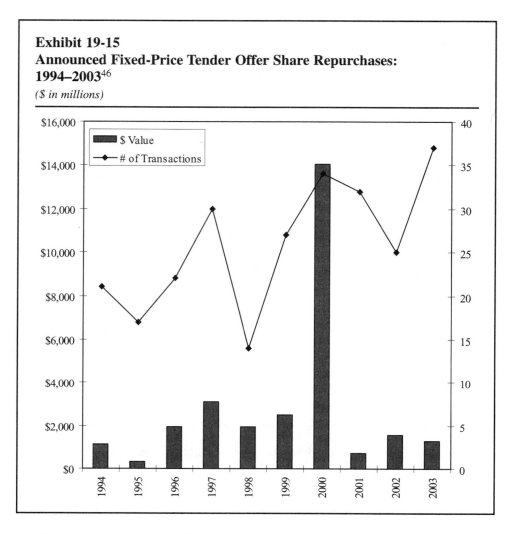

acquirer states the number of shares it proposes to acquire. In the event that more shares are tendered than can be purchased, the shares acquired are subject to pro-ration. The price paid by the acquirer is the lowest price that can clear the entire amount that is proposed to be repurchased. In a Dutch auction tender offer, the company acquires up to a predetermined number of shares, yet it will purchase these shares within a range of stock prices. In the Dutch auction, shareholders must decide at what price they are prepared to tender their shares and run the risk that the company does not purchase their shares.

Since 1994, there have been 206 announced Dutch auction self-tender share repurchases, representing $22 billion in value. In 2003, there were 20 Dutch auction self-tender repurchases, representing $2 billion in value. Exhibit 19-18 illustrates the trend in Dutch auctions.

---

46. Thomson Financial.

Exhibit 19-16
Recent Significant Completed Fixed-Price Self-Tender Offers[47]
($ in millions)

Auth. Date	Ending Date	Company	Amount	Synopsis
03/14/2003	04/11/2003	Van Kampen Prime Rate Income	$171	Van Kampen Prime Rate Income Trust completed its tender offer for up to 52 mil shares. The Trust purchased over 22 mil shares at a price of $7.78 per share.
02/24/2003	03/25/2003	Digitas Inc	$ 25	On March 25, 2003, Digitas Inc completed its self tender offer by acquiring 6.24 mil common shares, for $3.89 in cash per share or a total value of $25 mil. The program commenced in February 24, 2003.
04/23/2003	05/21/2003	Belk Inc	$ 27	On May 21, 2003, the company completed it self tender offer for 3 mil Class A and Class B shares, by accepting 2.809 mil shares, for $9.50 per share, or a total value of $26.685 mil. On April 23, 2003, the board of Belk Inc commenced a self tender offer to acquire 3 mil Class A and Class B common shares, at $9.50 in cash per share. The offer was to expire on May 21, 2003.
03/24/2003	05/22/2003	Keynote Systems Inc	$ 41	On May 22, 2003, Keynote Systems Inc completed its issuer tender offer for 7.5 mil common shares by accepting 4.3 mil common shares at a price of $9.50 in cash per share, or a total value of $40.85 mil. The tender commenced on March 24, 2003.
04/24/2003	05/22/2003	Templeton Dragon Fund Inc	$138	On May 30, 2003, Templeton Dragon completed its tender offer for 13,861,221 mil common shares at a price of $9.97 per share, or a total value of $138.1 mil. Originally, on April 24, 2003, Templeton Dragon Fund Inc commenced a tender offer for 6,656,425 mil, or 15% of its outstanding common stock, at of price per share of $9.98 per share.
08/04/2003	09/02/2003	Register.com Inc	$120	Register.com completed its tender offer for $120 mil of stock and warrants. The company accepted for purchase 17,910,347 mil common shares, and 987,283 in warrants for $6.35 per share. On August 4, 2004, the board of Register.com Inc commenced a tender offer to distribute $120 mil in cash to its security holders. The tender offer will be priced at $6.35 per share, and will include stock and warrants. The tender offer is expected to expire on September 2, 2003.
09/04/2003	10/08/2003	AMN Healthcare Services Inc	$180	AMN Healthcare completed its tender offer. On October 8, 2003, AMN accepted 10,098,251 common shares for a total cost of $180 mil. On September 4, 2003, the board of AMN Healthcare Inc commenced a tender offer to purchase up to $180 mil of its common shares outstanding, at a price of $18.00 per share. The offer will expire on October 1, 2003.
11/02/2003	11/03/2003	Journal Co	$300	On November 3, 2003, Journal Communications completed a tender offer by repurchasing 20 mil Class B common shares outstanding, for a total cost of $300 mil.
10/30/2003	12/04/2003	MBT Financial Corp	$ 30	MBT Financial completed its tender offer by purchasing 1,632, 475 mil common shares for a price of $18.50 per share, or $30.201 mil. The shares purchased included 1,250,000 shares that MBT Financial was obligated to purchase, and an additional 382,475 shares that the company purchased in accordance with the optional purchase provisions of the offer. On October 30, 2003, the board of MBT Financial Corp commenced a tender offer to repurchase up to 1.25 mil common shares outstanding for $18.50 per share. The tender offer is expected to expire on December 4, 2003.
11/26/2003	12/31/2003	MVC Capital	$ 31	MVC Capital completed its tender offer by accepting 23.9%, or 3,859,558 mil of the fund's outstanding common stock, at a price of $8.18 per share. On November 26, 2003, MVC Capital commenced a tender offer to acquire up to 25% of its outstanding shares of common stock. The offer is expected to expire on December 31, 2003.

---

47. Thomson Financial.

Exhibit 19-17
Premiums in Fixed-Price Self-Tender Offers[48]

Initial Auth. Date	Name	Price at Auth. Date	Purchase Price	Premium
06/10/1999	MGM Grand Inc.	$ 43.13	$ 50.00	15.9%
03/23/1999	Building One Services Corp.	$ 17.38	$ 25.00	43.9%
07/14/1999	EI du Pont de Nemours & Co.	$ 73.00	$ 80.76	10.6%
12/07/1999	International Game Technology	$ 19.94	$ 21.00	5.3%
11/08/1999	Washington Post Co.	$531.00	$575.00	8.3%
02/04/2000	United Parcel Service Inc.	$ 56.38	$ 60.00	6.4%

Exhibit 19-18
Announced Dutch Auction Tender Offers: 1994–2003[49]

($ in millions)

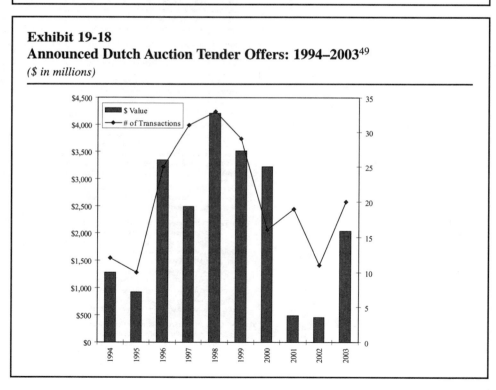

---

48. Public Company Documents.
49. Thomson Financial.

Exhibit 19-19 illustrates significant Dutch auction tender offers.

Mechanics of a Dutch Auction. In a Dutch auction, the company repurchasing stock offers to acquire a specific number of shares within a given price range. The shareholders may tender whatever shares they wish and may state a price at which they would be willing to sell their shares. After the tender offer period expires, the company repurchases the tendered shares up to a predetermined limit. The

---

Exhibit 19-19
Recent Significant Completed Dutch Auction Tender Offers[50]

Initial Auth. Date	Name	Price at Auth. Date	Synopsis
07/18/2002	Netro Corp	$ 2.46	Netro Corp completed its self tender by purchasing 23 million shares at a total cost of $82.8 million. In July 2002, Netro Corp launched a dutch auction self tender for up to 23 million shares of its outstanding commonstock. The offer will expire on August 16, 2002.
08/05/2002	Energizer Holdings Inc	$29.24	Energizer Holdings Inc. completed a dutch auction tender offer by acquiring 2.6 million shares at a total cost of $75.4 million. Shares were purchased at a price of $29 per share. In August 2002, Energizer Holdings Inc. launched a dutch auction tender offer for up to 6 million shares of its outstanding common stock. Shares will be purchased at a price range of $25.5 to $29 per share.
09/18/2002	Dress Barn Inc	$11.29	Dress Barn Inc completed its tender offer by acquiring 8 mil shares at a total cost of $120 mil. The shares were purchased at a price of $15 per share. In September 2002, Dress Barn Inc launched a dutch auction tender offer for up to 8 mil shares of its outstanding common stock.
02/04/2003	Brown-Forman Corp	$70.81	On March 4, 2003, Brown-Forman Corp completed its Dutch auction tender offer for 1.5 mil Class A shares and 6.8 mil class B shares, by accepting .471 mil Class A shares, at $73 per share, or a total value of $34.359 mil, and accepting 7.59 mil Class B shares at a price of $70.50, or a total value of $535.095 mil. Originally, on February 3, 2003, the board of Brown-Forman Corp authorized the repurchase of up to 1.5 mil Class A common shares and 6.8 mil Class B common shares, via a Dutch auction tender offer, for a price range between $63 and $73 each.

(Continued)

---

50. Thomson Financial.

Exhibit 19-19
(*Continued*)

Initial Auth. Date	Name	Price at Auth. Date	Synopsis
02/18/2003	Libbey Inc	$24.96	On March 17, 2003, Libbey Inc completed its modified Dutch auction tender offer for 1.5 mil of its common shares by accepting 1.65 mil shares, at an average price of $25.50, or a total value of $42.75 mil. Originally, in February 18, 2003, Libbey commenced the tender offer for 1.5 mil of its shares of outstanding common stock, at a price not greater than $26.50 and not less than $23.50 per share.
04/23/2003	Apogent Technologies Inc	$17.15	On May 21, 2003, Apogent Technologies Inc completed its Dutch Auction tender offer for 15 mil common shares, by accepting 6.023 mil shares, at an average price of $17.50 per share, or a total value of $105.402 mil. Originally, in April 2003, the board of Apogent Technologies Inc authorized a Dutch auction tender offer to repurchase 15 mil common shares, at a price between $15 and $17.50, to expire on May 21.
04/28/2003	Rent-A-Center Inc	$63.06	Rent A Center Inc completed its Dutch auction tender offer by purchasing 1,769,960 common shares outstanding for $73 per share, or $129.2 mil. On April 28, 2003, the board of Rent-A-Center commenced a Dutch auction self tender for 2.2 mil shares of its outstanding common stock at a price not greater than $73 and not less than $67 per share. The tender offer was to expire on , June 19, 2003. Orginal price was between $60 and $66, and was to expire on June 5, 2003.
07/01/2003	Zale Corp	$45.90	Zale Corp completed its tender offer by purchasing 4.7 mil common shares at a cost of $48.00 per share, or $225.6 mil. On July 1, 2003, the board of Zale Corp commenced a Dutch auction tender offer to repurchase 6.4 mil common shares or 20%, for a price not greater than $48.00 and not less than $42.00 per share.
11/03/2003	Intergraph Corp	$26.47	Intergraph Corporation completed its tender offer by accepting 23,732,032 mil common shares for $26 per share, or $617 mil. On November 3, 2003, Intergraph Corporation commenced a modified Dutch auction tender offer to buyback up to 10 mil common shares outstanding, at a price not greater than $28.00 and not less than $26.00 per share.

Exhibit 19-20
Dutch Auction Tender Example

Investor	Shares Tendered	Price Willing to Tender
Investor A	3,000,000	$23.00
Investor B	1,500,000	$22.75
Investor C	4,000,000	$22.50
Investor D	2,500,000	$22.25
Investor E	2,500,000	$21.00
Investor F	1,000,000	$20.50

company purchases the shares at the lowest price at which all of the shares it desires to purchase can be acquired.

As an example of a Dutch auction self-tender repurchase, let's assume that a company wishes to repurchase 10,000,000 shares. Its current stock price is $18.00 per share, and it proposes to acquire the tendered shares at a price from $20.00–$23.00 per share. Investors in the company are prepared to sell their stock at various price levels. For example, Investor A is prepared to sell 3,000,000 shares at $23.000 while investor F is prepared to sell 1,000,000 shares at $20.00. Exhibit 19-20 outlines the number of shares each investor is willing to tender and at what price.

Based on the shares tendered and the prices at which investors are willing to tender those shares, the company would repurchase the 10 million shares at a price of $22.50 — the lowest price that allows it to purchase the targeted number of shares. As set forth in Rule 13e-4 of the Securities Act of 1934, the company is obliged to pay all shareholders whose securities are purchased the same price. This is known as the "best price" rule, and it maintains that the consideration to be paid should be the highest consideration paid to any stockholder during the tender offer. Rule 13e-4 also states that if tender offer is oversubscribed, the company must acquire the shares on a pro rata basis. In addition, if the company chooses to repurchase more than 2% more than the specified number of shares, it may do so by extending the terms of its tender offer for an additional ten days.

From this example, it is possible to visualize why the Dutch auction approach has value to the company. In essence, while the shareholder would like to sell its stock at the highest price possible, it runs the risk that its shares are not repurchased because it submits a price that is too high. Therefore, the seller must make a determination of what the minimum price is that it is prepared to accept. Tender offer premiums in Dutch auctions are generally lower than those for fixed-price tender offers, but have been anywhere from 5%–16%. Exhibit 19-21 provides the tender offer premiums in a number of recent Dutch auction tender offers.

Exhibit 19-21
Premiums Paid in Dutch Auction Tender Offers[51]

Initial Auth. Date	Name	Price at Auth. Date	Purchase Price	Premium
05/11/1999	Conectiv Inc.	$24.19	$25.50	5.4%
05/03/1999	Limited Inc.	$44.63	$50.00	12.0%
07/27/1999	Gartner Group Inc.	$21.88	$21.65	−1.1%
06/16/1999	Cendant Corp.	$19.81	$22.25	12.3%
02/03/2000	DPL Inc.	$21.69	$23.00	6.0%
02/28/2000	Hasbro Inc.	$15.75	$17.50	11.1%
01/26/2000	Sempra Energy	$18.63	$20.00	7.4%
03/08/2000	Payless ShoeSource Inc.	$48.38	$52.83	9.2%
03/16/2001	Security Capital Group Inc.	$19.81	$20.50	3.5%

[c] Targeted Block Repurchase. Targeted block share repurchases are helpful in eliminating a large shareholder, most often one that is not management friendly. The benefit of this approach is that the selling shareholder may not be able to exit because of the illiquidity of its investment. In addition, it provides the company an opportunity to repurchase the blockof stock on potentially favorable terms. Targeted block repurchases are the least frequently used method of stock repurchase.

Since 1993 there have been approximately 391 targeted block repurchases, representing approximately $29 billion in value. In 2003, there were 14 targeted block repurchases representing $1 billion in value. Exhibit 19-22 illustrates the trend in announced block repurchases.

Exhibit 19-23 shows recent targeted block repurchase announcements.

[d] Share Repurchases in Response to Takeover Threats. Repurchasing stock in response to a takeover threat is a valid approach to subvert the transaction. The share repurchase serves to deliver value to shareholders and concentrates the stock in the hands of the remaining shareholders. In addition, when used with other defensive tactics, it can be very effective at stopping a takeover offer. An example of a share repurchase used in a defensive situation is the 1997 Dutch auction share repurchase of stock by WMX Technologies.

The share repurchase can be effected through an open market share repurchase program, an exchange offer or a self-tender such as a fixed-price or Dutch auction self-tender.

---

51. Public Company Documents.

Exhibit 19-22
Announced Targeted Block Repurchases: 1993–2003[52]
($ in millions)

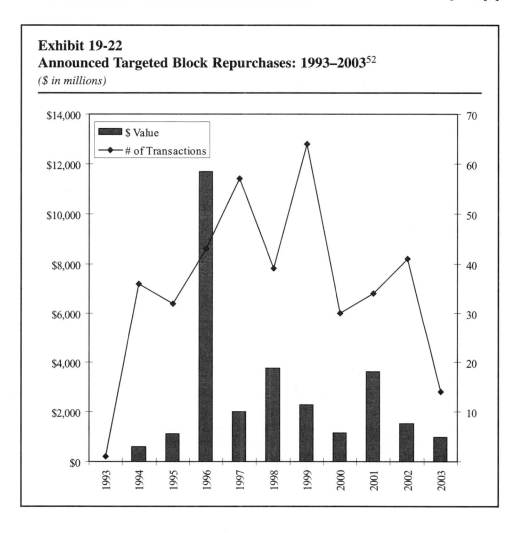

[3]   Leveraged Recapitalization

Of the various forms of recapitalization, the most aggressive is the leveraged recapitalization. A leveraged recapitalization entails the issuer offering a package of cash, debt and other securities, plus potentially stock in the surviving company, to shareholders in exchange for their stock in the company. The package of securities is often valued as high as 90% of the takeover value of the company, yet the shareholders may be able to continue to participate in the upside of the highly leveraged company post transaction. There are numerous advantages to this type of structure as outlined in Exhibit 19-24.

Leveraged recapitalizations are generally structured through two primary mechanisms: a reclassification of the company's charter or a merger of a subsidiary into the parent company.

---

52. Thomson Financial.

Exhibit 19-23
Recent Significant Targeted Block Share Repurchases[53]

Initial Auth. Date	Name	Price at Auth. Date	Synopsis
01/14/2002	Dun & Bradstreet Corp	$34.20	In January 2002, Dunn & Bradstreet Inc. repurchased 2.5 million shares from Berkshire Hathoway Inc. in a privately negotiated transaction for $34.04 per share.
10/08/2001	Rent-A-Center Inc	$25.00	Rent-A-Center, Inc. purchased 2.9 million shares of its outstanding common stock at a total cost of $59.7 million from its former Chairman and Chief Executive J. Ernest Talley via negotiated transactions.
06/05/2002	WebMD Corp	$ 6.51	In June 2002, the board or WebMD Corp. completed the repurchase of 14.1 million common shares at a total cost of $84.741 million, from Cerner Corp, in a privately negotiated transaction.
08/27/2002	UnionBanCal Corp,CA	$44.80	In August 2002, UnionBanCal Corp repurchased 7.1 million shares from the Bank of Tokyo Mitsubishi Ltd. in a block transaction at a total cost of $300 million.
08/28/2002	UTStarcom Inc	$12.57	UTStarcom Inc. bought back 6 million shares for about $72 million from its largest shareholder, Softbank Corp.
08/28/2002	Yahoo! Inc	$ 9.13	In August 2002, Yahoo Inc. paid about $100 million to repurchase almost 11.1 million shares of its common stock from Softbank America Inc. The transaction was made via a block purchase.
10/23/2001	Legg Mason Inc	$42.84	On October 23, 2001, the board of Legg Mason Inc. authorized the repurchase of up to 3 million common shares, through block transactions. As of December 31, 2002, the company repurchased 845,600 at a total cost of $40.570 million.
09/05/2003	UnionBanCal Corp,CA	$48.70	In August 2003, UnionBanCal Corp. repurchased 6,659,267 shares from the Bank of Tokyo-Mitsubishi Ltd in a block transaction at a total cost of $300 million.
10/20/2003	Winnebago Industries Inc	$52.61	On October 20, 2003, the board of Winnebago Industries Inc. repurchased 1,450,000 common shares outstanding, for a total cost of $63.979 million from Hanson Capital Partners LLC.

---

53. Thomson Financial.

Exhibit 19-24

Advantages and Disadvantages of Leveraged Recapitalizations

Advantages	*Disadvantages*
• Distributes up to 90% of the takeover value of the company to exiting shareholders	• May send signal to potential acquirers over company's possible takeover price
• Shareholders may retain upside in the remaining entity	• Leverage may constrain financial and operational flexibility to the point of financial distress
• Inside or large shareholders may obtain liquidity while retaining control of the company	
• Management, employees, and other insiders may be able to increase their stake in the company as a result of the transaction	
• Shareholders are all treated equally	

---

[a]   *Charter Reclassification.* In a reclassification recapitalization, the common stock of the company is reclassified into preferred stock, which is then redeemed for cash or some other form of consideration, plus new common stock in the surviving company. This form of transaction requires shareholder approval. In this structure, the management often elects not to receive the cash or debt components of the package and instead simply receive incremental shares, thereby increasing their stake in the company.

[b]   *Merger with a Subsidiary.* This is arguably the most common form of leveraged recapitalization and entails a complete overhaul of the company's capital structure. In this type of transaction, the company's shares of common stock are converted into cash or a combination of debt and cash plus new common stock of the surviving company. Requires shareholder approval. In this structure, the management often elects not to receive the cash or debt components of the package and instead simply receive incremental shares, thereby increasing their stake in the company.

[c]   *Example Leveraged Recapitalization.* By way of example, let's look at a company, UnderValued Co. that undertakes a recapitalization plan. UnderValued Co. has 10,000,000 shares outstanding and a stock price of $50.00 per share, representing a market value of $500 million. Approximately 25% of the company is owned by the founder, president and CEO of the company. An additional 15% is owned by the management team. A single large institution owns 10% of the company, and the remaining 50% is owned by the public. UnderValued Co. announces a recapitalization plan that will pay all shareholders

Exhibit 19-25
Terms of Illustrative Leveraged Recapitalization

| | Pre-Transaction | | Post-Transaction | | |
	Shares Owned	% Owned	Cash	Stock	% Owned
Founder	2,500,000	25%	$50.00/share	2,500,000	15%
Management	1,500,000	15%	$ 0/share	7,500,000	45%
Large Corporate Shareholder	1,000,000	10%	$44.00/share	1,600,000	10%
Public	5,000,000	50%	$50.00/share	5,000,000	30%
Total	10,000,000	100%		16,600,000	100%

$60.00 per share in value. For each share owned by an individual shareholder, it is offered the following package:

- Public Shareholders: $50.00 per share in cash plus one share of surviving UnderValued Co. stock;

- Founder, President, and CEO: $50.00 per share in cash plus one share of surviving UnderValued Co. stock;

- Management: No cash and five shares in surviving UnderValued Co. stock;

- Large Corporate Shareholder: $44.00 in cash plus 1.6 shares.

The stub share offered to the public and the founder is assumed to have a value of $10.00 per share, making up the difference between the $40.00 in cash and the $50.00 in value of the package. Exhibit 19-25 outlines the terms and impact of the transaction.

All shareholders benefit from the transaction:

- The value of the package yields an immediate increase in value of $10.00 per share;

- The founder, public shareholders, and large shareholder all receive the majority of their value in cash, with the founder and public shareholders receiving a 83% of their value in cash and the large shareholder receiving 73% of its value in cash;

- The founder, public shareholders, and large shareholder also retain an equity interest in the company and therefore maintain some equity upside;

- The founder is able to receive cash in the company, yet maintain a 15% ownership stake in the company;

- Management increases their equity stake from 15% to 45%.

From a tax perspective, the cash received by the large corporate shareholder is taxed as a dividend and therefore is subject to a dividend received deduction. The management is not taxed at all because it does not receive any cash.

[4]   Special Dividend

A special dividend is a one-time, non-recurring payment to shareholders. Unlike conventional dividends, there is no expectation on behalf of shareholders that a special dividend will be a recurring event. Historically, special dividends were quite common. Between 1926 and year-end 1995, "1,287 NYSE-listed firms paid a total of 10,008 special dividends with 9,636 specials paid by 942 firms that made special distributions in multiple years."[54] Special dividends have lost their popularity as a stand alone event, and are now thought of more in the context of recapitalizations. A study by Harry DeAngelo, Linda DeAngelo, and Douglas Skinner in February 2000, showed that in the 1940s, 61.7% of dividend-paying NYSE firms paid at least one special dividend, while only 4.9% of NYSE firms did so in the 1990s.[55] The special dividend typically averages 24.3% of the dollar value of total dividends paid.[56]

The DeAngelo study also suggests that the nature of special dividends have changed over the years, and today are more associated with restructuring and as a response to takeover pressure. An article in the Wall Street Journal reported that 81% of the special dividends announced in the 1980s and 1990s were a part of a corporate restructuring, and that 60% were related to takeover threats.

The special dividend involves paying a super dividend to shareholders, substituting most of its equity for debt. Often, the dividend is coupled with a "stub" in the company that represents their remaining interest in the company. The special dividend serves to pay out significant consideration to existing shareholders, thereby providing them with an attractive return on their investment, plus giving them the upside inherent in their stub shares in the company.

The payment of a special dividend has a primary advantage in that it can be issued immediately without shareholder approval. One of the drawbacks of the dividend is that it is paid to shareholders irrespective of their interest in receiving it, unlike in a share repurchase, where the shareholder may elect to sell its shares and receive cash.

Special dividends have been use as a basis for a comprehensive recapitalization as well as a means to simply pay out cash. Lie found that on average, absent a complete recapitalization of the firm, companies that paid a small special dividend, paid approximately 6.2% of the equity market value out to shareholders in

---

54. DeAngelo, Harry, Linda DeAngelo, and Douglas J. Skinner, "Special Dividends and the Evolution of Dividend Signaling," Marshall School of Business, USC, and University of Michigan School of Business, February 2000.

55. *Id.*

56. *Id.*

Exhibit 19-26
Announced ESOPs: 1990–2003
($ in millions)

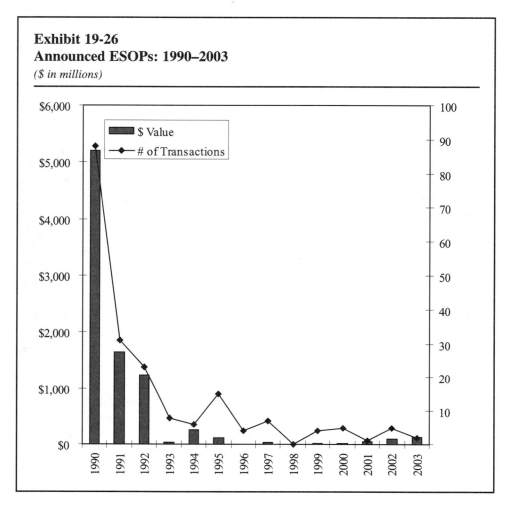

the form of a dividend, while companies that paid a large special dividend, paid 12% of their equity market value out to shareholders.[57]

[5]   ESOPs

Employee stock ownership plans have also been used as a means to recapitalize a company. The ESOP is used to acquire stock that is repurchased from public shareholders. The ESOP structure has a number of benefits including, the tax advantages of borrowing through the ESOP, allowing employees to share in the upside in the company, putting large blocks of company stock in the hands of friendly hands.

Since 1990, there have been approximately 199 announced ESOPs, representing $8.8 billion in value. Exhibit 19-26 illustrates the trend in ESOP announcements since 1990.

---

57. Lie, Erik, "Excess Funds and Agency Problems: An Empirical Study of Incremental Cash Disbursements," The Review of Financial Studies Vol. 13, No. 1, 219–248 (2000).

Exhibit 19-27
Significant Completed ESOPs[58]

($ in millions)

Ann. Date	Target	Deal Value	Transaction Overview
01/04/2002	Digital Transmission Systems	$ 0	The employee stock ownership plan of Digital Transmission Systems (DTS), a manufacturer of computer networking systems, acquired a 61.582% interest, or 10 mil common shares, in DTS, from Wi-LAN Inc (WLI), for $.166 mil in cash. Upon completion, WLI planned to retain .025 mil DTS common shares.
03/20/2002	Chromcraft Revington Inc	$ 20	The Chromcraft Revington Employee Stock Ownership Trust, acquired a 20.891% stake, or 2 mil common shares, in Chromcraft Revington Inc(CRI), a manufacturer and wholesaler of residential and commercial furniture, from Court Square Capital Ltd (CS), for $10 per share, or a total value of $20 mil, in a privately negotiated transaction. Concurrently, CRI repurchased 3.695 mil shares, or a 38.6% stake, in the company from CS.
06/30/2002	Spar Performance Group		The Spar Performance Group Employee Stock Ownership Plan acquired Spar Performance Group, a provider of group management services for travel, meetings, administrative, and merchandise fullfillment, from Spar Group Inc.
07/26/2002	Scitor Corp	$ 78	The Scitor Corp Employee Stock Ownership Plan acquired all the outstanding stock of Scitor Corp, a provider of computer consulting services, for $77.5 mil, in a leveraged buyout transaction.
01/07/2003	Alion Science & Technology	$130	The Alion Science & Technology Corp Empoyee Stock Ownership Plan acquired all the outstanding stock of Alion Science & Technology Corp, a provider of computer consulting services, for an estimated $130 mil, including the assumption of an undisclosed amount in liabilities, in a leveraged buyout transaction.
12/22/2003	BoatUS		The BoatUS Empoyee Stock Ownership Plan acquired all the outstanding stock of BoatUS, a boat retailer, in a leveraged buyout transaction.

Exhibit 19-27 provides summary terms of some of the largest ESOPs completed. In a leveraged ESOP, a trust acting on behalf of employees, acquires the company stock. The trust finances the acquisition with 50% tax-exempt ESOP loan which is guaranteed by the company. The company makes annual tax-deductible contributions

---

58. Thomson Financial.

Exhibit 19-28
Comparison Between Recapitalization Structures

	Special Dividend	Open Market	Dutch Auction	Fixed Price	Leveraged Recap
		Share Repurchase			
Requires Shareholder Approval	No	No	No	No	Yes
SEC Filings and Disclosure	No	No	Yes	Yes	Yes
Timing to Completion	Minimal	Flexible	Min. 20 business days	Min. 20 business days	Lengthy

to the ESOP which are used to repay the loan. As the loan is repaid, the shares are allocated to the individual accounts of the employees. ESOPs have certain issues, most importantly, that the ESOP loan is a company liability and that as the loan is repaid and the debt outstanding declines, the shares are allocated to employees.

[C]   Comparison Between Recapitalization Structures

Firms that undertake a recapitalization do so for a variety of reasons and choose a structure based on the objectives behind the transaction, the perceived takeover threat, and the time available to execute the deal. The simplest form of transaction is the open market share repurchase which does not require shareholder approval, and has no filing and disclosure requirements with the SEC. The same is true of a special dividend, which can be undertaken without shareholder approval and without the need to file with the SEC. A leveraged recapitalization typically is undertaken with shareholder approval and will entail making certain filings with the SEC. Self-tender offers, either Dutch auction or fixed-price tender offers, may not require shareholder approval, yet require the filing of certain documents with the SEC, such as Schedule TO. In addition, they are subject to Rule 13e-4 and in cases where the transaction results in a going private transaction, Rule 13e-3.

Exhibit 19-28 outlines the differences between the various forms of recapitalization discussed in this chapter.

§ 19.07   FINANCING

Recapitalizations are typically financed with excess cash on hand at the company and incremental debt assumed in the transaction. The cash usually is derived from the proceeds of divestitures or the accumulation of excess cash from the business. The debt portion of the financing can be in the form of bank debt assumed by the company, ESOP debt guaranteed by the company, and subordinated debt. In addition, it is feasible to give shareholders debt securities as a part of a package of cash, debt and/or other securities in exchange for their shares. One significant issue to consider in seeking debt financing is the timing associated with obtaining the debt. Bank debt may be quicker to obtain as, unlike public debt, it does not require prior approval from the SEC.

§ 19.08 TAX IMPLICATIONS

[A] Share Repurchases

From the perspective of the shareholder who sells its stock into the repurchase, the transaction is treated as either capital gain or as a dividend. In general, the sale is treated as a dividend, unless there is a complete redemption of the shareholder's shares in the company, i.e., all shares of the issuer that are owned by the shareholder are repurchased in the offer, in which case it is treated as capital gains. In addition, the transaction will be treated as capital gain if the sale is "substantially disproportionate" in relation to the stockholder or the sale is "not essentially a dividend." In the former case, the sale of shares will be "substantially disproportionate" if the ratio of the shares of stock of the issuer owned by the shareholder to all shares of the stock owned by all shareholders is less than 80% of the ratio immediately before the purchase of shares. In the latter case, the IRS Code requires a meaningful reduction in the shareholder's proportionate interest in the company. From the perspective of the issuer, there are few tax issues. The company generally does not recognize a gain or loss on the redeemed securities. The repurchase may have an impact on the earnings and profits of the company, however, and will depend on whether the shareholders receive capital gain or dividend treatment on their share sales. If the repurchase amount represents a dividend, the amount will reduce the earnings and profits of the company up to that amount, but not less than zero. If the amount represents capital gain, it will reduce earnings and profits of the company by the lesser of the amount of distribution or the pro rata share of earnings and profits attributable to the repurchased stock.

[B] Special Dividends

A special dividend is typically taxed as ordinary income. If the amount of the dividend exceeds the company's earnings and profits, its considered a return of capital. If the dividend serves to increase a shareholder's basis in its stock in the company, it is taxed as a capital gain.

[C] Leveraged Recapitalizations

A leveraged recapitalization in many ways is like a leveraged buyout: the company borrows substantially debt and distributes the proceeds to shareholders. At the same time, there may be a dramatic shift in the equity ownership of the structure, which is likely to dilute the current shareholders quite significantly. This dilution allows the transaction to be treated as capital gains to shareholders rather than ordinary income. For the transaction to receive this treatment, a shareholder cannot own more than 50% of the voting power of the company immediately after the transaction. In addition, the shareholders receiving cash must receive a "substantially disproportionate redemption." In other words, the shareholder's voting stock must be reduced to less than 80% of his/her original voting stock. In certain leveraged recapitalizations, it may be prudent to obtain a ruling from the Internal Revenue Service regarding the tax treatment of the transaction prior to undertaking the transaction.

§ 19.09   ACCOUNTING IMPLICATIONS

The accounting for special dividends, share repurchases and leveraged recapitalizations is fairly straight forward. The special dividend serves to reduce the cash on the company's balance sheet and thus reduce the company's book value as well. The shares that are repurchased are typically "redeemed" at a premium to book value and therefore, it is not uncommon for pro forma shareholder's equity to be negative and for the debt on the company to exceed 100% of the company's capitalization.

§ 19.10   RECAPITALIZATIONS VERSUS LEVERAGED BUYOUTS

Leveraged buyouts and recapitalizations share a number of similarities. They both rely on companies that share the same attributes in terms of cash flows, balance sheet strength, management expertise and company and industry dynamics. In addition, they both achieve a similar endgame, i.e., concentrating the equity of the target company in the hands of a small group of shareholders and creating value for those shareholders by using the cash flows of the company to repay excess quantities of debt assumed in the transaction. Once the debt is repaid, as the equity is owned by the same small group of shareholders, it is worth considerably more than when the transaction took place — the value of the debt is effectively transferred to shareholders by virtue of the debt being repaid down using the company's cash flows.

One of the more significant advantages of both transaction types is the shelter from taxes the debt provides the operating earnings. The interest expense assumed in the transaction is tax deductible and thereby preserves some of the cash flows that are available to repay debt.

As a defensive tactic, recapitalizations have certain benefits over recapitalizations. For example, if a company attempts a leveraged buyout at a given price, it is difficult for it to turn away a third party offer at a higher price. A recapitalization, on the other hand, gives current shareholders value at the time of the deal as well as an ongoing stake in the company post transaction. The recapitalization serves to sidestep the company's Revlon duties, i.e., the need to put the company up for sale to the highest bidder.

§ 19.11   CASE STUDIES

[A]   Leveraged Recapitalization Case Study: Caesar's World

In April 1987, Caesar's World was under takeover threat from the raider Martin Sosnoff. He had proposed a hostile acquisition at $28.00 per share. In response, Caesar's World announced a recapitalization plan that offered a special cash dividend of $25 per share yet it also allowed the shareholders to keep their stock. The plan also called for an immediate grant of 1.5 million shares of stock to the management team plus an future grant of 1.5 million shares to management under the long-term incentive plan.

Under the plan, Caesar's World would incur over $1 billion in new debt, making the company less desirable to Sosnoff as a takeover target. As a consequence of the announced recapitalization, Sosnoff withdrew his bid for the company. Interestingly, the courts subsequently rejected the company's recapitalization plan as imprudent.

[B]   Dutch Auction Case Study: The Limited

On May 3, 1999, the board of directors authorized the repurchase of up to 15 million shares of The Limited stock in a Dutch auction tender offer. The price offered was no greater than $55 per share and no less than $50 per share. The tender offer was expected to expire at midnight on June 1, 1999. The company's stock price the day prior to the announcement of the Dutch auction was $43.75 per share. At the range of prices offered in the Dutch auction, the premium offered shareholders would be 14.3% to 25.7%. The company would pay a single price for the shares tendered, taking into account the number of shares tendered, and its ability to acquire all of the 15 million shares at the lowest price to the company. The 15 million shares represented approximately 6.6% of the company's outstanding stock. All 15 million shares were tendered which the company purchased at $50 per share, representing approximately $750 million in value.

The purpose of the share repurchase was to distribute excess cash to shareholders. Over the past decade, the company had undertaken a number of steps to enhance shareholder value including spinning-off a division, selling various assets, and restructuring its business. The share repurchase was an additional attempt to distribute value to shareholders.

[C]   Fixed-Price Tender Case Study: United Parcel Service

On February 4, 2000, the board of United Parcel Service Inc. authorized the repurchase of up to 100.893 million shares. This represented approximately 27% of total United Parcel shares outstanding. The form of repurchase was a fixed-price tender-offer at $60 per share. The day prior to the announcement of the share repurchase, United Parcel's stock was trading at $57.44 per share. The $60 per share tender price represented a 4.46% premium over the pre-announcement price of the company's stock. The company repurchased 68 million shares in the tender offer, representing approximately $4 billion in value. The offer allowed each Class A-1 shareholder to tender up to 27% of its shares in the offer. The tender offer was designed to allow holders of the company's Class A-1 common stock to receive cash for their shares. The source of funds for the repurchase was the initial public offering of the company.

§ 19.12   SUMMARY

A recapitalization is an approach to restructuring that reconfigures a company's capital structure and ownership. There are multiple approaches to recapitalizations, including, share repurchases, special dividends, and leveraged recapitalizations. In most situations, cash is distributed to shareholders in the form of a special dividend or share repurchase, and the company either pays out incremental cash or assumes incremental debt.

Recapitalizations are effective at signaling a company's future prospects to the market or indicating the company is undervalued. In addition, recapitalizations are used to fend off an unwanted takeover threat and concentrate the company's equity in the hands of a few inside shareholders.

Recapitalizations have numerous benefits to the company and to shareholders. Benefits to shareholders include:

- Sell stock to issuer at a premium in an issuer tender offer;

- Receive substantial cash dividend yet retain equity upside;

- Receive cash, debt, and/or other instruments plus potentially some equity in remaining company in a leveraged recapitalizations, where the package represents close to the takeover value of the company.

Recapitalizations have benefits to the issuer corporation as well:

- Able to signal market regarding undervaluation or future prospects;

- Can distribute value to shareholders without selling company;

- May control fate of company in takeover situations;

- May opportunistically use share repurchase to enhance financial ratios.

This having been said, recapitalizations are also fraught with concerns, most notably:

- The company's financial and operating flexibility may be constrained because of significant leverage;

- The recapitalization proposal may stimulate a takeover offer for the company;

- The market may garner a negative perception of the motives behind the recapitalization announcement in that the company may not have better investment or growth opportunities.

Chapter 20

SPIN-OFFS, SPLIT-OFFS, EQUITY CARVE-OUTS, AND TRACKING STOCK

§ 20.01   OVERVIEW

Over the past few decades, restructurings utilizing spin-offs, carve-outs, and tracking stock have become quiet prevalent. A number of reasons have been put forth as to why these types of restructurings have been so successful in creating shareholder value; however, in general, each of these alternatives allows a parent company to focus on its core business, affords the equity markets a more efficient means to value the discrete components of a company, and provides subsidiary management with enhanced incentives tied to the performance of their business. The taxable private sale of stock or assets has also been successful at enhancing shareholder value, as it allows the acquirer to make more efficient use of the assets and other resources of the divested business than the parent. Taxable private sales are discussed more fully in Chapter 14.

[A]   Evidence Behind Restructurings

There has been significant academic research analyzing the impact of transaction-driven restructurings on parent companies and shareholder wealth. Most of these studies indicate there is a positive announcement effect from restructurings. In addition, numerous studies show that there is a marked increase in long-term value to shareholders as a result of a spin-off or equity carve-out. Tracking stock, the least utilized form of restructuring, tends to have mixed long-term results. Following is a brief summation of some of the more pertinent research relating to the different types of transaction restructurings.

In a study conducted in 1995 by Myron Slovin, Marie Sushka, and Steven Ferraro, they analyzed, among other things, the announcement effect of equity carve-outs, spin-offs, and sell-offs on the stock of parent companies involved in the transaction. The analysis showed that the average two-day returns post-restructuring announcement were positive in all cases, 1.22% for carve-outs, 1.32% for spinoffs, and 1.70% for sell-offs.[1] Their study also indicated that there is a negative impact on the rival firms of the parent and companies that are spun-off, if the surviving companies are stronger as a result of the transaction.

A 1999 McKinsey analysis showed that the announcement of a tracking stock or spin-off tended to raise the price of the parent by 2% or 3%.[2] They also found that in the long-term, spin-offs and equity carve-outs significantly outperformed their respective indices, with equity carve-outs having a two-year compound annual growth rate (CAGR) of 22.9% versus the Russell 2000 of 11.0%; spin-offs having a two-year CAGR of 26.9% versus 14.1% for the Russell 2000, and tracking stock having a 19.1% two-year CAGR versus 21.2% for the S&P 500.[3] The

---

1. Slovin, Myron B., Marie E. Sushka, and Steven R. Ferraro, "A Comparison of the Information Conveyed by Equity Carve-Outs, Spin-Offs, and Asset Sell-Offs," Journal of Financial Economics 37, 89–104 (1995).

2. The McKinsey Quarterly, 1999. No. 1.

3. *Id.*

parent companies outperformed their respective indices as well. The two-year CAGR was 18.2% for spin-off parents versus 17.5% for the S&P 500; 22.1% for equity carve-out parents versus 16.9% for the S&P 500, and 21.4% for tracking stock parents versus 21.5% for the S&P 500.[4]

The remainder of this chapter provides an overview of four restructuring approaches: spin-offs, split-offs, equity carve-outs, and tracking stock, and attempts to explain when and how to execute these transactions. It also addresses how each alternative is valued and in turn creates shareholder value.

§ 20.02 SPIN-OFFS

[A] Overview of Spin-Offs

A spin-off is a distribution of the stock of a subsidiary to shareholders. If the transaction meets certain requirements of the Internal Revenue Code, the distribution is tax free to shareholders, and the parent recognizes no gain or loss on the distribution. The stock is distributed pro rata to shareholders of record on a designated date, the record date, so that immediately after the spin-off, the ownership of the spun-off company is the same as that of the parent. The net result of the spin-off is to eliminate the parent management and board from the operation and control of the spun-off subsidiary.

Spin-offs are not a recent phenomenon, with major spin-off transactions having taken place in the 1970s and 1980s. Since 1990, there have been more than 673 spin-offs representing aggregate value of approximately $549 billion.[5] Exhibit 20-1 shows the overall trends in spin-off announcements since 1990.

Exhibit 20-2 provides a list of significant recent completed spin-off transactions.

To illustrate how a spin-off works, let's review the recent 2001 Pitney Bowes spin-off of its office systems business, Imagistics International. Before the spin-off, Pitney Bowes operated in three primary business segments: mailing and integrated logistics, office solutions, and financial services. The office systems business, the target of the spin-off, is a direct marketer, sales, and service organization offering document imaging solutions including copiers, facsimile machines, and other multi-functional products. For the nine months ended September 30, 2001, Pitney Bowes had estimated revenues of over $3.0 billion and a market capitalization of over $10.0 billion. At the time of the spin-off in December 2001, Imagistics International had estimated annual revenues in excess of $630 million.

Prior to the spin-off, the office systems business was a 100% owned subsidiary of Pitney Bowes. On December 3, 2001, Pitney Bowes' shareholders received 0.08 shares of Imagistics International stock for each share that they owned in Pitney Bowes, or one Imagistics share for each 12.5 shares of Pitney Bowes they owned.

---

4. The McKinsey Quarterly, 1999. No. 1.
5. Thomson Financial.

Exhibit 20-1
Announced Spin-Offs: 1990–2003[6]
($ in millions)

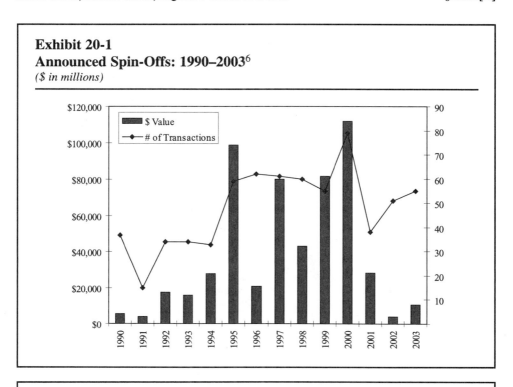

Exhibit 20-2
Recent Significant Spin-Offs[7]
($ in millions)

Date Announced	Date Effective	Target Name	Parent	Value
07/20/2000	06/03/2002	Agere Systems Inc	Lucent Technologies Inc.	$ 2,954
09/04/2001	07/09/2002	CompUSA Inc	Grupo Sanborns	$ 607
11/28/2001	08/13/2002	Monsanto Co	Pharmacia Corp.	$ 3,732
12/19/2001	08/20/2002	Travelers Property Casualty	Citigroup Inc.	$12,213
02/22/2002	09/30/2002	CarMax Group	Circuit City Stores Inc.	$ 1,068
11/14/2002	02/07/2003	Cognizant Technologies Solutions	IMS Health Inc.	$ 705
02/12/2003	12/02/2003	Genesis Health-Eldercare Bus	Genesis Health Ventures Inc.	$ 449
02/21/2003	12/22/03	US Bancorp Piper Jaffray Inc	US Bancorp	$ 829
04/22/2003	08/20/2003	Medco Health Solutions Inc	Merck & Co.	$ 6,809
07/10/2003	12/31/2003	First National Bankshares FL	FNB Corp.	$ 742

---

6. *Id.*
7. Thomson Financial.

Exhibit 20-3
Pitney Bowes Spin-Off of Imagistics International

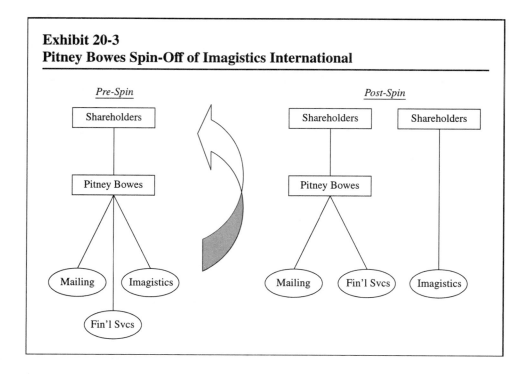

Post spin-off, Pitney Bowes would no longer have any interest in the subsidiary. Exhibit 20-3 outlines the spin-off.

In the restructuring, Pitney Bowes was motivated to "implement[ed] a plan to enhance its strategic focus to unlock and create greater value for stockholders."[8] The spin-off was designed to achieve the following benefits, as outlined in the Form 10 filing with the SEC. For Pitney Bowes, the spin-off would "allow Pitney Bowes to focus its resources on its other divisions where it can add more value."[9] The independent Imagistics International, the successor to the office systems business of Pitney Bowes, would enable Pitney Bowes to "enhance its focus on its core business and concentrate its financial, managerial and marketing resources on the aggressive development of the areas in which it has the strongest market position, the best expertise and the highest growth potential."[10] In addition, the spin-off would "allow Pitney Bowes to improve its profitability, stabilize its earnings growth and reduce its exposure to market fluctuations."[11]

The benefits to Imagistics International were numerous. The "separate management and ownership structure for [Imagistics] will liberate [Imagistics] from the constraints on its development currently imposed by reason of its inclusion in

---

8. Imagistics Form 10 Filing.

9. *Id.*

10. Imagistics Form 10 Filing.

11. *Id.*

Pitney Bowes."[12] In addition, the spin-off would "allow [Imagistics] to make substantial investments in systems, training and infrastructure; provide more targeted compensation to its management and work force; provide competitive benefits packages to its work force; and raise additional funds to pursue an expansion strategy in a consolidating industry."[13]

Prior to the spin-off, Pitney Bowes received a ruling from the Internal Revenue Service that the distribution would be tax free to shareholders, except in the case where a shareholder received cash for fractional shares.

[B]   Evidence Behind Spin-Offs

Spin-offs have been used extensively in the 1990s, and there is significant evidence that spin-offs have been effective at enhancing shareholder value. Spin-offs have been the subject of research and analysis in the past by academics, institutions, and investment banks.

Numerous studies have shown that there are positive returns to shareholders surrounding the announcement of a spin-off. The Slovin, Sushka, and Ferraro study showed that the stock price return for the two-day period surrounding the announcement of a spin-off was 1.32%.[14] Other older studies, such as those by Gailen Hite and James Owers in 1983,[15] James Miles and James Rosenfeld in 1993,[16] and Katherine Schipper and Abbie Smith in 1983,[17] all showed positive returns to parent companies surrounding the announcement of a spin-off.

In yet another independent study in 1997 by Lane Daley, Vikas Mehrotra, and Ranjini Sivakumar, the evidence showed that for parent companies spinning off subsidiaries in a different line of business, the stock price returns were higher than for those companies spinning off a subsidiary in a related business.[18] They found that the two-day announcement return for companies spinning off non-related businesses was 4.3% versus 1.4% for companies spinning off related businesses. This study helps reinforce the idea that the market rewards companies for focusing on their core business.

---

12. *Id.*

13. *Id.*

14. Slovin, Myron B., Marie E. Sushka, and Steven R. Ferraro, "A Comparison of the Information Conveyed by Equity Carve-Outs, Spin-Offs, and Asset Sell-Offs," Journal of Financial Economics 37, 89–104 (1995).

15. Hite, Gailen L., and James E. Owers, "Security Price Reactions Around Corporate Spin-Off Announcements," Journal of Financial Economics 12, 409–436 (1983).

16. Miles, James A., and James D. Rosenfeld, "The Effect of Voluntary Spin-Off Announcements on Shareholder Wealth," The Journal of Finance 38 (5), 1597–1606 (1993).

17. Schipper, Katherine, and Abbie Smith, "Effects of Recontracting on Shareholder Wealth: The Case for Voluntary Spin-Offs," Journal of Financial Economics 12, 437–467 (1983).

18. Daley, Lane, Vikas Mehrotra, and Ranjini Sivakumar, "Corporate Focus and Value Creation Evidence from Spinoffs," Journal of Financial Economics 45, 257–281 (1997).

The long-term stock price effects have been studied as well. A study by Patrick Cusatis, James Miles, and J. Randall Woolridge in 1993, found that the parent and subsidiary stock showed above-market returns as a result of a spin-off for up to three years following the transaction.[19] This study also concluded that "we observe superior long-term investment performance for spin-offs. In contrast to similar and more common newly traded security, the IPO, spin-offs provide abnormal returns over an extended period. Surprisingly, we find that parent firms also offer superior post-spin-off long-term investment performance."[20] Their study analyzed spin-offs from 1965 to 1988 by measuring the returns to the parent, the spin-off and the combination of the two from the time of the announcement of the spin-off to up to three years after the spin-off. It included 146 non-taxable spin-offs in 27 industries ranging from agriculture to retail and from mining to food.

The results of the study showed that for the spun-off companies, the mean common stock return over six, 12, 24, 36 months after the spinoff was −1%, 4.5%, 25.0%, and 33.6%, respectively. These returns were adjusted to show how the spin-offs outperformed their industry peer groups. For the parent firms, the mean common stock returns for the same time periods were 6.8%, 12.5%, 26.7%, and 18.1%, respectively.

In a more recent survey, Miles and Woolridge analyzed 199 spin-offs from 177 parent companies from the time period of 1965 through 1996.[21] Recognizing that there is a short-term positive abnormal return to the parent stock after the announcement of a spin-off, their approach was to evaluate the long-term performance of the parent and subsidiary after the spin-off. They concluded that for the spin-off itself, the long-term adjusted performance[22] of the stock for the 12, 18, 24, 36 months after the initial trade date were 6.8%, 14.6%, 24.7%, and 29.5%. For the parent company, the long-term adjusted performance for the same time periods was 5.9%, 9.8%, 15.9%, and 19.3%. This study is significant in that it establishes that while it is possible to generate immediate shareholder gains from the announcement of a spin-off, the long-term shareholder benefits are real and sustainable.

A study by Miles and Woolridge looked at takeover activity surrounding spin-offs and their parents. In their 1993 and 1996 studies, they found their was a high incidence of takeover activity amongst the parent and spin-off after the distribution date. In the 1993 study, of 146 spin-offs and 131 parents in the study, 21 spun-off companies and 18 parent companies had been acquired or merged within three years of the spin-off.[23] In the 1996 study by Miles and Woolridge, they found that

---

19. Cusatis, Patrick J., James A. Miles, and J. RandallWoolridge, "Restructuring through Spinoffs: The Stock Market Evidence," Journal of Financial Economics 33, 293–311 (1993).

20. *Id.*

21. Miles, James A., and J. Randall Woolridge, Spin-Offs and Equity Carve-Outs: Achieving Faster Growth and Better Performance, 22–34 (1999).

22. Adjusted to eliminate the returns to companies comparable to the spin-off.

23. Miles, James A., and James D. Rosenfeld, "The Effect of Voluntary Spin-Off Announcements on Shareholder Wealth," The Journal of Finance 38 (5), 1597–1606 (1993).

over one-third of the parent and spin-off companies were involved in merger activity within three years of the initial spin-off.[24]

The Cusatis, Miles and Woolridge study also looked at the combined returns to stockholders who held stock in the parent and subsidiary from six months prior to the distribution date to up to 36 months after the distribution date. They determined that the combined return to stockholders who held stock in both the parent and subsidiary for the six months prior to the distribution date to 12 months, 24 months, and 36 months after the distribution date would have been 12.6%, 24.2%, and 17.4% on a basis adjusted for the return to competitors.

[C] Creating Value Through Spin-Offs

In the eyes of the Internal Revenue Service, creating shareholder value through tax-free spin-offs is not a valid business purpose. Nevertheless, while the stated business reasons for spin-offs do not necessarily include the words "enhance shareholder value," the end result of a spin-off is usually the increase in value for the parent, subsidiary or both.

A good way to visualize the creation of value in a spin-off is to look at the combined value of the parent and spin-off pre and post spin. For example, if the prespin value of a parent trading with the subsidiary embedded in its financials is $100 million, once the spin-off has become effective, it is likely that the value of the parent may decline slightly, yet the value attributed to the spin-off may be sufficiently high that the combined valuation of the two entities post spin-off is greater than the value before the spin-off, say $120 million. Exhibit 20-4 illustrates this concept.

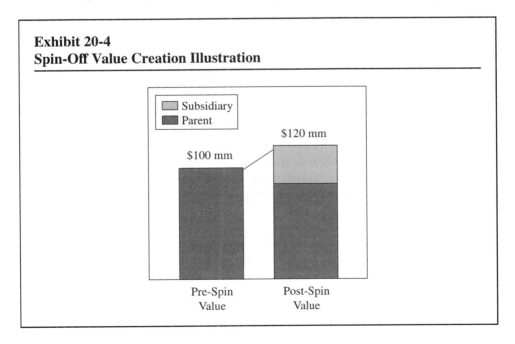

Exhibit 20-4
Spin-Off Value Creation Illustration

---

24. Miles and Woolridge (1999), *supra* n.21.

This is well illustrated in the AT&T spin-off of NC Rand Lucent, which generated approximately $7 billion in market capitalization. A year later, the difference in market capitalization between AT&T prior to the restructuring and the combined market capitalization of AT&T, NCR, and Lucent post restructuring, was over $100 billion.

The value created in spin-offs can be realized in a variety of ways and over differing time periods. As discussed in *Chapter 18: Overview of Corporate Restructurings*, the impact of a restructuring transaction will be felt in a company's capital structure, income statement, ownership and organization. Each of these effects will have a corresponding consequence on the parent and subsidiary's stock price. In addition, there is an "announcement effect" on a parent company in which it may see an immediate and sustained rise in its stock price immediately following the announcement of the spin-off.

From a financial perspective, the net result of the stock distribution of a subsidiary is that the income statement and balance sheet of the subsidiary are deconsolidated with that of the parent. The implications of this are numerous:

- The stand alone financial performance of the parent and subsidiary post spin-off are presented on a discrete basis, enabling the market to value the businesses based on their own growth rates and margins. Consequently, poorly performing subsidiaries will be eliminated from the parent, possibly leading to an increase in valuation of the parent's stock. Strong performing subsidiaries will be valued well in the marketplace. Under either scenario, for shareholders who owned stock in the parent pre spin-off, and thus became stockholders in the parent and subsidiary post distribution, the likely benefit is an increase in the overall value of their combined holdings in the two companies.

- The balance sheets of the parent and subsidiary are deconsolidated, allowing the market to assess the capital structure of each company independently. Also, the separation allows each company to finance itself at its own cost of capital, creating a more efficient use of capital. In the process of deconsolidating the companies, it is possible for the subsidiary to pay a dividend to the parent, increasing its leverage. Consequently, the parent can deliver its balance sheet and enhance its capital structure. For example, in the Pitney Bowes spin-off, Imagistics paid a $150 million dividend to Pitney Bowes prior to the spin-off.

By its nature, a tax-free spin-off has significant financial benefits to shareholders and the parent. Usually, a dividend is taxable to shareholders, yet in transactions that meet the requirements for tax-free status, shareholders may receive the dividend tax free. Their basis is carried over pro rata from the parent to the subsidiary. To the parent, the divestiture of a subsidiary is usually a taxable event, meaning, the parent ordinarily pays taxes on the difference between the fair market value or the business and its basis in the company. However, in a tax-free spin-off, the parent pays no taxes from the distribution.

From a balance sheet perspective, spin-offs can have a dramatic impact on the parent. First, the assets and liabilities of the subsidiary are deconsolidated from the parent. Second, prior to the spin-off, the subsidiary may pay a dividend to the parent which can be used to repay debt, repurchase stock or pay out as a special dividend to shareholders. Each of these will affect the company's leverage ratio and earnings per share, not to mention a possible impact on the company's ownership.

The same logic applies to the parent's income statement, where the subsidiary is deconsolidated. In addition, the altered capital structure of the parent will ripple through the income statement and alter the company's earnings per share and earnings growth rate. And, as the earnings per share change, the multiple applied to those earnings will change too: it will increase if the earnings growth rate expands and the leverage is optimized, and decrease if the earnings growth rate declines and the leverage deteriorates.

In the case of a company spinning off a business that is growing faster than the parent company, it is possible that the multiple applied to the new company's earnings is substantially higher than that of the parent, offsetting a potential decline in the growth rate and multiple of the parent post spin-off.

In some situations, the value created in a spin-off may only be witnessed once a poorly performing business is extricated from a parent's financials, and the market bears witness to the improved operating performance of the parent. In addition, shareholders may only see an increase in value if the spun-off entity is acquired a few years after the spin-off. As a result, it is wise to consider not only what specific events will enhance value, but over what time period those enhancements may take place.

From a market and strategic perspective, the distribution announcement is a strong signal that the parent is focusing on its core business or businesses, and is either getting rid of a poor performer or highlighting a star. The perceived breakup of the company facilitates the creation of pure play companies that can be easier valued in the market place.

Internally, creating a separately traded company allows management to establish incentives for managers and employees that are directly related to the performance of the business. For example, in the Pitney Bowes transaction, Imagistics adopted an employee incentive plan that tied performance goals to Imagistic's performance. In addition, the company established a separate directors, nonemployee option plan.

As an example, Exhibit 20-5 shows the stock prices for Pitney Bowes versus the S&P 500 from three months prior to six months post the announcement. Exhibit 20-6 shows Imagistic's stock price from December 4, 2001–April 30, 2002.

Pitney Bowes announced the spin-off of Imagistics on December 11, 2000. For the period two days prior to the announcement to the day when Imagistics began trading, the stock price increased 39.9% while the S&P 500 declined 14.8%. Imagistics began trading on December 4, 2001. In the six months since it started trading, the stock increased by 61%, while the market decreased 6%. The market capitalization of Pitney Bowes at the time of announcement was

Exhibit 20-5
Pitney Bowes Stock Price Versus the S&P 500:
October 11, 2000–June 11, 2001

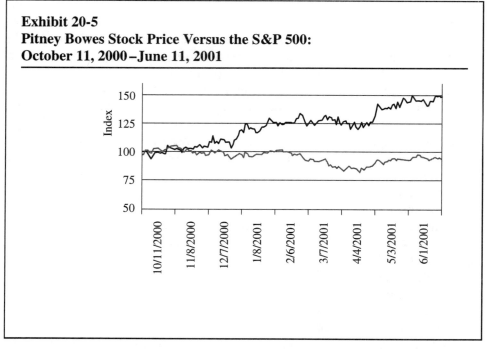

Exhibit 20-6
Imagistics Stock Price: December 4, 2001–April 30, 2002

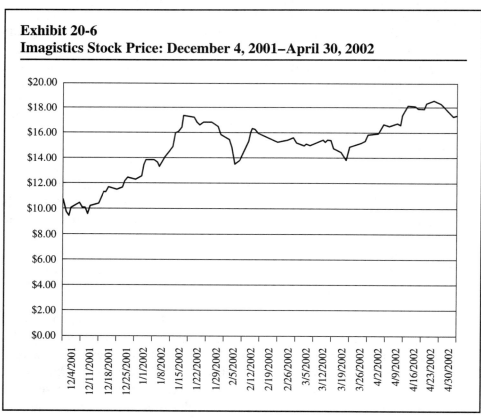

approximately $7.2 billion. Upon the distribution of the stock, the combined market capitalization of Pitney Bowes and Imagistics was $9.8 billion, an increase of $2.7 billion. While this is a single example of a spin-off, it should provide a roadmap of how to think about the timeline of value creation for a spin-off.

[D]   Motivation and Rationale

The overriding motivation behind spin-offs, like other modes of restructuring, is to enhance shareholder value. In addition, there are a number or other driving forces that are often used as valid business reasons.

[1]   Lack of Synergy or Strategic Fit

Synergies are the capitalization on joint opportunities between businesses to either generate increased revenue or reduce costs. As examples, synergies can be in the form of marketing arrangements, financial resources, overhead and operating costs, or operating cultures. In some companies, while various businesses may have been acquired or started as a result of synergies at the time, these joint economies may have disappeared and the two companies may no longer enjoy the benefits achieved from joint ownership. Numerous spin-offs have occurred for this reason.

Another form of synergy is the strategic fit that the parent may have with its subsidiary. In some cases, the risk profile—operating and financial—may be quite different for the two businesses. Some companies may require substantial capital investment yet generate attractive, albeit high, risk returns, while another company may require little capital investment yet generate stable, albeit low, returns. This lack of strategic fit may also be just cause for a spin-off.

Synergies can also be in the form of customer and supplier relationships. To the extent these constituents become the subject of internal conflicts or competing interests, it may make sense to separate the businesses.

Exhibit 20-7 lists a number of spin-offs where a lack of synergy or strategic fit were the primary motivation behind the transaction.

[2]   Focus on Core Business

Public company shareholders, in particular, institutional shareholders, have become increasingly vocal regarding their interests. They have been known to acquire stakes in companies to stimulate change, wage public campaigns to pressure management to improve performance, and place resolutions on proxies to incite change. Most of these tactics are designed to pressure management and the board to increase shareholder value. As the deconglomeration of the 1970s and 1980s gained momentum, there was an increased emphasis on shareholders pressuring companies to divest non-core assets and focus on core businesses, the rationale being that investors should be making investment decisions in different businesses, not management. Often, this pressure led to companies spinning off businesses that were non-core. Exhibit 20-8 provides a summary list of transactions where the primary business purpose was to focus on a core business.

Exhibit 20-7
Examples of Lack of Synergy or Strategic Fit as a Motivation Behind a Spin-Off

Parent	Subsidiary	Date	Rationale
Baxter International (Medical products)	Caremark (Home health care)	1992	Customer conflict
Quaker Oats (Foods)	Fisher Price Toys (Toys)	1992	Different operating and financial risk profiles
Marriott Corporation (Hotel business)	Marriott International (Management business)	1993	Different capital needs
General Mills (Prepared foods)	Darden Restaurants (Restaurants)	1994	Few cultural or operating synergies
Cooper Industries (Conglomerate)	Cooper Cameron (Oil and natural gas equipment)	1994	Different risk profiles
AT&T (Voice, data, and video communications)	1. NCR (Business information services) 2. Lucent (Communications systems)	1995	Focus on core business; divest poorly performing business
Kimberly Clark (Household, health, and personal care products)	Cigarette operations	1995	Cigarette operations had become highly litigious
Manor Care Inc. (Nursing homes)	Choice Hotels International (Hotels)	1996	Few operating synergies
ALCO Standard (Office technology systems)	Unisource Worldwide (Paper and supply distribution)	1996	Customer conflict
Kansas City Southern (Railroad)	Stilwell Financial (Financial Services)	2000	Lack of strategic fit

[3] Highlight Value, Monetize Assets, or Reduce Debt

While maximizing overall shareholder value is generally a business reason that, by itself, is not necessarily accepted by the IRS, a prime motivation behind spin-offs can be to highlight a particular business, and demonstrate value for a particular asset by allowing the market to value the business on a discrete basis.

Spin-offs have also been used opportunistically to allow a parent to realize value from a strong performing subsidiary and reduce debt. As the spin-off is a stock dividend, the parent can realize proceeds from the transaction by extracting a cash dividend from the subsidiary prior to the spin-off, thus realizing value from the transaction.

Numerous spin-offs have been undertaken for these reasons, as shown in Exhibit 20-9.

Exhibit 20-8
Examples of Focus on Core Business as a Motivation Behind Spin-Off

Parent	Subsidiary	Date	Rationale
Imperial Chemicals (Specialty chemicals)	The Zeneca Group (Pharmaceuticals)	1993	Focus on core chemicals business
Bally Entertainment (Gaming)	Bally Health and Fitness (Fitness clubs)	1994	Focus on core gaming business
Lilly (pharmaceuticals)	Guidant (Medical products)	1994	Focus on core pharmaceuticals business
AT&T (Voice, data, and video communications)	1. NCR (Business information systems) 2. Lucent (Communications systems)	1995	Focus on core business; divest poorly performing business
Annheuser-Busch (Brewing)	Earthgrains (Packaged goods division)	1995	Focus on core brewing business
ITT (Conglomerate)	1. ITT Industries (Automotive, defense, and electronics) 2. ITT Destinations (Hotels, gambling, entertainment) 3. ITT Hartford (insurance)	1995	Break-up of company allows each subsidiary to focus on its own business
Rockwell International (Industrial products and systems)	Automotive Components (Automotive)	1996	Focus on core industrial products business
Pepsi (Beverages)	Restaurant businesses (Pizza Hut, Kentucky Fried Chicken, Taco Bell)	1996	Focus on core soft drink business
Tenneco (Automotive products)	Newport News (Shipbuilder)	1996	Focus on core automotive business
Kansas City Southern (Railroad)	Stilwell Financial (Financial Services)	2000	Focus on core business; highlight value of Stilwell
Bristol-Myers Squibb (Pharmaceuticals)	Zimmer Holdings (Medical Devices)	2001	Focus on core business

[4]   Avoid Takeover

The requirements for tax-free status of spin-offs can sometimes serve as an effective deterrent to a takeover threat. In the event a parent or subsidiary is acquired post spin-off in a transaction that was anticipated at the time of the spin-off announcement, the parent becomes liable for the capital gains taxes on the difference between its basis in the spin-off and the fair market value of the

Exhibit 20-9
Examples of Spin-Offs Used to Highlight Undervalued Assets,
Monetize Assets, or Reduce Debt

Parent	Subsidiary	Date	Rationale
Marriott Corporation (Hotel business)	Marriott International (Management business)	1993	Allow Marriott to reduce its debt
W.R. Grace (Specialty chemicals)	National Medical Care (Kidney dialysis centers)	1995	Focus on core business; realize value from spin-off to reduce debt at W.R. Grace
Dial Corporation (Consumer products)	Viad Corp (Airline catering, convention, and leisure services)	1996	Allow markets to value businesses independently
Tenneco (Automotive products)	Newport News (Shipbuilder)	1996	Allow Tenneco to reduce debt
PepsiCo (Beverages)	Restaurant businesses (Pizza Hut, Kentucky Fried Chicken, Taco Bell)	1996	Reduce PepsiCo's debt
Rockwell International (Industrial products and systems)	Automotive Components (Automotive)	1996	Realize value from automotive business
Monsanto (Pharmaceuticals)	Chemicals (Chemicals)	1996	Realize value for chemicals business
AT&T Group (Telecommunications)	Liberty Media (Cable TV)	2000	Raise capital; build relationships with other companies
3Com Corp (Technology)	Palm Inc. (Handheld Devices)	2000	Highlight value of Palm
Hewlett-Packard (Computers)	Agilent Technologies (Test and Measurement)	2000	Highlight value of Agilent
AMR Corp (Airline)	Sabre Holdings (Reservations System)	2000	Highlight value of Sabre
Bristol-Myers Squibb	Zimmer Holdings	2001	Highlight value of Zimmer

company. Consequently, spin-offs have occasionally been used to fend off unwanted suitors. Exhibit 20-10 provides a few examples.

[5] Eliminate a Poor Performer

Poorly performing subsidiaries can often be subsumed by a company or drag down the parent's financial performance. A spin-off can be used to divest a poorly performing business, serving to enhance the value of the parent's remaining business. A poor performer may not simply under perform from a financial perspective,

Exhibit 20-10
Examples of Spin-Offs Used to Thwart a Takeover Threat

Parent	Subsidiary	Date	Rationale
ICI (Specialty chemicals)	Zeneca (Pharmaceuticals)	1991	Raise value in advance of potential takeover bid from Hanson
Commercial Intertec (Hydraulic systems manufacturer)	Cuno (TEC, Inc.) (Filtration products manufacturer)	1996	Fend off takeover threat from Union Dominion Industries

Exhibit 20-11
Examples of Spin-Offs of Poor Performers

Parent	Subsidiary	Date	Rationale
AT&T (Voice, data, and video communications)	1. NCR (Business information systems) 2. Lucent (Communications systems)	1995	NCR had not been a strong performer
Monsanto (Pharmaceuticals)	Chemicals (Chemicals)	1996	Eliminate the chemicals business which was not performing well
3M (Coatings and bondings)	Imation (Imaging and data storage)	1996	Imation was not very profitable
Corning (Telecommunications, materials, and information)	Clinical Laboratory (Clinical laboratories)	1996	Clinical laboratory business was a poor performer

it could also be in a sector where the overall opportunity is less attractive, or it may be quite small relative to the parent company's remaining businesses. In addition, it could be that while the subsidiary is able to trade on a stand alone basis, there are far larger, stronger competitors in the market in which it competes. History suggests that in cases of poorly performing businesses being spun-off, the subsidiary is usually acquired in the years following the spin-off. Exhibit 20-11 shows spin-offs of poorly performing businesses.

[6] Tax Efficiency

Once a company has made the strategic decision to divest a business, the logical question concerns what form of divestiture to use to maximize value to shareholders. While an outright private sale is a good option, one potential drawback is

Exhibit 20-12
Key Events in a Spin-Off

Event	Summary Description
Announcement	A press release is issued by the parent company to the public.
Seek IRS ruling on tax status	Letter to the IRS seeking a ruling on the tax-free nature of the transaction. May also seek a legal opinion from professionals.
File Form 10	The form, similar to an S-1 registration statement, that is required by the Securities and Exchange Act of 1934 to be filed with the SEC.
File application for exchange listing	Parent makes the exchange listing on behalf of the subsidiary.
Receive tax-free ruling	The IRS will notify the parent of its ruling prior to the Form 10 becoming effective.
Form 10 becomes effective	For the Form 10 to become effective, a number of conditions will need to be met, including the tax-free ruling from the IRS.
Shareholder meeting	A shareholder meeting is often required if the size of the business to be spun-off requires one.
Record date	Set by the parent once the Form 10 has become effective. Only shareholders of the parent on this date will receive the dividend of subsidiary stock.
Subsidiary begins trading on a when-issued basis	The spin-off will often trade in the market prior to the distribution becoming effective. The market place sets the stock-price of the spin-off stock. Investors not wishing to participate in the spin-off will often sell in this period.
Distribution becomes effective	Approximately 10 days after when-issued trading begins, the distribution becomes effective and the spun-off subsidiary begins to trade.
Parent trades ex-dividend	Once the spin-off has become effective, the parent then trades on an ex-dividend basis without the subsidiary.

the requirement for the parent to pay taxes on the gain on sale of the business. As a spin-off is often tax free to shareholders and the parent, it is an efficient method of divesting a business.

[7] Regulatory

Companies may be forced to divest businesses for regulatory reasons. One example is the break-up of AT&T in the early 1980s, whereby the Federal Trade Commission ordered the break-up of the company for competitive reasons.

[E] Key Timing Events in Spin-Offs

There are a number of important events in executing a spin-off. From start to finish, the process can take upwards of six months. Exhibit 20-12 outlines the key events in a spin-off. As an example, the key events and dates for the Pitney Bowes

```
┌─────────────────────────────────────────────────────────────────┐
│                                                                   │
│   Exhibit 20-13                                                   │
│   Key Events in Imagistics Spin-Off from Pitney Bowes[25]        │
│                                                                   │
│        Event                              Date                    │
│   ─────────────────────────────────────────────────────────      │
│   Announcement Date                   December 11, 2000           │
│   Incorporate Subsidiary[26]          February 20, 2001           │
│   Initial Form 10 Filing              April 18, 2001              │
│   Name Change[27]                     October 12, 2001            │
│   Final Form 10 Amendment             November 6, 2001            │
│   Record Date                         November 19, 2001           │
│   When Issued Trading Begins          November 20, 2001           │
│   Effective Date                      December 3, 2001            │
│                                                                   │
└─────────────────────────────────────────────────────────────────┘
```

spin-off of Imagistics are shown in Exhibit 20-13. From the announcement to the ex-dividend date for Pitney Bowes, the transaction took almost a year.

[F] Valuation of Spin-Offs

An overall spin-off analysis involves a number of steps, and includes not only the valuation of the business to be spun-off, but the valuation of the entire company pre-and post-spin, and the analysis of the impact of the spin-off on the parent. First, a break-up valuation should be performed in the manner proscribed in *Chapter 18: Overview of Corporate Restructurings*. This analysis is critical to understanding the stand alone value of a company and the value of the separate businesses in a transaction specific contest. The break-up valuation is performed to understand whether the parent company as a whole is undervalued in the market, and to determine what the stand alone values of each of the company's discrete businesses are. It enables us to determine whether a spin-off is a viable alternative, and helps us understand which divestiture approach to use. In the break-up valuation, remember that the corporate overhead and liabilities should be deducted from the combined values of the business segments.

Second, the subsidiary to be spun-off should be valued in the context of the transaction. In this framework, valuing a subsidiary for a spin-off is not materially different than valuing a subsidiary for an initial public offering, where standard valuation methodologies including discounted cash flow and comparable company analysis are used. As the subsidiary is "private," embedded inside the parent, the valuation should take into consideration the appropriate capital structure and cost of capital for the subsidiary, as discussed in *Chapter 10: Private Company Valuation*. Because the company will trade publicly once the spin-off has been

---

25. Public Company Documents.
26. Incorporated as Pitney Bowes Office Systems, Inc.
27. Name changed to Imagistics International.

completed, an emphasis should be placed on valuation using the comparable companies methodology, much the same way one would in the analysis of a company for an initial public offering. The one difference however, is that no IPO discount is applied to the company in determining its trading value.

There are other considerations to think of when valuing a subsidiary for a spin-off. First, the valuation is a reference range only. The true trading value of the stock will be determined during when-issued trading of the stock prior to the effective date of the distribution. The valuation analysis is used to determine the relative value of the subsidiary versus the parent, and calculate the number of shares of subsidiary stock to issue to parent shareholders. Second, while the parent company's tax basis in the subsidiary is not necessarily related to its value, the potential capital gains the parent could be liable for may determine whether or not the subsidiary is spun-off or sold.

The third step in the analysis is to determine the impact the spin-off will have on the parent. Accretion/dilution analysis is an important tool to use, as it allows us to understand the impact of the transaction on the parent company's earnings per share. Based on the revised earnings of the parent, it is possible to calculate an implied stock price post spin-off, based on multiples of comparable companies.

Based on these three approaches, it is feasible to calculate the theoretical value creation in a spin-off. Revisiting Exhibit 20-4, recall that prior to a spin-off, the parent is valued based on its combined earnings growth rate and leverage. Once the spin-off has been affected, it is likely that the parent's multiple will expand or contract, depending on the attractiveness of the subsidiary. However, the newly independent subsidiary will command a market valuation of its own based on its own growth and leverage characteristics. Theoretically, the sum of the market values of the two independent companies should be higher than the market capitalization of the parent prior to the spin-off.

[G]   Tax Requirements

Technically, a spin-off is a dividend to shareholders. For the dividend to be tax free to shareholders and the parent, it must meet a number of specific criteria as promulgated by Section 355 of the Internal Revenue Code. Following is a summary of these requirements:

(a) *Control:* The parent must have control of the subsidiary prior to the spin-off. For these purposes, the definition of control is at least 80% of each of the voting and non-voting classes of stock of the subsidiary.

(b) *Active Business:* After the spin-off, the parent and subsidiary must be engaged in an active trade or business that was actively conducted for five years prior to the distribution. In addition, neither of the businesses may have been acquired during that period in a transaction where any gain or loss was recognized.

(c) *Business Purpose:* The transaction must have a true business purpose. While there are numerous possible business purposes for a tax-free spin-off, some of the more common ones include: focus on core business, lack of strategic fit, reduce debt, monetize value of a subsidiary, or regulatory reasons.

(d) *Device Test:* The spin-off cannot be used as a means to distribute earnings and profits to shareholders.

(e) *Continuity of Interest:* The shareholders of the parent must continue to maintain adequate continuity of interest in the spun-off entity and the parent post distribution.

(f) *Continuity of Business:* Both the parent and spun-off entity must reasonably continue in the same lines of business as they did predistribution.

(g) *No Prior Acquisition:* The parent may not have acquired the subsidiary within five years prior to the distribution, in a transaction where a gain or loss was recognized.

(h) *No Tax Avoidance:* In some cases, the subsidiary to be distributed may have been a division of the corporation, and hence subject to a reorganization to create a subsidiary prior to the spin-off. These types of reorganizations are known as "D" reorganizations, and in such circumstances, a Section 355 spin-off also is subject to the requirements of Section 368 of the Internal Revenue Code that governs the tax-free nature of the D reorganization. The parent will need to establish that it distributed "control" in the subsidiary, and that any stock retained in the subsidiary was not as a result of the parent wishing to avoid any taxes. The issue stems from a continuity of interest test in D reorganizations that today mandate that there should be at least 50% continuity of interest between the parent and subsidiary shareholders.

In addition to these requirements, there are other provisions of Section 355 of the Code that govern post-distribution events.

(i) *No Plan to Acquire Parent or Subsidiary:* If after the distribution, 50% or more of the parent or subsidiary is acquired by a third party, and there was knowledge of the proposed acquisition on the date of the spin-off, the parent will have to recognize a gain on the distribution of the subsidiary stock.

(j) *Disqualified Distribution:* In the event that after the distribution, greater than 50% of the stock of the parent or subsidiary is controlled by one party or related group of parties, that stock having been acquired within five years of the distribution, the distribution becomes disqualified and is taxable to the parent. The parent will be required to recognize a gain on the distribution of stock that is equal to the fair market value of the stock minus the parent's basis in the stock.

Once the announcement of the spin-off has been made, it is common for the parent to seek a ruling from the IRS regarding the tax-free status of the spin-off.

The IRS will issue a letter to the company that states its position on the transaction. Usually, the receipt of this ruling is a condition to the Form 10 filing becoming effective. It is also fairly common for companies looking to undertake a spin-off to seek an opinion from a qualified tax lawyer who will issue a letter to the company stating the law firm's opinion as to the likely tax status of the transaction.

Spin-offs that meet the requirements of Section 355 of the Internal Revenue Code are tax free to shareholders. Unlike other dividends, shareholders don't pay taxes when they receive a tax-free distribution. Their pro rata basis in the subsidiary's stock carries over to the spun-off entity, and they only pay taxes when they sell their stock, at which point they pay taxes on the difference between the sale price and their basis in the stock. Shareholders will have a taxable gain or loss to the extent they receive cash in lieu of fractional shares in the subsidiary. The stockholders of the parent apportion their tax basis in the parent stock pre spin-off between two independent companies post spin-off on a pro rata basis. The holding period for shareholders who receive spun-off stock will include the period during which they owned the parent stock as well.

[H] Filing Requirements

Under the Securities and Exchange Act of 1934, the SEC requires that the company being spun-off file a form, Form 10, with the SEC in anticipation of the transaction. Form 10 is similar to a S-1 registration statement in that it contains much of the same information from a disclosure perspective. Some of the key items included in the Form 10 are: audited financial statements of the parent, unaudited pro forma financial statements of the subsidiary, the background of the transaction, and the reasons behind the spin-off. Exhibit 20-14 lists the Form 10 filing requirements in detail.

The distribution of subsidiary stock to shareholders cannot become effective until the Form 10 itself has become effective. For the Form 10 to become effective, a number of conditions need to be met, one of which is the ruling from the IRS that the transaction will be tax free to shareholders. There may be other conditions as well, for example, that the subsidiary has obtained bank financing sufficient to maintain its working capital needs. As an example, Exhibit 20-15 lists the conditions in the Pitney Bowes transaction.[28]

In some cases, if the subsidiary size is large enough, the parent will be required to seek shareholder approval. In these situations, the parent will also be required to file a proxy statement with the SEC and mail it to shareholders in anticipation of the shareholders meeting. In the case of Pitney Bowes, no shareholder approval was required for the spin-off of Imagistics, as the business did not represent a significant enough share of the company's assets or revenues.

---

28. Imagistics Form 10 Filing.

Exhibit 20-14
Partial List of Form 10 Filing Requirements[29]

Item	Description
Business Description	A general narrative of the development of the business, its subsidiaries and predecessors. Financial information regarding the company's business segments including revenues, profit, or loss and total assets for the past three years. Narrative description of the parent company and its subsidiaries. Financial information on the geographic break-down of the revenues and long-lived assets of the company, by domicile, all foreign countries, and foreign countries by themselves if material.
Financial Information	The last five fiscal years of financial statements for the registrant. Other fiscal years should be provided if necessary. Management Discussion and Analysis for all fiscal periods, addressing liquidity, capital resources and results of operations, and for interim periods, address any changes in financial condition or changes in results in operations.
Properties	The location and general characteristics of plants, mines, and other physical properties.
Security Ownership	The security ownership of beneficial owners and management. Information to be provided includes title of class, name of owner, amount, and percent of class owned.
Directors and Officers	The directors and officers, their positions and affiliations, terms and year nominated. Describe any relationships, arrangements or understandings between the director or officer and the company.
Executive Compensation	All plan and non-plan compensation awarded to, earned by or paid to executive officers. The CEO and his compensation as well as the four highest compensated individuals besides the CEO.
Other Items	In addition to the above, the Form 10 filling requires disclosures in the following areas: • Certain relationships and related transactions • Legal proceedings • Market price of and dividends on the registrant's common equity and related stockholder matters • Recent sales of unregistered securities • Description of registrant's securities to be registered • Indemnification of directors and officers • Financial statements and supplementary data • Changes in and disagreements with accountants on accounting and financial disclosure • Financial statements and exhibits

---

29. Securities and Exchange Commission public information.

Exhibit 20-15
Conditions to Spin-Off of Imagistics International[30]

- The Form 10 must have been declared effective by the SEC
- The New York Stock Exchange must have approved the listing of Imagistic's common stock
- Pitney Bowes' board of directors must have approved the spin-off and must not have abandoned, deferred, or modified the spin-off at any time before the record date for the spin-off
- Pitney Bowes must have contributed the necessary operations, assets, and liabilities to Imagistics
- Pitney Bowes must have elected Imagistics' board of directors
- The Imagistics certificate of incorporation and bylaws must be in effect
- Pitney Bowes and Imagistics must have entered into various ancillary agreements between the parties
- Pitney Bowes must have received a ruling from the IRS, or a legal opinion from its counsel, stating that the spin-off qualifies as tax-free to Pitney Bowes and its stockholders

---

[I]   Pricing of Spin-Offs

Spin-offs usually are priced in the market place when the subsidiary stock starts trading on a when-issued basis. After the Form 10 has become effective and, if necessary, shareholder approval has been received, the company sets a record date upon which shareholders who own parent stock as of that date will be entitled to receive the stock dividend. After the record date, the subsidiary stock starts trading on a when issued basis. This means that market makers and investors begin making a market in the stock in order to establish the initial trading range for the stock, and subsequently, the actual stock price for the company when the distribution becomes effective. At the outset of when-issued trading, the bid and ask on the subsidiary stock is usually quite large, as investors and market makers seek to establish an appropriate trading range. The when-issued period is approximately ten days, at the end of which, the distribution becomes effective and the stock trades on an exchange. Once the subsidiary stock is trading on a stand alone basis, the parent stock then trades on an ex-dividend basis, meaning it trades without the subsidiary.

[J]   Issues with Respect to Spin-Offs

[1]   Section 355

The most important concern in executing a tax-free spin-off is whether the transaction will meet the requirements of the Internal Revenue Code. While it is possible to go through the extensive check list of requirements for Sections 355

---

30. Imagistics Form 10 Filing.

and 368 of the Code, many of the requirements are subjective and may be up for interpretation. For example, the business purpose of the spin-off may sound reasonable to the parent and subsidiary, but may not be to the Internal Revenue Service. It is wise therefore, to seek a ruling from the Internal Revenue Service prior to the distribution.

[2] Management and Governance

While one of the motivations for undertaking a spin-off may be to facilitate better management and employee incentives, the management group should be chosen based not only on its understanding of the business to be spun-off, but also on its ability to manage the "new" company as a publicly traded entity. The issue to remember is that as a division or subsidiary, the management team was accountable to the parent and in many cases, did not have direct responsibility for managing the financing of the company. They possibly would not have had much, if any, contact with the public equity markets, institutional investors and equity research analysts. Therefore, the proposed management team should be well coached on the differences between managing a subsidiary and a public company.

The board of directors of a spun-off company initially is comprised of select board members of the parent, a few management employees from the spun-off company, and possibly one or two outside board members. The parent board members are charged initially with selecting the management team and overseeing the separation of the subsidiary from the parent. Once the company has been spun-off, the board composition is likely to change, as new outside board members are nominated and elected, and replace the board members from the parent.

[3] Separation of Assets

When deconsolidating the subsidiary from the parent, the companies may have trouble separating assets into appropriate categories that relate to each company. For example, the same inventory may be used in both companies, or the parent and subsidiary may be housed in the same office space and share joint resources.

[4] Capitalization

In many corporations with multiple business units, the financing of the divisions and subsidiaries takes place at the corporate level, and the balance sheets of the individual businesses do not reflect the capital allocated to them. Consequently, when the spin-off distribution is close at hand, there may be debate over how much debt the parent and subsidiary should each assume in the transaction. When evaluating this issue, it is wise to look at the capital structures of companies comparable to both the parent and subsidiary to determine the appropriate capital structure for each business. In some cases, the spin-off entity may pay a dividend to the parent at the time of the distribution. The effect of the dividend is to lever up the subsidiary and delever the parent.

[5] Contingent and Other Liabilities

Certain contingent and other liabilities may historically have been co-mingled in order to reap the benefits of critical mass. For example, 401(k) plans, health care benefits, and post-retirement benefits. Each of these items will have to be accounted for on a stand alone basis, and each company will need to have its own plans going forward that are reflective of the underlying business and human resources. One should bear in mind that the Pension Benefit Guaranty Corporation, the entity that oversees pension and retirement plans, has strict standards that will apply to how the assets and liabilities of pension plans are allocated in spin-offs.

To the extent there are any other contingent or other liabilities, it is wise to settle these potential claims prior to or at the time the spin-off becomes effective. It would be foolhardy to attempt to defer addressing these issues until after the spin, as you run the risk of "tainting" the benefits of the transaction.

[6]   Relations with Customers, Suppliers, and Shareholders

When a spin-off distribution is effective, often, there is significant turnover in the shareholder base of the parent and the newly independent company. This can take place for a number of reasons including, the automatic sale of stock in one of the companies as it no longer fits the investment criteria of the shareholder because of size or industry, or some other reason. It is wise therefore, to pursue good investor relations prior to and post-spin, to minimize the amount of turnover in the shareholder base.

The same logic applies to customers and suppliers. Both groups may have done business with either party — parent or subsidiary — because of the other. When the distribution is effective, the two companies are separated and the historical reasons may no longer exist. Therefore, it is prudent to be mindful of customer and supplier relationships throughout the spin-off process.

[7]   Subsequent Events

Spun-off companies often represent a small percentage of a parent company's assets or revenue. In addition, they may not be the strongest or largest competitor in their sector or industry. Further, in some cases, the spun-off subsidiary may not be a strong performer and its ability to stand alone as an independent entity may be in question over the long term. The Internal Revenue Code requirements mandate that for a Section 355 transaction to be tax free to the parent and shareholders, there cannot be an acquisition of the parent or subsidiary post-spin if there was knowledge of the proposed acquisition at the time of the distribution. Nevertheless, it is often the case that spun-off companies are acquired soon after the distribution is effective, and the only significant value that is created for shareholders is as a result of this acquisition.

In the 1993 Cusatis, Miles, and Woolridge study, they observed that "both spinoffs and parents experience an unusually high incidence of takeovers."[31] In

---

31. Cusatis, Patrick J., James A. Miles, and J. Randall Woolridge, "Restructuring through Spinoffs: The Stock Market Evidence," Journal of Financial Economics 33, 293–311 (1993).

addition, they observed that "spinoffs, by dividing a company into separate businesses and thereby effectively creating pure plays for prospective bidders, create value by providing a relatively low-cost method of transferring control of corporate assets to acquiring firms."[32] Their analysis showed that of the 146 spin-offs and 131 parents in the study, within three years of the spin-off, 21 spun-off companies had been taken over or merged while 18 parent companies had been taken over or merged.[33]

[8] Communications with Wall Street

Research suggests that upon the announcement of a spin-off, the parent's stock price will increase. Studies such as the one conducted by Cusatis, Miles, and Woolridge substantiate this fact. In addition, because the spun-off company will be publicly traded, it is likely that the equity research community will pick up coverage of the stock post spin-off.

As a result, prior to the announcement of the spin-off, it is incumbent on the management team of both the parent and the subsidiary to be spun-off, to formulate a well thought out and cohesive message that can be communicated to Wall Street regarding the proposed transaction. All the reasons for the distribution should be well rehearsed. In addition, the management team should have a clear idea of the earnings prospects of the company as an independent entity.

[K] A Variant on Spin-Offs: Split-Offs

A split-off is a form of corporate divestiture in which a company turns one of its subsidiaries into an independent company. The parent company issues stock of the subsidiary as a distribution to holder of, and in redemption of, some of the parent corporation's stock.

Since 1990 there have been approximately 13 announced split-offs representing approximately $30 billion in transaction value. Exhibit 20-16 shows the trend in split-off transactions since 1990.

Exhibit 20-17 illustrates a number of recent split-off transactions.

[L] Case Studies

[1] Coach Split-Off from Sara Lee

Coach, Inc. is a designer, producer, and marketer of fashion accessories for men and women. The company was founded in 1941 and is one of the most recognized brand names in the leather goods business. For the 2000 fiscal year, Coach generated net sales of $548.9 million and operating income of $56 million. The company had 106 retail stores in the United States, direct mail catalogs, an e-commerce web site, and 63 factory stores. In addition, the company sold its products through

---

32. *Id.*
33. *Id.*

Exhibit 20-16
Announced Split-Offs: 1990–2003[34]
($ in millions)

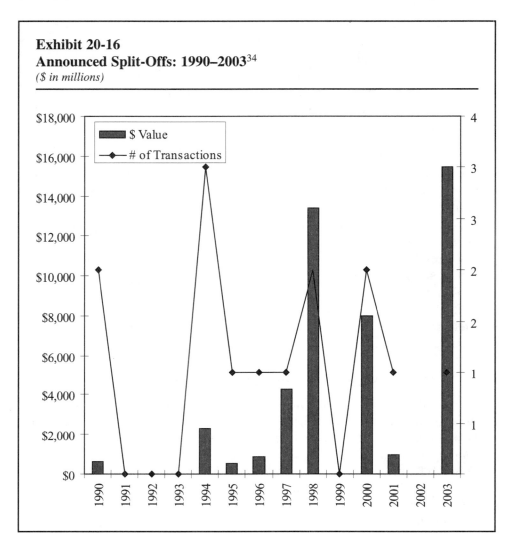

1,400 department stores and specialty retailers in the United States and 175 international department stores, retail stores, and duty free shops.

The company was acquired by Sara Lee Corporation in 1985, when the company's sales were $19 million, and grew the business to $540 million in sales in 1997. During 1997 through 1999, the company saw its sales and profitability decline as a result of changing consumer preferences and the economic downturn in Asia. The company thus embarked on a transformation of the Coach brand name. For the 2000 fiscal year, the company saw a dramatic turnaround in sales and profitability, with sales increasing 8.1% and operating income increasing 110%.

As a result of the turnaround in the business, Sara Lee made the decision to capitalize on the opportunity to take the company public in an equity carve out,

34. Thomson Financial.

Exhibit 20-17
Recent Significant Split-Offs[35]

($ in millions)

Date Effective	Parent / Target	Transaction Value	Overview
03/27/1991	Cabot Corp / Cabot Oil & Gas	$ 427	Cabot completed a self-tender offer to repurchase up to 6,978,359 of its common shares outstanding in a transaction valued at $427 mil. Cabot offered 2.4 common shares of its 82%-owned Cabot Oil & Gas (COG) unit for each Cabot share tendered. The value was based on Cabot's closing stock price of $25.50 on Oct 26, 1990, the day prior to the announced offer. The offer was conditioned upon a minimum of 6,280,523 shares being tendered. Following the offer, Cabot spunoff the remainder of COG to shareholders at a ratio of .79 COG shares per Cabot share held.
09/19/1995	Eli Lilly & CO / Guidant	$1,548	Eli Lilly (EL) completed an exchange offer for 16.5 mil common shares, or a 5.7% interest, through which it spun off 100% its Guidant (GT) unit to shareholders in a transaction valued at $1.547 bil. Under terms of the offer, EL exchanged 3.49 GT common shares, valued at $93.79, for each EL share tendered. The shares were valued based on GT's closing stock price of $26.875, the first full trading day of GT's shares. The exchange offer had been conditioned upon a minimum of 8.25 mil shares being tendered. GT consisted of five EL units.
07/03/1995	Cooper Industries Inc / Copper Cameron	$ 430	Cooper Industries(CI) completed its exchange offer for 9.5 mil common shares,

(Continued)

---

35. Thomson Financial.

Exhibit 20-17
(*Continued*)

Date Effective	Parent / Target	Transaction Value	Overview
			or 8.12% of its common stock outstanding, by accepting all 9.5 mil common shares sought in a transaction valued at $430.171 mil. Each CI sh was exchanged for 2.25 Cooper Cameron (CC) common shares, a newly formed subsidiary of CI consisting of Cooper Energy Services, Cooper Oil Tool, Cooper Turbo-compressor, and Wheeling Machine Products. Based on CC's stock price of $20.125 on 7/5,each CI sh was $45.28. Later, CI termi-nated its search for a buyer for its 14.4% stake in CC.
07/23/1996	Viacom Inc / TCI Pacific Communications	$550	Viacom completed a dutch auction exchange offer for 15.36 mil shares, or 4.18% of Viacom's Class A and B com-mon shares, in exchange for $550 mil TCI Pacific Communications (TPC) cumulative redeemable exchangeable preferred shares. Each share was exchangable into 4.81 common shares of Tele-Communications (TC) five years after completion. Concurrently, TC acquired all the common stock of TPC for $2.05 bil, including $1.7 bil in debt assump-tion. Also, InterMedia Partners acquired the Nashville cable television systems of TC.
10/21/1996	Lockheed Martin Corp / Martin Marietta Materials	$906	Lockheed Martin (LM) completed an exchange offer for 7.9 mil common shares, or about 3.9% of its common stock outstanding, through which it spun off its remaining 81% inter-est, or 37.35 mil common shares, in Martin Marietta Materials (MM) in a transaction valued at $905.73 mil. Under the terms of

(Continued)

Exhibit 20-17
(Continued)

Date Effective	Parent / Target	Transaction Value	Overview
			offer, LM exchanged 4.72 MM common share for each LM shares tendered. The transaction was valued based on MM's closing stock price of $24.25 on Oct 21, the first full trading day on which the shares were distributed. Earlier, LM split off 19% of MM via an IPO.
09/10/1997	Tele-Communications Inc / TCI Ventures	$4,276	Tele-Communications completed its self-tender exchange offer for up to 188,661,300 Class A common shares and 16,266,400 Class B common shares in a 1-for-1 exchange for new TCI Ventures Group Class A and Class B common shares valued at $4.276 bil. The shares were valued based on TCI Ventures Group Class A's and Class B's closing stock price of $20.875 and $20.75 respectively on September 19, the first full trading day on which the new shares were distributed.
05/14/1998	Limited Inc / Abercrombie & Fitch	$1,713	Limited (LT) completed an exchange offer for 47,075,052 common shares, or about 17% of its common stock outstanding, through which it spun off 78%, or 40,484,545 common shares, in its 84%-owned Abercrombie & Fitch subsidiary (AF) in a transaction valued at $1.713 bil. Under terms of the exchange offer, LT exchanged .86 AF common shares for each LT share tendered. The transaction value was based on AF's closing stock price of $42.3125 on May 15, the first full trading day on which the shares were distributed. Subsequently, LT spun off the remaining 6% stake, or 3,115,455 common shares, it still held in AF to its shareholders.

(Continued)

Exhibit 20-17
(*Continued*)

Date Effective	Parent / Target	Transaction Value	Overview
08/12/1999	EI du Pont de Nemours and Co / Conoco	$11,678	EI du Pont de Nemours and Co (EP) completed an exchange offer for 147.981 mil common shares, or about 13.14% of its common stock outstanding, through which it spun off its 69.513% interest in Conoco Inc (CI) to its shareholders in a transaction valued at $11.678 bil. EP offered to exchange 2.95 Class B CI common shares per EP share. The shares were valued based on CI's closing stock price of $26.75 on August 9, the first full trading day on which the shares were distributed. The offer was conditioned upon at least 6.6% of EP's shares being tendered. Previously, EP split off a 30.487% stake in CI through an initial public offering.
05/25/2001	AT&T Corp / AT&T Wireless	$ 7,971	US — AT&T Corp (AT) completed its exchange offer for 372.6 mil common shares, or 9.93% of the company's common stock outstanding, valued at an estimated $7.971 bil. AT offered 1.176 share or an estimated 438.2 mil AT&T Wireless Group (WG) tracking shares per AT share tendered. The shares were valued based on WG's closing stock price of $18.19 on May 24, the last full trading day prior to the announcement of the terms. Originally, in April 2001, AT launched an exchange offer for up to 427.737 mil of its common shares in exchange for up to 503.018 mil WS tracking shares, valued at an estimated $10 bil The offer was conditioned upon at least 1% of AT's shares being tendered. Previously, AT planned to spin off its remaining 71.95% stake in

(*Continued*)

Exhibit 20-17

(*Continued*)

Date Effective	Parent / Target	Transaction Value	Overview
			WG to its shareholders. Subsequently, AT planned to retain a 5% stake in WG for eventual disposition. The exchange offer was to take place prior to the spinoff.
04/11/2001	Sara Lee Corp / Coach	$ 982	US — Sara Lee Corp (SL) completed an exchange offer for 41.402 mil common shares, or about 4.97% of its common stock outstanding, through which it was to spin off its 80% interest in Coach Inc (CI)to its shareholders, in a transaction valued at $981.788 mil. SL offered to exchange .846 CI common shares per SL share. The shares were valued based on CI's closing stock price of $28.03 on March 5, the last full trading day prior to the announcement of exact terms. Previously in October 2000, SL split off a 20% stake in CI in an initial public offering.
12/22/2003	General Motors Corp / Class H Tracking Stock	$15,432	US — General Motors Corp (GMC), a manufacturer of motor vehicles, completed its self-tender offer for 1.109 bil Class H tracking shares in a transaction valued at $15.432 bil. GMC offered .8232 new Hughes Electronics Corp (HEC) common shares for each GMC Class H tracking share held. The shares were valued based on HEC's closing stock price of $16.90 on December 23, the first full trading day on which the shares were distributed. Concurrently, News Corp Ltd acquired a 34% stake in HEC, which comprised 19.8% from GMC and 14.2% from holders of GMC Class H common stock. Upon completion of the transactions, HEC became a publicly-traded, independent

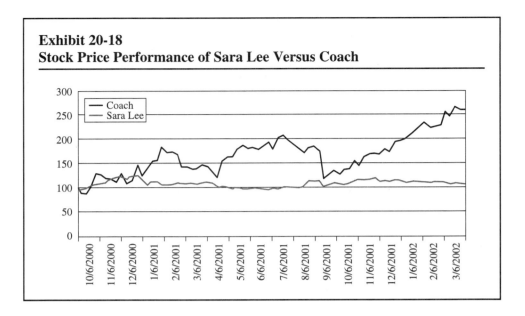

Exhibit 20-18
Stock Price Performance of Sara Lee Versus Coach

and then split-off the remaining stock to shareholders at a later stage. In June 2000, Sara Lee filed to take Coach public, with the offering initially filed at a range of $14 to $16 per share. The company priced the offering at $16 per share on October 4, 2000, selling 7.4 million shares to the public and raising $118 million. After the offering, Sara Lee owned approximately 82.6% of the company.

In early 2001, Sara Lee filed to split-off Coach and exchange 0.846 shares of Coach common stock for each Sara Lee share of common stock that was tendered and accepted by Sara Lee. Sara Lee proposed to accept up to 41.4 million shares of Sara Lee common stock and would distribute up to a total of 35.0 million shares of coach. Sara Lee's decision to split off the Coach business was driven by a desire to increase its focus on a smaller number of global branded consumer packaged goods businesses. Sara Lee believed that the separation would allow each company to offer approach incentives to employees that are more closely linked to each company's own performance; permit each company to focus its resources on its own lines of business; allow each company to target its own areas of strategic growth; and allow each company to independently access the capital markets. The split-off was chosen as the most tax-efficient means for shareholders to receive the value inherent in Coach.

Exhibit 20-18 shows the performance of Sara Lee relative to Coach since the split-off.

[2]   Zimmer Holdings Spin-Off from Bristol-Myers Squibb

Bristol-Myers Squibb is an $18 billion pharmaceutical and related health care products company. In an effort to increase shareholder value, the company announced the spin-off of Zimmer Holdings to shareholders on February 22, 2001. Zimmer designs, manufactures, and distributes orthopedic implants and related equipment and supplies. The company had worldwide sales of $1 billion in 2000 and 3,200 employees.

The company set the distribution date for August 6, 2001, to shareholders of record on July 27, 2001. Shareholders of Bristol-Myers stock would receive one Zimmer share for each ten shares of Bristol-Myers stock owned on the record date. The dividend distribution would be tax free to shareholders.

The spin-off of Zimmer from Bristol-Myers was undertaken to provide both companies with the opportunity to expand their business prospects and improve their operations. The tax-free spin-off was chosen because of the potential tax liability that would arise from a taxable sale. As outlined in the company's Form 10 filing, the key benefits of the transaction were as follow:

- Enhance the strategic focus of the two companies;

- Better target incentives for employees;

- Increase speed and responsiveness;

- Provide greater access to capital markets; and

- Allow investors to make better investment decisions based on the two separate companies.

Exhibit 20-19 shows the relative stock price performance of Zimmer Holdings versus Bristol-Myers Squibb since the spin-off of Zimmer.

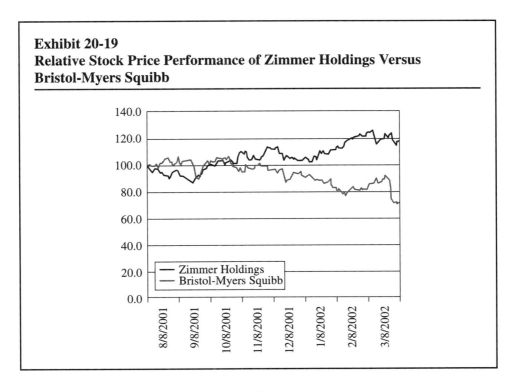

Exhibit 20-19
Relative Stock Price Performance of Zimmer Holdings Versus Bristol-Myers Squibb

Issue to Consider: When setting up the entity to be spun-off, it may be prudent to establish anti-takeover provisions at its inception. For example, the board of directors may be set up on a staggered basis, making it difficult for a potential acquirer to wage a proxy contest. Another possibility is to set up a shareholder rights plan, making it difficult for a potential hostile acquirer to acquire the company without negotiating with the board first.

§ 20.03   EQUITY CARVE-OUTS

[A]   Overview of Equity Carve-Outs

An equity carve-out is the initial public offering of subsidiary stock of a corporation. The sale can range from a small stake, i.e., less than 20%, of the subsidiary to the market, to the divestiture of 100% of the subsidiary. The sale of stock to the public generates cash proceeds for the parent and/or subsidiary. In a primary sale, the stock is sold by the subsidiary and the proceeds go to it. The subsidiary does not pay any taxes on the sale. In a secondary sale, the stock is sold by the parent and the proceeds go to it. In this case, the proceeds are taxable to the parent.

Equity carve-outs have become quite popular. Between 1990 and 2003, approximately 66 equity carve-outs were performed, representing approximately $11 billion in transaction value.[36] Exhibit 20-20 shows the history of equity carve-out announcements since 1990.

Exhibit 20-21 provides a list of recent significant equity carve-outs.

In most carve-outs, the parent company will continue to own an ongoing interest in the subsidiary. If its ownership percentage remains above 80%, the parent can continue to consolidate the subsidiary for tax and accounting purposes. Between 50% and 80% ownership, the parent can consolidate for accounting purposes but not for tax purposes. Between 20% and 50% ownership, the parent must use the equity method of accounting. Below 20% ownership, the parent must use the cost method of accounting for its investment in the company.

One fairly common approach is for the parent to take the subsidiary public by selling less than 20% of the company, and then divest the remainder at a later date in a tax-free spin-off. This mechanism achieves a few objectives. First, the parent can highlight the value of the subsidiary and possibly monetize a portion of the value created. Second, it also allows the parent to expand its own multiple by highlighting the growth characteristics of the subsidiary's underlying performance and its contribution to the parent, prior to the full divestiture.

Another approach is to use the carve-out as a way to opportunistically raise capital for the parent, as it sells down a portion of the subsidiary to the public over time. Each time it sells stock, its ability to consolidate the subsidiary for tax and accounting purposes may change.

---

36. Thomson Financial.

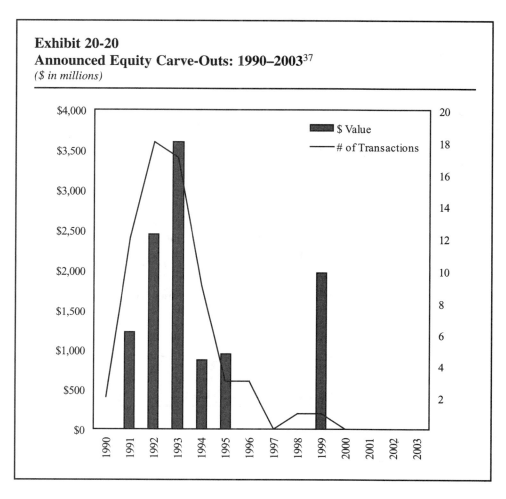

Exhibit 20-20
Announced Equity Carve-Outs: 1990–2003[37]
($ in millions)

To illustrate how an equity carve-out works, let's review the recent IPO of TyCom Ltd., a subsidiary of Tyco International. Tyco is a multi-national conglomerate that has multiples business units in health care, financial services, security and electronics, and fire protection and flow control. TyCom, with fiscal 2000 revenues of $2.54 billion, is one of the world's largest providers of advanced broadband communications capacity, systems, and services. TyCom is a leading fully integrated supplier of transoceanic optical networks, is the recognized world leader in undersea technology development and application, and operates one of the world's largest fleets of cable ships.

In the IPO, Tyco offered 61 million shares to the public, representing 11% of the total shares outstanding. Approximately $1.9 billion was raised by the subsidiary as primary capital. Of that amount, TyCom paid a dividend to Tyco of approximately $200 million. The IPO was priced at $32.00 per share.

Exhibit 20-22 illustrates how the equity carve-out of TyCom worked.

---

37. Thomson Financial.

Exhibit 20-21
Recent Significant Completed Equity Carve-Outs[38]

($ in millions)

Date Announced	Date Effective	Target	Parent	Value
11/20/85	05/27/86	Henley Group	Allied Signal	$2,234
05/06/87	07/02/87	E-II Holdings Inc.	Beatrice Co.	$ 420
10/15/91	08/04/93	Motor Coach Industries Intl.	Dial Corp.	$ 260
11/27/91	02/07/92	Margaretten Financial Corp.	Primerica Holdings	$ 300
12/01/91	06/26/92	Ultramar Corp.	LASMO	$ 495
04/02/93	06/17/97	Black Eyed Pea Restaurants	Unigate Holdings	$ 261
06/17/93	07/28/98	U.S. Enrichment Co.	U.S. Government	$1,425
11/23/93	01/26/94	TE Electronics-O'Sullivan Holdings	Tandy Corp.	$ 370
09/29/95	10/02/95	Prudential Reinsurance Holdings	PRUCO	$ 838
01/05/99	01/17/99	Pharmacia-Upjohn	Swedish Government	$1,967

Exhibit 20-22
Tyco International Equity Carve-Out of TyCom

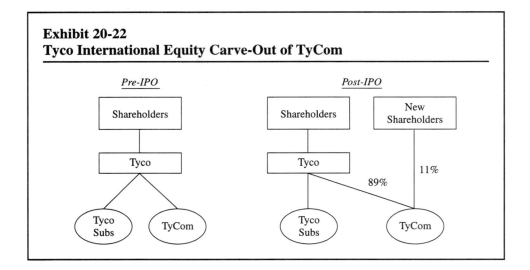

[B] Evidence Behind Equity Carve-Outs

Equity carve-outs have been studied quite actively through the years. They have been compared to each other to determine whether they create value for shareholders. They have been contrasted with other modes of divestiture including spin-offs and asset sales, to understand the comparative shareholder value creation relative to other comparable divestiture approaches. And, they have been analyzed

---

38. *Id.*

over the long term to understand the implications to parent and subsidiary share-holders.

Equity carve-outs, on the one hand, are similar to an initial public offering, yet also used as a divestiture method, on the other hand. In addition, in most cases, the parent company will retain a significant stake in the IPO candidate post carve-out, suggesting that the initial public offering is a pre-cursor to a future transaction whereby the parent may reduce its stake further or reacquire shares in the subsidiary. Consequently, there has been significant research on the subject that has focused primarily on two areas: the effect of the equity carve-out announcement on the parent's stock, and the follow-on merger, acquisition, and restructuring activity of the parent and subsidiary post initial public offering.

Various hypotheses have been proffered over why and how equity carve outs create value. Based on the literature, these theories include a number of different thoughts. First, an equity carve-out may signal that a parent company is undervalued and the subsidiary has a higher public market value than private market value. Second, equity carve-outs may have stronger growth opportunities when compared to companies that are spun-off. Third, an equity carve-out is often used to raise capital for the parent, in which case, the parent's balance sheet is made more efficient. These hypotheses have been tested, with surprisingly good results.

The announcement effect of carve-outs has been compared to the announcement effect of a follow-on equity offering. In a highly acclaimed 1986 study by Katherine Schipper and Abbie Smith, they found that parent firms have a positive abnormal return of about 2% for the five-day period around the announcement date of an equity carve-out.[39] While there are a number of explanations for this, one theory is that parent companies have confidential information on a subsidiary that is not necessarily known or shared with the public. The announcement of the equity carve-out signals that the parent's assets — and stock price — is undervalued, leading to the increase in parent stock price. Conversely, in follow-on equity offerings, often time these are undertaken when the parent's stock price is trading at or close to a high, signaling that the stock is possibly overvalued, leading to a decline in stock price.

In their recent study, James Miles and Randall Woolridge found that there is a significant difference between the long-term performance of the parent's stock and that of the carved-out subsidiary.[40] The study of 87 parent firms and their carved out subsidiaries showed that over an extended period, the carve-out substantially outperformed its peer group while the parent under performed its peer group. Specifically, for the period starting on the initial trading day of the carve-out to six, 12, 18, 24, and 36 months after the initial trade date, the parent company had

---

39. Schipper, Katharine, and Abbie Smith, "A Comparison of Equity Carve-Outs and Seasoned Equity Offerings," Journal of Financial Economics 15, 153–186 (1986).

40. Miles, James A., and J. Randall Woolridge, Spin-Offs and Equity Carve-Outs: Achieving Faster Growth and Better Performance, 22–34 (1999).

returns of −8.73%, −5.80%, −12.83%, −12.00%, and −10.35%, respectively. For the period one month after the initial trade date to six, 12, 18, 24, and 36 months after the initial trade date, the carve-out had returns of 5.04%, 11.89%, 8.21%, 11.83%, and 28.65%, respectively. All these returns were adjusted to reflect the performance of each company's peer group. In other words, these returns were the abnormal excess return for these stocks.

Other studies have focused on why parent stock prices behave in a certain way on the announcement of a carve-out. In a 1991 article by Vikram Nanda titled "The Good News in Equity Carve-Outs," the author provided explanations as to the information effect of carve-outs.[41] First, he proposed that a parent company announcing a carve-out is signaling that the subsidiary has a higher public market valuation than private market valuation, and that raising capital using the subsidiary implies that the market may provide capital at a value greater than its worth inside the parent. He also suggested that the announcement of an equity carve-out suggests a parent company is signaling that its own stock is undervalued, otherwise it would have raised capital using its public currency, not that of the private subsidiary. All this indicates that the parent company's stock should increase on the announcement of an equity carve-out.

As confirmation of the theory proposed by Nanda in 1991, a group of authors performed a study on the stock price returns of public companies in the same sector as the one being carved out. They hypothesized that if the equity carve-out signals that the subsidiary business is overvalued or its worth in the market is substantially higher than it is within the parent, then there could be a negative interpretation on the public stocks in the comparable universe. The study by Myron Slovin, Marie Sushka, and Steven Ferraro in 1995 concluded that for 36 equity carve-outs between 1980 and 1991, the firms in the same sector as the equity carve-out experienced significant negative returns during the period of the carveout announcement.[42]

As we saw earlier in the chapter on spin-offs, numerous studies have been conducted on the difference between equity carve-outs and spin-offs. The 1995 study by Slovin, Sushka, and Ferraro indicated that the return to the rivals of firms carved out were −1.11% surrounding the announcement of the carve-out versus 0.6% for rivals of spin-offs.[43] This study found that the rivals of the parent firms were not affected materially. The study suggests that companies undertake carve-outs when outside investors will price the equity of the carve-out favorably to the manager's own perspective on value. In another study by Jongbloed in 1992, the analysis compared the equity carve-out to a spin-off and found that subsidiaries

---

41. Nanda, Vikram, "The Good News in Equity Carve-Outs," The Journal of Finance 46 (5), 1717–1736 (1991).

42. Slovin, Myron B., Marie E. Sushka, and Steven R. Ferraro, "A Comparison of the Information Conveyed by Equity Carve-Outs, Spin-Offs, and Asset Sell-Offs," Journal of Financial Economics 37, 89–104 (1995).

43. *Id.*

that are taken public have higher growth opportunities than those that have been spun-off.[44]

Another area of interest has been the activity of the parent and subsidiary post equity carve-out. Some studies such as that by Schipper and Smith, found that a majority of carved-out subsidiaries underwent subsequent merger, acquisition, or restructuring activity. Of the 76 carve-outs studied between 1965 and 1983, 48 carved out subsidiaries did not have the same parent/subsidiary relationship as they did when they were initially carved out.[45] Of the 48 firms taken public, 26 were taken over, seven were spun-off entirely, and 15 were sold to another firm. A second study by Klein, Rosenfeld, and Beranek in 1991 confirms these findings.[46] They found that of a sample of 52 carve-outs, 42 became involved in a subsequent event. These events ranged from the parent reacquiring the public shares of the subsidiary, to selling off the interest in the subsidiary, either to the public or to another firm.

[C]   Creating Value Through Equity Carve-Outs

Carve-outs create shareholder value in a number of ways. Much like spin-offs, the value creation comes from the market's ability to value the subsidiary and parent independent of each other. The consequent impact is that the parent trades at a multiple that more closely resembles its growth rate, yet benefits from an expanded multiple based on the growth characteristics of the subsidiary. In addition, because the independent subsidiary is valued at a multiple based on its own characteristics, the remaining stake held within the parent is valued based on the value of the subsidiary's publicly traded stock. The implied value is likely to be reflected in the parent's stock price. As a result, the value of the subsidiary and parent on a combined basis is likely to be higher than the value of the parent alone, with the subsidiary fully embedded within its financials.

Carve-outs may also help create value by allowing the parent and subsidiary to bring efficiencies to their respective balance sheets. At both the parent and subsidiary, the cash proceeds raised can be used to reduce debt or may be paid out as a dividend. In addition, the proceeds may be used to finance the growth of either company, reducing the need to assume additional debt.

In a divestiture where an equity carve-out is the precursor to a spin-off, the initial public offering of the subsidiary serves a number of purposes, all of which help create shareholder value. First, the IPO allows the parent and subsidiary to

---

44. Jongbloed, Auke, "A Comparison of Spin-Offs and Equity Carve-Outs," Working paper, The University of Rochester (1992).

45. Schipper and Smith (1995), *supra* n.17.

46. Klein, April, James Rosenfeld, and William Beranek, "The Two Stages of an Equity Carve-Out and the Price Response of Parent and Subsidiary Stock," Managerial and Decision Economics 12, 449–460 (1991).

```
┌─────────────────────────────────────────┐
│                                           │
│   Exhibit 20-23                           │
│   Reasons Behind Carve-Outs               │
│   ─────────────────────────────────────   │
│   Lack of synergy or fit                  │
│   Focus on core business                  │
│   Highlight value of subsidiary           │
│   Monetize value of subsidiary            │
│   Reduce debt                             │
│   Avoid takeover                          │
│                                           │
└─────────────────────────────────────────┘
```

raise capital. Second, the IPO establishes an independent trading value for the subsidiary prior to the spin-off.

[D]   Motivation and Rationale Behind Equity Carve-Outs

The primary motivation behind equity carve-outs is much the same as that of spin-offs, to highlight the financial performance of the subsidiary business and allow the market to value the parent and subsidiary independently. Exhibit 20-23 summarizes the multiple reasons for why companies undertake carve-outs.

Unlike spin-offs, equity carve-outs usually does not entail a 100% sale of the subsidiary, and therefore, a few of the reasons behind spin-offs do not necessarily apply to carve-outs. First, carve-outs are usually undertaken with attractive businesses, whereas, spin-offs can also be achieved with poorly performing businesses. Because a subsidiary IPO requires new investors, it is difficult to take a poorly performing business public, whereas in a spin-off, it is possible to dividend a poor performer to existing shareholders. Second, an equity carve-out is not as tax efficient as a spin-off, because the cash proceeds, if any, to the parent are taxed. In addition, if after the carve-out, the parent owns less than 80% of the subsidiary, the parent is no longer in a position to perform a tax-free spin-off of the subsidiary, nor is it able to consolidate for tax purposes. This suggests that the tax efficiency is not necessarily a primary driver of a carve-out. Third, in most divestitures that have been mandated by regulatory requirements, the need is to divest 100% of the business which means that unless the IPO is for 100%, the transaction will likely not satisfy the regulatory body's demands.

Carve-outs may also be undertaken for reasons that are different from that of spin-offs. First, companies, such as Thermo-Electron, may incubate subsidiary businesses within the parent organization, providing them with parent company resources to build the company. At the point that the subsidiary is large enough to take public, the parent then takes the subsidiary public, highlighting the business to the market. Second, there may be instances where the subsidiary and parent share numerous resources, such as research and development or manufacturing, and where these synergies are highly efficient, yet the growth rates, risk profiles and capital needs of the businesses may vary. In these situations, the parent and subsidiary may desire an ongoing strategic or operating relationship, and therefore a carve-out is preferable over other divestiture alternatives.

A related reason why companies undertake carve-outs is to realize proceeds from the sale of the subsidiary's stock to the public. The proceeds may be used by the subsidiary, if the carve-out is performed as a primary offering, or by the parent, if performed as a secondary offering. The capital may be used by the subsidiary to finance itself or used by the parent to reduce debt or for other corporate purposes. In contrast to a pure spin-off, where the proceeds to the parent company typically come from a dividend paid by the subsidiary just prior to the spin-off, an equity carve-out usually relies on the sale of secondary shares to raise proceeds for the parent.

[E] Attributes of Equity Carve-Out Candidates

Candidates for a successful equity carve-out must have certain characteristics that will enable it to thrive as a public company. These characteristics are no different than those for an independent private company wishing to go public in an initial public offering. Unlike a spin-off, where the subsidiary is divested as a dividend of stock to existing shareholders, a carve-out's success relies on the subsidiary's ability to attract new investors, and like any other initial public offering, the company will need to go on a road show, presenting the company to investors.

[1] Critical Mass

For a company to go public, as a subsidiary of another public corporation or as an independent private firm, it must meet certain size requirements. These requirements are driven as much by the unwritten rules of each industry as they are by the listing requirements of the stock exchange(s) on which the company will trade.

From an industry perspective, there are sectors where a company need not have any revenue or profits to go public, e.g., the biotechnology or technology industries. Likewise, there are sectors where critical mass in revenues and earnings are required, e.g., the retail industry. For the market to appropriately value a company, it is typical for the IPO candidate to be either profitable, or to be able to establish that it will generate profitability in the upcoming quarters.

From a stock exchange listing perspective, each of the primary exchanges will have their own listing requirements as they relate to size. The New York Stock Exchange (NYSE) has basic requirements for minimum distribution of a company's shares in the United States. These criteria include a minimum number of shareholders, trading volume, and market value of public stock. In addition, there are minimum financial criteria that must be met. These criteria include a minimum threshold for pre-tax earnings and operating cash flow. Exhibit 20-24 provides a summary of NYSE listing requirements.

The American Stock Exchange has similar listing requirements, as shown in partial form in Exhibit 20-25. While these are the standard financial guidelines, there are other alternative guidelines that can be used in the event a company has unique circumstances.

Exhibit 20-24
New York Stock Exchange U.S. Listing Requirements[47]

Minimum Quantitative Standards: Distribution and Size Criteria

Round-lot Holders	2,000 U.S.
or	
Total Shareholders	2,200
. . . together with:	
Average Monthly Trading Volume (for the most recent 6 months)	100,000 shares
or:	
Total Shareholders	500
. . . together with:	
Average Monthly Trading Volume (for the most recent 12 months)	1,000,000
Public Shares	1,100,000 outstanding
Market Value of Public Shares:	
Public Companies	$ 100,000,000
IPO's, Spin-Offs, Carve-Outs	$ 60,000,000

Minimum Quantitative Standards: Financial Criteria
Earnings

Aggregate pretax earnings over the last three years of $6,500,000 achievable as:	
Most Recent Year	$ 2,500,000
Each of Two Preceding Years	$ 2,000,000
or:	
Most Recent Year (All three years must be profitable)	$ 4,500,000
or:	

Operating Cash Flow

For companies with not less than $500 million in global market capitalization and $100 million in revenues in the last 12 months:	
Aggregate for the Three Years	
Operating Cash Flow	$ 25,000,000
(each year must report a positive amount)	
or:	

Global Market Capitalization

Revenues for the Last Fiscal Year	$ 100,000,000
Average Global Market Capitalization	$1,000,000,000

The NASDAQ provides for three listing standards, one of which must be met in order to be quoted on The Nasdaq National Market. Exhibit 20-26 provides an overview of these three listing standards.

[2]   Strong Balance Sheet

For a company to stand alone, independent of its parent, it must have a balance sheet that can support its ongoing working capital and capital investment needs. While a carve-out may generate cash proceeds to the subsidiary, it is also

---

47. New York Stock Exchange public information.

Exhibit 20-25
American Stock Exchange U.S. Listing Requirements[48]

Regular Financial Guidelines

Pre-Tax Income	$750,000 latest fiscal year or 2 of most recent 3 fiscal years
Market Value of Public Float	$3,000,000
Price	$3
Stockholders' Equity	$4,000,000

Exhibit 20-26
NASDAQ Initial Listing Requirements[49]

Requirement	Standard 1	Standard 2	Standard 3
Stockholders' Equity	$15 million	$30 million	N/A
Market Capitalization			$75 million or
Total Assets	N/A	N/A	$75 million and
Total Revenue			$75 million
Pre-Tax Income (in latest fiscal year or 2 of last 3 fiscal years)	$1 million	N/A	N/A
Public Float (shares)	1.1 million	1.1 million	1.1 million
Operating History	N/A	2 years	N/A
Market Value of Public Float	$8 million	$18 million	$20 million
Shareholders	400	400	400
Market Makers	3	3	4
Corporate Governance	Yes	Yes	Yes

advisable for the newly public company to have sufficient debt capacity to be able to support the ongoing growth of its business. Prior to taking the company public, it is helpful to study the balance sheets of public companies in the subsidiary's universe to determine an appropriate capital structure.

[3] Strong Management Team

Prior to taking a subsidiary public, the parent company should ensure that the subsidiary has a management team able to manage the business as a public company. Often, there can be a difference between a management team that operates a division or subsidiary, and one that operates as a public company. Under the two scenarios, the management incentives may be different, the capital allocation process may not have been handled at the subsidiary level, the focus at the subsidiary may have been on targets that were not necessarily directly related to

---

48. American Stock Exchange public information.
49. NASDAQ public information.

earnings, or the culture of the subsidiary may have been driven by the parent. With each of these, the subsidiary's management team will have to be able to retool itself in the context of a public company: make corporate budgeting decisions, focus on quarter-to-quarter earnings, and build an independent culture.

[4] Attractive Financial Performance

Like any public company, a carved out subsidiary will have to withstand the scrutiny of the public equity markets. In addition, for the IPO of the subsidiary to create value for shareholders, its financial performance will need to be attractive: its growth rate should be high, its margins should be strong, and its balance sheet should be healthy. While it may be possible to carve out a poorly performing subsidiary, it is not the preferred approach to creating shareholder value, as it is common for the parent to continue to own a substantial stake in the subsidiary. One exception may be a 100% IPO of a subsidiary, in which the parent divests the entire business in a single transaction.

[5] Attractive Industry

A parent company should consider the timing of an IPO of a subsidiary in that certain industry segments may or may not be in favor at any given time. While a subsidiary may have attractive financial performance and other characteristics, there may be no appetite from potential shareholders due to industry dynamics.

[F] Key Timing Events of Equity Carve-Outs

Equity carve-outs follow the same general time line as an initial public offering of a private company. From announcement to pricing, the process can take upwards of six months. Exhibit 20-27 outlines key events in a carve-out. As an example, the key events and dates for the carve-out of Agilent Technologies, Inc. from Hewlett-Packard Company are shown in Exhibit 20-28.

[G] Valuation of Equity Carve-Outs

Much like the valuation of a spin-off, the valuation of an equity carve-out takes a number of stages. First, the parent company should be valued on a break-up basis to determine if it is undervalued in the market place. Second, the subsidiary must be valued stand alone to determine its going concern and acquisition value. Third, the impact of the equity carve-out must be analyzed to determine the effect on shareholder value.

On a break-up basis, each of the subsidiaries should be valued using comparable company, discounted cash flow, and comparable transaction methodologies, remembering to first include any adjustments required to account for the private nature of each subsidiary, and second, to adjust the overall valuation for the cost of the overhead and liabilities at the parent.

As the subsidiary to be carved out is valued, it is probably helpful to first look at the going concern value of the company using discounted cash flow and comparable company analysis, and then look at the value of the company under

Exhibit 20-27
Key Events in a Carve-Out

Event	Summary Description
Announcement	A press release is issued by the parent company to the public.
File Form S-1 Registration Statement	The registration statement is no different than that of an IPO of a private company.
File application for exchange listing	Parent makes the exchange listing on behalf of the subsidiary.
S-1 declared effective	The SEC provides comments on the S-1 over a period that can take up to six months. Once the S-1 has been reviewed and modified, it is declared effective by the SEC.
Shareholder meeting	A shareholder meeting may be required if the subsidiary to be carved-out is a 100% sold and is large enough to warrant the meeting.
Road show	Once the S-1 has been declared effective, the subsidiary stock can then be sold to investors. The subsidiary will be taken on a road show to meet with investors.
Pricing	After the road show, the subsidiary's stock is priced as a negotiation between the company, its underwriter, and the investors. After pricing, the stock trades publicly.

Exhibit 20-28
Key Events in the Equity Carve-Out of Agilent Technologies, Inc. from Hewlett-Packard Company[50]

Event	Date
Announcement Date	March 2, 1999
File S-1	August 16, 1999
Receive NYSE Listing Approval	October 4, 1999
S-1 Declared Effective	October 25, 1999
Pricing	November 17, 1999
Begin Trading	November 18, 1999

different scenarios, i.e., taxable sale, tax-free spin-off, and IPO. Under the initial public offering scenario, it is important to remember that the primary valuation driver will be the multiples of comparable public companies, and that it is likely there will be a discount to the valuation range, the IPO discount, proscribed by the market.

---

50. Public Company Documents.

When analyzing the impact of the transaction on shareholder value, there are a number of items to consider. First, determine the use of proceeds of the IPO. If the parent is to receive the proceeds from the sale, the proceeds are taxed, yet they may be used to realign the capital structure of the parent. Bringing efficiency to the parent's balance sheet may by itself enhance the value of the parent, by reducing interest expense and enhancing earnings. Second, depending on how much of the subsidiary is sold to the market, the parent may or may not be able to consolidate the subsidiary for tax and accounting purposes. These considerations should be taken into account when determining the pro forma accretion/dilution impact on the parent.

One issue to consider that is hard to quantify, is the impact the sale of a stake in the subsidiary will have on the parent's multiple. For example, in the case of a less than 20% carve-out, the parent may still consolidate for tax and accounting purposes. From this perspective, the consolidated financials look remarkably similar to that of the parent prior to the spin-off. The one exception is that the earnings of the subsidiary not owned by the parent, are adjusted for in the income statement as a deduction. The implication from this is that the public market value of the subsidiary will be driven by the multiple of the subsidiary. Since the subsidiary may, or may not, have a higher growth rate than the parent, its implied multiple may be higher, or less, than the parent. Consequently, the earnings of the subsidiary within the parent may be valued at a higher, or lower, multiple than those of the parent. This could — and should — lead to a multiple adjustment for the parent. If the characteristics of the subsidiary were not previously recognized within the parent, once the subsidiary is traded publicly, it should be valued more appropriately at the parent level as well, indicating that a subsidiary with more attractive attributes than the parent, should lead to multiple expansion at the parent level, and vice versa.

[H] Tax and Accounting Considerations

The percentage of stock the parent company retains in the subsidiary post carve-out will dictate how the parent must account for its ongoing ownership. If the parent owns greater than 80% of the subsidiary post carve-out, it may consolidate for tax and accounting purposes. If the parent owns between 50% and 80% of the carve-out, it may consolidate for accounting purposes but not for tax purposes. Between 20% and 50% ownership, and the parent may use the equity method of accounting for its ownership. Under 20% ownership, and the parent must use the cost method of accounting.

In the sale of subsidiary stock to the public, if the proceeds go to the parent in a secondary sale, those proceeds are taxable to the parent. If the sale of subsidiary stock is by the subsidiary in a primary sale, the proceeds are neither taxable to the parent or the subsidiary.

[I] Filing Requirements

Under the Securities and Exchange Act of 1933, companies must file a Form S-1 Registration Statement for the company to be taken public. This is no different than other private companies that are taken public. In general, the requirements for filing the registration statement are three years of audited income statements, two years of audited balance sheets, and five years of selected historical financial data. Following in Exhibit 20-29 is a more comprehensive list of the requirements for the registration statement.

Exhibit 20-29
Form S-1 Filing Requirements[51]

Item	Description
Risk Factors	Describe the risks associated with the company, including, if appropriate, its lack of operating history and financial position.
Use of Proceeds	State the use of proceeds of the offering and the amount of the offering allocated to each use.
Offering Price	Describe the various factors affecting the determination of the offering price.
Dilution	Describe the amount of dilution to net tangible book value that will result from the offering.
Selling Security Holders	Describe any securities to be sold by a security holder, including the amount and percent of class.
Plan of Distribution	Disclose the underwriters who are distributing the securities.
Business Description	Include a general narrative of the development of the business, its subsidiaries and predecessors. Provide financial information regarding the company's business segments including revenues, profit or loss and total assets for the past three years. Provide a narrative description of the parent company and its subsidiaries. Provide financial information on the geographic break-down of the revenues and long-lived assets of the company, by domicile, all foreign countries, and foreign countries by themselves if material.
Financial Information	Provide the last five fiscal years of financial statements for the registrant. Other fiscal years should be provided if necessary. Provide a Management Discussion and Analysis for all fiscal periods, addressing liquidity, capital resources and results of operations, and for interim periods, address any changes in financial condition or changes in results in operations.
Properties	Provide the location and general characteristics of plants, mines and other physical properties.
Security Ownership	Provide the security ownership of beneficial owners and management. Information to be provided includes title of class, name of owner, amount and percent of class owned.

(Continued)

---

51. Securities and Exchange Commission public information.

Exhibit 20-29
(*Continued*)

Item	Description
Directors and Officers	Identify the directors and officers, their positions and affiliations, terms and year nominated. Describe any relationships, arrangements or understandings between the director or officer and the company.
Executive Compensation	Describe all plan and non-plan compensation awarded to, earned by, or paid to executive officers. Disclose the CEO and his compensation as well as the four highest compensated individuals besides the CEO.
Other Items	In addition to the above, the registration statement requires disclosures in the following areas: • Certain relationships and related transactions • Legal proceedings • Market price of and dividends on the registrant's common equity and related stockholder matters • Recent sales of unregistered securities • Description of registrant's securities to be registered • Indemnification of directors and officers • Financial statements and supplementary data • Changes in and disagreements with accountants on accounting and financial disclosure • Financial statements and exhibits

Once the registration statement has been filed, the SEC makes comments on the filing that are then incorporated in the document. This process can take up to six months to complete. Once the amended registration statement has been filed, and the SEC has no further comments, the statement is declared effective, whereupon the stock in the subsidiary can be sold to investors.

[J]   Pricing of Equity Carve-Outs

Like conventional initial public offerings, equity carve-outs are priced based on a negotiation between the company, its underwriters and the investors. Initially, the registration statement is filed with a preliminary range of stock prices for the company. Once the S-1 has been declared effective, the company's underwriters take the management team on a road show to meet with investors. At the end of the road show, the underwriters, company, and investors will negotiate the pricing of the stock based on the initial pricing range, the current market conditions and the receptivity to the offering.

[K]   Issues with Respect to Equity Carve-Outs

There are a number of issues to consider prior to making a decision to undertake an equity carve-out.

[1]   Ownership

It is usual for parent companies to only carve out a small percentage of the subsidiary in an initial public offering. While this may have significant near-term advantages to the parent in terms of tax and accounting consolidation and information effect, the long-term impact may not necessarily be beneficial. First, for a public company to attract ongoing investor interest, it requires sufficient stock to be freely traded, i.e. public float. To the extent the stock does not have sufficient float, it is likely to lose investor interest and languish in the market place. There have been numerous instances where this has taken place, in which case, a likely outcome is that the stock is reacquired by the parent in a minority squeeze-out transaction.

One recent example of this is the recent acquisition of the 11% minority shares of TyCom Ltd. that were not owned by Tyco International. Tyco took TyCom public in August 2000 at a stock price of $32.00 per share, raising approximately $2.0 billion in proceeds from the offering. The offer to purchase the minority shares was valued at $15.42 per TyCom share, representing a 48% premium over the current stock price, and a 15% premium over TyCom's stock price for the prior three months. However, this was a 52% discount to the initial public offering price. The transaction was announced on October 4, 2001, and closed on December 18, 2001.

[2]   Intent

One sure way to impact the announcement effect of an equity carve-out, is to let the market know why the equity carve-out is being undertaken, and what the intent for the subsidiary is down the road. For example, indicating the use of proceeds may have an impact on the market's response. A company where the parent uses the proceeds to realign its balance sheet experiences higher returns post announcement than those where the proceeds go to the subsidiary. A second example would be the post carve-out intent. Does the company intend to spin-off the subsidiary at a future date, or does the company intend to sell down its stake further over time?

[3]   Integration

Despite the sale of a stake to the public, there still may be many areas where the parent and subsidiary have common processes and people. One should consider what functions and people need to be realigned to (a) prepare for any subsequent transaction and (b) provide attractive incentives to management and employees.

[4]   Management Incentives

One of the prime reasons to undertake an equity carve-out is to provide management and employee incentives that are tied directly to the performance of the subsidiary. These can come in the form of stock options or other bonus and financial incentives.

Exhibit 20-30
Example Carve-Outs Followed by Spin-Off or Split-Off [52]

Effective Date	Parent	Target	Overview
04/11/01	Sara Lee Corp.	Coach	Sara Lee took Coach public in an initial public offering and subsequently split-off the company to shareholders.
08/12/99	EI du Pont de Nemours	Conoco	DuPont took Conoco public in an equity carve-out, selling 30.4% to the public and subsequently split-off its remaining interest to shareholders.
10/21/96	Lockheed Martin	Martin Marietta Materials	Lockheed Martin took 19% of Martin Marietta Materials public in an equity carve-out. Lockheed subsequently exchanged 7.9 million shares, or about 3.9% of its common stock, for its remaining 81% interest in Martin Marietta Materials.

[5]   Taxable Nature of Transaction

The proceeds of a carve-out, if payable to the parent, are taxed. One should consider the overall tax efficiency of the transaction to determine if there are better ways to realign the parent's balance sheet. For example, in a spin-off, it is possible for the subsidiary to pay a dividend tax-free to the parent prior to the spin-off.

[L]   Subsequent Events

One common approach to undertaking a spin-off, is to first carve the subsidiary out in an initial public offering. The IPO serves to raise capital for the parent or subsidiary, provide an initial boost to the parent's stock price, and establish the initial trading range for the subsidiary's stock by pricing it with investors rather than on a when-issued basis. This approach can only be used to the extent the parent company owns greater than 80% of the subsidiary after the carve-out. Numerous companies have pursued this approach, including those outlined in Exhibit 20-30.

[M]   Case Study: Hewlett-Packard's IPO/Spin-Off of Agilent Technologies[53]

Hewlett-Packard Company is a leading provider of computing and imaging solutions and services for the business and the home. At year-end 1998, the

---

52. Thomson Financial, Public Company Documents.
53. Hewlett-Packard Company and Agilent Technologies, Inc. public information.

company had $47 billion in revenue and 122,000 employees worldwide. On March 2, 1999, Hewlett-Packard announced its intention to realign itself into two independent companies, by taking public its test and measurement, semiconductor products, chemicals analysis, and healthcare solutions businesses, ultimately named Agilent Technologies. Agilent had 1998 revenues of $7.6 billion and 48,000 employees.

Hewlett-Packard's motivation behind the IPO was to unleash the growth potential of Agilent, by separating it from the parent company. Even though Agilent had $7.6 billion in revenue, it was not significant enough to warrant attention from Hewlett-Packard shareholders or the Hewlett-Packard board of directors. In addition, Agilent's performance had little impact on the stock price of Hewlett-Packard. Finally, Agilent could not fund itself independently of Hewlett-Packard and was dependent on the parent company for growth capital.

Hewlett-Packard filed the preliminary S-1 registration statement for the IPO of Agilent on August 16, 1999, with the S-1 becoming effective on October 25, 1999. The offering was for 57 million common shares, all of which were offered by Agilent. The initial filing range was $19–$22 per share. At that price range, the IPO had a value of $1.1–$1.3 billion. After the transaction, there would be approximately 446 million shares outstanding, giving Agilent a market capitalization of $8.5 to $9.8 billion. The transaction was led by Morgan Stanley Dean Witter and Goldman, Sachs & Co.

On November 17, 1999, the initial public offering of Agilent was priced at $30 per share. The size of the offering had been increased to 72 million shares, and the pricing range exceeded the initial filing range of $19–$22 per share. The net proceeds of the offering were approximately $2.1 billion, all of which were paid to Hewlett-Packard as a dividend. After the offering, there were approximately 452 million shares outstanding, with Hewlett-Packard owning 84.1%. Hewlett-Packard had also announced at the time that it intended to distribute the remaining shares it owned in Agilent to shareholders in a tax-free dividend.

Subsequent to the IPO, Hewlett-Packard received a ruling from the IRS on August 3, 1999, that the proposed spin-off of Agilent would be tax free to Hewlett-Packard and to shareholders. Hewlett-Packard made a formal announcement on April 7, 2000, regarding the specific terms to spin-off its remaining Agilent shares to shareholders. The company set the distribution date of June 2, 2000, to shareholders of record on May 2, 2000. Prior to the distribution, on April 25, 2000, Agilent adopted a shareholder rights plan in anticipation of the spin-off. Hewlett-Packard's stock price, and that of Agilent, reacted to the restructuring at every milestone. Exhibit 20-31 provides an overview of Hewlett-Packard and Agilent's stock prices from two days prior to the announcement to three months after the spin-off, relative to the S&P 500.

Exhibit 20-32 shows Agilent Technologies stock price versus the S&P 500 from its IPO through June 30, 2000.

Just prior to the announcement of Agilent's IPO, Hewlett-Packard had a market capitalization of $34 billion. Once the IPO had priced, Hewlett-Packard had a market capitalization of $47 billion, including its 84% ownership in Agilent, which had a stand alone market capitalization of approximately $20 billion. The 16% of Agilent

Exhibit 20-31
Hewlett-Packard's Stock Price Versus S&P 500:
March 1, 1999–June 30, 2000

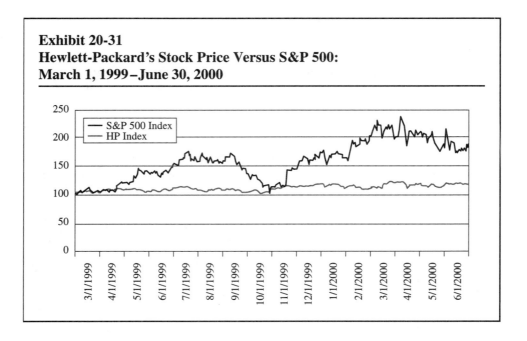

Exhibit 20-32
Agilent Technologies Stock Price Versus S&P 500:
November 17, 1999–June 30, 2000

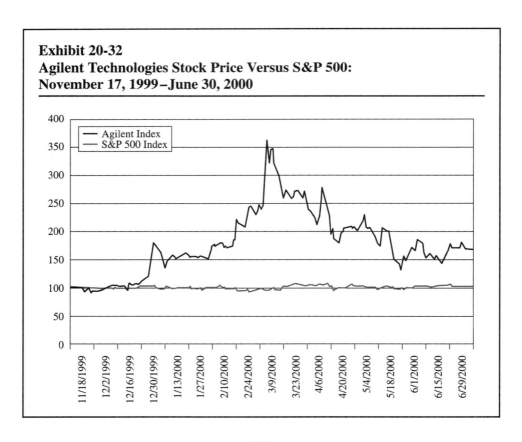

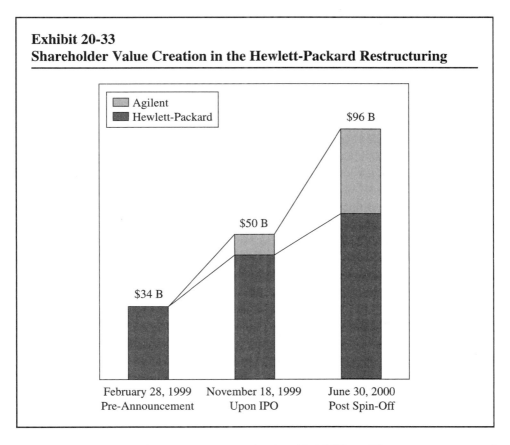

Exhibit 20-33
Shareholder Value Creation in the Hewlett-Packard Restructuring

that Hewlett-Packard did not own was valued at $3.2 billion. The announcement of the formalspin-off terms for Agilent saw Hewlet-Packard's market capitalization rise to $76 billion, while the stand alone market value of Agilent had risen to $55 billion. By June 30, 2000, when the distribution of the Agilent stock was complete, the combined market capitalization of the two companies was $94 billion. Exhibit 20-33 illustrates the value created in the Hewlett-Packard restructuring.

§ 20.04   TRACKING STOCK

[A]   Overview of Tracking Stock

Tracking stock, otherwise known as alphabet, letter, or targeted[54] stock, is a special class of common or preferred stock with earnings and/or dividends that are tied to a specific segment, division or subsidiary of a company's business. Tracking stocks are a way for companies to separate certain divisions of its business, allowing investors to receive dividends and capital appreciation based on the performance of that division, yet without the parent giving up control of the assets. The stock can

54. Attributed to Lehman Brothers.

be issued to existing shareholders as a dividend, the company may sell stock to the public in an initial public offering, or the stock can be issued to a target in an acquisition. Shares in a tracking stock represent only an economic interest in the unit, with its market value determined by the performance of the business.

Since 1990, there have been over 22 tracking stocks listed, representing over $17 billion in value.[55] Exhibit 20-34 shows tracking stock announcements since 1990.

Tracking stocks have been issued by some of the most notable names in corporate America including, Disney, AT&T, USX Corp., General Motors, and Sprint. Tracking stocks began in 1984 when General Motors Corp listed its Class E shares (GM-E), representing its newly acquired Electronic Data Systems Corp. (EDS). EDS was later spun-off in 1996; however, under the ownership of General Motors, the tracking stock appreciated more than 11-fold since it was created. General Motors liked the structure so much that it later used tracking stock to track its Hughes Aircraft division.

Exhibit 20-35 provides a list of recent tracking stock issues.

While on the surface, tracking stocks may appear similar to spin-offs and equity carve-outs, there are some material differences. First, in spin-offs and

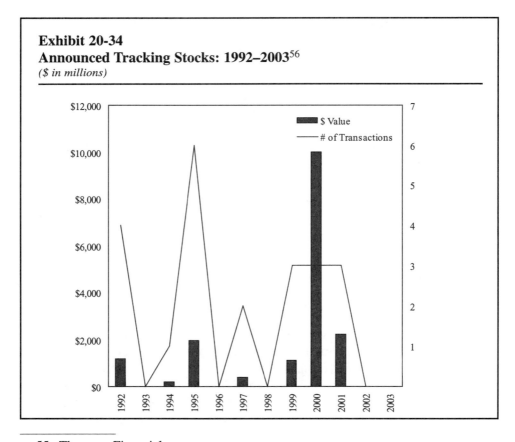

Exhibit 20-34
Announced Tracking Stocks: 1992–2003[56]
($ in millions)

---

55. Thomson Financial.
56. Thomson Financial.

Exhibit 20-35
Recent Significant Completed Tracking Stocks[57]

Issuer	Tracking Stock	Issue Date	Comments
General Motors	GM-E (Electronic Data Systems)	1984	Spun-off in 1996
General Motors	GM-H (Hughes Electronics)	1985	Has undergone restructuring through asset sales
NL Industries	Series C	1986	
USX	USX-Steel	1991	Spun-off in 2001
USX	USX-Marathon	1991	Separated from USX-Steel in 2001
USX	USX-Delhi	1992	Separated from USX-Marathon in 1992. Assets sold and net proceeds were exchanged for Delhi shares
Pittston	Pittston Minerals	1993	Tracking stock eliminate in 1999 when Minerals shares were exchanged for Pittston shares
Ralston Purina	Continental Baking	1993	Tracking stock redeemed in 1996 when the assets of Continental Baking were sold
Fletcher Challenge	Forest Division	1993	Unwound in 2000 with sale of forest division
Genzyme	Genzyme Tissue Repair	1994	Restructured in 2000
American Health Properties	Psychiatric Group	1995	
CMS Energy	Consumer Gas	1995	Consumer Gas shares exchanged for CSM shares in 1999
Tele-Communications	Liberty Media	1995	Split-off in 2001
U.S. West	MediaOne Group	1995	Spun-off
Pittston	Brinks Group	1996	
Fletcher Challenge	Building Division	1996	Energy business sold in 2001;
	Energy Division	1996	energy and paper division
	Paper Division	1996	became separate public companies

(Continued)

---

57. Thomson Financial, Public Company Documents.

Exhibit 20-35
(*Continued*)

Issuer	Tracking Stock	Issue Date	Comments
Circuit City	CarMax	1997	
Genzyme	Molecular Oncology Division	1998	Issued in connection with merger with Pharmagenics
Georgia-Pacific	Timber Group	1997	Timber Group stock eliminated through merger with Plum Creek Timber Company in 2000
Tele-Communications	TCI Ventures	1997	
Atlantic Energy	Class A	1998	Issued to Delmarva Power & Light in merger
Sprint	PCS Group	1998	
Disney	Go.com	1999	Eliminated in 2001 when Go.com closed
Donaldson, Lufkin, & Jenrette	DLJDirect	1999	Converted to CSFBDirect tacking stock in merger with CSFB
Genzyme	Genyzme Surgical Products	1999	
Quantum Corp.	Quantum HDD	1999	
PE Corp.	Celera Genomics	1999	
Snyder Communications	Circle.com	1999	Redeemed in 2001 when Snyder purchased by Havas
Ziff-Davis	ZD Stock ZDNet	1999	Eliminated in 2000 in merger with CNET
Cendant	Move.com	2000	Eliminated when Move.com was acquired by Homestore.com in 2001
AT&T	AT&T Wireless	2000	Split-off in 2001
Electronic Arts	EA.com	2000	Integrated back into Electronic Arts in 2001
WorldCom	MCI Group	2001	Eliminated in 2002
Cablevision	Rainbow Media Group	2001	

carve-outs, a new corporate entity is created that is legally separated from the issuer or parent and then begins to trade publicly. The spin-off is executed by dividing the stock of the subsidiary to shareholders, with the parent company giving up control of the asset. In a carve-out, the parent company establishes a new corporate entity and sells part or all of the entity to the public, either by selling its

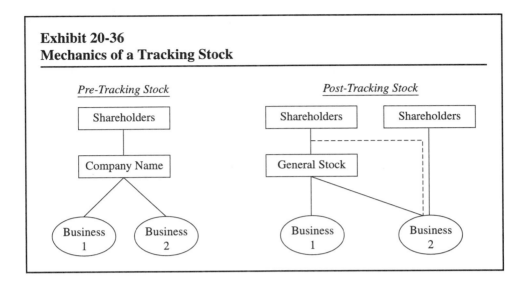

Exhibit 20-36
Mechanics of a Tracking Stock

own shares in the company or by the subsidiary selling new shares to the market. Exhibit 20-36 illustrates the mechanics of a tracking stock.

Under both a spin-off and an equity carve-out, the shareholders have the rights that they would have in any other conventional common equity security, i.e., the right to vote on shareholder matters, such as electing a board of directors or voting in favor or against a certain transaction. The board of directors, in both cases, is accountable to the shareholders of the publicly traded corporation.

In contrast, tracking stocks are not newly created entities. Companies that issue tracking stocks still own the assets of the business being tracked, i.e., there is no legal separation of the division from the corporate parent. The economic or financial interests in the business are sold to investors who have an interest in the pure play of the tracking stock. The assets, liabilities, revenues, expenses, and cash flows of the corporation are allocated between the tracking stock and the remaining parent company business.

Tracking stocks allow a company with business units that have different risk and return profiles to attract different investors that may prefer one economic unit over another. Tracking stocks also enable investors to value the independent segments differently.

Tracking stocks achieve many of the same end goals as a spin-off, among them, the ability to raise capital for the parent or division, a way for investors to value the discrete businesses independently, and a means to provide strong incentives for management. However, tracking stocks offer a few other features as well: the parent company maintains control of the subsidiary; capital can be raised, yet the funds raised at the tracking stock may be used for other businesses within the parent's umbrella; companies need not change their corporate structure to issue a tracking stock; and, there is no need for a new board, no need for a name change, and no need to incorporate a new business.

Tracking stocks can be created by either issuing a dividend to shareholders, by undertaking a public offering or by issuing the tracking stock as currency in an acquisition. The IPO route can often be preceded by a dividend distribution to help establish a market. This avenue also usually ends up with only a portion of the tracking stock trading publicly, with the remainder retained as a part of the other stock.

Other key characteristics of tracking stocks are as follows:

Voting, Dividend, and Liquidation Rights. The voting and liquidation rights of holders of tracking stock differ from those of holders of ordinary common stock. Shareholders of tracking stock usually have voting rights that relate to the overall company, not the tracking stock in particular. In addition, the voting rights of one of the tracking stocks is usually fixed while the voting rights of the other tracking stock is usually adjusted periodically based on the relative market values of the different stocks.

Holders of tracking stock do not have a special claim on the assets of the tracked business; rather, they share in all of the assets of the issuer, or parent. The liquidation rights are often based on the relative values of the tracked stock and total assets of the parent at the time of issuance, but also can be based on the relative market values just prior to liquidation.

Much like ordinary common stock, if the tracking stock pays a dividend, it is usually at the discretion of the board of directors; however, the dividend usually tracks the earnings of the tracking stock.

Conversion Rights. The parent company that issued the tracking stock usually retains the right to convert the tracking stock into another class of stock subject to certain restrictions. This conversion may often be at a premium to its then current stock price.

Financial. Separate financial statements are prepared for the tracking stock and for the parent excluding and including the tracking stock.

Legal. Tracking stocks are not necessarily legally separated from the parent. The stock is a separate class of stock where the holders of different classes of stock of the parent corporation own the entire equity interest in the corporation. The tracking stock "tracks" the financial performance of a specific business unit operated by the corporation. The tracking is accomplished by certain provisions being inserted into the corporation's certificate of incorporation. These provisions define the rights that the holders of the tracking stock have. Therefore, there is cross-over risk in that legal obligations of one entity are by default the joint obligation of the other parties. Investors in the tracking stock are investors in the parent as a whole and own a undivided interest in the parent. Investors have no claim on specific assets of the parent. The parent is free to dispose of assets of a business unit that is being tracked without shareholder approval. Assets should be held in the divisional form not in a single entity to ensure that the stock is that of the parent or issuer.

Governance. Like any other corporation, tracking stocks companies are governed by a single board of directors who are accountable to shareholders. Unlike conventional corporations however, tracking stock companies usually have more

---

Exhibit 20-37
Pros and Cons of Tracking Stock

Advantages

- Enables the market to value respective businesses more accurately
- Parent company does not have to give up control
- Allows synergies to continue, e.g., internal capital markets, shared overhead
- Maintain board control
- Allows separate financing of business
- Generates greater analyst coverage and garners greater attention from investors
- Potentially generates cash from sale of stock
- Allows creation of incentives for management that align objectives
- Allow parent company to retain tax benefits of consolidation and avoids the tax cost of separation.
- Tracking stock can be used as acquisition currency
- Allows parent company to fund high growth businesses without suffering dilutive impact at other divisions
- Provides for separate accounting for tracked business

Disadvantages

- Creates potential conflict at board level
- Shareholders have no specific claim on tracking stock assets or business
- Shareholders usually only have voting rights in overall company, not tracking stock alone
- No legal separation, therefore cross-over liabilities exist whereby each tracking stock is liable for overall liabilities of the company
- Competition between shareholder groups can create internal conflict

---

than one class of shareholders, each representing ownership in the tracking stocks and/or the parent company. As a result, the board of directors is accountable to multiple groups of shareholders who may have divergent interests.

Tracking stocks differ from spin-offs and carve-outs in that the latter two separate a company into two separate firms with distinct legal boundaries, whereas tracking stock keeps the legal boundary in tact, with no separation of firms. In this distinction lies much of the controversy over the long-term benefits of tracking stock to shareholders. The controversy arises from a few areas. First, with no legal separation, there is cross-over liability risk. Second, there is the risk that the board of directors of the company faces an ongoing conflict in managing two different businesses with no direct accountability for anything other than the overall parent.

There are a number of advantages and disadvantages to tracking stock, as outlined in Exhibit 20-37.

[B]   Evidence Behind Tracking Stock

Numerous studies have shown that, like spin-offs and carve-outs, there is a significant abnormal positive return surrounding the announcement of a tracking stock. A study by John Elder and Peter Westra in 2000 showed that the 35 tracking stock announcements in the analysis had a mean abnormal return surrounding the announcement date of over 3%.[58] An independent study conducted in 2000 by Thomas Chemmanur and Imants Paeglis of 19 companies that announced tracking stocks through 1999 showed that the mean abnormal return surrounding the announcement of the tracking stock was approximately 3.09%.[59] In a 2000 study by Matthew Billet and David Mauer, they found that there was a positive relationship between the announcement returns and the preservation of internal capital markets of the combined firm, meaning that the parent and tracking stock were able to benefit from the combined power of the two businesses in terms of raising capital.[60]

Beyond the initial announcement effect of tracking stocks, there is significant controversy surrounding the long-term benefits of tracking stocks. In a paper published in the Michigan Law Review in 1996 entitled "Directorial Fiduciary Duties in a Tracking Stock Equity Structure: The Need for a Duty of Fairness," the author, Jeffrey Hass, cites numerous reasons why tracking stocks may have negative long-term performance.[61] Mostly, he argues, tracking stocks suffer because of the lack of legal separation between the different classes of stock in the issuing corporation. The boards of directors in tracking stock companies are not accountable to the individual shareholders of a particular business unit and shareholders do not have voting rights tied directly to the specific business being tracked. Consequently, there are significant conflicts that arise internally, between managers and business units, at the board level, and with shareholders. These conflicts all lead to a lack of understanding on how tracking stocks work and a poor perception of the shareholder value that can be created.

In early 2001, Matthew Billet and Anand Vijh performed a study on tracking stocks that confirm many of Hass' suspicions. While it is well-established that the announcement effect of tracking stocks is positive, their analysis looked at the long-term performance of tracking stocks and how the market reacted to subsequent events.[62] They found that tracking stocks had significantly negative returns

---

58. Elder, John, and Peter Westra, "The Reaction of Security Prices to Tracking Stock Announcements," Journal of Economics and Finance 24(1), 36–55 (Spring 2000).

59. Chemmanur, Thomas J., and Imants Paeglis, "Why Issue Tracking Stock? Insights from a Comparison with Spin-Offs and Carve-Outs," Working Paper, Boston College (March 2000).

60. Billet, M., and D. Mauer. "Diversification and the Value of Internal Capital Markets: The Case of Tracking Stock," Journal of Banking and Finance 24, 1457–1490 (2000).

61. Hass, Jeffrey J., "Directorial Fiduciary Duties in a Tracking Stock Equity Structure: The Need for a Duty of Fairness," Michigan Law Review Vol. 94, 2089–2177 (June 1996).

62. Billet, Matthew T., and Anand M. Vijh, "The Market Performance of Tracking Stocks," February 2001.

during the three-year period following the issue date. In the study, Billet and Vijh analyzed 28 tracking stocks and 29 issuers between 1984 and 1998. They found that post-tracking stock issuance, the issuing company, on average, had negative but insignificant returns for the three years post-issuance. On the other hand, the tracking stocks underperformed their respective benchmarks quite significantly. They compared the tracking stock returns to a market benchmark, an industry benchmark and a size benchmark. The average annual raw return on the tracking stocks was 7.3%, which compared to returns on the market, the industry and the size benchmarks of 19.3%, 16.0%, and 14.7% respectively.

Billet and Vijh made a number of other observations in this study. First, the smaller tracking stocks earned significantly worse returns than the larger tracking stocks. Second, tracking stocks that separate growth businesses from value businesses perform better, albeit insignificant returns, when compared to tracking stocks that do not separate value from growth businesses. Third, tracking stock issued as acquisition currency earn significantly poor returns.

The authors also studied post-issuance events and the effect these had on stock prices. They found that eight of the tracking stocks had been eliminated in favor of the "old stock structure," two had been sold and two had been spun off. In addition, two of the tracking stocks had been acquired along with the issuer and one had been restructured after acquiring another firm. In most cases, the announcement of these events resulted in a strong positive announcement effect. For example, the eight tracking stocks that reverted back to their prior ownership structure had an average market adjusted return of 19%, while the issuer stock had an average market adjusted return of 7.4%. This study also found that there was a significant positive announcement effect with the elimination of a tracking stock.

The long-term shareholder effects of tracking stock were also analyzed by Chemmanur and Paeglis, who concluded that firms issuing tracking stock underperform their respective indices and the market. In addition, they showed that the performance of tracking stocks was significantly worse than that of spin-offs. Their conclusion is that the primary motivation behind tracking stock is the "preservation of the synergies between business units involved and the control benefits accruing to firm management, while reaping the benefits of the better reflection of "hidden value" in the combined firm's equity market valuation."[63]

[C] Creating Value Through Tracking Stock

Value creation through issuing a tracking stock is theoretically little different than a spin-off or equity carve-out. Investors and research analysts are better able to value the discrete businesses of a company. Therefore, for example, if a company trading at a P/E multiple of ten has a high growth subsidiary, the company might issue a tracking stock tied to that business, so the market could value the attractive business separately from the parent. The resulting market capitalization

---

63. Chemmanur (March 2000), *supra* n.59.

of the two classes of stock combined should be greater than that of the parent by itself with the division included in its financial statements.

[D]   Motivation and Rationale Behind Tracking Stock

Many of the reasons behind implementing a spin-off, carve-out, or split-off also apply to tracking stock, namely, lack of synergy or fit, focus on core business, highlight value, monetize assets or reduce debt, and avoid takeover. However, tracking stocks are undertaken for two fundamental reasons: to enhance shareholder value and to create an acquisition currency. One additional motivation behind tracking stock is to avoid takeover.

[1]   Enhance Shareholder Value

To create value, tracking stocks attempt to unlock the value of attractive or high growth businesses while retaining the benefits of consolidation. Much like spinoffs and carve-outs, tracking stocks enable a company to separate the financial performance of a particular asset from that of the rest of the company, allowing the market to value the discrete business independently of the parent. However, in addition, the tracking stock format allows the parent and division to continue to enjoy the benefits of the combined company.

For example, since there is no legal separation, the companies continue to benefit from the combined economies of both businesses balance sheets, thereby making the task of raising debt capital that much easier. The companies presumably benefit from a lower cost of debt financing. Also, when the tracking stock raises equity capital, it can access the capital markets using its own valuation that is based on its financial characteristics and performance, and not that of the slower growing or less attractive parent. In theory, this structure enables the parent and tracking stock to get the best of both worlds, i.e., lower debt cost of capital for parent and tracking stock, and lower cost of equity for the tracking stock.

A second consolidation benefit is from the sharing of costs and resources such as manufacturing, marketing, or overhead. These costs can be spread across both organizations, which brings substantial savings to the parties.

By unlocking the value in the tracking stock, theoretically, the market will apply a multiple to the tracking stock that is more attractive than the multiple applied to the parent, resulting in a higher overall market value for the combined companies.

There have been numerous high profile tracking stock transactions that have been used to unlock the value of a division, as outlined in Exhibit 20-38.

Tracking stocks allow parent companies to continue to enjoy the benefits of internal capital markets, if desired, yet access the public debt and equity markets if more feasible at the division or business level. This approach allows the separate businesses to access public equity markets using the cost of capital most closely associated with the division's growth characteristics. Tracking stock has also been used to raise capital for the parent company, as shown in Exhibit 20-39.

Exhibit 20-38
Tracking Stock Used to Highlight a Business Division[64]

Tracking Stock	Parent	Date	Rationale
Marathon Group (Oil) Steel Group (Steel)	USX	1991	Reflect the different steel and oil businesses.
Delhi Group		1992	Marathon Group was subdivided into two, adding Delhi Group.
TCI Group Liberty Media Group	Tele-Communications Inc.		Separate media business from communications business.
Circuit City (Electronics and appliances) CarMax (Cars)	Circuit City	1997	Separated car business from electronics and appliance business.
Georgia Pacific Group (Manufacturing) Timber Stock (Timber)	Georgia Pacific[65]	1997	Separated manufacturing from timber business.
PE Biosystems (Life sciences) Celera Genomics (Genomics)	Applera	1998	Separated the life sciences business from the genomics business.
Rainbow Media Group (Media content)	Cablevision	2001	Separated cable business from media content business.
WorldCom Group (Commercial voice, data, Internet, and International services)	WorldCom	2001	Separated consumer, long-distance voice from commercial voice, data and International services.

Exhibit 20-39
Tracking Stocks as Vehicles for Raising Capital

Tracking Stock	Parent	Date
DLJDirect	DLJ	1999
ZDNet	Ziff-Davis	1999
AT&T Wireless Group	AT&T	2000

---

64. Thomson Financial, Public Company Documents.
65. In 2000, Georgia Pacific announced the spin-off of the timber group.

[2]   Create Acquisition Currency

Stock-for-stock transactions are quite commonplace. Sellers, however, are often concerned with taking an acquirer's stock as consideration, if they do not feel that the acquirer's stock has the potential to maintain the same type of return that their own stock has provided them in the past. In addition, they may be concerned about giving away the upside in their company. Furthermore, for large corporations making smaller acquisitions, the seller may be concerned that their company may not be able to have a significant impact on the financials of the parent, implying that the market may not recognize the value of the acquisition. Consequently, a few companies have formed tracking stocks to create an acquisition currency that reflects the underlying attributes of a division that is similar to that of the target.

By using tracking stock, the seller is able to receive consideration tax free and participate in the upside of the company once the acquisition has closed. The participation is not simply that of the acquirer; rather, it is directly tied to the entity that will assume the financial performance of the target.

Tracking stock as an acquisition currency has been used in a number of transactions, beginning with the first tracking stock ever done, General Motor's acquisition of EDS, whereby GM created the GM-E tracking stock to serve as the currency in the acquisition of Electronic Data Systems. This approach gave Ross Perot, the largest shareholder in EDS, the ability to continue to benefit from the upside in EDS while realizing value from the sale of the company to GM. After the transaction, Ross Perot continued to be a part of the management team at EDS; the tracking stock allowed him to continue to enjoy the benefits of appreciation in stock options tied to the performance of the GM-E stock. For GM, the tracking stock made certain that it controlled the asset.

A more recent situation of note is in the use of tracking stock by Genzyme in its acquisition of BioSurface Technology in 1994. In this transaction, the shareholders of Genzyme approved a new stock, the TR Stock (Tissue Repair Division Common Stock) and the General Stock (General Division Common Stock). The TR Stock was used to create the Tissue Repair Division, which combined the tissue repair business of Genzyme with the newly acquired BioSurface business. The General Stock reflected all the other businesses at Genzyme.

One of the major issues in using tracking stock as acquisition currency is that, to the extent the tracking stock is created to facilitate the transaction, there is no market for the tracking stock. Therefore, in addition to having to negotiate a purchase price for the target, the acquirer must negotiate the value of the shares that are given to the target as consideration. In the Genzyme situation, for example, the tissue repair division assets that went into the tracking stock along with the newly acquired BioSurface technology, did not have any income or cash flow, and consequently, the tracking stock was difficult to value.

A second issue with tracking stocks as acquisition currency is that tracking stocks have rights that are dramatically different that conventional common stock. For example, their voting rights are for that of the entire company, not of

```
┌──────────────────────────────────────────────────────────────────────┐
│  Exhibit 20-40                                                         │
│  Tracking Stock as Acquisition Currency                               │
```

Tracking Stock	Target	Parent	Date
GM-"E"	Electronic Data Systems[66]	General Motors	1984
	Delmarva Power & Light	Atlantic Energy	1998
FON	PCS	Sprint	1998
TR Stock	BioSurface Technologies	Genzyme	1994
Genzyme Biosurgery	Biomatrix	Genzyme	2000
AT&T LMG	Tele-Communications, Inc.	AT&T	1999

the business being tracked. This raises issues of operating control and management oversight. Thus, prior to the acquisition, the acquirer and target must negotiate what rights the shareholders of the tracking stock have with respect to the business being tracked.

Exhibit 20-40 provides a list of cases where tracking stock has been used as acquisition currency.

[3] Avoid Takeover

Much like other restructuring alternatives, tracking stock has been used as a means to thwart takeover. As an example NL Industries, in response to a tender offer from Simmons Group, NL anticipated undertaking a spin-off of NL Chemicals, a subsidiary. In contemplation of the spin-off, it issued Series C preferred stock that tracked the chemicals business. The spin-off did not get executed.

[E] Key Timing Events in Tracking Stock

The timing for issuing a tracking stock will depend on how the stock is issued: as a dividend to existing shareholders, as acquisition currency in a transaction, or in an initial public offering. Each form of issuance will impact the timing because of the various filings that need to be made. For example, if the tracking stock is issued through an initial public offering, an S-1 registration statement will have to be filed, in which case the timing will be driven by the preliminary filing and subsequent effectiveness of the registration statement. In other words, the timing will be very much like that of an equity carve-out. To the extent the tracking stock is issued as acquisition currency, the timing is likely to be driven by the negotiations and filings relating to the merger or acquisition transaction. If the transaction requires shareholder approval, there will be a need to file a proxy statement which must be approved by the SEC prior to mailing to shareholders. If the tracking

---

66. EDS was split-off from GM in 2000.

Exhibit 20-41
Key Dates in the AT&T Issuance of AT&T Wireless Tracking Stock[67]

Date	Event
October 25, 2000	AT&T announces restructuring plan.
December 22, 2000	AT&T files with the SEC for the AT&T Wireless tracking stock.
April 18, 2001	AT&T announces terms of the AT&T Wireless tracking stock exchange offer.
June 19, 2001	AT&T Wireless names initial board.
July 9, 2001	AT&T Wireless split-off becomes effective.

---

stock is issued as a dividend to shareholders, depending on the size of the transaction, it could require shareholder approval, in which case, it will be subject to a proxy statement filing.

As an example, following in Exhibit 20-41 are the key dates in the AT&T issuance of AT&T Wireless tracking stock in 2000.

[F]   Valuation of Tracking Stock

The valuation of tracking stock is theoretically no different than that of a spinoff, i.e., the division is valued independently of the parent or issuer as if it is a separate entity. Therefore, the steps to evaluating the tracking stock transaction follows the same process as that of a spin-off. First, perform a break-up valuation of the issuer to determine if the company is undervalued. Second, value the business to be tracked to determine if its public company valuation is higher than its private market valuation. Third, evaluate the impact of the transaction on the parent company's earnings. The results of this analysis should support the premise that the separation of the division from the parent will enhance shareholder value.

[G]   Tax and Accounting Issues

The IRS has a no-ruling policy on tracking stock classification; however, the IRS does have the power to retroactively address tax issues in tracking stock transactions. For tax purposes, the tracking stock is generally considered stock of the issuer or parent. In consideration of the tax issues with respect to tracking stock, a determination is made as to whether the tracking stock is stock of the issuer (or parent) or stock of the subsidiary owning the tracked business. For a tracking stock to meet the issuer classification, for state law purposes, it should be treated as stock of the issuer. The voting rights are as shareholders of the issuer, not the subsidiary. The dividend rights are those of the issuer, declared by the board of directors and subject to the state law limitations on dividends paid by the issuer on its

---

67. Public Company Documents.

capital stock. The liquidation rights must reflect the net of the issuer's assets in excess of liabilities, and have no security interest in or special liquidation rights to receive the tracked assets.

If the tracking stock is deemed to be that of the issuer, the distribution of the tracking stock to the issuer's shareholders qualifies as a non-taxable dividend. The distribution of the tracking stock is also tax free to the issuer. A public offering by the issuer of tracking stock is non-taxable to the issuer. In addition, the tracked assets remain a part of the consolidate group for tax purposes. Finally, conversion by the issuer of tracking stock into residual stock or into another tracking stock is tax free.

If the tracked stock is deemed to be stock of the subsidiary, the dividend to shareholders is taxable as dividends, if the transaction does not qualify for Section 355 spin-off. If it does not qualify under 355, then the difference between the fair market value and the basis of the stock distributed would be recognized as gain to the issuer. In this case, a public offering of the tracking stock would be taxable to the issuer. If the tracking stock constitutes more than 20% of the stock or value of the subsidiary, then the parent or issuer would be forced to deconsolidate for federal tax purposes. If issued as a dividend, the dividend is non-taxable to shareholders. In a tax-free transaction, a shareholder's basis is allocated between the tracking stock and that of the parent.

The tax status of tacking stock transaction has come under scrutiny for many years. The IRS has taken a position of not commenting on the transaction which means that it reserves the right to challenge the tax-free nature of the transaction at future date.

[H]   Filing Requirements

The filing requirements for tracking stock will depend on the form of issuance of the tracking stock. Under most circumstances, tracking stock will require shareholder approval, in which case the issuer will have to file a proxy statement. In the case of an initial public offering, the issuer will have to file an S-1 registration statement. In the event the tracking stock is used as acquisition currency, the transaction is likely to be subject to shareholder approval by both parties, in which case a proxy statement will have to be filed. Chapter 22 provides detailed information on the filing, disclosure and dissemination of the registration and proxy statement.

[I]   Pricing of Tracking Stock

The pricing of a tracking stock will depend on the mode by which it is issued: as an initial public offering, as a dividend to shareholders, or as currency in an acquisition.

As an IPO, the tracking stock is priced as a negotiation between the company, its underwriters, and the investors. As a dividend to shareholders, the stock begins trading on a when-issued basis no different than in a spin-off. As currency in an acquisition, there is significant negotiation that takes place between the target and the acquirer with respect to the valuation of the tracking stock being issued as currency.

[J]   Issues with Respect to Tracking Stock

While tracking stocks may allow issuers to unlock the value of a hidden division, they can create numerous problems. The issues arise because of the structure that is used to create them. Since a tracking stock "tracks" the earnings and dividends of a particular business, rather than represents an equity stake in that business, there are divergent interests between the shareholders of the different classes of stock in the company. Therefore, the divergence of interests between classes of stock creates a conflict between shareholders, the board and between the management of the companies and the board.

From a legal standpoint, there is no separation between the tracking stocks. Legally, a shareholder of the tracking stock is a shareholder in the corporate entity that issued the tracking stock. From a financial standpoint, the goal of tracking stock is to separate the financial or economic benefits of different businesses. The different entities share a board of directors, and shareholders of the tracking stock do not have an independent board looking out for their interests. The board of directors cannot look out exclusively for the interests of one business; rather, they need to work on behalf of all shareholders.

[1]   Conflicts

Tracking stocks can create conflicts between shareholder groups and within the board of directors. These conflicts relate to capital allocation, corporate resource allocation, dividend policies, intercompany and intracompany dealings, capital raising and use of proceeds, and tracking stock redemption or exchange features. One way to solve this is to have an operating committee that oversees the tracking stock. The operating committee reports to the board of directors. In certain circumstances, the issuer has set up a separate board of directors for the tracking stock. This however, creates the possibility that the stock will not be treated as issuer stock, and therefore will trigger significant punitive tax issues.

[2]   Difficult to Maintain

Because a tracking stock continues to be controlled by the parent, consolidated for tax and accounting purposes, and many of its operations are still interconnected, the task of buying and selling or even altering assets becomes quite difficult, as the issuer and the tracking stock are forced to allocate assets and liabilities to one or the other entity. In addition, capital raised at the tracking stock through an asset sale or otherwise, presents a problem with respect to who uses that capital.

[3]   Financial Statements

The tracking stock and issuer are consolidated for tax and accounting purposes, yet the issuer is required to report separate financial results for each. While this is one of the prime benefits of tracking stock — allowing the market to value the businesses independently — it also creates a significant burden on the issuer, to maintain financial records that accurately reflect the businesses.

[4]   Shareholder Approval

Shareholder approval is required to issue tracking stock. This increases the risk that the transaction may not get approved. Shareholder approval may be avoided by creating the tracking stock as preferred stock not common stock.

[5]   Cross-Over Liabilities

As there is no legal separation between issuer and tracking stock, and the parent maintains control of the assets of the tracking stock, there is no segregation of the liabilities of the parties. The tracking stock remains on the hook for the liabilities of the parent and vice versa.

[K]   Subsequent Events

In certain circumstances, tracking stock may become too cumbersome for the issuer, or it may wish to divest the business completely or reacquire it. There are a number of ways to execute the unwinding of a tracking stock. First, the tracked assets can be sold, in which case the parent pays a gain on sale of the assets and the shareholders pay a gain on the receipt of the net sales proceeds, regardless of whether the proceeds are paid in the form of a dividend or as a redemption of their stock. An example of this is the 1997 issue of Timber Group tracking stock by Georgia-Pacific, which was subsequently eliminated when the Timber Group merged with Plum Creek Timber Company in 2000. Second, the tracking stock can be converted into another class of common stock of the company, either in contemplation of a sale, or after the sale has been completed. For example, the Circle.com tracking stock of Snyder Communications was eliminated when Snyder was purchased by Havas in 1999. Third, the issuer can redeem its tracking stock in exchange for stock of a subsidiary that holds the tracked assets. The subsidiary can then be split-off as a public company. The split-off will qualify for tax-free treatment to the company and its shareholders provided the requirements of Section 355 are met. As an example, AT&T created the AT&T Wireless tracking stock in 2000, and then split off the Wireless tracking stock in 2001.

A recent example of a tracking stock that went awry, is the WorldCom and MCI Group tracking that were implemented in 2001. In May 2002, the company announced it was eliminating the tracking stocks and dropping the MCI dividend, which would save the company $284 million annually. In addition, the tracking stock would simplify the company's corporate structure, enabling the market to better understand the company. The transaction was expected to become effective on July 12.

[L]   Case Study: Genzyme Corporation

Genzyme Corporation is a biotechnology company that develops and markets innovative products and services designed to address significant unmet medical needs. Beginning in 1994, the company underwent a series of restructurings that were designed to highlight the value of individual businesses and create shareholder value. The first business to be highlighted was Genzyme Tissue Repair (GZTR), a business focused on tissue and biomaterials engineering. GZTR was restructured as a tracking stock. At the time that Genzyme created the tracking stock, the combined market capitalization of the two businesses was approximately $230 million.

Over the subsequent seven years, the company created separate tracking stocks for its oncology business — Genzyme Molecular Oncology (GZMO) and its surgical products business — Genzyme Surgical Products (GZSP). In March of 2000, the board of Genzyme reorganized the three tracking stocks, GZTR, GZMO, and GZSP, into two tracking stocks. The company created a new tracking stock named Genzyme Biosurgery (GZBX) that was used to acquire a company named Biomatrix. As a part of the merger, GZTR and GSP were exchanged for GZBX tracking stock, eliminating the GZTR and GZSP tracking stocks. As a result, Genzyme had three primary divisions, each of which having its own series of tracking stock. The three divisions are: Genzyme General, Genzyme Biosurgery, and Genzyme Molecular Oncology. There is not stock that represents the overall Genzyme Corporation as a whole.

Genzyme General develops and markets therapeutic products in the areas of genetic disorders and chronic debilitating diseases. The business also manufactures and markets diagnostic products, genetic testing services, and pharmaceutical intermediates. Genzyme Biosurgery develops and markets devices, advanced biomaterials and biotherapeutics. It focuses primarily in the cardiothoracic, orthopedic, and general surgery markets. Genzyme Molecular Oncology develops new generation cancer products, focusing on vaccines and angiogenesis inhibitors.

The three divisions operate under the same general guidelines, having a common board of directors that act on behalf of the three businesses. Genzyme Corporation files financial statements with the SEC on behalf of each division by itself, and on behalf of Genzyme Corporation on a consolidated basis. Genzyme Corporation files a consolidated tax return and pays taxes based on the earnings and profits of the combined divisions. While each division can raise capital on its own, they have full access to the resources of Genzyme Corporation. The cost of utilizing these resources is allocated among the divisions.

In its public filings, Genzyme stated the following reasons why the company uses tracking stock:[68]

- It allows each Genzyme business to focus on a distinct market;

- It accelerates the growth of Genzyme's development stage businesses;

- It broadens the investor base and provides financing flexibility;

---

68. Genzyme Corporation Public Filings.

- It creates entrepreneurial environments;

- It maximizes resource; and,

- It offers tax and cash flow benefits.

Genzyme's history of creating tracking stocks to highlight divisions has created substantial shareholder value. In 1994, when Genzyme initiated the tracking stock program, the company's stock had lagged the performance of the S&P 500. At the time of the Genzyme Tissue Repair transaction, the company had a market capitalization of approximately $240 million. By March 31, 2001, the combined market capitalization of the three principal tracking stocks was approximately $4.2 billion. Exhibit 20-42 highlights the timeline and shareholder value creation the various Genzyme related tracking stocks.

In mid-2003, the tracking stocks for Genzyme Biosurgery and Genzyme Molecular Oncology were eliminated. Shares in each tracking stock were exchanged for Genzyme stock.

Exhibit 20-43 shows a visual representation of Genzyme's stock price performance versus the S&P 500 from the beginning of 1994 to the completion of the tracking stocks. Exhibit 20-44 shows the stock price performance of the three present tracking stocks of Genzyme.

Exhibit 20-42
Genzyme Tracking Stock Time Line and Value Creation[69]
($ in millions)

Date	Event	Combined Market Capitalization
1994	Genzyme Tissue Repair begins trading as a tracking stock	$ 231
June 18, 1997	Genzyme reclassifies company into three divisions stocks: Genzyme General Division (GGD), Genzyme Tissue Repair (GTR), and Genzyme Molecular Oncology (GMO). Genzyme Molecular Oncology is created in the reclassification by combining GGDs oncology programs and the acquired assets of PharmaGenics, a company engaged in the development of cancer therapeutics.	$1,037
		(Continued)

---

69. Public Company Documents.

Exhibit 20-42
(*Continued*)

Date	Event	Combined Market Capitalization
October 15, 1998	Genzyme's board authorizes a tax-free dividend of Genzyme Molecular Oncology to shareholders of record on November 2, 1998.	$1,561
October 27, 1998	Genzyme announces the declaration of a tax-free dividend of shares of Genzyme Molecular Oncology payable on November 16, 1998.	$1,571
November 16, 1998	Genzyme Molecular Oncology begins trading on Nasdaq.	$1,801
March 4, 1999	Genzyme announces the distribution of Genzyme Surgical Products (GSP) stock to shareholders.	$1,999
May 27, 1999	Genzyme declares dividend of GSP stock to shareholders.	$1,697
June 14, 1999	Record date for distribution of a tax-free dividend of GSP.	$1,984
June 28, 1999	Distribution date for GSP stock to shareholders.	$2,340
March 2, 2000	The board of Genzyme authorizes the reorganization of GMO, GSP, and GTR tracking stock.	$3,256
March 6, 2000	Announced the merger between a subsidiary of Genzyme and Biomatrix to create a new series of tracking stock known as Genzyme Biosurgery (GBX). As a part of the merger, GTR and GSP were to be exchanged for GBX stock eliminating the GTR and GSP tracking stocks.	$3,466
December 18, 2000	The Genzyme merger with Biomatrix was completed.	$4,312
December 19, 2000	The stock of GSP and GTR are cancelled and GBX is created.	$4,672

Exhibit 20-43
Genzyme General Stock Price Performance Versus S&P 500:
January 3, 1994–March 31, 2001

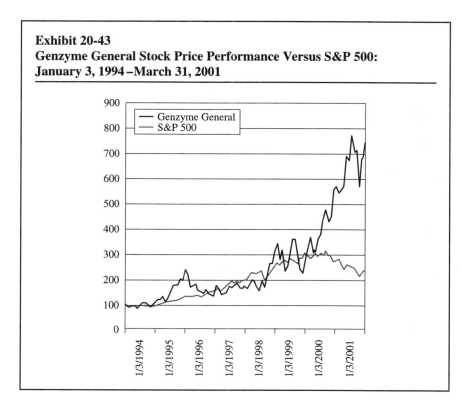

Exhibit 20-44
Genzyme Group of Companies Stock Price Performance:
January 2, 1992–March 31, 2001

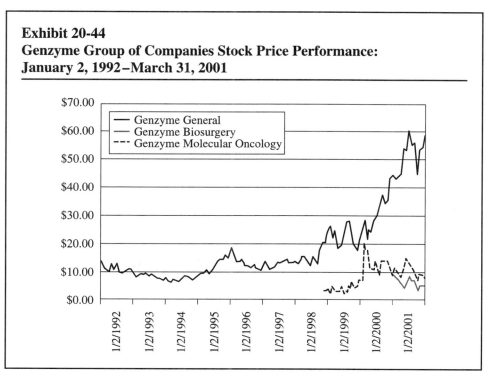

§ 20.05 SUMMARY

Transaction driven restructurings occur because parent companies are aiming to enhance shareholder value. The motivation and rationale discussed in this chapter behind these transactions tell us the specific details behind a particular company's ownership and performance. They do not however explain all the reasons why a divestiture may make sense.

Based on this chapter, we have learned that it is possible to create significant shareholder value through restructurings. The evidence supports value creation with almost all the transaction driven divestiture alternatives, with long-term positive returns to shareholders created with spin-offs, split-offs, and equity carve-outs, and mixed returns to shareholders with tracking stock. The question facing an executive considering a restructuring is when to restructure and how to do it.

In answer to the first question, we have seen that a restructuring makes sense under the following conditions, not all of which need to be present: (1) the parent and subsidiary operate in dissimilar industries or sectors; (2) the strategic fit and risk profiles of the two businesses are different; (3) the subsidiary or division is hidden behind the financials of the parent; (4) the subsidiary is either performing better or worse than the parent; (5) subsidiary management is lacking motivation; (6) the parent wishes to avoid takeover; and (7) the parent needs to realign its balance sheet.

The question how to restructure, is driven by a number of factors: (1) the tax basis the parent has in the subsidiary or division; (2) the need or desire to maintain certain joint synergies such marketing, manufacturing, and overhead; (3) the degree to which the strategic interests of the parent and subsidiary diverge; (4) the need for the parent to raise capital; (5) the need to raise capital at the subsidiary level in order to fund growth; and (6) the degree to which the parent and subsidiary need to rely on debt capital.

Based on these drivers, a spin-off would make sense under the following conditions: (1) the parent and subsidiary are in different businesses, have poor strategic fit and dissimilar risk profiles, (2) the tax basis in the subsidiary is low, indicating an outright sale would be tax inefficient; (3) there is little benefit derived by the subsidiary from resources provided by the parent; (4) the parent needs to raise capital; and (5) the subsidiary has strong operating and financial performance. In addition, a spin-off makes sense when the subsidiary needs its own currency to raise capital and make acquisitions. Furthermore, a spin-off may be a good alternative for a business that is not performing well relative to the parent. Finally, like other divestiture alternatives, spin-offs are a sound means to provide incentives for management.

An equity carve-out is an appropriate alternative under the following circumstances: (1) when both the parent and subsidiary need better access to capital; (2) when managers need motivation tied to their business unit; (3) when the businesses of the parent and subsidiary are dissimilar and can be separated; and (4) when the subsidiary business has strong growth prospects that are being overshadowed by the parent. Equity carve-outs may also be a good alternative to the extent the parent company wishes to retain a majority interest in the subsidiary and take advantage of the tax and accounting consolidation benefits. In addition, an equity carve-out of less than 20% allows the parent to potentially pursue a tax-free spin-off at a later stage. Equity carve-outs are not recommended for poorly performing subsidiaries.

Tracking stock makes sense under the following conditions: (1) when the subsidiary business needs its own currency to make acquisitions; (2) when the parent and subsidiary need better access to capital; (3) when there are still significant synergies between the business units that it does not make sense to divest the subsidiary completely; (4) when the parent and subsidiary can take advantage of debt capital raising based on the strength of the combined company; and (5) when there are net operating losses at the parent or tracking stock that can be used to the benefit of both parties in consolidation for tax purposes.

Tracking stocks can have benefits over spin-offs. First, the overall corporation can benefit from lower cost of debt financing, while the spun-off subsidiary must secure its own financing. Second, tracking stocks can spread the cost of overhead and other resources over a large entity while spin-offs must stand alone. Third, tracking stocks are simpler to affect on a tax-free basis, while spin-offs require a tax-free ruling from the IRS. Finally, tracking stocks cannot be taken over as they are a part of a larger entity.

Drawbacks of tracking stocks are the conflicts that may arise between shareholders, management, and the board of directors of the issuer and tracking stock, and the mixed long-term evidence that tracking stocks create shareholder value.

In terms of how the different divestiture approaches can be compared, Exhibit 20-45 provides a simple matrix to think about.

The execution of a spin-off differs somewhat from that of other alternatives. It does not require a new group of equity investors like an equity carve-out; rather, the subsidiary stock is issued as a dividend to shareholders, thus minimizing the execution risk of a spin-off. Conversely, in equity carve-outs, the transaction is dependent on the parent company's ability to sell stock to new investors in the market, increasing the potential risk in the transaction. A split-off, like a spin-off, is not reliant on new investors investing in the company; rather, it depends on the ability of the company to swap stock in one company for stock in another. Tracking stock, like a spin-off, is often executed as a dividend to shareholders and thus has less execution risk than an equity carve-out.

Despite the lack of execution risk associated with spin-offs, split-offs, and tracking stock, they must still be carefully considered. While it may be possible to execute the transaction, the true test of deal's success will be the market's reaction to the announcement and the long-term ability of the restructuring to create shareholder value.

Shareholder value creation in these types of restructurings comes from a number of sources. First, by separating business units into discrete entities with their own financial statements, the market is better able to value the pieces. This attracts new investors as well as new research analysts. Second, the mere act of undertaking

Exhibit 20-45
Comparison Between Spin-Offs, Carve-Outs, and Tracking Stock

Category	Spin-Off	Carve-Out	Tracking Stock
Ownership by Parent	• Usually no ongoing ownership	• Parent may sell 100% or very little • Common for parent to own substantial stake	• Parent usually owns 100% yet may sell some in IPO.
Governance	• New Board of Directors	• New Board of Directors	• Usually same Board of Directors as parent
Liabilities	• Separate	• Separate	• Cross-over liabilities
Tax	• Tax-free if meet requirements	• Taxable of proceeds go to parent. Non-taxable if proceeds got to subsidiary. • Can consolidate if own greater than 80%.	• Non-taxable if tracking stock is "issuer stock."

the restructuring sends a strong signal to the market that either the parent is under-valued or the divested or restructured business is undervalued. Third, the creation of an independent entity provides an opportunity to create attractive incentives for management which may ultimately lead to enhanced operating performance of the business. Fourth, the independent entities are better able to finance themselves at a cost of capital that is based on their unique risk profiles.

PART V

LEGAL ASPECTS OF MERGERS & ACQUISITIONS

Chapter 21

BUSINESS JUDGMENT RULE

§ 21.01 OVERVIEW AND PURPOSE OF THE BUSINESS JUDGMENT RULE

A board of directors is a group of individuals legally charged with overseeing a corporation from a governance perspective. It has a fiduciary duty to act in the best interests of the corporation and its shareholders, whether daily, in strategic, operational, and financial oversight, or in the context of a merger, acquisition, or other transaction. The business judgment rule is a collection of laws, standards, and doctrines that together form a framework that articulates a director's duties to shareholders. Generally, a director has a responsibility to act in good faith, with due care, and with loyalty to shareholders.

On a day-to-day basis, a board of directors has numerous responsibilities, including selecting and monitoring the progress of the chief executive officer and the senior management team, providing governance and oversight to the corporation, overseeing financial responsibility for the company, evaluating itself, and being accountable to shareholders for the performance of the company and the conduct of its employees. In general, however, a board is responsible for the day-to-day and long-term well-being of the corporation.

In contrast to a director's conventional day-to-day responsibilities, it has specific duties in the context of mergers, acquisitions and restructurings, in particular in situations where the company is subject to takeover. And, in some instances, the board must set aside its normal day-to-day responsibilities in favor of its duties in the context of a transaction. These obligations are generally measured by a principle known as the "business judgment rule." The business judgment rule is a standard that is used to judge a board of directors when exercising its fiduciary duties in the context of a takeover or some other form of M&A transaction. The courts rely on the business judgment rule when shareholders sue a corporation and its board of directors for having violated its fiduciary duties to shareholders, or when directors are seen to have a conflict of interest in a transaction.

Under the business judgment rule, sometimes also referred to as the "business judgment doctrine," there is a presumption that directors act in the best interests of stockholders, and that their behavior is consistent with their fiduciary obligations to shareholders. To the extent a board's behavior in the context of a transaction is consistent with what is considered acceptable business judgment rule practices, it is generally protected from liability. Likewise, to the extent the board is found to have violated its duties to shareholders, it may lose the specific protections provided by the business judgment rule. In general, a board is presumed to be acting in accordance with the business judgment rule if it acts in good faith on an informed basis, shows due care, and is loyal to shareholders. Any party contesting the actions or behavior of the board must be able to demonstrate that the board violated its fiduciary duties.

Three principle duties — good faith, care, and loyalty — form the basis of the business judgment rule. They do not, however, offer the entire picture surrounding a board's duties under the business judgment rule in all cases; they merely form a framework for evaluating a board's behavior in the context of a transaction. To fully appreciate the breadth and scope of the business judgment rule requires a deeper understanding of the history of the business judgment rule, the development of the Model Business Corporations Act, and the evolution of case law surrounding the actions of boards in the context of M&A transactions. Based on these precedents, various standards and duties, such as the "Revlon" duties and the "Unocal Standard," have developed that provide a detailed framework within which a board's actions are judged in the context of a deal.

The business judgment rule exists for a number of reasons. First, the business judgment rule affords a board of directors the opportunity to manage a corporation on behalf of shareholders knowing that they have the flexibility to make decisions unencumbered by daily or frequent shareholder questioning. If shareholders legally questioned each and every action a board takes, shareholders would ultimately run the corporation or the board would continually be in litigation. The business judgment rule gives the board comfort that if it acts in the best interests of shareholders, it will be protected from liability.

Second, the business judgment rule enables the courts to avoid getting involved in corporate decision-making. The business judgment rule establishes a framework for behavior; it does not enable the courts to make decisions on behalf of the board, the corporation or shareholders. The board makes decisions on behalf of shareholders and with protection of the business judgment rule. Third, the courts have recognized that a board of director's role can often be fraught with risk and uncertainty, and that without the often difficult decisions made by a board, a corporation may not be able to grow and prosper. The business judgment rule provides the board with sufficient protection to make decisions that may entail vast amounts of risk, but may also provide significant upside. Fourth, and arguably most important, the protections provided by the business judgment rule encourage individuals to take on the immense task of board director, which an individual may otherwise not be willing to do without the business judgment rule protection.

Beyond the standard business judgment rule that applies in most M&A related transactions, there are enhanced levels of scrutiny that apply in specific circumstances. For example, in cases where directors take a defensive action in response to a takeover threat, enhanced scrutiny is applied. The test the courts apply in these circumstances is often referred to the "Unocal" test. Another level of scrutiny is articulated in a set of duties known as the "Revlon" duties. This test essentially says that if a board of directors authorizes the sale of the company, it has a duty to seek the highest price possible for shareholders. The highest level of scrutiny a board can come under is known as the "entire fairness test." This applies in cases where directors have either been found to breach their duty of loyalty and/or care to shareholders, or in cases where directors have a material conflict or economic interest in the transaction. Each of these specific types of enhanced scrutiny are discussed in greater depth later in this chapter.

[A] The Sarbanes-Oxley Act of 2002

On July 30, 2002, the Sarbanes-Oxley Act was signed into law. In essence, the Sarbanes-Oxley Act redesigns federal regulation of public company corporate governance and reporting obligations, tightens the accountability standards for directors, officers, auditors, securities analysts and legal counsel, and outlines specific securities violations as crimes. The Act is aimed at responding to the public outcry over the numerous corporate scandals of the past few years and is designed to curb corporate fraud and abuse. While the Act is not targeted specifically at mergers and acquisitions, it is bound to have significant implications on M&A as board of directors and managers are going to be held accountable to a standard that is consistent with the Act.

In principal, there are five main components of the Act. First, the Act requires more frequent and enhanced financial and other disclosures by public companies. The Act requires the SEC to set forth stronger disclosure requirements on all aspects of a company's financial statements, including off-balance sheet and other obligations that may have a material impact on the business.

Second, it requires the CEO and CFO of public companies to certify their financial reports. The certification must specify that the CEO and CFO have reviewed the annual and quarterly reports, that the reports do not contain any material misstatements or omissions, and that the reports present the financial condition of the company fairly. In addition, the CEO and CFO are responsible for establishing and maintaining internal controls and disclosing to the company's auditors and audit committee all significant control deficiencies and any fraud involving management or other employees.

Third, the Act creates an independent board to oversee the accounting industry from an auditing perspective. The board, the Public Company Accounting Oversight Board, operates under the supervision of the Securities and Exchange Commission, and is charged with regulating the public accounting industry.

Fourth, it ensures the independence of public accounting firms that audit public companies. As a part of this provision, the Act provides for mandatory separation of the audit function from the consulting function provided by accounting firms. This was a situation that was seen in the recent Enron scandal.

Finally, the Act specifies and increases penalties for those who violate the securities laws. In addition, the Act highlights new crimes and specifies penalties for those crimes. For example, the Act makes it a crime to knowingly alter or destroy documents with the intention of obstructing or impeding an investigation. The crime is punishable for up to 20 years plus fines. A second federal crime that has been highlighted is securities fraud in which a person knowingly engages in a scheme to defraud in connection with a registered security or obtain money or property through false pretenses. This crime is punishable by fine and up to 25 years in prison. A third federal crime that results from the Act is the certification of false or misleading financial statements, which is subject to a $1 million fine and ten years imprisonment. Willful violations of this provision are subject to $5 million in fines and 20 years imprisonment.

§ 21.02   GENESIS OF THE BUSINESS JUDGMENT RULE

The business judgment rule has evolved from over a hundred years of legal precedents in which the actions of board members have been challenged by shareholders and other corporations. However, it is only in the past four or five decades that an overall framework has been developed and is now embodied loosely in the business judgment rule.

There are numerous repositories for the standards that are outlined in the business judgment rule. First, the state of Delaware, where over 40% of New York Stock Exchange companies are listed, has well-developed case law surrounding the fiduciary responsibilities of directors. Thus, Delaware case law serves as a backdrop for much of the corporate litigation in the United States. Second, each state has developed its own set of corporate statutes that govern the behavior of directors. Third, the Model Business Corporation Act was established to form a general framework for the business judgment rule that can be used by states in formulating their own standards. Fourth, the *Principles of Corporate Governance: Analysis and Recommendations* was created by the American Law Institute to help analyze the business judgment rule and establish a further framework for directors' duties.

[A] The Model Business Corporation Act

The Model Business Corporation Act (MBCA) and the Revised Model Business Corporation Act (RMBCA) are documents that have attempted to codify the business judgment rule. The Acts are the work of two legal organizations, the Committee on Corporate Laws of the Section of Business Law and the American Law Institute. The Acts attempt to put in place a framework for states to follow in modeling their own business corporation statutes.

As 50% of Fortune 500 companies are incorporated in Delaware, this state has the most developed corporate law. The MBCA and RMBCA provide up-to-date guidelines that mimic in many respects the case law and precedents that have evolved in Delaware. Many states have already adopted the MBCA and/or RMBCA.

The MBCA and RMBCA articulate the elements of the business judgment rule and allow the opportunity for continued evolution of the standards as they develop over time. Section 8.30(a) of the Model Business Corporation Act provides the following concise summation of a director's duties:

A director shall discharge his duties as a director, including his duties as a member of a committee:

(1)   in good faith;
(2)   with the care of an ordinarily prudent person in a like position would exercise under similar circumstances; and
(3)   in a manner he reasonably believes to be in the best interests of the corporation.[1]

The revised version, adopted in 1998, restated the above duties in the following way:

(a)   Each member of the board of directors, when discharging the duties of a director, shall act: (1) in good faith, and (2) in a manner the director reasonably believes to be in the best interests of the corporation.
(b)   The members of the board of directors or a committee of the board, when becoming informed in connection with their decision-making function or devoting attention to their oversight function, shall discharge their duties with the care that a person in a like position would reasonably believe appropriate under similar circumstances.[2]

---

1. Model Business Corporation Act 8.30.
2. Revised Model Business Corporation Act 8.30.

In addition to framing the duties of directors, the Model Business Corporation Act outlines the liability faced by directors in the face of a breach of duties. The language reads as follows:

(a)   A director shall not be liable to the corporation or its shareholders for any decision to take or not to take action, or any failure to taken any action, as a director, unless the party asserting liability in a proceeding establishes that:

    (2)   the challenged conduct consisted or was the result of:
      (i)   action not in good faith; or
      (ii)   a decision

        (A)   which the director did not reasonably believe to be in the best interests of the corporation, or
        (B)   as to which the director was not informed to an extent the director reasonably believed appropriate in the circumstances; or

      (iii)   a lack of objectivity due to the director's familial, financial or business relationship with, or lack of independence due to the director's domination or control by, another person having a material interest in the challenged conduct:

        (A)   which relationship or which domination or control could reasonably be expected to have affected the director's judgment respecting the challenged conduct in a manner adverse to the corporation, and
        (B)   after a reasonable expectation to such effect has been established, the director shall not have established that the challenged conduct was reasonably believed by the director to be in the best interests of the corporation; or

      (iv)   a sustained failure of the director to be informed about the business and affairs of the corporation, or other material failure of the director to discharge the oversight function; or
      (v)   receipt of a financial benefit to which the director was not entitled or any other breach of the director's duties to deal fairly with the corporation and its shareholders that is actionable under applicable law.[3]

---

3. *Id.* at 8.31.

[B]   The Principles of Corporate Governance: Analysis and Recommendations

The Principles of Corporate Governance: Analysis and Recommendations was developed in the 1980s and set forth in 1993. It was the work of the American Law Institute, and was created to "serve the analytical and descriptive functions of the [American Law] Institute's restatements of the law and also to propose desirable changes in prevailing legal norms or corporate practice when such judgments can be made."[4]

Much like the Model Business Corporation Act, the Principles of Corporate Governance has promulgated the duties of directors and set forth a definition of the business judgment rule.

Section 4.01(a) of the Principles of Corporate Governance states the overall duties of directors:

> A director or officer has a duty to the corporation to perform the director's or officer's functions in good faith, in a manner that he or she reasonably believes to be in the best interests of the corporation, and with the care that an ordinarily prudent person would reasonably be expected to exercise in a like position and under similar circumstances.[5]

Sections 4.01 (c) and (d) dictate the business judgment rule and who must establish adherence to the business judgment rule:

(c)   A director or officer who makes a business judgment in good faith fulfills his duty if the director or officer:

    (1)   is not interested in the subject of the business judgment;

    (2)   is informed with respect to the subject of the business judgment to the extent the director or officer reasonably believes to be appropriate under the circumstances; and

    (3)   rationally believes that the business judgment is in the best interests of the corporation.

(d)   A person challenging the conduct of a director or officer under this Section has the burden of proving a breach of the duty of care, including the inapplicability of the provision as to the fulfillment of duty under subsection ... (c), and in a damage action, the burden of proving that the breach was the legal cause of the damage suffered by the corporation.[6]

---

4. Principles of Corporate Governance and Structure: Restatement and Recommendations, Introductory Note at xxi.

5. Principles of Corporate Governance: Analysis and Recommendations, 4.01(a) (1994).

6. *Id.* at 4.01(c), (d).

§ 21.03   GENERAL PRINCIPLES OF THE BUSINESS JUDGMENT RULE AND DUTIES OF DIRECTORS

The business judgment rule relies on broad principles that translate into directors' duties. First, for the business judgment rule to apply, there must be an actual business decision. The business judgment rule will only protect a director to the extent there is a business decision, or in cases where a lack of decision was a conscious effort on the part of the directors.

Second, for the board to receive the protection of the business judgment rule, the directors may not be tainted by the personal interests or potential financial benefit of any one director. A director may have a personal interest in a transaction and make a personal decision regarding his/her own shares in a company, but must disregard this interest when acting on behalf of the corporation and all shareholders. In addition, the board may have protection of the business judgment rule if a majority of the disinterested directors approved the action that is under question.

Outside of these two preconditions that outline the circumstances under which directors are protected by the business judgment rule, there are three basic duties that a director has to shareholders in the context of merger and acquisition transactions: (1) a duty of care, (2) a duty of loyalty, and (3) to act in good faith.

[A]   The Duty of Care

A director's duty of care entails an obligation to act on behalf of shareholders by making well-informed decisions. The director should only make a decision after due consideration of all facts and circumstances material to a situation. Directors must "inform themselves of all information reasonably available to them and relevant to their decision to recommend" the merger.[7] The Model Business Corporation Act proscribes how a director must perform his duties "in a manner he reasonably believes to be in the best interests of the corporation, and with such care as an ordinary person in like position would use under similar circumstances."[8] The courts will look to both the process that was undertaken and the decision itself in evaluating whether directors acted with due care.

A board may rely on the advice and counsel of third parties such as lawyers and investment bankers in making a decision; however, implicit in this acknowledgement is that the board may not "delegate" the responsibility of being informed or decision making to a third party. Under Delaware law, the board of directors is permitted to rely upon certain information and materials:

> A member of the board of directors, or a member of any committee designated by the board of directors, shall, in the performance of such member's duties, be fully protected in relying in good faith upon the records of the corporation and upon such information, opinions, reports or

---

7. *Smith v. Van Gorkom*, 488 A.2d 893.
8. Business Model Corporation Act 8.30.

statements presented to the corporation by any of the corporation's officers or employees, or committees of the board of directors, or by any other person as to matters the member reasonably believes are within such other person's professional or expert competence and who has been selected with reasonable care by or on behalf of the corporation.[9]

For a plaintiff to determine that a board has breached its duty of care, it must demonstrate that the board has been grossly negligent, the standard for gross negligence having been articulated in the *Smith v. Van Gorkom* case, among others.[10]

[1]   *Smith v. Van Gorkom*

In *Smith v. Van Gorkom*, the court found that Trans Union Corporation, and in particular, the CEO of the company, were personally liable for recommending and approving a cash merger proposal. The court found that the board was not entitled to the protection of the business judgment rule, even though the company had obtained a substantial premium over the current stock price for shareholders.

In 1980, Trans Union Corporation was considering its alternatives to utilizing excess equity capital and considered four options, a stock repurchase, dividend increases, a major acquisition program, or combinations of the above. In addition, the chief financial officer of the company had considered the feasibility of a leveraged buyout (LBO). Initially, the CEO of Trans Union, Jerome W. Van Gorkom, rejected the idea of a LBO because of a potential conflict of interest of management; however, he indicated his willingness to sell his own 75,00 shares at $55 per share. Nevertheless, Van Gorkom subsequently approached Jay Pritzker, a well-known corporate takeover specialist, regarding a possible cash-out merger of Trans Union at $55 per share.

Pritzker agreed to acquire the company in a leveraged buyout at $55 per share on the condition that he could acquire 1,750,000 shares of Trans Union stock at the market price such that in the event a third party bidder surfaced and won the company away from him, he could sell this stock to the higher bidder. Ultimately, the number of shares that Trans Union agreed to sell to Pritzker was reduced to 1,000,000, and the purchase price was at $38 per share, 75 cents higher than the current stock price.

Van Gorkom informed very few members of his management team or board of the LBO transaction prior to scheduling a board meeting to vote on the transaction. In addition, he had not included the company's investment banker in the discussions. At the September 20 board meeting, he did not disclose to the board how the $55 per share offer had been derived, or the fact that he had initiated the negotiations. Van Gorkom rationalized the offer to the board by maintaining that there would be a 90-day period during which the company could receive third party offers, thus allowing the "free market" to judge the $55 per share price.

---

9. Delaware Code, 141(e).
10. *Smith v. Van Gorkom*, 488 A.2d 858, 873.

In the meantime, the chief financial officer of the company had prepared an analysis suggesting a range of LBO prices that could be paid for the company as high as $65 per share.

The board approved the offer on the condition that Trans Union reserve the right to accept any better offer that was made during the 90-day market test period and that Trans Union could share proprietary information with third party bidders. The merger agreement was subsequently executed and the company issued a press release announcing the transaction. Subsequent to the press release going out, the company was faced with widespread disenchantment among the management team who threatened resignation. In an attempt to preserve the transaction, Van Gorkom and Pritzker agreed to modify the terms of the deal. The company then issued a further press release stating that Pritzker had obtained the financing for the transaction, that he had acquired 1 million shares of the company at $38 per share, that the company was free to solicit other offers, and that if other offers were not received by February 1, 1981, then Trans Union's shareholders would vote on the Pritzker proposal.

It was not, however, until after the press release went out that the amendments to the merger agreement were completed reflecting the board's two conditions. As might be expected, the amendments differed from what the board's wishes were. The amendments placed significant constraints on Trans Union's ability to seek third party offers.

The company and its bankers were only able to find one other strategic buyer, General Electric Credit Corporation, who ultimately backed away from the transaction. It was unwilling to make an offer unless Trans Union first rescinded its merger agreement with the Pritzker group.

Litigation resulting from the transaction commenced on December 19. At issue was whether Trans Union's board of directors acted with due care in making their decision to support the Pritzker proposal. In other words, did the board of directors make an informed decision? The Delaware Supreme Court found that the directors did not "reach an informed business judgment on September 20, 1980 in voting to 'sell' the company for $55 per share pursuant to the Pritzker cash-out merger proposal," and consequently evidenced a lack of due care to shareholders.[11]

Their rationale was as follows:

1. The directors did not adequately inform themselves of Van Gorkom's role in forcing the sale and in establishing the $55 price;

2. The directors were uninformed as to the intrinsic value of the company;

3. The directors were "grossly negligent" in approving the sale with only two hours of consideration;

4. The board's efforts to amend the merger agreement were ineffectual; and

5. The board did not deal with candor with shareholders and reveal all material facts.

---

11. *Smith v. Van Gorkom*, 488 A.2d 858.

The court also maintained that the mere fact there was a significant premium in the transaction was not sufficient reason to recommend the transaction, as it did not assess the fairness of the price that was offered. The court found that the amendments to the merger agreement did not give the company the freedom to solicit third party bids and therefore the 90-day market test was not a true condition to the transaction. An additional finding was that the significant premium and the board's belief were not sufficient evidence of the board's collective experience and sophistication, and therefore they found that the gross negligence of the board outweighed their experience.

The significance of the *Smith v. Van Gorkom* case is that it underscores the duty of care a director has in acting on behalf of stockholders. It requires that directors be well-informed of all material facts and circumstances and take them into consideration in making a decision. Importantly, it did not focus on the premium that shareholders received in the transaction — arguably a very attractive one — but rather on the process the board went through in coming up with its decision.

[B] The Duty of Loyalty

A director's duty of loyalty to a corporation and its shareholders is a responsibility to act in their best interests. The courts have generally maintained a broad view of the definition of a director's duty of loyalty, and require that a plaintiff demonstrate that the board engaged in "self-dealing" in the transaction in order to show a breach of loyalty. For example, if a director is seen to be on both sides of a transaction or personally benefit from the deal, it does not immediately establish that the director has breached his duty of loyalty; rather, it exposes the director to meet the "entire fairness test" and the burden of proof shifts to the board member.

A shareholder seeking to establish a breach of loyalty must establish sufficient facts to overcome the presumption that the directors were disinterested in the transaction and acted in good faith. If successful, the burden of proof shifts to the directors who must then establish that the action was approved by the disinterested directors or that the action was fair to shareholders. The courts will focus not only on the process employed by the directors, but also on the substance of the decision itself.

[C] Act in Good Faith

A fundamental presumption of the business judgment rule is that directors will act in good faith when discharging their duties to shareholders, and the business judgment rule will not provide protection to directors who act in bad faith. There have been numerous attempts to define "good faith" in the case law; likewise, the case law has served up many definitions of "bad faith." Good faith has been thought of as synonymous with a director's duty of loyalty, in that good faith presumes that a director has the best interests of the company and its shareholders in mind when taking an action.

Bad faith, on the other hand, has been given multiple definitions, ranging from a conscious act of wrongdoing,[12] to a decision that is outside the bounds of reasonable judgment.[13]

§ 21.04   BUSINESS JUDGMENT UNDER ENHANCED SCRUTINY

In situations where the board adopts a defensive posture in response to a takeover threat or it approves a transaction involving a sale of control or the breakup of a company, the board is subject to "enhanced scrutiny" rather than merely the traditional business judgment rule. The courts will look at both the process the board went through in coming up with its decision, as well as the action it took. The court will also assess the reasonableness of the decision. Unlike the scrutiny of the traditional business judgment rule, under enhanced scrutiny, the board will have to prove that their process and conduct satisfy standards known as the "Unocal Standard."

[A]   The Unocal Standard

The Unocal standard arose from the Delaware Supreme Court's landmark decision in 1985 in *Unocal v. Mesa Petroleum Co.*, a case surrounding the 1985 $54 per share offer for Unocal by Mesa Petroleum. It is applied in situations where directors are acting as fiduciaries where a company is subject to takeover. For the Unocal Standard to apply, it is not necessary for a company to be under a specific takeover threat; it also applies in cases where a company has taken preemptive measures to ward off unwanted takeover offers.

The Unocal Standard applies enhanced scrutiny to the actions of directors, prior to the application of the business judgment rule. A board's duty in defensive situations is enhanced because a board may act in its own interest rather than in the interest of the shareholders or the corporation. And, as such, unlike the traditional business judgment rule where there is a presumption of care, loyalty and good faith, the board must establish that it has acted reasonably and that the action taken in defense of the corporation was in proportion to the threat posed to the company.

These two ideas are embodied in the Unocal Standard, which articulates that a board of directors has a two-part responsibility that includes a reasonableness test and a proportionality test. The reasonableness test maintains that the board of directors must demonstrate that their actions were "reasonable" in relation to the danger to the corporate policies of the company. The proportionality test maintains that the board must demonstrate that the defensive action was proportionate to the magnitude of the perceived threat.

---

12. *Potter v. Pohlad*, 1996.
13. Model Business Corporation Act 8.31. Comments.

The board may satisfy its burden under the Unocal Standard by showing that it acted in good faith and had performed a reasonable investigation into the proposed threat. If the board satisfies these standards, then it is offered the protections of the business judgment rule.

[1] *Unocal v. Mesa Petroleum Co.*

In 1985, Mesa Petroleum, an entity controlled by T. Boone Pickens, announced an unwanted offer for Unocal at $54 per share. The offer was a two-tiered, front-end loaded cash offer for 64 million shares of Unocal, representing 37% of the shares outstanding. Mesa already owned 13% of the company. The remainder of the stock would be frozen-out for junk bonds. In response to the offer, Unocal offered to repurchase 50 million shares excluding the shares owned by Mesa. The $72 per share consideration was made up of notes.

In *Unocal v. Mesa Petroleum*, the question before the Delaware Supreme Court was whether the board of directors of Unocal had acted appropriately in defending itself from the Mesa Petroleum offer by undertaking a self-tender of Unocal's shares in competition with the offer from Mesa. The court noted their concern that the board of directors of Unocal acted in their self-interest in that they favored the self-tender offer over the Mesa offer, instead of simply seeking the highest value deal for shareholders. Ultimately, Unocal prevailed, with the court finding that the action was reasonable in light of the threat the company saw from Mesa Petroleum.

This having been said, the result of this case was that a board of directors must establish that its actions are in the best interests of shareholders. In addition, the Securities and Exchange Commission limited discriminatory offers like Unocal's, and they are no longer permitted under SEC Rule 13e-4.

[2] *Unitrin v. American General Corp.*

In the mid 1990s, Unitrin, Inc. repurchased its own shares to thwart a takeover bid from American General Corp. Directors of Unitrin owned 25% of the company's stock. The tender offer had the effect of concentrating the stock owned by the directors, as they did not sell into the tender offer. The result was that they could block the merger because Unitrin had a provision that precluded a merger with anyone owning greater than 15% of the stock, unless the transaction was approved by a majority of the incumbent directors or by a 75% shareholder vote. Accordingly, the directors could block the deal with American General even if they were replaced as directors, because they owned 28% of the company after the share repurchase.

In the case, *Unitrin v. American General Corp.*,[14] the Delaware Supreme Court found that the defensive measure that was taken by the directors was reasonable in relation to the threat. It was a limited self-tender offer that did not preclude a tender offer by another third party, and it was not coercive. In addition, it did not

---

14. *Unitrin, Inc. v. American General Corp.*, 651 A.2d (Del. 1995).

preclude a proxy fight and a merger was still possible. The court found that the directors had met its obligation of reasonable investigation and good faith.

What was interesting about this case from a proportionality perspective, is that the Chancery court found the self-tender to be disproportionate to the threat, while the Delaware Supreme Court found that the threat was reasonable, reaffirming that a board should be given broad latitude in the context of a takeover threat.

§ 21.05   APPLICATION OF THE ENTIRE FAIRNESS STANDARD

A level of scrutiny known as the "entire fairness standard" applies in situation where the board of directors is found to have a conflict in a transaction, stands to benefit personally from the deal, for example, in a leveraged buyout or minority squeeze-out where a controlling shareholder acquires the shares it does not own, or where a board of directors has been found to breach its duty of loyalty and/or duty of care.

In the case of the leveraged buyout, directors and management have a conflict of interest in that, the management team and directors stand to benefit at the expense of shareholders who may be bought out in the transaction. In the case of the minority squeeze-out by a controlling shareholder, the controlling corporation stands on both sides of the transaction. These conflicts make the duty of loyalty, and in certain situations, the duty of care, standards much more difficult to establish, and thus directors come under a much greater level of scrutiny. In these cases, the traditional business judgment rule is bypassed, and the transaction is subject to the entire fairness standard, in which the parties that have entered into the transaction must prove the entire fairness of the transaction.

In the case where it is alleged that the board breached its duty of loyalty or care, the plaintiff must give the courts reasonable basis for invoking the entire fairness standard, and must show not only that the transaction involved self-dealing or was a self-interested transaction, but that there is a reasonable basis for the transaction to be unfair to shareholders. The entire fairness standard is applied in these cases where directors have been found to breach their duty of care and loyalty, or in cases where a transaction that has a director with a conflict, i.e., an interested director, has not been approved by disinterested directors or disinterested shareholders. Section 1.23(a) of the Principles of Corporate Governance defines an interested director as one that is a party to the transaction, has a business, financial or familial relationship with a party to the transaction, has a monetary interest in the transaction, or is subject to controlling influence by a party to the transaction.[15]

The entire fairness standard entails determining if the transaction is "entirely" fair to stockholders. Two concepts underlie the entire fairness standard: fair dealing and fair price. In practice, for example, a controlling shareholder in a squeeze out

---

15. Principles of Corporate Governance: Analysis and Recommendations, 1.23(A) (1994).

transaction, must establish for the courts that the transaction had both a fair price and was the subject of fair dealing. Fair price was given the following definition in the *Cede & Co v. Technicolor, Inc.*, case.

A fair price does not mean the highest price financeable or the highest price that fiduciary could afford to pay. At least in the non-self-dealing context, it means a price that is one that a reasonable seller, under all the circumstances, would regard as within the range of fair value; one that such a seller could reasonably accept.[16]

In *Weinberger v. UOP*, the Delaware courts gave the following interpretation of fair dealing and fair price.

The concept of fairness has two basic aspects: fair dealing and fair price. The former embraces questions of when the transaction was timed, how it was initiated, structured, negotiated, disclosed to the directors, and how the approvals of the directors and the stockholders were obtained. The latter aspect of fairness relates to the economic and financial considerations of the proposed merger, including all relevant factors: assets, market value, earnings, future prospects, and any other elements that affect the intrinsic or inherent value of a company's stock. However, the test for fairness is not a bifurcated one as between fair dealing and price. All aspects of the issue must be examined as a whole since the question is one of entire fairness.[17]

Fair price relates to all the different factors that influence the valuation of the entity under consideration, and is not limited to the assets, market values, earnings, and future prospects of the corporation. Fair dealing relates to the overall process that the directors went through in approving the transaction, including the timing, initiation, negotiation, and structuring of the transaction.

Transactions that have been subject to the entire fairness standard include *Cede & Co. v. Technicolor, Inc.*, and *Weinberger v. UOP.*

[A] *Cede & Co. v. Technicolor, Inc.*

Technicolor, Inc. was a company engaged in a number of different businesses in the film and audio-visual industries, ranging from a professional services group to a duplicating division to a manufacturing business. In 1980, the Chairman of the company, Morton Kamerman, concerned with the lack of growth in its principal theatrical film processing business, proposed entering into the consumer film development business with a chain of One Hour Photo stores. Over the course of the next few years, the company's progress towards opening 50 stores was slow, having only opened 21 of the stores by late 1982. At that time, the board decided to close one division and seek a buyer for another. Meanwhile, the core theatrical film processing business continued to decline, and the company's financials continued to deteriorate.

---

16. *Cede & Co. v. Technicolor, Inc.*, 634 A.2d 31.
17. *Weinberger v. UOP*, 547 A.2d 701 (Del. 1993).

Ronald Perelman of MacAndrews & Forbes Group Incorporated, indicated a willingness to acquire the company at $22 per share. At this time, Kamerman retained an investment bank and outside counsel. He gave the bank instructions to prepare a fairness opinion over a short time frame, and limited their contact to himself and two other officers of Technicolor. The investment bank indicated a price of $20–$22 per share would be a feasible range of values for Kamerman to pursue. After a few rounds of meetings, Kamerman and Perelman agreed to a deal whereby MacAndrews & Forbes would acquire Technicolor for $23 per share. At the time, Kamerman had not disclosed these meetings to other board members. Prior to the board meeting three directors had no prior knowledge of the deal, while four directors had limited knowledge of the deal.

At the board meeting, a few specific terms of the deal became clear. First, a director was to receive $150,000 as a finder's fee for initiating the transaction. Second, Kamerman would have an employment agreement with MacAndrews & Forbes. Third, MacAndrews & Forbes had a lock-up option on 18% of Technicolor's shares.

Kamerman recommended the deal to the board on the basis that the transaction was preferable to the company continuing to take the risk on the One Hour Photo project. MacAndrews & Forbes commenced its tender offer in November 1982 and upon closing of the tender offer, had gained control of 81% of the company's stock. The merger of the two companies was formally completed on January 24, 1983. Cinerama, Inc. and its shareholder of record, Cede & Co., owned approximately 4.4% of the outstanding stock of Technicolor. In 1983, Cinerama challenged the Technicolor board's decision to approve the transaction, and claimed the board had breached its fiduciary duties to shareholders.

The Delaware Supreme Court found that the board of Technicolor had breached its fiduciary duty to shareholders and could be held personally liable for the breach of duty. The board had failed to inform itself adequately of the merger prior to approving the deal. The central issue in the case was whether or not the board had discharged its duty of care when it approved a transaction immediately upon presentation by the chairman who had personally negotiated the deal. While the board was able to rely on a fairness opinion presented by an investment bank, the court questioned whether the board had a reasonable basis for believing that it had obtained the best price for the company.[18]

The Delaware Supreme Court also showed that the "directors were grossly negligent in failing to reach an informed decision when they approved the merger."[19] Therefore, they held that the board's lack of due care was sufficient to eliminate the presumptions of the business judgment rule. Ultimately, the Delaware Supreme Court required the transaction to be reviewed subject to the entire fairness standard because there was no search for alternative merger partners prior to the agreement being signed with MacAndrews & Forbes, the

---

18. *Cede & Co. v. Technicolor, Inc.* 542 A.2d 369.
19. *Id.* at 366.

directors had no basis for determining if a better offer would arise after contract signing, the directors knew very little — and in some cases nothing — prior to the board meeting that approved the deal, the stock lock-up option as well as other side stock purchase agreements effectively locked up the transaction, and the board was found to have failed its Revlon duties.[20]

While the board became subject to the entire fairness standard, the Delaware Court finally determined that the board had satisfied its fiduciary duties because (1) the CEO had sought the highest price from the bidder, (2) he had sold his stock at the same price as all other shareholders, (3) the management team had refused to undertake a leveraged buyout at a higher price, (4) the board and CEO had been informed of the transaction by a leading investment bank and law firm, (5) the price paid was in excess of 100% of the company's stock price, and (6) the CEO was experienced and knowledgeable.[21]

[B] *Weinberger v. UOP*

In *Weinberger v. UOP*, Signal Companies, Inc. proposed a cash-out merger for the shares it did not own in UOP, Inc. Signal had acquired 50.5% of UOP's stock two years previously for $21 per share — the stock had traded at $14 per share prior to the offer. Signal offered $21 per share for the minority shares and agreed to have the transaction subject to the positive vote of a majority of the minority shareholders. The offer price was a 50% premium to UOP's stock price upon announcement. UOP's minority shareholders approved the transaction, with 51.9% of the minority voting in favor of the transaction. In addition to receiving a majority of the minority voting in favor of the deal, the UOP board also received a fairness opinion from its investment bankers.

The disgruntled minority shareholders filed suit claiming a lack of entire fairness. The Delaware court found a lack of fair dealing in the transaction on a number of bases. First, two Signal directors who were also UOP directors had prepared a report indicating a price up to $24 per share would be a good investment for Signal. The report had not been disclosed to the independent directors of UOP or the shareholders. This indicated a lack of fair dealing. Second, the fairness opinion provided by the investment bank had been hurriedly prepared under Signal's insistence that the transaction be approved quickly. In addition, Signal had initiated the transaction and set the process for timing. The time constraints and lack of negotiations further established the lack of fair dealing, and suggested a lack of arm's-length negotiations. Third, the court noted that UOP had not appointed a special independent committee of outside directors to negotiate the transaction on behalf of shareholders. Fourth, the court showed that while the company had obtained approval of a majority of the minority shareholders, the lack of disclosure of the report prepared by the two Signal directors rendered the vote irrelevant, as the vote was not well-informed.

---

20. *Cede & Co. v. Technicolor, Inc.*, 634 A.2d 368.
21. *Id.*

As for the matter of fair price, the Delaware Supreme Court remanded the case back to the Court of Chancery for further consideration. It concluded that shareholders were entitled to $1 per share award as a measure of compensation for the wrong done to minority shareholders.

§ 21.06 FIDUCIARY DUTIES IN THE CASE OF SALE OF CONTROL

In the context of a sale or change of control of a company, a board of directors is subject to a number of obligations that have evolved over time as precedents have been established in the courts. In general, the courts, whether in Delaware or elsewhere, have applied the business judgment rule to cases in which shareholders have challenged the actions taken by a board of directors in the context of a sale or change of control of a company. In particular, the courts have focused on situations where a company is under threat of an unwanted takeover or is in the midst of a battle for control of the company, and in situations where a negotiated transaction is challenged by a third party.

The courts have generally tried to remain quite flexible in their interpretation of various precedents, most often looking to ensure that the actions taken by the board of directors were in the best interests of shareholders. Therefore, in many circumstances, the board has not rendered certain defensive mechanisms invalid if they are perceived to be in the best interests of shareholders. Likewise, they have overturned various defensive mechanisms if they have further entrenched management or do not allow the directors to serve their fiduciary duties to shareholders.

[A] Revlon Duties

One of the more significant sets of directives to fall out of M&A case law is known as the "Revlon" duties. Two primary decision by the Delaware Supreme Court helped establish the framework for the Revlon Duties: *Paramount Communications Inc. v. QVC Network, Inc.*, and *Revlon, Inc. v. MacAndrews and Forbes Holdings*. The essential premise of the Revlon duties is that in the context of a sale of a company, the board has a duty to maximize value of the company for the benefit of the shareholders. In a sense, this is contrary to the board's day-to-day obligations, as the board is now faced with an immediate decision to maximize shareholder value rather than a long-term strategic process to deliver shareholder value. The board's responsibility shifts from preserving the corporation for long-term benefit to maximizing the value of the company in the sale to the shareholders' benefit.

[1] *Revlon, Inc. v. MacAndrews and Forbes Holdings*

One of the seminal cases that established the Revlon duties was the Delaware Supreme Court's 1986 decision in *Revlon, Inc. v. MacAndrews and Forbes Holdings*. In this case, the Delaware Supreme Court ruled on the obligations of a board of directors in the context of an offer for control of a company. The court noted that "the duty of the board ... is the maximization of the company's value at a sale for the stockholders' benefit."[22]

The transaction was initiated in mid-1985 when Pantry Pride approached Revlon regarding an acquisition at $40–$42 per share. The board initially found that the bid was inadequate, and advised shareholders to reject the offer as it began the search for a white knight. In addition, Revlon began putting in a shareholder rights plan. It ultimately found that white knight in the form of Forstmann Little & Co., the leveraged buyout firm. Revlon began negotiating with Forstmann Little, providing it with financial information that it did not provide to Pantry Pride. In addition, it did not include Pantry Pride in the negotiations. As a response, Pantry Pride increased its offer to $47.50 per share, which prompted an increase by Forstmann Little to $56 per share. The ultimate deal with Forstmann Little was at $56 per share. The Forstmann Little offer, however, was conditioned on a lock-up option and a no-shop provision, as well as Revlon agreeing to redeem the poison pill. The lock-up option gave Forstmann Little the right to purchase two of Revlon's divisions at a price substantially below the value of the businesses established by Revlon's bankers. The no-shop provision prohibited Revlon from considering any other third party bids, including the bid from Pantry Pride. There was also a $25 million cancellation fee for Forstmann. The board of Revlon accepted the offer from Forstmann Little, while Pantry Pride offered $58 per share and sued to enjoin the Forstmann transaction.

In the case, the courts were faced with two fundamental questions: whether the lock-up agreements were permitted under Delaware law, and whether the Revlon board of directors acted in the interests of shareholders. The court found that the no-shop provision and lock-up option stifled the competitiveness of the process and were detrimental to shareholder value. In this context, the court found that the board had violated its duty to shareholders. The court maintained that the board should act as a "neutral auctioneer" once the decision has been made to sell a company.

The court ruled that certain anti-takeover defenses that favored a particular bidder were invalid. The court found that these defenses served to inhibit the auction process, rather than help to maximize value for shareholders. The defenses in particular were a lock-up option and a no-shop provision. The court did not rule that lock-up options and no-shop provisions as defensive tactics were invalid; rather, it maintained that the defenses should be used to promote the auction to benefit the value gains of shareholders.

As a result of this case, the Revlon duties evolved. These duties are material in the instance where it is clear that a company is for sale or the breakup of a company is unavoidable. In this situation, the board of directors has a duty to maximize shareholder value in the context of the transaction. As articulated in the court's decision, if a sale or breakup of a corporation becomes "inevitable," the board's duty changes "from the preservation of the corporation as a corporate entity to the maximization of the company's value at a sale for the stockholder's

---

22. *Revlon, Inc. v. MacAndrews and Forbes Holdings, Inc.*, 506 A.2d 182.

benefit."[23] Specifically, the Revlon case established that the courts will not allow a board of directors to grant a lock-up option to a favored bidder that in effect cuts out other bidders from the process.

[2]   *Paramount Communications Inc. v. QVC Network, Inc.*

A second case that helped set the framework for the Revlon duties was the Delaware Supreme Court's 1994 decision in *Paramount Communications Inc. v. QVC Network, Inc.*

In late 1993, Paramount Communications Inc. and Viacom Inc. announced that they were merging. Viacom had offered $69.14 per share in cash for a controlling interest in the company, the balance of the purchase price was in Viacom stock. Soon after the deal was announced, QVC Network offered $80 per share for Paramount in a similarly structured transaction. The board of directors rejected the QVC offer maintaining that the financing of QVC's bid was too uncertain. QVC subsequently raised its offer to $90 per share, whereupon the Paramount board once again rejected it on the grounds that the bid was too conditional. During the course of the negotiations and the increased offers from QVC, Paramount's offer increased to approximately $85 per share. In the process, Paramount granted Viacom an option to acquire Paramount stock in the event Paramount rejected Viacom's offer in favor of another bidder. It also agreed to pay a termination fee if it rejected Viacom's offer. Paramount also began the process of rescinding its shareholder rights plan.

As a consequence, QVC sued Paramount and Viacom in the Delaware Chancery courts. The courts sided with QVC in that it rejected the stock lock-up option. However, it upheld the termination fee as it found the fees to be a reasonable amount to cover Viacom's expenses. The opinion by the courts in the QVC case confirmed the Revlon duties. The courts stated that "when a corporation undertakes a transaction which will cause: (a) a change in corporate control or (b) a breakup of the corporate entity, the director's obligations is to seek the best value reasonably available to the stockholders."[24]

As a result of the litigation, Paramount initiated a bidding process between the prospective purchasers that was to be decided by shareholders. Ultimately, the shareholders favored a transaction with Viacom who offered shareholder $105 per share.

§ 21.07   SUMMARY

A board of directors has a fiduciary duty to act in the best interests of shareholders, whether in the day-to-day operation of the company or in the context of a transaction. These duties are articulated by the business judgment rule that makes a presumption that directors will satisfy their fiduciary duties to shareholders. The

---

23. *Id.* at 182.
24. *Paramount Communications v. QVC Network Inc.*, 637 A.2d 48.

basic duties entail the duty of care, the duty of loyalty, and acting in good faith. For the board to receive the protection of the business judgment rule, however, there must have been an action or decision that the board has taken against which the business judgment rule can be applied. In addition, the board may not have been tainted with the personal interests of any one director. Under the business judgment rule, there is a presumption that directors act in the best interests of shareholders.

The business judgment rule has evolved from over 100 years of case law and development of state corporate law, most notably the Delaware Code, which has numerous precedents that outline the responsibilities of directors. There have been attempts to codify the business judgment rule, most notably, the Model Business Corporation Act and the Principles of Corporate Finance: Analysis and Recommendation, both of which provide a framework for the business judgment rule, yet leave the definition broad enough to allow the courts on a state-by-state basis to continue to interpret the business judgment rule based on a specific set of circumstances.

There are different levels of scrutiny placed on a board of directors depending on the form of M&A transaction, and how the directors respond to certain events. For example, in the sale or breakup of a company, the board is typically subject to the Revlon duties, a set of guidelines that essentially state that in the context of a sale, a board's fiduciary duty is to maximize the value of the company for shareholders.

A second set of standards, known as the Unocal standards, apply in the case where a board of directors is in a defensive situation because the company is under takeover threat. In this circumstance, the board has a two-part responsibility test that it must meet, including a reasonableness test and a proportionality test. In other words, the courts will question whether the response the board took in light of the takeover threat was reasonable, and whether it was proportional to the threat at hand. The most onerous scrutiny a board will face is where the courts find that the board had a conflict in rendering a decision, for example, where directors are on both sides of a transaction such as a leveraged buyout. In this type of situation, the board is subject to the entire fairness standard. When determining whether the transaction meets the entire fairness standard, it will look to both the process that the board took in making its decision — fair dealing — and the price that the board negotiated on behalf of shareholders — fair price.

While each of the different standards may apply individually to certain specific circumstances, it is not inconceivable that multiple standards may apply. Specifically, while a board may be subject to the most basic duties — due care, loyalty, and good faith, based on the board's actions in response to a transaction — they could be subject to enhanced scrutiny, and even the entire fairness standard, if the courts find the board has a personal benefit or conflict in the transaction. Based on the standards developed in the business judgment rule, the Revlon duties, Unocal Standard, and the enhanced level of scrutiny that is placed on a board in certain circumstances, there are a number of guidelines that can be proffered which can assist a board in pursuing good decision making in the context of a transaction.

First, a board should follow a fair process in approving a transaction or making a material decision that impacts shareholders. This includes being well-informed, forming an independent, outside committee to structure and negotiate a transaction, obtaining a fairness opinion that establishes the fairness in the transaction, acting reasonably in the context of a transaction, and ensuring the response to a given situation is proportionate to the perceived threat. Second, the board should act in good faith and make decisions that are absent of material conflicts of interests. If conflicts exist, steps should be taken to ensure that appropriate protections, checks and balances are put in place to allow an objective decision on behalf of shareholders.

Third, the price paid or received in the transaction should be fair. In certain circumstances, it does not necessarily have to be the highest price possible; however, the directors should ensure the price is fair to shareholders. In the context of an authorized sale of the company, the directors should seek the highest price possible.

Fourth, the board of directors, despite receiving the protections of the business judgment rule, should be aware that to the extent they are found to have breached their duties of shareholders, they will be subject to the entire fairness standard, in which case the burden is on them to prove the transaction was fair to shareholders.

Chapter 22

LEGAL ASPECTS OF MERGERS & ACQUISITIONS

§ 22.01 OVERVIEW

The business judgment rule provides a framework for how a board of directors should act in a merger or acquisition transaction. In addition to the business judgment rule, there are other rules, regulations and disclosure requirements that are designed to protect corporations and shareholders in the context of a transaction and ensure that transactions are conducted in an appropriate manner. The primary framework surrounding the legal and disclosure requirements of mergers and acquisitions is articulated by the Securities and Exchange Commission in the Securities Act of 1933 and the Securities Exchange Act of 1934.

[A] The Securities and Exchange Commission

The Securities and Exchange Commission (SEC) is an entity whose mission is to "protect investors and maintain the integrity of the securities markets."[1] The SEC was established in 1934 to oversee two securities acts that were put in place to protect investors — the Securities Act of 1933 (1933 Act) and the Securities Exchange Act of 1934 (1934 Exchange Act).

Leading up to the enactment of these Acts, the country had been through significant turmoil and loss of investor confidence as a result of the post-war investment boom of the 1920s and the subsequent stock market crash of 1929. Up until this time, Congress had been reluctant to implement any federal regulation of securities. However, with the stock market crash, the subsequent run on banks, and the ensuing depression, the securities industry was primed for reform. Investors had lost confidence in the securities markets, and Congress was motivated to restore its credibility.

Through the efforts of Congress, the 1933 Act and 1934 Exchange Act were passed. The laws were designed to bring structure and oversight to the capital markets in an effort to restore investor confidence. In essence, the Acts protect investors by forcing companies offering securities for public sale to make appropriate disclosures regarding their businesses, the securities to be sold, and the pertinent risks to potential investors. In addition, the Acts force brokers, dealers, and exchanges to treat investors fairly.

In 1934, Congress established the Securities and Exchange Commission to enforce the rules and regulations set forth in the 1933 Act and the 1934 Exchange Act. Today, the SEC is seen as an entity that protects investors, whether large financial institutions or private individuals. The SEC ensures that investors have access to basic information regarding a company prior to making an investment in it. It requires disclosure of all material, relevant information such that investors may make an informed investment decision. The SEC is concerned with enforcing the securities laws of the United States, promoting disclosure of information to investors, protecting investors who participate in the securities markets, and monitoring behavior of the organizations that interact with investors, such as broker-dealers and exchanges.

---

1. Securities and Exchange Commission.

[B]   The Securities Act of 1933

The Securities Act of 1933 requires companies to disclose to investors financial and other pertinent information for securities that are being offered for sale. In addition, the 1933 Act prohibits "deceit, misrepresentations, and other fraud in the sale of securities." As a result of these two premises, the 1933 Act is also sometimes referred to as the "truth in securities" laws.

Underlying the 1933 Act is the registration of securities and the concomitant disclosure of information to investors. The information allows investors to make educated, informed decisions with respect to investing in a company's securities. Of noted importance, is that the SEC requires the disclosure of information, it does not guarantee the accuracy of the information. Therefore, investors may have significant claims against a company if it determines that information was inaccurate or incomplete.

The registration of securities applies in general to all companies that offer securities to the public. However, there are a number of exceptions to the rule that allow companies to avoid registration. In particular, offerings that are limited in size and/or are private offerings limited to a small number of private investors or institutions are exempt from registration. In addition, intra-state offerings and the securities of municipal, state and federal governments are exempt from registration.

Even with exempt offerings, there are strict rules in place designed to ensure that the investors purchasing securities are informed, sophisticated investors. In general, through the registration of securities, companies must provide basic facts on the company, its securities and the risks of an investment to investors.

Information required in the registration forms includes:

- A description of company, its business and assets
- A description of the securities that are for sale
- Information on the management of the company
- Significant financial information
- The use of proceeds of the sales of securities.

The registration documents are publicly available to all investors free of charge, and may be found through numerous sources, including the SEC itself.

[C]   The Securities Exchange Act of 1934

The Securities Exchange Act of 1934 oversees the trading of securities once they have been registered. It also regulates exchanges and broker-dealers. All corporations are required to register with the SEC once its assets and shareholders reach a specified level. All broker-dealers and exchanges must register with the SEC as well.

With respect to mergers and acquisitions, the 1934 Exchange Act has three primary functions: it governs the disclosure of materials used to solicit shareholder votes in annual meetings or in special meetings for the election of directors or other corporate action; it requires disclosure of information by any party seeking to acquire greater than 5% of a company's securities by direct purchase or tender offer; and it prohibits fraudulent activities in connection with the offer, purchase, or sale of securities. Outside of these three functions, there are numerous tangential rules, regulations and disclosure requirement that pertain to mergers and acquisitions.

[D]   The Williams Act of 1968

Up until the late 1960s, tender offers were largely unregulated. Until this time, tender offers had not been frequently used as a means for acquisition. In the 1960s, tender offers became more prevalent. While the 1933 Act as well as the 1934 Exchange Act required disclosure of information regarding securities, there was little regulation or disclosure in cash tender offer situations. Consequently, cash tender offers became ripe for abuse as a takeover tactic.

In 1968, The Williams Act was passed as an amendment to the 1934 Exchange Act. The Williams Act added a number of new provisions that regulated tender offers, required substantial disclosure in takeover situations, and allowed investors to make informed decisions in a transaction. In essence, The Williams Act protected shareholders from abusive tactics that were inherent in cash tender offers. As a result of the Williams Act, five new subsections were added to the 1934 Exchange Act.

Section 13(d) of the 1934 Exchange Act requires that any purchaser acquiring greater than 5% of a target company's securities disclose itself and its intentions to the target and shareholders through the filing of a Schedule 13D form with the SEC. Schedule 13D must be filed within ten days of the purchase, and copies of the form must got to the target and to all the exchanges where the target's stock is traded. Schedule 13D must disclose some basic information, including, the identity of the acquirer, the sources of financing, and the purpose of the acquisition.

Section 13(d) was enacted to alert a company and its shareholders to the possibility of a takeover threat. The disclosure must take place even if there is no tender offer. In other words, once a purchaser reaches the 5% threshold, regardless of whether it is in conjunction with a tender offer or not, it must file Schedule 13D.

Section 14(d) of the 1934 Exchange Act requires disclosure of information in tender offers in which the acquirer would obtain more than 5% of the target company's securities in the tender offer. The disclosure must be made on Schedule 14D-1 and must include the intentions of the acquirer and its plans for the target, as well as any past relationships or agreements between the acquirer and the target. Recently, Schedule 14D-1 was simplified with Schedule TO, Tender Offer Statement, that must be filed in all tender offer situations, whether by a third party, an affiliate of the issuer, or the issuer itself. Schedule TO must be delivered to the target firm and any competitive bidders.

Section 14(d) also specifies the timing and procedures for a tender offer. In general, Section 14(d) requires that a tender offer remain open for at least 20 business days, and that the tender offer period must be extended if there is a modification in the terms of the tender offer. In addition, Section 14(d) dictates how shares are to be accepted in a tender offer and what withdrawal rights tendering shareholders have.

Section 14(e) prohibits "misrepresentation, nondisclosure, or any fraudulent, deceptive, or manipulative acts or practices in connection with a tender offer."[2]

Section 14(f) requires substantial disclosure any time a change in share ownership results in the change or replacement in a board of directors without shareholder approval.

Section 13(e) regulates the purchase of an issuer's stock by the issuer or an affiliate of the issuer in a going private transaction.

The remainder of this chapter looks at the principal forms of mergers and acquisitions in the context of the legal and disclosure framework set forth by the SEC. It also reviews the framework surrounding the regulation of mergers and acquisitions from an antitrust perspective.

§ 22.02   TENDER OFFERS

There are several ways to acquire significant amounts of stock in a public company, including, open-market purchases, targeted block purchases, and tender offers. Open-market purchases can be made simply by acquiring stock of the target company in the open market at the then current market price. There are limitations on a company's ability to buy significant amounts of the target's stock without it knowing. First, once the acquirer has purchased greater than 5% of the target's stock, it must file a Schedule 13D form with the SEC in order to acknowledge the fact it acquired the stock and to disclose its intentions with respect to the stock. Second, certain states, such as Delaware, have statutes that prevent acquirers from incrementally increasing their ownership without first seeking the approval of the target company's board of directors (control share acquisition statutes). In addition, states such as Delaware, also have other statutes such as the business combination statute and fair price statute, which place constraints on an acquirer's ability to pursue this approach as an effective means to taking over a company.

The second approach is to acquire a large percentage of the company in a targeted block purchase. Like the open-market purchase, there are certain limitations on the acquirer's ability to take over a company by purchasing a large block or series of large blocks. These limitations include the disclosures required by the SEC once the acquirer reaches a certain threshold, as wells as the various state statutes that govern business combinations.

Tender offers are the most effective means for an acquirer to take over a company on a cash basis. A tender offer is a transaction where an offer is made directly to the shareholders of a company. In a tender offer, the acquirer offers to purchase some or all of their stock at a certain price and under certain terms and conditions.

---

2. Securities and Exchange Commission.

There are two principal types of tender offers: an offer for all of the shares of a company's stock, and an offer for part, but not all, of a company's stock. In a tender offer, it is typical for the offer to be conditioned upon a minimum number of shares being tendered in the transaction.

A tender offer can be conducted by a third party acquirer for the target's shares, a party affiliated with the target, or by the target itself. A third party tender offer would be used, for example, in a case where a company acquires an unrelated company in a cash transaction. An example of an affiliated tender offer is in a minority squeeze-out transaction, where a public parent tenders for the public stock it does not own in a subsidiary business. Two common examples of a self-tender offer are a share repurchase, where a company tenders for a specified number of shares in order to adjust its capital structure or use up excess cash, and a going private transaction where a public company tenders for its own stock.

Tender offers have a number of benefits as outlined in Exhibit 22-1.

Tender offers are subject to Section 14(d), which outlines the procedures for commencing a tender offer. In order to commence a tender offer, the bidder must file Schedule TO with the SEC, publish an advertisement regarding the tender offer, and mail the tender offer materials to shareholders.

The target company must respond to the tender offer by filing a form 14D-9 within ten business days of the commencement of the offer. In the 14D-9, the target must indicate whether it recommends acceptance or rejection of the offer. The target may also take no position on the offer, yet even in this case, it must state

---

Exhibit 22-1
Advantages and Disadvantages of Tender Offers

Advantages	*Disadvantages*
• *Speed:* Quick way to acquire control of a public company. Tender offers are usually open for 20 business days. By obtaining at least 90% of a company in a tender offer, it is possible to close the transaction using a short form merger.	• *Fully Financed:* By their nature, tender offers are cash transactions, and therefore must be fully-financed.
• *Highly Effective:* Tender offers present a definitive proposal to shareholders that is financed, conveying a commitment to completing the transaction.	• *Risk of Third Party Intervention:* Tender offers are directed at shareholders. In addition, the offer must remain open for 20 business days. Further, the disclosure requirements are significant. These facts may afford a third party acquirer the ability to prepare a bid that is more attractive for shareholders, resulting in a bidding war for the company.
• *Usually No Board Approval Required:* A tender offer is directed at shareholders directly and therefore usually does not involve board approval.	
• *Fast Anti-Trust Review:* Review under a tender offer is usually faster than that under a long-form merger.	

its reasons why. The target must file the 14D-9 with the SEC and must also submit copies of the filing to each of the exchanges where its stock is traded.

A tender offer must remain open for a minimum of 20 business days. During this period, it must accept all shares that are validly tendered; however, it may not actually purchase the tendered shares until after the tender offer has expired. The bidder may extend the offer if it feels like it needs more time to secure additional shares. In addition, it must extend the tender offer period if it changes the terms of the offer.

Shareholders are able to withdraw their shares anytime during the tender offer period as long as the tender offer is still open. The bidder must accept shares tendered on a pro rata basis. In other words, all shares tendered during the tender offer period must be accepted on a pro rata basis. The implication from this is that in the case of partial tender offers, the bidder must acquire the pro rata portion of shares tendered based on the entire offer period. If the tender offer period is extended, the proration period is extended along with it, such that shareholders who tender their shares later in the tender offer process are included in the proration.

It is possible for a bidder to place certain conditions on a tender offer, for example, the meeting of antitrust approval. In addition, a bidder may make a tender offer subject to the receipt of a minimum number of shares. However, waiver of a minimum condition near or at the end of a tender offer is considered a material change in the offer and requires an extension of the tender offer period for at least five business days, but possibly as many as ten business days.

[A] Schedule TO

Schedule TO, Tender Offer Statement, must be filed in the case of tender offers, and applies to third party tender offers subject to Rule 14d-1, issuer tender offers subject to Rule 13e-4, going private transactions subject to Rule 13e-3, and to amendments to Schedule 13D under Rule 13d-2.

Schedule TO requires the disclosure of the following information as outlined in Exhibit 22-2.

Exhibit 22-2
Schedule TO Disclosure Requirements[3]

Item	Summary Description
1. Summary Term Sheet	The summary term sheet must briefly describe the material terms of the proposed transaction, in sufficient detail to allow shareholders to understand the "features" and "significance" of the transaction.
	(Continued)

---

3. Securities and Exchange Commission.

Exhibit 22-2
(*Continued*)

Item	*Summary Description*
2. Subject Company Information	The subject company information must include the name and address of the target company as well as its telephone number and place of principal offices. The information should state the title and number of shares of equity securities outstanding of the most recent date. The principal market in which the securities are traded as well as the high and low sales prices for each quarter of the past two years should be stated.
3. Identity and Background of Filing Person	For third party and issuer tender offers, Item 3 must include the name and address of each filing person, and if the filing person is an affiliate of the target company, the nature of relationship. For a third party tender offer, the information should also include the business and background of the entities, if the filing person is "not a natural person," or the business and background of the filing person if it is a "natural person."
4. Terms of the Transaction	For third party and issuer tender offers, the terms of the transaction should include the material terms for both tender offers and mergers or similar transactions. Material information to be included for tender offers includes, among other things, the total number and class of securities sought in the offer; the type and amount of consideration to be offered; and the scheduled expiration date. For mergers and similar transactions, the material information that should be provided includes, among other things, a brief description of the transaction, the consideration to be offered, the reasons for engaging in the transaction, and the vote required for approval. For an issuer tender offer, the information should also include a statement as to whether any securities are to be purchased from any officer, director or affiliate of the subject company.
5. Past Contacts, Transactions, Negotiations, and Agreements	For a third party tender offer, the information should disclose any transaction between the filing person and the subject company, any of its affiliates or any executive officer, director or other natural person affiliate in the past two years. The information should also disclose any significant corporate events, negotiations, transaction, or material contracts during the prior two years regarding any merger, consolidation, acquisition, tender offer, election of the subject company's directors, or the sale or transfer of a material

(*Continued*)

Exhibit 22-2
(*Continued*)

Item	Summary Description
	amount of assets of the subject company. For issuer tender offers, Item 5 requires disclosure of any agreements involving the subject company's securities.
6. Purposes of the Transaction and Plans or Proposals	Third party tender offers require disclosure of the purpose of the transaction, and any plans that would result in (i) an extraordinary transaction, (ii) a material purchase, sale or transfer of assets; (iii) a material change in the dividend rate or policy, indebtedness, or capitalization of the company; (iv) a material change in the present board of directors or management; (v) a material change in the corporate structure of business; (vi) any class of equity securities to be delisted from an exchange or cease to be quoted; and (vii) any class of equity securities becoming eligible for termination of registration. Issuer tender offers require disclosure of the purpose of the transaction, the use of the securities acquired, any plans that would result in (i) an extraordinary transaction; (ii) a material purchase, sale, or transfer of assets; (iii) a material change in the dividend rate or policy, indebtedness or capitalization of the company; (iv) a material change in the present board of directors or management; (v) a material change in the corporate structure of business; (vi) any class of equity securities to be delisted from an exchange or cease to be quoted; (vii) any class of equity securities becoming eligible for termination of registration; (viii) the suspension of any obligation to file reports under Section 15(d); (ix) the acquisition or disposition of any additional securities; and (x) any changes in the charter, bylaws or other governing instruments of the company.
7. Source and Amounts of Funds and Other Considerations	The source and amount of funds for the transaction should be disclosed, along with any material financing conditions, and if any of the funds for the transaction are to be borrowed.
8. Interest in Securities of the Subject Company	This item should disclose the number and percentage of securities that are owned by each filing person, natural, and non-natural. In addition, all transactions in the subject securities during the past 60 days should be disclosed and described.
9. Persons/Assets Retained, Employed, Compensated or Used	Item 9 requires that all persons that are directly or indirectly employed, retained, or to be compensated to to make solicitations or recommendations be disclosed.

(*Continued*)

Exhibit 22-2
(*Continued*)

Item	Summary Description
10. Financial Statements	The schedule should disclose audited financial statements for the two most recent fiscal years. In addition, the document should provide unaudited balance sheets, comparative year-to-date income statements and related earnings per share data, and statements of cash flows. The ratio of earnings to fixed charges for the two most recent fiscal years and the interim periods should be stated. Pro forma information should be included that discloses the effect of the transaction on the company's balance sheet, income statement, earnings per share and ratio of earnings to fixed charges. The company's book value per share should be disclosed. Summary information of the above should be provided as well.
11. Exhibits	Numerous exhibits should be filed along with the schedule including, (i) tender offer materials, solicitation or recommendations, going private disclosure documents, prospectuses; (ii) any loan agreements; (iii) other documents that related to agreements, arrangements or understandings; (iv) any instructions, forms or other materials used in a solicitation or recommendation; and (v) any written opinion pertaining to the tax consequences of the transaction.
12. Information Required by Schedule 13E-3	If Schedule TO is combined with Schedule 13E-3, the additional information required by Schedule 13E-3 that is not covered by Schedule TO should be set forth.
13. Additional Information	The additional information includes an agreement, regulatory requirements and legal proceedings, as well as any other material information.

[B]   Regulation 14D

Regulation 14D pertains to any tender offer by an affiliate of the issuer or a third party and governs the filing, disclosure, and dissemination of information in tender offers commenced by a person other than the issuer. Following are some of the more significant provisions of Regulation 14D.

- A tender offer is deemed to have commenced at 12:01 a.m. on the date on which the bidder first publishes, sends, or gives the tender offer material to security holders. Specifically, the tender offer material must include the means for the security holder to tender their shares. In addition, the bidder will have filed Schedule TO with the SEC no later than the date of the communication to shareholders, and the bidder must have delivered to the target company the communications related to the transaction.

- A bidder may not tender for the shares of a company unless it has filed a Schedule TO with the SEC as soon as practicable on the date of the commencement of the tender offer, and delivered copies to the target company and to any other bidders that have filed Schedule TO. The bidder must also inform by telephone and send copies of Schedule TO to each exchange where the target company's securities are listed or quoted.

- The bidder must also promptly file any amendments to Schedule TO and then file a final amendment to the schedule that reports the final results of the tender offer.

- The bidder must publish, send, or give disclosure of the tender offer as soon as practicable on the date of commencement of the tender offer. For cash tender offers and exempt securities offers, the bidder must publish a long-form publication in a newspaper. If the tender offer is not a going private transaction, the bidder may publish the tender offer in summary form and mail the tender offer materials to security holders who request the material. For tender offers where the consideration is securities registered under the Securities and Exchange Act of 1933, a registration statement must be filed.

[1] Rule 14d-9 and Schedule 14D-9

If the third party uses solicitations or recommendations of third parties, it must file a Schedule 14D-9, which is governed by Rule 14D-9. Schedule 14D-9 requires disclosure of the person making the solicitation or recommendation and the relationships between that party and the party making the offer. In addition, the schedule requires disclosure of a transaction in the target's stock within the prior 60 days.

Schedule 14D-9 requires disclosure of the following items, as shown in Exhibit 22-3.

[2] Rule 14d-10

Rule 14d-10 is designed to ensure that all shareholders receive equal treatment in a tender offer. The rule mandates that a tender offer is open to all security holders of the class of securities that is subject to the tender offer (the "all holders" rule), and the consideration that is paid to any security holder is the highest consideration paid to any other security holder during the tender offer (the "best price" rule). Therefore, if during the tender offer, the bidder increase the consideration that is offered to shareholders, the increased consideration must be paid to all tendering shareholders, irrespective of whether they have previously tendered their shares or not.

Exhibit 22-3
Schedule 14D-9 Disclosure Requirements[4]

1. Subject Company Information	The subject company information must include the name and address of the target company as well as its telephone number and place of principal offices. The information should state the title and number of shares of equity securities outstanding of the most recent date. The principal market in which the securities are traded as well as the high and low sales prices for each quarter of the past two years should be stated. If the subject company pays dividends, the frequency and amount of dividends paid during the past two years should be stated. If the subject company has had and underwritten public offering for cash by the filing person during the past three years, the date of the offering, amount of securities offered, offering price per share, and aggregate proceeds received should be disclosed. If the filing person has purchased any of the subject's securities in the past two years, the amount of the securities purchased, the range of prices paid, and the average purchase price for each quarter during that period should be stated.
2. Identity and Background of Filing Person	Item 3 must include the name and address of each filing person, and if the filing person is an affiliate of the target company, the nature of relationship. The information should include the business and background of the entities, if the filing person is "not a natural person," or the business and background of the filing person if it is a "natural person."
3. Past Contracts, Transactions, Negotiations, and Agreements	The information should disclose any transaction between the filing person and the subject company, any of its affiliates or any executive officer, director, or other natural person affiliate in the past two years. The information should also disclose any significant corporate events, negotiations, transaction, or material contracts during the prior two years regarding any merger, consolidation, acquisition, tender offer, election of the subject company's directors, or the sale or transfer of a material amount of assets of the subject company. Finally, Item 5 requires disclosure of any agreements involving the subject company's securities.
4. The Solicitation Recommendation	If the filing person or any executive officer, director, affiliate, or subsidiary intends to tender, sell, or hold the securities of the subject company, it should be disclosed. If there are recommendations of others,

(Continued)

---

4. Securities and Exchange Commission.

Exhibit 22-3
(*Continued*)

---

	those recommendations and the reasons for them should be disclosed.
5. Persons/Assets Retained, Employed, Compensated or Used	Item 14 requires that all persons that are directly or indirectly employed, retained or to be compensated to make solicitations or recommendations be disclosed. All employees, officers or corporate assets that are to be used by the filing person in connection with the transaction should be disclosed.
6. Interest in Securities of the Subject Company	This item should disclose the number and percentage of securities that are owned by each filing person, natural, and non-natural. In addition, all transactions in the subject securities during the past 60 days should be disclosed and described.
7. Purposes of the Transaction and Plans or Proposals	Item 6 requires disclosure of the purpose of the transaction, the use of the securities acquired, and any plans that would result in (i) an extraordinary transaction, (ii) a material purchase, sale or transfer of assets; (iii) a material change in the dividend rate or policy, indebtedness, or capitalization of the company, (iv) a material change in the present board of directors or management; (v) a material change in the corporate structure of business; (vi) any class of equity securities to be delisted from an exchange or cease to be quoted; (vii) any class of equity securities becoming eligible for termination of registration; (viii) the suspension of any obligation to file reports under Section 15(d); (ix) the acquisition or disposition of any additional securities in the company, and (x) any changes in the company's charter, by-laws, or governing instruments.
8. Additional Information	The additional information includes any other material information.
9. Exhibits	Numerous exhibits should be filed along with the schedule including, (i) tender offer materials, solicitation or recommendations, going private disclosure documents, prospectuses; (ii) any loan agreements; (iii) reports, opinions, or appraisals; (iv) other documents that related to agreements, arrangements or understandings; (v) detailed statement of the unaffiliated shareholders' appraisal rights and the procedures for exercising the rights; (vi) any instructions, forms, or other materials used in a solicitation or recommendation; and (vii) any written opinion pertaining to the tax consequences of the transaction.

[C] Regulation 14E

Regulation 14E pertains to all tender offers and governs the procedures and prohibitions of certain tender offer practices. Some of the material provisions of Regulation 14E are as follows:

- The tender offer must remain open for no less than 20 business days from the date the tender offer is first published or sent to security holders;

- If there is an increase or decrease in the percentage of the class of securities being sought, or the consideration offered, the tender offer must remain open for at least ten days from the time the notice of the increase or decrease is given to security holders;

- The person making the tender offer must promptly pay for the securities or return the securities deposited after the termination or withdrawal of a tender offer;

- The length of the tender offer may not be extended without issuing a notice of the extension; and,

- Within ten days of the commencement of the tender offer, the subject company must publish or send to security holders a statement disclosing whether the company recommends acceptance or rejection of the bidder's tender offer, expresses no opinion as to the tender offer, or is unable to take a position with respect to the tender offer.

[D] Tender Offers by Affiliates and Issuers

[1] Rule 13e-4

Rule 13e-4, Tender Offers by Issuers, governs tender offers by issuers, and outlines the filing, dissemination, and disclosure requirements for cash tender offers or exchange offers that are made by the issuer for its own securities. Per the SEC, an issuer tender offer refers to a tender offer for, or a request or invitation for tenders of, any class of equity security, made by the issuer of such class of equity security or by an affiliate of such issuer. Rule 13e-4 applies not just to going private transactions, by also in cases that are irrespective of the intent to go private.

Rule 13e-4 requires that the issuer or the affiliate making the tender offer file with the SEC, Schedule TO, Tender Offer Statement, all written communications by the issuer or affiliate relating to the issuer tender offer, any amendments Schedule TO, and the final amendment to Schedule TO reporting the results of the issuer tender offer.

The issuer or affiliate making the tender offer must disclose a summary term sheet for the transaction, as well as the other information in Schedule TO, except Item 12. If there are any material changes in the information previously disclosed, the changes must be promptly disclosed to security holders.

The information to be disclosed should be disseminated to security holders in the following ways. If the consideration in the issuer tender offer is exclusively cash and/or securities exempt from registration, then the information is disseminated by (i) long-form publication in a newspaper or newspapers on the date of commencement of the tender offer; (ii) mailing or furnishing a statement containing the information to each security holder, by contacting each participant on the most recent security position listing of any clearing agency who represents the security holders, by furnishing to the participant enough copies of the information to make it available to the beneficial owners, and by agreeing to reimburse each participant for forwarding the information to beneficial owners. If the transaction is not a going private transaction, then the information can be disseminated by summary publication and by mailing or furnishing the statement and transmittal letter to any security holder who requests a copy of such.

If the tender offer consideration consists solely or partially of securities registered under the 1933 Act, a registration statement containing all the required information, a prospectus, and a letter of transmittal is delivered to shareholders.

Under Rule 13e-4, the issuer tender offer must remain open for at least 20 business days from commencement, and at least ten business days from the date of an increase or decrease in the percentage of the class of securities being sought or the consideration offered. In addition, securities that are tendered pursuant to the issuer tender offer may be withdrawn at any time during which the tender offer is open, and if not yet accepted for payment, after the expiration of 40 business days from the commencement of the tender offer.

If the issuer or affiliate tenders for less than all of the securities of a class, and a number of shares is tendered that exceeds the amount sought, the issuer or affiliate will accept and pay for those securities on a pro rata basis. Much like the requirements under Rule 13d-10, if the issuer or affiliate increases the amount of consideration to be paid pursuant to the tender offer, the issuer or affiliate shall pay the increased amount to all security holders who have tendered their shares. The issuer or affiliate making the tender offer shall either pay for the securities or return the tendered securities promptly after the termination or withdrawal of the tender offer. In addition, the issuer or affiliate may not make any purchases of securities subject to the tender offer until at least ten business days after the date of termination of the issuer tender offer.

§ 22.03 TRANSACTIONS REQUIRING SHAREHOLDER APPROVAL

[A] Regulation 14A

In the event the transaction does not have enough votes to carry shareholder approval, and/or shareholder approval is required, it is governed by Regulation 14A which establishes the rules for the filing and dissemination of a proxy statement on Schedule 14A and the solicitation of proxies. The proxy statement is designed to ensure that shareholders are given the information they need to make a reasonably informed decision. It must be filed in preliminary form with the SEC at least ten days before the date definitive copies are sent to the shareholders.

The final proxy must be filed or mailed for filing with the SEC no later than the date it is first distributed to the shareholders. Copies of the proxy must be sent to each of the national exchanges where the company is listed or quoted.

In the context of Regulation 14A, a solicitation of proxies includes "any request for a proxy whether or not accompanied by or included in a form of proxy; any request to execute or not to execute, or to evoke, a proxy; or the furnishing of a form of proxy or other communication to security holders under circumstances reasonably calculated to result in the procurement, withholding or revocation of a proxy."[5] While there are certain exceptions, Rule 14A applies to every solicitation of securities of a registered company subject to Section 12 of the Act.

[B]   Schedule 14A

The proxy must disclose the material features of the proposed merger/acquisition, a description of the businesses of the purchaser and the target, and detailed financial information on each.

Exhibit 22-4 provides an overview of the material disclosure items in the proxy statement.

Exhibit 22-4
Proxy Statement Disclosure Requirements[6]

Item	Summary Description
1. Date, Time, and Place Information	Includes the date, time, and place of the meeting of security holders and the primary address of the registrant. Also includes the date upon which the proxy statement are first sent to security holders.
2. Revocability of Proxy	Any right to revoke the proxy or limitation on the security holder's ability to exercise the proxy should be described.
3. Dissenters' Right of Appraisal	The rights, if any, of dissenting security holders should be outlined with any limitations thereon.
4. Persons Making the Solicitation	This item calls for the disclosure of the parties making the solicitation, how the solicitation is made, what the cost of the solicitation is, and who is bearing the cost of the solicitation.
5. Interest of Certain Persons in Matters to be Acted Upon	Includes the identification of persons making the solicitation that own a substantial interest, direct or indirect, in the securities of the

(Continued)

---

5. Securities and Exchange Commission.
6. *Id.*

Exhibit 22-4
(*Continued*)

Item	*Summary Description*
	registrant. Under certain conditions, disclosure should be made regarding the certain relationships between the person, its affiliates and the registrant company.
6. Voting Securities and Principal Holders Thereof	Disclose each class of securities subject to the solicitation and entitled to vote on the matters, the number of shares outstanding in each class, and the number of votes each class is entitled too. State the record date for the solicitation.
7. Authorization or Issuance of Securities Otherwise than for Exchange	If securities are to be issued or authorized to be issued except for an exchange of outstanding securities of the registrant, disclose the title and amount of securities to be issued or authorized and the purpose of the issuance.
8. Modification or Exchange of Securities	If securities of the registrant are to be modified or issued or authorized for issuance in exchange for outstanding securities of the registrant, the title of the class of the securities should be stated, an if an exchange, the basis for the exchange. The difference between the outstanding securities and the modified or new securities should be stated and the reasons for the exchange or modification should be identified.
9. Mergers, Consolidations, Acquisitions and Similar Matters	In the context of a merger or consolidation or acquisition of securities by another person, among other transaction types, numerous disclosures need to be made including: (i) summary term sheet, (ii) contact information for the principal offices, (iii) a description of the business, (iv) terms of the transaction, (v) regulatory approvals required for the transaction, (vi) any third party reports, opinions or appraisals pertaining to the transaction, (vii) any past contacts, transactions or negotiations between the parties, (viii) detailed financial information including summary financial data, pro forma financial data, and other pro forma information.
10. Voting Procedure	State the vote required for approval, and disclose the method by which the vote will be counted.

§ 22.04 TRANSACTIONS NOT REQUIRING SHAREHOLDER APPROVAL

[A] Regulation 14C

In the event the transaction does have enough votes and shareholder approval is not required, then it is governed by Regulation 14C and an information statement must be filed. An information statement must be filed if the issuer chooses not to solicit proxies. The information statement requires essentially the same information as the proxy statement. In addition, it requires an item that states that proxies are not being solicited and that security holders are asked not to send in a proxy.

§ 22.05 GOING PRIVATE TRANSACTIONS

Going private transactions are governed by the disclosure requirements of the Securities and Exchange Commission, while the matters of fairness of the transaction are governed by the corporate laws of individual states. In many states, well-established precedents make it clear that minority shareholders cannot block going private transactions, except in cases where fraud can be demonstrated. The sole and exclusive remedy for dissenting stockholders is appraisal proceedings, whereby stockholders can seek a court determination of the fair value of their shares. Shareholders that tender their shares into a transaction forego their appraisal rights. Under the concept of "fair dealing," however, there is an obligation on the part of the majority stockholder to provide full and accurate disclosure. The adequacy of disclosure is thus the subject of almost all litigation that arises in a going private transaction. Courts generally inquire into the fairness of the process pursuant to which the public shares were acquired. Thus, "procedural fairness" becomes a key focus. Certain procedural devices have been recognized by the courts as helpful in assuring procedural fairness: establishment of an independent process and the creation of an independent board or special committee to review the transaction, and receipt of a fairness opinion by an independent investment banker.

The role of the SEC is to ensure that the going private transactions provide adequate disclosure of the transaction in order to allow shareholders to make an informed decision regarding the transaction. Going private transactions are subject to a great deal more disclosure than other transactions. These requirements relate not just to the going private transaction, but also to the form of going private transaction, whether through tender offer or merger, or whether the transaction is by an affiliate or a third party. Exhibit 22-5 provides an overview of the rules and regulations as well as the filings required under each type of going private transaction.

The disclosure requirements for going private transactions are governed by Rule 13e-3 which requires detailed disclosure about the going private transaction, including:

- Whether the company believes the transaction is fair to stockholders and the basis for that belief.

Exhibit 22-5
Rules, Regulations, and Schedules for Going Private Transactions

	Rule 13e-3 Schedule 13E-3[7]	Rule 13e-4 Schedule 13E-4	Regulations				Forms & Schedules	
			14A[8]	14C	14D Schedule 14D-9	14E	Schedule TO	Schedule 13D
Issuer Tender Offer	X	X	X	X[9]	X		X	X
Third Party Tender Offer	X		X		X	X	X	X[10]
Affiliate Tender Offer	X		X		X	X		
Long-Form Merger	X		X					

- Whether the transaction is structured to require the approval of a majority of disinterested shares.

- Whether the independent directors have retained an independent representative to negotiate on behalf of the public stockholders.

- Whether the transaction was approved by a majority of disinterested directors.

- Whether the company has received any report, opinion or appraisal from an outside party related to the 13e-3 transaction.

SEC disclosure requirements are particularly strict about disclosure of third party valuations that have been prepared within the last two years. In essence, the SEC seeks to force the party seeking to go private to disclose all information that might be relevant to a determination of whether the price being offered is "fair" to the stockholders.

The goal of Rule 13e-3 and the companion Schedule 13E-3 is to provide enough information to public shareholders that they can make an informed decision over whether the board of directors, management, and/or the controlling shareholder are performing their fiduciary obligations to public shareholders in the

---

7. Any transaction that qualifies as a going private transaction must comply with Rule 13e-3.

8. Any transaction that seeks or requires shareholder approval is subject to Regulation 14A and must file and disseminate a proxy statement.

9. In the event the issuer does not solicit proxies, it must file an information statement.

10. Filed if third party acquires greater than 5% of the target.

going private transaction. The rule does not require that the board of directors establish an independent committee to review the going private transaction or other third party offers. In addition, it does not require that the board obtain a fairness opinion to support the transaction. Rather, it mandates disclosure of the process the board took in evaluating the transaction and in establishing the fairness of the price paid. This would suggest, that even though a board is not required to take the aforementioned steps, it behooves them to do so, because if they cannot establish the fairness of process and price, they may be exposed to litigation.

Some going private transactions are not subject to Rule 13e-3. These include the second step of a transaction where the going private transaction occurs within one year of a tender offer by or on behalf of a third party bidder that then becomes an affiliate of the issuer.[11] The bidder may only be exempt however if it previously made the requisite disclosures of Rule 13e-3. The rule also does not apply to situations where the stock of the minority shareholders is exchanged for stock having essentially the same rights as those exchanged.[12]

[A] Rule 13e-3

Going private transactions are governed by Rule 13e-3, Going Private Transactions, promulgated under the Securities Exchange Act of 1934. Under Rule 13e-3, a transaction qualifies as a going private transaction if it meets the following criteria:

(1) The equity securities of the target are acquired by the issuer or an affiliate of the issuer;

(2) The equity securities of the target are acquired through a tender offer by the issuer or an affiliate of the issuer; or

(3) The equity securities of the target are acquired through a proxy or consent solicitation, or the mailing of an information statement by the issuer or an affiliate of the issuer in connection with a merger, recapitalization, sale of assets to an affiliate of the issuer, or a reverse stock split in which the issuer acquires fractional shares.

In addition, the transaction will qualify as a going private transaction if, as a result of the previous criteria, the target has less than 300 shareholders remaining after the transaction, or the target is delisted from an exchange or no longer quoted on the NASDAQ.[13]

The entity engaged in a going private transaction must file Schedule 13E-3 with the SEC, including any ongoing amendments as well as the final amendment that includes the results of the going private transaction.

---

11. Exchange Act Rule 13e-3(g)(1).
12. Exchange Act Rule 13e-3(g)(2).
13. Section 12(g) or Section 15(d) of the Exchange Act of 1934.

If the going private transaction involves a solicitation of proxies subject to Regulation 14A, if there are securities to be issued in the transaction, or the going private transaction is the result of a third party tender offer, the material disclosures required of Rule 13e-3 must be combined with the proxy statement, information statement, prospectus or tender offer material sent to shareholders.

If the going private transaction involves a purchase of securities by the issuer or an affiliate, or through a vote, consent, authorization, or distribution of information statements, the issuer or affiliate must disseminate the relevant 13e-3 disclosure information no later than 20 days prior to any purchase, vote, consent or authorization, or prior to any meeting date with respect to the distribution of information statements, or prior to the earliest date on which a corporate action is taken by means of a written authorization or written consent of shareholders. However, if the purchase of securities in the going private transaction is subject to a tender offer, the disclosure information must be disseminated subject to Rule 13e-4, Tender Offers by Issuers, no later than ten business days prior to any purchase under the tender offer. This information must be disseminated to shareholders who are record holders of the securities on a date not more than 20 days prior to the dissemination of the information.

If the going private transaction is subject to a tender offer subject to Regulation 14D or Rule 13e-4, the tender offer containing the Rule 13e-3 disclosure information must be published or disseminated subject to Regulation 14D or Rule 13e-4 to shareholders.

[B] Schedule 13E-3

Rule 13e-3 requires the filing of Schedule 13E-3 in conjunction with a going private transaction. The document contains the required disclosures regarding the transaction. The schedule must be filed with the SEC at the times that correspond below to the type of going private transaction that is undertaken.

- Regulation 14A or 14C Solicitations or Information Statements: Schedule 13E-3 must be filed at the same time as the filing is made for the preliminary or definitive soliciting materials or information statement.

- Registration Statement under Securities Act of 1933: Schedule 13E-3 must be filed at the same time as the registration statement is filed.

- Tender Offer: Schedule 13E-3 must be filed as soon as practicable on the date the tender offer is published, sent, or given to shareholders.

- Purchase of Securities: Schedule 13E-3 must be filed at least 30 days prior to the purchase of any securities subject to the going private transactions, if the transaction does not involve a solicitation, information statement, registration of securities, or a tender offer.

- Series of Transactions: If the going private transaction involves a series of transactions, Schedule 13E-3 must be filed at the initiation of each of the prior transactions and then updated upon the occurrence of each subsequent transaction.

If the going private transaction involves a tender offer, then a combined statement on Schedule 13E-3 and Schedule TO may be filed.

The material information that must be disclosed in Schedule 13E-3 can be found in Exhibit 22-6.

§ 22.06   OTHER REGULATIONS AND DISCLOSURE FILINGS

[A]   Regulations 13D and 13G

Regulation 13D requires that any person, or group of persons acting together, who acquired directly or indirectly greater than 5% of the class of any equity security,[14] must file a report on Schedule 13D within ten days disclosing that acquisition with the SEC, and send a copy of the report to the company. Certain entities or persons may file a 13G in lieu of the 13D if, among other things, the person acquired the securities in the ordinary course of his business and not with the purpose of changing or influencing control in the company. At any point that there is a material change in the facts set forth in the 13D, or the intent of the party filing the 13G changes, the party must file an amendment to the original filing, in the case of the 13D, or the party becomes subject to the rules of Regulation 13D, and must file a 13D.

Exhibit 22-6
Schedule 13E-3 Disclosure Items[15]

Item	Summary Description
1. Summary Term Sheet	The summary term sheet must briefly describe the material terms of the proposed transaction, in sufficient detail to allow shareholders to understand the "features" and "significance" of the transaction.
2. Subject Company	The subject company information must include the name and address of the target company as well as its telephone number and place of principal offices. The information should state the title and number of shares

(Continued)

---

14. As per the SEC, an equity security is "any equity security of a class which is registered pursuant to section 12 of the Act, or any equity security of any insurance company which would have been required to be registered except for the exemption contained in section 12(g)(2)(G) of the Act or any equity security issued by a closed-end investment company registered under the Investment Company Act of 1940: provided, such term shall not include securities of a class of non-voting securities."

15. Securities and Exchange Commission.

Exhibit 22-6
(Continued)

Item	*Summary Description*
	of equity securities outstanding as of the most recent date. The principal market in which the securities are traded as well as the high and low sales prices for each quarter of the past two years should be stated. If the subject company pays dividends, the frequency and amount of dividends paid during the past two years should be stated. If the subject company has had an underwritten public offering for cash by the filing person during the past three years, the date of the offering, amount of securities offered, offering price per share, and aggregate proceeds received should be disclosed. If the filing person has purchased any of the subject's securities in the past two years, the amount of the securities purchased, the range of prices paid, and the average purchase price for each quarter during that period should be stated.
3. Identity and Background	Item 3 must include the name and address of each filing of person, and if the filing person is an affiliate of the target company, the nature of relationship. The information should include the business and background of the entities, if the filing person is "not a natural person," or the business and background of the filing person if it is a "natural person."
4. Terms of the Transaction	The terms of the transaction should include the material terms for both tender offers and mergers or similar transactions. Material information to be included for tender offers includes, among other things, the total number and class of securities sought in the offer; the type and amount of consideration to be offered; and the scheduled expiration date. For mergers and similar transactions, the material information that should be provided includes, among other things, a brief description of the transaction, the consideration to be offered, the reasons for engaging in the transaction, and the vote required for approval. In addition to the above information, the disclosure should include: a description of any terms of arrangements that treats any equity security holders different from other security holders; a statement of whether or not any dissenting security holders are entitled to any appraisal rights; a description of any provision granting unaffiliated security holders access to the corporate files of the filing person or to obtaining counsel or appraisal services at the expense of the filing person;

(Continued)

Exhibit 22-6
(*Continued*)

Item	Summary Description
	and, if the transaction involves the issuance of securities by the filing person for equity securities of unaffiliated shareholders, a description of whether any steps have been taken to ensure the offered securities are or will be eligible for trading.
5. Past Contracts, Transactions, Negotiations and Agreements	The information should disclose any transaction between the filing person and the subject company, any of its affiliates or any executive officer, director, or other natural person affiliate in the past two years. The information should also disclose any significant corporate events, negotiations, transaction, or material contracts during the prior two years regarding any merger, consolidation, acquisition, tender offer, election of the subject company's directors, or the sale or transfer of a material amount of assets of the subject company. Finally, Item 5 requires disclosure of any agreements involving the subject company's securities.
6. Purposes of the Transaction and Plans or Proposals	Item 6 requires disclosure of the purpose of the transaction, the use of the securities acquired, and any plans that would result in (i) an extraordinary transaction; (ii) a material purchase, sale, or transfer of assets; (iii) a material change in the dividend rate or policy, indebtedness, or capitalization of the company; (iv) a material change in the present board of directors or management; (v) a material change in the corporate structure of business; (vi) any class of equity securities to be delisted from an exchange or cease to be quoted; (vii) any class of equity securities becoming eligible for termination of registration; (viii) the suspension of any obligation to file reports under Section 15(d); (ix) the acquisition or disposition of any additional securities in the company, and (x) any changes in the company's charter, by-laws or governing instruments.
7. Purposes, Alternatives, Reasons, and Effects	The purpose of the transaction should be stated, and should include any alternatives that the subject company or affiliate considered, with the reasons for the structure of the going private transaction and the reasons for undertaking the transaction. In addition, the effects of the going private transaction on the subject company should be described.
8. Fairness of the Transaction	Item 8 requires that the filing person state whether it believes that the going private transaction is fair or unfair to unaffiliated security holders. It should

(*Continued*)

Exhibit 22-6
(*Continued*)

Item	Summary Description
	disclose if any director dissented or abstained from voting, and who that director is as well as the reasons for the dissention or abstention. In addition, the disclosure should include the material factors that were considered in determining the fairness of the transaction. It should also state whether the transaction will seek approval of at least a majority of the unaffiliated shareholders. In addition, it should state whether a representative has been retained to represent the unaffiliated shareholders. Furthermore, it should disclose whether the transaction was approved by a majority of the directors of the subject company who are not employees. Finally, if any other offers have been received, those should be disclosed, as well as the reasons for their rejections.
9. Reports, Opinions, Appraisals, and Negotiations	The item should disclose whether a report, opinion, or appraisal had been received. In addition, it should disclose the identity of the party that prepared the report, opinion, or appraisal, along with that party's qualifications, the methods that were used to select the party, and any relationship between the party during the past two years and the subject company and its affiliates. If the report, opinion or appraisal concerns the fairness of the consideration, it should be disclosed whether the subject company or affiliate determined the amount of consideration to be paid or whether the outside party recommended the amount of consideration to be paid. A summary of the report, opinion, or appraisal should be furnished.
10. Source and Amounts of Funds and Other Considerations	The source and amount of funds for the transaction should be disclosed, along with any material financing conditions, the expenses incured in the transaction, and if any of the funds for the transaction are to be borrowed.
11. Interest in Securities of the Subject Company	This item should disclose the number and percentage of securities that are owned by each filing person, natural and non-natural. In addition, all transactions in the subject's securities during the past 60 days should be disclosed and described.
12. The Solicitation or Recommendation	If the filing person or any executive officer, director, affiliate, or subsidiary intends to tender, sell, or hold the securities of the subject company, it should be disclosed. If there are recommendations of others,

(*Continued*)

Exhibit 22-6
(Continued)

Item	Summary Description
	those recommendations and the reasons for them should be disclosed.
13. Financial Statements	The schedule should disclose audited financial statements for the two most recent fiscal years. In addition, the document should provide unaudited balance sheets, comparative year-to-date income statements and related earnings per share data, and statements of cash flows. The ratio of earnings to fixed charges for the two most recent fiscal years and the interim periods should be stated. Pro forma information should be included that discloses the effect of the transaction on the company's balance sheet, income statement, earnings per share, and ratio of earnings to fixed charges. The company's book value per share should be disclosed. Summary information of the above should be provided as well.
14. Persons/Assets, Retained, Employed, Compensated, or Used	Item 14 requires that all persons that are directly or indirectly employed, retained, or to be compensated to make solicitations or recommendations be disclosed. All employees, officers, or corporate assets that are to be used by the filing person in connection with the transaction should be disclosed.
15. Additional Information	The additional information includes any other material information.
16. Exhibits	Numerous exhibits should be filed along with the schedule including, (i) tender offer materials, solicitation or recommendations, going private disclosure documents, prospectuses; (ii) any loan agreements; (iii) reports, opinions or appraisals; (iv) other documents that related to agreements, arrangements or understandings; (v) detailed statement of the unaffiliated shareholders' appraisal rights and the procedures for exercising the rights; (vi) any instructions, forms, or other materials used in a solicitation or recommendation; and (vii) any written opinion pertaining to the tax consequences of the transaction.

[B] Schedules 13D and 13G

Schedule 13D has a number of items that must be disclosed as outlined in Exhibit 22-7.

Schedule 13G includes much of the same information required in Schedule 13D, however in summary form.

Exhibit 22-7
Schedule 13D Disclosure Requirements[16]

Item	Summary Description
1. Security and Issuer	This item includes the title of the class of equities that have been acquired and the principal executive offices of the issuer.
2. Identity and Background	Item 2 requires disclosure of the name, residence, or business address and principal occupation of the person filing the statement. This information relates both to the natural person filing and the corporation, general partnership, limited partnership, syndicate or other group of persons that may be filing. In addition, the disclosure should include whether the person has been convicted of a criminal or civil proceeding in the past five years. It should also state the citizenship of the person.
3. Source and Amount of Funds or Other Consideration	This item requires the disclosure of the source and amount of funds that were used in making the acquisition. In addition, if any part of the purchase price was borrowed funds, this too must be disclosed.
4. Purpose of Transaction	The filing person must state the purpose of the acquisition of the securities of the issuer, and describe any plans with respect to the issuer. In particular, it should disclose, among other things, if it intends to acquire additional or dispose of equity securities in the issuer; if it has any plans for a corporate transaction such as a merger; if it has plans for a sale or transfer of assets of the issuer; or if it has plans for a change in the board of directors or management of the issuer.
5. Interest in Securities of the Issuer	The filing person should state the aggregate number and percentage of the class of equity securities of the issuer it owns, and detail the ownership by each person named in the filing.
6. Contracts, Arrangements, Understandings, or Relationships with Respect to Securities of the Issuer	All arrangement, contracts, understandings, or relationships between the persons named in the filing should be disclosed.
7. Material to Be Filed as Exhibits	Numerous exhibits should be filed including: copies of written agreements relating to joint acquisitions, and agreements, understandings, plans or proposals relating to the borrowing of funds for the acquisition, the acquisition of issuer control, and the transfer or voting of the securities.

---

16. Securities and Exchange Commission.

§ 22.07   ANTITRUST LAWS

Any time an acquisition or merger is announced, it comes under the scrutiny of the antitrust laws of the United States. Prior to the consummation of the transaction, it must receive approval from the Department of Justice (DOJ) and/or the Federal Trade Commission (FTC). Federal antitrust law prohibits the acquisition of stock or assets that may substantially lessen competition. In addition to the DOJ and FTC, transactions may also be scrutinized by each of the 50 states as well as private enterprise, each of which may file suit to enjoin the transaction.

Transactions between competitors — horizontal acquisitions — are most usually subject to antitrust concerns, in particular in industries that are dominated by a handful of companies. Transactions between companies and their suppliers or purchasers — non-horizontal or vertical acquisitions — are also likely to be reviewed, if as a result of the transaction, competition is reduced. In cases where the transaction is seen to lessen competition, the DOJ or FTC may seek to enjoin the transaction or cause the parties to divest certain assets or businesses to make the transaction less anti-competitive.

The laws governing the restriction of competition in mergers and acquisitions have evolved over many years, and are designed to prevent firms from entering into transactions that may limit competition. Legislation has changed over the past few decades, which of late, has resulted in less governmental intervention in transactions from an antitrust perspective.

A number of acts have been passed over the past 100 years that have evolved into the antitrust legislation of today.

[A]   The Sherman Antitrust Act

The Sherman Antitrust Act of 1890 (Sherman Act) formed the initial framework behind antitrust legislation in the United States. The Sherman Act prohibited the formation of monopolies and any contract or combination that restrained trade. Violations of these provisions were punishable by law. Under the Sherman Act, both individuals and the government may file suit to prohibit a transaction, and the courts may then choose the requisite resolution to rectify the situation, whether a simple injunction or other more serious forms of punishment including fines and imprisonment.

The Sherman Act was unusual in that it made illegal all contracts that restrained trade. It was broad enough in its mandate that most contracts could be interpreted to restrain trade, and thus could be deemed illegal. The breadth of the Sherman Act resulted in a need for further clarification, culminating in the Clayton Act.

[B]   The Clayton Act

The Clayton Act was established in 1914 to provide clarification to the Sherman Act, and in particular, to reinforce certain types of anticompetitive behavior. Specifically, the Clayton Act clarified which business acts under the Sherman Act were unfair practices and restrained trade. In particular, the Clayton act defined a number of categories of anti-competitive acts: price discrimination, the tying of contracts, the acquisition of stock in a competitor if it lessened competition, and overlapping boards of directors in competing firms.

[C]   The Federal Trade Commission Act of 1914

One of the primary drawbacks of the Clayton Act and the Sherman Act, was that there was no agency to enforce the legislation set forth in the two acts. In 1914, the Federal Trade Commission Act (FTC Act) was passed. It created the Federal Trade Commission to oversee the enforcement of antitrust legislation under the Clayton Act and the Federal Trade Commission Act. Specifically, the FTC was given the power to enforce the antitrust laws of the United States, as well as prohibit firms from engaging in anticompetitive practices.

With respect to mergers and acquisitions, the FTC Act further clarified what was deemed as an anti-competitive transaction. Specifically, the FTC Act prohibited acquisitions for stock that resulted in lessening competitions. The FTC Act also gave the FTC broader reign over the impact of transactions in various industries. It allowed the FTC to consider the impact of a transaction on multiple lines of business, not necessarily only the line of business in which the two companies participated. Further, the FTC Act allowed it to consider transactions from a geographic perspective in addition to an industry perspective. Finally, it gave the FTC broad latitude in looking at how a transaction could lessen competition.

[D]   The Celler-Kefauver Act of 1950

The Celler-Kefauver Act was drafted to close certain loopholes that had evolved as a result of the Clayton Act. While the Clayton Act gave the FTC broad discretion with respect to defining anti-competitive behavior and transactions that lessened competition, it left open a number of methods or structures around which transactions could be structured so as to bypass the antitrust regulations. For example, the Celler-Kefauver Act clarified that an acquisition of assets in a competing company was the same, in effect, as the acquisition of stock in a competing company, if the result was to lessen competition.

The Celler-Kefauver Act also continued to develop the government's thinking on antitrust legislation. For example, historically, antitrust legislation had focused on horizontal mergers. As merger and acquisition activity picked up during the middle of the century, vertical and non-horizontal acquisitions became more prevalent. The Celler-Kefauver Act established that vertical mergers that lessened competition would be subject to the same antitrust restrictions as horizontal mergers.

[E]   The Hart-Scott-Rodino Antitrust Improvements
Act of 1976

The Hart-Scott-Rodino Antitrust Improvements Act (HSR Act) was implemented in 1976 and had a material impact on the way transactions were reviewed.

The HSR Act mandates that the DOJ and FTC be given the opportunity to review transactions for antitrust considerations prior to their consummation. In general, a transaction may not close unless a specified period known as the "waiting period" has expired. Once the waiting period has expired, and the DOJ and/or FTC have not objected to the transaction, it may then close. The HSR Act was enacted to ensure that transactions did not close when there was a likelihood that it would result in a reduction in competition. It preempts the potential retroactive dismantling of a completed transaction for antitrust reasons.

[1]   Implications of the HSR Act on Mergers and Acquisitions

The HSR Act can have a significant effect on the timetable of an acquisition. Under the HSR Act, transactions over a certain size cannot be completed until certain information is supplied to the federal enforcement agencies and until the Hart-Scott-Rodino waiting period elapses.

There are two principal tests that determine whether a transaction is subject to the HSR Act requirements. These tests are: (1) the size-of-parties test and (2) the size-of-transaction test.

The size-of-parties test is met if (1) the transaction is over $200 million or (2) if the transaction is less than $200 million, the parent of one of the entities party to the transaction has at least $10 million in total assets or annual net sales and another party to the transaction has at least $100 million in total assets or annual net sales. The size-of-transaction test is met if the transaction involves the acquisition of stock and/or assets having an aggregate value in excess of $50 million. If the two tests are met, the target and acquirer must complete and file a form that provides basic information about the transaction, the companies and their lines of business.

The waiting period under the HSR Act is 30 days, except for a tender offer where it is 15 days from the filing of the information. The acquisition cannot be consummated until the expiration of the waiting period. If, prior to the expiration of waiting period, the DOJ or FTC requests further information, consummation cannot be effected until 20 days after the additional information requested has been submitted. The FTC, however, is able to grant early termination of the waiting period in cases where it is apparent that the acquisition raises no problems under the antitrust laws.

[2]   Non-HSR Concerns in Mergers and Acquisitions

In addition to the constraints on mergers and acquisitions presented by the FTC and DOJ, companies should consider possible private suits brought by individuals and other entities that are designed to enforce the antitrust laws. Of particular note, are suits brought by the targets of hostile takeovers, who use this strategy as an approach to thwarting an unwanted takeover bid. In addition to private suits and the federal regulation of antitrust laws, the attorney generals of the 50 states may challenge transactions on a state-by-state basis, when they feel that federal merger policies are not restrictive enough.

[F]   Merger Guidelines

Although the private or state enforcement of mergers and acquisitions is a possibility, the principal enforcement of the antitrust laws with respect to mergers and acquisitions is the DOJ and the FTC. The DOJ has issued merger guidelines to enable companies to better assess the likelihood that particular business combination may be challenged under the federal antitrust laws. The FTC also has issued a policy statement indicating views similar to those reflected in the DOJ guidelines.

The federal antitrust guidelines surrounding mergers and acquisitions attempts to balance the need to promote M&A as a valuable means to growing the economy yet minimize the risk that a particular transaction will limit competition. Of principal concern is a transaction's impact on the combined company's market power, which increases substantially as the number of competitors in a market diminishes.

As a result, the guidelines focus primarily on horizontal acquisitions involving direct competitors. However, vertical acquisitions are heavily scrutinized as well.

[1]   Horizontal Acquisitions

The DOJ and FTC review a number of factors in determining whether transactions between companies in the same market will lessen competition. Principally, the federal agencies look at the individual market shares of the combining companies, the resulting market share of the combined company, and the degree of market concentration post transaction. Market concentration is the distribution of market shares among competitors in the market.

Clearly, the definition of the market in which the companies operate is a real question. The federal guidelines attempt to address the issue by including in the definition of market, all the products and production facilities which are capable of exercising a constraint on market power. Once the market is defined, the guidelines attempt to measure the extent to which the transaction will increase market concentration.

The most common measure of market concentration is known as the Herfindahl-Hirschmann Index (HHI). The HHI for a given market is the sum of the squares of the market shares of all the companies in that market. For example, a market consisting of ten companies, each with a 10% share of the market, will have an HHI of 1,000. The HHI classifies degrees of concentration in terms of HHI levels. As the index increases, so does the competitive significance of the transaction.

The DOJ is unlikely to challenge an acquisition where the market's postacquisition HHI is below 1,000. In addition, the DOJ considers a market with an HHI between 1,000 and 1,800 as moderately concentrated. If the post-acquisition HHI falls within that range, the DOJ will consider challenging the transaction if it increases the HHI by more than 100 points, unless there are other factors that may indicate the transaction will not lessen competition. For example, a combination of two companies with market shares of 5% each would increase the HHI by only 50 points and is not likely to be challenged.

The DOJ considers a market with an HHI of 1,800 to be highly concentrated. If post-acquisition, the HHI is greater than 1,800 or more, the DOJ is likely to challenge the transaction if it produces an increase of 50 points in the HHI, unless there are other factors that indicate the transaction will not lessen competition.

In addition to market shares and market concentration, the federal agencies will consider other factors in its review of a transaction. First, it will consider the ease of entry into a given market. If barriers to entry are low, and companies can enter the market with little cost or little know-how, a transaction may not be subject to scrutiny even if the market has a high HHI or the transaction creates a substantial increase in the HHI. The federal agencies will also look at the changing dynamics of each industry, the financial condition of the firms party to the transaction, and any efficiencies that might result from the transaction.

[2]   Vertical Acquisitions

Horizontal transactions between competitors in a market are not the only forms of transaction that are subject to review. Acquisitions that involve suppliers or customers also may come under scrutiny for lessening competition. Significant concern has been raised regarding the anti-competitive effect of such transactions as they can limit competitors' access to suppliers or customers.

§ 22.08   SUMMARY

The legal framework behind mergers and acquisitions is quite broad. It encompasses not just the rules, regulations and disclosure requirements of tender offers, and stock-for-stock transactions that may or may not require shareholder approval, but also a myriad of other situations where the interests of corporations and their investors must be protected. The SEC guidelines are designed to force adequate disclosure of information in transactions such that investors can make well-informed decisions with respect to their investment in a company's securities, and that investors are well-informed in making a decision with respect to voting in favor of a transaction or tendering their shares into a deal.

Outside of the disclosure requirements of transactions, there are other laws that govern takeovers. For example, the antitrust laws of the United States restrict transactions that will result in lessened competition. Prior to the completion of a transaction, the waiting period under the HSR Act must have expired and the DOJ and FTC may not have requested further information on the transaction or objected to the deal.

Chapter 23

ANTI-TAKEOVER MEASURES

§ 23.01   OVERVIEW

Anti-takeover measures protect corporations and shareholders from unsolicited takeover offers that are deemed by the board of directors not to be in the best interests of shareholders. The optimal defensive program entails a number of facets: optimizing shareholder value, proactive mechanisms put in place in advance of any perceived takeover threat, and active responses to a real threat. A well-conceived program will give comfort to shareholders, the board and the market that a company is not vulnerable to opportunistic attempts to take over a company.

A board's best defense is a full stock price coupled with sound underlying performance and a strong capital structure. Satisfaction of these criteria results in shareholders that have little reason to seek a change in control, and limits the risk that a third party may find an opportunity to takeover a company. However, in many cases, a strong stock price and solid financial and operating performance is not a sufficient deterrent to takeover. In fact, strong performance can often be a catalyst for takeover. For this reason, there are legal and structural approaches that can be taken to appropriately prepare a company for an unwanted takeover threat.

Preemptive anti-takeover programs include devices that are put in place before an offer materializes, and include such defense mechanisms as charter and by-law amendments, shareholder rights plans, and certain structural modifications.

Reactive responses are those that occur when a company has been approached regarding a potential acquisition, and include both active and passive responses. Active responses can include such actions as recapitalizations and restructurings, seeking a white knight, or implementing a poison pill. The most notable passive response is to simply not respond to the offer or "just say no."

Certain devices are used to control the pricing and timing of a takeover offer. For example, a shareholder rights plan is designed to encourage a potential acquirer to talk to the board of directors prior to undertaking an offer for a company. Another device, such as a fair price provision is designed to ensure a potential acquirer is not able to easily make a two-tiered offer for a company's stock, acquiring a given percentage of the company at one price, and the remainder of the stock at a lower price.

Exhibit 23-1 provides an overview of the many different forms of anti-takeover measures that can be used preemptively or in response to an unwanted takeover threat.

Defense plans have become quite sophisticated as a result of the increase in hostile takeover activity in the 1980s. The number of contested acquisitions led to many innovated defensive strategies that today have now rendered the well protected company almost impossible to penetrate. Companies with under performing stock prices but solid cash flows, low levels of debt and saleable assets are particularly vulnerable to takeover. Astute anti-takeover measures alter the defensive profile of a company and either make the hostile acquirer think twice before launching an offer, or make the transaction financially and structurally unattractive in the event the takeover offer is successful.

Exhibit 23-1
Anti-Takeover Measures

Preemptive Measures	Responsive Measures
• Staggered board	• Acquisitions and divestitures
• Supermajority provision	• Recapitalizations or leveraged buyout
• Fair price provision	• Spin-off, split-off or tracking stock
• Shareholder rights plan	• Joint venture and limited partnerships
• Anti-greenmail provisions	• Share repurchase
• Blank check preferred stock	• Sale/leaseback
• Golden and silver parachutes	• Pac-Man Defense
• ESOPs	

§ 23.02   OVERVIEW OF DIRECTORS' FIDUCIARY DUTIES[1]

In the context of mergers and acquisitions, a board of directors has a duty to act in the best interests of shareholders. A board's duty to shareholders is driven by the business judgment rule, a doctrine that provides a framework for assessing a board's fiduciary obligations. Under the business judgment rule, a director has a duty of care and loyalty, and an obligation to act in good faith. The business judgment rule presumes that directors will act in such a manner on behalf of shareholders.

In certain circumstances, the board is subject to a higher standard than the traditional business judgment rule. In particular, in cases where directors have a financial or personal interest in a transaction and thereby have a conflict of interest, the board is subject to a greater level of scrutiny than the business judgment rule. In cases where the board has been found to have breached its duty of care or loyalty to shareholders, it becomes subject to the entire fairness standard, which means that the board must establish that the transaction was "entirely" fair to shareholders. Fairness in this context means that the price was fair and that the transaction was subject to fair dealing.

In defensive situations, the board is subject to enhanced scrutiny, meaning that the board's decisions will be judged according to a two-pronged test: a reasonableness test and a proportionate test. In other words, were the board's actions reasonable in light of the proposed threat, and was the action taken proportionate to the magnitude of the threat. These notions have been set forth in the Unocal Standard, a set of precedents arising from the 1985 *Unocal v. Mesa Petroleum Co.* case.

With the business judgment rule and its corollaries as a backdrop, it behooves the average board of directors to put in place a program of reasonable defensive measures that will not raise into question its fiduciary duties in the context of a takeover. For example, a board should consider implementing certain charter amendments, a poison pill and other structural defenses prior to the reality of a takeover proposal rather than in the face of an offer, where the boards actions may come under greater scrutiny of the enhanced test.

§ 23.03   STATE TAKEOVER STATUTES

The state in which a company is incorporated dictates the corporate governance of a company. It articulates a board's fiduciary duties to shareholders and spells out director liability and indemnification of directors. Furthermore, through the various corporate statutes, state corporate law establishes the framework for a company's legal defensive posture.

State laws are significant in the context of a takeover in that they will influence how a potential unwanted acquirer may approach a company and the likely success of a given approach. In addition the statutes afford the target the ability to respond

---

1. The business judgment rule and a board's duties are discussed in more detail in *Chapter 21: Business Judgment Rule.*

to the offer, and better control the timing of the transaction and the effectiveness of its response. Much like specific corporate defenses that a company can implement, state takeover laws are not an absolute deterrent to a takeover overture. In addition, for companies that have instituted a shareholder rights plan, state takeover laws have taken on less importance in the defensive scheme.

The primary state statutes that are discussed below include: business combination statutes, control share acquisition statutes, fair price statutes and cash out statutes.

[A] Business Combination Statutes

A business combination statute generally prevents a hostile acquirer from merging with a target company after the bidder has acquired a substantial stake in it without having obtained prior approval from the target's board. Specifically, if a bidder crosses over a defined threshold, say 10%–20%, it is prohibited from entering into a business combination with the target for a proscribed period of time unless prior to reaching the threshold, the bidder had received approval from the target's board to acquire the stock or to enter into the business combination.

Business combination statutes are arguably the most prohibitive of the state statutes that can help prevent a company from unwanted takeover. In particular, business combination statutes are significant for companies without a poison pill.

The most recognized of the business combination statutes is Section 203 of the Delaware General Corporation Law. Delaware's statute is significant in that more than 50% of the companies listed on the New York Stock Exchange are incorporated in Delaware. The Delaware statute prohibits business combinations between "interested stockholders" and the target corporation for three years after a stockholder becomes interested, unless one of the exceptions to the statute applies.[2] The statute defines an interested stockholder as one who owns at least 15% of the company's outstanding voting stock.[3] Companies incorporated in Delaware are able to opt out of Section 203 by amending their charter, however it does not become effective for a year after the amendment.

Section 203 has a number of exceptions whereby it does not apply. It does not apply in cases where the interested stockholder obtains permission from the board for the business combination or to purchase the 15% stake in the company. It also does not apply if, in crossing the 15% threshold, the bidder is able to obtain 85% of the company's voting stock. Finally, it does not apply if the business combination is approved by the board of directors and 66% of the stockholders, excluding the interested party.

Numerous other states have business combination statutes besides Delaware. The terms of the statute vary from state to state, but will typically differ in terms of the definition of interested stockholder, i.e., the threshold required to reach interested stockholder status, and the period of time the bidder is prohibited from merging with

---

2. Delaware Code, 203(a).

3. *Id.* 203(c)(5).

the target after becoming an interested stockholder. Each state may too have its own exceptions to the applicability of the business combination statute.

[B]   Control Share Acquisition Statutes

Control share acquisition statutes generally require that a bidder receive shareholder approval prior to acquiring a significant stake in a company. The benefit of a control share acquisition statute to the target company is that it potentially delays the time period during which an unwanted acquirer may purchase the company. For example, in a tender offer, the offer is open for 20 business days, while in certain states the control share acquisition statute can extend that time period for 50 days or more. Control share acquisition statutes may also have acquisition thresholds above which the bidder must obtain shareholder approval.

These statutes have mixed success in fending off unwanted suitors for a number of reasons. First, in companies that have a poison pill, the bidder must be mindful of triggering the pill if it acquires over a certain percentage of the target's stock. Additionally, in certain circumstances, the control share acquisition statute may actually work in the bidder's favor in that the board may be required to show the bidder's offer to shareholders. In addition, the statutes may force the board to hold a shareholder meeting to review the transaction, and at that meeting, the bidder may be able to implement other meaningful change to aid in its takeover of the company.

[C]   Fair Price Statutes

Fair price statutes generally state that in the event an acquirer is able to purchase a significant stake in a company, the remaining shareholders are entitled to receive a "fair price" for their shares. Fair price in this context typically means a price that is at least as high as the current market price or the highest price paid by the bidder for shares acquired previously. The fair price statute prohibits a business combination with the target company unless it has paid a fair price or received approval from the board and a supermajority vote of approval from shareholders.

[D]   Cash Out Statutes

A less well-recognized statute is the cash out statute which maintains that a stockholder acquiring over a certain percentage of a target's stock, e.g., 20%, must notify the other shareholders and they must be given the right to have their shares acquired at the highest price paid by the acquirer in the last 90 days.

§ 23.04   ASSESSING A COMPANY'S VULNERABILITY TO TAKEOVER

There are a number of elements that go into assessing a company's vulnerability to takeover. The analysis performed is no different than that performed by a potential hostile acquirer looking to launch an unsolicited takeover. You are looking for all the potential access points into a company's armament and ways a potential acquirer might influence the board or shareholders. You should look for what obstacles there may or may not be that could prevent or allow a potential acquirer to launch a successful offer. These include the following:

[A] The Current M&A Environment

During the 1980s, hostile takeover activity became quite prolific. Companies and raiders had easy access to capital and stock prices after the 1987 crash in particular were quite accommodating, making aggressive takeover behavior quite commonplace. In addition, what was once considered taboo by large, blue-blood organizations, became quite acceptable as a legitimate means of acquiring a competitor. Since the 1980s, hostile activity has slowed down, partly because of the onset of sophisticated anti-takeover legislation and corporate legal and structural defensive techniques. Nevertheless, hostile transactions continue and are now viewed as an accepted means to acquire a company.

The state of the current M&A environment will partly dictate the form of consideration that is paid in a transaction and the potential price that may be paid. When interest rates are low and the financial markets are providing access to capital, cash transactions tend to be more prevalent. However, in markets where stock price currencies are attractive, stock is commonly used as a form of consideration.

[B] Defensive Posture Analysis

A company's defensive posture is multi-faceted, and includes a review of its current stock price and valuation, an analysis of its financial and operating performance, a review of the company's shareholder profile and trading in the company's stock, and an extensive review of the company's legal and structural defenses, including its charter and by-laws, relevant state law and other defense mechanisms such as golden parachutes and the like.

[1] Financial Statement and Valuation Analysis

There are numerous financial attributes that make a company vulnerable to takeover. For example, the combination of strong cash flow, low levels of debt, saleable assets and an underperforming stock price, makes for an easy target of an unwanted takeover offer.

Does the company have any financial constraints in its loan covenants that could restrict it from pursuing various restructuring options in the face of a takeover? Does the company have any off-balance sheet assets or undervalued assets that could be used by an acquirer to finance an acquisition? Are there business lines that do not necessarily fit with the company's core strategy and which could be sold off by a potential acquirer?

[2] Stock Price Evaluation and Trading

There are two aspects to consider when looking at a company's stock. The first is the level at which the company's stock is trading compared to its historical trading range. To the extent the stock has traded down recently or has been depressed for a period of time, it may indicate that existing shareholders may be in favor of a sale of the company. It also may indicate that the company is potentially vulnerable to takeover from a stronger counterparty. This stock price analysis should also be performed in conjunction with the company's overall valuation analysis. To the extent the company is trading at a discount to its theoretical value and at a discount to its peer group, it may indicate a vulnerability to takeover.

The second consideration is the level of trading activity in the company's stock — who has been selling and who has been buying. One should question whether long-term shareholders, such as the mutual funds and other institutional shareholders, are adding to their holdings or reducing their holdings. Are there new funds that are coming in to the stock and what are the characteristics of these funds? Are they long-term investors, or do they have a reputation for acquiring stock in companies and then stimulating a takeover?

Outside of who is buying and selling, paying attention to the volume of stock price trades may give an early warning as to a potential unwanted suitor. Have there been recent block trades that could have gone into unfriendly hands? Has a potential acquirer been able to acquire stock without being noticed because of an increase in overall trading volume?

[3]   Charter and By-Laws and State Corporate/ Takeover Law

A company's charter and by-laws and its state corporate law go hand-in-hand in determining its legal defensive posture. There are numerous items that should be analyzed in this context.

Staggered Board: Does the company have a staggered board, and if not should the company put one in place such that only a portion of the board can be re-elected in any given year? The staggered board prevents an unwanted suitor from successfully launching a proxy fight and replacing a majority of the board in a single year.

Supermajority Voting Provisions: Does the company have a supermajority voting provision that calls for a supermajority of the shareholders voting in favor of a merger or for an amendment to the charter and by-laws? Some states have statutory requirements to approve a merger unless otherwise stated in the charter. For example, in Delaware, the threshold is a majority.

Fair Price Provision: Does the company have a fair price provision that requires a potential acquirer with a stake in the target to pay the remaining shareholders no less than the price that was paid in the initial purchase?

Authorized Common and Preferred Stock: Does the company have authorized but unissued common or blank check preferred stock that can be used to issue to a white knight or backstop a poison pill?

Special Meetings: The company's by-laws typically allow special meetings to be called by shareholders. Can a potential acquirer call a special meeting? What minimum number of shareholders is required to call a special meeting? Various states have different provisions for calling special meetings. For example, Delaware only allows persons authorized in the by-laws to call special meetings.

Action by Written Consent: Can shareholders act by submitting a written consent rather than at the annual meeting or a special meeting called by shareholders? One can remove the action by written consent by amending the company's charter.

Greenmail: Does the company's charter prohibit the payment of greenmail to a potential unwanted suitor who owns a stake in the company? If not, it may be wise to enact the amendment in order to remove the incentive for an acquirer to purchase a stake in the company.

State Law Considerations: While a large proportion of companies in the United States are incorporated in Delaware, there are also many companies incorporated in other states. It is prudent to review the state laws where the target company is incorporated to assess the company's vulnerability. In some instances, it may be advisable for a company to reincorporate in a different state if the current state of incorporation does not have adequate protections in place in its corporate code. Typically, reincorporating in a new state requires shareholder approval.

In many instances, a state statute may be overridden by the company's charter. For example, the number of shareholders required to vote in favor of a transaction may have one threshold in Delaware — a majority — but a different threshold in the company's charter. Delaware also has an interesting provision in Section 203 of the Delaware General Corporation Code which prohibits a merger with a 15% shareholder for three years after the acquirer has purchased the stake, unless the board of the target approves the merger or the acquisition of the 15% prior to the acquisition. It is possible for a company to opt out of Section 203.

Certain states have control share acquisition statutes which prohibit a shareholder acquiring greater than a threshold percentage of a target company from having voting rights in the company unless shareholders approve the acquisition.

[4] Structural and Other Defenses

There are a number of other defenses that are not charter amendments and do not necessarily require shareholder approval. The most of these is the poison pill or shareholder rights plan. If the company does not have one, it should consider implementing one as it does not require shareholder approval, and can be put in place fairly quickly. Other defenses to look for are special compensation plans such as golden parachutes and silver parachutes, employment agreements that call for a trigger payment to be paid to executives, in the former case, and employees, in the latter case, in the event a potential acquirer purchases over a certain threshold of a target company or is able to gain control of the company.

Structurally, a company may wish to examine all of its business lines. Does it have business lines that are not central to its strategy and could be sold off by a potential suitor to finance the acquisition? Does it have one core business that overrides the other business lines and is particularly attractive to potential suitors? Does it have undervalued assets that can be monetized?

Other structural impediments to a company defending itself adequately are its loan covenants, leases and other agreements that may restrict the company's flexibility in assuming additional debt, selling businesses or restructuring the company. These should be reviewed and modified accordingly.

There are other not-so-obvious defenses that a company can look to for protection in the event of an unwanted takeover offer. First, the company may operate in a regulated industry or one where antitrust considerations are paramount. There have been various cases in the past where a company has fought a takeover on these grounds.

[5]   Shareholder Profile

A very important indicator of a company's defensive position is the composition of its shareholder base. An analysis of the shareholder base will reveal how much stock is in the hands of "friendly" shareholders, how much is owned by unwanted shareholders, and how much is freely traded. Typically, one might find stock in the hands of directors, management and employees. In addition, there may be stock owned by institutional investors and hedge funds, called "beneficial owners," if they own more than 5% of the company's stock. Furthermore, there is likely to be stock in the hands of public shareholders that trades quite frequently. Finally, there may be stock in the hands of an unwanted suitor.

Section 13(d) of the Williams Act requires that any shareholder acquiring more than 5% of a company's stock file a Schedule 13D even if there is no offer for the company. Schedule 13D must be filed even if no one person owns the 5%. The law requires that a group of persons acting in concert file the Schedule 13D if collectively they own more than 5%. The filing must be made within ten business days of acquiring the stock. In addition, Section 13(d)(2) requires that the filing person make an additional filing within ten days of any material change in its ownership in the company.

Schedule 13D mandates, among other things, that the filing person disclose the name and address of the firm subject of the filing. In addition, it must disclose information on the filing person and what types of securities have been acquired. It must also disclose how many shares it owns, the purpose of the transaction and the sources of funds used to finance the purchase of the stock.

Schedule 13G is filed by those investors who acquire greater than 5% of a company's stock, yet have no interest in taking control of the corporation. An additional condition for this filing is that no more than 2% of the stock can have been acquired in the past twelve months. Schedule 13G must be filed by February 14 of each year.

[6]   Possible Suitors

As important as it is to understand a company's internal defenses, its corporate state law protections, and the current M&A environment, it is also important to review who potential acquirers may be, what their appetite is for making the acquisition, and how it would be financed. You may learn a lot about a target's vulnerability simply by knowing which companies would benefit strategically from an acquisition and which companies have the financial capacity to acquire the target.

This analysis could also include current aggressive or opportunistic individuals or financial purchasers with a reputation for making hostile acquisitions.

[7] Other

Outside of assessing a company's defensive posture, the company should actively monitor the daily trading in its stock price and who is purchasing and selling its stock. Some ways to do this include actively monitoring filings with the Securities and Exchange Commission and working with the company's transfer agent. Both of these entities will be able to help the company determine who is massing a stake in the company.

Based on the outcome of this analysis, it is possible to devise a strategy for effectively shoring up a company's defenses. Recommendations could range from financial and operating strategies to enhance shareholder value, to acquisitions, mergers and restructurings in order to optimize a company's business lines, capital structure and operating performance, and legal and structural approaches to fending off an unwanted takeover offer.

§ 23.05 PROACTIVE ANTI-TAKEOVER MEASURES

Building a strong defense entails putting in place a number of mechanisms or devices that serve to thwart an unwanted takeover offer or limit the ability of a potential acquirer to come in and make a potential offer in the first place. These devices are sometimes referred to as "shark repellants."

Exhibit 23-2 provides an overview of certain shark repellants that have been used in the past.

[A] Shareholder Rights Plans

[1] Overview of Shareholder Rights Plans

A shareholder rights plan is a common anti-takeover defense mechanism that is highly effective in allowing a target company time to respond to an unwanted takeover proposal, and encourage bidders to negotiate with the company. Otherwise known as poison pills, rights plans work by causing significant dilution to the acquirer if it is successful in acquiring a given percentage of a target. In a

---

Exhibit 23-2
Illustrative Shark Repellants

Staggered Board of Directors	Special Meetings
Supermajority Provisions	Director Qualifications
Fair Price Provision	Common and Preferred Stock
Dual Capitalization	Executive Compensation
Consent Procedure	Cumulative Voting
Shareholder Rights Plans	Anti-Greenmail Amendments
Employee Compensation and ESOPs	Increase in Authorized Shares

basic poison pill, each shareholder is granted a right to acquire stock in their company at a steep discount, in the event that the acquirer is able to acquire, or announces an intention to acquire, stock in the target that if successful, would let it own over a predefined percentage of the company. Everyone except the hostile bidder may exercise the rights. For the rights to be exercised, the target must issue a significant number of new shares, thereby creating significant dilution to the acquirer.

In and of itself, a rights plan will not prevent an unsolicited takeover offer or proxy contest. It will, however, enable the target company to control the timing and process of unwanted proposals. Rights plans attempt to level the playing field between parties in takeover situations. They help a board of directors maximize shareholder value by preventing and/or seeking alternatives to a hostile or unfriendly offer that may be for a price that is too low or may not be in the best interests of the company. The mere existence of the plan is enough to encourage the would-be acquirer to talk to the target prior to making an offer.

Shareholder rights plans have become the defense of choice for corporate America. More than 2,200 companies have adopted shareholder rights plans, with more than 50% of Fortune 500 companies having adopted them. They are simple to adopt in that they do not require shareholder approval, and can be implemented by the board of directors.

Poison pills are effective in enhancing shareholder value. In most situations, companies that have poison pills in place when an offer is made result in the offer being increased substantially. From a legal perspective, the validity of poison pills has been upheld, and the board's right to use a pill to seek alternative offers or force a bidder to negotiate with the board has been supported. Pills therefore, are instrumental in protecting shareholder interests and maximizing value.

In addition to helping maximize value in the face of a takeover proposal, the adoption of a pill has a de minimis impact on the stock price of the adoptee at the time the pill is adopted, implying that shareholders accept poison pills as a legitimate defense technique.

[2] How Do Shareholder Rights Plans Work?

Most rights plans are known as "call plans," in which the holder of the right has the right to buy stock in the target — and in some cases the acquirer — under certain circumstances. Call plans work by causing the acquirer to suffer significant stockholder dilution if it is successful in acquiring a given percentage of the company on a hostile basis, or without the approval of the board of directors.

In a call plan, there are two basic types of triggers, a flip-in trigger and a flip-over trigger. In a flip-in, in the event the unwanted bidder is successful in acquiring over a certain percentage of the company, the rights holder has the right to acquire stock in the target company. In a flip-over, if the unwanted bidder is successful in acquiring over a certain percentage of the company, the rights holder has the right to acquire stock in the acquirer. Flip-over triggers usually work in tandem with a flip-in whereby, if the flip-in does not work, the flip-over will. They are used to ward off squeeze-out mergers.

The rights become triggered if the unwanted bidder is able to acquire a threshold percentage, usually between 10% and 20%, or if the hostile bidder announces its intention to acquire stock in the company that if successful would result in the would-be bidder going over the threshold percentage. If after the rights are triggered, the acquirer is successful in merging with the company, then the rights flip over, enabling the target shareholders to purchase stock in the acquirer at a steep discount.

The stock acquired in the target as a result of shareholders exercising their rights, is purchased at a price known as the exercise price, most often two to eight times the price of the company's stock when the rights plan is implemented. The rights holder may acquire stock at the exercise price usually having a value of twice the exercise price.

Once the rights have been exercised, to meet the demand for the shares to be acquired, new shares have to be issued by the target — in the case of the flip-in — and by the acquirer — in the case of the flip-over. All shareholders that are beneficiaries of the rights plan, excluding the unwanted bidder, have the right to acquire stock. In this way, the stockholder interest of the hostile acquirer is diluted dramatically, making the acquisition economically unattractive.

Prior to the earlier of the expiration of the poison pill or the exercise of the rights, the board has the ability to redeem or modify the plan. In addition, in the face of a friendly transaction, the board may approve the transaction, effectively bypassing the pill.

Ultimately, while poison pills may be effective in preventing an overtly hostile transaction, they are little match against a carefully planned and executed offer at an attractive price. Thus, when making an offer for a company with a rights plan in place, it is common to see the offer conditioned upon the board redeeming the pill.

There are a number of advantages and disadvantages of poison pills. The most significant advantages are that they are very effective in forcing hostile bidders to negotiate with the target's board and they create a level playing field among bidders, allowing the board time to formulate a response to a bid and encourage third party bidders to enter the process. The most significant disadvantages are that ultimately, rights plans will not prevent all hostile actions, and certain shareholders and the courts may view them negatively in the event they are viewed as a management entrenchment tool.

Exhibit 23-3 provides an overview of many of the pros and cons of poison pills.

[3] Implementation, Structure, and Mechanics of Shareholder Rights Plans

Rights plans follow a typical sequence of events, as outlined in Exhibit 23-4.

Step 1: Adoption

At the inception of the poison pill, the board of directors approves an issue of rights to existing shareholders. The rights are issued as a dividend distribution pursuant to a rights indenture entered into between the corporation and a trust

Exhibit 23-3
Advantages and Disadvantages of Shareholder Rights Plan

Advantages	*Disadvantages*
• Entices a hostile acquirer to negotiate with the board prior to making an offer	• Ultimately will not thwart a well-thought out acquisition plan
• Allows the board to level the playing field between bidders	• May be perceived negatively by certain shareholders and the courts as they could be viewed as a management entrenchment device
• Allows the board to make informed decisions regarding potential offers	
• Can be adopted, implemented and removed by the board of directors without shareholder approval	• May give management a false sense of security
• Effective in forcing unwanted bidders to pay a fair price for a company	
• Companies with pills receive higher acquisition premiums than those without pills	
• Prevents a hostile acquirer from acquiring a significant stake in a company without warning	
• May be implemented in advance of a takeover proposal without indicating a sale price for the company	
• Inexpensive to implement	
• No up-front adverse accounting and tax implications	

Exhibit 23-4
Overview of Shareholder Rights Plans

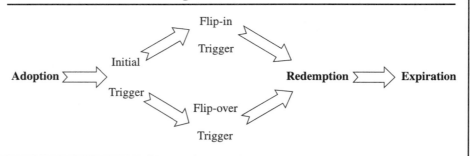

company. One right is issued per share that the shareholder owns. The issue of rights is exempt from prospectus and registration requirements.

A rights plan typically has a term of ten years, during which time, the rights may be redeemed or the pill modified unless the poison pill is triggered.

If the rights are redeemed, the redemption price is usually $0.001 to $0.05 per right.

The rights grant shareholders the right to purchase additional shares at an exercise price that is typically an estimate of the long-term trading value of the common stock. Upon the triggering event, the rights entitle holders to purchase common stock of the company—flip-in trigger—or common stock of the acquirer—flip-over—at a predetermined exercise price.

Until a triggering event occurs, the rights are represented by the common share stock certificate. The rights are initially attached to and trade with the common stock. This is known as being "stapled" to the common stock. There are no separate certificates that represent the rights. Anytime the stock trades, the rights trade along with it.

The underlying security can be either common stock or preferred stock of the target. If preferred stock, the amount of stock that can be acquired, its voting rights and other terms are such that it is equivalent to the common stock of the target. The Securities and Exchange Commission does not require that the stock to be issued be registered with the SEC upon adoption of the pill; however, once the rights are exercised, the stock does have to be registered.

The board of directors determines the exercise price. It is based on an estimate of the price the company's stock may reach over the term of the poison pill. Most exercise prices are set at roughly two to eight times the price of the company's common stock when the poison pill is adopted. The multiples used in determining the exercise price will depend on the sector within which the company operates, and can be based off precedent transactions.

The acquirer is excluded from the use of the rights so that substantial dilution of the acquirer's ownership results.

Step 2: Initial Trigger

The rights are triggered at the first sign that a bidder has made an unwanted approach. This is known as a triggering event. Typically, the trigger kicks in upon the occurrence of one of two events: (1) acquisition of a predetermined amount — usually 10% to 20% — of the company's common stock or (2) the announcement to acquire through tender or exchange offer of the threshold amount, the result of which, if successful, would give the acquirer beneficial ownership of a predetermined percentage — usually 20% to 30% — of the company's common stock.

Until a triggering event occurs, the rights only represent a right to acquire common stock at what is an uneconomic, "out-of-the-money" price. Upon a triggering event, the rights detach and become transferable apart from the company's common stock and become exercisable. At the time the rights become exercisable, the rights trade separately from the common stock. Separation of the rights is generally deemed never to have occurred if a takeover bid is unsuccessful or withdrawn.

Step 3: Flip-In Trigger

When a triggering event occurs, the rights become exercisable, or "flip-in." A flip-in trigger gives the rights holder the right to acquire, at the exercise price, common stock of the target company having a market value of some multiple, usually twice the exercise price. In addition, the rights owned by the unwanted bidder cannot be exercised.

The flip-in plan was given its name because of the ability for shareholders to flip their rights into positions in the target company. The flip-in provision works by diluting the economic interest that the acquirer would have in the target, because all shareholders other than the acquirer are able to exercise their flip-in rights.

Example Flip-In Provision. Let us look at the economic impact of a flip-in trigger provision. Assume that Company A is successful in acquiring 30% of a target company, Company B, just prior to the rights being exercised. Further assume that at the time the rights are exercised, Company A's stock price is $20 per share and it has 30 million shares outstanding. The exercise price on Company A's stock is $100 per share.

As a result of the flip-in provision, 210 million shares would be issued, diluting the acquirer's ownership in Company A from 30% to 3.75%. Initially, Company B owned 30% of Company A, or 9 million shares. After the flip-in, Company B continued to own 9 million shares out of a total of 240 million shares, thus diluting itself to 3.75%. Exhibit 23-5 illustrates the above flip-in example.

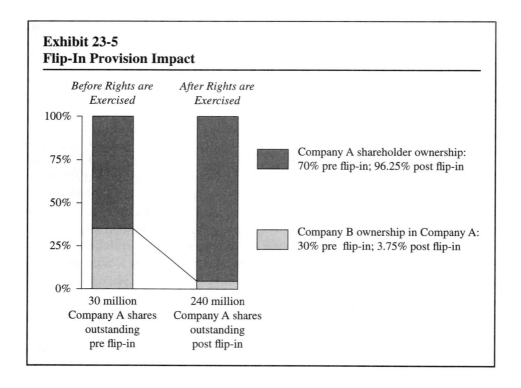

Exhibit 23-5
Flip-In Provision Impact

Before Rights are Exercised / After Rights are Exercised

Company A shareholder ownership: 70% pre flip-in; 96.25% post flip-in

Company B ownership in Company A: 30% pre flip-in; 3.75% post flip-in

30 million Company A shares outstanding pre flip-in

240 million Company A shares outstanding post flip-in

The formula for calculating the number of shares issued is as follows:

New shares issued = (Company A shares outstanding)
$\quad \times$ (% Shares not owned by acquirer)
$\quad \times$ (2× exercise price/Company A stock price)

Step 4: Flip-Over Trigger

A flip-over trigger usually initiates with an unwanted merger proposal, and kicks in, in the event the unwanted acquirer is able to merge with the target. A flip-over provides rights holders the right to purchase stock of the acquiring corporation. Each right "flips-over" into the right to acquire, at the exercise price, common stock of the acquiring corporation having a value of some multiple, generally twice the exercise price. Generally speaking, most companies with poison pills have both flip-in and flip-over provisions such that, if the flip-in provision does not work, the flip-over will.

Example Flip-Over Provision. In the case of a flip-over provision, the acquirer's ownership position is diluted because the rights holders have the ability to acquire the stock of the acquirer once the rights are exercised.

Let's assume that the acquirer's — Company B's — stock price is $15.00 per share just prior to the exercise of the rights. In addition, assume that the exercise price is $60 and the shares of the target — Company A — that Company B owns are 20%. Further, assume that Company B has 25 million shares outstanding pre flip-over.

Once the exercise of the rights has taken place, the acquirer's ownership of Company B is diluted dramatically. In this example, 48 million new acquirer shares are issued, all of which are assumed by Company A's shareholders. Exhibit 23-6 illustrates the above flip-over example.

The formula for calculating the number of share of Company B that are issued is as follows:

New Shares Issued = (Company B shares outstanding)
$\quad \times$ (% Shares not owned by acquirer)
$\quad \times$ (2× exercise price/Company B stock price)

Step 5: Redemption

Between the time that the rights are issued, and the earlier of a triggering event or the expiration of the rights plan, the rights may be redeemable, in whole but not in part, at the option of the target's board of directors. The redemption price is usually between $0.001 and $0.05 per right. In addition to being able to redeem the poison pill, the board may also have the ability to amend the plan unless one of the triggering events has occurred. The rights agreement may be amended or supplanted without the approval of any rights holders, so long as they are redeemable, and thereafter if the rights holders are not adversely affected.

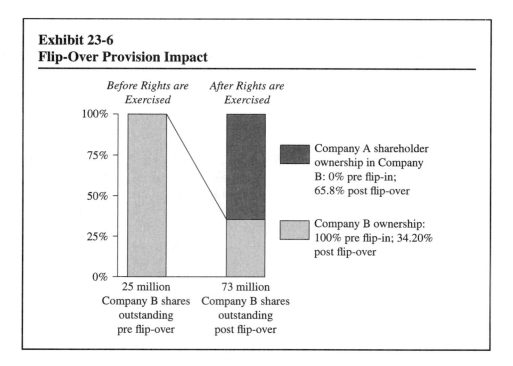

Exhibit 23-6
Flip-Over Provision Impact

During this timeframe, the rights have no voting rights and are not entitled to receive any dividends. In theory, the rights may receive dividends in the event they are exercised.

Once a pill has been triggered, the board has limited ability to redeem the rights. However, in certain cases, the rights plan will specify a period of time after the trigger event during which the board may still be able to redeem the pill. Known as the redemption period, this mechanism provides the board with flexibility to negotiate with the potential acquirer. In addition, it helps avoid potential inadvertent triggers of a poison pill by creating a delay between trigger and exercise.

Step 6: Expiration

The typical life of a shareholder rights plan is ten years. In the event the rights are not exercised or redeemed, they will expire. As a result, the rights plan terminates as well.

[4]   Accounting and Tax Treatment of Shareholder Rights Plans

When a shareholder rights plan is implemented, there is no immediate accounting impact to the company or shareholders. The rights are not included in the target company's earning per share calculation, as the possibility of the rights being exercised in the near future is remote. When the rights are issued, because the exercise price is above the market price of the stock, the rights are considered "out-of-the-money," and therefore they cannot dilute the company's earnings per share.

The actual issuance of shares upon exercise of the rights may have an impact on the accounting for a potential transaction. Historically, the share issuance would have precluded a pooling of interests transaction; however, since pooling transactions have been phased out, there is no concern here any longer. The exercise or redemption of the rights will be treated as a capital transaction.

No taxable income is recognized either by shareholders or the company when the rights are issued. Rights should be treated as a non-taxable stock dividend after issuance. Income is only recognized when the shares are sold. The redemption of rights generates a gain to the holder of the rights, which is treated as dividend income.

[5]   The View from the Courts

Given the effectiveness of poison pills, it is not surprising that they have been aggressively challenged over the years. Since the initial landmark case on rights plans, *Moran v. Household International, Inc.*,[4] there has been extensive litigation by bidders and various shareholder groups who have disputed the validity of shareholder rights plans. Despite the litigation, the courts have upheld the validity of pills and the authority of the board of directors to implement them.

More recently, litigation has shifted from the validity of pills to the duties of the board of directors in redeeming a pill in the face of a takeover offer. The scrutiny therefore has focused on the board of director's adherence to the business judgment rule and, in the face of a given takeover threat, whether or not the board acted with due care and loyalty in exercising its fiduciary duties to shareholders.

In the 1985 case, *Moran v. Household International, Inc.*, the Delaware Supreme Court upheld the pill yet left open the question of how a board responds to a takeover offer. Household International was a diversified company with a large portfolio of securities. The board felt that the company was vulnerable to a takeover offer, and in 1984, it adopted a shareholder rights plan. The plan included only a flip-over provision which was triggered upon two events: (1) the acquisition of greater than 20% of the company's stock or (2) the announcement of a tender offer for over 30% of the company.

The validity of the Household shareholder rights plan was upheld using the following arguments:

- The rights issued under the pill were authorized by Section 157 of the Delaware General Corporation Law;

- The pill did not prevent a bidder from acquiring the company in other ways; and

- The pill did not alter the shareholder's ability to vote their shares, for example, in the case of a proxy contest.

---

4. *Moran v. Household International, Inc.*, 500 A.2d 1346 (1985).

While the validity of the pill itself was upheld and the board's authority to implement the pill was established, these arguments did not necessarily address the board's decision to adopt the pill, how the pill was used and whether in the face of a takeover threat, the board used the pill appropriately to further the interests of shareholders.

In the *Moran v. Household International, Inc.* case, the courts focused on the applicability of the business judgment rule to the circumstances, concluding that the burden on the board of directors was to establish that the takeover offer posed a real threat and that the implementation of the pill was a reasonable response to the threat posed. The court found that the board had met these burdens under the business judgment rule, in that it had been well informed thereby acting with care, and that its response had been reasonable relative to the threat and therefore had discharged its duty of loyalty to shareholders.

As a result of this case, pills and the authority of the board to adopt them have been upheld consistently in the courts. However, the focus of the courts and litigation has shifted to the use of the pill as a means to further shareholder interests and whether the use of the pill by the board is consistent with the business judgment doctrine. At the conclusion of the Household case, while the court upheld the pill, it stated that the board would come under further scrutiny if and when the board had to respond to an actual takeover bid. In other words, the board would not be relieved of its duty to shareholders in the face of a real offer.

Since *Moran v. Household International, Inc.*, legal attention has focused on the circumstances under which a board should redeem a pill in the face of an offer. Generally, the courts have allowed pills to remain in effect if the board acts with care in determining if additional offers are available for shareholders. In other words, the courts have afforded the board the opportunity to seek alternatives to a potentially unfriendly offer or force the would-be bidder to negotiate with the board.

[6] Bells and Whistles

Rights plans have a number of variants, additional provisions and nuances that can make them more or less attractive to the target and acquirer.

Redemption period: Most plans call for the rights to be exercised as soon as the threshold percentage has been reached. Some plans however allow for a redemption period between the time the threshold percentage is reached and the time the rights are exercised. This period enables the board to potentially negotiate with the unwanted party, or other third parties, and possibly redeem or modify the shareholder rights plan.

Shareholder redemption: While plans may be adopted and redeemed by the board of directors, some plans enable shareholders to redeem a poison pill.

Chewable pill: One variant on the typical poison pill is that the pill may be nullified or "chewed" in the case of an all cash tender offer that is conditioned on the acquirer acquiring a majority of the target's shares. This variation was designed to appeal to the institutional investor community. All cash tender offers must remain open for 20 business days; however, a chewable pill variant mandates that the offer must remain open for a period substantially longer than that, e.g., 120 days. While this variation has appeal to certain shareholders, it may expose the company to risk by effectively putting the company in play once the offer has been made.

Dead hand pill: One of the potential downsides of a poison pill is that the board of directors may redeem the pill without shareholder approval. Consequently, in the event a hostile acquirer is able to remove the board of directors through a proxy contest, the new board may redeem the pill, thus enabling the unwanted bidder to succeed in its takeover efforts. As a result, the dead hand pill provision emerged. This provision mandates that only the continuing directors, i.e., those directors in office before the proxy contest, may redeem the pill. The net effect of this is that even though the unwanted bidder may be able to replace the board, it may not be able to remove the pill. Dead hand pill provisions have been upheld in certain states yet struck down in others.

[7]   Poison Pill Summary

Poison pills are arguably the most effective tool in a company's defense arsenal. They are simple and quick to implement, and can be enacted by a board of directors without shareholder approval. Shareholder rights plans deter third party hostile bidders from attempting to acquire a company without board approval by threatening massive dilution to the acquirer in the event its takeover bid is successful. They are not designed to make a company completely takeover proof; rather, they are designed to prevent abusive or coercive takeovers.

Rights plans are valuable in enhancing value for shareholders in the face of a takeover threat. Studies have shown that companies with poison pills receive higher takeover premiums than those without poison pills. Fundamentally, because pills help prevent unwanted bidders from making offers without board approval, they allow a board to level the playing field between bidders, seek alternatives to an unwanted offer, or encourage bidders to negotiate with the board.

The use of a shareholder rights plan will generally be upheld by the courts if it meets certain criteria. First, it should not be designed to prevent all takeovers. Second, the implementation of the pill is reasonable in response to the potential threat of takeover. Third, the board has exercised its duty of care and loyalty in implementing and utilizing the plan. Fourth, the board's use of the pill was appropriate in the face of a real takeover offer and the board was found to have discharged its duties under the business judgment doctrine.

A carefully drafted shareholder rights plan that complies with state laws and is consistent with the company's charter, is the most effective defensive device to prevent unwanted takeover offers.

[B]   Charter and By-Law Amendments

Corporate charter amendments as anti-takeover measures are fairly common. Amendments to a charter require shareholder approval, but more often than not, these amendments are voted upon favorably. Amendments to a company's by-laws, on the other hand, can be adopted without shareholder approval. No charter or by-law amendment is an absolute defense against hostile takeover, but in general, they provide a board of directors additional time to consider alternatives and develop a negotiating strategy.

[1] Staggered Board of Directors

A board of directors is elected by shareholders to oversee the day-to-day corporate governance of the company. It is responsible for hiring the CEO and overseeing the financial and strategic performance of the company. The board is ultimately accountable to shareholders for the performance of management and the company, and is also accountable for its own actions. Typically, directors are nominated and elected to one-year terms.

One approach to taking over a company is for a potential acquirer to have its own slate of directors nominated to the board and replace the existing directors of the company, the logic being that the directors friendly to the acquirer will vote in favor of a transaction and/or remove any road blocks to the transaction, such as a poison pill.

Amending the charter to provide for a staggered board is one attractive means to shoring up the defenses of a company. A staggered board will vary the terms of each of the board members such that only one or two directors may be re-elected in any given year. In this way, it is impossible for a potential acquirer to replace enough board members in a single year to affect a transaction. And, the bidder may not be interested in attempting to gain control over a multi-year period.

Typically, amending a charter to include a staggered board requires shareholder approval. In addition, the ability of a company to implement a staggered board may also be dependent on the state corporate law where the company is incorporated. A conventional staggered board is one where the board is divided into three groups, with one-third of the board members to be elected in each year. Thus, each board member is elected for a three-year term. This form of staggered board is often referred to as a "classified" board.

Staggered boards meet with some success in providing takeover protection. First, it will force a potential acquirer to think twice before launching a proxy fight to replace a board. The time and expense in replacing a majority of a board of directors over a multi-year period can be prohibitive. However, a staggered board does prevent an acquirer from launching a cash tender offer for a company and taking its offer directly to shareholders. In addition, if the acquirer is successful in obtaining control of the stock of the company, despite not having board control, it is in a good position to affect an acquisition or merger.

[2] Supermajority Provisions

Various important decisions require a shareholder vote, for example, an amendment to a company's charter or the sale of the company. Other transactions that require a shareholder vote might include a liquidation of the company or a transaction with an interested party. Typically, shareholder approval requires a majority, or 50.1%, of the shareholders voting in favor of the transaction or amendment.

A supermajority provision is an amendment to the charter that provides for a substantially higher threshold for shareholder approval. Generally, supermajority provisions range from 66% to 80%, with a few instances where supermajority thresholds have been seen as high as 95%.

In some cases, the supermajority provision is enacted with various caveats that allow the board to circumvent the higher level required for shareholder approval under certain circumstances. For example, the board may be able to sidestep the supermajority provision in the case where a merger has been approved by the board. These provisions are carefully worded to avoid situations where a potential suitor may replace the board and then bypass the supermajority provision.

It is not common for supermajority provisions to stand by themselves in a company's defensive arsenal. They are typically enacted along with other charter amendments, or after other amendments have been put in place. And, like a staggered board, a supermajority provision by itself does not prevent an acquirer from successfully making a fully financed cash tender offer for a company.

[3] Fair Price Provisions

A fair price provision is a charter amendment that requires a potential acquirer that owns stock in a company to pay the remaining shareholders at least the maximum price that was paid for the initial holdings. This provision is most effective in two-tiered offer situations where, for example, an acquirer tenders in cash for control of a company and then offers a lower price to the remaining shareholders. The idea behind this approach is to encourage shareholders to tender early in the process to receive the high price. A fair price provision, in this case, forces the bidder to pay the remaining shareholders the same price as it paid for acquiring its initial stake, thereby removing the financial incentive for launching a two-tiered offer.

A fair price provision can also be structured to ensure that shareholders receive a fair price for their stock. The price can be stated in terms of the company's stock price or in terms of its price/earnings multiple, and is usually triggered when a potential acquirer makes an offer for the company.

Fair price provisions are a deterrent to two-tiered tender offers, however, by themselves, they are not an effective anti-takeover measure, as they simply require that the bidder pay fair value for the company's stock.

[4] Blank Check Preferred Stock

Blank check preferred stock is preferred stock that is issuable in series. The terms of blank check preferred stock can be dictated by the board of directors and can be used for multiple purposes. For example, it can be used to backstop a shareholder rights plan, or it can be issued to a white knight in the face of a takeover offer. Authorizing blank check preferred stock is a charter amendment that requires shareholder approval.

[5] Increase in Authorized Shares

Similar to blank check preferred stock, a company may wish to have additional authorized but unissued shares that can be used to offer as consideration in a defensive acquisition or provide to a white knight.

[6]   Dual Capitalization

A dual capitalization company is one with two classes of stock, each class having different voting rights. Historically, companies were able to amend their charters to create the two classes of stock, where the voting control of the company was concentrated in the hands of a select group of shareholders. That class of stock might have more votes per share than the other class of stock. For example, one class of stock might have ten votes per share while the other class might have one vote per share. The low-vote class of stock might pay a dividend that is higher than the class with higher voting rights.

The Securities and Exchange Commission has prohibited companies that do not have dual capitalizations from adopting one; however, companies that historically have had dual capitalization are allowed to continue them.

[7]   Anti-Greenmail Amendments

An anti-greenmail provision prohibits a company from paying greenmail to a potential hostile bidder. Greenmail is the repurchase of a block of stock owned by an unwanted suitor at a premium. Certain variations of the blanket anti-greenmail provision allow the target company to pay greenmail if it receives shareholder approval, or it may limit the amount that can be paid to the shareholder.

[8]   Special Meetings

Most states require companies to allow shareholders to call a special meeting if a required number of shareholders demand it. This ability has given unwanted acquirers the opportunity to call special meetings in order to revoke certain anti-takeover devices, rescind poison pills or launch proxy fights. A by-law amendment is possible whereby the ability of shareholders to call a special meeting is limited. For example, the threshold required to call the meeting may be increased, or the issues that may be brought up at a special meeting may be limited. Alternatively, the amendment may simply restrict the ability to call special meetings to the board of directors.

[9]   Action by Written Consent

Action by written consent is the ability for shareholders to take an action by submitting a written action supported by shareholders rather than by submitting the proposal for approval at the shareholders meeting. This is a by-law amendment that does not require shareholder approval, only the approval of the board of directors. An amendment prohibiting shareholders from approving an action by written consent can stop a potential suitor from bypassing the scrutiny of the board.

[10]   Notice

Working in tandem with calling a special meeting and submitting proposals for approval at the meeting, the company may amend its by-laws to state that any proposals to be submitted for vote at the shareholder meeting must be submitted within a defined period of time prior to the meeting, for example, 60 or 90 days prior the meeting. The advanced notice gives the company, board and management the opportunity to formulate a response to the proposal and gives shareholders the ability to hear both points of view, i.e., that of the proposer and that of management.

[11]   Cumulative Voting

Cumulative voting is the ability for a shareholder to vote all of his/her stock for one or a handful of directors, rather than allocating the votes among the directors. In other words, the shareholder would take the number of shares it owns and multiply that by the number of directors to be elected to yield a total number of possible votes that can be cast by that shareholder. The shareholder may then cast all those votes behind one director or may split them up among the directors.

A board may consider amending its certificate of incorporation to allow for cumulative voting as it can assist management in fending off a potential suitor that has a large stake in the company.

[C]   Other Preemptive Defenses

[1]   Executive Compensation

Special compensation is often used as a way to retain employees in the face of a takeover offer. There are two principle forms of special compensation: "golden parachutes" and "silver parachutes." Neither provision typically requires shareholder approval.

The golden parachute is a form of compensation that is targeted to the corporate executive. It is highly lucrative to the manager in the event there is a change of control in the company. While on the surface, golden parachutes are not necessarily put in place as a defense mechanism, they can often serve as a minor anti-takeover tool.

In the context of a takeover, target management may often be vulnerable to losing their position. As a result, the anxiety may encourage managers to seek alternate employment during a takeover process. Golden parachutes serve to keep management interested in the transaction until the transaction has taken place, and hopefully work for a better deal on behalf of shareholders. Companies therefore adopt golden parachutes during the normal course as well as in the context of a takeover.

The typical golden parachute agreement calls for a lump-sum payment upon the voluntary or forced termination of the manager. The payment is based on the individual's existing compensation and his years of employment service. The lump sum is often a multiple of the person's annual compensation. A golden parachute's term can range from a one-year contract with automatic one-year renewals to defined fixed-term contracts.

Golden parachutes can be triggered thanks to a number of scenarios, but most typically, they are triggered when a potential acquirer purchases over a certain threshold of a target company's stock.

The second form of special compensation is the silver parachute. This is generally provided to all employees and is often a trigger payment of one times the person's annual salary or annual compensation.

[2] Structural Defenses

In addition to protection from various state corporate statutes, amendments to a company's charter and by-laws, and the implementation of a poison pill, a company can take additional action to ward off an unwanted takeover offer. These structural defenses are precautionary, and are prudent to consider regardless of the takeover threat faced by the company.

[a] Protect Crown Jewel Assets. Companies can sometimes come under attack because they have disparate lines of business or one of the company's businesses is an outlier in terms of performance. In addition, a potential acquirer may be after only one of the target's businesses, and may sell off the remaining assets to finance the acquisition of the attractive business. Protecting certain assets may be a good move for companies vulnerable to attack. One way to approach protecting the business includes turning it into a subsidiary so that if the company is attacked, the business or the other businesses can be readily sold, spun-off or taken public. In this way, the target is ready to respond appropriately to an unsolicited offer and does not have to begin this process once the takeover is in progress.

[b] Review Loan, Lease, and Other Documents for Constraints. Bank debt, public debt, leases, and other legal agreements can often contain restrictive covenants that prohibit a company from undertaking certain actions such as incurring additional debt or selling assets. It is wise to be mindful of these constraints and to attempt to minimize the number of restrictions placed on the company in order to afford it maximum flexibility in the face of a takeover.

[c] Obtain Additional Financial Capacity. In the face of a takeover, a target company may require capital to undertake a stock repurchase, recapitalization, special dividend, or defensive acquisition. It is prudent to ensure that the company has adequate room in its credit facilities or obtains sufficient additional credit capacity to have maneuverability in the face of a takeover.

[d] Implement Share Repurchase Program. Prior to the threat of takeover becoming real, a company should consider a share repurchase. A share repurchase achieves a number of objectives. First, it sends a clear signal to Wall Street that the target company sees its stock as a good investment and therefore, the share repurchase may stimulate the purchase of shares. Second, it helps to shrink the company's equity base and therefore increase earnings per share, thereby helping to increase the company's stock price. Third, it eliminates disloyal shareholders as well as those shares that may be easily acquired by a potential suitor. Share repurchases effectively help to reduce the threat of takeover by enhancing shareholder value.

One caution however, certain types of share repurchases, such as fixed-price tender offers, may signal to the market a price at which the company could be acquired, and therefore it could stimulate aggressive behavior toward the company.

[e] Issue Stock to an ESOP or Friendly Party. Employee stock ownership plans have been used for many years to create a vehicle for

employee ownership of a company's stock. There are a number of benefits to ESOPs. First, by placing the stock in the ESOP, the company can be somewhat assured that the stock is in "friendly" hands. Second, an ESOP has numerous financial benefits for the company undertaking the ESOP, most significantly, it receives a deduction for the principal and interest payments that are used to fund the ESOP.

In December 1987, Delaware passed an anti-takeover statute that provides that if a bidder acquires greater than 15% of a target's stock, it is prohibited from merging for three years unless (1) the purchaser acquires greater than 85% of the target's stock, (2) two-thirds of the shareholders—excluding the bidder—approve the transaction, or (3) the board of directors and shareholders elect to opt out of the provisions of the statute.

As many companies in the United States are incorporated in Delaware, the implications from this are that a company may establish its own ESOP as a means to thwart a takeover bid. The ESOP serves to place stock of the company in friendly hands, effectively preventing a bidder from acquiring 85% of its stock. In addition, it may eliminate the possibility that two-thirds of the shareholders approve the transaction.

ESOPs have been used effectively as a means to thwart takeover, in particular in the 1988 Polaroid-Shamrock Holdings takeover battle. In that transaction, the Polaroid ESOP borrowed approximately $285 million to fund the ESOP and acquire shares of Polaroid in the face of a takeover offer from Shamrock Holdings. The ESOP acquired new shares from Polaroid that was financed by a reduction in pay of the Polaroid employees. In addition to the ESOP, Polaroid undertook a share repurchase that ultimately resulted in the ESOP owning greater than 20% of the company's shares outstanding, and the total outstanding shares in Polaroid dropping substantially.

Ultimately, while Shamrock Holdings challenged the use of the ESOP, the courts upheld its use, making it impossible for Shamrock to complete its purchase. Shamrock subsequently dropped its takeover bid and entered into a standstill agreement with Polaroid, with Polaroid reimbursing Shamrock for some of its expenses incurred in the transaction.

While the use of ESOPs to thwart takeovers has become more commonplace, there have been restrictions placed on the use of ESOPs in the context of takeovers, most importantly, that the ESOP must have been planned prior to the takeover attempt. In the event that the ESOP is implemented as a result of the takeover, there is a fair chance that the ESOP structure could be struck down by the courts.

Another approach is to issue stock to a friendly party such that there is enough stock in the hands of that one party to block the takeover of the company by an unwanted suitor.

[f]   Make a Defensive Acquisition. One consideration for a company reviewing its defenses is to go on the offensive and acquire a competitor or shore up its market position with niche acquisitions. If these acquisitions are attractive, the market should respond favorably, making it more difficult for a potential acquirer to pose a threat.

§ 23.06   RESPONDING TO A TAKEOVER PROPOSAL

When a company is under takeover threat and has received an unsolicited acquisition proposal, it is bound to formulate some form of response to the potential acquirer. In preparing to respond, the company should be mindful of the potential outcomes of its decision-making. In addition, there are varying degrees of response that can be tailored to the specific circumstances. The company must recognize that once an offer has been made, there are certain outcomes that are almost guaranteed. First, if the company is successful in fending off the unwanted suitor, the company does have a good chance of remaining independent. Second, if the target does not have adequate defenses in place, it may be forced to restructure, sell assets or undergo a recapitalization. Third, there is the real possibility that the potential buyer is successful in its attempts, and the company is taken over, either by the unwanted suitor or by a white knight.

Regardless of the response, the board of directors should be aware of its fiduciary duties to shareholders and that the transaction will come under enhanced scrutiny by the courts. The directors will likely be scrutinized for the reasonableness and proportionality of the response as outlined under the enhanced scrutiny standard.

[A]   Passive Responses

[1]   Just Say No

At the one end of the spectrum is a response, known as the "just say no" defense, whereby the target refuses to be taken over and lets its defenses, such as a poison pill and other provisions, do their work. The just say no defense has been used on numerous occasions and can be quite effective at the early stages of a takeover game, in particular, where the offer for the company is not as high as it could be. The management team is perfectly justified in refusing to take any steps to negotiate with the potential acquirer as it can make the case that the offer is inadequate and the company can create more value for shareholders by remaining independent. This approach, however, does become harder to maintain as an offer is increased and the gap between the fair value of the company and the offer price narrows. At some point, the board is bound to take the offer to shareholders or else be concerned with having breached its duty to shareholders.

[B]   Active Responses

Under most unsolicited takeover scenarios, it is likely that the target will have a difficult time saying no to an offer. In today's environment, hostile acquirer's are quite sophisticated, and perform extensive analysis of a target's defenses prior to making an offer, and thus have a well-crafted plan that they adhere to in making the offer. Therefore, it is more likely that the target will have to undertake various active responses to counter the threat of takeover, with the objective of either gaining the maximum price for the company, restructuring the company to deliver greater value to shareholders, or reconfiguring the company to prevent the takeover and preserve certain assets.

As we have seen from earlier in the chapter, there are a number of charter and by-law amendments that can be implemented to help shore up the defenses of a company. Many of these however, are difficult to implement once a takeover offer has been launched, partly because many of them require shareholder approval, and because a lot of them are moot once the takeover offer has been launched. One alternative that has been used in the past in the midst of a takeover offer is a shareholder rights plan. This however, has been challenged in court, and therefore the use of a poison pill in the face of an offer must be thought through wisely prior to implementing.

There are a number of structural defenses that can be implemented in the midst of a takeover offer, including finding a white knight, restructuring the company or undertaking a recapitalization, forming an ESOP, fighting the transaction on antitrust grounds, issuing stock to a friendly third party, or turning the tables on the unwanted suitor and attempting to acquire it.

[1] White Knights

A white knight is a company that is friendly to the target corporation and which enters into a merger agreement with the target to prevent it from being acquired by the hostile acquirer. The white knight is approached during the takeover process and is given financial and other information on the target. The purchase price paid by the white knight would need to rival that or be superior to that of the hostile acquirer, but it is fair for the target to enter into an agreement with the white knight, such as a crown jewel lock up, to provide the white knight with an incentive to pay a higher price for the company.

[2] White Squires

A white squire defense is similar to a white knight defense. However, the primary difference is that instead of merging the entire company with a white knight, the target merely sells a significant block of stock to a friendly party who becomes a long-term shareholder in the company.

[3] Restructuring, Recapitalizations, and LBOs

Often it is feasible for a company subject to a takeover offer to use the offer as a catalyst to restructure. The company may pay a special, one-time dividend to shareholders.

It could undertake a complete leveraged recapitalization of the company. Under certain circumstances, the company could undertake a leveraged buyout, although a LBO is difficult to execute in the face of a fully financed strategic offer. The company could also undertake a spin-off, split-off, or sale of select assets and change the entire configuration of the company. The purpose of each of these alternatives is to deliver value to shareholders while at the same time preventing the unwanted suitor from getting its hands on the company.

[4] ESOPs

ESOPs have been used as a preemptive measures to thwart a takeover, and in certain circumstances, an ESOP can be put in place in the face of a takeover offer.

It should be noted however, that there is a reasonable chance that the ESOP may be struck down by the courts if implemented at the latter stages of a takeover. The optimal time to put an ESOP in place is prior to the receipt of any offer.

[5]   Antitrust Considerations

In certain industries, the merger of two companies, whether in a hostile or friendly transaction, may create antitrust concerns. One avenue for the board under takeover threat to explore is the possibility of fighting the acquisition or merger on antitrust grounds.

[6]   Pac-Man Defense

The Pac-Man defense is one where the company subject to the takeover offer turns the tables on the acquirer and makes an offer to acquire it. This can lead to quite an interesting battle, as the shareholders of each company must decide their preference — to be acquired at a premium, or acquire someone else for a premium in hopes that the combined company can create greater value down the road.

§ 23.07   SUMMARY

Takeover defense is a complicated art and sophisticated science. It revolves around the interplay between state takeover statutes in the target company's state of incorporation, the target's charter and by-laws, and other structural impediments the target has in place. In addition, a company's vulnerability to takeover will depend on its current valuation, the strength or weakness of its balance sheet and operating performance, the availability of undervalued or hidden assets that can be sold, and importantly, whether or not the company has a poison pill in place.

Various state statutes in many states provide basic protections for a company in the form of business combination statutes, control share acquisition statutes, fair price statutes and cash-out statutes. These statutes place limitations on a bidder's ability to acquire a stake in the target and then merge with it without shareholder approval, acquire a stake at one price and pay less for the remaining interest, acquire a stake without shareholder approval, or if it does acquire a stake in the target, offer the remaining shareholders the opportunity to sell their stock at the same price. State statutes are helpful, yet they do not stand up to a fully financed, fully priced offer for a company.

A company's charter and by-laws may be amended to provide a number of attractive protections. For example, a company may implement a staggered board or supermajority voting provisions. It may have a fair price provision and limit shareholders' ability to call special meetings. It may authorize additional common and/or preferred stock that can be used to support a poison pill or be issued to a friendly third part. Finally, charter amendments may limit the company's ability to pay greenmail, and they can limit a shareholder's ability to have an action approved by written consent. Like state takeover laws, charter and by-law amendments provide some but not absolute protection. And, rarely are the charter and by-law amendments used by themselves. They usually work together with state takeover laws and other defensive mechanisms. In addition, charter amendments are difficult to put in place as they require shareholder approval.

The most effective form of defense is the shareholder rights plan. A rights plan may be put in place without shareholder approval; it is be approved by the board of directors. To date, no poison pill has been triggered. In the event a company has a poison pill in place, it renders other legal and state defenses as less important.

In the face of a takeover offer, a company must devise a response that is proportionate to the threat and reasonable given the circumstances. Otherwise, the board of directors may be faced with a breach of duty to shareholders, or the defensive action may be struck down by the courts. However, with an offer afoot, a company has numerous structural defensive actions it may take including seeking a white knight or squire, recapitalizing or restructuring the company, or implementing a Pac-Man defense.

Chapter 24

HOSTILE ACQUISITIONS

§ 24.01 OVERVIEW

Hostile acquisitions gained in popularity in the 1980s. Thanks to the significant increase in merger and acquisition activity, companies developed strong anti-takeover measures, forcing potential acquirers to pursue aggressive means to taking over a competitor. The availability of high-yield debt and overall acceptance of aggressive takeover behavior drove the levels of hostile takeovers.

Today, hostile transactions have gained in acceptance, as they have become a common tool to gain market share, access new technology, or consolidate a market.

Since 1990, there have been approximately 833 hostile transactions, representing approximately $720 billion in value. In 2001 alone, there were 32 transactions representing $121 billion in value. Exhibit 24-1 illustrates the trend in hostile acquisitions since 1990.

Some of the largest M&A transactions undertaken have been through hostile means, and have involved some of the better known companies in America. For example, companies that have been the target of a hostile takeover include Federated Department Stores, Kraft, RJR Nabisco, and NCR. In some cases, the original hostile bidder was not the ultimate acquirer, while in others, the hostile bidder won the transaction. Exhibit 24-2 shows some of the more significant completed hostile transactions in the past few decades.

Exhibit 24-1
Announced Hostile Acquisitions: 1990–2003[1]
($ in millions)

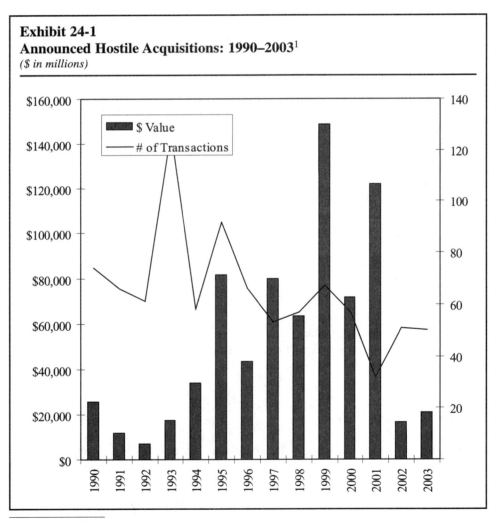

1. Thomson Financial.

Exhibit 24-2
Significant Completed Hostile Transactions[2]
($ in millions)

Date Effective	Target/Acquirer	Value of Transaction	Synopsis
06/24/88	Federated Department Stores/Campeau Corp	$ 6,512	Campeau acquired Federated for $73.50 per share, or $6.5 billion cash. Campeau had originally launched a hostile offer at $47 per share, and raised its bid several times before RH Macy emerged as a white knight with a two-tier offer of cash and stock. Campeau revised its offer to also be two-tier, and it and Macy sweetened their bids several times, with Macy finally bidding $78.92 cash per share for 80% and $60 cash per share of stock for 20%. Eventually, Campeau and Macy agreed that Campeau would buy Federated for $73.50 cash per share and sell 2 Federated units to Macy for $1.1 billion.
12/07/88	Kraft Inc./ Philip Morris Inc.	$13,444	Philip Morris acquired Kraft through a cash tender offer of $106 per share, or $13.44 billion. Philip Morris had launched a tender offer valued at $90 cash per share, or $11.41 billion, which Kraft rejected as inadequate. In response to the bid, Kraft adopted a poison pill that would have been enacted when anyone acquired 20% of its shares and a golden parachute plan worth $14.5 million. Kraft also announced a recapitalization plan valued at $13.95 billion in cash, common stock and debentures. Philip Morris sought the merger to diversify beyond its core tobacco business.
04/28/89	RJR Nabisco Inc./ Kohlberg Kravis Roberts & Co.	$30,599	Kohlberg Kravis Roberts (KKR) acquired RJR Nabisco in a hostile, two-tiered offer valued at $109 per share, or $30.6 billion. KKR paid $109 cash per share for 165.5 million shares and 2.803 cumulative preferred shares

(Continued)

---

2. Thomson Financial.

Exhibit 24-2
(*Continued*)

Date Effective	Target/Acquirer	Value of Transaction	Synopsis
			plus $31.14 in senior convertible debentures for the remaining shares, as well as $108 cash per preferred share. KKR also assumed $5.5 billion of RJR liabilities. RJR was put in play when its management, Shearson and Salomon bid $75 per share and made further bids of $92 to $112 each. KKR's earlier bids, ranging from $90 to $106 per share, were rejected by RJR.
09/19/91	NCR Corp./ American Telephone & Telegraph	$7,893	American Telephone & Telegraph (AT&T) acquired NCR in a stock swap valued at a sweetened $110.74 per share, or $7.8934 billion. NCR holders received 2.839 shares of AT&T stock for each NCR share held. The deal included an extra 6.3 million NCR shares sold to Capital Group. This offer was made after several others, including a hostile tender offer at $90 in cash per share, were rejected. NCR increased its poison pill trigger to 20% and took steps to protect itself in a proxy fight, as AT&T fought to take control of the board, although it had succeeded in gaining only 4 seats.
12/21/94	American Cyanamid Co./ American Home Products Corp.	$9,561	American Home Products (AHP) completed its hostile merger with American Cyanamid (AC) in a transaction valued at $9.56 billion. Earlier, AHP completed its tender offer to acquire AC for an amended $101 in cash per share, by accepting 89.6 million shares, or about 97.6% of AC's fully-diluted share capital. Originally, AHP had offered $95 per share, or a total value of $8.7 billion. Also, AC rejected AHP's special 24-hour $100 per share offer. In August 1993, AC was to exchange its drug and consumer brands units with Smithkline Beecham's vaccine and animal health units.

(*Continued*)

Exhibit 24-2
(*Continued*)

Date Effective	Target/Acquirer	Value of Transaction	Synopsis
04/01/96	First Interstate Bancorp, CA/ Wells Fargo Capital	$10,930	Wells Fargo (WF) acquired First Interstate Bancorp (FIB) in a sweetened hostile stock swap merger valued at an amended $10.929 billion. FIB common shareholders received .67 WF common share, amended from .625 WF share, for each FIB share held. Based on WF's closing stock price of $215.37 on Nov 10, the last full trading day prior to the disclosure of amended terms, each FIB share was valued at $144.30. Earlier, First Bank System, acting as a white knight, terminated its agreement to acquire FIB for $10.01 billion.
06/19/00	Warner-Lambert Co/Pfizer	$89,168	Pfizer Inc (PI) acquired all the outstanding common stock of Warner-Lambert Co (WC), a pharmaceutical company, in a hostile challenging stock swap transaction valued at a sweetened $89.167 billion, creating the world's second largest drug maker. PI offered a sweetened 2.75 common shares per WC share. Based on PI's closing stock price of $35.75 on February 4, 2000, the last full trading day prior to the increase in terms, each WC share was valued at $98.31. Originally, PI offered 2.5 common shares per WC share. PI's shareholders were to hold a 61% interest in the merged company with WL's shareholders owning the remaining 39%. Concurrently, American Home Products Corp agreed to walk away from its mergers of equals transaction with WC, which had been valued at $75.563 billion, in return for a break-up fee of roughly $1.8 billion.
05/31/00	Mirage Resorts Inc/MGM Grand Inc (Tracinda)	$ 6,483	MGM Grand Inc (MGM), a majority-owned unit of Tracinda Corp, acquired all the outstanding common stock of Mirage Resorts Inc (MR), an owner and operator of casino hotels, for a sweetened $21 in cash per share, or a total

(*Continued*)

Exhibit 24-2
(*Continued*)

Date Effective	Target/Acquirer	Value of Transaction	Synopsis
			value $6.483 billion, including the assumption of approximately $2 billion in liabilities. Originally, MGM offered a choice of $17 in cash or a combination of $7 in cash and $10 in common stock per MR share. MR's board rejected the original offer, and adopted a poison pill plan giving shareholders the right to purchase stock at a deep discount in the event of an acquisition or an attempt to acquire a stake of 10% or more of the company. Upon completion, this acquisition was to create the second largest US gaming company behind Park Place Entertainment Corp.
10/04/00	Bestfoods/ Unilever PLC	$25,065	Unilever PLC (UL) acquired all the outstanding common stock of Bestfoods (BF), a producer of consumer foods, via an unsolicited hostile offer, for a sweetened $73 in cash per share, or a total value of $25.065 billion, including the assumption of $4 billion in liabilities. UL first made an unsolicited written proposal on April 20, stating its interest to purchase all outstanding shares of BF common stock, par value $0.25 per share, at $61 to $64 cash per share. BF informed UL that its management would study the proposal and would submit it to its Board of Directors for its review at a special Board meeting on May 2. On May 1, unsolicited, UL increased its proposal, subject to certain conditions, to $66 per share. After careful consideration of UL's latest proposal, including consultation with independent financial and legal advisors, the BF Board of Directors rejected the offer.
03/14/02	Willamette Industries Inc./ Weyerhaeuser Co	$ 7,857	Weyerhaeuser Co (WY) acquired all the oustanding common stock of Willamette Industries Inc (WI), a

(*Continued*)

Exhibit 24-2

(*Continued*)

Date Effective	Target/Acquirer	Value of Transaction	Synopsis
			provider of timber forestry services and manufacturer of wood products, for a thrice sweetened $55.5 in cash per share, or a total value of $7.857 billion, including the assumption of an estimated $1.7 billion in liabilities.
01/18/02	Newport News Shipbuilding Inc./ Northrop Grumman Corp	$3,057	Northrop Grumman Corp (NG) acquired all the outstanding stock of Newport News Shipbuilding Inc (NN), a manufacturer of and maintenance provider for aircraft carriers, in a stock swap transaction valued at $3.057 billion, including the assumption of an estimated $500 million in liabilities. Earlier, NG completed its unsolicited, challenging tender offer for NN by accepting 26.469 million shares, or 74.779% of NN's outstanding shares. NG offered a choice of $67.50 in cash or NG common stock per share, subject to a collar agreement. The shares were valued based on NG's closing stock price of $92.50 on May 7, the last full trading day prior to announcement. The offer was conditioned upon at least a majority of NN's shares being tendered, the termination of the General Dynamics Corp's (GD) agreement to acquire NN and the redemption of NN's anti-takeover defense. Subsequently, GD withdrew its tender offer to acquire all the outstanding common stock of NN, upon which NG and NN reached a definitive agreement in the offer.
12/11/02	TRW Inc./ Northrop Grumman Corp	$6,678	Northrop Grumman Corp (NG) merged with TRW Inc (TRW), a manufacturer of advanced technology products, in a stock swap transaction valued at $6.678 billion. NG offered .5357 shares per TRW share. Based on NG's closing stock price of $96.62 on December 10, the last full trading day prior to the

(*Continued*)

Exhibit 24-2

(*Continued*)

Date Effective	Target/Acquirer	Value of Transaction	Synopsis
			announcement of the exact exchange ratio, each TRW share was valued at $51.76. Previously, NG offered a twice-sweetened $60 in common stock per TRW share, subject to a collar agreement, which was subsequently breached. Previously, in July 2002, NG launched an unsolicited, hostile tender offer to acquire all the outstanding common stock of TRW for a sweetened $53 in common stock per TRW share. Originally, in February 2002, NG offered $47 in common stock per TRW share. As a result of the definitive merger agreement announced on July 1, 2002, NG did not extend its tender offer for all the outstanding common stock of TRW, which expired on Friday June 28, 2002, and was not to accept any shares tendered.
03/18/03	CoorsTek Inc./ Investor Group	$223	A management led investor group (IG), comprised of the Coors Family, acquired the remaining 73% interest, which it did not already own, in CoorsTek Inc (CT), a manufacturer of electronic components, for a sweetened $26 in cash per share, or a total value of $222.783 million. Originally, IG launched an unsolicited offer to acquire CT for $21 in cash per share, or a total value of $179.94 million.
08/22/03	Ribapharm Inc./ ICN Pharmaceuticals	$187	ICN Pharmaceuticals Inc (ICN) acquired the remaining 19.9% stake, or 29.85 mil common shares, which it did not already own, in Ribapharm Inc (RPI), a biotechnology company, for a sweetened $6.25 in cash per share, or a total value of $187.273 million. Earlier, ICN completed its hostile tender offer for RPI by accepting 20.729 million shares, or 13.731% of RPI's common stock outstanding. Originally, ICN

(*Continued*)

Exhibit 24-2

(*Continued*)

Date Effective	Target/Acquirer	Value of Transaction	Synopsis
			offered $5.60 in cash per share, or a total value of $167.238 million in an unsolicited bid. The offer was conditioned upon at least 90% of RI's shares being tendered.
10/27/03	Elder-Beerman Stores Corp./ Bon-Ton Stores	$ 98	Bon-Ton Stores Inc (BTS) acquired all the outstanding common stock of Elder-Beerman Stores Corp (EBC), an owner and operator of department stores, for a sweetened $8.00 in cash per share, or a total value of $97.831 million. Earlier, BTS completed its tender offer for EBC by accepting 10.893 million shares, or 94% of EBC's common shares outstanding. Previously, in July 2003, BTS offered $7.00 in cash per share, or a total value of $85.124 million, in a challenging bid. The offer was conditioned upon at least 67% of EBC's being tendered on a fully diluted basis. Previously, Wright Holdings Inc, a unit of Goldner Hawn Johnson & Morrison Inc, definitively agreed to acquire all the outstanding common stock of EBC. Originally, EB Acquisition Ltd planned to launch a tender offer to acquire all the outstanding common stock of EBC.
6/3/02	NRG Energy Inc. /Excel Energy Inc.	$673	Xcel Energy Inc (XE) acquired the remaining 25.65% stake, or 54.689 mil common shares, which it did not already own in NRG Energy Inc (NRG), a provider of electric & gas utility services, in a stock swap transaction valued at $672.556 million. Earlier; XE completed its unsolicited tender offer for NRG, by accepting 42.990 million shares, or 21.654% of NRG's common shares outstanding, equivalent to 84.41% of NRG's shares not owned by XE. XE offered a sweetened .5 common shares per NRG share. Based on

(*Continued*)

Exhibit 24-2
(*Continued*)

Date Effective	Target/Acquirer	Value of Transaction	Synopsis
			XE's closing stock price of $25.72 on April 3, the last full trading day prior to the announcement of amended terms, each NRG share was valued at $12.86. Originally, XE offered .4846 shares per NRG share. Based on XE's closing stock price of $23.73 on February 14, the last full trading day prior to the announcement, each NRG share was valued at $11.50. The offer was conditioned upon at least 90% of the total NRG shares outstanding being tendered or 60% of NRG shares not owned by XE.

§ 24.02   TACTICAL ALTERNATIVES FOR GAINING CONTROL

Whenever contemplating a merger or acquisition, there are a variety of approaches that a potential acquirer must consider when evaluating how to successfully complete a transaction. The chosen approach will depend on a number of factors including whether or not the target company is actively for sale, whether the target and acquirer have an existing relationship, whether the target is amenable to a transaction, and how critical the acquisition is for the buyer.

Tactical alternatives differ based on their level of aggression towards the target, from a friendly, negotiated deal to an unsolicited, hostile tender offer. Exhibit 24-3 illustrates the range of alternatives.

[A]   Friendly Approaches

A friendly approach should always be considered, as aggressive or hostile approaches can be quite costly and raise numerous issues. Friendly transactions most often take place when the acquirer is not prepared to undertake a hostile or unsolicited deal, where the industry is such that an unsolicited transaction may jeopardize business or customer relationships, and where retention of the target's senior management team is essential.

While in most situations, a friendly transaction is preferred, there are also numerous disadvantages of a friendly deal. Exhibit 24-4 outlines the advantages and disadvantages of friendly transactions.

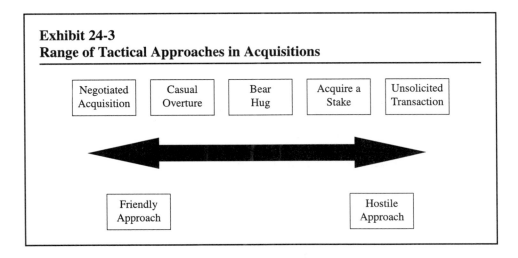

Exhibit 24-3
Range of Tactical Approaches in Acquisitions

| Negotiated Acquisition | Casual Overture | Bear Hug | Acquire a Stake | Unsolicited Transaction |

Friendly Approach   Hostile Approach

Exhibit 24-4
Advantages and Disadvantages of Friendly Transactions

Advantages	*Disadvantages*
• Encourages discussion on joint opportunities and synergies	• Limits the flexibility of the acquirer
• Allows both parties to transaction to perform complete due diligence	• Target may require the acquirer to enter into a standstill agreement
• Greater potential for acquirer to pay reasonable, uncontested price	• Target management may "entertain" discussions while it prepares defense
• Likely to receive support of target management and board of directors	• Success is partly dependent on the right people from both parties leading the negotiations
• Friendly transaction may be better received than hostile transaction	
• Does not preclude more aggressive approach later, if warranted	

[1]   Negotiated Transaction

The friendliest approach is to simply undertake a negotiated transaction with the counterparty. This most often occurs between companies where members of the management team or board of directors know each other or where the strategic merits of the transaction as so compelling that the parties recognize the value of undertaking the transaction.

[2]   Casual Overture

In situations where the acquirer does not know the target's management team or board of directors, or the target is not actively for sale, a slightly more aggressive approach is to proactively suggest a potential combination to the target. This may be well-received in which case, the transaction may proceed to a negotiated deal. Alternatively, it may not be well-received, in which case, the acquirer may reserve the ability to become more aggressive.

The overwhelming benefit of this approach is the significant public relations benefit in that the acquire may ultimately let it be known that at first it attempted to pursue a friendly transaction, but was "rebuffed" by the target, and therefore had no choice but to go hostile. An additional benefit of this approach is that the target's management team may ultimately support the transaction if, and when, it becomes friendly. The downside to the casual overture is that it may alert a company and its management team to the potential value of the company and that it is a sought after asset. Thus, the target may put itself up for sale, jeopardizing the transaction that was initiated by the initial acquirer.

[B] Aggressive Approaches

Once it has been determined that a friendly, negotiated transaction is not possible, or that the casual overture has been rebuffed, it is feasible to consider more aggressive tactics. These tactics range from sending the target's board of directors a "bear hug" letter, to acquiring a stake in the company.

[1] Bear Hug

A bear hug is an overture to a company that is made directly to the board of directors with the overt suggestion that the acquirer may take its offer directly to shareholders if the board does not consider its offer. The bear hug letter is designed to force the board of directors and management to take a position, one way or the other, on a given proposal. It is usually sent to the chairman or chief executive officer with a copy to the board of directors. A highly effective, albeit aggressive, approach is to submit a bear hug letter to the target along with a public announcement of the acquirer's intentions. This approach forces the board to respond to the acquirer's proposal through a public response, in the process, subjecting the board to the scrutiny of shareholders who will be ever mindful of the board's fiduciary duties. Implicit in both forms of bear hug is the notion that if the board does not seriously consider the proposal, the acquirer may be forced to pursue a hostile tender offer for the target.

The most significant benefit of a bear hug is that it serves as the first step in a takeover process. It effectively may initiate the transaction and put the company in play. It places pressure on the board of directors and management to consider the offer, yet there is no obligation on the part of the board other than their normal fiduciary responsibilities. A bear hug usually by itself will not trigger a shareholder rights plan, although, the acquirer should be careful to word the offer in a way that it does not unwittingly trigger the plan.

One of the downsides of the bear hug, if sent without a public release, is that the target may not be required to disclose the letter to its shareholders or the public. Therefore, if the target chooses to ignore the overture, the acquirer's letter may become worthless unless pursued further. The target may also turn down the bear hug which may force the acquirer to take even more aggressive action such as launching a tender offer. In the event the acquirer delivers a bear hug letter along with a public announcement, and the target rejects the overture, it may leave the acquirer with no choice but to launch the tender offer or other form of hostile approach. In this case, the acquirer must be prepared to "go hostile" in the event its bear hug is rejected.

[2] Stake Acquisition

In the event a more aggressive posture is required, for example, in situations where a casual approach or a bear hug are not successful in eliciting a positive response from the target, acquiring a stake in the target may be a feasible alternative. Sometimes called a "toe hold" purchase, this approach accomplishes a number of objectives. First, it allows the acquirer to purchase a small stake in the company without paying a premium for the shares, thus lowering the acquirer's overall cost of the acquisition, if successful. And, in the event the acquirer loses out to a third party, it may sell its stock at a premium, compensating for its expense involved in the transaction. Second, it provides the acquiring shareholder with the same rights as other shareholders in the company, forcing the target's board of directors to be aware of its fiduciary responsibilities in the context of all shareholders. Third, as a shareholder, it is able to obtain the target company's shareholder list which may help it in a proxy contest.

Acquiring a toe hold position can be effective as a first step in launching a hostile acquisition; however, acquiring companies should be cognizant of a number of issues that arise out of toe hold acquisitions. First, once a company owns more than 5% of a target's securities, it must file a Schedule 13D that forces it to disclose its identity, its ownership in the target, and its intentions with respect to the target. Second, there are numerous state business combination statutes that prohibit combinations if an acquirer purchases more than a certain percentage of a target without the target board's consent. For example, Section 203 of the Delaware General Corporation Law prohibits an acquirer from merging with a target for three years if the acquirer had previously acquired over 15% of the target's stock without prior board authorization. Third, certain states have control share acquisition statutes that prohibit a company from acquiring a stake in a target without first receiving board approval. Fourth, under antitrust guidelines, a filing is required for transactions where the stock or assets acquired is over $50 million, unless the stock is acquired solely for investment purposes. Fifth, the acquirer should be cognizant of the target's shareholder rights plan, if any, and the threshold at which the plan is triggered.

If the acquirer decides to purchase target stock, it should establish a buying strategy and procedure for monitoring its purchases. It should monitor the volume and price levels at which it has purchased stock, and the effect these purchases have on the target's stock. It should be careful to avoid unnecessary disclosure that could cause a run-up in the price of the stock. One important note is that the bidder must cease its purchase of stock if and when a tender or exchange offer commences.

[C]   Hostile Approaches

To the extent the friendly or even mildly aggressive approaches are not impactful, an acquirer may consider overt hostile action which includes tender offers, exchange offers and proxy contests. An overtly hostile transaction should be evaluated carefully, as it can be quite costly to the acquirer and target, it can "put the target in play" and thereby force the originating bidder to pay a higher premium than it ordinarily might if the transaction were friendly, and it can create a public relations debacle. Exhibit 24-5 illustrates the advantages and disadvantages of unsolicited approaches.

[1]   Tender Offer

Tender offers are an effective approach to taking over a company, in particular in a hostile situation. A tender offer is an acquisition where an offer is made directly to the shareholders of a target company by the acquirer. In a tender offer, the acquirer offers to purchase some or all of the shareholders' stock in the target at a certain price and under certain terms and conditions.

Tender offers are typically used in hostile transactions when a friendly transaction fails to materialize and/or a bear hug has proven ineffective. The overwhelming benefit of a tender offer is that it enables the acquirer to evade management and the board and go directly to shareholders, even if the management team objects to the transaction. Tender offers have a number of benefits as outlined in Exhibit 24-6.

The mechanics of tender offers and hostile transactions have gone through significant changes over the years. There have been numerous abusive situations, where acquirers have effectively "tendered" for a target's shares, but technically, the acquisition did not constitute a tender offer. The Williams Act of 1968 was enacted to regulate tender offers. It put in place provisions that forced an acquirer with a 5% or greater stake in a company to file a Schedule 13D, identifying itself

---

Exhibit 24-5
Advantages and Disadvantages of Unsolicited Approaches

Advantages	Disadvantages
• Acquirer maintains the advantage of surprise	• May become a protracted process
	• May be costly to effect
• Acquirer reserves ability to go directly to shareholders and bypass the board	• May subject the acquirer and target, to unattractive public relations issues
	• May require that acquirer pay high premium, especially in contested situations
	• Due diligence may be limited
	• May be difficult to obtain buy-in from target management

Exhibit 24-6
Advantages and Disadvantages of Tender Offers

Advantages	Disadvantages
• Able to acquire control of target quickly	• Must be fully financed
• Effective approach	• May put target in play
• No board approval typically required	• May result in initial bidding party paying high premium for target
• Short time frame for antitrust approval	• Not possible to acquire stock of target during tender offer
	• More costly than a negotiated transaction

to the target and its shareholders. Today it requires the filing of Schedule TO which provides substantial disclosures regarding the acquirer, its plans for the target, and any prior relationship between the target and acquirer. The Williams Act also provides an overall timeframe for tender offers, mandating that tender offers remain open for 20 business days, describes how tendering shareholders may withdraw their shares, and elicits how the acquirer must pay for the tendered shares. All these requirements are designed to treat investors and the target company fairly.

The Williams Act however, does not actually define what constitutes a tender offer, and this is where the abuse has taken place in the past. Companies have acquired stock in the open market, and even though the company must file a Schedule 13D once it reaches the 5% threshold, it is not necessarily forced to file the more detailed tender offer documents. This approach is known as a "creeping tender offer."

Over the years, as companies have taken advantage of the lack of definition of a tender offer, the courts have developed various definitions that have subsequently been applied by the SEC in an "eight-factor test." A tender offer is commonly viewed as a general, public bid for the shares of a public company by a group of individuals. The eight-factor test supports this notion as shown in Exhibit 24-7.

One approach for an acquirer to consider when contemplating a tender offer, is to first purchase a toe hold stake in the target. When the acquirer's ownership reaches the 5% level, it is bound to file a Schedule 13D within ten business days of reaching the 5% threshold. During that ten-day period, the purchaser has the ability to continue to acquire stock in the target at the market prior to launching a tender offer. This affords the acquirer the opportunity to acquire a substantial amount of the target's stock without paying a significant premium, unless, of course, the market realizes that the acquirer is purchasing the stock and the stock price begins to rise on speculation.

The acquirer should be aware of the risks inherent in this approach. First, it should evaluate the state combination and control share statutes in the state in which the target is incorporated, as these may prevent it from acquiring a substantial stake and/or prevent it from merging with the target for a period of time in

---

Exhibit 24-7
SEC Eight-Factor Test[3]

A transaction is considered a tender offer if it:

1. involves an active and widespread solicitation of security holders;
2. involves a solicitation for a substantial percentage of the issuer's stock;
3. offers a premium over the market price;
4. contains terms that are fixed as opposed to flexible;
5. is conditioned upon the tender of a fixed number of securities;
6. is open for a limited period of time;
7. pressures security holders to respond; and
8. would result in the bidder acquiring a substantial amount of securities.

---

the event it acquires over a given threshold of stock in the target. Second, it should check to see whether the target has a poison pill and if the acquisition of stock may trigger the pill. Third, an acquirer that pursues the strategy of purchasing a stake in a target, runs the risk that it is not able to purchase the company and ends up owning a stake in the target that it does not want. Owning this minority position may force the acquirer to sell the stake at a discount in order to exit the investment. Fourth, the strategy has the potential to backfire on the acquirer to the extent the market determines that the acquirer has accumulated a large stake in the company. If the target's strategy comes to light, other shareholders may "hold out" on their investment, driving the stock price higher and eventually resulting in the acquirer paying a significant premium for the company, either in the open market, or through a tender offer. Finally, the target must tender for enough shares to satisfy state takeover statutes and the target's charter and by-law requirements.

[2]   Exchange Offer

An alternative to the cash tender offer is the exchange offer, in which the acquirer offers to exchange its stock for shares in the target. The stock consideration may represent 100% of the transaction consideration or a part of the consideration. By offering securities, the acquirer gives the target shareholders options in terms of receiving consideration. In certain circumstances, securities that are received in a tender offer may be tax free, while the cash received in a tender offer is not.

One significant drawback of the exchange offer is that the securities offered in the transaction need to be registered with the SEC, introducing a significant time delay. Another negative of the exchange offer approach is that it is harder for investors to value than a cash tender offer. An exchange offer is also able to trigger a shareholder rights plan, if applicable.

Exhibit 24-8 provides an overview of tender offers versus exchange offers.

---

3. Securities and Exchange Commission.

Exhibit 24-8
Tender Offers Versus Exchange Offers

	Tender Offer	Exchange Offer
Form of Consideration	Cash	Securities
Value to Target Shareholder	Same as cash, simple to value	Requires valuation of security offered
Timing	Minimum of 20 days	Minimum of 50 days, subject to extension for SEC review
Documentation	Tender offer materials Schedule TO Schedule 13D HSR filing	Tender offer materials Schedule TO S-4 Registration Statement Blue Sky Survey Schedule 13D HSR filing
Financing	• Must be arranged • Rating agency considerations • Indenture of target and acquirer must be examined	• Securities offered provide all or portion of financing
Merger Process	Two step • Tender and merger • Short form merger after tender completed, depending upon percentage of target's shares acquired	Two step • Depends upon percentage of target's shares acquired

Tender offers are typically subject to certain conditions in hostile, and other transactions. Exhibit 24-9 provides an overview of the types of conditions found in tender offers.

[3] Proxy Solicitation

In a proxy solicitation or "proxy context," a group attempts to effect change in a company through the mechanisms inherent in the proxy process. Typical proxy contests entail seeking to take control of a company through the ousting of its board of directors. The insurgent group goes directly to shareholders with its proposal and seeks sufficient votes from shareholders for its proposal to be enacted. Groups conducting proxy contests spare no expense and go to great lengths to persuade shareholders to support their cause. To the extent the group conducting the proxy contest is a shareholder, it may use its own voting rights to drive support for its proposal. Proxy contests essentially pit the incumbent board and/or management team against the insurgent group of shareholders.

Exhibit 24-9
Conditions in Tender Offers

Topic	Consideration
Financing	• Acquirer may wish to obtain financing prior to commencing offer
	• Contingent financing may raise regulatory concerns, or may make offer appear uncertain
Poison Pill	• Offer should be conditioned upon redemption of target's plan
Regulatory Condition	• Offer should be conditioned upon receipt of regulatory approvals
	• Must take into account possible solutions to regulatory problems, e.g., sale of assets to satisfy antitrust concerns
No Material Adverse Change	• Provisions can relate to material adverse changes in the target company, as well as certain litigation or a competing offer

---

Proxy contests take advantage of the process surrounding the election of a board of directions. Elections are usually held once a year, at a company's annual shareholders meeting. The time and place of the annual meeting are stated in the company's articles of incorporation.

The regulation of disclosure of information pertaining to proxy information comes under Section 14 of the Securities and Exchange Act. The SEC required that companies mail their annual report to stockholders in advance of the annual meeting. Therefore, annual shareholder meetings are usually held after the company's fiscal year and after the annual report has been sent to shareholders. Section 14 also requires that a proxy statement on Schedule 14A be filed with the SEC. Schedule 14A requires extensive disclosure on the proposal and the target company.[4] Information included in the proxy statement includes detail behind the transaction structure, the tax and accounting consequences of the deal, and detailed financial statements and analysis including any fairness opinions provided by investment bankers.

At annual meetings, shareholders vote on numerous items ranging from the election of board members, to the authorization of an increase in shares, to the approval of a merger. Proposals may be submitted to the company in advance of the shareholder meeting for inclusion in the proxy material. These proposals may in certain circumstances be counter to the desires of the incumbent board and management team. For example, in a proxy contest for control, a dissatisfied shareholder may submit its own slate of directors for nomination to the board of directors.

The voting itself takes place at the meeting or through proxy voting, a mechanism whereby shareholders may vote with the use of proxies. In other words, shareholders authorize somebody else to vote on their behalf.

---

4. *See Chapter 22: Legal Aspects of Mergers & Acquisitions* for a detailed description of the Schedule 14A disclosure requirements.

A proxy contest can be used to achieve a number of objectives. First, it may be used by a group interested in taking control of a company. For example, the insurgent group may attempt to oust the board of directors by proposing its own. If the group is successful in replacing the board, it may then replace management at its discretion. The management team may then be supportive of the insurgent's transaction, causing the change of control in the company.

Second, it may be used to submit a proposal to shareholders to affect change. For example, the group may attempt to have a shareholder rights plan rescinded. Or, it may attempt to block certain anti-takeover mechanisms that the incumbent board is trying to put in place.

Third, it may be used as a weapon to encourage shareholders to vote against a proposal submitted by management. For example, the insurgent group may be in favor of a sale of the company while the incumbent board may not.

Proxy contests have a number of advantages. First, the timing may coincide with that of the target company's regularly scheduled annual shareholder meeting. Second, minimal investment is required by the acquirer in the target in order to conduct a proxy contest. In addition, a proxy contest can be run in conjunction with a tender or exchange offer.

Proxy contests take advantage of a number of facets of the proxy process. First, they capitalize on the public process surrounding the submission of proposals to the company and to shareholders prior to the annual meeting. To the extent the insurgent group is able to submit its material on time, the company is bound to include the proposal in the proxy material going to shareholders. Proxy material must be sent to shareholders of record of a certain date, usually around 60 days prior to the shareholders' meeting. The significance of the record date is that only shareholders of record on that date may vote on a proposal.

Second, the dissident group may be able to call a special meeting of shareholders to vote on its proposal, unless otherwise prohibited by the company's charter. The purpose of calling a special meeting may be to replace the board of directors such that the insurgent-friendly board can vote in favor of a transaction with the insurgent group, or to have shareholders vote on the insurgent's proposals. This is most typically undertaken when a group has acquired a stake in a target company, and then desires to complete the acquisition against the target's wishes. The ability to call the special meeting is dictated by the company's article of incorporation which will specify the process for doing so. In certain instances, companies will amend their charter and by-laws to prohibit or severely restrict shareholders' ability to call a special meeting.

Third, the proxy solicitation process allows the dissident group of shareholders to contact shareholders in advance of the shareholder meeting to encourage them to vote in favor of the insurgent's proposal or against the proposals of management. Based on this solicitation process, which may entail extensive media campaigns, the shareholders vote on the transaction or proposal.

     [a] Proxy Contests in Conjunction with Tender Offers. A proxy contest may be used with a tender offer to purchase a target, and may in fact

be an effective means to taking control of a company. From a practical standpoint, the most likely approach under this scenario is for an acquiring group to purchase a stake in a company and then publicly announce an offer coupled with the initiation of a proxy contest. The proxy contest may have a number of objectives in this context including the removal of the board of directors and the dismantling or rescinding of various anti-takeover measures, such as poison pills. Subject to the success or failure of the proxy contest, the acquirer may then follow up the proxy contest with a cash tender offer.

§ 24.03 KEY CONSIDERATIONS FOR HOSTILE TRANSACTIONS

There are a number of factors to consider when evaluating a potential hostile takeover. These include the target board's fiduciary duties, the target's defense posture, the price and form of consideration for the transaction, any potential antitrust issues that may arise out of the deal, the need to perform due diligence, the need to maintain the existing management team in place, and the accounting and tax aspects of the transaction. Essentially, prior to embarking on a hostile strategy, the acquirer must anticipate all the issues that ordinarily would arise during the course of a friendly transaction. As a gut check, the acquirer must be fully prepared to undergo the hostile deal.

[A] Fiduciary Duties of Target's Directors

In the context of mergers and acquisitions, a board of directors has a fiduciary duty to act in the best interests of shareholders. Under the business judgment rule, a board of directors has a duty to act with care and with loyalty. In other words, a board must make sure that its decisions are well-informed, and that they have no conflicts and act in good faith in a transaction. In the event the board acts accordingly, it is afforded the protections of the business judgment rule. If it does not, and is found to have breached its fiduciary duties to shareholders, it may lose its protections under the business judgment rule and become personally liable for their actions.

A board of directors may take extra steps to support their position in a transaction and to substantiate that they have acted responsibly. For example, the board may retain legal counsel and financial advisors. In addition, it may appoint a special committee to review a transaction. Finally, it may obtain a fairness opinion that substantiates the financial terms of a transaction.

The fiduciary obligations of a target's board of directors are material for a variety of reasons. First, as the potentially hostile acquirer evaluates a transaction, it should structure its approach so as to force the target's board of directors to act on an offer, thereby compelling the board to recognize its fiduciary duties. Second, the board's duties will dictate how it responds to an offer, whether simply saying no to the proposal, at the one extreme, or putting the company up for sale and seeking the highest price, at the other extreme.

The target's board of directors will assess a number of factors in determining whether an acquirer's proposal is acceptable, and whether other defensive actions should be taken. First, the board of directors will consider the overall financial fairness of the consideration offered in the transaction. Typically, a board will ultimately receive a fairness opinion from an investment banker opining as to the fairness of the transaction. Second, the board will consider the merits of the transaction and the attractiveness of the consideration relative to other possible transactions or against simply maintaining status quo. In so doing, it will consider its current business plan and future prospects, and the likelihood that it can achieve its milestones on a stand alone basis or in partnership with the acquirer, or other third party acquirers. Third, it will consider the likelihood that the hostile transaction under consideration can be consummated. To do so, it will evaluate not only the structure of the transaction, but the sources of financing for the transaction and the likely regulatory hurdles to consummation of the deal. Fourth, it will consider the ramifications of either entering into discussions with the hostile bidder, fighting the transaction to remain independent, or entering into negotiations with third parties to sell the company outright. Finally, it must assess the impact of the transaction on employees, customers and other constituents.

Implicit in this thinking is that the acquirer must anticipate the target board's response to each of these questions and prepare accordingly.

[B] Price and Form of Consideration

Of central importance in all transactions, hostile or friendly, is the purchase price to be paid to the target and the form of consideration. Of unique significance in hostile transactions are two factors: hostile bids are usually made without the benefit of detailed due diligence on the target, and hostile transactions are often contested, resulting in high premiums in the transaction. Therefore, potential hostile acquirers must reason through the proposed initial offer price as well as the highest price it can reasonably pay and still realize value in the transaction.

The form of consideration is also important to consider. First, deciding on whether to use cash or stock or a combination will have a significant impact on the timing of the transaction. Where stock is issued in a transaction will often require the filing of detailed disclosure information that increases the length of time required to close the deal. Second, cash transactions are often easier to execute than stock transactions. Exhibit 24-10 illustrates the advantages and disadvantages of stock and cash as consideration in hostile transactions.

[C] Target's Defensive Posture

A target company's posture has numerous components. The acquirer's purpose in evaluating the target's defensive posture is to build the case for acquiring the company on a hostile, or other, basis. First, like friendly transactions, the financial and strategic merits must be present to support the deal. Second, an evaluation

Exhibit 24-10
Advantages and Disadvantages of Stock and Cash as Consideration in Hostile Transactions

	Advantages	Disadvantages
Cash	• Simple to value • Certain in terms of price • Short time frame to completion • High probability of success • Shareholders take premium and "walk away"	• May require financing • Financing risk may introduce uncertainty • Taxable transaction to shareholders
Stock	• Self-financing transaction • Typically "relative" valuation approach • Downside risk shared with target's shareholders	• Slower process than cash transaction – Requires registration statement to be effective with SEC prior to consummation • Requires management/shareholders of target to conduct due diligence on acquirer • Upside shared with target's shareholders
Other	• Same benefits as common stock • May bridge value "gap" between acquirer and target • Limits the extent to which target shareholders share in upside or downside	• Involves a slower process than cash – Requires registration statement to be effective with SEC prior to consummation • Same valuation considerations as common stock of acquirer/combined company but more complicated to value

of the target's financial performance will build a case for why the company should be acquired and how the acquirer can justify support from the target's shareholders. Third, it will establish how vulnerable the target is to takeover and the likelihood of success of launching the attack.

[1] Target Financial Performance

A company's historical stock price performance by itself and relative to the market and its peer group will be a good indicator of whether or not a company is the potential victim of a hostile takeover attempt. Underperforming companies are ripe for change, and the case can quickly be made with shareholders that management and/or the board should be replaced in order to "breathe new life" into the company. As a part of this analysis, it is helpful to track a number of performance measures.

First, evaluate the company's stand alone financial performance relative to its peer group. Determine how it compares from a growth, margin and return on capital perspective. Why is it lagging behind competitors?

Second, evaluate its stock price performance relative to its peer group and the market. Is there a correlation between its financial performance and its stock price performance?

Third, compare the target's trading values relative to its peer group. For example, evaluate its enterprise value as a multiple of revenues, EBITDA and EBIT, and its equity value relative to net income both on a historical and projected basis. Also evaluate its price earnings multiple to its growth rate to determine if it is undervalued or overvalued relative to its projected growth rate.

Each of these analyses will help establish whether the company is vulnerable from a valuation standpoint, and will help bolster the hostile acquirer's proposal if it comes to fruition.

[2] Structural Defenses

Structural defenses are those legal and other attributes that make it difficult for a potential buyer to pursue the target. Solid structural defenses will help protect a company from being unwittingly taken over, increase the board of director's negotiating leverage and flexibility, and cause the bidder to increase its price in order to complete the transaction. However, despite the strength of a company's defensive arsenal, it will not protect a company from a fully financed cash offer. In addition, even though a hostile bidder may have the upper hand initially, a board may still consider endorsing a friendly transaction.

There are a number of structural defense components to review. First, one should consider the concentration of ownership in the target's stock, including shares owned by management and insiders as well as institutions. One should also attempt to evaluate the quality of the target's institutional relationships, and whether there are key institutional shareholders that may be amenable to the hostile transaction and not in support of the target's management and board.

A second element is to review the company's own defenses, i.e., those defenses that are embedded in the company's charter and by-laws and articles of incorporation. These defensive tools are outlined in Exhibit 24-11.

The implications from this analysis are two-fold. First, it may suggest to a potential hostile acquirer how difficult it may be to successfully undertake a hostile acquisition. Second, it may indicate what structural defenses must be eliminated or overcome in order to successfully complete the transaction.

Except for a shareholder rights plan, most structural defenses by themselves have relatively little deterrence effect in hostile transactions, especially when used by themselves. Shareholder rights plans however, have a strong deterrent effect. By launching an offer for a company, the pill is triggered, causing significant financial dilution to the acquirer, rendering the transaction financially uneconomic to complete.

As many of the structural defenses are amendments to the target company's charter and by-laws, they are difficult to remove, as they require shareholder approval. Therefore, potential suitors looking to take control of a company may wish to consider the difficulty entailed in removing these impediments. Defenses that require shareholder approval to be removed include: action by written

Exhibit 24-11
Target Company's Defensive Arsenal[5]

Defense Provision	Description
Shareholder Rights Plan	A shareholder rights plan is a common anti-takeover defense mechanism that is highly effective in allowing a target company time to respond to an unwanted takeover proposal, and encourage bidders to negotiate with the company. Poison pills work by causing significant dilution to the acquirer if it is successful in acquiring a given percentage of a target. In a basic poison pill, each shareholder is granted a right to acquire stock in their company at a steep discount, in the event that the acquirer is able to acquire, or announces an intention to acquire, stock in the target that if successful, would let it own over a pre-defined percentage of the company. Everyone except the hostile bidder may exercise the rights. For the rights to be exercised, the target must issue a significant number of new shares, thereby creating significant dilution to the acquirer.
Staggered Board	A staggered board will vary the terms of each of a target company's board members such that only one or two directors may be reelected in any given year. In this way, it is impossible for a potential acquirer to replace enough board members in a single year to affect a transaction. And, the bidder may not be interested in attempting to gain control over a multi-year period.
Shareholder Ability to Call Meeting	Most states require companies to allow shareholders to call a special meeting if a required number of shareholders demand it. This ability has given unwanted acquirers the opportunity to call special meetings in order to revoke certain anti-takeover devices, rescind poison pills or launch proxy fights. Companies may amend their by-laws to restrict the ability of shareholders to call a special meeting.
Action by Written Consent Permitted	Action by written consent allows shareholders to submit an action to the board and shareholders by written consent.
Blank Check Preferred	Blank check preferred stock is preferred stock that is issuable in series. The terms of blank check preferred stock can be dictated by the board of directors and can be used for multiple purposes. For example, it can be used to backstop a shareholder rights plan, or it can be issued to a white knight in the face of a takeover offer. Authorizing blank check preferred stock is a charter amendment that requires shareholder approval.

(Continued)

---

5. See *Chapter 23: Anti-Takeover Measures* for a detailed review of anti-takeover defensive provisions.

Exhibit 24-11
(*Continued*)

Defense Provision	*Description*
Cumulative Voting	Cumulative voting is the ability for a shareholder to vote all of his/her stock for one or a handful of directors, rather than allocating the votes among the directors. In other words, the shareholder would take the number of shares it owns and multiply that by the number of directors to be elected to yield a total number of possible votes that can be cast by that shareholder. The shareholder may then cast all those votes behind one director or may split them up among the directors.
Supermajority Provisions	A supermajority provision is an amendment to the charter that provides for a substantially higher threshold for shareholder approval. Generally, supermajority provisions range from 66% to 80%, with a few instances where supermajority thresholds have been seen as high as 95%.
Fair Price Provision	A fair price provision is a charter amendment that requires a potential acquirer that owns stock in a company to pay the remaining shareholders at least the maximum price that was paid for the initial holdings.
Anti-Greenmail Provision	An anti-greenmail provision prohibits the payment of greenmail to a potential unwanted suitor who owns a stake in the company.

---

consent, blank check preferred stock, staggered board, and special meetings. Other defenses, such as a poison pill, only require board action.

[3]   State Statutes

Working hand-in-hand with a company's own internal defenses are the various state statutes that have been enacted to protect companies and shareholders from abusive takeover tactics. These statutes include control share acquisition statutes, business combination statutes, fair price statutes and cash out statutes. Exhibit 24-12 summarizes the various types of state statutes.

These statutes should be evaluated in conjunction with a target company's structural defenses to determine an approach that will not be undermined by the company's defensive posture. For example, if the acquirer chooses to make a toehold acquisition in the target, how much stock can it acquire before it runs afoul of the company's shareholder rights plan, if any, and the states control share and business combination statutes.

[4]   Antitrust and Other Regulatory Constraints

Hostile transactions, like friendly transactions, are subject to federal and state regulation. Principally, these include the antitrust laws of the United States and

Exhibit 24-12
Summary of State Anti-Takeover Statutes

Type of Statutes	Overview
Control Share Acquisition Statute	Control share acquisition statutes generally require that a bidder receive shareholder approval prior to acquiring a significant stake in a company. The benefit of a control share acquisition statute to the target company is that it potentially delays the time period during which an unwanted acquirer may purchase the company.
Business Combination Statute	A business combination statute generally prevents a hostile acquirer from merging with a target company after the bidder has acquired a substantial stake in it without having obtained prior approval from the target's board. Specifically, if a bidder crosses over a defined threshold, say 10%–20%, it is prohibited from entering into a business combination with the target for a proscribed period of time unless prior to reaching the threshold, the bidder had received approval from the target's board to acquire the stock or to enter into the business combination.
Fair Price Statute	Fair price statutes generally state that in the event an acquirer is able to purchase a significant stake in a company, the remaining shareholders are entitled to receive a "fair price" for their shares.
Cash Out Statute	A cash out statute maintains that a stockholder acquiring over a certain percentage of a target's stock, e.g., 20%, must notify the other shareholders and they must be given the right to have their shares acquired at the highest price paid by the acquirer in the last 90 days.

requirements under the Securities Act of 1933 and the Securities Exchange Act of 1934.

Antitrust regulation is enforced by the Federal Trade Commission or the Department of Justice. Cash tender offers as well as long-form mergers are subject to review. Antitrust concerns should be viewed from the perspective of the acquirer and the target. Inasmuch as the acquirer wishes to undertake the acquisition, it should anticipate any potential antitrust issues that may arise, first, because the transaction, if successful, may not close until it has been reviewed, and second, because the target may fight the transaction on antitrust grounds.

The Securities and Exchange Act enforces the provisions of the Securities Act of 1933 and the Securities Exchange Act of 1934. Under these acts, an acquirer and target must make certain filings in order to provide shareholders with sufficient information in order to make an informed decision with respect to a transaction. The various rules pertaining to hostile transactions are summarized in Exhibit 24-13.

[5] Employees and Other Constituents

Given the nature of a hostile transaction, it is wise to consider the impact of the potential transaction on employees and other constituents. Senior management and key employees are likely to be ambivalent at best, and opposed at worst, to a

---

Exhibit 24-13
SEC Rules and Disclosure Requirements Applying to Hostile Transactions

Rule	Impact
Regulation 13D	Regulation 13D requires that any person, or group of persons acting together, who acquire directly or indirectly greater than five percent of the class of any equity security, must file a report on Schedule 13D within 10 days disclosing that acquisition with the SEC.
Regulation 14D	Regulation 14D pertains to any tender offer by an affiliate of the issuer or a third party and governs the filing, disclosure and dissemination of information in tender offers commenced by a person other than the issuer.
Rule 14(d)-9	If the third party uses solicitations or recommendations of third parties, it must file a Schedule 14D-9, which is governed by Rule 14D-9. Schedule 14D-9 requires disclosure of the person making the solicitation or recommendation and the relationships between that party and the party making the offer.
Rule 14(d)-10	Rule 14d-10 is designed to ensure that all shareholders receive equal treatment in a tender offer. The rule mandates that a tender offer is open to all security holders of the class of securities that is subject to the tender offer (the "all holders" rule), and the consideration that is paid to any security holder is the highest consideration paid to any other security holder during the tender offer (the "best price" rule).
Section 14(e)	Prohibits insider trading, misstatements and certain other practices in connection with tender offers.
Schedule TO	Schedule TO, *Tender Offer Statement*, must be filed in the case of tender offers.
Regulation 14E	Regulation 14E pertains to all tender offers, and governs the procedures and prohibitions of certain tender offer practices.
Regulation 14A	Regulation 14A establishes the rules for the filing and dissemination of a proxy statement on Schedule 14A and the solicitation of proxies. The proxy statement is designed to ensure that shareholders are given the information they need to make a reasonably informed decision. It must be filed in preliminary form with the SEC at least 10 days before the date definitive copies are sent to the shareholders.

hostile transaction, and therefore, the acquirer should consider the loss of these key individuals if the transaction is successful. Unions and other organized groups of employees may have similar strong negative feelings regarding a hostile transaction, and therefore the business may suffer as a result of the deal. This is of particular importance in services businesses where the employees are the key assets of the company. In certain companies, there might be numerous severance agreements or parachutes in place that could increase the cost of the transaction to the acquirer substantially.

Like the management and employees of a company, there may be other key constituents that are likely to have a negative view of a hostile transaction. These could include customers and suppliers, as well as banks and other financial institutions.

[6] Public Relations

Prior to commencing a hostile transaction, the bidder must have a sound strategy in place to address the communications aspects of the transaction and respond to enquiries from third parties. Of critical importance is formulating the acquirer's key messages assembled prior to launching the attack. It should speak consistently regarding its rationale for the transaction and the benefits of the transaction to shareholders and the company. The company should assemble a group of advisers that are able to address various aspects of the deal and speak authoritatively on the matters. The acquirer should formulate a strategy for handling enquiries, and the team should direct the calls accordingly.

In addition to communications with the media, the company should develop similar strategies for communicating with the target, the target's shareholders, and regulatory bodies such as the SEC and FTC.

[7] Divestiture Risk and Non-Core Assets

One often overlooked aspect of a hostile transaction is the potential impact the transaction may have on the complexion of the assets of both the target and the acquirer. As a result of potential antitrust action, the acquirer may be forced to divest certain portions of its own assets, or certain assets of the target. This analysis should be carefully thought through, in particular, its effect on the company's operating performance and capital structure.

[8] Litigation

A review of the target's structural defenses as well as the state legal framework will bring to light the defenses that are available to a target in fending off a deal. However, an acquirer also has the benefit of legal action to promote a transaction. The acquirer may use litigation to supplement its offensive strategy in order to defeat certain structural defenses. The acquirer should work with its legal counsel to determine what appropriate legal action may be taken to facilitate the transaction.

Of particular note are a number of claims or attacks that the acquirer may make. It may litigate claiming that the target's board of directors has breached its duties to shareholders. This can come up in a number of contexts, for example, in the context of certain structural defenses that are designed to prohibit third party bids. It may also attack other specific defenses on a case-by-case basis. It may sue to prevent the management of the company from taking action that may prevent a transaction from occurring. It may challenge other bids and the process that the target company went through in obtaining those bids to the detriment of the hostile acquirer. It may also use litigation as a less-expensive means to fighting a full proxy fight.

The target may also pursue the same strategy as the acquirer, by filing suit to fight a hostile transaction. The litigation may force the acquirer to reconsider its approach as the litigation can result in significant expense and time delay, regardless of the outcome. Nevertheless, the litigation process will inevitably buy the target time to analyze its options and potentially bring in a white knight.

[9]   Bidding Strategy

There is considerable debate regarding the bidding strategy in hostile acquisitions. The debate centers around the market's expectations for pricing in contested transactions, and whether once a bid has been made, additional bids will be received by the target. There are essentially three approaches to bidding a hostile transaction: the preemptive strike, the low-ball offer, and the planned bid.

A preemptive strike entails the acquirer putting its highest and best offer first and sticking with that offer. If it is high enough, it has the potential to discourage other bidders from entering the process. It also likely not to be as subject to criticism as a low offer might. The disadvantage of this approach is that the acquirer may end up paying more than it possibly could have if it had started at a lower price. In addition, its ability to increase price is limited.

The second approach is to deliberately propose a low offer knowing full well that the acquirer will have to negotiate price. The intention however is to attempt to set the bidding low and thereby possibly acquire the company for less than it may have to in a hotly contested situation. While this approach does allow the acquirer to increase its bid substantially, it may be negatively received by management and the board, and it may encourage third party bidders. The low offer puts the third party offers in a positive light further undermining the acquirer's attempts to take over the target.

The third approach is a combination of the above that entails a moderately high offer that still affords the acquirer room to increase its offer. This approach may be better received by shareholders, and may discourage some third party bidders. Because it allows for an increase, it may also give the target's board the opportunity to exercise their fiduciary duties by negotiating a higher price for the company.

§ 24.04   TARGET'S POTENTIAL REACTIONS TO TAKEOVER PROPOSALS

A target company has numerous options available to it to respond to a hostile takeover proposal. First, it can simply "say no." Using this approach, the board of directors simply rejects the proposal, standing behind its charter, and by-laws and state statute protection, as well as its shareholder rights plan, if present. This approach may simply be a negotiating tactic on behalf of the target, as a means to obtain a higher price from the acquirer. Typically, the target will say no to the acquirer by alleging that its offer is inadequate, unfair to shareholders, or that the company and shareholders are better off by remaining independent.

A second approach is for the target to fight the offer on antitrust grounds, accusing the bidder of violating antitrust or regulatory rules. This is most effective however, in regulated industries such as banking, insurance and utilities.

A third approach is for the target to implement a restructuring or recapitalization. Using this approach, the target may dispose of assets, repurchase its stock or take the company private in a leveraged buyout. An additional option is to undergo a leveraged recapitalization whereby the target assumes significant debt and either repurchases stock or issues a special dividend to shareholders. Another restructuring approach is for the target to divest certain of its "crown jewel" assets. These are attractive assets that may have made the transaction appealing to the acquirer. By selling these assets, the acquirer may lose interest in the transaction.

Another approach is for the target to seek a white knight or white squire. A white knight is a third party that the target merges with or sells to in a friendly transaction. A white squire is a third party to whom the target issues a large block of shares, sufficient to thwart the takeover efforts of the hostile party.

Less common is an approach whereby the target makes an acquisition of another third party in lieu of being sold to the hostile bidder. This may make the transaction less attractive or financially infeasible to the acquirer. Similar to this strategy is for the target to turn around and acquire the hostile acquirer. Known as the "Pac-Man" defense, this approach has not been used that frequently.

Finally, the target may approach the hostile acquirer and offer to purchase its stake in the company at a premium, as an incentive to back away from the transaction, known as "greenmail." The IRS imposes a large excise tax on greenmail payments.

§ 24.05　SUMMARY

Hostile transactions should be viewed as the transaction approach of last resort. They are expensive to undertake, can cause a significant public relations backlash, and are all-consuming from a management perspective. Nevertheless, hostile deals have become quite commonplace and are now an accepted weapon in a company's takeover arsenal.

There are numerous types of hostile transactions that range in complexity according to their degree of hostility. Bear hugs and the acquisition of a stake in the target are the most benign forms of aggressive transaction, while tender offers and proxy contests are the more extreme forms of hostile approaches. It is common for these different approaches to be used in sequence or in tandem in a transaction, with the acquisition of a stake often coupled with a bear hug and then followed by a proxy contest and tender offer.

PART VI

STRUCTURING, NEGOTIATING, AND EXECUTING THE DEAL

Chapter 25

THE FUNDAMENTALS OF NEGOTIATION

§ 25.01 OVERVIEW

If ever you have bought a home or car, or gone to war with your children over an increase in allowance, chances are, you've already mastered many of the basics of negotiation. These same skills—leverage, knowledge, trust and judgment—can be applied to negotiating merger and acquisition transactions.

To set the stage for understanding some of the finer points of negotiations, imagine the following scenario. Early on in your career, you have the privilege of selling a Major League professional baseball team. As the agent in the sale process, you are in the envious position of having a premium business to sell and multiple potential buyers for the property. Your client and you have significant leverage in the negotiations.

Representing the buyer is a tenured senior member of a prestigious law firm. His style is to make every issue in the negotiation a point of contention, and consequently, emotions run high and tempers flare.

During the course of the contentious purchase agreement negotiation, the discussions reach a point where your counterpart's lack of leverage becomes crystal clear. Unable to build a case for why he needs to "win" a point, he stands up, grabs his hair, and promptly pulls off and throws his toupee on the table. While his antics do little to advance the deal, they provide a number of interesting morals from which to learn. Keep this story in mind as you read on.

This chapter combines some of life's lessons with fundamental M&A negotiation principles, and integrates them into a framework that is central to structuring and negotiating deals.

§ 25.02   THE BASICS OF NEGOTIATION

As you embark on a transaction, it is important to keep in mind a few key principles:

A.   Be informed.

B.   Formulate a negotiation plan.

C.   Have a backup strategy.

D.   Be creative.

E.   Listen.

F.   Build trust.

G.   Separate the people from the issues.

H.   Seek common ground.

[A]   Be Informed

The better educated you are on all dimensions of a proposed transaction, the greater opportunity you have to realize a deal that meets your expectations. Your knowledge should come from many sources and perspectives, but starts the moment you consider embarking on a transaction, and builds over time.

Know your company: Understand your company's objectives in doing the transaction. Are they to grow, consolidate a market or eliminate competition? Are they to acquire new technology or products, or enter a new market? Determine what, if any, leverage your company has in the negotiation, and what gives rise to that leverage. Where does your company rank in the industry relative to competitors? As a buyer, is there likely to be formidable competition for the transaction under contemplation? As a seller, are there multiple buyers for your company? Analyze the impact of the proposed transaction on your organization from a financial, strategic and human resource perspective. Is it likely to be accretive to earnings? How will the equity markets react to an announcement? How will customers respond to the deal? Know all the players on your team well, and understand their areas of expertise to enable you to draw on their capabilities as needed.

Know your counterparty: Learn everything you can about their company and objectives. What is their motive for doing the deal? Determine what leverage, if any, they may have in the negotiation and what gives rise to that leverage. Read all public information on the company including annual reports, 10-K's, 10-Q's, proxy statements, and registration statements. Peruse analyst research reports, S&P and Moody's reports, press releases, and news articles. Understand what other deals the company has done in the past, and read the public documents that contain the definitive agreements for those deals. Research the management team and understand each person's character and background.

Know the market and competition: Research and be up to speed on all your competition as well as that of the other side. Research all the comparable deals that have been done in the sector. What were the critical issues in those deals? How have they worked out? What companies are most likely to compete with you for the deal? How would they approach the transaction differently than you? Do they have any different leverage points? What is their ability to pay? How would it impact your company if a competitor won the transaction away from you?

Know the transaction: Thoroughly review all the financial, strategic and business merits and pitfalls of the transaction. Look at it from both your company's and the counterparty's perspective. What are their alternatives to doing this transaction with you? Review all the comparable deal and trading multiples, the discounted cash flow analysis, and all the other types of analyses relevant to your transaction. Know intimately the financial projections for your company as well as the counterparty. Understand the impact of key assumptions on the valuation analysis and the accretion/dilution in the transaction. Develop a sense for how various outcomes of the negotiation may impact the financialand strategic merits of the transaction. Remember, the idea behind a successful negotiation is to ensure that the expected value creation is realized by protecting all the assumptions that were made going into the deal. Also, analyze the transaction from the point of view of your competition. Look at their ability to pay and the impact it may have on you if they won the deal.

[B] Formulate a Negotiation Plan

You should develop a strategy for negotiating the transaction. What issues are most important to you? What issues are you prepared to compromise on? Where should the negotiation be held? Who should draft the contract? What is the timeframe for the process? Who are the principal negotiators? Who makes the final decision on different issues? Should there be a letter of intent or should you go straight to a contract? If possible, establish with the principal negotiator for the other side a framework that lays out the process, time line and ground rules for the negotiation. Establish objective criteria for how issues should be resolved.

[C] Have a Back-Up Strategy

In any deal, it is always good to have alternatives. You never want to be in a position where the deal on the table is your only option. Even in the event that it actually is your only option, you should have a strategy that allows you to negotiate from a position of strength. A back-up plan can be as simple as knowing under what conditions you would not do the deal, i.e., walk away, or as complex as a completely different deal that becomes more attractive under certain parameters.

Knowing when to walk away from a deal is critical to maintaining your negotiating leverage in a transaction. However, in order to do so, you need a comprehensive understanding of the financial and strategic terms of the transaction, and to know at what point the deal no longer makes sense to do. It could be that while the financial terms of the deal are attractive, the treatment of employees is less than hoped for. It could be that the non-compete agreements are onerous. It could be that there is no collar in the transaction and there is uncertainty in the merger partner's stock. Irrespective of the reason, or reasons, you should have a good sense for your company's bottom line going into a negotiation. As the negotiation progresses, it is possible that the bottom line may change; however, be mindful of what the initial objectives were in undertaking the deal, and make sure that the final terms of the deal support the objectives.

Understanding your bottom line can enhance leverage in a negotiation. First, it allows you to negotiate from a position of strength, knowing that your back-up plan is to walk away if the deal terms are not satisfactory. Second, it enables you to convey with confidence your desired outcome and stick with it. Third, it gives you an internal benchmark against which to check the deal's progress at every juncture. Finally, a bottom line provides you with protection that you won't get into a deal that is not advantageous for shareholders.

As an example of knowing when to walk away, in the sale of a division by a diversified conglomerate, the parent company should thoroughly understand the valuation of the business based on its future growth prospects. It should know how much capital is required to realize those growth plans. This information will enable the parent to evaluate potential offers in an objective light and allow it to negotiate from a position of strength.

Having a strong back-up transaction in addition to knowing your bottom line can significantly add leverage to your negotiating posture. For example, in the case of a company for sale, negotiating with multiple parties allows the seller to optimize the price for the company as well as realize a contract that provides maximum benefit for the seller's shareholders.

[D] Be Creative

Many transactions die because the different sides cannot find a solution to a problem or bridge a gap. The most creative solution to many problems is compromise. As you go into a negotiation, know what issues you have the ability to compromise on and those where you need to remain firm. Be prepared to trade value in one part of a deal for value in another part of a deal. For example, you might assume a liability but give up on cash purchase price. This may be more valuable to a seller than a higher cash purchase price with no assumption of liabilities. You might also consider different forms of consideration besides stock and cash. For example, it is possible to bridge valuation gaps with earnouts, options, warrants, notes, preferred stock and the like. Try to be a problem solver, not a problem.

[E] Listen

One of the most important rules of negotiation is to listen—you will be amazed at what you hear. Negotiators often send signals or cues for the other side to pick up. They float ideas and test things out. They propose hypothetical situations. You should take each of these cues and process them along with all the other information you learn in a transaction. Ask questions. Clarify statements. Try and truly understand what your counterpart is saying.

Inasmuch as you should listen well, you should also be careful what you say. If your counterparty is doing his job right, he will be looking for the same cues from you as you are from him.

[F] Build Trust

Trust is something that serves one well in all walks of life. However, in deal negotiations, trust serves not only to build credibility with the other side, but also to enhance your leverage. Each step along the way, you should be building your trust capital since you may very well need to use it at some point in the transaction. Using your capital with the other side may come in many forms. It could be they are asking you to make a representation on information you have not yet provided. It could be there was confusion on some aspect of the transaction that was undertaken by someone else on your team, and you need to backtrack the transaction a little. When using this capital, use it wisely and don't use it too often. In addition, be careful not to breach the trust, as it may never be recovered.

Building trust and credibility begins before the negotiation. It starts the first day you have contact with your counterparty. It takes place between all members of both teams and builds each day as expectations are met and erodes as either side is disappointed. Credibility is very quickly gained or lost in a transaction. It is important to establish the other side's trust in you early on and to maintain it throughout the process.

[G] Separate the People from the Issues

The personalities involved in a deal can often get in the way of successful execution. Emotions can run high, tempers can flare, and egos can be bruised. To minimize emotional trauma, it is important to focus on the interests of the parties and to separate the interests from the individuals. Keep your cool and facilitate the other side in keeping their cool. Be sure not to express your regret or glee over losing or winning on a point. Use objective criteria in evaluating an issue and keep the emotions of the individuals out of the negotiation. Remember, you very well may have to work with your counterparty and their team after the transaction has been finalized. At the end of the negotiation, both sides should feel like they would be prepared to sit across the table from each other again.

[H] Seek Common Ground

At every opportunity, find ways to meet your counterparty on common ground. Focusing on these issues allows you to build a groundswell of deal momentum and push the transaction forward. Creativity and compromise are sure ways to bring the parties closer together.

These basic negotiation principles are merely guidelines for developing a negotiation framework. Deals can be accomplished using a variety of styles and approaches. And, successful contracts can be defined in many different ways depending on the objectives and circumstances of the deal. Legally, a contract should protect the business and legal interests of all parties to the transaction. Spiritually, even though a contract exists, a successful outcome is where both sides feel like they have "won." This is difficult to achieve; however, it means that both sides have to be willing to compromise, be fair and look beyond the transaction at hand to the post-closing relationship between the various constituents in the deal.

§ 25.03 TRICKS OF THE TRADE

[A] Do's

- *Compromise* — The power of compromise is one of the most important lessons a negotiator can learn. Fundamentally, negotiation is all about compromise. Compromise comes in many forms. You can back away from an issue in order to move the process forward. You can trade an issue that is important to you for one that is important to the other side. Knowing your bottom line on an issue allows you to compromise in order to get the deal done, but not give away the entire deal.

- *Keep a list* — Throughout the deal process, including the negotiation, keep a running list of the significant issues that arise. Make sure that you track issues that are of importance to you, and those that are important to the other side as well. In addition, keep a record of your conversations. You will learn that a lot of information is passed between the parties during negotiations, and it is easy to forget who's responsible for tracking down information or what the resolution of a certain issue was.

- *Appoint a lead person* — Regardless of the situation, you should have a point person designated to lead the negotiations. That individual could be the senior-most executive involved in the deal, the second in command or an agent such as a lawyer or an investment banker. The lead negotiator should be well-versed in all the deal facts as well as those pertaining to the counter party.

- *Have a backup* — Make sure that there is more than one person on the team for each conversation or meeting. That individual should be as knowledgeable on the details of the transaction as the lead negotiator. A partner serves a number of purposes. First, a partner helps keep the other side honest by letting them know there are two sets of ears listening to every conversation. Second, in most conversations, it is possible for two people to hear two different messages. Thus, having more listeners allows one to formulate a broader perspective on a given issue. Third, in the event you are not able to participate in a meeting or call, your partner is equally educated to take the lead.

- *Keep your cards close to your chest* — Focus on the issues that need to be addressed. Try not to add additional commentary on the deal, the people or tangential topics. If your counterparty is doing their job well, they are listening to everything you say, and could glean valuable information from you that could be used against you later.

- *Be consistent* — Be firm on those things that are important. Try not to go to battle on issues. Set the expectation with the other side that you are objective, fair and reasonable. Back up your statements with evidence or strong rationale. You should also be able to judge the overall temperament of the deal negotiation in order to know when to stick a stake in the ground on a certain issue.

- *Don't give away the less important stuff too early* — If you come to terms too soon on all the simple points, you may not have something to trade later on. You should have a good enough understanding of all the issues in the deal that you learn which are important to the other side. While these points may not be important to your team, you are able to maintain a certain amount of leverage by not conceding these issues to the other side too soon.

- *It's OK to be a jerk every once in a while* — Depending on the deal circumstances, it may be appropriate to get emotional during a negotiation. Reasons to make a bold statement would include if the other side is not hearing your concerns loud and clear, if they are veering off course, if their own behavior becomes intolerable, or if you need to ensure that an issue of importance turns in your favor. Be careful with this strategy, since while it can be effective, it also can reveal your own negotiating strategy and leverage position.

- *Consider an agent* — There are a number of reasons to consider an agent such as an investment banker or lawyer to act as the lead negotiator on your behalf. First, bankers and lawyers negotiate for a living and have already encountered many of the issues that you will face in your deal. Second, they shelter you from the possible negative side effects of a negotiation, and help preserve your relationship with the counterparty. Third, they enable you to keep more focused on your underlying business while they focus on the deal itself.

- *Stop to take the temperature* — In every step of the negotiation, it is important to revisit the original objectives and expectations of the deal, and make sure that the direction of the discussions is consistent with those intentions. From a business perspective, you should be concerned that the evolving contract supports the valuation and financial analysis performed in the deal.

- *Track progress* — At the end of each negotiation session, agree on the open items with the other side, what is required to resolve them, and what the next steps should be. Every step of the way you should be pushing the ball closer to the finish line.

- *Ask questions* — If you do not understand something, ask questions. One party may say something that is interpreted entirely differently by the other side than was originally intended. If you think an issue is difficult to understand, it is alright to spell it out and ask the other side if they understand what you are saying. Misunderstandings do not move a deal forward.

- *Learn*—Each statement or reaction elicits a corresponding response from the other side. Learn how the other side responds to your approach and adjust your style accordingly. Also, be careful how you respond to their style.

- *Educate* — A well-informed counterparty is more likely to see things your way. Spend time investing in your counterparty by providing them with information that educates them and is supportive of your position. Let them know why certain items are of importance to you; likewise, don't force issues that are not as important to you.

- *Use your judgement*—While judgement is a difficult skill to teach, your gut feeling about an issue should more often than not accrue to your benefit. Do not be afraid to go with your instincts.

- *Decide on the tough issues*—Many times, the difficult issues are not just price and structure. In fact, those points are often the easiest to tackle, since without agreement in these fundamental areas, there would be no basis for a deal. The tough issues are often those that don't appear until after the negotiation is already underway. It behooves you to try and preempt the process by ferreting out the difficult issues as soon as possible. You should then decide when you want those issues to be addressed. For example, there may be a lawsuit or regulatory issue that is pending, the premature resolution of which may scare away the other side. However, if left to the end of the negotiation, the counterparty may not perceive the issue to be quite as severe if they have made substantial progress on most other aspects of the deal.

[B] Don'ts

- *Don't get hung up on issues*—No transaction ever gets done unless both parties push the process forward. This means that neither side has the luxury of getting hung up on issues. If a particular point looks like it is not going to get resolved on a given day, agree to put it aside and revisit it later. You will be amazed at how quickly the list of unresolved, or open, issues dwindles.

- *Don't keep raising new issues*—You should get all the issues out on the table as quickly as possible in a negotiation, partly to understand the overall magnitude of the process, but also to prevent both sides from introducing new issues during the deal. New issues that are left too late in the process can negatively affect the entire process and damage your credibility, since these points may alter a party's viewpoint on issues already negotiated.

- *Be careful when trying to bluff*—People sometimes liken certain aspects of deal negotiation to a game of poker. This is a risky strategy, since in a transaction the whole deal is as stake rather than a single round of cards.

If you are caught bluffing, you should be prepared to walk away from the deal, otherwise you run the risk that you damage your credibility with the other side. While bluffing comes in different shades of gray and certainly can have its place in a negotiation, it is not for the faint of heart.

[C]   Tactics to Look Out For

- *Deceit*—In most cases, peoples' natural tendency is to give the other side the benefit of the doubt and to assume that they are acting in a forthright manner. While I'm not suggesting that you treat every counterparty as a criminal, you should be astute in your interactions with the other side and observe their approach to negotiations. Did they deliver on their promise? Have they provided the information you asked for? Does the term sheet or contract accurately reflect what you discussed and agreed to?

- *Calling on a higher authority*—A common strategy is for a lead negotiator to have the responsibility to negotiate certain issues but not others. While this strategy can work, the principal dealmaker runs the risk of undermining his credibility with the other side, because they become unsure over what issues the dealmaker has authority. They thus become reluctant to resolve an outstanding point for fear that a "resolved" or "closed" issue may get reopened.

- *Good guy/bad guy*—Much like the higher authority approach, a bad guy may play tough on issues in order to make as much progress as quickly as possible. To the extent the bad guy goes too far or fails in his efforts, the good guy then steps in and backtracks if necessary. However, if the bad guy's approach is successful, the good guy simply steps in to continue the deal. This high-risk approach can work under certain circumstances, but can damage credibility if used as an overriding tactic.

- *Intimidation*—Another tactic to be wary of is intimidation, where the negotiator tries to bully the other side into conceding on an issue. Intimidation may suggest a lack of leverage or a masking of issues that are not desired to be revealed. Common signs of intimidation are when the point person introduces personal attacks or tries to pull seniority over the negotiator for the other side.

- *Beware of the trial balloon*—Often, a party may float an idea or propose a solution to a problem. While in many circumstances, this is a legitimate means to exploring the other side's flexibility on an issue, you should be careful about giving too much away in responding to a proposal positioned as a "trial balloon."

All of these tactics may have their rightful use, place and time in a negotiation, and can be effective if not abused. However, misuse of any of these tactics is high risk and is certain to reveal weakness or damage credibility. So, just as you should be wary of using these approaches, you should be aware when others are using them on you.

§ 25.04 SUMMARY

Negotiating a transaction is the most exciting part of any deal. It is where peoples' personalities shine through, and where all the fruits of one's labor are put down on paper and memorialized in perpetuity. There are no hard and fast rules that mandate how deals must be negotiated, only a few guidelines for shepherding you through the process. Each deal is different and every negotiator has a different approach.

You too will develop your own style, not just for negotiating in general, but also for each type of situation in particular. Some styles work well for certain people in particular situations while the same style may not work for other people in the same or different circumstances.

Be wary of transactions where the negotiation is too simple and every issue seems to fall in your favor. This may be an indication that you are getting into a bad deal. Likewise, be wary of situations where you are beaten at every turn. This too may be a circumstance where you are being used as a stalking horse or taken advantage of.

At every juncture, step back from the negotiation and take stock of the deal. Evaluate it in terms of your initial objectives and expectations and make sure that the contract supports the expected creation in shareholder value.

Many people assume that the transaction is over when the term sheet has been done and turned over to the lawyers to develop a contract. Or, they relax once the contract has been signed. Many deals also fall a part at the same stage, often, because the parties to the transaction assume that the deal will miraculously "get done." Don't be fooled. No transaction gets closed unless each member of the team continues to contribute to the deal and ensures that every last detail is sewn up at the closing of the transaction.

If all else fails, keep calm and maintain a level head. Don't stop talking to the other side. Keep on listening and asking questions. Believe in compromise and creativity, and, taking one day at a time, move the ball closer to the end zone.

Chapter 26

FORMULATING AN OFFER

§ 26.01 OVERVIEW

An initial offer is based on the combined financial and strategic analysis performed in a transaction, and is presented at the point where the parties consider formalizing negotiations. Many times, an opening offer is presented in the form of a letter of intent. It is not simply comprised of price; rather, it includes a number of additional material terms and conditions that help support the offer price. However, determining the offer price, in particular the initial bid, is the most difficult aspect of preparing an offer. This chapter focuses primarily on determining the initial offer price. *Chapter 27: Structuring the Letter of Intent and Definitive Agreement* discusses the other terms and conditions that are included along with price in the letter of intent.

Various transactions require different approaches to determining the initial offer. However, common to most deals are a number of financial and strategic analytical tools that can be used to establish the preliminary offer price. At the outset, it is important to define what the offer price is and how it differs from the value placed on a company.

The offer or purchase price is the amount that is paid for a target company in a transaction, while the value of a company is its worth under different scenarios. Price depends on a number of factors, including the current M&A environment and the acquirer's ability to pay. The value of a target company is independent of a buyer's ability to pay and depends on the target company's ability to realize its expected future results. When formulating an offer, presumably there is a correlation between a company's worth and the price paid for it; however, there are many circumstances where the two are not necessarily well coordinated.

In formulating an offer, it is important to realize that the ability of an acquirer to create value for shareholders is dependent not only on the price paid for a company, but also on the target company's ability to realize its potential value in the future. The trick therefore is to present an offer that is high enough to win the deal but also sufficiently low enough to not overpay and jeopardize future value creation.

A number of factors should be analyzed in order to formulate an initial offer for a company. Each of these elements provides a different perspective on both a company's ability to pay and its need to pay a certain price for a target. Many of the elements are quantitative, yet the critical skill is to understand the subjective issues and apply critical business reasoning in formulating the offer. The key areas where to focus include:

1. Industry trends.

2. Competitive environment.

3. Stand alone values of the target company.

4. Historical trading prices and share ownership of the target company.

5. Acquisition premiums in the sector.

6. Shareholder value impact analysis.

7. Synergies.

8. The seller's objectives.

9. Your objectives.

§ 26.02   INDUSTRY TRENDS

Understanding the industry in which your company operates as well as that of your counterparty is important for a number of reasons. First, it provides you a view of what sectors may be maturing and where the growth opportunities are. Second, it allows you to evaluate the target company and its opportunity in the context of industry trends and the competitive environment. Third, it offers you insight into why a seller may be interested in exiting the business. Is it because they lack the capital to take advantage of a growing market? Could it be the sector is maturing and they are interested in redeploying the capital raised from the sale into higher growth businesses. Is it because the opportunity for the combined company is greater than each company by itself?

This information helps build an overall framework for developing a bid. It sets the stage for reconciling the company's worth and the proposed offer price with the industry opportunity. For example, sectors with high growth potential may command acquisition premiums much higher than current valuations or trading prices, whereas maturing sectors may command purchase prices at or lower than current trading values.

§ 26.03   COMPETITIVE ENVIRONMENT

Another factor influential on the preliminary purchase price is the competitive landscape. Highly competitive industries may indicate a number of potential buyers for a property, suggesting a competitive bidding environment. In this case, a buyer may be inclined to bid at the high end of its price range in order to win the deal. Alternatively, a bidder may wish to back away from a deal for fear of overbidding. Concentrated industries may suggest a lack of potential bidders for a property; however, it could also indicate that the few remaining competitors may be just as eager as you to get their hands on the target.

Other competitive factors to review include each competitor's strategic focus, their product lines and market penetration, and their need to make the acquisition. This analysis should reveal the likelihood that you are faced with competition in the transaction.

Certain industries are highly acquisitive while others are not. Reviewing the acquisition history of, and the prices paid, by other companies may give you a view as to the likely interest of other parties in the target as well as the potential prices that may pay for the business. This is helpful in that it may reveal a price you may have to pay to win the business, rather than a price you want to pay.

§ 26.04   STAND ALONE VALUATION OF THE TARGET COMPANY[1]

The stand alone value of a company is determined in a number of ways. Using the methodologies described in this book, you can establish this value and understand how the company's theoretical valuation compares to its public price in the market. It also allows you to place the theoretical value of the company in perspective with its peers.

Discounted Cash Flow Valuation: Using the projected cash flows of the target, the analysis derives a range of values for the company by discounting its cash flows using a discount rate reflecting its cost of capital. Typically this value represents the stand alone, going concern value of the company that can be realized if the future projections are met.

Comparable Trading Analysis: Using the trading multiples of the target's peer group, it's own metrics are analyzed and translated into a stand alone range of values. This range can then be compared to the target company's own trading value to determine if it is undervalued or overvalued in the market.

---

1. For a more detailed description of stand alone valuation analysis, please refer to Chapters 1–6.

Leveraged Buyout Analysis: This type of analysis places a valuation on the target company based on the acquisition of the company using its own cash flows to pay down debt. It assumes the purchase price is comprised partly of equity and mostly of debt. The debt is repaid using the cash flows generated by the company. Clearly the purchase price generated in this analysis is constrained by two principal factors: the debt capacity of the target, and the equity investors' investment return criteria. This analysis serves as a hypothetical floor on the purchase price, since at prices below this floor, the management team could deliver greater value to shareholders by undertaking a leveraged buyout.

The stand alone valuation and leveraged buyout analysis give you a means to initiate the purchase price analysis because, if you have an understanding of the stand alone valuation, you probably have a good sense for the target's own perception of its value and expectations in the deal.

§ 26.05 HISTORICAL TRADING PRICES AND SHARE OWNERSHIP OF TARGET COMPANY[2]

A public company's trading history is a fairly good indicator of how the company has been perceived over time in the marketplace. Comparing the last few years of trading history with the company's stand alone value can provide a wealth of information. First, it may suggest why the company is selling. To the extent the stock price has languished, the management team may be looking to achieve an exit for shareholders and move on. To the extent the stock price has done exceedingly well, the company may be trying to lock in the value it has created by selling the company. Second, it provides a baseline price range against which to compare the proposed offer price. For example, if the company's stock price has traded in a range of $18 to $22 per share for the past two years, and is currently trading at the lower end of that range, it may suggest that shareholders would be quite thankful to receive a price at the mid-to-upper end of that range.

A second aspect is to analyze the target's shareholder base. First, analyze the entire shareholder base to determine how much stock is owned by the board, management, employees, institutions and other entities. This will enable you to understand who may be driving the transaction, whether it is management who owns 40% of the company and is looking to realize a return, or a large institutional shareholder whose goal is to maximize a return on its portfolio holding. Second, analyze when each investor acquired stock in the company and at what price they acquired the stock. This will give you a good sense for what price each investor may be prepared to sell their stock at a gain.

This information can typically be found through public databases and filings, as large shareholders, management and insiders typically have to report their holdings in a public company.

---

2. For a detailed description of stock price and shareholder analysis, please refer to *Chapter 9: Stock Price Analysis.*

§ 26.06 TAKEOVER VALUATION[3]

Many public transactions are benchmarked off the premiums paid in and the acquisition multiples of comparable public transactions. Applying the premiums and multiples from comparable deals to the target company yields a range of values for the target that is indicative of the target company's expected purchase price. For example, if comparable acquisitions in an industry were announced with an average one-day premium of 15%, it is reasonable to believe that a 15% premium for the target in question is likely. Clearly the specific circumstances of the transaction should be taken into consideration, but transaction multiples and premiums tend to be good indicators of purchase price.

§ 26.07 IMPACT OF TRANSACTION ON SHAREHOLDER VALUE[4]

Based on the stand alone and takeover values for the target company, as well as the stock price and shareholder analysis, it is possible to derive a preliminary range of prices to evaluate the impact of an acquisition on the acquiring company. Using this range, there are two analyses that should be performed.

Accretion/Dilution Analysis: Using this analysis, an acquiring company is able to determine the potential impact of the acquisition on its future earnings. The income statements of the two consolidated and the impact of the financing for the transaction are reflected as adjustments to the income statement. Therefore, if stock is issued in the deal, the number of shares issued by the acquirer is added to its total number of shares outstanding. Likewise, if cash or debt is used to finance the acquisition, the interest cost of the debt or the diminution in interest income is reflected in the income statement. The earnings that result from this combination are then compared to the original stand alone earnings of the acquirer in order to assess whether the transaction has an overall accretive or dilutive impact on the acquirer.

While there are circumstances where dilutive deals can be well-received by the market, accretive transactions are good indicators that value is likely to be created in a transaction. The expected accretion or dilution in a deal provides a strong signaling message to the market, with accretion generally providing a positive signal and dilution indicating the possibility for paying too much. However, be careful not to fall into the P/E trap, where companies announce accretive deals, only to realize later that the core earnings growth rate of the combined company has declined, leading to a contraction of their multiple.

Contribution Analysis: As an adjunct to accretion/dilution analysis, contribution analysis serves as a check on the potential price offered in a transaction. It is most

---

3. For a more detailed description of takeover valuation, please refer to *Chapter 6: Comparable Transactions Analysis.*

4. For a more detailed description on accretion/dilution and contribution analysis, please refer to *Chapter 7: Merger Analysis.*

applicable in stock-for-stock transactions, where each party's ownership of the combined company post deal can be compared with their relative contribution of revenues, cash flow and earnings. Transactions where the relationship between the two is inconsistent should be questioned.

§ 26.08   SYNERGIES

Synergies are an important component of every analysis. To be prudent, you should understand synergies as well as you can, but ignore them in the purchase price analysis if at all possible. You may be forced to include synergies in the valuation analysis to the extent you are at a competitive disadvantage in the process. Experience suggests that synergies are difficult to achieve and therefore increasing a purchase price by utilizing synergies may result in the target's shareholders reaping more than their fair share of the combined company — in a stock-for-stock deal — or a greater purchase price than warranted in a cash deal. In stock-for-stock transactions in particular, the synergies should accrue to the benefit of shareholders of both companies. And, it is difficult to determine who "brings" the synergies to the transaction.

§ 26.09   SELLER'S OBJECTIVES

A seller's objectives can be determined through a variety of means. First, it makes sense to simply ask them why they are interested in doing the transaction and what they expect to get out of it. Asking the question may give you a clear indication of where you need to be in purchase price to win the transaction. It also gives you a sense for what other items, besides purchase price, are important. For example, a seller may wish to cash out part of their holdings in a company, yet retain some of the upside afforded by ownership in the combined company. It may suggest that the seller would like a continuing role in the company and therefore an employment contract could provide some value in the deal.

Second, a seller's objectives can be weighted against the industry and competitive analysis and either validate or invalidate what you were told.

§ 26.10   YOUR OBJECTIVES

Completely understanding your objectives will give you a roadmap for how aggressive you want to be in offering a given price. To the extent your company needs to do the deal for competitive reasons, you may wish to be more aggressive on price. Alternatively, if the acquisition is not essential, you may wish to be more opportunistic on price. You should thoroughly understand how the transaction is going to impact your own culture, management team and employees. How does it enhance market share, your relationship with customers, revenue, and earnings? Will it create a more competitive organization? Or, are you simply acquiring the business to prevent it from being acquired by someone else?

§ 26.11   FORMULATING THE OFFER ITSELF

Once you have formulated a range of prices in your own mind, the question becomes what do you put down on paper and offer as an opening bid? First, the offer should typically be presented as a range of values that predicates the upper and lower ends of the range on the satisfaction of certain types of due diligence and the resolution of certain points. Evaluate the strategic message your initial offer sends the other side. A low offer may put you at competitive advantage yet it may offend the seller and cause them to back away from the deal. A high offer may be attractive to the seller, but it can also suggest desperation on the part of the acquirer, resulting in lost leverage. If realized, it could hurt the buyer dearly in terms of the financial ramifications of the deal to shareholders.

Formulating the offer therefore, must be based on the overall financial and strategic analysis. It melds the subjective assessment of the industry, competitors and the seller's objectives, with the objective financial valuation of the target company and the assessment of the transaction's impact on the acquirer.

§ 26.12   CASE STUDY: TROPICAL PRODUCTS CORP. ACQUISITION OF GLOBAL SNACKS, INC.

In order to translate the theoretical framework into a practical application, let's revisit the hypothetical valuation case study we analyzed in Chapter 11. This potential transaction revolved around the possible acquisition of Global Snacks by Tropical Products.

The first step is to evaluate the industry and the competitor. From the case study we know that the snack food industry is highly competitive, with a number of large players that dominate the sector. Growth rates have been declining throughout the industry as overall demand for snack foods has been waning and the larger companies mature. Revenue growth comes from new product development and accessing markets outside of the U.S. In addition, earnings growth can be derived from lowering product costs and operating expenses.

Tropical's desire to make the acquisition is driven by its declining margins, slowing growth rate, and a need to access external markets. Global, as the leading player outside the United States, is an innovative, research driven company. The combination of the two companies creates the worldwide leader in the global snack food business. The two companies have complementary product lines and have little overlap in their own markets.

On a stand alone basis, Global Snacks has a going concern valuation of $15.43–$29.62 per share, with the trading multiples analysis yielding the low end of the range and the DCF analysis suggesting the high end of the range. On a takeover basis, Global Snacks has a valuation range of $15.53–$25.11 per share, based on transaction multiples and transaction premiums, with the transaction premiums yielding a fairly tight range of values of $19.71–$25.11 per share. From the stock price analysis, we know that Global Snacks has traded in a range of $18–$32 per share in the past 12 months, and has a current stock price of $18 per share. Exhibit 26-1 summarizes the range of values derived for Global Snacks based on different valuation methodologies.

Aside from the stand alone and transaction based valuation of Global Snacks, it is important to analyze the impact of the proposed transaction on Tropical Products. From the accretion/dilution analysis performed in Chapter 11, we know that at a chosen range of $18–$24 per share, and a current stock price of $38 for Tropical Products, in 2002 the transaction would be accretive by $0.27 per share at the low end of the range, and dilutive by $0.02 per share at the high end of the range, excluding any impact of synergies. Exhibit 26-2 shows the accretion/dilution sensitivity to purchase price.

In terms of formulating an offer, the accretion/dilution analysis reveals substantially more than the valuation analysis. The stand alone analysis yields a wide range of values, approximately $15.50–$30.00 per share, while the transaction analysis too provided a range of approximately $15.50–$30.00 per share. Within this range of values, the transaction premiums valuation range showed a somewhat narrow range of $29.71–$25.11 per share.

Exhibit 26-1
Global Snacks Summary Valuation Analysis

Current Stock Price:	$18.00
Stock Price Range for Last Twelve Months:	$18.00–$32.00
Trading Multiples Valuation Range:	$15.43–$25.93
Discounted Cash Flow Valuation Range:	$20.78–$29.62
Transaction Multiples Valuation Range:	$15.53–$30.53
Transaction Premiums Valuation Range:	$19.71–$25.11

Exhibit 26-2
Accretion/Dilution Analysis: Tropical Products
Acquisition of Global Snacks

Tropical Share Price	Global's Purchase Price/Premium to Current Share Price				
	$18.00 0.0%	$20.00 11.1%	$22.00 22.2%	$24.00 33.3%	$26.00 44.4%
$34.20	$0.16	$0.05	($0.05)	($0.15)	($0.24)
$36.10	$0.22	$0.11	$0.01	($0.08)	($0.17)
$38.00	$0.27	$0.17	$0.07	($0.02)	($0.11)
$39.90	$0.32	$0.22	$0.12	$0.03	($0.06)
$41.80	$0.36	$0.26	$0.17	$0.08	($0.01)

Interpreting this data, we know that the trading multiples range implies a value for Global based on the trading multiples of comparable companies. By their nature, trading multiples reflect the earnings growth, operating performance and capital structure of a company and therefore, these financial metrics and their resulting multiples are imposed on the financial metrics of Global, yielding a wide range of values, reflecting the wide range of performance of its peer group. The discounted too shows a wide range of values with a per share value that is high at the upper end. This approach also has its limitations in that the analysis depends on a number of a assumptions that can have a significant impact on value: revenue growth, margins, working capital requirements, capital expenditures, terminal value and discount rate. Even small variations in one of these assumptions can result in a dramatic shift in the range of values. For example, a 1% change in the long-term growth rate can impact the valuation by approximately $800 million, or roughly 20% of the entire equity value!

The transaction analysis, too, has certain anomalies. First, each transaction in the peer group was announced under its own set of circumstances — one may have been a negotiated transaction, another may have been hotly contested. In each case, the overall stock market and the snack food sector may have been trading based on market and industry specific factors such as changes in interest rates or other external events. In addition, each company's stock price may have been influenced by company specific events such as earnings announcements, management changes or analysts reports. Second, there are differences between the transaction premiums and the transaction multiples. The multiples analysis allows one to compare transactions based on the overall market value and equity value of a transaction, whereas the transaction premiums reflect the timing of the announcement of the transaction relative to a company's stock price at the time.

The accretion/dilution analysis goes beyond the valuation ranges by assuming a purchase price — in this case, $18 to $24 per share — and evaluates the impact of the transaction on the acquirer. Based on this analysis, we can draw a few observations.

First, Tropical's ability to pay for Global is limited given its own stock price constraints. From Exhibit 26-3, we know that the average and median projected P/E multiple for the sector, excluding Global Snacks, is 15.6× and 14.6×. Global and Tropical trade at 11.0× and 14.1× projected net income, respectively.

While Tropical trades at a premium to Global, Tropical nevertheless trades at a discount to the peer group. In addition, Tropical trades at 220% of its projected growth rate, the second highest in its peer group, suggesting that even though its multiple is below the average, it may be fairly valued in the market. In other words, investors may be giving Tropical more credit in its stock price that it should really get. Global on the other hand, trades at a mere 130% of its growth rate, suggesting that the market may not appreciate the growth and performance of the company.

While this dynamic is suggestive of why there is a financial opportunity to acquire Global, it also highlights the limitations that Tropical has in terms of paying for Global. One thing to consider when you perform this type of analysis is to

Exhibit 26-3
Snack Food Comparable Multiples

	Enterprise Value to:			Equity Value to:		
	LTM Revenues	LTM EBITDA	LTM EBIT	LTM Net Income	Projected Net Income	P/E/G[5]
Global Snacks	1.5×	6.6×	8.3×	11.5×	11.0×	130%
Tropical Products	1.6×	7.5×	9.4×	15.0×	14.1×	220%
Crunch Corp.	1.6×	8.9×	11.7×	20.4×	20.4×	240%
Fried Food Hldgs	0.9×	4.4×	5.6×	11.3×	11.1×	120%
Health Nut, Inc.	1.2×	8.7×	11.7×	15.3×	15.1×	150%
Salty Seasons	1.4×	9.8×	12.7×	20.3×	20.0×	180%
Sweeties, Inc.	1.2×	7.3×	7.7×	13.7×	12.8×	180%
Excluding Global:						
Average	1.3×	7.8×	9.8×	16.0×	15.6×	180%
Median	1.3×	8.1×	10.5×	15.1×	14.6×	180%
Excluding Global and Tropical:						
Average	1.3×	7.8×	9.9×	16.2×	15.9×	180%
Median	1.2×	8.7×	11.7×	15.3×	15.1×	180%

consider building separate accretion/dilution models for each of the potential acquirers of Global to determine each company's respective ability to pay. This may give you a sense for the probability of Tropical's success in acquiring Global at the estimated price range.

Once the accretion/dilution analysis has been performed, it is prudent to double check the analysis by performing a contribution analysis. This analysis compares the contribution of each company to the revenues and EBITDA of the combined company, with the pro forma ownership of each company's shareholders post transaction. Exhibit 26-4 recalls this analysis from Chapter 11. In this contribution analysis, we assume a purchase price of $25.50 per share, at the top end of our valuation range.

Given the $25.50 per share proposed purchase price, we know that Tropical shareholders would own approximately 63% of the combined company. From Exhibit 26-4, we know that Tropical is contributing 65.5%, 65.1% and 65.7% of revenues, EBITDA and operating income, respectively. This suggests that for the transaction to be viewed more equitably, Tropical should pay less than the $25.50 per share. Adjusting the price downward may be appropriate. From Exhibit 26-5 below, we know that at a purchase price between $22 and $24 per share, Tropical would own approximately 65% of the company, and at $22 per share, it would own

---

5. P/E/G is the price earnings multiple as a percentage of the company's projected earnings growth rate. It provides a relative valuation of a company by comparing its earnings multiple to its growth rate.

Exhibit 26-4
Contribution Analysis

	Tropical	Global	Adj.	Pro forma	% Contribution Tropical	Global
Revenue	$7,515.5	$3777.6	$ –	$11,293.1	65.5%	33.5%
Cost of Sales	4,471.7	2013.4	–	6,485.1		
Gross Profit	3,043.8	1764.2	–	4,808.0		
Operating Expenses	1,434.4	900.2	–	2,334.6		
EBITDA	1,609.4	864.0	–	2,473.4	65.1%	34.9%
Depreciation Expense	205.1	158.3	–	363.4		
Goodwill	89.1	20.0	(20.0)	89.1		
Transaction Expense	0.0	0.0	8.5	8.5		
Amortization						
Operating Income	1,315.2	685.7	11.5	2,012.4	65.4%	34.1%
Other Income (Net)	(23.1)	8.9	–	(14.2)		
Interest Expense (Net)	228.3	122.4	6.8	357.5		
Pre-Tax Income	1,063.8	572.2	4.7	1,640.7	64.8%	34.9%
Income Taxes	372.3	200.3	(2.4)	570.2		
Net Income	$ 691.5	$ 371.9		$ 1,070.5	64.6%	34.7%

Exhibit 26-5
The Impact of Price on Tropical's Ownership of
Pro Forma Combined Company

Tropical Share Price	Global's Purchase Price/Premium to Current Share Price				
	$18.00 0.0%	$20.00 11.1%	$22.00 22.2%	$24.00 33.3%	$26.00 44.4%
$34.00	68%	66%	63%	61%	59%
$36.00	69%	67%	65%	63%	61%
$38.00	70%	68%	66%	64%	62%
$40.00	71%	69%	67%	65%	63%
$42.00	72%	70%	68%	66%	64%

66% of the company post transaction. Therefore, based on the contribution analysis, a top price for Tropical to pay for Global, excluding any impact of synergies, may be approximately $22 per share.

With the contribution analysis complete, we need to assimilate all of our financial information. We know from the valuation analysis that Global has a stand alone value that could reach as high as $30 per share. In addition, we know that the transaction analysis yields a value as high as $25 per share. Further, we know that Global has a current stock price of $18 per share and has traded as high as $32 per share in the past twelve months.

From the accretion/dilution analysis, we know that the transaction is accretive at $18 per share and becomes marginally dilutive at $24 per share. We also know from the contribution analysis that at $24 per share, and Tropical's current stock price of $38 per share, Tropical's shareholders would own approximately 64% of the combined company, less than the 65%–66% of revenues, EBITDA and operating earnings that it contributes to the combined company.

Therefore, on the one hand, at a price of $24 per share, Tropical would own less of the company than it contributes, yet on the other hand, the transaction is marginally dilutive in 2002. This could suggest a few concerns. First, it implies that if Tropical could secure the transaction at less than $24 per share, it may be getting a good deal for shareholders. However, it could also suggest that the market may not like the deal because it is slightly dilutive at $24 per share. Second, it may suggest that Tropical should wait to make a bid until its stock price is higher. For example, if Tropical's stock price increased $2 to $40 per share, it could offer almost $2 per share more in consideration before the transaction becomes dilutive.

At $40 per share for Tropical and $26 per share for Global, the transaction is accretive to Global in 2002 by $0.03 per share. Third, the overall analysis raises a concern over the likelihood that Tropical is successful in its bid for Global in the event of competition from third parties. Since Tropical trades at a multiple that is substantially below that of the peer group, it could be that one of its competitors has a greater ability to pay for the company that it does.

Given the overall analysis, Tropical may wish to take a hard look at the synergies that are achievable in the transaction. While I do not necessarily recommend "using" synergies to increase purchase price, it may be worthwhile understanding the magnitude of the synergies in order to substantiate the long-term value creation opportunity. For example, from Exhibit 26-6, we know that at a proposed purchase price of $24 per share, an increase in operating margin of $75 million, or approximately 2.5% of combined operating income, would result in 2002 accretion of

Exhibit 26-6
2002 Accretion/Dilution Sensitivity to Margins

Operating Synergies (in millions)	Global's Purchase Price/Premium to Current Share Price				
	$18.00 0.0%	**$20.00** 11.1%	**$22.00** 22.2%	**$24.00** 33.3%	**$26.00** 44.4%
$ 0.0	$0.27	$0.17	$0.07	($0.02)	($0.11)
$ 75.0	$0.42	$0.31	$0.20	$0.11	$0.02
$150.0	$0.56	$0.45	$0.34	$0.24	$0.14
$225.0	$0.71	$0.59	$0.48	$0.37	$0.27

$0.11 per share. This may suggest that Tropical could "stretch" to $24 per share for the transaction, and make sure it communicates a strong story to the market regarding the combined opportunity for the company.

Based on the valuation analysis for Global Snacks, its stand alone valuation reached as high as $30 per share. As we have learned, the stand alone valuation by itself does not suggest an appropriate range of values for Global. The accretion/dilution analysis indicates Tropical's ability to pay for Global based on the value of its own stock currency. At $24 per share, the transaction would be marginally dilutive to Tropical in 2002 by $0.02 per share, excluding any synergies. Including $75 million in synergies, the transaction would be accretive by $0.11 per share in 2002. In addition, we know that at $24.00 per share, Tropical would own approximately 66% of the combined company, greater than the 65%–66% of the revenues, EBITDA and operating earnings it contributes to the combined company.

This overall analysis indicates that at this price, Tropical shareholders would own more of the combined company than Global shareholders, yet the Global shareholders would be receiving a 33.3% premium to the current $18 stock price for Global. This purchase price compares to the average comparable one-day prior premium paid in prior transactions of 12.9%.

Armed with this information, Tropical must then focus on critical strategic issues before finalizing its price for the initial offer. It needs to balance its need to make the acquisition in order to access Global's foreign markets, obtain its research and development capability and shore up its own margins, with the potential that another company may be in a position to pay more for the company, and the fact that at $20 per share, the transaction is slightly dilutive to its 2002 earnings.

Assuming a $20 per share initial offer, the task ahead for Tropical's management is to convince Global's board that it is the best acquirer, or strategic merger partner, for Global and its shareholders.

§ 26.13   SUMMARY

Formulating an offer is a difficult task. It requires assimilating valuation analysis with transaction impact analysis and strategic analysis. In addition, it requires evaluating the ability of third party competing bidders to potentially intercede with a proposed transaction. It mandates that a buyer balance the difference between paying a winning price while ensuring that enough value is created for its own shareholders to warrant the deal. It requires that the buyer evaluate and understand what happens if it is not successful in winning the transaction.

As a review, following are a number of guidelines to use in formulating the financial terms of an offer.

1. Calculate a preliminary range of stand alone values for the target. This includes the trading multiples and DCF analyses.

2. Determine a potential purchase price based on comparable transactions. This includes the transaction multiples and transaction premiums analyses.

3. Formulate the maximum price your company could pay within those range of values by assessing the acquirer's ability to pay. This is accomplished using the accretion/dilution analysis.

4. Double check the maximum purchase price to assess the rational for the purchase price. This is performed using the contribution analysis.

5. If necessary, determine the maximum price the most likely competitors could pay using the same accretion/dilution and contribution analyses.

6. Evaluate the competitive landscape to determine the relative impact of the proposed transaction on your company and your competitors. Ask yourself what the impact would be if you did not win the deal?

Chapter 27

STRUCTURING THE LETTER OF INTENT AND DEFINITIVE AGREEMENT

§ 27.01   OVERVIEW

Most M&A transactions follow a similar overall plan from inception to closing. However, the specific steps in certain transactions can vary depending on a number of factors including, whether the transaction is between public or private companies, requires financing, or is not a plain vanilla merger or acquisition. Generally speaking, an M&A transaction progresses according to the following steps, some of which are concurrent:

1. The parties enter into a confidentiality agreement and exchange confidential information.

2. The acquirer formulates an initial offer.

3. The acquirer submits an initial non-binding offer in a letter of intent.

4. The parties perform due diligence.

5. The acquirer submits a revised letter of intent.

6. The first draft of the definitive agreement is prepared.

7. Financing is secured if required.

8. The parties negotiate and execute the definitive agreement.

9. Relevant filings are made with the SEC and other regulatory bodies.

10. Regulatory and other approvals are received.

11. Shareholder approval is received if necessary.

12. The transaction closes.

Two critical aspects of the process, and the subject of this chapter, are the structuring of the letter intent and the definitive agreement. A letter of intent (LOI) is a non-binding letter provided by a prospective acquirer to the seller. It outlines the macro financial and legal terms of the acquirer's offer. The definitive agreement is the binding document that includes all the financial and legal terms that will govern the transaction.

§ 27.02   THE CONFIDENTIALITY AGREEMENT

The confidential process of evaluating a transaction between two parties begins with signing a confidentiality agreement. This agreement is designed to protect the misuse of proprietary information shared between the parties, and prohibit disclosure of that information. In addition, a confidentiality agreement can also set guidelines for behavior during the transaction process. For example, a confidentiality agreement may restrict an acquirer's right to solicit the target's employees or prevent the acquirer from purchasing stock in a target without the prior approval of the target's board of directors. A confidentiality agreement is also known as a non-disclosure agreement.

Confidentiality can be in the form of "one-way" or "two-way" agreements. A one-way agreement is where information is provided from one party to another and the party in receipt of the information signs the agreement and is bound not to misuse the information it has been provided. A two-way agreement is used in instances where both parties in a transaction share information with each other, each becoming bound by the terms of the agreement. For illustrative purposes, a one-way confidentiality agreement is discussed in this chapter.

There are a number of legal terms in a confidentiality agreement that require explanation.

[A]   Definition of Information

In an M&A transaction, there are many different types of information pertaining to the business, operations and financial performance of a company that are shared between the parties. The principal concern of the parties is to protect the proprietary nature of this information and to limit the possibility of misuse and disclosure. Typically there is a period of time during which the information must remain confidential, and in some cases, a time frame for maintaining confidentiality of certain information can be in perpetuity. Following are pertinent excerpts from a sample confidentiality agreement that pertain to the definition of information.

> In connection with a possible transaction between you and XYZ, Inc. (the "Company"), the Company will make available to you certain information concerning its business, financial condition and operations. You and your Representatives ("Representatives" means the directors, officers, employees, agents or advisors (including without limitation, attorneys, accountants and financial advisors), respectively, of you and the Company) agree to treat all Information (as defined below) in accordance with the provisions of this letter agreement.
>
> The term "Information" means any information concerning the Company (whether prepared by the Company, its Representatives or otherwise and irrespective of the form of the information or the manner in which it is communicated) furnished to you or to your Representatives by the Company or its Representatives. The term "Information" does not include information which (i) is or becomes generally available to the public other than as a result of a disclosure by you or your Representatives, or (ii) was within your possession prior to its being furnished to you by the Company or its Representatives, or (iii) becomes available to you on a nonconfidential basis from a source other than the Company or any of its Representatives, provided in each case that the source of such information was not prohibited from disclosing such information to you by a legal, contractual or fiduciary obligation to the Company.

There are a number of elements that can often come up for negotiation in this definition. First, it is possible to see multiple parties named in the agreement, not just the parent company. For example, if a partially owned subsidiary is working with the parent company to evaluate the transaction, one may see all the parties named in the confidentiality agreement. Second, the parties may wish to include or exclude certain types of representatives in the definition of Representatives. It is more typical to witness the definition expanding to include other specific types of representatives that have a relationship with the signatory to the confidentiality agreement. For example, this could include a named individual or a specific firm. Third, the definition of information may be clarified to avoid misunderstandings over what information was in the public domain or not, and what information specifically is subject to the confidentiality agreement. For example, if an information memorandum was prepared, it may be referenced specifically in the confidentiality agreement.

[B]   Disclosure of Information

Once the proprietary information has been defined, the confidentiality agreement then specifies how the information may be used and to whom the information may, or may not, be disclosed. Following is illustrative language pertinent to the disclosure of information.

> You agree that you and your Representatives shall use the Information solely for the purpose of evaluating a possible transaction between the Company and you, that the Information will be kept confidential and that you and your Representatives will not disclose any of the Information in any manner whatsoever, in whole or in part, provided, however, that you may make any disclosure of such information to regulatory authorities having jurisdiction over you and to your Representatives who need to know such information for the purpose of evaluating a possible transaction, provided, further, that you shall inform each such Representative of the confidential nature of the Information and of the terms of this letter agreement. You agree, at your sole expense, to take all reasonable measures (including, without limitation, court proceedings) to restrain your Representatives from prohibited or unauthorized disclosure or use of the Information.

The party bound by the agreement may wish to have the individual representatives sign separate agreements, as it may not wish to be responsible for the behavior of each of the representatives.

Despite the aforementioned restriction on disclosure of proprietary information, the confidentiality agreement may provide for disclosure that is required by law. The agreement specifies the process for complying with this disclosure as seen below.

> In the event that you or any of your Representatives are requested or required to disclose any of the Information, you shall provide the Company with prompt written notice of such request or requirement so that the

Company may seek a protective order or other appropriate remedy and/or waive compliance with the provisions of this letter agreement. If, in the absence of a protective order or other remedy or the receipt of a waiver from the Company, you or any of your Representatives are nonetheless, in the opinion of your counsel, legally compelled to disclose the Information, you or any such Representative may, without liability hereunder, disclose only that portion of the Information which such counsel advises you is legally required to be disclosed, provided that you exercise your best efforts, but without cost to you, to preserve the confidentiality of the Information, including, without limitation, by cooperating with the Company (at the Company's cost and expense) to obtain an appropriate protective order or other reliable assurance that confidential treatment will be accorded the Information.

In some cases where there is potential for forced disclosure, the parties may negotiate stricter or less onerous terms depending on the potential threat.

[C]   Discussion with Other Parties

Included in the proprietary information is the fact that discussions are taking place between the parties. The confidentiality agreement typically prohibits disclosure regarding the discussions and negotiations as evidenced in the example below.

In addition, you agree that, without the prior written consent of the Company, you and your Representatives will not disclose to any person or entity (other than bank regulatory authorities having jurisdiction over you) the fact that the Information has been made available to you, that discussions or negotiations are taking place or have taken place concerning a possible transaction involving the Company or any of such transaction's terms, conditions or other facts (including its status), unless in the opinion of your counsel such disclosure is required by law and then only with as much prior written notice to the Company as is practical or allowed under the circumstances.

The confidentiality agreement requires that all proprietary information be destroyed or returned in the event the transaction is not consummated. Regardless however, the parties are still bound by the obligations under the agreement, as outlined below.

If you decide that you do not wish to proceed with a transaction with the Company, you will promptly inform the Company of that decision. In that case, or at any time upon the request of the Company for any reason, you will promptly deliver to the Company or, at your option, certify as to the destruction of all Information (including all copies thereof and any notes, analyses, studies, interpretations or other documents prepared by you or your Representatives which contain, reflect or are based on any of the Information) furnished to you or your Representatives. Notwithstanding the return or destruction of the Information, you and your Representatives will continue to be bound by your obligations of confidentiality and other obligations under this letter agreement.

While the party providing the information typically does so in good faith, it is not uncommon for the disclosing party to ensure that it does not make any representation as to the accuracy or completeness of the information, and as such shall have no liability to the other party resulting from the use of the information. The language would read as follows.

> Although the Company has endeavored to include in the Information, information and materials which the Company believes to be relevant for the purpose of your investigation of the Company, you acknowledge that neither the Company nor any of its Representatives makes any representation or warranty as to the accuracy or completeness of the Information. You agree that neither the Company nor any of its Representatives shall have any liability to you or to any of your Representatives relating to, or resulting from the use of, the Information by you or any of your Representatives.

[D]   Non-Solicitation of Employees

Often, confidentiality agreements contain provisions that prohibit the parties from soliciting the employees of the other. This provision may not only limit the solicitation, but also prevent the parties from hiring any employees that may not have been solicited, but approached either party independently. The provisions may be general and pertain to all employees and management, or they may be specific and name certain levels of employees, for example, Vice Presidents and above, or go so far as to identify individual employees by name. Following is illustrative non-solicitation language.

> You further agree that for a period of one year from the date of this letter agreement, neither you nor any of your subsidiaries or affiliates will directly or indirectly solicit for employment or employ any persons who are employees of the Company that are involved in the due diligence process or that you learn of through such process; provided, however, that if any such employee has been dismissed by the Company, or solicits you, you may freely solicit and employ such person; and provided, further, that advertisements or other solicitations made to the public generally shall not be restricted by this letter agreement.

[E]   Survival of the Terms of the Confidentiality Agreement

The terms of a confidentiality agreement may survive in perpetuity, or in certain circumstances, the terms of part or all of the agreement may survive for a limited period of time. The survival period will depend on the nature of the life of the proprietary information and the degree to which the information may hurt the disclosing company if it becomes public. For example, it is often the case that the terms protecting financial information survive for a limited period of time, say one year, because financial information becomes old fairly quickly. Alternatively, information relating to proprietary technology may have a perpetuity life and not be subject to any survival termination provisions.

[F]   Standstill Provisions

For public companies, the confidentiality agreement typically contains what is known as a standstill provision. This prohibits a potential acquirer from purchasing the stock of the target or seeking to control the target company without having been specifically requested by the target company. While the topic of standstill provisions merits an entire book of its own, following is a sample standstill for a public company acquisition.

> Unless specifically requested by the Company, you will not for a period of one year from the date of this letter agreement, (A) directly or indirectly (whether alone or in concert with another person, entity or group) acquire, offer to acquire, or agree to acquire, or make any proposal with respect to the acquisition, by purchase or otherwise, from the Company or from any other person or entity, of any securities or assets of the Company or direct or indirect rights or options to acquire any securities or assets of the Company or any of its subsidiaries, or (B) otherwise act (whether alone or in concert with another person, entity or group) to seek to control or influence the management, Board of Directors, or policies of the Company.

In addition to limiting an acquirer's ability to purchase the target company's stock without permission, the confidentiality agreement may also prohibit the acquirer from seeking control of the target company through a proxy solicitation.

Following in Exhibit 27-1 is an illustrative confidentiality agreement that could have been prepared for the Tropical Products Corp. acquisition of Global Snacks, Inc.

Exhibit 27-1
Illustrative Confidentiality Agreement Between Tropical Products Corp. and Global Snacks, Inc.

February 1, 2001

Tropical Products Corp.
1 Main Street
Suite 100
Orlando, FL 32820

Attention: Howard Baker, President & CEO

Gentlemen/Ladies:

In connection with a possible transaction between you and Global Snacks, Inc. (the "Company"), the Company will make available to you certain information concerning its

(Continued)

Exhibit 27-1
(*Continued*)

business, financial condition and operations. You and your Representatives ("Representatives" means the directors, officers, employees, agents or advisors (including without limitation, attorneys, accountants and financial advisors), respectively, of you and the Company) agree to treat all Information (as defined below) in accordance with the provisions of this letter agreement.

The term "Information" means any information concerning the Company (whether prepared by the Company, its Representatives or otherwise and irrespective of the form of the information or the manner in which it is communicated) furnished to you or to your Representatives by the Company or its Representatives. The term "Information" does not include information which (i) is or becomes generally available to the public other than as a result of a disclosure by you or your Representatives, or (ii) was within your possession prior to its being furnished to you by the Company or its Representatives, or (iii) becomes available to you on a non-confidential basis from a source other than the Company or any of its Representatives, provided in each case that the source of such information was not prohibited from disclosing such information to you by a legal, contractual or fiduciary obligation to the Company.

You agree that you and your Representatives shall use the Information solely for the purpose of evaluating a possible transaction between the Company and you, that the Information will be kept confidential and that you and your Representatives will not disclose any of the Information in any manner whatsoever, in whole or in part, provided, however, that you may make any disclosure of such information to bank regulatory authorities having jurisdiction over you and to your Representatives who need to know such information for the purpose of evaluating a possible transaction, provided, further, that you shall inform each such Representative of the confidential nature of the Information and of the terms of this letter agreement. You agree, at your sole expense, to take all reasonable measures (including, without limitation, court proceedings) to restrain your Representatives from prohibited or unauthorized disclosure or use of the Information.

In addition, you agree that, without the prior written consent of the Company, you and your Representatives will not disclose to any person or entity (other than bank regulatory authorities having jurisdiction over you) the fact that the Information has been made available to you, that discussions or negotiations are taking place or have taken place concerning a possible transaction involving the Company or any of such transaction's terms, conditions or other facts (including its status), unless in the opinion of your counsel such disclosure is required by law and then only with as much prior written notice to the Company as is practical or allowed under the circumstances.

In the event that you or any of your Representatives are requested or required to disclose any of the Information, you shall provide the Company with prompt written notice of such request or requirement to the extent permitted by law so that the Company may seek a protective order or other appropriate remedy and/or waive compliance with the provisions of this letter agreement. If, in the absence of a protective order or other remedy or the receipt of a waiver from the Company, you or any of your Representatives are nonetheless, in the opinion of your counsel, legally compelled to disclose Information, you or any such Representative may, without liability hereunder, disclose only that portion of the Information which such counsel advises you is legally required to be disclosed, provided that you exercise your best efforts, but without cost to you, to preserve the confidentiality of the Information, including, without limitation, by cooperating with the Company (at the Company's cost and expense) to obtain an appropriate protective order or other reliable assurance that confidential treatment will be accorded the Information.

(*Continued*)

Exhibit 27-1
(*Continued*)

If you decide that you do not wish to proceed with a transaction with the Company, you will promptly inform the Company of that decision. In that case, or at any time upon the request of the Company for any reason, you will promptly deliver to the Company or, at your option, certify as to the destruction of all Information (including all copies thereof and any notes, analyses, studies, interpretations or other documents prepared by you or your Representatives which contain, reflect or are based on any of the Information) furnished to you or your Representatives. Notwithstanding the return or destruction of the Information, you and your Representatives will continue to be bound by your obligations of confidentiality and other obligations under this letter agreement.

Although the Company has endeavored to include in the Information information and materials which the Company believes to be relevant for the purpose of your investigation of the Company, you acknowledge that neither the Company nor any of its Representatives makes any representation or warranty as to the accuracy or completeness of the Information. You agree that neither the Company nor any of its Representatives shall have any liability to you or to any of your Representatives relating to, or resulting from the use of, the Information by you or any of your Representatives.

Unless specifically requested by the Company, you will not for a period of one year from the date of this letter agreement, (A) directly or indirectly (whether alone or in concert with another person, entity or group) acquire, offer to acquire, or agree to acquire, or make any proposal with respect to the acquisition, by purchase or otherwise, from the Company or from any other person or entity, of any securities or assets of the Company or direct or indirect rights or options to acquire any securities or assets of the Company or any of its subsidiaries, or (B) otherwise act (whether alone or in concert with another person, entity or group) to seek to control or influence the management, Board of Directors, or policies of the Company.

You further agree that for a period of one year from the date of this letter agreement, neither you nor any of your subsidiaries or affiliates will directly or indirectly solicit for employment or employ any persons who are employees of the Company that are involved in the due diligence process or that you learn of through such process; provided, however, that if any such employee has been dismissed by the Company, or solicits you, you may freely solicit and employ such person; and provided, further, that advertisements or other solicitations made to the public generally shall not be restricted by this letter agreement.

It is understood and agreed that no failure or delay by the Company in exercising any right, power or privilege shall operate as a waiver, nor shall any single or partial exercise preclude any other or further exercise or the exercise of any other right, power or privilege.

It is further understood and agreed that money damages would not be a sufficient remedy for any breach of this letter agreement by you or any of your Representatives and that the Company shall be entitled to equitable relief, including injunction and specific performance, as a remedy for any such breach, and that you shall not oppose the granting of such relief. Such remedies shall not be the exclusive remedies for a breach by you of this letter agreement but shall be in addition to all other remedies available at law or equity to the Company.

This letter agreement shall be governed by and construed in accordance with the internal laws of the State of New York without reference to its conflict of laws rules.

It is agreed that you have no obligation to the Company, except as described in this letter agreement, unless and until a definitive and mutually acceptable agreement is executed by you and the Company. It is further agreed that you may, at any time and for any reason, cease any consideration of any business relationship or transaction with the Company.

(*Continued*)

Exhibit 27-1
(*Continued*)

Please confirm your agreement by signing and returning one copy of this letter, whereupon this letter agreement shall become a binding agreement between you and the Company.

Very truly yours,
GLOBAL SNACKS, INC.

By:_____
Ernest Henry

Chairman

Accepted and agreed as of the date first written above:
TROPICAL PRODUCTS CORP.

By:_____
Howard Baker

President & CEO

---

§ 27.03 FORMULATING THE OFFER

Once an initial round of due diligence has been performed, the parties kick off the formal negotiation process by having the acquirer submit an initial offer or bid for the business, company or assets under consideration. The initial offer is based on the combined financial and strategic analysis done in a transaction. Many times, an opening offer is presented in the form of a letter of intent. It is not simply comprised of price; rather, it includes a number of additional material terms and conditions that help support the offer price. However, determining the offer price, in particular the initial bid, is the most difficult aspect of preparing an offer. While this section provides an overview of formulating an offer, Chapter 26 provides a detailed analysis of the topic.

Formulating the initial offer is based on a number of variables. It takes into consideration the current M&A environment as well as the acquirer's ability to pay for the business or assets. While it considers the value of the target, the offer may or may not necessarily mimic the value of the business. The value of a business is independent of the acquirer's ability to pay; likewise, the offer is dependent as much on the acquirer's ability to pay as it is on the acquirer's ability to realize a return on the investment. Formulating an initial offer therefore, is a balancing act between the value of the target, which could lead to a high purchase price, and the price that the acquirer may pay and still realize a return.

A number of factors should be analyzed in order to formulate an initial offer for a company. Each of these elements provides a different perspective on both your ability to pay and your need to pay for the target. Many of the elements are quantitative, yet the critical skill is to understand the subjective issues and apply business judgement in formulating the offer. These key elements are as follows:

Industry Trends: Analyzing industry trends allows one to understand where the growth in the business is going to come from, what some of the potential issues are that the company is facing, and allows one to evaluate the target business in the context of the competitors in the sector. Understanding the industry may also offer insight into why a seller is divesting a business. Having a good grasp on the industry trends allows one to frame the entire transaction in the context of the industry.

Competitive Environment: The competitive environment may yield a view of how prized the target business is. Competitive industries may indicate a number of potential buyers for a property, suggesting a competitive bidding environment. In this case, a buyer may be inclined to bid at the high end of their price range in order to win the deal. Concentrated industries may suggest a lack of potential bidders for a property; however, it could also indicate that the few remaining competitors may be just as eager as you to get their hands on the target. Evaluating the competitive landscape may also reveal the strengths and weaknesses in the target business.

Stand Alone Valuation of the Target Company: The stand alone value of the company should be determined using discounted cash flow analysis, comparable trading multiples analysis, and if appropriate, leveraged buyout analysis. The stand alone valuation and leveraged buyout analysis gives one a means to initiate the purchase price analysis because, if you have an understanding of the stand alone valuation, you probably have a good sense for the target's own perception of its value and expectations in the deal.

Historical Trading Prices and Share Ownership of Target Company: A public company's trading history is a fairly good indicator of how the company has been perceived over time in the marketplace. Comparing the last few years of trading history with the company's stand alone values can provide a wealth of information. First, it may suggest why the company is selling. To the extent the stock price has languished, the management team may be looking to achieve an exit for shareholders and move on. To the extent the stock price has done exceedingly well, the company may be trying to lock in the value it has created by selling the company. Second, it provides one with a roadmap of what events have led to changes in the company's stock price and why the company is valued at a given level in the current environment.

A second element of the target company's stock price is to analyze its shareholder base. First, analyze the entire shareholder base to determine how much stock is owned by the board, management, employees, institutions and other entities. This will enable you to understand who may be driving the transaction, whether it's management who owns 40% of the company and is looking to realize a return, or a large institutional shareholder whose goal is to maximize value for shareholders. Second, analyze when each investor acquired stock in the company and what their going-in basis is. This will give you a good sense for what price each investor may be prepared to sell their stock at a gain.

Acquisition Premiums and Multiples: Many public transactions are benchmarked off the premiums paid in and the acquisition multiples of comparable public transactions. Applying the premiums and multiples from comparable deals to the target company yields a range of values for the target that is indicative of the target company's expected purchase price.

Impact on Shareholder Value: Based on the stand alone and acquisition values for the target company, it is possible to derive a preliminary range of prices to evaluate the impact of an acquisition on the acquiring company. Using this range, one should perform and accretion/dilution analysis and a contribution analysis. The accretion/dilution analysis will yield a price at which the transaction is accretive or dilutive to the acquirer. This price is a strong indication of the level at which the acquirer can pay for the target yet not suffer earnings dilution and possibly shareholder value loss. The contribution analysis serves as a check on whether a proposed purchase price for a target translates into pro forma ownership that is consistent with each company's contribution of revenues and earnings to the combined company.

Synergies: Synergies are a vital aspect of every transaction. It is likely that most transactions will generate synergies of one sort or another, for example, in the form of cutting overhead costs, or generating incremental revenue as a result of the combination. The value created through the synergies should be viewed as "cushion" in the deal to the acquirer, not necessarily as a means to increase purchase price.

Seller's Objectives: A seller's objectives can be determined through a variety of means. First, it makes sense to simply ask them why they are interested in doing the transaction and what they expect to get out of it. Asking the question may give you a clear indication of where you need to be in purchase price to win the transaction. Second, the industry and competitive analysis may provide further insight into the seller's objectives and either validate or invalidate what they told you.

Your Objectives: Completely understanding your objectives will give you a roadmap for how aggressive you want to be in offering a high price. To the extent your company needs to do the deal for competitive reasons, you may wish to be more aggressive on price. Alternatively, if the acquisition is not essential, you may wish to be more opportunistic on price.

Based on the above factors, you should be able to formulate the initial offer as it relates to the proposed purchase price. Once you have formulated a range of prices in your own mind, the question becomes what do you put down on paper and offer as an opening bid? The offer should typically be a range of values that predicates the upper and lower range on the satisfaction of certain types of due diligence and the satisfactory resolution of certain points. Evaluate the strategic message your initial offer sends the other side. A low initial offer may put the buyer at a competitive disadvantage and may not motivate the seller to do the deal. A high initial offer suggests eagerness and may result in lost leverage and if realized, could cost the buyer dearly in terms of the financial ramifications of the deal to shareholders.

§ 27.04   SUBMITTING THE INITIAL NON-BINDING LETTER OF INTENT

In many transactions, it is common to memorialize an initial offer in a letter of intent or memorandum of understanding. This document typically outlines the major terms of the deal such as price, a description of the business or assets to be acquired, the major conditions to closing, and any other terms that may be material to a negotiation.

The letter of intent serves a number of purposes. First, it outlines the major issues in the deal and forces the parties in the deal to focus on their common points as well as their differences. Second, it serves as a foundation for the formal contract and the basis for the negotiations. Finally, the letter of intent can be used to initiate certain approval processes such as financing waivers or antitrust clearance.

The letter of intent is usually addressed to the individual who is to receive the offer and briefly outlines the key terms of the offer or proposal. The common elements in a letter of intent are as follows:

[A]   Purchase Price

The price is the actual purchase value for the stock or assets of the company. It may be stated as a price per share or it could be stated as an aggregate dollar value. It also may or may not include a statement regarding the assumption of certain liabilities. For example, in a stock-for-stock merger, a typical price would be stated as, say, $25.00 per share. Implicit in this statement is the assumption of the liabilities on the balance sheet, since the acquirer is acquiring the stock of the company. Alternatively, in a cash acquisition of a company's assets, the price could be stated as, say, as $100 million plus the assumption of $25 million in liabilities.

The purchase price would be based on all the work performed in formulating the initial offer. However, one should be cognizant of the relationships between the offer price of the deal and all the other terms and conditions of the letter of intent.

[B]   Consideration

The consideration is the currency that is offered to the seller by the buyer. It can range from the seller's stock in a stock-for-stock transaction, to cash, or to other forms of consideration such as a note or convertible preferred stock. For example, a buyer could offer a combination of $75 million in cash plus a $15 million note plus stock in the buyer worth $10 million.

[C]   Transaction Structure

The structure of a transaction typically relates to the manner in which the transaction is accomplished. It can refer to the accounting for the transaction. It can refer to the tax and legal structure of the transaction, for example, a tax-free reorganization. It can identify a subsidiary that would be used to merge into the acquirer. It may refer to the acquisition of stock or assets of the company.

[D]   Conditions to Closing

These conditions are designed to ensure that the parties to the contract fulfill them prior to the closing of the deal. If the conditions are not met, then the party who did not fulfill the condition runs the risk that it loses the deal as the counterparty has no obligation to close the transaction. Typical closing conditions include: (a) no material adverse change in the business between signing an closing, (b) all representations and warranties of the buyer and seller are true, and (c) all documents requested by the buyer and seller have been delivered.

[E]   Due Diligence

Typically one or both of the parties to a transaction will want to perform extensive due diligence prior to signing a contract. The due diligence provision provides that the target company will cooperate with the counterparty in conducting due diligence and provide it with the requisite information and personnel to complete its due diligence.

[F]   Timing

It is common to specify in the letter of intent the expected time frame for conducting due diligence, negotiating the definitive agreement and signing the documents. It may also be appropriate to define a date upon which the offer as outlined in the letter of intent is no longer valid if a contract has not been signed. The purpose of this provision is to encourage both sides to work diligently toward the signing of a definitive agreement.

[G]   Approvals

Most transactions require a number of approvals in order to close. These approvals range from government such as antitrust, to corporate such as Board of Director, to shareholder approval, to the approval of lenders. The letter of intent can specify the required approvals in detail, or can refer to all required approvals.

[H]   Non-Binding

Most letters of intent are non-binding, meaning that they are not legally binding on the parties until a formal contract has been executed. One exception is the confidentiality provision that usually remains in effect even if a deal is not consummated. The letter of intent typically contains language that states that they are non-binding.

[I]   Confidentiality

Even though the parties to the transaction usually have already entered into a confidentiality agreement, a confidentiality provision is often included in the letter of intent to reinforce the proprietary nature of the discussions. The confidentiality provision may include many of the same provisions contained in the stand alone confidentiality agreement including non-solicit provisions, standstill provisions, and the like.

Following in Exhibit 27-2 is a hypothetical initial non-binding letter of intent sent from Tropical Products Corp. to Global Snacks, Inc.

Exhibit 27-2
Hypothetical Letter of Intent for the Tropical Products Corp. Acquisition of Global Snacks, Inc.

March 30, 2001

Mr. Ernest Henry
Chairman
Global Snacks, Inc.
65 Center Street
New York, NY 10025

Dear John:

Tropical Products Corp. ("Tropical") is delighted to submit this offer to acquire the capital stock Global Snacks, Inc. ("Global" or the "Company"). This letter of intent is intended to summarize the principal terms of our proposal and establish a basis for further negotiations of a merger agreement ("Agreement"). This letter contains non-binding terms and conditions of the proposed business combination and is intended only to assist the parties in negotiating a comprehensive, binding Agreement to be signed by the parties.

The principal terms are as follows:

1. *Acquirer.* The acquirer shall be Tropical Products Corp, Inc., a Delaware corporation.

2. *Price.* Tropical proposes to acquire all the outstanding common stock of Global for a purchase price of $22.00–$24.00 per share.

3. *Structure.* The transaction shall be structured as a "tax-free reorganization" and shall be accounted for under the purchase method.

4. *Consideration.* The form of consideration shall be Tropical common stock. Based on the average closing stock price of Tropical's common shares for the prior twenty trading days of $38.00 per share, the number of shares that would be issued to Global shareholders would equal to 110.5 million.

5. *Continuing Relationship With Ernest Henry and Frank Stellar.* Mr. Henry and Mr. Stellar will enter into consulting and non-competition agreements with Tropical that will include mutually acceptable terms and conditions. Mr. Henry and Mr. Stellar will be offered Board seats on the Tropical Board of Directors.

6. *Representations and Warranties.* Global and Tropical shall give such representations and warranties as are customary with respect to similar transactions.

7. *Definitive Agreement; Closing.* The parties shall commence immediately to finalize a mutually acceptable Agreement with the goal of closing the transaction before June 30, 2001.

8. *Conditions to Closing.* In addition to the other conditions described herein, Tropical shall require the following conditions to closing: (i) approval of the Tropical Board of Directors, (ii) shareholder approval, (iii) Hart-Scott-Rodino approval,

(Continued)

Exhibit 27-2
(*Continued*)

---

and (iv) the management team of Global shall have entered into employment contracts acceptable to Tropical.

9. *Due Diligence.* Global shall make available to Tropical all officers, directors and key employees as well as grant Tropical full access to the Company's properties, records, personnel, facilities, books, financial and operating data and contracts and other documents. In addition, the Company shall furnish to Tropical all books and records that Tropical may reasonably request in order to complete its due diligence prior to the signing of a definitive agreement.

10. *No Shop.* Through the later of three months from the signing of this letter of intent or June 30, 2001, you agree not to solicit, negotiate or accept any offer for Global, or to cause Global to solicit, negotiate or accept any offer for a merger or sale of part or all of the Company.

11. *Non-Binding.* This letter of intent is intended to be non-binding on the parties. Only those terms contained in a definitive merger agreement shall be binding on the parties.

12. *Publicity.* The parties agree not to make any public announcement regarding this transaction without the other's prior written approval. The parties shall agree to issue a joint press release at a time to be mutually agreed upon.

13. *Confidentiality.* We refer you to that certain confidentiality agreement dated February 1, 2001, and remind you of the confidentiality of these discussions.

If the foregoing terms are acceptable, please sign as indicated below on the enclosed duplicate original of this letter and return the same to us.

Very truly yours,

Tropical Products Corp.
Howard Baker, President & CEO

Agreed and Accepted this ____ day of April ___, 2001.
Global Snacks, Inc.

By:_____
   Ernest Henry, Chairman

§ 27.05   ADVANTAGES AND DISADVANTAGES OF LETTERS OF INTENT

Letters of intent can serve a number of good purposes yet may have drawbacks as well. Before undertaking the effort of drafting a letter of intent, it is wise to determine if the proposed transaction warrants one at all and if the letter by itself creates any issues.

[A]   Advantages

There are significant benefits to both sides to a transaction in drafting a letter of intent. First, it helps develop a framework for the negotiation. Second, it forces the parties to the transaction to focus on the issues and determine where the common ground is or what issues need to be explored further. Third, while a letter of intent is non-binding, it does create a sense of commitment between the parties. Fourth, for a seller, a letter of intent provides a fairly reliable benchmark against which to compare other transactions.

[B] Disadvantages

There are many disadvantages to drafting a letter of intent. First, a letter of intent may be perceived as an unnecessary step in the process, since the definitive agreement will have the same terms as the letter of intent but it will be binding. Second, to the extent the letter of intent has binding features, the degree of certainty of the transaction is high, and the parties to the transaction are public, federal securities law may oblige the parties to disclose the existence of the transaction discussions prematurely, undermining the ability to get the deal done. Deals often fall apart prior to the signing and closing of the definitive agreement, in which case the early disclosure of the deal could be embarrassing.

§ 27.06   THE REVISED LETTER OF INTENT

The letter of intent forms the basis for a negotiation and provides a vehicle for identifying those issues where the parties have common ground and those where the parties need to come together. In addition, the letter of intent identifies issues that may be important to one party but are as yet unrecognized by the counterparty. Once the initial non-binding letter of intent is submitted, it is common for the parties to discuss their common ground and try and agree on the very broad terms of the transaction. To the extent certain provisions in the letter of intent need to be revised, a second letter is drafted that includes the modified terms. All terms in the letter of intent may be modified and it is not unusual for a letter of intent to go through multiple drafts.

§ 27.07   PERFORM DUE DILIGENCE

Once the letter of intent has been agreed to by both sides, it is typical for the lawyers to initiate the drafting of the definitive agreement and for the parties to the transaction to begin their in-depth due diligence. Due diligence is covered in detail in Chapter 31.

§ 27.08   THE DEFINITIVE AGREEMENT

Most M&A transactions result in a definitive, legally binding contract that documents the agreed upon terms of the deal. An agreement is only signed when both parties to the contract believe that the terms of the deal protect them from a business and legal perspective. In a negotiation, it is important to differentiate between the business and the legal issues. The business issues are those that relate to the financial aspects of the transaction and affect valuation, price and shareholder value. The legal aspects of the transaction are those that govern contractual terms of the relationship between signing and closing, and provide for protection mechanisms for the parties post closing.

[A] Business Issues

Price: The purchase price in the transaction and the mechanic for delivering the purchase price. The purchase price may indicate a dollar amount to be paid or it may indicate an implied purchase price based on a number of shares to be issued.

Consideration: The corm of currency that is to be paid to the seller upon closing. It may include stock, cash, or a combination thereof.

Collar: The collar may specify the parameters around which the buyer may pay a given price for the target. For example, it may indicate a price range of the acquirer's stock such that in that price range, the acquirer may issue to the seller a given number of shares, yet outside that range, the number of shares issued fluctuates.

Assumption of Assets and Liabilities: In a stock acquisition, the buyer generally assumes the liabilities. In most other cases where other than the stock is acquired, the buyer and seller must detail in the contract what liabilities and assets are acquired or assumed. The outcome of this negotiation can impact the overall economics of the transaction by increasing or decreasing the purchase price. For example, paying cash for the assets of $100 and assuming liabilities of $20 results in purchase price of $120.

[B] Legal Issues

Representations and Warranties: In any contract, it is typical for the parties to make various representations about their respective businesses, in particular with respect to ownership, financial operations and condition of the operations. Standard representations include: (a) the buyer and seller are duly organized and in good standing in their respective states of incorporation, (b) the buyer and seller are authorized to enter into the proposed contract, (c) the financial information presented by buyer and seller are fairly presented, (d) the assets and liabilities presented by buyer and seller are fairly represented, (e) the contracts presented by buyer and seller are accurate and complete lists of all contracts, (f) neither of the businesses of buyer or seller are in compliance with environmental and other safety regulations, (g) all benefit plans of buyer and seller are in compliance, and (h) there is no threatened litigation or governmental proceeding against buyer or seller.

Closing Conditions: Conditions to closing may include (1) the receipt of all necessary approvals, including shareholder, board, lender, regulatory, etc.; and (2) the representations and warranties having been found to be true.

Indemnification: Buyers and sellers will typically indemnify each other for risks assumed or not assumed, pre-closing and post-closing obligations and breaches of representations and warranties. For example, if a buyer assumes the liabilities of the seller, it is typical for the seller to ask the buyer to indemnify it from the risk that the buyer does not fulfill its obligations under the assumed liabilities. The indemnification provisions also often state the remedies in the event one of the conditions needs to be enforced.

Termination: A termination provision specifies the conditions under which a contract can be terminated and by whom. It also often describes what happens in the event there is a default under one of the many other provisions in the contract. As an example, a termination provision could state that if a transaction is not concluded by a certain date in the future, both parties have the right to terminate the contract without recourse.

Covenants: Buyers and sellers often agree to take or refrain from taking certain actions. These agreements are known as covenants and can cover the period between signing and closing the transaction or can pertain to after the deal closes. Examples of covenants include: (a) the agreement to jointly seek approval from certain agencies or institutions, (b) the seller's agreement not to compete for a period of time after the deal closes, (c) the agreement to maintain the secrecy of the contract, the terms of the deal and proprietary information, and (d) the agreement to make certain filings post closing.

§ 27.09   FINANCING

During the course of a transaction, financing may be necessary. The financing may be in order to fund a part of the purchase price or to refinance existing debt at the target that have to be refinanced as a part of the deal. It is common for any required financing to be committed prior to the signing of a transaction; however, it is not unheard of for the closing of a transaction to be subject to the acquirer receiving the required financing to close a transaction.

Clearly, having the financing commitment in place prior to the signing of the binding contract reduces the risk that the transaction does not close. Allowing the transaction to be signed with the financing not in place introduces tremendous risk and puts the seller in a disadvantageous position in the deal.

§ 27.10   NEGOTIATION AND EXECUTION

The process of negotiating and executing the definitive agreement can take anywhere from a few days to a few weeks. It is typical for one of the parties to prepare the first draft of the definitive agreement based on the letter of intent or preliminary offer. In the case of an auction of a business, it is common for the seller to prepare a standard agreement that is distributed to the potential buyers in advance of a final bid. In the case of a negotiated merger or acquisition, it is common for the purchases to prepare the first draft of the definitive agreement.

The first draft is circulated to the parties to the transaction and is marked up based on the counterparty's view of the transaction and its desires with respect to seeking certain protections. The first draft and the preliminary comments form the basis of the negotiation on the definitive agreement. The draft and comments thereto form the parameters for the negotiation. For example, the draft may ask for certain representations that are quite comprehensive, yet the counterparty may not be quite as willing to provide such comprehensive representations.

The parties may or may not get together face-to-face at this point to negotiate the revisions to the definitive agreement. However, with each draft, the agreement should converge on one that is acceptable to both sides. At the end of the negotiation, the contract is ready to be signed. However, during the course of the negotiation, it is common for due diligence to continue, and the finding of any new information may have an impact on the terms or structure of the agreement.

§ 27.11 REGULATORY APPROVALS

Once the document is signed, it is common to seek certain approvals. Shareholder approval may be sought through the filing and dissemination of a proxy statement and the solicitation of shareholder approval. Antitrust clearance may be sought through the filing of required documents. Other approvals may be required such as that of the lenders.

§ 27.12 CLOSING

The closing of the transaction takes place as soon as all approvals have been met and all relevant documents have been filed with the authorities.

§ 27.13 SUMMARY

The key behind the successful execution of a transaction is establishing the right framework for the deal. From the initial dialogue to the final negotiation of contract terms, it is essential to have a well-thought out strategy for conducting the process, coordinating due diligence, formulating the initial offer and letter of intent, and negotiating the definitive agreement.

There are a number of factors that can influence the successful negotiation and execution of the LOI and definitive agreement. First, it is important to establish early on who will be the primary negotiator for both parties to the transaction. They should serve as the primary contact on the transaction and should have the authority and flexibility to make decisions that can drive the process forward.

Second, it is advisable to set realistic expectations early on in the process and only revise those expectations if absolutely necessary. This is paramount to establishing trust and credibility between the parties and it allows the parties to conduct up-front, candid discussions. Breaching trust, not meeting expectations, or revising expectations frequently, can create an adverse negotiating environment and put the transaction at risk.

Third, make sure you and your team are well-informed of the specifics of the industry, the parties to the transaction and the nuances of the transaction.

An intimate knowledge of the details will allow you to react quickly as circumstances change or new information comes to light.

Fourth, in many cases, a letter of intent is not necessary and may in fact be a hindrance to completing the transaction. Nevertheless, it is advisable to prepare some form of term sheet that outlines the major business and legal terms of the transaction. Preparing a term sheet helps to crystallize one's thinking and forces the parties to focus on any potential transaction issues early on in the process. Good analysis and preparation prior to drafting a definitive agreement can help expedite the contact phase of a transaction.

Fifth, it is helpful to maintain a running list of the key business and legal issues. Beginning with the first discussions on a potential transaction, possible issues will crop up. It is important to keep track of these, as ultimately, every one will need to be addressed in some fashion or another. Without a record of these issues, it is difficult to determine what detailed due diligence to perform, and it is virtually impossible to develop a term sheet, LOI or definitive agreement. As you record these issues, it is always helpful to separate out the business issues from the legal issues, the due diligence items from the contract items, and the issues that should be addressed in a term sheet versus those that should be addressed in a binding contract.

Sixth, one helpful strategy for developing an initial offer and letter of intent is to outline the key strategic and financial rationale for the transaction at the outset of the discussions. Then, as the transaction develops, and assumptions change or new information is introduced, you should revisit the initial outline to either validate, modify or nullify the original assumptions. This is a fine way to keep a check and balance on your thinking and determine if, after due diligence and some of the negotiation, the transaction still makes sense. As a part of this thinking, it is typical to see the major assumptions reflected in the financial model for the transaction. However, there will be issues and due diligence items that come up which cannot be reflected in the model. It is important to revisit these assumptions and continue to make sure the transaction works from this perspective.

Finally, having control of the contract is always helpful. While in many cases, the buyer prepares the contract, there are also numerous examples where either party to the transaction may assume that role, for example, in mergers-of-equals. Maintaining control of the contract may cost you a little more, but the control is worth the cost.

Chapter 28

COLLARS AND WALK-AWAYS

§ 28.01   OVERVIEW

Stock-for-stock transactions can take a long time to close, often subjecting the deal to market risks resulting from the delay. A drop in an acquirer's stock price during the pre-closing period can lead to selling shareholders receiving less value for their company than expected, or it can lead to increased earnings dilution for the acquirer. Consequently, pricing structures used in stock-for-stock transactions have become increasingly complex, as companies and their investment bankers have perfected various means to protect the parties to the transaction from various risks.

One approach to coping with market risks is to use a collar. A collar is a mechanism in the purchase or merger agreement whereby the buyer and seller are protected in the event there are significant changes in either party's stock price, such that the negotiated terms of the transaction are no longer attractive to the parties. Collars are typically used in conjunction with two stock-for-stock pricing structures: fixed price and fixed exchange ratio transactions.

To put this in perspective, let's assume that a company has offered to acquire a competitor for $100 million in the form of the acquirer's stock. The agreed-upon price is based on the acquirer's stock price of $20 per share at the time the agreement is signed. Based on this, the acquirer would issue 5 million shares to the seller's shareholders, assuming its stock price remains at $20 per share upon closing. However, between signing and closing the transaction, the acquirer's stock price takes a dramatic turn, and upon closing of the transaction, its stock price is $9 per share. Because the acquirer agreed to pay a fixed price of $100 million, it would be required to give 11.1 million shares to the seller instead of the original 5 million shares. As a result, the seller would own significantly more of the surviving company than it had originally expected, and the transaction would change from being accretive to dilutive to the acquirer.

In this situation, through the use of a collar, it is possible to protect the acquirer from possible adverse swings in its stock price prior to closing. The transaction would be entered into subject to a collar that articulates a range of stock prices for the acquirer within which the fixed price of $100 million would apply. Outside the collar, the number of shares issued is fixed, exposing the value selling shareholders receive to negative or positive swings in the acquirer's stock price. For example, the acquirer could offer to pay $100 million if its stock price is between $18.50 and $21 per share. Below $18.50 per share, it would pay a fixed 5.4 million shares, and above $21 per share, it would pay a fixed 4.8 million shares. In this way, the acquirer knows that in no event will it have to issue more than 5.4 million shares. This form of collar is known as a "fixed price" with floating exchange ratio collar.

As an alternative to the fixed-price approach, the parties could structure the transaction as a fixed number of shares or "fixed exchange ratio" with a floating price collar. In this case, the acquirer could offer 5 million shares to the seller, based on recent trading ranges for the acquirer's stock of $18 to $22 per share. Assuming the collar of $18.50 to $21 per share, within the collar, the seller receives 5 million acquirer shares, and outside the collar, the seller receives a value fixed at the upper or lower bounds of the collar, the number of shares issued adjusted upwards or downwards to maintain the value. In this way, both the acquirer and seller know how many shares the seller will get, yet the value of the transaction could fluctuate depending on the price of the acquirer's stock at closing. Within the collar, the seller bears the risk of a downward swing in the acquirer's stock price, receiving a minimum of $90 million in stock consideration, but would also benefit from an upswing in the acquirer's stock price by receiving a maximum of $110 million in stock consideration at the top end of the range.

The decision to use either the fixed-price or fixed-exchange ratio approach is based on a number of factors, including among others, the outlook for the acquirer's stock, the potential market response to the transaction, and the size of the seller relative to the acquirer. Critical to the choice is which of the risks is most important to protect against.

In many cases, in addition to a collar, transactions are structured with a "walkaway" provision, whereby outside the collar, the parties to the transaction have the right to terminate the transaction without penalty.

§ 28.02   FIXED-EXCHANGE RATIO WITHIN PRICE COLLAR

Using a fixed-exchange ratio in a stock-for-stock transaction is often viewed as the simplest form of pricing mechanism. For the acquirer, the advantage of a fixed-exchange ratio is that it is able to determine at the signing of the transaction how much stock it will have to issue to the seller and the potential impact on its earnings with a fair degree of certainty.

Exhibit 28-1
Advantages and Disadvantages of Fixed-Exchange Ratio Pricing

Advantages	*Disadvantages*
• Allows acquirer to determine at outset how many shares are to be issued	• Value seller receives is not determined until closing
• Gives acquirer a degree of certainty with respect to earnings impact of the transaction	• Seller is at risk to adverse stock price moves of acquirer
• Market likely to reflect the value of the transaction in both stocks	• Value seller receives on the upside is capped
• Shares risk between two stockholder groups party to the transaction	• Transaction is at risk to not receiving shareholder approval or
• Market and industry risk may affect both stocks similarly	inviting third party bids if acquirer's stock drops dramatically between signing and closing

---

With a fixed-exchange ratio however, the seller's shareholders, if they choose to hold their stock through to the closing, are at risk to the market and swings in the acquirer's stock price. In the event that the acquirer's stock price declines dramatically, the value that selling shareholders receive may decline to such a level that the deal runs the risk that it does not receive shareholder approval, or it may attract attention from competing bidders who can outbid the existing acquirer. Nevertheless, fixed exchange ratio transactions are the most common pricing structure used in stock-for-stock deals, especially in situations where the two parties are of equal size, commonly known as a "merger of equals."

Exhibit 28-1 provides a summary of the advantages and disadvantages of fixed-exchange ratio transactions.

In fixed-exchange ratio transactions, the collar is set using predetermined upper and lower bounds on the acquirer's stock price, such that if its stock price increases or decreases beyond the upper or lower bounds, the exchange ratio is adjusted to maintain the minimum or maximum values the acquirer would receive. The implications of the collar are that, between the upper and lower bounds on the acquirer's stock price, the acquirer knows that it will have to issue a fixed number of shares to the seller; however, below the lower bound, the number of shares issued is adjusted upward to protect the value the seller receives on the downside, and above the upper bounds, the number of shares issued is adjusted downward to cap the value the seller receives on the upside.

[A] Mechanics of Fixed-Exchange Ratio Within Price Collar

A fixed-exchange ratio with floating price collar has three components: the initial exchange ratio, the bounds of the value on the exchange ratio (the collar), and the mechanism for adjusting the exchange ratio if the minimum or maximum bounds are exceeded.

Set the initial exchange ratio: The initial exchange ratio is set by taking the price per share that the acquirer is willing to pay for the seller and dividing it into the average stock price of the seller for a predetermined period prior to signing. For example, if the proposed purchase price for a target is $100 million, and the company has 10 million shares outstanding, the implied acquisition price is $10 per share. Further, if the acquirer's stock has traded at an average of $15 per share for the two weeks prior to signing the transaction, the acquirer would issue 6.7 million shares of its stock to seller stockholders ($100 million/$15 per share = 6.7 million shares). In other words, the exchange ratio would be 0.667 ($10 per share/$15 per share = 0.667). What this means, is that for each share that a selling shareholder owns in the target, it would receive 0.667 shares in the acquirer.

Determine the collar: A collar is usually based on a range around the estimated price of the acquirer's stock just prior to signing. Often the collar is between 10% and 15% of the estimated price. Alternatively, the collar can based off a reasonable trading range for the acquirer prior to signing the transaction. For example, if for the two weeks prior to signing, the acquirer's stock has traded between $13 per share and $17 per share, it is reasonable for the upper and lower bounds of the collar to be set using this range.

Establish the adjustment mechanism: Above and below the collar, the number of shares issued to selling shareholders is adjusted upwards or downwards in order to maintain a minimum and maximum value. In our illustration, below $13 and above $17 per share, the number of shares issued would be adjusted to maintain minimum and maximum values of $87 million and $114 million, respectively. To illustrate, if the acquirer's stock price is at $12 per share upon closing, the number of shares issued to maintain the minimum value of $87 million would be increased from 6.7 million to 7.3 million.

An alternate way to calculate the number of shares to be issued is to determine the new exchange ratio below or above the collar. In the case of the acquirer's stock price closing below the lower bound of the collar, take the exchange ratio of 0.667, multiply it by the lower bound on the collar of $13 per share, and then divide it by the new closing stock price for the acquirer of $12 per share. This results in a new exchange ratio of 0.723. In other words, at the $12 per share price, selling shareholders now receive 0.723 shares of the acquirer's stock for each share in the target.

[B] Example of a Fixed-Exchange Ratio Within Price Collar

Company A, the acquirer, has a current stock price just prior to signing an acquisition agreement of $34 per share. During the preceding month, the acquirer's stock has traded in a range of $30 to $38 per share.

Company B has a stock price of $22 per share. It has 20 million shares outstanding.

Company A has offered to acquire Company B. The transaction offer was priced using an exchange ratio of 0.8235, implying that for each share of Company B a selling shareholder owns, it would receive 0.8235 shares in Company A. The implied value of the deal for Company B is $560 million or $28 per share.

The collar was set at the $30 and $38 bounds on the acquirer's stock price, such that, within the collar, the number of shares issued is fixed at 16.47 million shares. If the acquirer's stock decreases or increases outside of those bounds, the number of shares issued would be adjusted upwards or downwards to maintain a minimum value of the deal of $24.71 per share or a maximum value of the deal of $31.29 per share.

Exhibit 28-2 illustrates the value received by and the number of shares issued to the seller above, below, and within the collar in a fixed exchange ratio transaction.

Exhibit 28-2
Fixed-Exchange Ratio Within Collar Illustration

Acquirer's Stock Price At Closing	Exchange Ratio	Value of Stock Received Per Seller Share	Aggregate Value of Deal (in millions)	Shares Issued (in millions)
Below Collar				
$27.00	0.9150	$24.71	$494	18.30
$28.00	0.8823	$24.71	$494	17.64
$29.00	0.8519	$24.71	$494	17.03
Within Collar				
$30.00	0.8235	$24.71	$494	16.47
$31.00	0.8235	$25.53	$511	16.47
$32.00	0.8235	$26.35	$527	16.47
$33.00	0.8235	$27.18	$544	16.47
$34.00	0.8235	$28.00	$560	16.47
$35.00	0.8235	$28.82	$576	16.47
$36.00	0.8235	$29.65	$593	16.47
$37.00	0.8235	$30.47	$609	16.47
$38.00	0.8235	$31.29	$626	16.47
Above Collar				
$39.00	0.8024	$31.29	$626	16.05
$40.00	0.7823	$31.29	$626	15.65
$41.00	0.7632	$31.29	$626	15.27

§ 28.03   FIXED-PRICE WITH FLOATING EXCHANGE RATIO COLLAR

An alternative to using fixed-exchange ratio pricing with a collar is to offer selling shareholders a fixed value for their stock, such that within the collar around the acquirer's stock price, the selling shareholders receive that number of shares required to ensure they receive the fixed value. Outside of the collar, the exchange ratio is set at its upper or lower bounds, and the seller bears the risk in the value decline or participates in an increase in value.

In a fixed-price transaction, the number of shares issued by the acquirer at closing is determined based on the value of the acquirer's stock at the time of closing. Specifically, the value is based on the average price of the acquirer's stock over a predetermined period prior to closing, e.g., 20 business days.

Exhibit 28-3 provides the advantages and disadvantages of fixed price transactions.

When a fixed price is offered, a collar can mitigate certain risks associated with adverse stock price moves. A collar provides protection to the acquirer, limiting the amount of stock it will have to issue in the event of a decline in the price of its stock between signing and closing. The collar protects the selling shareholders by placing a minimum on the number of the acquirer's shares they receive in the event of a price increase over the same period.

Between the upper and lower bounds of the collar, usually 10–15% around the acquirer's stock price at signing, selling shareholders will receive that number of shares required to deliver the deal price determined at the signing. Therefore, as the acquirer's stock price increases, the number of shares requiredto be issued declines. Likewise, as the acquirer's stock price declines, the number of shares to be issued increases. Outside of the collar, the exchange ratio is fixed, and therefore the value of the transaction to the seller declines if the acquirer's stock price is below the lower bounds of the collar, and the value of the transaction increases if the acquirer's stock is above the upper bounds of the collar.

[A]   Mechanics of Fixed Price Within Collar

Much like fixed-exchange ratio transactions, fixed-price transactions with a collar have three components: establishing the initial price, defining the collar, and setting the mechanism for adjusting the price outside of the collar.

Exhibit 28-3
Advantages and Disadvantages of Fixed-Price Pricing

Advantages	*Disadvantages*
• Seller guaranteed a fixed price as long as the acquirer's stock stays within the collar	• Acquirer bears the risk of a decline in its stock price
• Seller knows the value shareholders will receive within the collar	• Exposes the acquirer to dilution

---

The initial price: The acquirer offers the seller a fixed price based on its valuation and other analysis. For example, if the value of the deal is $100 million and the seller has $10 million shares outstanding, the offer price per share is $10 per share.

Defining the collar: The collar is usually set between 10% and 15% around the acquirer's stock price at the signing of the merger or acquisition agreement. For example, if the acquirer's stock is $15, the collar could be $13 to $17 per share. Within the collar, the acquirer would pay a fixed price of $10 per share for the seller, and consequently, the number of shares the acquirer issues would increase as its stock price declines or decrease as its stock prices increases.

Establishing the adjustment mechanism: In a fixed-value transaction, outside the upper and lower bounds of the collar, the number of shares issued becomes fixed at the bounds, and the value the seller receives is based on the increase or decrease in the acquirer's stock price.

[B] Example of Fixed Price Within Collar

Company A, the acquirer, has a current stock price just prior to signing an acquisition agreement of $34 per share. During the preceding month, the acquirer's stock has traded in a range of $30 to $38 per share.

Company B has a stock price of $22 per share. It has 20 million shares outstanding.

Company A has offered to acquire Company B for a fixed value of $560 million or $28 per share.

The collar was set at the $30 and $38 bounds on the acquirer's stock price, such that if the acquirer's stock declines or increases outside of those bounds, the number of shares issued would be fixed, resulting in a minimum and maximum number of shares issued of 14.74 million and 18.67 million, respectively. Within the collar, the seller is guaranteed a price of $28 per share.

Exhibit 28-4 illustrates the value received by and the number of shares issued to the seller in a fixed price within collar transaction.

§ 28.04 WALK-AWAYS

In many transactions, in addition to a collar, the parties also negotiate a walk-away provision that gives them the right to walk away from the transaction without penalty, upon certain conditions. Most commonly, the seller has the right to walk-away from the transaction if the acquirer's stock price goes below a certain level. In some cases, the walk-away right may be at the bottom of the collar; in others, it may be lower.

There are different ways to structure a walk-away right, most common of which are "absolute" walk-away and "relative" walk-away rights. In an absolute walk-away, the seller has the absolute right to walk away from the transaction if the acquirer's stock goes below a predetermined level. In a relative walk-away, the seller has the right to back away from the transaction if the acquirer's stock price

Exhibit 28-4
Fixed Price Within Price Collar Illustration

Acquirer's Stock Price at Closing	Value of Stock Received Per Seller Share	Exchange Ratio	Aggregate Value of Deal (in millions)	Shares Issued (in millions)
Below Collar				
$27.00	$25.20	0.9333	$504	18.67
$28.00	$26.13	0.9333	$523	18.67
$29.00	$27.07	0.9333	$541	18.67
Within Collar				
$30.00	$28.00	0.9333	$560	18.67
$31.00	$28.00	0.9032	$560	18.07
$32.00	$28.00	0.8750	$560	17.50
$33.00	$28.00	0.8485	$560	16.97
$34.00	$28.00	0.8235	$560	16.47
$35.00	$28.00	0.8000	$560	16.00
$36.00	$28.00	0.7778	$560	15.56
$37.00	$28.00	0.7568	$560	15.14
$38.00	$28.00	0.7368	$560	14.74
Above Collar				
$39.00	$28.74	0.7368	$575	14.74
$40.00	$29.47	0.7368	$890	14.74
$41.00	$31.21	0.7368	$604	14.74

declines by a predetermined percentage relative to a set of comparable companies or indexes. However, in this case, it is usually not permitted for a seller to walk away if there is an overall market correction. In some transactions, the walk-away may be structured to have both an absolute and a relative walk-away, for example, if the stock of the acquirer declines by greater than 15% from the announcement of the transaction, and the acquirer's stock declines by more than 5% relative to its peer group. This situation is known as a "double-trigger."

In the situation where a walk-away level has been reached, an acquirer may sometimes be allowed to adjust the merger or acquisition price by grossing up the number of shares to be issued. This is done to ensure that the parties continue to negotiate the transaction before unilaterally terminating it.

§ 28.05 FACTORS INFLUENCING CHOICE OF PRICING STRUCTURE

There are a number of factors that influence the pricing structure used in a given transaction. The resulting choice will help decide how to allocate the risk between the respective parties and their shareholders. The most common factors are the size and relative bargaining strength of the parties, and the specific terms of the transaction. A given pricing structure used for a merger-of-equals, for example, may not be appropriate for a transaction where the parties are of significantly different sizes. In a merger-of-equals, the shareholders of both parties are generally participating equally in the benefits of the merger and therefore, their interests are largely aligned. Conversely, in an acquisition, the selling shareholders are at greater risk since they have little ongoing say in the ownership and management of the combined company.

In addition to choosing a pricing structure, the parties will need to decide whether a collar is appropriate. The decision to use a collar will be based on a number of factors including the potential earnings impact of the transaction on the acquirer, the possible reaction of the market to the deal's announcement, the relative sizes of the companies, and whether or not it makes sense to create floors and caps on the price or shares offered. On important consideration is how closely held the companies are, and whether there is any arbitrage risk. Arbitrage is most common in mergers-of-equals, and therefore, collars may not be appropriate.

§ 28.06 SUMMARY

Because of the length of time taken to complete stock-for-stock acquisitions or mergers, the protection of the parties and their shareholders is of paramount importance. Setting the appropriate pricing structure, fixed-price or fixed-exchange ratio, and coupling it with an appropriate collar and walk-away mechanism, can help allay concern, protect against downside, and ensure the parties continue to work in good faith to bring a transaction to conclusion. It is important to recognize that there are a variety of approaches and combinations to achieving similar objectives, and it is folly to simply pick a transaction structure that has been used before on which to model a new situation. Make sure that each aspect of the pricing structure and the associated bells and whistles are carefully thought through beforehand.

Chapter 29

TERMINATION FEES, LOCK-UP OPTIONS, AND NO-SHOP CLAUSES

§ 29.01 OVERVIEW

Transactions can fail to close for a number of reasons: shareholders may not approve the deal; a third party acquirer may emerge with a higher offer, or either party may terminate for no particular reason. In most situations, both parties to a transaction have every incentive to ensure their deal closes, and in that spirit, there are a number of mechanisms that can be used to protect the deal, ranging from fees that are paid by the terminating party, to lock-up options, to clauses that prevent the seller from soliciting third party offers.

While each of these approaches may be effective in protecting a transaction, they need to be structured carefully so as to avoid the scrutiny of the courts. In all cases, the courts will look to how the deal protection mechanism serves to enhance shareholder value. Generally, the courts will allow those deal protection devices that serve to ensure a transaction is completed without jeopardizing shareholder upside in the event a third party bidder attempts to intervene in the transaction.

§ 29.02 TERMINATION FEES

Both parties to a transaction may be concerned that if the transaction does not close, they could suffer irreparable harm. In particular, acquirers may be concerned that a seller does not try to use its offer as a way to boost the valuation of the company to another acquirer and start a bidding war. On the other hand, the seller may be worried that its customers could become disloyal if they disapprove of the deal. Employees of both companies may become concerned over the transaction's merits, and therefore, either company can be damaged if the deal fails. As a way to address the risk in the deal, both sides can propose termination fees. There are two types of termination fees: topping fees and break-up or bust-up fees.

Topping Fees: This type of fee is an agreement between the target and the acquirer designed to compensate the acquirer in the event it's offer is exceeded by a third party. The topping fee is the obligation of the target, and therefore, ultimately becomes a cost to the third party acquirer. Topping fees serve to deter third party acquirers by making the transaction more expensive to that bidder.

Break-Up Fees: Also known as "bust-up" fees, these are arrangements between the buyer and seller that call for a fee to be paid by the party who terminates the transaction without cause. A break-up fee requires that the party responsible for the break up pay to the other party a negotiated amount of liquidated damages. The amount of the break-up fee should reflect the damages likely to be sustained by the damaged party. In many cases, the break-up fee includes reimbursement for expenses. Some parties dislike break-up fees because they believe that they imply permission not to close (as long as the break-up fee is paid) and they would prefer an unequivocal obligation to close.

Exhibit 29-1 provides the advantages and disadvantages of break-up and topping fees.

Termination fees can vary widely in size; however, as a benchmark, for transactions greater than $1 billion, termination fees approximate 2%–3% of the equity value of the deal. Below $1 billion in size, the fee may be higher than 2%–3% of the equity value, while the reverse may apply for transactions that are substantially higher than $1 billion. For example, if the equity value of a target company is $100 million, the estimated termination fee would be approximately $4–$5 million. While on a percentage basis, the fee is double that of one for a $1 billion transaction, it is common to see this size fee for smaller deals.

Transaction fees will also differ depending on whether the proposed transaction is a sale of control or a merger-of-equals. In control transactions, boards of directors may be unwilling to impose a high termination fee for fear of impeding other potential bidders, and subjecting themselves to the scrutiny of the courts.

Exhibit 29-1
Advantages and Disadvantages of Break-Up and Topping Fees

Advantages	*Disadvantages*
• Entices either or both parties to complete the deal	• Makes it less likely that a competing bidder will emerge
• Makes it more expensive for other potential bidders to acquire the target	• Subject to scrutiny by the legal community if fees are not reasonable
• May be used to induce a higher bid from a third party	

On the contrary, in merger-of-equal transactions, termination fees may be higher as they are not necessarily viewed as intervening in a board's fiduciary duty to shareholders.

[A]   Termination Fee Example

In 2002, Cardinal Health, Inc. acquired Boron, LePore & Associates, Inc. for approximately $195 million. As a part of the transaction, Cardinal and Boron, LePore entered into a termination provision whereby in the event of a termination of the transaction, Boron, LePore would pay to Cardinal an amount equal to the aggregate amount of Cardinal's costs — including legal, accounting and investment banking fees — incurred in connection with the transaction up to a $1,750,000, plus a termination fee in the amount equal to $9,000,000.[1] The combined amount represented approximately 5.4% of the equity value.

§ 29.03   LOCK-UP OPTIONS

Lock-up options are provisions drafted to favor an acquirer with whom the target company has signed a definitive agreement. They give the acquirer the right to purchase stock or assets of the target under certain circumstances. The goal of a lock-up is to discourage third party offers, in particular hostile third parties. There are two types of lock-up options: stock and asset.

[A]   Stock Lock-Ups

In a stock lock-up option, the target gives the favored bidder the right to acquire authorized but unissued shares of the target. In the event the acquirer exercises the option, it enables it to vote those shares in favor of a deal. If the favored acquirer is outbid by a third party, the acquirer may then sell the shares in the transaction, reaping the benefit of the higher price. The mechanic for this is often through a put whereby the favored bidder may sell the shares to the competing bidder and collect the spread between its bid and that offered by the competitor.

Stock lock-up options are not viewed favorably by shareholder advocate groups or the legal community as they may limit selling shareholders' ability to reap the benefits of a higher third party offer. While stock lock-ups are not illegal, the courts have maintained that they may inhibit a board of director from fully exercising its fiduciary duties to.

Stock lock-ups are usually for less than 20% of a target's shares outstanding, since in most cases, for amounts higher than 20%, shareholder approval is usually required. In many merger-of-equal transactions, the stock lock-up option is reciprocal, i.e., each company grants the other an option to acquire stock in the other company.

---

1. Source: Public documents.

Stock lock-up options have received intense scrutiny, in particular in defensive situations where the option is used to deter third party bidders. Of key consideration is the extent to which the acquirer benefiting from the option proceeds receives compensation from the spread on the transaction. As a result, in the event stock lock-up options are used, it is not uncommon for them to have a financial limit on the amount that can be garnered by the favored bidder.

An alternative to the stock-lock up option is the reverse lock-up option in which a group of shareholders agree not to vote or tender their shares in the target to a third party, or unfavored, acquirer. This type of lock-up option is not subject to the same scrutiny as stock lock-up options, since it is not an agreement that is necessarily driven by the board; invariably, reverse lock-ups are signed between the selling shareholders and the acquirer directly.

[B]   Asset Lock-Ups

In an asset lock-up option, the target gives the favored bidder the right to acquire certain assets in the target. Typically, these are attractive or "crown jewel" assets that are offered to the acquirer at a price below their presumed fair market value. This type of option may also be effective in deterring third party bidders, since the assets subject to the lock-up may either be crucial to the ongoing financial performance of the target, or the third party bidder may have a particular interest in those assets. Fairness is a central issue in asset lock-up options, in particular in the case of the crown jewel option where the courts can bring in to question the appropriateness of the pricing of the option.

Exhibit 29-2 provides the advantages and disadvantages of lock-ups.

Lock-up options are not necessarily illegal, however, in some cases, the courts may invalidate the provision as not being in the best interests of shareholders. Ever since the Revlon case in which a board's duties to shareholders in a control transaction were clearly stated, lock-up options have come under heavy scrutiny. Lock-up options can be construed as impeding a third party bidder by making the target less attractive to the suitor.

Exhibit 29-2
Advantages and Disadvantages of Lock-Ups

Advantages	*Disadvantages*
• Provides acquirer with assurance that proposed offer will be consummated, if transaction is completed • If a competing third party offer is successful, the lock-up provides compensation for initial acquirer for its efforts • May be used to induce a higher bid from a third party	• Frowned upon by the courts as they may prevent selling shareholders from reaping the benefit of a higher price from a competing third party • Limits competitive bidding

---

In situations where the Revlon duties are not applicable, such as in mergers-of-equals, lock-ups can also be subject to the same level of scrutiny. Courts will look at the pricing of the option relative to the fair value of the assets. On the one hand, if the option undervalues the assets, it may act as a strong deterrent to a third party bidder. On the other hand, if the option is fairly priced, it may not deter competing offers and therefore may be ineffectual as a deal protection device.

In the case of asset or crown jewel lock-ups, the courts will try to determine whether the asset is one that would be sold in the normal course or if the target had previously attempted to sell the asset. A situation may also arise where the crown jewel may constitute the bulk of the assets of the target, or at least the most important assets in the company, which, if sold, would render the target financially unviable. In this case, the courts may question whether the issuance of a crown jewel option is possible without shareholder approval.

Despite the scrutiny of lock-ups from the legal community, the courts may allow lock-up options that are reasonable, and also may allow lock-up agreements to induce a higher offer from a third party bidder.

§ 29.04   NO-SHOP PROVISIONS

Many merger and acquisition agreements may contain language that is designed to stop the target company from soliciting other potential buyers. Referred to as "no-shop" provisions, these clauses not only prevent the target from seeking other buyers, but in some cases, they may prevent the target from sharing information with another party that is unsolicited.

The first form of no-shop provision, which prohibits the target from soliciting other buyers, usually is drafted in a way that provides the target's board with little flexibility in exercising fiduciary judgment. In other words, the board has minimal ability to seek third party bidders without breaching the agreement. This is typically viewed as not providing the target board with a fiduciary out, which means that the board cannot exercise its fiduciary duties by soliciting third party bidders.

The second form of no-shop provision does not allow the target to share information with a competing bidder. While restrictive, it does allow the board to exercise its fiduciary duties, i.e., it does have a fiduciary out. In this case, the target's board has the ability to use its judgment that if an unsolicited bidder approaches the target, it may be able to provide the information to the third party if it deems that, by not doing so, it would violate its duties to shareholders.

Much like termination fees, no-shop provisions have come under tremendous scrutiny from the courts. There have been numerous cases that support no-shop provisions, the argument in support of the provision maintaining that it is permissible for an acquirer to not want the target to seek third party bidders as a good faith gesture required to conclude the transaction. On the other hand, the courts have not been as clear on provisions limiting a target's ability to talk to an unsolicited third party and provide it with information. While they may support the contention that it is fair to request that a target not seek a third party bidder, they may not support the contention that it is fair to prohibit a target from talking to an unsolicited third party.

As a consequence of the intense legal scrutiny of no-shop provisions, it is typical to see them drafted to prevent solicitation of competing bidders, yet allowing the target to share information with an unsolicited bidder.

[A]   No-Shop Example

In the 2002 acquisition of Boron, Lepore & Associates, Inc. by Cardinal Health, Inc., the companies agreed to a no-shop provision whereby Boron, LePore would not "directly or indirectly solicit, initiate, encourage or facilitate, or furnish or disclose nonpublic information" to any party that would result in it abandoning, terminating or failing to consummate the transaction with Cardinal, subject to certain conditions that gave Boron, LePore the right to entertain discussions with other third parties under a predefined set of circumstances. These conditions were designed to afford the Boron, LePore Board of Directors to pursue an alternate transaction on behalf of shareholders if they deemed it to be on more favorable terms.

The key provisions of the non-solicitation agreement were as follows:

- Boron, LePore would not directly or indirectly solicit, encourage or facilitate, or furnish or disclose non-public information to a third party that would result in Born, LePore abandoning the transaction with Cardinal;

- Prior to the point that Cardinal pays for shares tendered in the transaction, Boron, LePore could engage in discussions for a competing transaction if it was not solicited by Boron, LePore, under the condition that the Boron, LePore Board of Directors determines that, if they did not engage in the discussions, it would be a breach of their fiduciary duties and that the competing transaction is on terms more favorable to Boron, LePore shareholders; and,

- Boron, LePore was required to notify Cardinal if it were approached with a competing transaction.

Following is the text of the non-solicitation provision in the Cardinal Health Boron, LePore merger agreement.[2]

> *No Solicitation.* [Boron, LePore ("BLP")] agrees that, during the term of this Agreement, it shall not, and shall not authorize or permit any of its subsidiaries or any of its or its subsidiaries' directors, officers, employees, agents or representatives, directly or indirectly, to solicit, initiate, encourage or facilitate, or furnish or disclose nonpublic information in furtherance of, any inquiries or the making of any proposal with respect to any recapitalization, merger, consolidation or other business combination

---

2. Source: Public documents.

involving BLP, or acquisition of any capital stock (other than upon exercise of BLP Options that are outstanding as of the date of this Agreement) or a material amount of the assets of BLP and any of its subsidiaries, taken as a whole, in a single transaction or a series of related transactions, or any acquisition by BLP of any material assets or capital stock of any other person, or any combination of the foregoing (a *"Competing Transaction"*), or negotiate, explore or otherwise engage in discussions with any person (other than Cardinal, Subcorp or their respective directors, officers, employees, agents and representatives) with respect to any Competing Transaction or enter into any agreement, arrangement or understanding requiring it to abandon, terminate or fail to consummate the Merger or any other transactions contemplated by this Agreement; *provided* that, at any time prior to the Appointment Time, BLP may furnish information to, and negotiate or otherwise engage in discussions with, any individual or entity that delivers a written proposal for a Competing Transaction that was not solicited, encouraged or facilitated after the date of this Agreement if and so long as the BLP Board determines in good faith by a majority vote, taking into account the advice of its outside legal counsel, that failing to take such action would constitute a breach of its fiduciary duties under Applicable Laws and determines that such a proposal is, after consulting with Bear Stearns (or any other nationally recognized investment banking firm), more favorable to the BLP Stockholders than the transactions contemplated by this Agreement (including any adjustment to the terms and conditions proposed by Cardinal in response to such Competing Transaction) taking into account, among other things, the likelihood and anticipated timing of consummation and all legal, financial, regulatory and other aspects of the proposal and the individual or entity making the proposal and of the transactions contemplated by this Agreement and the parties hereto (a *"Superior Proposal"*), *provided, further*, that, prior to furnishing any information to such individual or entity, BLP shall enter into a confidentiality agreement that is no less restrictive, in any respect, than the confidentiality agreement between Cardinal and BLP, dated September 20, 2001 (the *"Confidentiality Agreement"*). BLP immediately will cease all existing activities, discussions and negotiations with any individual or entity conducted heretofore with respect to any proposal for a Competing Transaction and request the return of all confidential information regarding BLP provided to any such individual or entity prior to the date of this Agreement pursuant to the terms of any confidentiality agreements or otherwise. In the event that, prior to the Appointment Time, the BLP Board receives a Superior Proposal that was not solicited, encouraged or facilitated after the date of this Agreement and the BLP Board, taking into account the advice of outside legal counsel, determines that failure to do so would constitute a breach of the fiduciary duties of the BLP Board under Applicable Laws, the BLP Board may (subject to this and the following sentences) withdraw, modify or change, in a manner adverse to Cardinal, the BLP Board Recommendation and/or comply with Rule 14e-2 under the Exchange Act with respect to a Competing Transaction, *provided* that BLP gives Cardinal five business days prior written notice of its intention to do so (*provided* that the foregoing shall in no way limit or otherwise affect Cardinal's right to terminate this Agreement pursuant to Section 8.1(d)). Any such withdrawal, modification or change of the BLP Board Recommendation shall not change the approval of the BLP Board for purposes of causing any state takeover statute or other state law to be inapplicable to the transactions contemplated by this Agreement, including the Offer, the Merger or the transactions contemplated by this Agreement. From and after the execution of this Agreement, BLP shall immediately advise Cardinal in writing of the receipt, directly or indirectly, of any inquiries, discussions, negotiations, or proposals relating to a Competing Transaction (including the specific terms thereof and the identity of the other individual or entity or individuals or entities involved) and promptly furnish to Cardinal a copy of any such written proposal in addition to a copy of any information provided to or by any third party relating thereto. In addition, BLP shall immediately advise Cardinal, in writing, if the BLP Board shall make any determination as to any Competing Transaction as contemplated by the proviso to the first sentence of this Section 6.3(b). Nothing contained in this Section 6.3(b) shall prohibit BLP from, at any time, taking and disclosing to the BLP Stockholders a position contemplated by Rule 14d-9 or Rule 14e-2 under the Exchange Act or making any disclosure required by Rule 14a-9 under the Exchange Act so long as the requirements set forth in this Section 6.3(b) are satisfied.

§ 29.05   DEAL PROTECTION MECHANISMS AND THE BUSINESS JUDGMENT RULE

Deal protection devices, although not necessarily prohibitive by themselves, can often be viewed by the courts as intervening in the best interests of shareholders. For example, in the case of a change of control sale of a company, termination fees may prevent a third party from submitting a higher offer for the target, because of the cost associated with having to absorb the termination fees. In so doing, the termination fee has effectively "protected" the deal at the expense of the target's shareholders. In this case, where the target has clearly been put up for sale, the courts could strike down the termination fee using two precedent-setting cases, Revlon and QVC-Paramount. Under Revlon, a board of directors has a duty to seek the best price for a company once it is determined that the company is for sale. In this transaction, the Revlon board agreed to provide Forstmann Little & Co. with a lock-up option and a no-shop provision in exchange for providing a higher bid. The third party bidder, Pantry Pride, Inc. sued Revlon and ultimately won the litigation, with the courts siding with Pantry Pride, maintaining that Revlon's board had violated its fiduciary duty of loyalty to shareholders by inhibiting Pantry Pride's ability to submit a higher offer. In this case, it was determined that once a board has chosen the path of selling a company, its duty to shareholders is to seek the best price. Deal protection mechanisms may, taken together, serve to subvert this duty. In QVC-Paramount, it was determined that the stock option, termination fee and no-shop provisions taken together were designed to limit the ability of third party bidders to make a viable competing bid.

There are numerous legal precedents that support termination fees, no-shop clauses and lock-up provisions, and provide guidance as to their appropriateness under various circumstances.

§ 29.06 SUMMARY

Deal protection devices can be an effective means to inhibiting a third party from intervening in a signed transaction. Likewise, they can be successful in preventing a target from soliciting third party bids once a deal has been signed. However, there are numerous legal precedents that either support or refute the different types of deal protection provisions. These precedents are driven by case law on a state-by-state basis, and therefore, it is wise to consult with a legal practitioner that is knowledgeable in the state where the target is incorporated, prior to entering into a transaction.

In structuring deal protection devices in a merger or sale transaction, it is important to remember that the more reasonable the fee, option or no-shop provision, the less likelihood there is that the transaction and its protection mechanisms will be challenged. Each of the termination fee, lock-up or no shop-provisions by themselves can be based on precedent and thus can be somewhat protected from the scrutiny of the courts. However, they should also be taken together in the context of the transaction and the tradeoffs balanced between the objective of closing the transaction and their impact on a board's ability to exercise its fiduciary duties.

Transactions that are not change of control transactions may not necessarily be subject to the same level of scrutiny as control transactions, and consequently, it may be possible to structure stronger deal protection mechanisms than their counterpart control transactions. Boards of directors are subject to the duties set out in precedent cases such as Revlon and QVC-Paramount.

Conflicts of interest will help compound the problems with any court action. In particular, in cases where management shareholders serve to benefit directly from the deal protection mechanism, at the possible expense of other shareholders, the courts will heavily scrutinize any termination fees, lock-ups and no-shop provisions. For example, in the case of leveraged or management buyouts.

Deal protection mechanisms that are used to induce a higher bidder that will directly benefit shareholders will generally be looked upon more favorably than deal protection mechanisms that are designed to hinder third party offers.

Chapter 30

EARNOUTS AND CONTINGENT PAYMENTS

§ 30.01 OVERVIEW

Many proposed transactions stall because the buyer and seller are not able to agree on price, most often, because of a mismatch in the two parties' perception of the seller's ability to realize its projected financial performance. In these situations, there is a mechanism to bridge the gap in purchase price by paying part of the consideration if the seller achieves certain milestones. This future payment is known as an "earnout" or contingent payment.

While an earnout is a contingent payment, a distinction can also be drawn between the two. An earnout is typically closely linked to the achievement of financial goals, in particular, projected financial performance, while a contingent payment is more often associated with non-financial objectives. For simplicity, in this chapter, the terms earnout and contingent payment will be used interchangeably.

While an earnout is usually structured as a way to bridge the gap in price expectations between buyers and sellers, they can also be structured for other reasons. Exhibit 30-1 summarizes key reasons for an earnout.

Earnouts and contingent payments have become more popular in recent years. In 2001, there were 225 announced contingent payment deals, an increase of 16.6% over 2000. Exhibit 30-2 illustrates the trend in contingent payment deals.

Exhibit 30-1
Reasons for an Earnout or Contingent Payment

Buyer's Reasons	*Seller's Reasons*
Increase value to seller	Increase value
Seller forecasts are too aggressive	Seller forecasts are attainable
Motivate management shareholders	Seller forecasts can be exceeded
Mitigate risk of acquisition	
Encourage realization of financial and non-financial milestones	
Align seller incentives with buyer objectives	

Exhibit 30-2
Contingent Payment Transactions: 1990–2001[1]

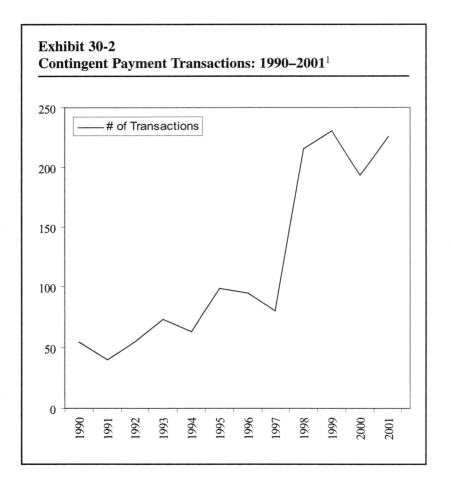

1. Mergerstat.

§ 30.02 ADVANTAGES AND DISADVANTAGES OF EARNOUTS

There are advantages and disadvantages to earnouts and contingent payments, so it is wise to analyze the risks and objectives of the earnout structure prior to proceeding. The principal advantage of an earnout is that it allows the buyer to increase the purchase price without necessarily increasing its risk. At the same time, it is possible to use the earnout to motivate management and thereby align the incentives of management with the objectives of the buyer. In addition, ensuring that non-shareholder managers have an equity stake in the transaction, a buyer should consider contingent bonus payments tied to certain financial targets.

Another advantage of the contingent payment structure is that it reduces the amount of cash or stock consideration that is paid up front in the transaction. Consequently, the impact of the transaction on the buyer's earnings is mitigated.

The most significant disadvantage of earnouts is that they are difficult to monitor on an ongoing basis. For example, in the case of an acquisition where there are considerable synergies from revenue enhancements or cost savings, and where the operations of the two companies are "merged" operationally, it is virtually impossible to determine from where the revenue enhancements or cost savings came, making it difficult to evaluate the true financial performance of the target against the original performance goals set out in the earnout agreement. By default, monitoring the future financial performance goals of the target requires that its financials be kept independent of those of the acquirer.

In addition to the aforementioned advantages and disadvantages, there are others that should be kept in mind. Exhibit 30-3 details additional advantages and disadvantages of earnouts.

Exhibit 30-3
Advantages and Disadvantages of Earnouts and Contingent Payments

Advantages	Disadvantages
• Can motivate shareholder employees	• May de-motivate non-shareholder employees
• Allows seller to increase price without dramatically increasing risk	• May create divergent objectives between management and shareholders
• Ensures seller that buyer is paying a fair price	• Difficult to monitor
• Provides the seller with upside in the event certain performance goals are met	• Seller shares in future downside
• Reduces immediate cash or stock payment and consequently dilution to earnings	
• Allows seller to share in future upside	
• Aligns objectives of seller and buyer post transaction	

---

§ 30.03   SIZE OF THE EARNOUT

The amount of an earnout is typically dependent on the magnitude of the gap between the buyer and seller's perception of value. Often, this gap is attributed to a mismatch in perception of the seller's ability to realize its projections. An earnout serves to reduce the value gap by compensating the seller if it realizes certain financial, or other, milestones. Therefore, the size of the earnout will depend on the parties agreeing on the value attributable to the realization of the performance goals.

Buyers will ordinarily try to increase the size of the earnout to minimize the amount of cash paid out at closing, while sellers may try to reduce the amount of the earnout in order to receive more up-front consideration. Overall, the amount of the earnout will depend on the parties' willingness to receive more or less consideration at closing, the risk that each party is willing to assume, the performance and other criteria used for monitoring the earnout, and the overall operational objectives of the parties.

While it is possible to structure an earnout for part, or all, of the purchase price, it makes little sense for the parties to structure a contingent payment at the two extreme ends of the spectrum. For example, if the value gap in purchase price is less than 10%, it may not make sense to structure an earnout, since the possible human resource and financial cost of monitoring the earnout could outweigh the benefits of the earnout. It would be far more beneficial for the parties to try and reach an agreement on price up front. If the value gap is greater than 60% or 70% of the purchase price, this could very well indicate that a transaction is not worth pursuing. Both buyer and seller would be bearing huge risk in the transaction: the value the buyer would like to receive is too dependent on the milestones to be reached; likewise, the seller's consideration is largely dependent on the attainability of the performance goals. Most earnouts fall somewhere in between the two extreme examples above, say, 20% to 60% of the purchase price.

In addition to identifying the value gap and the earnout amount today, it is wise to take into consideration the contingent nature of both the performance goals and the earnout payments. This is done by using the time value of money concept and utilizing discount rates to calculate the projected payment. For example, if the value gap today is $10 million, and the negotiated earnout that would result if future goals are met is $10 million, the earnout amount would be adjusted upwards if the payment would be made in three years. While the discount rate is usually negotiated between the parties, one fair approach is to match the discount rate for the earnout amount with the interest rate on a government security with a maturity corresponding to the time period of the earnout. In this case, the discount rate would match the interest rate on the three-year note. If the interest rate on the government note is 6%, the payment made to the seller if the performance goals are met would be $10 \times (1.06)^3 = \$11.9$ million.

Inasmuch as the buyer and seller may agree on the size of the earnout, there should also be a mechanism in the earnout documentation that provides for floors, or minimum payments, partial payments, and caps or limits.

A minimum payment could make sense if seller management reaches a certain threshold that is below the ideal performance level. This might occur if there are factors that could influence the achievability of the goal. The seller may be reluctant to have the entire earnout subject to an "all or nothing" approach.

A second approach is to consider making partial payments based on the seller's ability to meet pre-defined levels of performance within the ideal performance goal. This could also be time based, for example, making a payment every six months or every year for three years. Payments can be made on a scale that corresponds to the degree to which seller management achieves the performance goal. However, recognize that there may be a distinction between shareholder and non-shareholder management. The buyer should continue to be prepared to reward management, apart from shareholders, for exceptional performance; otherwise, it runs the risk of demotivating management.

Finally, if a staged approach is used, with minimum payments as well as staged or partial payments, the buyer could very well insist on some type of maximum payment. In this way, even if seller management far exceeded the ideal performance goal, the earnout payment would be capped at a certain amount.

§ 30.04 PERFORMANCE GOALS

Between earnouts and contingent payments, there are innumerable different measurable performance criteria, and there are no hard and fast rules that dictate what benchmarks need to be used. The criteria used will be determined by the objectives of the buyer and the willingness of the seller. For the earnout to provide maximum benefit to the parties, the criteria should be clearly identified and defined in the earnout agreement. They should be attainable, measurable, and understood by both parties. It is important to remember that the more criteria used, the more complex the earnout is, and the harder it is to administer.

Revenues: Often regarded as the easiest financial metric to monitor, revenues are frequently used as an earnout benchmark. The primary advantage of using revenues is that the operations of the target can be consolidated with the acquirer while the revenues can be kept apart. However, there are downsides to relying exclusively on revenues. As an example, seller management may sacrifice margins to enhance revenues, thereby meeting, or exceeding, the performance criteria, yet actually harming shareholder value for the acquirer by hurting margins.

In order to mitigate the risk in a revenue-only earnout, the acquirer may require that the target maintain certain margins or profitability during the earnout period. Likewise, the target may be concerned that the buyer has the financial and operational capacity to support the growth of the target's revenue base. Consequently, the seller may require certain commitments on the part of the acquirer to ensure that the revenue targets can be met.

Gross Profit: On the surface, gross profit may appear to be the metric of choice to monitor in addition to revenues. It ensures that the target does not sacrifice production costs or cut prices to boost revenue, and therefore protects the integrity of the revenue stream. However, in many transactions, the purchasing cost savings that can be achieved in the deal are a key driver, and the future cost of goods is dictated by the acquirer. In the former case, the acquirer may be concerned that it is paying the seller an earnout based on savings that are brought to the transaction by the acquirer. In the latter case, the seller may be concerned that the acquirer will not help maintain cost structure or may hurt the purchasing power of the target. It is likely that in any gross profit driven earnout structure, the acquirer and seller will require strict guidelines for how the product costs are defined and monitored.

Operating Profit: Much like the gross profit benchmark, operating profit is a difficult metric to monitor. After the closing of a transaction, the acquirer is likely to merge certain selling, general and administrative expenses of the target into that of the acquirer. Consequently, it is difficult to identify the discreet operating expenses of the target post closing. Likewise, it is unlikely that the acquirer will be willing to pay the benefit of the operating expense improvements to the seller. To the extent operating profit is used as a key criteria in determining an earnout, the buyer and seller will need to keep the operational structure of the target distinct from that of the acquirer. Consequently, successfully monitoring operating profit may go against the overall consolidation benefits of the transaction.

There are other financial metrics that can be monitored in an earnout, including earnings before interest and taxes, cash flow and capital expenditures. Each of these have merit in that they may encourage the seller to perform at an optimal or predetermined level. However, like gross profit and operating profit, they force the acquirer to keep the target unconsolidated in order to monitor the discreet performance of each metrics.

Other Metrics: While financial benchmarks are one means for structuring an earnout, there are other non-financial benchmarks that can form the basis of an earnout or contingent payment stream. For example, a seller's financial projections may be predicated on the introduction of certain products. The acquirer may offer a contingent payment based on the achievability of this milestone. Exhibit 30-4 provides an overview of common non-financial benchmarks used in earnouts and contingent payments.

**Exhibit 30-4
Common Non-Financial
Benchmarks Used in Earnouts
and Contingent Payments**

Project completion
Product introduction
Contract signing
Time

---

§ 30.05   TIMEFRAME

The time period for an earnout depends on the criteria used for the contingent payment structure. Financial performance goals are typically set against the seller's projected financial results and will coincide with the financials used to determine the base purchase price. For example, to the extent the seller presents three-year forecasts that it is willing to stand behind, it is common to structure the earnout for the three-year time period.

Experience suggests that the longer the earnout timeframe, the more difficult it is for the acquirer to monitor the metrics, and the more difficult it is for seller management to perform against the benchmark. Managers and employees turn over, markets change, and technology shifts. The longer the earnout period, the greater the risk that the earnout structure falls apart. Consequently, acquirers are well advised to try and keep the earnout timeframe as short as possible.

§ 30.06   OTHER STRUCTURAL CONSIDERATIONS

While the most critical aspects of an earnout are its size, the performance criteria used for determining the payment, and the time period over which it is paid, there are other structural issues that should be considered in order to optimize the overall complexion of the earnout. Since there are no legal constraints to structuring an earnout, the buyer and seller have flexibility to structure the earnout to meet both parties' objectives.

Consolidation: In most acquisitions and mergers, the parties to the transaction are able to take advantage of revenue and cost improvements by consolidating certain operations of the two companies. In transactions that incorporate an earnout, the buyer and seller should be aware of the potential limitations that an earnout places on the companies' ability to consolidate operations. The principal reason for the constraints is the need to monitor the results of the seller to satisfy the performance goals for the earnout. For example, if the earnout's performance goal is based on revenue and gross profit, the buyer and seller may be restricted in their ability to take full advantage of revenue enhancements from a stronger combined sales force. Likewise, the parties may be limited in their ability to capitalize on cost savings. In the event the parties decide to integrate certain operations, they are well advised to clearly define the performance criteria and the mechanism for monitoring them.

Management Incentives: In many cases, there are shareholder and non-shareholder managers and employees in a company. While the earnout payments are targeted at seller shareholders, the buyer should also be aware that seller management and employees need to be co-opted into the process, independent of shareholders. The buyer should therefore be prepared to set up bonus plans and employment agreement with key managers and employees; otherwise, the buyer and seller shareholders run the risk that they create conflict between selling shareholders and employees.

Capital Allocation: In most acquisitions, it is typical for the acquirer to assume control of the financing of the seller post transaction. The acquirer makes capital available to fund expansion plans and growth, pay employees and vendors, and support the working capital of the target. In order to meet the financial goals set out in the earnout, the seller may require some form of assurances that the acquirer will provide the capital necessary to fund the targeted financial performance.

Earnout Protection: Selling shareholders face two key risks when entering into an earnout: the buyer's ability to fund the earnout and the risk that the buyer itself gets acquired during the earnout period. In both cases, the seller may request some form of deal protection, such as the funds to pay the earnout be put into escrow. In addition, the seller may ask for a provision that protects the earnout payment or accelerates the payment if the acquirer is purchased during the earnout period.

Monitoring: Quite important is the agreement over how the performance goals are monitored. In addition to precisely defining the criteria, the parties will want to agree on the mechanism for monitoring them. For example, the parties may agree that the seller continue to produce independent audited financial statements. They should also understand any differences in accounting methodology between the companies, so there is no misunderstanding in the definition of performance criteria. For example, expenses that are included in cost of goods sold versus operating expenses. The parties should also define some form of dispute resolution mechanism, for example, a third party auditing firm.

§ 30.07   WORDS OF CAUTION

Earnouts are quite difficult to administer. First, they potentially limit the parties' ability to integrate their companies. Second, establishing performance criteria that are easily monitored is tricky. Third, they can create a conflict between shareholder and non-shareholder management and employees. Fourth, the corporate and personal objectives of the companies and seller shareholders may change once a transaction is signed. Fifth, if there are disputes over the earnout structure, the mere fact that the earnout exists may jeopardize the success of the acquisition. Finally, no agreement can provide absolute protection to both parties; there are too many variables.

Given the complexities of earnouts, in many cases they are restructured soon after their inception. Options for restructuring an earnout include modifying the performance criteria to facilitate easier administration or afford operational integration between the parties, accelerating earnout payments, or buying the earnout out completely. Both the buyer and seller should look for opportunities to restructure an earnout as soon as possible after its inception to bring the transaction to a close.

A buyer may wish to terminate an earnout and buy out the payments prematurely, for a variety of reasons. For example, if it deems the earnout as too restrictive on its ability to integrate the operations of the seller with its own. Or, the buyer may opportunistically recognize that the seller can easily achieve the performance targets and thus be interested in capitalizing on the opportunity early. On the other hand, a seller may wish to terminate an earnout structure if it's corporate and personal objectives change, or if it opportunistically recognizes that it may not be able to meet the performance goals.

§ 30.08   LIMITATIONS ON THE USE OF EARNOUTS

Earnouts as a structuring mechanism are quite flexible, and can be tailored to meet the objectives of the buyer, seller shareholders and seller management. However, the use of earnouts is limited by the type of transaction and form of consideration used for the upfront portion of the purchase price.

Taxable versus Tax Free Transactions: In many transactions, stock is the most desired form of consideration, in that it allows the buyer to conserve its cash, and the seller to receive tax-free consideration and participate in the upside of the combined organization. Cash that is used as part or all of the consideration in a deal is taxable — this includes cash earnout payments. Therefore, in order for an earnout to be structured as a part of a tax-free transaction, there are a number of issues to consider.

First, for a stock-for-stock acquisition to be tax free, all of the consideration must be paid in stock. Therefore, any consideration paid as a part of the earnout must be in the form of stock. The Internal Revenue Service mandates that in a tax-free acquisition, the earnout cannot exceed more than 50% of the total consideration, and the earnout period cannot exceed five years. Second, in a straight or forward triangular tax-free merger, at least 50% of the total consideration must be paid in the form of stock. In a reverse triangular tax-free merger, at least 80% of the total consideration must be paid in stock.

For the seller, taxable payments can be recognized on the installment sale basis that allows the income tax on the earnout amount to be deferred until the payment is received.

Accounting: Taxable and tax-free transactions incorporating earnouts are typically accounted for using purchase accounting.

As a result of the accounting treatment for earnouts, the acquirer must recognize the goodwill associated with the transaction. Since earnout payments are considered a part of the transaction purchase price, the amount of the earnout will serve to increase the amount of goodwill that is recognized by the acquirer in the transaction.

§ 30.09   SUMMARY

Earnouts and contingent payments are an effective tool for bridging a valuation gap between buyer and seller. They are also valuable in motivating key shareholder managers and mitigating risk in a transaction. Earnouts work best when the incentives of the selling management team are aligned with the objectives of the acquirer. In addition, they function well when the performance criteria are well defined and are easily monitored. Entering into an earnout, the buyer and seller are well advised to keep the structure as simple as possible and to be realistic about the limitations and risks of incorporating an earnout in the overall transaction.

Chapter 31

DUE DILIGENCE

§ 31.01 WHAT IS DUE DILIGENCE?

One of the most overlooked and poorly executed aspects of any M&A or restructuring transaction is due diligence. Transactions are frequently penciled out on paper, models are run, and high-level strategic discussions are held. Yet, often, little attention is paid to the validation of the underpinnings of the deal through sound due diligence. Due diligence not only serves to unearth potential problems in a transaction, it also validates one's thinking and provides a roadmap for ensuring that post-transaction follow-up is well-executed.

Due diligence is the methodical investigation of all the legal, financial and strategic facets of a company and a transaction. It is a process that involves obtaining and verifying very detailed information about a company that is not usually found in its public documents.

[A]   Why Perform Due Diligence?

Companies, bankers, accountants, lawyers and consultants perform due diligence for a variety of reasons. However, in concept, due diligence has three central purposes:

1. *Validate Transaction Assumptions:* Initial deal assumptions are often based on public information. Due diligence allows one to verify the initial assumptions based on confidential discussions and documents. As an example, in the sale of a company, the seller must "package" the company to sell it. Therefore, most sales memoranda will show the company in a positive light that paints an attractive future for the business. As we know, this is often not the case, and most companies have their unique problems, skeletons and warts. The due diligence process helps ensure that any representations the seller makes are true, for example, that the financial statements accurately reflect the historical financial performance of the company. As one performs due diligence, it enables us to better understand the risks inherent in the transaction and assume those risks based on an informed decision. Finally, due diligence allows us to truly understand the extent of the opportunity.

2. *Unearth Possible Problems:* In the course of validating initial assumptions, by digging deeper into a company's legal and financial framework, and by challenging strategic assumptions, it is often possible to identify errors, omissions or factual misrepresentations. In addition, there may be items not previously disclosed that are material to the transaction.

3. *Plan for Transition:* Based on the in-depth knowledge gained from the due diligence exercise, it is possible to craft a detailed transition plan that ensures the assumptions in the transaction are seen to fruition, manages any problems that have arisen in the course of the due diligence, and integrates the companies or ensures the successful conclusion of the transaction.

Due diligence also provides a board of directors and management a measure of security that they have protected shareholder's interests by diligently evaluating a proposed transaction. Essentially, once a transaction has reached the point where it appears likely the deal may be consummated, due diligence will either confirm that the transaction should proceed on the terms discussed, or indicate that the parties should restructure the transaction or part ways. Due diligence is necessary to protect a company from liability. Without having conducted proper, thorough due diligence, the board of directors could be found to have been negligent in its efforts when undertaking a transaction.

[B]   When to Perform Due Diligence

Due diligence is performed in a variety of circumstances; however, it is usually undertaken in every transaction. A fundamental question is when in the life cycle of a deal is due diligence performed? While there are multiple answers to this question, due diligence is usually performed at different levels of intensity and detail all through the deal life cycle. Due diligence begins with a cursory overview of the company, the industry and the management team, and ends with an in-depth legal and financial analysis of the company's contracts and financial statements.

Initial due diligence begins with the first telephone call or communication between the parties. During this initial phase, it is important to listen and observe how the other parties behave, what they say, and how they respond to your questions. It is helpful to make a mental note of who performs the work or has the interaction. Is this a high level person or has the transaction been delegated to a junior person? Does it receive high priority in the organization? Are you dealing with a person who has the authority to make decisions? Are they up front and responsive, or are they cagey and not direct? Do they answer the question you ask or do they circumvent the question with tangential answers? All of these signs during the early stages of communication on a deal help form a picture of whether the counterparty is credible.

Preliminary due diligence will ordinarily involve a review of public information, verbal and written. Despite the public nature of the information, it is possible to uncover very detailed facts regarding the company. Thanks to various accounting and securities disclosure requirements, companies are required to disclose certain information regarding their businesses in their operations. For example, an accounting auditor may have concerns regarding the solvency of a company or the company's accounting for certain items. These concerns can often be found in the auditor's opinion or the footnotes to the financial statements.

As the transaction progresses, the pace and detail of the due diligence will increase, as more and more confidential information is sought from the parties involved. As the confidential material is divulged, it is important to separate the information and issues into categories, for example, issues that affect the valuation of the transaction, issues that affect the structure of the transaction, or issues that affect the strategic merits of the transaction.

Due diligence is usually performed in every transaction, whether merger, acquisition or restructuring, or a variant thereof. In addition, due diligence will be conducted for various purposes within each transaction by different parties. For example, in an acquisition, the acquirer will perform due diligence on the target to validate the transaction and determine if there are any reasons not to do the deal. In the same transaction, potential lenders may perform due diligence on the target to determine specifically if there is sufficient cash flow to pay back a loan or if there are sufficient assets to serve as collateral for the loan. As another example, investment bankers may perform their own due diligence on a target company in order to provide a fairness opinion to the acquirer's board of directors.

[C] Forms of Due Diligence

Regardless of who performs the due diligence, it will fall into three broad categories: legal due diligence, business due diligence and strategic due diligence.

Exhibit 31-1
Legal Documents to Be Reviewed

Charter and By-Laws	10-K's (past five years)
Certificate of Incorporation	10-Q's (past two years)
Employment and Compensation Agreements	Annual Reports (past five years)
	Proxy Statements (past five years)
401(k) and other Benefit Plans	Registration Statements
Option Agreements	8-K's
Significant Contracts	Insurance Contracts
Legal Settlements or Pending Claims	Acquisition, Merger and Divestiture Agreement
Loan Agreements	
Patents and Trademarks	Leases and Real Estate Agreements
Franchise Agreements	Shareholder Agreements

[1] Legal Due Diligence

Legal due diligence entails the review of a company's legal contracts and other documents. Many of these documents will be filed as exhibits or attachments to the company's public filings. Exhibit 31-1 provides an illustrative list of the types of legal documents that should be reviewed.

[2] Business Due Diligence

Business due diligence is the detailed evaluation and analysis of the operating and financial performance of the company and the factors that influence the performance of the business. It includes an assessment of the past, present and future performance of the business by analyzing financial statements, business plans, and other documents that relate to the business.

[3] Strategic Due Diligence

Strategic due diligence is the analysis of those factors that influence the strategic merits of the transaction and affect the company's strategic position in the industry. It includes a thorough review of the industry, the competitive environment and the company's position within the industry.

[D] Who Performs Due Diligence?

Due diligence is performed by a number of different parties. Lawyers will typically review the legal aspects of the transaction and the company under discussion, and are responsible for determining whether there is any legal exposure in the transaction. They are also responsible for verifying whether the representations and warranties made by the counter party are true.

Accountants will usually be responsible for assessing the integrity of the company's financial statements. In addition, they will often review the business implications of contracts to ensure the historical and projected financial statements correctly reflect the contractual relationships.

Bankers, in particular investment bankers, will usually perform financial, business and strategic due diligence in conjunction with accountants and lawyers and other parties involved in the due diligence. Much of their due diligence is used to support the financial and strategic analysis underlying the transaction negotiations. In addition, their due diligence will be in support of a fairness opinion, if any, delivered to their client's board of directors.

Consultants can play different roles in a merger and acquisition transaction, but often are engaged to perform due diligence on products or intellectual property. They can also provide expert third party opinions on markets, sectors, or industries.

Internal management and employees are the most important people in the due diligence process. While service firms retained by a company to provide advice and perform due diligence can be very effective and helpful, it is the management team and employees who have the ultimate burden of having to recommend a transaction to senior management and the board of directors. It is based on their knowledge and understanding of a transaction that the board may decide to pursue a transaction. In addition, since the management and employees of a company are intimately involved in the industry, they are best positioned to perform due diligence.

Finally, there is the individual who is responsible for the transaction. He or she must have full knowledge of the transaction, the parties to the transaction, and all the issues that affect the business and legal terms of the deal. In order for the transaction to proceed to the board approval stage, this person must have complete confidence in the breadth, scope and outcome of the due diligence. Without it, the board of directors and senior management may not have a sound basis on which to proceed.

[E] Where to Get Information

Whether it is written or verbal information, it is usually maintained by individuals that have current, past or potential future relationship with the company in question. There are a number of individuals who may have the requisite information, depending on the type of information you are seeking. Exhibit 31-2 outlines the key people who may be involved in the due diligence process as a source of information.

Besides information that can be garnered from these individuals, there are additional insights that can be gained by going to a variety of public sources including, databases such as Edgar. Other public sources include Dun and Bradstreet, Multex, Yahoo, Moody's, Standard and Poors, and other industry specific publications. Additionally, public equity research analysts often provide valuable opinions on companies. Furthermore, there are numerous sources for industry research such as Frost & Sullivan that can be purchased.

Valuable information can also be gathered by simply visiting a plant or other facility, where the operations of a company may be observed first hand

Exhibit 31-2
Sources of Information

Source(s)

Internal Management	Chairman & CEO
	Chief Operating Officer
	President
	Chief Financial Officer
	Controller
	Treasurer
	Head of Human Resources
	Head of Marketing
	Chief Legal Officer
	Division or Subsidiary Management
	Corporate Development Officers
External Insiders	Auditors
	Outside Law Firm
	Consultants
Third Parties	Customers
	Suppliers
	Bankers
	Insurance Agents
	Regulatory Officials

Exhibit 31-3
Document Request

Market Studies	Marketing Plans
Management Reports	Long-Range Operating Plans
Engineering Reports	Board Minutes
Detailed Business Plans and Budgets	Committee Reports
Historical Financial Statements	

and the culture of an organization may be assessed. While there is no way to "quantify" this information, it is often the glue that cements that transaction.

While substantial information can be obtained from internal management and employees, third parties, and by visits to the company and its facilities, the most likely places to find detailed information are the internal documents of the company. Many of these documents may not be legal documents and they probably are not filed along with the regulatory filings of the company. Exhibit 31-3 outlines some of the more common documents that should be requested in a due diligence review, outside of the standard legal documents.

§ 31.02   THE DUE DILIGENCE PROCESS

Every transaction is different and the need to perform due diligence will vary accordingly; however, the overall process of conducting due diligence remains largely the same. In general, the due diligence process falls into six categories or phases:

1. Establish a plan and assemble the team

2. Identify key issues

3. Prepare the information request and obtain information

4. Translate issues into value

5. Resolve issues

6. Plan for transition

[A]   Establish a Plan and Assemble the Team

At the outset of any transaction, it is important to understand what the objectives are. In particular, when performing due diligence, it is critical to determine why due diligence is being conducted. What are you trying to achieve? What issues are you attempting to clarify? What concerns do you wish to ameliorate? Do you have any time constraints? Where are there likely to be problems? What potential "deal breakers" are on the horizon? What issues in the transaction are important to you and to the counter party? What issues have less significance?

In so doing, it is helpful to identify the people who will be involved in the process and to form a team that is responsible for various facets of the due diligence. In putting together the team, it is helpful to appoint a team leader or point person on the overall project as well as point people or team leaders for individual components of the due diligence. The team should discuss the most appropriate means to communicate to each other and to disseminate information throughout the due diligence process. One approach is to conduct once daily meetings in person or by telephone whereby each team leader presents their significant findings to the rest of the due diligence team members. This communication is effective at identifying areas of concern that may overlap with other areas where different teams are conducting an investigation. The team should discuss the timing and scope of the due diligence inquiry, and lay out a timetable and responsibility chart with which to manage the transaction.

Setting forth a framework for performing due diligence clearly establishes ground rules for the process and sets an expectation among members of the teams as to what is required of the process, what the objectives are and what the deliverables are. It can save the company time in analyzing, structuring and negotiating the transaction, and establishes a framework for post-merger or post-transaction integration.

In general, it is important to include those members from the company who post transaction will have responsibility for certain aspects of the integrated businesses. They are best qualified to understand and evaluate issues in the transaction as well as oversee their resolution and implementation once the transaction is complete.

[B] Identify Key Issues

Issues, concerns and questions will arise at every phase of the deal process. One should keep a running list of these items to make sure they are resolved along the way. However, lists of issues have a way of taking on a life of their own and can often result in pages and pages of unanswered questions. For this reason, it is helpful to sort the issues into different baskets.

First, identify the major items or deal breakers. Rarely are there more than ten significant items in a deal. If there are more, you should be concerned. "Deal" issues are those where unless they are completely resolved to your satisfaction, the deal should not go through. For example, making sure that a key employee's employment and non-competition agreement is sound. Another example may be establishing the extent to which a pension plan is underfunded. Deal issues are usually those issues that affect the pricing of the transaction or the legal terms of the contract. Even as you develop the list of deal breakers, it is important to prioritize those in order to know where to focus attention and on what issues one can compromise, if at all.

Second, separate out the business issues from the remaining concerns. Business issues are those that relate to the ongoing business. While they may not have a direct impact on the price or contract, they will help confirm the feasibility of the transaction in that they substantiate the ongoing viability of the business. For example, confirming terms of a customer contract.

Third, identify the legal issues. For example, to what extent is there litigation in the company? Is it threatened or actual? Or, does the company have the required licenses and permits to do business? While these issues will often not affect price or contract terms, they may be pre-requisites to closing a transaction. Regardless of the issue or concern, it is important to always go back and reevaluate the original intent of the transaction and determine how the resolution, or lack of resolution of an issue affects the transaction.

[C] Prepare the Information Request and Obtain Information

[1] The Preliminary Information Request

The inception of the discovery phase of due diligence begins with a formal request for information. The information request is sent to the company that is subject of the investigation. It includes very general questions and seeks preliminary information to assist the requestee in evaluating the business. Documents and topics that are typically requested in a preliminary information request are outlined in Exhibit 31-4 below.

Exhibit 31-4
Typical Information Request Topic List

I. *Business Information*

Management and Employees
- Organization Chart
- Management Profiles
- Employment Contracts
- Labor Contracts

Products
- Product Lines
- Revenue and Operating Performance by Product Line
- Profitability Analysis
- Volume Analysis
- Catalogues

Industry and Competition
- Market Studies and Analyses
- Industry Characteristics: Size, Competitors, Growth, Trends

Marketing
- Key Customers
- Pricing/Terms
- Marketing Strategy
- Organization
- Cost Structure
- Variation by Regions, Seasons, etc.
- Key Salesmen

Production Facilities
- Physical Description
- Capacity/Utilization
- Leases
- Significant Capital Expenditures, Historical/Projected

Manufacturing
- Cost Structure—Fixed vs. Variable
- Process
- Quality Control
- Suppliers/Raw Materials
- Capacity

Research and Development
- Budget
- Human Resources
- History of New Product Introduction

(Continued)

Exhibit 31-4

(*Continued*)

II.   *Financial Information*

Historical
- Latest Available Financial Statements
- Sources and Uses of Funds
- Management Discussion and Analysis for Last Two Years
- Historical Budgets

Current
- Analysis of Budget vs. Actual
- Contribution Analysis
- Asset Utilization

Projections
- Near Term Budget
- Long Range Plan
- Assumptions

III. *Supplementary Information*

Employee Benefits
- Pension Plan
- Salaries and Other Compensation
- Health Care and Other Benefits

Insurance Coverage

Product Liability

Litigation History

Inter-Company Transactions

Previous Inquiries/Efforts to Sell

In addition to the various topics outlined above, it is not uncommon to provide a counterparty with a detailed document request list. Items that would ordinarily be found on a document request list are shown below in Exhibit 31-5.

[2]   The Detailed Due Diligence Review

Based on the preliminary information, the due diligence team will be in a better position to understand pertinent issues and identify areas for further investigation. A more formal detailed due diligence review list is prepared and discussed with management of the target business. Clearly such a review will vary by transaction type, the unique aspects of each company, and industry in which it participates. An example of a detailed due diligence review list can be seen below in Exhibit 31-6.

Exhibit 31-5
Typical Detailed Document Request List

I. *Documents to Review*
    1. Annual reports for last 5 years
    2. 10K's for last 5 years
    3. Latest 10Q
    4. Proxy statements for last 5 years
    5. Last 5 years of auditor's reports to management together with management response
    6. Board minutes for last 2 to 3 years
    7. Executive and other committee minutes for last 2 to 3 years
    8. Two to three years of internal monthly interim reports
    9. Business plan including projected financial statements for 5 years
    10. Description of any significant pending litigation or contingent liabilities
    11. Pension plans; employee benefit coverage; executive compensation agreements
    12. Summary of major leases
    13. Schedule of insurance carried
    14. R&D plans and budgets
    15. Major loan agreements

II. *Topics to Review*
    Industry Overview
    1. Description of industry segments, size and growth of each
    2. Competitors
    3. Nature of competition
    4. Major trends affecting each segment
    5. History of mergers, acquisitions and joint ventures by segment

    Company
    1. Description of products and services of each segment
    2. Detailed breakdown of revenues, profits, expense structure by line of business for past 5 years together with 5-year projections
    3. Analysis of revenues, profits, expense structure by geographic region
    4. Environmental issues, if any
    5. Labor issues, if any
    6. Any legal or other constraints to trade, including regulatory, anti-trust or other injunctions?
    7. What are significant governmental issues facing company?

    Technology
    1. Summary of owned or licensed technology, if any
    2. List of patents, trademarks, copyrights
    3. Discussion of technology and risks inherent in technology, e.g., obsolescence risk

    Organization and Management
    1. Organizational chart: ages, length of service
    2. Management biographies

(Continued)

Exhibit 31-5

(*Continued*)

---

3. Senior management team
4. Stock option and other non-cash compensation plans
5. Management cash and bonus compensation
6. Management objectives 1, 5, and 10 years in future
7. Compensation structure, of each business segment, of employees

Markets and Marketing

1. Size of markets, growth rate over last 5 years, projected growth rates for each segment
2. Major trends influencing growth or decline of segment
3. Company's market share, trend/projection
4. Description of cyclicality, if any
5. Pricing policy, how set, by whom
6. Major suppliers to each business, degree of reliance, major contract terms
7. Description of how product is sold and by whom, key decision maker to be influenced, key buying factors
8. Sales force size, geographic coverage, compensation structure coverage compensation
9. Major differentiation points of products
10. Training methods for sales force
11. Age/experience of sales force; qualitative assessment
12. Advertising budget, emphasis, method, vehicles
13. Summary of distribution practice (e.g. direct sales vs. OEM sales vs. distributors vs. franchises, etc.)
14. Summary of key buying factors: quality, price, delivery, service, ancillary benefits, reputation, financing terms, favored relationships, etc.
15. Summary of decision making process and duration
16. Major customers by segment; what percentage of sales to top customer, what number of customers account for 80% of sales; what percentage of sales to top 10 customers
17. Summary of long term contracts either to buy materials or to sell products or services
18. Summary of warranty/guarantee policy; costs to implement and maintain

Competitors

1. List of competitors, by segment, including market share over last 5 years
2. Basis for competition
3. Competitor technology differentiation
4. Competitor manufacturing differentiation
5. Competitor marketing, sales and distribution differentiation
6. Competitor product differentiation
7. Competitor product differentiation
8. Profitability (gross, operating, and net) product line for competitors

(*Continued*)

Exhibit 31-5

(*Continued*)

Manufacturing Process

1. Number and location of plants; age of plants
2. Function of each plant
3. Plant capacity and utilization
4. Overview of manufacturing process
5. Suppliers of raw materials and availability, terms of arrangement, alternative suppliers
6. Stages of value-added
7. Overview of quality control
8. Cost advantages: low-cost producer?
9. Technology employed at plants
10. State-of-art technology available in the industry or in development
11. Unionization of work force; wage costs relative to locale
12. Capital expenditure plans and programs: anticipated benefit
13. Research and Development activities
14. Distribution; warehousing
15. Number of shifts; simultaneous product line production
16. Manufacturing organization
17. Description of inventory: controls, terms, dead inventory

Financial and Other Assets:
Real Estate

1. Recent real estate appraisals
2. Data on recent real estate sales in area
3. Description of holdings — maps, location, etc.

Assets — by business

1. Description of physical assets
2. Appraisals
3. Replacement cost data
4. Market value of inventories/LIFO value/FIFO value
5. Loan agreements, including major conditions/restrictions
6. Summary of major financings of customer purchases
7. Backlog by product line
8. List of major banks used; nature and amount of credit extended; summary of past usage and anticipated usage
9. If company has changed auditors, why?
10. Summary of major accounting policies (cash vs. accrual, tax vs. book, completed contract vs. percentage of completion, etc.)
11. What significant items are there off balance sheet?
12. What operating reports (e.g., operating and capital budgets, shipping reports, manufacturing reports, sales reports, variance analysis, monthly summaries, etc.) are prepared for management?

Exhibit 31-6
Detailed Due Diligence Review List

A.   *Industry Review*

  1. Develop a comprehensive view of the industry: who the competitors are by business segment, what their respective market share is, what the trends are that affect the business, and what the basis for competition is.

  2. In performing the review, you should be concerned with the following:

    (a) Ten-year historical growth and profitability of the industry in relation to the performance of the company in question. Look at the company's market share, margins and financial performance over the ten-year time period relative to the industry.

    (b) Assess successes and failures in the industry. Why have certain companies gained market share while others have not? Has any company gone out of business? Which companies were sold and why?

    (c) Has there been any legal or regulatory shifts that have impacted competition? Who survived and/or thrived after the shift?

    (d) Have there been any new entrants? How has the new competition affected the industry?

    (e) Has the nature of competition changed?

    (f) Is the industry dependent on any proprietary technology? Does anyone own key patents that may limit future competition?

    (g) Have there been any significant technological changes that have affected competition? How have competitors adjusted to the change and have they made investments to protect against the future?

    (h) How has manufacturing changed in the industry? Is it a source of competitive advantage?

    (i) How is marketing, sales and distribution done in the industry? Have there been any changes in the nature of sales, marketing and distribution in the last ten years?

    (j) Are there any labor issues in the industry? How does the target company's labor situation compare to that of the industry?

    (k) Is there any seasonality in the industry? How have competitors adjusted to the seasonality?

B.   *Accounting and Valuation*

  1. Gain a thorough understanding of the company's accounting and valuation practices and determine their impact on the company's earnings. For example:

    (a) Inventory valuation (FIFO, LIFO, average).

    (b) Depreciation (straight-line, machine hours, units produced, sum-of-the-years digit, double declining).

    (c) Provision for pension costs.

    (d) Research and development costs — what is expenses and what is amortized?

    (e) Goodwill impairment.

    (f) Realization of income:

      (1) Sale of products, services, or real property — at time of sale, upon collection of sales price, or completion of product.

(Continued)

Exhibit 31-6

(*Continued*)

---

    (2)   Sales to joint ventures or other affiliated type companies.

    (3)   Long-term construction or contracting operations — at time contract is completed or proportionately over performance of contract.

    (4)   Cash discounts taken by customers on sales and effect on income — at time of sale or at time of collection.

    (5)   Unamortized discount and expenses on debt or refunded debt.

    (6)   Capitalization of assets.

    (7)   Accounting for foreign exchange translation gains and losses.

    (8)   Property, plant and equipment depreciation.

    (9)   Long-term investment valuation.

    (10)   Leases — operating or capitalized.

2. How does the company's accounting and valuation methods differ from those of the industry?

3. Do the Board Minutes reflect any material transactions and have these transactions been accounted for in accordance with the company's practices? Are these practices in line with generally accepted accounting practices? Are these accounting practices consistent with those of the industry?

4. Have there been any reports by internal or third party auditors that recommend a change in accounting practices?

5. Gain a thorough understanding of the company's accounting and budgeting procedures. Obtaining a copy of the company's accounting manual and determine whether the company has adhered to these procedures.

6. Understand how the internal and external audit process is undertaken, who has responsibility, what staff has been involved.

7. Review prior acquisitions, what accounting policies were involved, what due diligence was performed.

8. Reconcile all material electronic and other funds transfers for the past two to three years.

9. What cash is restricted? What receivables, inventory and other assets are pledged as collateral for debt?

10. Are there any non-standard receivables? Are there any internal receivables?

11. Understand how assets and real estate is valued and carried on the balance sheet? Are there any hidden assets?

12. Review historical capital expenditures and assess these expenditures relative to the property, plant and equipment on the balance sheet. Compare historical levels of capital expenditures to future projections.

13. Assess financial investments and how these investments are carried on the balance sheet.

14. Assess intangible assets and goodwill, as well as goodwill impairment.

15. Determine if there are any contingent or other liabilities that are not recorded on the balance sheet.

(*Continued*)

Exhibit 31-6

(Continued)

---

16. Examine the company's debt outstanding to determine what, if any, debt needs to be refinanced in the transaction, what covenants there are and what other constraints the debt may have on the transaction.

17. Understand the company's credit lines, how much is available, and any constraints, if any.

18. Understand all reserves and other balance sheet commitments.

19. What dividend requirements are there?

20. Review the company's treasury stock. What is the company's history of stock repurchases?

21. Analyze the company's shareholder base. Who are the significant shareholders? Who has purchased and sold over the past two years?

22. Are there any net operating losses?

23. Are there any commitments or contingencies that are not reflected on the balance sheet?

24. Understand the nature of the lease commitments. When do they expire?

25. Understand all issuance of equity and other securities.

26. Are there any obligations for retirement benefit plans? Is there a funding need for underfunded pension plans?

27. Is the company subject to any pending changes in accounting rules?

28. Have there been any transactions between management or insiders and the company that may give rise to any conflicts of interest?

29. Have there been any questions raised by accountants or the SEC on any prior filings?

30. Are interim statements prepared on the same basis as year-end financial statements?

C. *Earnings*

1. Review the company's public financial statements for the last ten fiscal years and for the most recent interim period. Note any unusual matters, including footnotes that may suggest anything out of the ordinary.

2. Focus on the independent public accountant's opinion on the financial statements and note any qualifications, exceptions or disclaimers.

3. Evaluate the operating performance of the company by product line or service for the past ten years and note any significant trends or changes in the business.

4. Establish where growth has come from—organic or same store, new product or service, acquisition, etc. Why has the company grown this way?

5. Review the same information by product line on a quarter-to-quarter basis, paying particular attention to gross margins, operating margins and any seasonality in the product lines.

6. Evaluate cost of goods sold for the past ten years on a product-by-product basis or by service, noting any negative or significant trends.

(Continued)

Exhibit 31-6

(*Continued*)

---

7. Analyze sales and cost of goods sold by product line for the past year on a monthly basis to determine if there have been any unusual changes in the past 12 months.

8. What percentage, if any, of the company's sales are to affiliated entities?

9. Look at the top ten customers for the company and determine how dependent the company is on any one customer.

10. Have any customers provided an opinion or feedback with respect to problems or any other issues with the company's products?

11. Review the company's revenue recognition policies by product.

12. Understand what, if any, other or miscellaneous income is.

13. Understand the different channels of distribution for the company's products. Review product pricing as well as margins for products by channel.

14. What percentage of sales does returns and allowance represent? Is it reasonable in relation to the level of sales? How does it compare to competitors?

15. Review the company's current backlog to determine how real the backlog is. Review the company's backlog for the past two years on a quarter-by-quarter basis to determine how the current backlog compares during similar past time periods.

16. Understand the methodology for calculating cost of goods sold. Is it the same for interim periods?

17. Has the company made any purchases from affiliated entities? Are these terms consistent with what the affiliated entity is charging other third parties?

18. Look at the company's top 25 suppliers. Is the company dependent on any one or two suppliers?

19. Review any significant supplier contracts.

20. Review detail behind the company's selling, general and administrative expenses for the past ten years on a yearly basis, for the past two years on a quarter-by-quarter basis and for the last year on a monthly basis. Note any significant changes or trends.

21. Review the detail behind the company's sales and marketing plan for the past ten years, past two years on a quarter-by-quarter basis and for the past year on a monthly basis. Note any significant changes or trends. Have there been any recent increases or decreases in spending on sales and marketing?

22. Evaluate the company's historical budgets by product line versus the actual results for the past three to five years. Also, review the consolidated budget in relation to actual results.

23. Analyze the company's projections and projection assumptions in light of the company's prior budgets and history of meeting or not meeting its plan.

24. Establish the availability of labor to support the growth of the company. Are there any material labor issues that may impact growth?

25. Establish the availability of raw materials to support the growth of the company. Are there any material raw material issues that may impact growth?

(*Continued*)

Exhibit 31-6

(Continued)

26. Establish that the company has sufficient capacity to meet production demands in support of the company's projections.

27. Evaluate the company's geographic concentration by product line and determine the dependency of the company on any one country or region. Are there any unique issues with that company or region that may affect growth?

28. Have there been any material changes in accounting policies or practices in the past ten years? How have these changes affected earnings? Are there any other changes on the horizon that may affect earnings?

29. Are there any items in the income statement that have been recorded in current or prior periods that could have, or should have, been recorded earlier?

30. Evaluate all non-recurring, extraordinary and one-time charges. Are they appropriate? Should any of these charges be viewed as on-going expenses?

31. Analyze inventory for the past year on a monthly basis and for the past two years on a quarterly basis. Have there been any adjustments to inventory? Are they reasonable? Is there any obsolete inventory? How does the company prepare its inventory valuations? What is the process for determining if inventory is obsolete?

32. Analyze accounts receivable on a monthly basis for the past year and on a quarterly basis for the past two years. Look at the aged accounts summary and evaluate any reserves. To what extent are there any bad or uncollectible receivables? Look at the company's history of write-offs. Is it consistent with past periods? Is there any unusual build-up of receivables in recent periods?

33. Review receivables by customer and by product line for the past year on a monthly basis and for the past two years on a quarterly basis.

34. Evaluate research and development expenses. Understand the company's methodology for determining what is expensed and what is amortized. How much is allocated to research and development for the next few years? How does this amount relate to prior years? Are the human resources in place to undertake the research and development?

35. Understand what other assets are on the balance sheet. Are there any deferrals that should be noted?

36. Does the company have any provisions for lost sales? Understand to whom they are for and why they were made. Analyze relative to prior periods.

37. Inquire as to whether all appropriate accruals, were made for such items as advertising, retroactive wage adjustments, litigation, warranties under contracts, sales allowances and credits, provisions for environmental problems and foreign currency losses.

38. Review all contingent liabilities, whether on or off balance sheet. Are there items that should be on the balance sheet that are not?

39. Obtain any third party appraisals of real estate and other assets. Establish the fair market value of such assets in relation to the depreciated value.

40. Analyze intangible assets, goodwill and all amortization and goodwill impairment amounts. Are they reasonable? Are prior period amortization and impairment consistent with current periods and future projections?

(Continued)

Exhibit 31-6

(*Continued*)

41. Review the company's tax rate. Establish how the tax rate has changed for each period analyzed. Are the assumptions underlying the forecasts consistent with prior experience?

42. Has the company closed any plants in the past ten years? Does it expect to close any plants in the near future?

43. Does the company have any plans to open any plants in the near future?

44. Evaluate the profitability of each plant. Are there any plants that should be shut down?

45. Is the company in discussions regarding the sale or any product, division or business? Is it in discussions regarding the purchase of any product, division or business?

46. Analyze the company's cash flow statement for the past two years on a quarterly basis and for the past year on a monthly basis. Evaluate in the context of the company's budget and projections. Are there any material variances that should be noted? Any unusual expenditures, changes in working capital or funding needs?

47. Evaluate the company's prior capital expenditures. How do they compare to future capital plans? Are there any unusual recent expenditures? Are there any unusual projected expenditures?

48. Review the company's intellectual property portfolio. Are there any patents that are close to expiration? What is the company's vulnerability to its intellectual property position?

49. Evaluate the senior management team of the company. Are there any holes in the management team? Is present management equipped to build the business? Has there been any recent turnover in the management team? Are there any unusual contracts between any member of management and the company?

50. Does the company have a succession plan in place?

51. In the event of a downturn in the industry, what management could be let go and the company still be in a position to survive?

52. Evaluate all employment contracts and severance agreements. Determine the impact these agreements may have on the transaction.

53. Review the company's manufacturing and quality control procedures.

54. Review the company's safety and emergency procedures.

55. Evaluate the efficiency of the company's manufacturing processes.

56. Assess the company's property taxes. Determine if any tax increases are in order and the impact of such on the company.

57. Review the company's investments. Is the company's cash invested in appropriate investments? How does the company carry its investments? Do current carrying values reflect market value? What is the value of the company's investments?

58. Review all non-cash compensation. Are there any unusual arrangements with management and insiders?

59. To what extent are there items on the balance sheet that are estimated or subjective? What is the basis for such estimation?

These due diligence questions are a broad overview of the types of questions that should be asked in a due diligence review session. Essentially, in conducting due diligence, it is advisable to review all items on the company's historical and projected income statements, cash flows and balance sheets to determine how current and projected periods relate to prior experience. In addition, it is appropriate to question how items are valued and accounted for. Furthermore, it is important to question the trends, shifts and changes in the business to determine how such differences will affect future performance.

[3] Meeting with Management

The next step is to meet with management in their offices to discuss the information that was received. At these meetings, it is appropriate to go through all the items on the due diligence list as well as any new concerns or questions that have arisen in the course of the due diligence process. Often, it is appropriate for one or both parties to initiate the management meetings with an overview presentation of their respective businesses. For example, in a merger-of-equals transaction, it is common for both management teams to present their company to the other side.

[4] Follow-Up Questions

Once the management meetings have been had, further issues may come to light, while many issues have hopefully been put to rest. It is common to see additional exchanges of due diligence material and to arrange for additional face-to-face meetings if necessary.

[D] Translate Issues into Value, Structure, and Terms

One of the most important facets of due diligence is to translate the outcome of the issues into value and terms of the transaction. Most in-depth due diligence phases begin after a preliminary term sheet has been agreed to by the parties. Any new items or unresolved issues may have to be addressed in the term sheet. For example, if there are liabilities that were not previously disclosed. Or, there is litigation that has arisen since the term sheet was agreed to.

One should look at how each issue affects the earnings, cash flows and balance sheets of the parties. It is important to consider if the issues will in any way impede the parties to the transaction's ability to operate the business going forward or if the issues will undermine the financial performance of the parties. While certain issues may not have a direct impact on the company today, will they affect the operations or balance sheet in the future, e.g., potential or threatened litigation?

All of these issues may require an adjustment to the purchase price or the structure of the transaction. For example, a cash deal could become part stock or part earnout, or the equity value of a deal may go down because of unforeseen liabilities. It may be necessary to impose an escrow account to cover certain items that may not be concluded at closing.

Identified issues may also impact the legal structure of the transaction and impact the parties' representations and warranties or the conditions to closing.

Each of these mechanisms will serve to protect the parties between signing and closing and, in many cases, post closing.

[E] Resolve Issues

Often, it is possible to resolve issues prior to signing a transaction or prior to closing the deal. One example of an issue that can be resolved before signing is an employment contract with a key employee. An example of an issue that could be resolved prior to closing is a transfer of a license or permit to a buyer. One way or another, due diligence issues must be addressed, either as a modification to the price or structure of the deal, as a clarification to the legal terms of the transaction, or by "fixing" the issue prior to signing or closing.

[F] Plan for Follow-Up, Integration, or Transition

There are many benefits to performing quality due diligence, including the ability to validate a transaction and ensure that the parties are entering into a transaction well-informed of the issues. However, one of the additional benefits of due diligence is that it brings to light those areas where the parties have the greatest opportunity to create value or the greatest risk of failure. It highlights organizational and structural issues that will need to be addressed in order to integrate the firms. It identifies individuals from all organizations and departments that are potential leaders or potential problems. It arms one with meaningful information with which to create a post-merger integration plan.

§ 31.03 SUMMARY

Due diligence is time consuming. It must be well-organized and managed by individuals with an intimate knowledge of their respective fields. It should include multiple members of the management teams of all parties to the transaction, and should be conducted in coordination with outside consultants, lawyers, investment bankers and accountants. Due diligence is invaluable in validating the proposed terms of a transaction and providing a board of directors with enough information to make a well-informed decision regarding a deal. Due diligence is also important in planning an appropriate transition and post-merger integration.

INDEX

[References are to sections.]

A

A reorganizations, 13.06[A][1]

Accounting. *See also* Accounting standards;
      M&A accounting
  asset sales, 14.08
  divestitures, 14.08
  earnouts, 30.08
  equity carve-outs, 20.03[H]
  leveraged recapitalizations, 19.09
  recapitalizations, 19.09
  shareholder rights plans, anti-takeover
      measures, 23.05[A][4]
  share repurchase, 19.09
  tracking stock, 20.04[G]

Accounting Principles Board (APB) Opinions
      16, 12.02[A]
      18, 12.02[B][1]

Accounting standards
  private company valuation, 10.04[C]

Accretion/dilution analysis, 7.01, 7.02
  asset sales, 14.05[C]
  basic forms of consideration, Exhibit 7-2
  corporate restructuring, 18.06[C]
  deal valuation, 2.03[C]
  divestitures, 14.05[C]
  example, 7.02[B]
  fairness opinions, 17.03
  financing, determination, 7.02[B]
  form of consideration, sensitivity to,
      7.02[B]
  goodwill, 7.02, 7.02[B]
  income statements, combining, 7.02[B]
  margins, sensitivity to, 7.02[B]
  methodology, 7.02[A]
  offer, formulating, Exhibit 26-2,
      Exhibit 26-6, 26.07
  offer price, sensitivity to, 7.02[B]
  pro-forma shares outstanding, calculation,
      7.02[B]
  valuation case study, 11.10[A]

Acquisition at various prices (AVP)
      analysis, 7.01

Active business requirement
  spin-offs, 20.02[G]

Affiliates
  tender offers by, 22.02[D]

Agilent Technologies, 20.03[M]

Alliances, 15.01–15.08
  adjustments, 15.06[D]
  announced, Exhibit 15-1
  case studies, 15.07
  competitive advantage, 15.04[F]
  cost sharing, 15.04[G]
  diversification, 15.04[B]
  efficiencies, maximizing, 15.04[H]
  employee attraction and retention, 15.04[I]
  incentives, aligning, 15.06[C]
  joint ventures versus, 15.01[A]
  leverage partner's competencies, 15.04[C]
  markets and, 15.04[E]
  motivation behind, 15.04
  overview, 15.01
  planning ahead, 15.06[A]
  recently completed, Exhibit 15-2
  Renault SA Alliance with Nissan Motor
      Corp., 15.07[A]
  risk sharing, 15.04[G]
  simplicity, necessity for, 15.06[B]
  success factors, 15.06
  synergies, exploitation of, 15.04[D]
  technology, accessing new, 15.04[A]
  valuation, 15.05
    cash flows, potential, 15.05[B]
    initial contribution of the parties,
      15.05[A]
    internal rate of return, Exhibit 15-3
    outcome, 15.05[C]
    overall value, calculation, 15.05[D]
  Vodafone Airtouch Wireless
      Operations/Bell Atlantic Wireless
      Operations, 15.07[B]